# Lecture Notes in Computer Science 15259

Founding Editor

Juris Hartmanis

The series Lecture Notes in Computer Science (LNCS), including its subseries Lecture Notes in Artificial Intelligence (LNAI) and Lecture Notes in Bioinformatics (LNBI), has established itself as a medium for the publication of new developments in computer science and information technology research, teaching, and education.

LNCS enjoys close cooperation with the computer science R & D community, the series counts many renowned academics among its volume editors and paper authors, and collaborates with prestigious societies. Its mission is to serve this international community by providing an invaluable service, mainly focused on the publication of conference and workshop proceedings and postproceedings. LNCS commenced publication in 1973.

Jan L. Plass · Xavier Ochoa
Editors

# Serious Games

10th Joint International Conference, JCSG 2024
New York City, NY, USA, November 7–8, 2024
Proceedings

 Springer

*Editors*
Jan L. Plass 🅾
New York University
Brooklyn, NY, USA

Xavier Ochoa 🅾
New York University
Brooklyn, NY, USA

ISSN 0302-9743          ISSN 1611-3349 (electronic)
Lecture Notes in Computer Science
ISBN 978-3-031-74137-1          ISBN 978-3-031-74138-8 (eBook)
https://doi.org/10.1007/978-3-031-74138-8

This Springer imprint is published by the registered company Springer Nature Switzerland AG
The registered company address is: Gewerbestrasse 11, 6330 Cham, Switzerland

If disposing of this product, please recycle the paper.

# Preface

The Joint Conference on Serious Games 2024 (JCSG 2024) took place at New York University in New York, USA, from November 7–8, 2024. This year's conference once again served as a gathering point where participants with a wide variety of backgrounds, including researchers, designers, developers, writers, health practitioners, and artists, could present and discuss innovative topics and challenges related to the field of serious games.

For JCSG 2024, we received 63 submissions from 17 countries. After a comprehensive double-blind peer-review process with an average of 2.6 reviews per submission, we selected 19 full papers, 5 short papers, 12 posters and 5 demos. Reviewers' feedback was provided to the authors to facilitate the subsequent revisions and improvement of their final manuscripts. The selected papers covered various topics, including: Artificial intelligence and analytics (six papers), serious games design (six papers), health and wellbeing (four papers), extended realities (four papers), and impact studies (four papers). The contributions were presented through traditional talks and presentations.

Furthermore, the program was enriched with the concurrent presentation of 17 contributions in diverse topics related to serious games. These posters, demos, and exhibits were displayed within the exhibition area at the conference.

The theme for the 2024 edition of JCSG was leveraging current AI technologies, such as large language models and multi-agent architectures, to enhance the design, implementation, and operation of serious games. While some papers reflected the theme, this collection of papers reflects the wide range of topics that are relevant for serious games. The conference theme was reflected in the conference keynotes, which were given by Val Shute and Julian Togelius. Val Shute, Mack and Effie Campbell Tyner endowed professor of education emerita at Florida State University, is an expert in student modeling, evidence-centered design, and stealth assessment in serious games. Julian Togelius, Associate Professor of Computer Science at New York University Tandon, is an expert investigating artificial intelligence techniques for making computer games more fun, and on games for making artificial intelligence smarter, and is a co-director of the NYU Game Innovation lab.

We would like to express our gratitude to the authors for submitting their papers and participating in engaging discussions. Additionally, we thank the keynote speakers for providing inspiring insights into the field. We also thank the program committee members for their diligent reviews, and thank the dedicated volunteers who contributed during the event. We also thank the Steering Committee members who played a key role in shaping the conference.

November 2024

Jan L. Plass
Xavier Ochoa

# Organization

## General Chairs

Jan L. Plass                    New York University, USA
Xavier Ochoa                    New York University, USA

## Program Committee Chairs

Jan L. Plass                    New York University, USA
Xavier Ochoa                    New York University, USA

## Demo and Poster Chairs

Fabian Froehlich                New York University, USA
Charles Raffaele                New York University, USA

## Steering Committee

Minhua Eunice                   Ma University of Oxford, UK
Stefan Göbel                    TU Darmstadt, Germany
Jannicke Baalsrud Hauge         University of Bremen, Germany
Manuel Oliveira                 KIT-AR, UK
Heinrich Söbke                  Bauhaus-Universität Weimar, Germany
Pia Spangenberger               TU Berlin, Germany
Tim Marsh                       Griffith University, Australia
David White                     Staffordshire University, UK
Jan L. Plass                    New York University, USA

## Program Committee

Sobah Abbas Petersen            Norwegian University of Science and Technology,
                                  Norway
Per Backlund                    University of Skövde, Sweden
Jannicke Baalsrud Hauge         University of Bremen, Germany

| Licia Calvi | Breda University of Applied Sciences, Netherlands |
| Polona Caserman | TU Darmstadt, Germany |
| Michael Christel | Carnegie Mellon University, USA |
| Karin Coninx | Hasselt University, Belgium |
| Ralf Dörner | RheinMain University of Applied Sciences, Germany |
| Kai Erenli | University of Applied Sciences BFI Vienna, Austria |
| Baltasar Fernandez-Manjon | Universidad Complutense de Madrid, Spain |
| Fabian Froehlich | New York University, USA |
| Augusto Garcia-Agundez | Brown University, USA |
| Tom Gedeon | Australian National University, Australia |
| Pascual Gonzalez | Castilla-La Mancha University, Spain |
| Pedro González Calero | Universidad Politécnica de Madrid, Spain |
| Stefan Göbel | TU Darmstadt, Germany |
| Mads Haahr | Trinity College Dublin, Ireland |
| Helmut Hlavacs | University of Vienna, Austria |
| Petar Jerčić | Graz University of Technology, Austria |
| Michael Kickmeier-Rust | Graz University of Technology, Austria |
| Tim Marsh | Griffith University, Australia |
| Wolfgang Mueller | University of Education Weingarten, Germany |
| Alenka Poplin | Iowa State University, USA |
| Charles Raffaele | New York University, USA |
| Alberto Rojas-Salazar | Universidad de Costa Rica, Costa Rica |
| Nikitas Sgouros | University of Piraeus, Greece |
| Nada Sharaf | German International University, Egypt |
| Pia Spangenberger | University of Potsdam, Germany |
| Heinrich Söbke | Bauhaus-Universität Weimar, Germany |
| Thrasyvoulos Tsiatsos | Aristotle University of Thessaloniki, Greece |
| David White | Staffordshire University, UK |
| Josef Wiemeyer | TU Darmstadt, Germany |

## Additional Reviewers

Maurice Boothe
Jeff Brenneman
Josephine Jahn
Alvaro Olsen
Yuli Shao

# Contents

## Extended Realities

## Healthcare and Wellbeing

## Applications

# Artificial Intelligence in Serious Games

# AI as a Co-creator: A Survey on AI Support for Educational Game Authoring Tools

Florian Horn(✉) and Stefan Göbel

Serious Games Research Group, Technical University of Darmstadt, 64289 Darmstadt, Germany
{florian.horn,stefan_peter.goebel}@tu-darmstadt.de
https://www.etit.tu-darmstadt.de/serious-games

**Abstract.** The emergence of educational games in teaching environments has shown significant potential to engage and educate students effectively. However, the technical challenges associated with developing such games often deter educators, particularly those without a background in programming. This paper focuses on the role of artificial intelligence (AI) in empowering educators to overcome these barriers by facilitating the creation of educational games. Central to our approach is a comprehensive survey conducted with educators to ascertain their preferences and the features they value most in AI-driven authoring tools. This study explores several AI capabilities, including the generation of 3D models from text or images, the automatic arrangement of spatial layouts from descriptions, and the creation of interactive storylines and dialogues. Participants of the survey universally found the presented AI features desirable. Our research demonstrates how tailored AI features can make educational game development more accessible. Integrating such features helps bridge the gap for educators, enabling them to utilize these tools more confidently and efficiently.

**Keywords:** Educational games · Authoring tool · Artificial Intelligence · Large-Language Models · Survey

## 1 Introduction

In recent years, educational games have emerged as a pivotal tool in modern pedagogy, known for their ability to enhance student engagement and facilitate a deeper understanding of complex subjects [8]. Studies consistently demonstrate that well executed educational games have a positive impact on player's engagement [14] and can significantly improve learning outcomes by merging educational content with interactive elements that captivate students' interests and cater to various learning styles. The immersive nature of 3D educational games, in particular, offers a dynamic and visually stimulating learning environment that is often more engaging than traditional educational methods [10].

© The Author(s), under exclusive license to Springer Nature Switzerland AG 2025
J. L. Plass and X. Ochoa (Eds.): JCSG 2024, LNCS 15259, pp. 3–18, 2025.
https://doi.org/10.1007/978-3-031-74138-8_1

Despite their potential, the creation of educational games presents considerable challenges, primarily due to the technical expertise required. Many educators possess strong pedagogical knowledge but lack the programming skills and game design experience necessary to develop these resources. This gap between educational intent and technical capability can significantly hinder the adoption and integration of game-based learning in educational settings, as the development process becomes too daunting or resource-intensive for most educators.

Artificial Intelligence (AI) holds transformative potential across various sectors, including education. In recent years, especially since the emergence of Large-Language Models, AI has begun to play a crucial role in enhancing educational processes, from personalized learning algorithms to AI-driven content creation tools. For educational game development, AI can particularly be a game-changer, offering tools that simplify the creation of complex game environments and interactive narratives. These tools can generate 3D models, automate layout designs, and even write educational content, thereby bridging the gap between the pedagogical goals of educators and the technical demands of game development.

The primary objective of this paper is to explore how AI can support educators in creating educational games by directly addressing their specific needs and preferences. To achieve this, we conducted a comprehensive survey to gather insights from educators regarding the features they find most valuable regarding AI-support in authoring tools. This feedback is instrumental in guiding the development of AI solutions that are both user-friendly and effective in facilitating the creation of educational games.

This research provides insights into which AI tools are desired by educators in creating educational games, thereby democratizing the game development process and potentially expanding the use of game-based learning in educational settings.

## 2   Related Work

### 2.1   Introduction to the Field

Artificial Intelligence has made a remarkable perceptible impact on everyday life since the emergence of Large-Language Models. Students increasingly use AI to complete their homework, benefiting from tools that provide instant feedback and personalized explanations. However, educational systems are struggling to adapt to this new reality, facing challenges in integrating these advanced tools into their curricula effectively.

One potential solution to this challenge is the use of immersive educational games, which can shift the focus from traditional homework to interactive and engaging learning experiences. These games have the potential to make learning more dynamic and enjoyable, fostering a deeper understanding of educational content. However, many educators encounter significant technical challenges in creating these games, primarily due to a lack of programming skills and the time required to develop such content.

This section reviews the integration of AI in education, the effectiveness of game-based learning, the importance of educational game authoring tools, and the potential of AI to transform game authoring. By examining these areas, we identify the potential gaps and opportunities in using AI to create immersive educational games and discuss the research that addresses these challenges.

## 2.2    AI in Education

Over the past decade, AI has steadily integrated into various educational practices. From 2010 to 2020, substantial advancements have been made in personalized learning algorithms and AI-driven content creation tools [15]. For example, AI algorithms could tailor educational content to meet individual students' needs, providing personalized learning experiences that traditional methods cannot match [1]. AI's ability to adapt learning processes to individual students' strengths and weaknesses has a profound impact on educational outcomes [2]. This transformative potential is one of the main reasons why AI is becoming increasingly prevalent in education [3].

Additionally, Holmes et al. reviewed the state of the art and practice of AI in education comprehensively, highlighting various applications and their impacts [6]. Intelligent Tutoring Systems provide personalized instruction and feedback to students, simulating the one-on-one interaction with a human tutor. AI can also be used to adapt the learning content and pace individually and finally also for grading [6]. Furthermore, The discussion on AI in education highlights both its potential and challenges, particularly in terms of the hype versus the practical use of AI-driven educational tools [9].

## 2.3    Game-Based Learning

Well executed educational games are particularly effective in engaging students and enhancing their understanding of complex subjects. An example of such games are the Discovery Tour games by Ubisoft. These games combine educational content with interactive elements that cater to different learning styles, making learning more appealing and effective [11]. However, the technical skills required to develop educational games pose a significant challenge for many educators. Tokarieva et al. [13] discusses the gap between educators' pedagogical knowledge and the technical demands of game development, which often hinders the adoption of game-based learning. This is where AI could play a pivotal role by simplifying the game development process.

## 2.4    Educational Game Authoring Tools

Creating educational games often requires - besides the programming and artistic knowledge - a significant investment of time. However, the use of authoring tools specifically designed for educational games can drastically reduce the time as well as knowledge needed. Therefore, these educational game authoring tools have become increasingly important in creating interactive, multimedia-rich learning experiences. These tools enable educators to design complex educational scenarios without needing extensive programming skills, making game-based learning more accessible and effective.

Two notable examples for such tools are *CoSpaces Edu*[1] and *GameTULearn* [7]. These tools provide a user-friendly editor that allows educators and students to build interactive narratives through a visual interface. By allowing various media inputs such as text, images, audio, and video, they simplify the process of creating engaging educational content.

*StoryTec* [5] exemplifies how such tools can enhance student engagement and learning outcomes by enabling the creation of personalized and adaptive learning experiences. Although StoryTec is no longer actively maintained, its pioneering approach provides a solid foundation for the development of future authoring tools. By leveraging the insights and innovations from StoryTec, new educational technologies can continue to evolve, offering even more sophisticated and effective solutions for personalized learning.

## 2.5   AI in Game Authoring

AI can transform the process of creating educational games by automating complex tasks such as spatial layout design, narrative generation, and 3D modeling or 2D asset generation. For example, AI tools can generate 3D models from text descriptions or images, as demonstrated by *Tripo SR* [12]. They can also arrange spatial layouts based on descriptions, as shown in *LayoutGPT* [4], and create interactive narratives, as exemplified by GameTULearn [7]. These capabilities could make it easier for educators to develop educational games without needing advanced technical skills. This not only saves time but also allows educators to focus more on the educational content and less on the technical aspects of game development.

## 2.6   Gaps and Opportunities

Despite the significant progress made in AI and educational game development, there are still gaps that need to be addressed. One of the main challenges is the seamless integration of AI in 3D game authoring tools for educational purposes. While many tools for various AI usages already exist, they often require a level of technical expertise that most educators might not possess and are not seamlessly integrated into an authoring tool designed for educators and educational games.

## 2.7   Conclusion

In conclusion, the literature reviewed highlights the transformative potential of AI and immersive technologies in education. AI-driven authoring tools can potentially democratize the creation of educational games, making it easier for

---

[1] https://www.cospaces.io/, last accessed on July 18, 2024.

educators to develop engaging and effective learning experiences. By focusing on the specific needs of educators, we can further enhance the usability and effectiveness of these tools. This research aims to find out which AI-supported functionalities are desired by educators and which concerns educators have regarding AI in education.

## 3 Questionnaire

### 3.1 Preface

To systematically assess educators' preferences for various AI-driven features in 3D educational game authoring, we employed a 5-point Likert scale survey. This scale ranged from 1 (Strongly Disagree) to 5 (Strongly Agree) and was designed to measure the perceived usefulness of specific AI features. The features evaluated included 3D model generation from text or image, automated room layout, 3D object and animation creation, narrative creation and extension, and dialogue writing.

The survey consisted of several sections, each dedicated to one of the AI features mentioned. The questions asked and the mean and standard deviation of the response values are listed in Table 1. The questions were presented with adequate example images, so the participants had a visual understanding of the questions. These questions were crafted to directly assess the appeal and perceived practicality of various ways AI could help in educational game development.

We distributed the survey electronically through various networks. The aim was to reach a broad demographic of educators across different educational levels and subject specializations. We got a total of **18 participants** ranged from 23 to 60 years old, with a mean of approximately **29.5 years old**.

After collecting the responses, the data was analyzed to determine the average rating for each feature, which provided an initial understanding of the overall sentiment towards these AI features. To gain deeper insights, we also performed various analyses on the collected responses in Sect. 5.

## 4 Summary of Interest in AI Features

The survey data provides valuable insights into the participants' interest in various AI features that could enhance the usability of educational authoring tools. This section elaborates on each survey question and its outcomes. Figure 1 displays a stacked bar chart of the survey answers, showing that most AI-related features were highly desired.

The most-desired feature was the ability to create animations via text descriptions, with a mean rating of 4.61 and a standard deviation (SD) of 0.7. This was closely followed by an AI feature that expands and improves dialogue, with a mean rating of 4.56 and an SD of 0.78. The least-desired feature was the creation of a room by providing a reference image, which had a mean rating of 3.83 and

**Table 1.** Survey questions and average responses

| No. | Question | Mean | SD |
|---|---|---|---|
| **Demographics** | | | |
| 1 | How would you rate your programming skills? (1 = No skills, 5 = Advanced skills) | 2.28 | 1.56 |
| 2 | How interested are you in developing small learning games for your students independently, without programming knowledge? | 3.72 | 1.23 |
| **Questions about the world design** | | | |
| How interested are you in a feature that allows you to... | | | |
| 3 | ...describe a room through text input and automatically generate a fully designed room? | 4.33 | 0.74 |
| 4 | ...generate a room through an image? | 3.83 | 0.99 |
| 5 | ...select a specific area in a room to automatically generate objects based on a text input? | 4.11 | 0.81 |
| 6 | ...automatically fill an existing room with additional objects? (e.g., to prevent it from looking empty) | 3.94 | 0.97 |
| 7 | ...generate new objects through textual description when the object you want is not available in the object library? (e.g., a wolf figure) | 4.11 | 0.85 |
| 8 | ...generate new objects based on an image when the object you desire is not available in the object library? | 3.56 | 1.08 |
| 9 | How important is it to you that AI-generated objects match the style of the rest of the already built room? | 4.00 | 0.91 |
| 10 | How interested are you in using AI to create animations for characters through a text description? (e.g., to have a character pour a chemical from one bottle into another) | 3.72 | 0.70 |
| **Questions about story/dialogues** | | | |
| How interested are you in a feature that allows you to... | | | |
| 11 | ...automatically generate the entire game logic based on text input? | 4.06 | 0.93 |
| 12 | ...expand the existing game logic based on text input? | 4.06 | 0.89 |
| 13 | AI tools that automatically generate game logic would reduce the time I spend developing game plots and scenarios. (1 = Strongly disagree, 5 = Strongly agree) | 3.72 | 0.92 |
| 14 | I believe that AI-generated game logic would help me develop more engaging narratives. (1 = Strongly disagree, 5 = Strongly agree) | 3.67 | 0.96 |
| 15 | How interested are you in the possibility that AI creates complete dialogues? | 3.89 | 0.96 |
| 16 | How interested are you in an AI feature that extends and improves existing dialogues? | 4.17 | 0.83 |
| **Other questions** | | | |
| 17 | How concerned are you about the rise of AI in the educational sector? (1 = not concerned, 5 = very concerned) | 2.25 | 0.86 |
| 18 | (if you previously answered 2–5) Which specific concerns do you have? | N/A | N/A |
| 19 | Which other possible uses for AI can you imagine? | N/A | N/A |

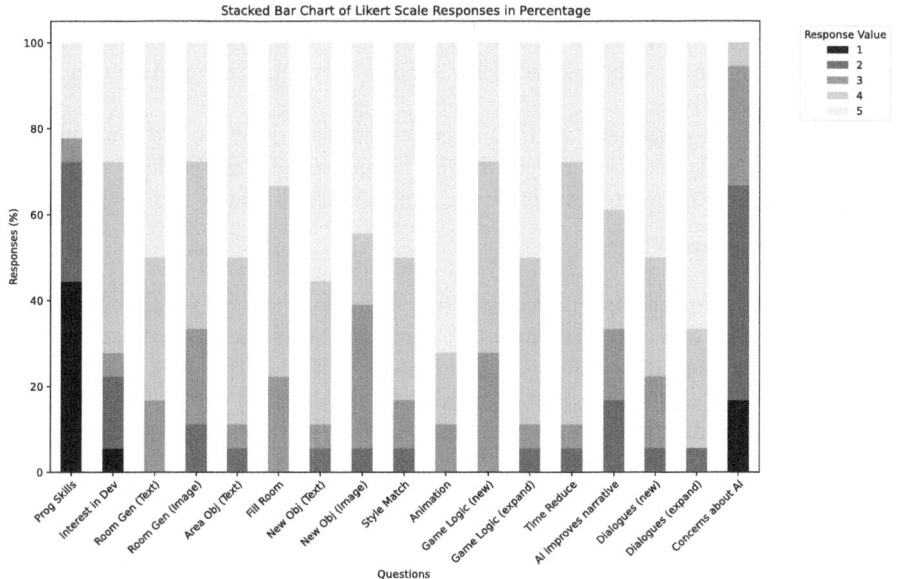

**Fig. 1.** Stacked bar chart of Likert scale responses from Table 1 in percentage. All AI-related features are at least moderately liked, with the majority of them being universally wanted.

an SD of 0.99. Despite being the least preferred among the listed options, it still garnered a moderate level of interest among respondents.

Participants rated their programming skills on a scale from 1 (no skills) to 5 (advanced skills). The average rating was 2.28, with an SD of 1.56 and a variance of 2.42. Most participants indicated they had minimal to no programming knowledge (ratings 1–2) or good knowledge (ratings 4–5), with the majority falling on the lower end of the spectrum. This underscores a significant demand for user-friendly tools that do not require advanced technical expertise, making AI features particularly valuable for this group.

There was also considerable interest in creating small learning games without programming knowledge, with an average rating of 3.72. This highlights a strong demand for tools that enable educators to develop educational content without needing advanced programming skills.

## 4.1 Concerns About AI in Education

The survey also asked about concerns regarding AI in the educational sector, with an average rating of 2.25 and a standard deviation of 0.856. This indicates moderate concern, suggesting that while there are some worries about AI's role in education, they aren't overwhelmingly high. Addressing these concerns through clear communication about AI's benefits and limitations, along with ethical considerations, will be crucial for successfully integrating AI technologies in educational settings.

Educators have expressed a range of concerns regarding the integration of AI in educational settings, focusing on both the potential drawbacks for teachers and students. The concrete concerns are summarized below:

### Over-Reliance on AI

- **Educators' Concerns**: There is a fear that teachers might overly rely on AI, trusting it to always provide the correct answers and solutions without critically assessing its outputs. This reliance could lead to a lack of thoughtful engagement with teaching materials and methods.
- **Implications for Students**: Students might also depend too heavily on AI for completing assignments, which could undermine their learning process and development of critical thinking skills.

### Resistance to Technology

- **Older Teachers**: Older educators are often more skeptical and resistant to adopting new technologies, including AI. This resistance can create a divide between different generations of teachers and their comfort levels with integrating AI into their teaching practices.

### Flexibility and Adaptability

- **Systemic Inflexibility**: Concerns were raised about the inflexibility of the educational system in Germany and teachers' ability to adapt to new AI-driven methods. There is a worry that AI tools might make traditional teaching methods, assessments, and student evaluations less effective.

### Ethical and Fair Use

- **Supportive Role**: AI should remain a supportive tool rather than a primary one. Excessive reliance on AI can make it difficult to verify facts and maintain the integrity of educational content.
- **Fairness**: It's important to ensure fairness by not allowing double standards-such as prohibiting students from using AI for their work while teachers use it extensively to generate assignments.

### Quality and Accuracy of AI Outputs

- **Verification**: AI systems can sometimes produce incorrect or overly simplistic answers. Ensuring the accuracy and depth of AI-generated content is crucial to maintain educational quality.

**Student Dependency and Skill Development**

- **Loss of Critical Thinking Skills**: Students might lose their initiative and critical thinking skills if they become too dependent on AI for completing their tasks. This dependency could hinder their ability to independently summarize, research, and understand complex topics.
- **Competence Development**: Students might struggle to develop essential academic skills independently, which could reduce their ability to engage in self-directed learning and effective problem-solving.

**Teacher Preparedness**

- **Training Needs**: Teachers may lack the necessary knowledge and training to effectively integrate AI into their teaching. This could lead to ineffective use of AI tools and potential frustration among educators.
- **Societal Concerns**: Broader societal issues involve the risk of people becoming too dependent on AI and the spread of shallow or incorrect information, based on the AI's limitations.

**Balance Between AI and Human Effort**

- **Critical Engagement**: There is a concern that both teachers and students might not critically engage with AI-generated content, leading to passive acceptance of information without proper evaluation.

In summary, while AI offers significant potential to enhance educational practices, educators are wary of over-reliance on these technologies, the ethical implications, the accuracy of AI-generated content, and the impact on students' development of critical academic skills. Additionally, there are concerns about the systemic inflexibility in adapting to new and emerging AI tools. Balancing AI's supportive role with traditional teaching methods and ensuring adequate training for educators are crucial steps to address these concerns.

## 4.2   Conclusion

Overall, the survey data reveals a strong interest in various AI features that facilitate the creation and enhancement of educational content, particularly for users with basic to intermediate programming skills. The findings underscore the importance of developing intuitive, user-friendly AI tools that support creative freedom and efficiency. Additionally, while there is enthusiasm for these AI capabilities, it is crucial to address the moderate concerns about AI's impact on education. By acknowledging these concerns, developers can create AI-powered educational tools that are both effective and widely accepted by educators. This approach can potentially bridge the gap for educators, enabling them to create their own educational games and fostering broader acceptance and integration of AI in educational settings.

## 5   Evaluation

To explore the relationships between various factors, we conducted various analyses. Specifically, we examined the link between participants' programming skills and their desire for an easy-to-use tool for creating small learning games, as well as age-related differences.

Additionally, we checked how educators' answers differ based on their current job status - whether they are still studying or already working. These relationships are presented below:

### 5.1   Programming Skills and Interest in Developing Learning Games

To explore the relationship between programming skills and other factors, we conducted a t-test comparing the mean responses of participants categorized as proficient and not proficient in programming skills. Participants were considered proficient if they had a Likert score of 3 or higher in the "Programming Skills" category.

The results of the t-test showed that all p-values were above the threshold for statistical significance ($p > 0.05$), except for three factors: Individuals with programming knowledge had higher interest in Room Generation via text description, while non proficient individuals had a higher level of interest in room generation via image, as well as higher concerns regarding AI in education. This indicates that, in most cases, there were no significant differences in interest levels across the different programming skill groups. Participants with high programming skills and those with little to no programming skills exhibited similar levels of interest in tools that allow them to develop educational games without programming knowledge.

The lack of significant difference in most factors is noteworthy as it suggests that the appeal of AI tools for developing educational games is widespread, regardless of programming proficiency. The similar interest levels across all groups highlight a universal recognition of the potential benefits these tools can provide in educational settings, irrespective of an individual's technical background. The exceptions, where significant differences were found, provide specific insights into areas where programming proficiency may influence user perceptions and concerns.

The survey data reveals several key observations about the relationship between self-assessed programming proficiency and responses to various questions, as highlighted in Fig. 2.

**Similarity in Average Responses** The average responses from both groups, those who consider themselves "Not Proficient" (14) and those who consider themselves "Proficient" (4) in programming, are quite similar across most questions. This suggests that programming proficiency might not significantly influence their general perceptions or experiences related to the topics covered in the survey. However, it is important to note that a larger sample size might yield different results.

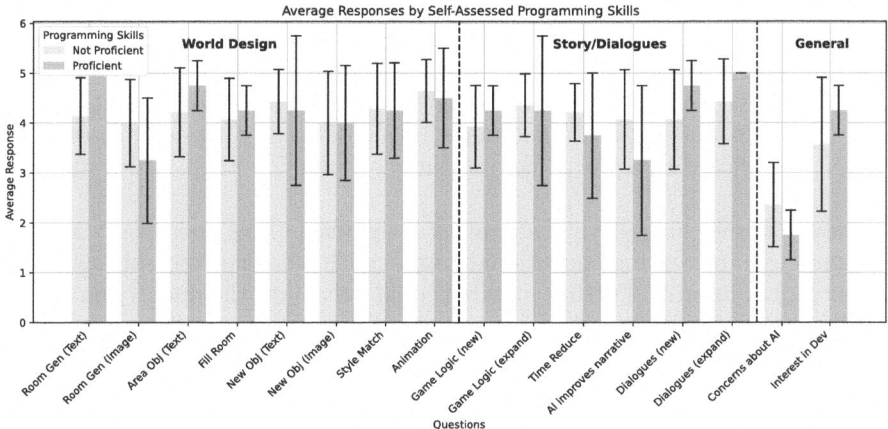

**Fig. 2.** Average responses to survey questions by self-assessed programming proficiency.

**Programming Proficiency and AI Feature Valuation** While the overall trends are similar, there are specific questions where the average responses show more noticeable divergence between the two groups. These differences could point to particular areas where programming proficiency has a more substantial impact. Specifically, individuals with programming skills seem to have a clearer understanding of which AI-related features they value more, while those with less proficiency tend to have a more general appreciation for all AI-related features.

**Implications for Support and Training** The observed similarity in responses suggests that programming proficiency may not be the primary factor shaping participants' views on the surveyed topics. This implies that support and training interventions could potentially be equally effective for both groups, regardless of their self-assessed programming skills.

In summary, the survey data indicates that self-assessed programming proficiency does not drastically alter participants' general responses. However, it does suggest that those with programming skills have a more defined sense of which AI-related features they value, whereas those less proficient in programming tend to appreciate all features more generally.

## 5.2   Age-Related Differences

An analysis was conducted to explore variations in various educational interests and skills across different age groups among participants. The participants were categorized into three age groups: under 25, 25–40, and over 40. The average interest levels in learning games for these groups were 2.20, 4.27, and 4.50, respectively.

The data indicates that older participants tend to exhibit a higher interest in learning games. To determine if these observed differences were statistically significant, an ANOVA test was performed. The results showed an F-statistic of 12.76 and a p-value of 0.00058, demonstrating that the differences in interest levels among the age groups are statistically significant.

Further ANOVA tests were performed for all other questions, including programming skills and various AI features. None of these categories showed statistically significant differences across the age groups, with p-values all above 0.05.

These findings suggest that age plays a significant role specifically in influencing interest in creating educational games, with older participants showing a notably higher interest. Further research could delve into the underlying reasons for this trend and examine other demographic factors that may affect educational interests and skills.

## 5.3    Relevance of Job Status (Studying vs. Working)

We separated the survey participants by their current status-whether they are still studying or already working-to examine any significant differences between these two groups. Figure 3 presents the survey responses categorized by these groups.

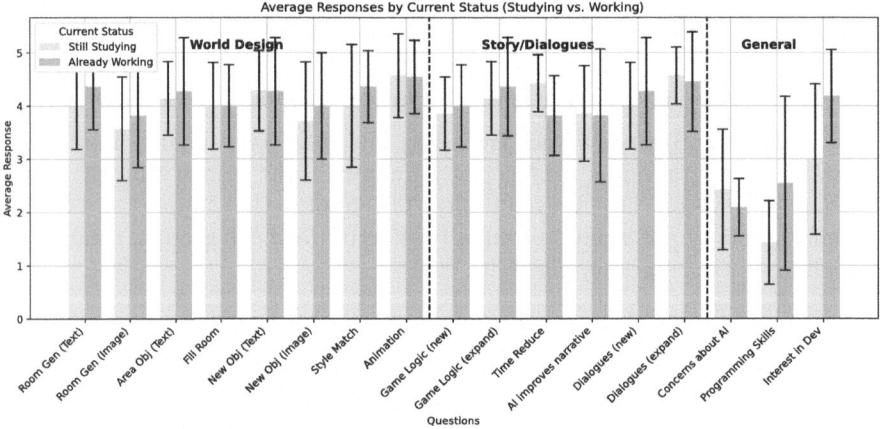

**Fig. 3.** Average responses to survey questions by current status (studying vs. working).

Overall, both groups exhibited a high level of interest in the presented AI features and showed moderate concern regarding the integration of AI in education. The studying group displayed slightly higher concern, possibly due to their lack of classroom experience and uncertainty about AI's role in education.

To identify significant differences in the responses between the two groups, independent samples t-tests were performed for each of the Likert scale questions. The results indicated a statistically significant difference in the level of interest in developing small learning games without programming knowledge ($p = 0.042$). Specifically, the working group showed a higher interest (mean = 4.18) compared to the studying group (mean = 3.0). This finding aligns with the observed age-related differences and suggests that those who are already working in educational settings see more value in creating educational games, likely because of their experience in personalizing learning experiences for their students. The ability to tailor educational content to meet the specific needs and preferences of their students may make the development of small learning games particularly relevant and valuable to them.

For other questions, the t-tests did not reveal statistically significant differences between the studying and working groups. This indicates that, overall, both groups have similar attitudes towards the majority of AI features and their potential integration into educational contexts.

## 5.4    Analysis Summary

The evaluation investigates the relationships between various factors and participants' interest in developing learning games. The key findings are as follows:

1. **Programming Skills and Interest in Developing Learning Games**: A t-test revealed that most factors showed no significant differences between participants proficient in programming and those who are not, except for three areas. Proficient individuals showed higher interest in Room Generation via text description, while non-proficient individuals were more interested in room generation via image and had higher concerns regarding AI in education. This indicates a broad appeal for AI tools across all proficiency levels, with proficient individuals valuing specific features more clearly.
2. **Age-Related Differences**: Participants were categorized into three age groups: under 25, 25–40, and over 40. Older participants exhibited a higher interest in learning games, with statistically significant differences confirmed by an ANOVA test (F-statistic = 12.76, p = 0.00058). Other categories, including programming skills and AI features, showed no significant differences across age groups. This suggests that age significantly influences interest in educational games, with older individuals showing greater enthusiasm.
3. **Relevance of Job Status (Studying vs. Working)**: Participants were divided into studying and working groups. Both groups showed high interest in AI features and moderate concern about AI integration in education. The working group displayed a significantly higher interest in developing learning games without programming knowledge, likely due to their experience in personalizing learning experiences. Other questions showed no significant differences, indicating similar attitudes towards most AI features and their educational potential.

Overall, the findings suggest that while programming proficiency and job status influence specific areas of interest, there is a general widespread appeal for AI tools in educational game development, with older participants and those already working in education showing higher interest. AI features were highly regarded; experienced programmers had a better understanding of their specific preferences, while others generally appreciated the concept of AI supported educational game creation.

# 6   Conclusion

The research presented in this paper elucidates the transformative potential of AI in educational game development, particularly for educators who may lack advanced technical skills. By systematically surveying educators to understand their needs and preferences, this study highlights the significant interest in AI-driven authoring tools that can facilitate the creation of educational games. The key findings from this research underscore the following points:

**Importance of AI in Education** AI has shown considerable promise in various educational applications, from personalized learning algorithms to content creation tools. This study extends this potential to the realm of educational game development, demonstrating that AI can help bridge the gap between educators' pedagogical goals and the technical challenges of game creation.

**Educational Game Development Challenges** Despite the pedagogical advantages of educational games, their development remains a daunting task for many educators due to the technical skills required. This gap hinders the broader adoption of game-based learning in educational settings.

**AI-Driven Authoring Tools** The survey results indicate strong interest among educators in AI features that can simplify game development. Key features such as generating 3D models from text or images, automating spatial layouts, and creating interactive narratives and dialogues were highly rated by participants. Integrating such features can democratize game development, making it more accessible to educators without programming backgrounds.

**Survey Insights** The data collected from the survey provides valuable insights into which AI functionalities are most desired by educators. The most popular features included creating animations via text descriptions and enhancing dialogues. All features were highly valued by educators. Those who considered themselves proficient in programming had more specific preferences for certain AI features, while others generally liked all of the features equally.

**Statistical Analysis** The analyses conducted revealed several insights into the factors influencing educators' interest in AI tools for educational game development.

Firstly, programming skills do not significantly impact educators' overall interest in developing their own educational games. This suggests that AI tools designed for educational game development have a broad appeal, regardless of the users' programming proficiency.

Secondly, age and interest in developing educational games showed significant differences among age groups. Specifically, younger educators (under 25) demonstrated significantly less interest in developing educational games compared to their older counterparts.

Lastly, whether participants were still studying or already working, they exhibited strong interest in AI tools, while studying participants are less interested in developing own educational games. This aligns with the findings regarding age. However, their specific preferences and concerns varied slightly based on their practical experience and current roles.

This highlights the importance of tailoring AI tools to meet the diverse needs of educators at different stages of their careers.

**Concerns and Considerations** While there is enthusiasm for AI in educational game development, there are also moderate concerns about AI's role in education. These concerns include over-reliance on AI, potential loss of critical thinking skills among students, and the need for adequate training for educators. Addressing these concerns is crucial for the successful integration of AI technologies in educational settings.

In conclusion, the findings from this research highlight a significant demand for AI-supported authoring tools that can enable educators to create engaging and effective educational games. By addressing the specific concerns and preferences of educators, AI has the potential to make game-based learning more accessible and widespread. The positive reception of AI features among educators suggests that integrating AI features into educational authoring tools can enhance the development and use of educational games, ultimately benefiting the learning experiences of students.

**Acknowledgment.** This invested research has been partially funded in the course of the zQSL project "3DVirtualCampus4GamifiedOnlineTeaching" to improve the quality of study conditions and teaching at the Technical University of Darmstadt.

**Disclosure of Interests.** The authors have no competing interests to declare that are relevant to the content of this article.

# References

1. Aggarwal, D.: Integration of innovative technological developments and AI with education for an adaptive learning pedagogy. China Petrol. Process. Petrochem. Technol. **23**(2) (2023)
2. Cardona, M.A., Rodríguez, R.J., Ishmael, K., et al.: Artificial intelligence and the future of teaching and learning: insights and recommendations (2023)
3. Chen, L., Chen, P., Lin, Z.: Artificial intelligence in education: a review. IEEE Access **8**, 75264–75278 (2020). https://doi.org/10.1109/ACCESS.2020.2988510
4. Feng, W., et al.: LayoutGPT: compositional visual planning and generation with large language models. Adv. Neural Inf. Process. Syst. **36** (2024)

5. Göbel, S., Salvatore, L., Konrad, R.: StoryTec: a digital storytelling platform for the authoring and experiencing of interactive and non-linear stories. In: 2008 International Conference on Automated Solutions for Cross Media Content and Multi-Channel Distribution, pp. 103–110 (2008). https://doi.org/10.1109/AXMEDIS.2008.45

6. Holmes, W., Tuomi, I.: State of the art and practice in AI in education. Eur. J. Educ. **57** (2022). https://doi.org/10.1111/ejed.12533

7. Horn, F., Vogt, S., Göbel, S.P.: GameTULearn: an interactive educational game authoring tool for 3D environments. In: Haahr, M., Rojas-Salazar, A., Göbel, S. (eds.) Serious Games, pp. 384–390. Springer Nature Switzerland, Cham (2023). https://doi.org/10.1007/978-3-031-44751-8_32

8. Li, Y., Chen, D., Deng, X.: The impact of digital educational games on student's motivation for learning: the mediating effect of learning engagement and the moderating effect of the digital environment. PLoS ONE **19**(1), e0294350 (2024). https://doi.org/10.1371/journal.pone.0294350, https://www.ncbi.nlm.nih.gov/pmc/articles/PMC10783726/

9. Nemorin, S., Vlachidis, A., Ayerakwa, H.M., Andriotis, P.: AI hyped? A horizon scan of discourse on artificial intelligence in education (AIED) and development. Learn. Media Technol. **48**(1), 38–51 (2023). https://doi.org/10.1080/17439884.2022.2095568

10. Ştefan, L.: Immersive collaborative environments for teaching and learning traditional design. Procedia Soc. Behav. Sci. **51**, 1056–1060 (2012)

11. Steinkuehler, C., Squire, K.: Videogames and Learning, pp. 377–394 (2014). https://doi.org/10.1017/CBO9781139519526.023

12. Tochilkin, D., et al.: TripoSR: fast 3D object reconstruction from a single image. arXiv preprint arXiv:2403.02151 (2024)

13. Tokarieva, A.V., Volkova, N.P., Harkusha, I.V.: Educational digital games: models and implementation (2019)

14. Yu, Z., Gao, M., Wang, L.: The effect of educational games on learning outcomes, student motivation, engagement and satisfaction. J. Educ. Comput. Res. **59**, 073563312096921 (2020). https://doi.org/10.1177/0735633120969214

15. Zhai, X., et al.: A review of artificial intelligence (AI) in education from 2010 to 2020. Complexity **2021**, e8812542 (2021). https://doi.org/10.1155/2021/8812542, https://www.hindawi.com/journals/complexity/2021/8812542/

# Students' Use of an LLM-Powered Virtual Teaching Assistant for Recommending Educational Applications of Games

Mamta Shah[1,2](✉) ⓘD, Maciej Pankiewicz[1] ⓘD, Ryan S. Baker[1] ⓘD, Jiahui Chi[1] ⓘD,
Yue Xin[3] ⓘD, Hetali Shah[4] ⓘD, and Dangela Fonseca[1] ⓘD

[1] University of Pennsylvania, Philadelphia, PA 19104, USA
m.shah@elsevier.com
[2] Elsevier, Philadelphia, PA 19103, USA
[3] University of Maryland, College Park, MD 20742, USA
[4] Raritan Valley Community College, Branchburg, NJ 08876, USA

**Abstract.** In this paper, we discuss the application of JeepyTA – a virtual teaching assistant (TA) powered by a large language model (LLM) - within a graduate-level course on games and learning in Spring 2024. Specifically, we describe how JeepyTA was integrated in two "play journal" assignments where twenty-two students documented their observations of playing classic and contemporary digital games, shared insights from assigned readings, and proposed educational applications of the respective games through consultation with JeepyTA. We (a) report students' overall communication patterns with JeepyTA and (b) identify five ways in which students incorporated JeepyTA's recommendations for Minecraft. We conclude this paper with directions for future research and practice on supporting students in using LLMs for reflecting on their experiences and creatively adapting games for learning.

**Keywords:** Virtual teaching assistant · Large language models · Games · Minecraft · Game-based learning

## 1 Introduction

Repurposing commercial entertainment games for education is not new [1, 2]. However, navigating the complex mechanics and vast environments of popular games (e.g., Legend of Zelda Breath of the Wild) can be overwhelming for educators who are new to the study and application of games for education. Researchers have proposed analytical and pedagogical frameworks for making game analysis and integration accessible to educators and customizable to their ecological conditions [3, 4]. The genre of 'Let's Play' videos on YouTube have expanded opportunities to learn about a game from novice and expert players [5]. Training teachers and disseminating educational curricula based on popular games has also become common both through community driven efforts (e.g., Common Sense Media) and through major companies recognizing the need for training teachers (e.g., Teach with Minecraft). We argue that the use of large

J. L. Plass and X. Ochoa (Eds.): JCSG 2024, LNCS 15259, pp. 19–24, 2025.
https://doi.org/10.1007/978-3-031-74138-8_2

language models (LLMs) can advance these academic and socio-technical contributions by assisting students and educators in leveraging their knowledge of a particular game for educational use. This provided the impetus for the project described in this paper involving the application of JeepyTA in a course on games and learning.

## 2   Application of JeepyTA in EDUC5152 in Spring 2024

EDUC5152 Video Games and Virtual Worlds as Sites for Learning and Engagement introduces students to the interdisciplinary scholarship of game studies. Practices in gaming ecologies such as playing, making, and remixing digital and analog games inspire course activities and assignments [See 6 for a detailed description]. JeepyTA was developed at the Penn Center for Learning Analytics [7] to interact with students in conversations on a course discussion forum as one of the forum's users. To generate specific responses in each course, JeepyTA's available context is based on materials provided by an instructor such as course syllabus and examples of feedback from the past. It uses embeddings to store these materials and performs semantic search to generate a precise response. JeepyTA's responses are published with a short delay, to reflect the characteristics of a discussion forum (and allow for server latency).

JeepyTA was deployed in EDUC5152 using OpenAI's GPT-3.5 model (gpt-3.5-turbo-16k-0613) to (a) respond to students' questions about the course, (b) summarize discussion board posts for the instructor, and (c) serve as a discussion partner for two play journal assignments (A1 and A5). For A1, students chose two classic games, preferably released before 1980 (e.g., Donkey Kong, Frogger). For each game, they documented their play experience from first impressions to final thoughts. Almost identical requirements guided A5, the play journal involving Minecraft, except for different assigned readings [8, 9 for A1 and 10, 11 for A5], and an additional requirement of including how YouTube supported/enhanced their game play experience.

## 3   Instructions and Prompt for Consulting with JEEPYTA

Three former students (one from Spring 2020, and two from Spring 2023) volunteered to test the prompt for consulting with JeepyTA and provided feedback for modifying it. As a result, the following instructions and prompt were provided to the full class of Spring 2024 students for consulting with JeepyTA (see Fig. 1).

Below we present findings for the following research questions, "How did students consult with JeepyTA?" (RQ1) and "How did students incorporate JeepyTA's recommendations for repurposing Minecraft?" (RQ2).

## 4   Findings

### 4.1   Findings for RQ1

A1 required the students to seek JeepyTA's guidance on applying two classic games in education. For the first game, 54.5% (12/22) students followed the prompt and 50% (11/22) of students asked follow-up questions. For the second game, 50% (10/22) students followed the prompt and 45% (9/20) students asked follow-up questions. A5

*Hello!*
*For A5, Dr. Shah has asked you to seek my; that is, JeepyTA's assistance in recommending educational applications of Minecraft. Follow the instructions and tips to engage in a 1:1 dialog with me.*

*You will need the following info ready from your journal:*
- *A description of the key elements (e.g., story, interface, gameplay, graphics, characters, music, art style, design, genre) affected/influenced/impacted your experience.*
- *Interesting details/anecdotes that you noticed while playing the game (e.g., character, discussion with a play partner) or learnt about through a secondary source (e.g., fan page, discussion board, YouTube).*
- *Connections between your play experience with insights gained from the readings (Ito, 2008; Malliet & de Meyer, 2005)*

*You will also need the following for your dialog with me:*
- *Desired Educational Objectives: A description of your specific educational objectives or areas of interest for how Minecraft can be used. For instance, you may highlight aspects like critical thinking, creativity, collaboration, or subject-specific learning you wish to address through Minecraft.*
- *Desired Educational Application: An articulation of the type of educational application you wish to explore using Minecraft. Let me know if you're interested in inquiry-based learning, narrative creation, skill development, or any other specific educational focus.*
- *Begin with this multi-step prompt and use your judgment to insert relevant excerpts from your journal. Give me a few minutes between the steps. Use your time judgment to move to the next prompt.*

*JeepyTA, please act like a coach. I will provide you with excerpts from my Minecraft play journal and directions for how I wish to explore the application of Minecraft in education. I would appreciate your suggestions.*
- *First, please familiarize with the key elements that influenced my experience. <insert text from your journal>*
- *Now, learn about an interesting detail/anecdote that I noticed/documented while playing the game. <insert text>*
- *Let me share the connections I made between my experience playing and the readings assigned by [your instructor]. <insert text>*
- *I would like to explore the use of Minecraft for fostering <insert texts related to desired educational objectives and application>*
- *JeepyTA, please remember the context I have provided you thus far and provide your suggestions for implementing Minecraft in education.*

*Once you arrive at this step, let's engage in a 1:1 dialog. Former students of this class have found it useful to ask follow-up questions and offer clarification until they've reached a point of satisfaction with the outcome. Make sure you use insights from our dialog to recommend (in 500 words) what knowledge, skill(s) or attitude(s) can a particular audience/user learn/practice using Minecraft (as a whole or one of the key elements) in a formal or informal setting? Include that in your journal before you hit submit on Canvas!*

**Fig. 1.** Instructions and prompts provided to the students for consulting with JeepyTA

required students to seek JeepyTA's guidance on applying Minecraft in education. 40.9% (9/22) students followed the prompt and 54.5% (12/22) students asked follow-up questions. 13.6% (3/22) students followed the prompt only for A1 and 9.1% (2/22) followed the prompt only for A5. 27.5% (6/22) students followed the prompt and 31.8% (7/22) did not follow the prompt for both assignments. Of the students who did not follow the prompt, some students omitted a portion of the prompt, while other students chose to modify the prompt. Example of a modification includes: "Hi JeepyTA, have you heard of the game, The Legend of Zelda? Can you recommend an educational use for this game? What knowledge, skill(s) or attitude(s) can a particular audience/user learn/practice using this game?" For both A1 and A5, elaboration was the most frequently used question type for follow-ups with JeepyTA (e.g., "Can you expand on the first point that you made? Write a more fleshed-out detailed lesson plan on how you think that sort of thing would work"). Other question types included feedback, summary and clarification.

## 4.2   Findings for RQ2

We identified five patterns in students' play journals for A5 that illustrate how they acknowledged, integrated, rejected or built upon JeepyTA's recommendations for using Minecraft for education.

*Thirty-six percent students (8/22) found JeepyTA's recommendation insightful and/or in alignment with their own idea(s).* These students intentionally sought JeepyTA's guidance to brainstorm Minecraft's application in a specific domain. Their journals also suggested that students took a collaborative approach with JeepyTA to recommend implementation strategies. For instance, "My passion for math inspired me to ask JeepyTA to recommend how one can use Minecraft as a resource for students to build their knowledge base…I must align all Minecraft activities with the learning objectives and math standards to properly reach the learning goals. To do this, I can integrate explicit math instruction and game-based activities to help students make connections between the game and mathematics. Here are the following implementation strategies that JeepyTA recommends…"

*Eighteen percent students (4/22) acknowledged the role of 1:1 communication with JeepyTA in their recommendations.* In these journals, students embraced a cooperative stance. They demonstrated some level of personalization but refrained from commenting about whether JeepyTA's guidance was helpful/not helpful. For instance, "After consulting JeepyTA, I have gained insights into two possible educational adaptations for Minecraft. First, to foster creative thinking with Minecraft, teachers could formulate a class for students to create their virtual worlds or build structures in Minecraft that encourage them to use their imaginations…Plus, with the abundance of online MODs for Minecraft, students may also be asked to create their MODs featuring adventures in Minecraft by engaging in creative-writing or storytelling to strengthen and practice their creativity."

*Eighteen percent students (4/22) referred to JeepyTA but seemed detached or did not express ownership of the idea(s) proposed.* Phrases such as 'All above info provided by JeepyTA', 'JeepyTA provided some educational use for this game' and 'Educational Use for Minecraft Recommended by JeepyTA' were used in their journals. In this category, students' proposals for applying Minecraft were mostly generic and copy-pasted from the interaction logs without much modification. For instance: "Problem-solving and Critical Thinking: In the vast, open-world environment of Minecraft, players are required to engage in continuous decision-making. From gathering resources to building structures, the game compels players to think critically and solve problems creatively… This aspect of gameplay nurtures an analytical mindset, encouraging players to assess situations, anticipate outcomes, and devise innovative solutions."

*Eighteen percent students (4/22) made no reference to JeepyTA in their journal.* These students foregrounded their knowledge/experiences of the game and insights from the readings in describing their proposal. The following is an illustration: "Minecraft offers a unique environment for students interested in interior design, mirroring the challenges faced by professionals like those at IKEA…Through connected gaming, students not only learn about design but also become creators of their virtual spaces, actively applying and reflecting on the design principles they learn, which deepens their engagement and understanding of interior design concepts (Kafai, 2017). Educators can introduce concepts of modern design, such as minimalism or sustainability, and ask students to incorporate these ideas into their Minecraft projects." The only way to know if JeepyTA contributed to the recommendations was to refer to the interaction logs.

*Thirteen percent students (3/22) were critical of JeepyTA's recommendations.* These students described JeepyTA's proposed idea, critiqued it, and offered an alternative or built upon it in their journals. For instance, "JeepyTA's suggestions also include the idea of incorporating storytelling in Minecraft. Storyline is something that I think Minecraft missed in its design. But a completely blank storyline gives students the opportunity to write their own story. What I think about this idea is that students can brainstorm a storyline, build different scenes in Minecraft, and tell their own story."

## 5   Discussion, Conclusions, and Implications

The use of LLMs for game-based learning is gaining traction [12]. In this paper, we illustrated the application of an LLM-based teaching assistant in a course on games and learning. Specifically, we reported findings for students' use of JeepyTA as part of two play journal assignments to recommend educational applications of classic and contemporary games.

Interaction logs examined in RQ1 illustrated that students are not likely to exactly follow the recommended prompt, omitting portions or modifying the prompt. Students' follow-up questions (i.e., elaboration, clarification, summary, feedback) were reflective of three types of intentions that guide users in human-AI collaborative conversations: describing information need, understanding received information, and maintaining conversation [13]. In this study, no feedback was provided to students between A1 and A5 to observe naturally occurring shifts in student-JeepyTA communication patterns. In future courses, we may consider providing feedback between the play journal assignments and assess its impact on student-JeepyTA interactions. We may also introduce in-class activities where students can practice questioning and messaging JeepyTA using the categories and examples provided by Wei and colleagues [13]. This may benefit both students that prefer the structure of a pre-written prompt and those who prefer freedom to lead their communication with the virtual TA.

Across the five patterns described for answering RQ2, students' recommendations of applying Minecraft were most novel when they were intentional about integrating insights from readings, experience of the game and/or their domain expertise. This corroborates with reports of when teachers and students have used their deep knowledge of a game along with their understanding of instructional goals for a targeted user group to innovatively repurpose games such as RollerCoasterTycoon3 and Animal Crossing New Horizons [e.g., 14]. Future studies warrant a deeper examination of these patterns using approaches such as thematic analysis [15].

Findings from RQ2 also illustrate that student-JeepyTA interaction resulted in a variety of potential educational applications for Minecraft. Specifically, sixty-eight percent students proposed more than one educational application for Minecraft in their play journals for A5. This finding is promising in relation to the intent of our study; that is, to examine the use of LLMs for assisting individuals (students and educators alike) in leveraging their knowledge of a particular game for educational use. As next steps, we will examine similarities and differences in the number and the kinds of educational applications students of Spring 2024 proposed for Minecraft as compared to students from previous cohorts of EDUC5152.

# References

1. Charsky, D., Mims, C.: Integrating commercial. TechTrends **52**(5), 39 (2008)
2. Schrader, P.G., Deniz, H., Keilty, J.: Breaking SPORE: building instructional value in science education using a commercial, off-the shelf game. J. Learn. Teach. Digit. Age **1**(1), 63–73 (2016)
3. Aarseth, E.: Playing research: methodological approaches to game analysis. In: Proceedings of the Digital Arts and Culture Conference, Melbourne, Australia, May 2003, pp. 28–29
4. Shah, M., Foster, A.: Developing and assessing teachers' knowledge of game-based learning. J. Technol. Teach. Educ. **23**(2), 241–267 (2015)
5. Dezuanni, M.: Peer Pedagogies on Digital Platforms: Learning with Minecraft Let's Play Videos. MIT Press (2020)
6. Kafai, Y., Shah, M.: Video games as sites for learning and engagement. In: Ferdig, R., Baumgartner, E., Gandolfi, E. (eds.) Teaching the Game: An Interdisciplinary Collection of Game Course Syllabi, vol. 2, pp. 244–259. ETC Press (2021)
7. Liu, X., Pankiewicz, M., Gupta, T., Huang, Z., Baker, R.S.: A Step Towards Adaptive Online Learning: Exploring the Role of GPT as Virtual Teaching Assistants in Online Education (under review)
8. Ito, M.: Education vs. entertainment: a cultural history of children's software. In: Salen, K. (ed.) The Ecology of Games: Connecting Youth, Games, and Learning, pp. 89–116. The MIT Press, Cambridge, MA (2008)
9. Malliet, S., de Meyer, G.: The history of the video game. In: Raessens, J., Goldstein, J. (eds.) Handbook of Computer Game Studies, pp. 23–45. MIT Press, Cambridge, MA (2005)
10. Kafai, Y.B.: Connected gaming: an inclusive perspective for serious gaming. Int. J. Serious Games **4**(3), 5–14 (2017)
11. Dezuanni, M.: Minecraft and children's digital making: implications for media literacy education. Learn. Media Technol. **43**(3), 236–249 (2018)
12. Huber, S.E., Kiili, K., Nebel, S., Ryan, R.M., Sailer, M., Ninaus, M.: Leveraging the potential of large language models in education through playful and game-based learning. Educ. Psychol. Rev. **36**(1), 1–20 (2024)
13. Wei, Y., Lu, W., Cheng, Q., Jiang, T., Liu, S.: How humans obtain information from AI: categorizing user messages in human-AI collaborative conversations. Inf. Process. Manage. **59**(2), 102838 (2022)
14. Xin, Y., Shah, M.: Analyzing the affordances of animal crossing: new horizons for middle school life-science education. Paper Presented at the 2021 AERA Annual Meeting, Virtual, 8–12 Apr 2021
15. Guest, G., MacQueen, K.M., Namey, E.E.: Applied Thematic Analysis. Sage, Thousand Oaks, California (2012)

# Serious Games Analytics

# A Taxonomy for Enhancing Metacognitive Adaptivity and Personalization in Serious Games Using Multimodal Trace Data

Roger Azevedo[1]([envelope]) [iD], Daryn Dever[2] [iD], Megan Wiedbusch[1] [iD],
Annamarie Brosnihan[1] [iD], Tara Delgado[1] [iD], Cameron Marano[1] [iD], Milouni Patel[1] [iD],
and Kevin Smith[1] [iD]

[1] School of Modeling, Simulation, and Training, University of Central Florida, Orlando,
FL 32826, USA
roger.azevedo@ucf.edu

[2] College of Education, School of Teaching and Learning, Institute for Advanced Learning
Technologies, University of Florida, Gainesville, FL 32611-704, USA

**Abstract.** This paper presents a theoretically-driven and empirically-based preliminary taxonomy for optimizing metacognitive adaptivity and personalization in
serious games by leveraging multimodal trace data. By integrating diverse sources
of multimodal trace data, such as eye tracking, log files, concurrent verbalizations,
facial expressions of emotions, physiological sensors, and screen recordings, the
taxonomy aims to capture nuanced insights into learners' metacognitive processes
during gameplay. Our taxonomy focuses on six specific metacognitive processes,
including judgments of learning (JOLs), feelings of knowing (FOKs), content evaluations (CEs), monitoring progress towards goals (MPTG), and monitoring use
of strategies (MUS), and self-questioning (SQ). These metacognitive processes
are critical in learning, reasoning, and problem solving across several learning
technologies, including serious games. We provide operational definitions and
examples of how each process can be captured by each multimodal data channel
during gameplay. More specifically, the taxonomy facilitates the development of
serious games that dynamically adjust difficulty levels, provide personalized feedback, and offer tailored scaffolding to enhance metacognitive development using
advanced machine learning techniques, including generative AI, for real-time multimodal analysis. Through this taxonomy, researchers and developers can design
and evaluate adaptive serious games that optimize metacognitive awareness, monitoring, regulation, and reflection, contributing to advancing the science of learning
with serious games. Lastly, future research needs to empirically test these recommendations, and we expect further refinements based on such testing with different
serious games across various learners, tasks, domains, and educational contexts.

**Keywords:** Serious games · Metacognition · Adaptivity · Personalization ·
Multimodal data · Taxonomy

© The Author(s), under exclusive license to Springer Nature Switzerland AG 2025
J. L. Plass and X. Ochoa (Eds.): JCSG 2024, LNCS 15259, pp. 27–40, 2025.
https://doi.org/10.1007/978-3-031-74138-8_3

# 1  Introduction

Serious games are potent tools for instruction, harnessing immersive and captivating environments to facilitate learning [1]. However, within these games lies an untapped potential in their capacity to adapt and personalize the learning experience to individual needs, preferences, and motives. While existing taxonomies for adaptivity and personalization in serious games often concentrate on cognitive, motivational, and socio-cultural aspects of learning [2, 3], our research takes a novel approach. We argue that metacognition, the awareness of, monitoring, regulation, and reflection of one's own cognitive processes [4, 5], is a critical yet overlooked aspect of learning, reasoning, and problem solving within serious games. Metacognitive processes need to be captured, modeled, inferred and used dynamically during gameplay to adapt and personalize game elements to meet the metacognitive challenges, demands, and opportunities learners face [6, 7].

Metacognition, a key aspect of effective learning, enables learners to become aware of, monitor their understanding, evaluate their progress, and employ appropriate strategies to regulate aspects of the task, self, and context [8]. Ultimately, metacognition facilitates reflection on their learning and other key self-regulatory processes, such as learners' cognitive, affective, metacognitive, and motivational states (e.g., interest) and beliefs (e.g., self-efficacy). By incorporating metacognitive processes into adaptive and personalized serious games, we can create learning experiences that impart knowledge and foster self-regulated learning and metacognitive development [9, 10].

Moreover, the rise of multimodal and multichannel learning data presents new opportunities for detecting and inferring metacognitive processes [11–13]. Data sources such as concurrent think-alouds, eye movements, screen recordings, facial expressions of emotions, and physiological signals can provide rich data streams of learners' cognitive and metacognitive states, enabling more nuanced and effective adaptations.

This paper proposes a novel preliminary taxonomy for adaptivity and personalization in serious games centered on metacognitive processes and leveraging multimodal and multichannel learning data. By integrating these elements, we can create a framework that enables games to adapt to learners' metacognitive needs dynamically, providing personalized support, feedback, and challenges tailored to their individual learning processes and strategies.

The paper is organized as follows: (1) It presents and operationally defines six specific metacognitive processes, illustrating how each is identified across several multimodal multichannel data channels; and (2) It provides theoretically-based and empirically-driven recommendations for adaptivity and personalization in serious games.

# 2  Metacognitive Processes During Game-Based Learning: Definitions, Multimodal Data, and Adaptivity and Personalization

In this section, we operationally define each of the six metacognitive processes that have already been identified using concurrent think-alouds protocols (e.g., [14–24]) when learning with various learning technologies (e.g., [6, 25]). As such, each sub-section is structured in the following manner: operational definition of the metacognitive process, followed by examples[1] of how each metacognitive process can be identified, measured, and inferred using think-alouds, log files, eye movements, facial expressions of emotions, screen recordings, and physiological data during learning with serious games and be used to adapt and personalize learning.

## 2.1  Judgments of Learning (JOL)

JOL refers to individuals' subjective assessments of their learning, memory performance, or emerging understanding of a concept, topic, or domain. During concurrent think-alouds, students verbalize assessments of their learning progress and understanding. For instance, a student might say, "I need to review this topic later," indicating a low JOL, or "I understand this concept well enough to move on," suggesting a high JOL. High and low does not refer to the accuracy or "ground truth" of how well a learner actually has progressed, but rather their perception of their progression. JOLs can also be identified from log files by tracking students' interactions with the game and their performance on learning tasks. For example, suppose a student revisits certain sections of the game multiple times or spends extra time on practice activities related to specific concepts. In that case, it may suggest higher confidence and positive JOL. Additionally, eye-tracking technology can capture patterns of visual attention associated with JOLs. For example, if a student exhibits focused and prolonged fixations on key information or checkpoints within the game, it may suggest higher confidence and positive JOL. In contrast, facial expression analysis can reveal emotions linked to JOL, such as when a smile or relaxed expression might indicate confidence in one's learning progress. Simultaneously, a frown or furrowed brow (i.e., Action Unit [AU] 4) might suggest uncertainty or doubt. JOLs can also be inferred from screen recordings by analyzing students' behavior and interactions with learning content. For example, a student demonstrating self-assurance and minimal hesitation while progressing through tasks or levels may suggest a positive JOL. Lastly, different physiological responses, such as pupil dilation or electrodermal activity, can reflect arousal levels associated with JOL. Students may exhibit larger pupil dilation or higher EDA levels when they are more engaged or confident in their learning progress, reflecting their JOL.

Once JOLs are identified, detected, and inferred, they can be used to adapt and personalize learning within serious games based on multimodal data. For example, *adaptive feedback* can be provided if a student expresses low JOL, and serious games can provide targeted feedback or additional practice opportunities to reinforce learning, such as offering explanations or scaffolding in areas where the student feels less confident. In addition, the serious game can also provide *personalized challenges* whereby students with high JOL may benefit from more advanced or challenging tasks to maintain cognitive and affective engagement and motivation by using adaptive algorithms that can adjust the difficulty level of game tasks based on students' self-assessed learning progress. By tracking students' JOLs over time, *progress monitoring* can help educators monitor their learning trajectories and identify areas where additional support may be needed (e.g., understanding complex diagrams). This data can inform instructional interventions and adjustments to optimize learning outcomes. In addition, helping students develop accurate and calibrated JOLs can enhance their metacognitive awareness and self-regulation skills by using *metacognitive training* using NPCs or other artificial agents. Simultaneously, educators can reinforce this type of training by providing additional guidance and scaffolding to help students better assess their learning progress and make informed decisions about their study strategies. Lastly, acknowledging and validating students' positive JOLs can boost their confidence and motivation to continue learning by using *motivational support*. Celebrating achievements and progress milestones can foster a positive learning environment and encourage students to persist in learning.

In summary, by leveraging multiple data sources to identify, measure, and infer JOLs during learning with serious games, educators can adapt and personalize learning experiences to better support students' self-regulation and metacognitive development, ultimately enhancing their learning outcomes.

## 2.2   Feeling of Knowing (FOK)

FOK refers to an individual's subjective sense of whether they can retrieve or recognize information stored in memory. During concurrent think-alouds, students verbalize their uncertainty or confidence in their knowledge. For instance, a student might say, "I'm not sure if I remember this correctly, but I've learned it before," indicating a low FOK. Learners can state "I feel confident about this answer," or "I remember reading this previously" or "I remember coming across this diagram while playing the game," suggesting a high FOK. FOKs can also be identified from log files by tracking students' interactions with the game content, such as accessing hints, skipping questions, repeating levels, or prematurely terminating interactions with NPCs describing instructional content. For example, suppose a student repeatedly accesses hints or help features. In that case, it may indicate a low FOK versus terminating an NPCs explanation of how a virus is transmitted to a human. Eye movements can also be used to capture patterns of visual attention associated with FOK, such as when increased fixations on certain game elements or prolonged gaze durations may indicate uncertainty or low confidence, respectively. Similarly, analysis of facial expressions can reveal emotions linked to FOK, such as furrowed brows or a tense jaw suggesting uncertainty, while a relaxed smile might indicate confidence. Screen recordings can also provide insight indicating FOKs when analyzing hesitation or confidence in gameplay. For instance, if a student hesitates before making choices or exhibits smooth and confident interactions, it may indicate a high or low FOK. Lastly, physiological responses such as heart rate variability (HRV) or electrodermal activity (EDA) can reflect arousal levels associated with FOK. Increased arousal may indicate uncertainty, while decreased arousal may suggest confidence.

Serious games can use several strategies based on multimodal data to adapt and personalize game-based learning to reflect learners' FOKs. For example, serious games can provide *adaptive feedback, targeted feedback, or additional resources to support memory retrieval by offering hints or explanations for challenging questions* if a student exhibits low FOK. The serious game can also provide *personalized challenges* to students with high FOK who may benefit from more advanced or challenging tasks to encourage deeper engagement and learning by using adaptive algorithms that can adjust the difficulty level of game tasks based on FOK assessments using various game elements such as NPCs. For students with low FOK, the game can provide *adaptive scaffolded* learning experiences by breaking down complex concepts into smaller, manageable chunks, or providing step-by-step guidance can help build confidence and improve FOK over time. In some cases, supporting *emotion regulation* by recognizing and addressing emotions associated with FOK can help students regulate their learning experiences, such as cognitive reappraisal to enhance FOK [26]. Another possibility is the use of *real-time interventions* based on physiological data indicating heightened arousal linked to low FOK, whereby the game can prompt students to take a break or engage in self-regulation strategies before continuing, as this proactive approach can prevent frustration and optimize learning outcomes.

In summary, by leveraging multiple data sources to identify, measure, and infer FOKs during learning with serious games, educators can adapt and personalize learning experiences to better support students' cognitive and emotional needs, ultimately enhancing their learning outcomes.

### 2.3 Content Evaluation (CE)

CE involves assessing the relevance, importance, and quality of learning materials or information relative to the student's goals, objectives, and plans. CEs can be identified from concurrent think-alouds when students verbalize their thoughts and evaluations of the learning content. For instance, they may express opinions on the clarity of explanations and the relevance of examples, text, or diagrams, such as "I do not think this diagram is relevant to my current learning goals." As such, the frequency, nature, and positive or negative verbalized CEs can be measured to assess the extent of content evaluation. CEs can also be identified from log files by tracking students' interactions with the game content. For example, if a student skips over text sections or spends more time on certain topics, it may suggest engagement in content evaluation. CEs can be measured by quantifying the frequency and duration of interactions with different game elements, such as reading explanations, accessing help features, exploring optional content, or searching for relevant content. Inferences about CEs could also be made based on increased time spent on specific topics, instructional content, or repeated accesses to help features. Eye-tracking technology can capture visual attention patterns associated with CEs. For example, suppose a student spends more time reading certain sections or fixates on specific elements such as an NPC explaining the next level of the game. In that case, it may indicate an evaluation of content relevance or importance. As such, CEs can be measured by quantifying fixation durations and gaze patterns on different game elements related to learning content. Increased fixations on key information or visual content scanning may infer active content evaluation. In addition, facial expressions can reveal emotions linked to CE. For example, positive expressions such as joy, surprise, nodding, or smiling may indicate agreement or satisfaction with the content. In contrast, negative expressions such as frowns or puzzled looks may suggest confusion. The occurrence and intensity of facial expressions associated with CEs can be measured, and inferences about positive or negative facial expressions may infer favorable or critical evaluations of the learning content. Screen recordings may help identify CEs by observing students' behaviors and interactions with the learning content. For instance, a CE may be identified if a student engages in active notetaking or pauses to reflect on presented information in a scientific notebook. CEs can be measured by quantifying observable cognitive strategy use such as note-taking, pausing or replaying content segments, and asking NPCs for explanations. Lastly, CEs can be calibrated by quantifying physiological responses linked to arousal levels during interactions with learning materials. Physiological responses such as changes in heart rate or skin conductance may indicate arousal levels associated with CE, as exemplified by heightened arousal when students encounter challenging or unfamiliar relevant or irrelevant instructional content.

Serious games can use several strategies based on multimodal data to adapt and personalize game-based learning constructed around learners' CEs. For example, based on detected levels of content evaluation, the serious game can provide tailored *feedback and support*. For instance, if a student shows low engagement in CE, the game can offer additional explanations or examples to enhance understanding. Also, serious games can modify and adjust the challenge level by using adaptive algorithms that can adjust the difficulty or complexity of learning tasks based on students' demonstrated levels of CE, thus ensuring that students are appropriately challenged and engaged. Similarly, the *allocation of resources* such as hints or supplementary instructional materials can be allocated based on students' CEs behaviors. For example, students who demonstrate high levels of CE may benefit from advanced resources or extension activities.

In summary, by leveraging multimodal data sources to identify, measure, and infer CE during learning with serious games, educators can adapt and personalize learning experiences to better support students' engagement, comprehension, and critical thinking skills.

### 2.4   Monitoring Progress Towards Goals (MPTG)

MPTG involves individuals tracking their advancement, learning, and performance based on their learning objectives within specific constraints such as limited time to play the game, a level, or a scenario. MPTG can be identified, measured, and inferred using various data sources during learning with serious games, along with adaptations to personalize learning. During think-alouds, students may verbalize their awareness of their progress towards their goals. Statements like "I'm halfway through the level," "I need to complete this task before moving on," or "I have 10 min left but still need to interact with the NPCs in order to understand how to better engage in scientific reasoning" can indicate monitoring of progress. The frequency and nature of verbalized statements related to goal progress can be measured to assess the extent of this type of metacognitive monitoring. Active verbal tracking of progress or task completion may infer effective goal monitoring. MPTGs can be identified from log files by tracking students' interactions with the game and their progress through levels or tasks. Progress logs and completion rates can indicate the monitoring of goals. As such, they can be measured by quantifying progress metrics such as level completion time, task completion rates, or points earned relative to set goals. Inferences made about MPTGs include consistent progress, completion of tasks promptly, or reaching milestones, which may infer effective monitoring of goals. Eye trackers can capture visual attention patterns associated with progress monitoring, including increased fixations on progress indicators, timers, skill-o-meters, or completion bars that may indicate monitoring of goals. MPTGs can be measured by quantifying fixation durations and gaze patterns on game elements related to progress tracking and inferences about their presence, including prolonged fixations on progress-related elements or frequent glances at timers, which may infer effective monitoring of goals. During gameplay, analyses of facial expressions can reveal emotions linked to progress monitoring. For example, positive expressions such as smiles or determination may indicate satisfaction with progress or efforts toward goals. The occurrence and intensity of facial expressions associated with progress monitoring can be measured, and inferred positive or determined facial expressions may suggest effective monitoring of goals and engagement in progress-tracking behaviors. In addition, screen recordings of MPTG can be identified by observing students' on-screen behaviors and interactions related to progress tracking, such as checking in-game progress menus, reviewing objectives, or referencing completion criteria. MPTGs can be measured by quantifying observable behaviors such as menu navigation, objective review, or interactions with progress indicators. Active engagement with progress-related features or behaviors, such as frequent checking of objectives, may infer effective goal monitoring. Lastly, physiological responses such as changes in heart rate or skin conductance may indicate arousal levels associated with progress monitoring, such as heightened arousal, which may occur when students actively track their progress toward goals. While MPTGs can be measured by quantifying physiological responses linked to arousal levels during interactions with progress-related game elements, they may be inferred from effective goal monitoring and engagement in goal-oriented activities.

Adaptation and personalization of MPTGs within serious games can be accomplished using several methods, including providing *feedback and guidance* based on identified levels of progress monitoring; the serious game can provide tailored feedback and guidance. For instance, if students demonstrate low awareness of their progress, the game can offer reminders or updates to keep them on track. In addition, *goal adjustment* of learning objectives or task difficulty based on students' demonstrated progress monitoring abilities ensures that goals are appropriately challenging and aligned with students' monitoring skills. Given the temporal nature of MPTGs, recognizing and reinforcing students' progress monitoring efforts through *motivational support* by providing positive feedback or rewards can enhance motivation (e.g., increase interest or task value) and engagement in goal-oriented behaviors. Lastly, providing explicit instruction and scaffolding on effective progress monitoring strategies using *metacognitive training* can help students develop and refine their metacognitive skills, improving their ability to track and manage their learning goals effectively.

In summary, by identifying, measuring, and inferring MPTG by leveraging multiple data sources during learning with serious games, educators can adapt and personalize learning experiences to better support students' learning, reasoning, problem-solving, and performance.

## 2.5   Monitoring the Use of Strategies (MUS)

MUS involves individuals actively overseeing, monitoring, and adjusting their application of cognitive strategies during learning tasks. Here are examples of how MUS can be identified, measured, and inferred using various multimodal data sources during learning with serious games, along with potential adaptations to personalize learning.

For example, during think-alouds, students may verbalize their thoughts and decision-making processes related to strategy use. Think-alouds may discuss their reasoning behind selecting certain approaches or reflect on the effectiveness of their strategies. More specifically, "I now know that making accurate inferences about the complex biology diagrams are allowing me to move levels in the game," or "I have tried several learning strategies, including talking to the scientists and collecting evidence, but I am still struggling to determine which of these cognitive strategies is helping me diagnose the biological case in this game." The frequency and nature of verbalized statements regarding strategy selection and adjustment can be measured to assess the extent of MUS, and active verbalization of strategic decisions or reflections on strategy effectiveness may infer effective monitoring and adaptation of cognitive strategies. On the other hand, log files can be used to identify MUS by tracking students' interactions with the game content and their utilization of strategic features or tools. Examples include accessing hints or tutorials, using problem-solving approaches, or employing memory aids. MUS can be measured by quantifying the frequency and duration of interactions with strategic elements, such as accessing help features or using specific game mechanics. Increased utilization of strategic features or repeated application of problem-solving methods may infer effective monitoring and adjustment of cognitive strategies. Eye movements can capture visual attention patterns associated with strategy use with increased fixations on strategic elements within the game interface, such as hints or instructional prompts, which may indicate monitoring the utilization of cognitive strategies. While MUS can be measured by quantifying fixation durations and gaze patterns on game elements related to strategic decision-making and execution, it may be prolonged fixations on strategic cues or visual scanning of relevant information that allows for inferences about effective monitoring and adjustment of cognitive strategies. Similarly, facial expression analysis can reveal emotions linked to strategy use, such as positive expressions (e.g., smiles or expressions of satisfaction such as joy), which may indicate successful strategy implementation. In contrast, expressions of frustration or confusion may suggest ineffective strategy application. The occurrence and intensity of facial expressions associated with strategy use can be measured. Positive or negative facial expressions may infer effective or ineffective monitoring and adjustment of cognitive strategies, respectively. MUS can be identified from screen recordings by observing students' behaviors and interactions related to strategy execution, such as active engagement with problem-solving tasks, utilization of in-game tools, or adaptation of strategies in response to challenges. MUS can be measured by quantifying observable behaviors such as problem-solving approaches, tool usage, or adjustments made during gameplay, and active and adaptive engagement with strategic elements or behaviors may infer effective monitoring and adjustment of cognitive strategies. Lastly, physiological responses such as changes in arousal levels or cognitive load may indicate engagement in strategy use. For example, increased arousal or cognitive effort may occur during active problem-solving or strategic decision-making. MUS can be measured by quantifying physiological responses linked to arousal levels or cognitive load during interactions with strategic game elements. Higher arousal levels or cognitive load during strategic activities may infer effective monitoring and adjustment of cognitive strategies.

Adaptation and personalization of MUS with serious games can be accomplished using several techniques, including providing *feedback and guidance* based on identified levels of strategy use. For instance, if a student demonstrates ineffective strategy application, the game can offer alternative approaches or additional support to enhance understanding. Also, *adaptive interventions* can provide explicit instruction and practice opportunities for developing and refining effective cognitive strategies based on students' demonstrated needs and preferences. In addition, *strategic support* by providing access to adaptive tools or resources that align with students' preferred learning strategies can facilitate their engagement and success in learning tasks. Lastly, *progress monitoring* by continuously tracking and analyzing students' strategy use can inform ongoing adaptations and refinements to learning experiences, ensuring that instructional strategies are optimized for individual needs and preferences.

In summary, by identifying, measuring, and inferring MUS during learning with serious games, educators can reinforce the conditional knowledge and skills needed to adequately monitor and assess the selection, use, and transfer of various learning strategies and adapt and personalize learning experiences to support better students' learning, reasoning, problem solving, and performance.

### 2.6 Self-questioning (SQ)

SQ involves individuals generating and asking themselves questions to monitor their understanding and guide their learning process. Here are examples of how SQ can be identified, measured, and inferred using various data sources during learning with serious games, along with potential adaptations to personalize learning. During think-alouds, students may verbalize their self-generated questions or internal dialogue as they navigate the serious game. They may ask questions like, "OK, I've spent the last 15 min learning about viruses and bacteria; let me try to generate some situations to see if I comprehend the differences?" The serious game can measure the frequency and nature of verbalized self-questions or reflective statements to assess the extent of SQ and inferences of active verbalization of self-generated questions or reflective dialogue may infer engagement in metacognitive regulation through SQ. SQs can be identified from log files by tracking textual inputs or interactions where students pose questions to themselves or engage in reflective dialogue, such as logging instances where students type or select questions within the game interface. SQ can be measured by quantifying the frequency and complexity of self-generated questions or reflective statements recorded in the log files, with increased instances of SQ or reflective statements that may infer active engagement in metacognitive monitoring and regulation. Eye-trackers can capture patterns of visual attention associated with SQ. For example, increased fixations on textual prompts, game elements related to problem-solving, or gameplay pauses may indicate self-questioning moments. SQ can be measured by quantifying fixation durations and gaze patterns on game elements related to self-generated questions or reflective thinking. Prolonged fixations on textual prompts or visual scanning of relevant information may infer engagement in self-questioning activities. Facial expression analysis can reveal emotions linked to SQ, where positive expressions such as concentration or determination may indicate active engagement in reflective thinking, while expressions of frustration may suggest difficulty generating effective questions. The occurrence and intensity of facial expressions associated with self-questioning can be measured with positive facial expressions or expressions indicative of cognitive effort that may infer engagement in self-questioning processes. SQ can be identified from screen recordings by observing students' behaviors and interactions related to reflective thinking. For example, pausing during gameplay to consider options, accessing help features for clarification, or verbally articulating questions. SQ can be measured by quantifying observable behaviors such as pauses in gameplay, interactions with game elements related to SQ, verbal expressions of questions with active engagement in reflective behaviors, or verbal articulation of questions that may infer engagement in SQ activities. Lastly, physiological responses such as changes in heart rate or skin conductance may indicate arousal levels associated with SQ. Heightened arousal may occur during moments of cognitive effort or reflective thinking. SQs can be measured by quantifying physiological responses linked to arousal levels during interactions with self-questioning activities, with increased arousal levels during reflective thinking or problem-solving tasks that may infer engagement in self-questioning processes.

Adaptation and personalization of SQs with serious games can be accomplished using several approaches, including providing tailored *feedback and guidance* based on identified levels of SQ. For instance, if a student demonstrates limited engagement in self-questioning, the game can offer prompts or scaffolding to encourage more reflective thinking. Additionally, *questioning strategies* can provide explicit instruction and practice opportunities for developing effective SQ strategies based on students' demonstrated needs and preferences. *Metacognitive training* can also provide targeted support, and modeling of effective SQ techniques that can help students develop and refine their metacognitive skills, enhancing their ability to monitor and regulate their learning effectively. Lastly, allocating resources such as hints or additional information based on students' self-questioning behaviors can support their cognitive processes and enhance their learning outcomes.

In summary, SQs are generally easier to detect and infer given their verbal nature and, in some cases, either written behaviors or selection from a pull-down menu, depending on the serious game's features and interface elements. Regardless of how they are expressed, SQs are critical in determining what, when, how, and why to adapt and personalize resources during game-based learning.

## 3   Recommendations for Adaptivity and Personalization for Serious Games

Based on the empirical literature on metacognition, self-regulated learning (SRL), multimodal multichannel data, and serious games cited above, we offer the following key recommendations for enabling adaptivity and personalization in serious games:

*Leverage multimodal data sources*: Integrate diverse data sources such as eye-tracking, facial expressions, physiological signals, and user interactions to gain a comprehensive understanding of learners' cognitive, affective, metacognitive, and motivational states [9, 11, 27–29].

*Foster metacognitive awareness and SRL skills*: Design serious games that actively promote and support the development of metacognitive skills and SRL strategies, such as goal setting, planning, metacognitive awareness, monitoring and regulation, reflection, and strategy use [9, 30, 31].

*Implement intelligent pedagogical agents*: Incorporate intelligent virtual agents or tutors that can leverage multimodal data to provide personalized feedback, scaffolding, and support for enhancing learners' metacognitive awareness and SRL knowledge and skills using accurate and sophisticated student models capable of "understanding" the evolution of learners' metacognitive development, knowledge, and skills [6, 11, 29, 32, 33].

*Adapt game mechanics and content*: Use multimodal data and learners' metacognitive and SRL processes to dynamically adapt game mechanics, difficulty levels, and learning content in real-time, creating personalized and engaging learning experiences [9, 34].

*Enable real-time adaptations*: Develop computational models and algorithms that can process and interpret multimodal data in real-time, especially concurrent verbalizations using NLP, enabling dynamic and personalized adaptations based on learners' metacognitive states [35, 36].

*Facilitate transfer of SRL strategies*: Incorporate mechanisms to transfer SRL strategies and metacognitive skills acquired within serious games to other learning contexts and real-world scenarios [13, 30, 31].

*Foster human-AI co-evolution*: Design serious games that facilitate a co-evolutionary relationship between human learners and AI, where the system adapts to learners' needs, and learners develop stronger SRL and metacognitive skills [37–39].

*Conduct longitudinal evaluations*: Implement longitudinal studies and large-scale evaluations in authentic educational settings to assess the long-term impacts of multimodal data and metacognitive support on learners' academic achievement, engagement, and overall metacognitive development [30, 31].

*Promote inclusive and equitable approaches*: Integrate culturally responsive and equitable approaches into using multimodal data and metacognitive support within serious games to ensure inclusive and accessible learning experiences for diverse populations [34].

By incorporating these recommendations, serious games can leverage multimodal multichannel data and metacognitive processes to create adaptive, personalized, and effective learning experiences for students that foster self-regulated learning, metacognitive development, and overall academic success. Lastly, we emphasize several key issues: (1) the recommendations included in this paper are theoretically-based [e.g., 5, 39] and based on an extensive review of the empirical literature [e.g., 1, 2, 6] that cannot be fully cited due to space constraints, and (2) future research needs to empirically test these recommendations and we expect further refinements to the recommendations, based on such testing with different GBLEs, learners, tasks, domains, and educational contexts.

## Notes

1. In this paper, we do not discuss several key issues related to metacognitive processes, including (i) valence (either positive or negative) associated with each metacognitive

process when illustrating think-alouds (e.g., JOL$^+$ and JOL$^-$) due to the space limitations (see [6, 39] for details); (ii) frequency, duration, sequencing and recurrence of each process about each other and other self-regulatory cognitive, affective, and motivational processes during gameplay; and, (iii) how to handle adaptivity and personalization over time during gameplay based in (i) and (ii) and several other factors, variables, and serious games' affordances.

**Acknowledgments.** This work was partially supported by funding from the National Science Foundation (DRL #1916417, BCS #2128684, IIS #2302778), National Institutes of Health (1R25GM150142-01), and CELLA Project funded by the Jacobs Foundation.

**Disclosure of Interests** The authors have no competing interests to declare relevant to this article's content.

# References

1. Plass, J., Mayer, R., Homer, B.: Handbook of Game-Based Learning. MIT Press (2019)
2. Plass, J.L., Pawar, S.: Toward a taxonomy of adaptivity for learning. J. Res. Technol. Educ. **52**(3), 275–300 (2020). https://doi.org/10.1080/15391523.2020.1719943
3. Mayer, R.E.: Computer games in education. Annu. Rev. Psychol. **70**, 531–549 (2019). https://doi.org/10.1146/annurev-psych-010418-102744
4. Nelson, T.O., Narens, L.: Metamemory: a theoretical framework and new findings. Psychol. Learn. Motiv. **26**, 125–173 (1990). https://doi.org/10.1016/S0079-7421(08)60053-5
5. Winne, P.H.: Cognition and metacognition within self-regulated learning. In: Schunk, D.H., Greene, J.A. (eds.) Handbook of Self-Regulation of Learning and Performance, 2nd edn., pp. 36–48. Routledge, New York (2018). https://doi.org/10.4324/9781315697048-3
6. Azevedo, R., Wiedbusch, M.: Theories of metacognition and pedagogy applied to AIED systems. In: du Boulay, B., Mitrovic, A., Yacef, K. (eds.) Handbook of Artificial Intelligence in Education, pp. 45–67. Edward Elgar Publishing, Cheltenham, UK (2023). https://doi.org/10.4337/9781800375413.00013
7. Dever, D.A., Azevedo, R.: Scaffolding self-regulated learning in game-based learning environments based on complex systems theory. In: Rodrigo, M.M., Matsuda, N., Cristea, A., Dimitrova, V. (eds.) Artificial Intelligence in Education 2022. LNCS, vol. 13356, pp. 41–46. Springer, Cham (2022). https://doi.org/10.1007/978-3-031-11647-6_7
8. Tarricone, P.: The Taxonomy of Metacognition, 1st edn. Psychology Press, London (2011). https://doi.org/10.4324/9780203830529
9. Dever, D., et al.: Identifying the effects of scaffolding on learners' temporal deployment of self-regulated learning operations during game-based learning using multimodal data. Front. Psychol. **14** (2023). https://doi.org/10.3389/fpsyg.2023.1280566
10. Taub, M., Sawyer, R., Smith, A., Rowe, J., Azevedo, R., Lester, J.: The agency effect: the impact of student agency on learning, emotions, and problem-solving behaviors in a game-based learning environment. Comput. Educ. **147** (2020). https://doi.org/10.1016/j.compedu.2019.103781
11. Azevedo, R., Taub, M., Mudrick, N.V.: Using multi-channel trace data to infer and foster self-regulated learning between humans and advanced learning technologies. In: Schunk, D., Greene, J.A. (eds.) Handbook of Self-Regulation of Learning and Performance, pp. 254–270. Routledge, New York (2018)

12. Azevedo, R., Mudrick, N.V., Taub, M., Bradbury, A.: Self-regulation in computer-assisted learning systems. In: Dunlosky, J., Rawson, K. (eds.) Handbook of Cognition and Education, pp. 587–618. Cambridge University Press, Cambridge, MA (2019)
13. Azevedo, R.: Reflections on the field of metacognition: issues, challenges, and opportunities. Metacogn. Learn. **15**, 91–98 (2020). https://doi.org/10.1007/s11409-020-09231-x
14. Azevedo, R., Cromley, J.G.: Does training on self-regulated learning facilitate students' learning with hypermedia? J. Educ. Psychol. **96**, 523–535 (2004). https://doi.org/10.1037/0022-0663.96.3.523
15. Azevedo, R., et al.: Lessons learned and future directions of MetaTutor: leveraging multi-channel data to scaffold self-regulated learning with an intelligent tutoring system. Front. Psychol. **13** (2022). https://doi.org/10.3389/fpsyg.2022.813632
16. Duffy, M.C., Azevedo, R.: Motivation matters: interactions between achievement goals and agent scaffolding for self-regulated learning within an intelligent tutoring system. Comput. Hum. Behav. **52**, 338–348 (2015). https://doi.org/10.1016/j.chb.2015.05.041
17. Engelmann, P., Bannert, M.: Fostering students' emotion regulation during learning: design and effects of a computer-based video training. Int. J. Emot. Educ. **11**(2), 3–16 (2019)
18. Fan, Y., et al.: Towards a fuller picture: triangulation and integration of the measurement of self-regulated learning based on trace and think aloud data. J. Comput. Assist. Learn. 1–22 (2023). https://doi.org/10.1111/jcal.12801
19. Greene, J.A., Azevedo, R.: A macro-level analysis of SRL processes and their relations to the acquisition of a sophisticated mental model of a complex system. Contemp. Educ. Psychol. **34**, 18–29 (2009). https://doi.org/10.1016/j.cedpsych.2008.05.006
20. Greene, J., Bolick, C., Jackson, W.P., Caprino, A.M., Oswald, C., McVea, M.: Domain-specificity of self-regulated learning processing in science and history. Contemp. Educ. Psychol. **42**, 111–128 (2015). https://doi.org/10.1016/j.cedpsych.2015.06.001
21. Lajoie, S.P., Zheng, J., Li, S., Jarrell, A., Gube, M.: Examining the interplay of affect and self-regulation in the context of clinical reasoning. Learn. Instr. **72** (2021). https://doi.org/10.1016/j.learninstruc.2019.101219
22. Li, S., Lajoie, S.P.: Cognitive engagement in self-regulated learning: an integrative model. Eur. J. Psychol. Educ. **37**, 833–852 (2022). https://doi.org/10.1007/s10212-021-00565-x
23. Molenaar, I., de Mooij, S., Azevedo, R., Bannertd, M., Järveläe, S., Gaševicf, D.: Measuring self-regulated learning and the role of AI: five years of research using multimodal multichannel data. Comput. Hum. Behav. **139** (2022). https://doi.org/10.1016/j.chb.2022.107540
24. Sonnenberg, C., Bannert, M.: Discovering the effects of metacognitive prompts on the sequential structure of SRL-processes using process mining techniques. J. Learn. Anal. **2**, 72–100 (2015). https://doi.org/10.18608/jla.2015.21.5
25. Azevedo, R., Dever, D.: Metacognition in multimedia learning. In: Mayer, R.E., Fiorella, L. (eds.) The Cambridge Handbook of Multimedia Learning, 3rd edn., pp. 132–142. Cambridge University Press (2022). https://doi.org/10.1017/9781108894333.013
26. Gross, J.J.: Conceptual foundations of emotion regulation. In: Gross, J.J., Ford, B.Q. (eds.) Handbook of Emotion Regulation, 3rd edn., pp. 3–12. The Guilford Press (2024)
27. Giannakos, M., Spikol, D., Di Mitri, D., Sharma, K., Ochoa, X., Hammad, R. (eds.): The Multimodal Learning Analytics Handbook. Springer (2023)
28. Wiedbusch, M., Dever, D., Li, S., Amon, M.J., Lajoie, S.P., Azevedo, R.: Measuring multidimensional facets of SRL engagement with multimodal data. In: Ifanthaler, D., Azevedo, R., Gibson, Kovanonic, V. (eds.) Unobtrusive Observations of Learning in Digital Environments. Advances in Analytics for Learning and Teaching (AALT), pp. 141–173. Springer, Cham (2023)
29. Wiedbusch, M., Lester, J., Azevedo, R.: A multi-level growth modeling approach to measuring learner attention with metacognitive pedagogical agents. Metacogn. Learn. **18**, 465–494 (2023). https://doi.org/10.1007/s11409-023-09336-z

30. Muldner, K., Wixon, M., Rai, D., Burleson, W., Woolf, B., Arroyo, I.: Exploring the impact of a learning dashboard on student affect. In: Conati, C., Heffernan, N., Mitrovic, A., Verdejo, M. (eds.) Artificial Intelligence in Education. LNAI, vol. 9112, pp. 207–317. Springer, Cham (2015). https://doi.org/10.1007/978-3-319-19773-9_31
31. Roll, I., Russel, D.M., Gašević, D.: Learning at scale. Int. J. Artif. Intell. Educ. **28**, 471–477 (2018). https://doi.org/10.1007/s40593-018-0170-7
32. Lester, J., Bansal, M., Biswas, G., Hmelo-Silver, C., Roschelle, J., Rowe, J.: The AI institute for engaged learning. In: Goel, A., Ou, C. (eds.) AI Mag. **45**, 69–76 (2024). https://doi.org/10.1002/aaai.12161
33. Mavrikis, M., Cukurova, M., Di Mitri, D., Schneider, J., Drachsler, H.: A short history, emerging challenges and co-operation structures for artificial intelligence in education. Bild. Erzieh. **74**, 249–263 (2021). https://doi.org/10.13109/buer.2021.74.3.249
34. Aleven, V., McLaughlin, E.A., Glenn, R.A., Koedinger, K.R.: Instruction based on adaptive learning technologies. In: Mayer, R.E., Alexander, P. (eds.) Handbook of Research on Learning and Instruction. Routledge (2016)
35. D'Mello, S.K., Graesser, A.C.: Feeling, thinking, and computing with affect-aware learning technologies. In: Calvo, R.A., D'Mello, S.K., Gratch, J., Kappas, A. (eds.) The Oxford Handbook of Affective Computing, pp. 419–434. Oxford University Press (2015). https://doi.org/10.1093/oxfordhb/9780199942237.013.032
36. Worsley, M., Blikstein, P.: A multimodal analysis of making. Int. J. Artif. Intell. Educ. **28**, 385–419 (2018). https://doi.org/10.1007/s40593-017-0160-1
37. Molenaar, I., Wise, A.F.: Temporal aspects of learning analytics - grounding analyses in concepts of time. In: Lang, C., Siemens, G., Wise, A.F., Gašević, D., Merceron, A. (eds.) Handbook of Learning Analytics, 2nd edn., pp. 66–76. Society for Learning Analytics Research (2022)
38. Järvelä, S., Nguyen, A., Hadwin, A.: Human and artificial intelligence collaboration for socially shared regulation in learning. Br. J. Educ. Technol. **54**, 1057–1076 (2023). https://doi.org/10.1111/bjet.13325
39. Azevedo, R., Dever, D.: Metacognition in multimedia learning. In: Mayer, R.E., Fiorella, L. (eds.) Cambridge Handbook of Multimedia, 3rd edn., pp. 132–141. Cambridge University Press, Cambridge, MA (2022)

# An Architecture for Repeatable, Large-Scale Educational Game Data Analysis: Building on Open Game Data

Luke Swanson[✉] and David J. Gagnon

University of Wisconsin-Madison, Madison, WI 53706, USA
lwswanson2@wisc.edu, djgagon@wisc.edu

**Abstract.** Given the incredible popularity of video games in contexts from entertainment to education, and the capacity of internet-connected games to record fine-grained telemetry data, there exists an unprecedented opportunity to investigate gameplay behaviors, outcomes, and their relationships to learning processes. However, with these opportunities come the need for technical infrastructures to manage the collection and analysis of massive amounts of game event data. In this work, we build upon existing literature to develop an architectural design for such infrastructure. We address issues of play data collection across many games; regular, repeatable extraction of gameplay features from raw data; and access to data for secondary analyses. In addition, we describe an implementation of this infrastructure and provide real-world examples of the implementation's usage in prior large-scale analysis work.

**Keywords:** Software architectures · Interactive learning environments · Computer games · Open source software

## 1 Introduction

Unfortunately, but not unexpectedly, collection and analysis of game data requires a significant amount of infrastructure and a diversity of expertise. A complete games-based research project must cover game design and development, distribution, data collection, data storage, data processing, visualization, analysis, and communication of research results. Thus, there are many potential barriers for new researchers or small teams to participate in game data research.

These barriers are exacerbated by the often closed nature of educational research. Closed science refers to a process of scientific inquiry where research questions, data, findings and results are kept confidential until publication, which still may limit access to subscribers or purchasers. This approach may lead to delayed dissemination, inaccuracy, lack of transparency and reproducibility, and inequality [11,17]. Open science attempts to confront these limitations, offering enhanced accessibility and equity [30], improved reproducibility and transparency [16], and better facilitation of collaboration [15]. The barriers to entering

© The Author(s), under exclusive license to Springer Nature Switzerland AG 2025
J. L. Plass and X. Ochoa (Eds.): JCSG 2024, LNCS 15259, pp. 41–55, 2025.
https://doi.org/10.1007/978-3-031-74138-8_4

games research may be lowered by reducing the breadth of expertise required for each project. If game studios can simply be game studios, and researchers can simply be researchers, with shared infrastructure ensuring each group has the resources they need, it becomes easier for newcomers to participate in their area of expertise.

To this end, Open Game Data has been developed as a technical and social infrastructure for game data logging and analysis, which is used and developed by a growing number of educational video game researchers [4]. It is designed to support the general needs for data collection and processing across all kinds of video game, as well as the unique forms of learning data created by game environments. This infrastructure provides modular components for data collection, processing, access and analysis that support open science practices. Most importantly, it enables an open exchange of data between the studios that develop learning games, and the researchers that study them. As of the time of writing, the system processes 5–10M events daily from 17 games that use the system for analysis and distribution of public data sets.

However, there are issues that face such an initiative, and the simple pipeline described in past work on the subject. As the collection of games using shared infrastructure grows, there is a greater need for standards to ensure compatibility across games and over time. A need also arises to support diverse data analysis tools and techniques. Across the entire pipeline, an increasing scale in games, gameplay sessions, and analyses increases the number of points of failure in the analysis pipeline and thus creates a need for adequate monitoring of system performance. In this work, we expand upon the general pipeline described in the prior work, presenting an architecture for logging and processing of telemetry data across many games, and an implementation thereof.

## 2   Background

The commercial video game industry has a long tradition of leveraging data and using analytics approaches. A collection of several dozen industry and academic case studies were published in a volume edited by Seif El-Nasr et al. [1] demonstrating the value of using player data for topics such as ensuring game quality, maximizing success, understanding player behavior and enhancing the quality of the player experience. In educational contexts, the descriptive capacity of event log data affords many theoretical and methodological approaches. In games, learner performances can be conceptualized as both descriptive and procedural, and game researchers have adopted theories such as embodiment [3], socio-cultural learning [25], and situated learning [7]. Similarly, game studies using log data adopt a wide range of quantitative and qualitative methods such as discourse analysis [26], epistemic network analysis [22], player clustering [24,28], educational data mining [20], replay coding [19], learning engineering [2], and evidence centered design [12].

While many of these data mining and analytics projects leveraged their own proprietary systems and infrastructures, there are several examples of commercially available game analytics systems that are available for any researcher or developer today. One of the most popular systems is Google Analytics (GA). GA was initially developed for website analytics, specifically to understand user demographics, user behaviour and user acquisition. Game Analytics is a game-specific platform that is also widely used, and provides similar functionality to GA. Both platforms provide client libraries to work with popular programming languages and game engines as well as web-based visualization and reporting tools. However, both platforms focus on increasing monetization rather than understanding deeper features of the players' thinking or learning.

Several education-focused projects have also been developed in recent years that enable large-scale analytics and data mining. The ADAGE (Assessment Data Aggregator for Game Environments) game research platform was designed to collect and analyze data from digital game environments. Its purpose was to facilitate the study of player interactions, learning outcomes, and behavior within educational games, providing valuable insights for game designers and educators [27]. Unfortunately, the platform was never widely adopted beyond its developers, and is no longer in operation.

Successful tools for large-scale learning analytics include DataShop, a repository for educational data initiated by Carnegie Mellon University [13], and MORF (Massive Open Online Courses Research Framework), a platform for analyzing and sharing data from Massive Open Online Courses (MOOCs) [6]. DataShop has yielded numerous datasets, analytical tools, and insights into learning processes, significantly contributing to the fields of educational data mining and learning analytics. MORF provides a unique structure based in the use of Docker containers, which are self-contained virtual machine images, designed to ensure complete reproducibility while allowing the use of any software or language.

## 3 Architecture

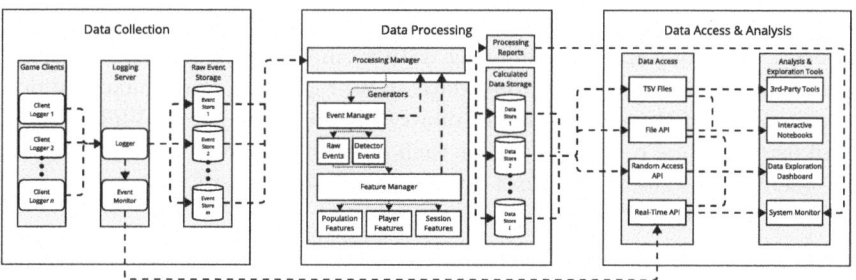

**Fig. 1.** Full architecture diagram, including all three blocks of the architectural design. Dashed lines indicate the primary flow of data from module to module. Dotted lines specifically indicate the flow of event data through the various generator modules.

With the projects discussed in 2 as a guide, we propose a modular infrastructure capable of serving large-scale data collection and analysis needs across many game projects. Our proposed system utilizes a layered architecture, allowing each layer can use different technical solutions at increasing scales of use, requiring only that the data exchanged between layers have a standardized format. There are three major layers, corresponding to primary phases of game data analysis. These are represented as top-level blocks within Fig. 1:

- Data Collection
- Data Processing
- Data Access and Analysis.

We describe each part of the architecture, and the relationships between them, in the following sections.

### 3.1    Data Collection

Data analysis necessarily begins with the collection of the data to be analyzed. In the case of game telemetry data, any number of players may interact with the game at any time. To enable consistent deployment of logging across many games and large numbers of players, we adopt a model using a single endpoint to route data from multiple game clients to one or more storage locations. This single entry point allows for the separation of event logging logic from the details of event storage. That is, changes in storage location or technology can be made without incurring maintenance costs to modify and re-deploy games that have not otherwise been changed. Only the entry point must be modified to redirect incoming data to a new storage endpoint.

**Game Clients** On the game/client side, a reusable logging package is imported by each game, rather than using ad-hoc implementations per-game. The package must adopt a standard event schema, such as the one proposed by Gagnon and Swanson [5]. Using a standard allows for the logging package to be ported to different game platforms without fear of diverging formats. Further, use of a single standard complements the single-point-of-entry system described in the "Logging Server" section; allowing differing data formats would necessarily increase the processing time needed to route data to storage, and may make the downstream portions of the data pipeline more difficult to manage. While the flexibility of using ad-hoc data formats for each game may offer some gains in initial development time, these are offset by the increased cost of long-term maintenance and support.

**Logging Server** As discussed above, our architecture uses a single server endpoint to collect all event logs sent by game clients. This creates a single entry point into the system for all clients across games and players, enabling monitoring of all data sources regardless of scale. The trade-off here is an emphasis on lightweight processing of incoming data, to avoid server overload. Thus, this server endpoint should act as a simple "router," identifying the source of an event, mapping it to a storage location, and generating an appropriate insertion request to the storage system. Optionally, this component of the architecture may be augmented with a load-balancing system, which reroutes incoming events to different logging server instances.

*Real-Time Event Stream Monitoring* One additional feature for the logging server is a mechanism for real-time monitoring of incoming events. The logging "router" mentioned above forwards each event to a monitor server, in addition to requesting insertion into the storage system. This monitor can then filter and/or process event data based on any active system monitor clients at the data access level (discussed in 3.3). While any server technology can potentially be used to implement such a monitor, we recommend a sockets-based server application, allowing for multiple concurrent connections to a single, persistent server instance.

**Raw Event Storage** We distinguish storage of raw event data from later, calculated events and data features. Data collected in this part of the architecture is treated as a series of objective, immutable events that occurred in the game. The logging server translates event data as directly as possible from the request sent by a logging client to the format of whatever storage technology is used. Once an event has been logged, it should only (at most) be moved to another location; event content is never modified or edited. Instead, post-processing may create and use "annotated" copies of these game-generated events (discussed in 3.2).

## 3.2  Data Processing

Given large-scale datasets of fine-grained game events have been collected and recorded, additional processing of the data may be performed at any time and for purposes of any analysis. By cleanly separating logging from processing and inference, we minimize the risk of changes to the game being required as research needs grow and change. However, there are difficulties to address with processing event data at scale; our primary concern is feature engineering. Feature engineering is often performed in an ad-hoc manner, tightly coupled to specifics of a given game's event logs, with little attention paid to repeatability of an analysis. This approach can lead to problems when attempting to replicate results over time or across similar games. Further, poorly-designed feature engineering processes can lead to prohibitive processing times on large-scale datasets. To address this, our architecture includes structures for a consistent, repeatable feature engineering system.

**Generators** This segment of the data processing architecture is responsible for the generation of post-hoc data, based on the game telemetry captured during data collection. The output of this processing infrastructure includes the following:

- Copies from the raw event data
- Newly-generated events, called "calculated" or "detector" events

- Session-level features
- Player-level features
- Population-level features.

Our data generation process uses small code modules, rather than monolithic implementations of ad-hoc, project-specific calculations. This directly enables support for reusable and reproducible analyses. Because of the choice to enforce a single event data schema in 3.1, these modules can be executed on any event data, even across games. While a small cost may be paid in initial implementation time, generator modules may be easily swapped in and out of any given data processing task, and may be applied to new data as it is collected.

*Event Manager and Event Detectors* The event manager is responsible for copying the raw input data for a distributable output dataset, and for passing the raw data to what we term "event detectors." An event detector is a small code module that accepts events as input and generates new events as output. For example, an "idle detector" might generate `begin_idle_behavior` and `end_idle_behavior` events based on long gaps in "meaningful" player interactions with the game, for some definition of "meaningful" chosen by a researcher. This definition could be based on an arbitrary threshold for gaps between any two game events, or on labels generated by a machine learning model, trained on human-coded observations of players.

In this way, our architecture supports post-hoc generation of game-referenced events with arbitrary complexity, from simple hand-written if-else logic to full machine learning models. This eliminates the need for logging clients to report anything other than objective, in-game actions and system responses.

*Feature Manager and Feature Extractors* The second component of data generation is feature extraction. The process here is similar to that described for event detectors. In this case, however, the individual modules are called "feature extractors," and each extractor generates a value summarizing the set of events it has observed, rather than new events. We do not place any specific constraints on the type of value generated by an extractor; the value could be boolean, numeric, a string, or even a JSON object, though numeric values tend to be most common.

The feature manager creates and tracks instances of each extractor module, and routes their outputs to the rest of the processing pipeline. This may include directing outputs to what we term "higher-order" feature extractors, which accept other features' values as inputs, in addition to event data. Extractors may operate at the level of a population, a player, or a gameplay session. Population-level features generate values based on all events in the given processing task, while session-level extractors use all events for a given session ID. In cases where a game provides user identifiers (discussed in ??), the architecture produces player-level extractors using all events for each given player ID. This creates further flexibility in the feature engineering process.

**Processing Management** Above the generators segment of our architecture sits a *processing manager*. This manager is responsible for organizing the common, high-level process of moving data through the pipeline, separating that process from the details of any given game's data or feature set. It maps inputs, in the form of raw event data, to the lower-level managers, described in the "Generators" section above. It also maps outputs into the calculated data storage. Finally, the processing manager is responsible for recording reports on the success or failure of processing tasks.

**"Calculated Data" Storage** Here, we distinguish storage of all data calculated post-hoc from raw event data logged from game clients. Unlike game telemetry data, in which events objectively occur once and are recorded for analysis, the inferences made about data are subject to change. This may be due to bugfixes during feature engineering, or changes in how an inference is made. By separating "calculated" data in our architecture, we allow such data to be governed by an invalidation scheme, which in turn allows re-calculation of data to be scheduled. The details of such a scheme are left to implementation, depending on researchers' needs for specific projects or games.

### 3.3   Data Access and Analysis

There are two primary concerns for access to data generated by the system. Namely, we must consider endpoints for the system, which deliver data in a specific format, as well as the analysis tools that will connect with those endpoints. While there are many technologies and formats that could theoretically be used, we identify several broad categories of tools for data exploration and analysis, not as a comprehensive summary but as a means to describe and account for common use cases. We then discuss four main endpoint types that cover a significant portion of use cases.

Due to the great variety of analysis tools and technologies for data access, this is the least prescriptive segment of our proposed architecture. Rather than present a specific set of relationships between components, we provide major categories of tools and show how different endpoints naturally map to different analysis tools, and how existing analysis pipelines can be improved by integrating our proposed architecture.

#### Analysis and Exploration Tools

– *Interactive Notebooks*
  Notebook environments organize executable code into individual "chunks" that can be independently edited and executed in any order. Jupyter Notebooks are a very popular implementation, supporting Python and other statistics-oriented programming languages in one environment [18]. Several other programming languages, including R and Matlab, provide their own notebook environments.
– *Data Dashboards*
  Dashboards are typically data visualization tools that display pre-set visual summaries of a selected dataset. Google's Looker Studio is a popular dashboard creation tool that integrates with Google-Cloud-based data stores.

Another commonly-used tool for dashboard design is Tableau, which provides general-purpose data visualization features.

- *System Monitors*
This class of tool addresses the case of analyzing an analysis system itself. Many popular web service providers offer monitoring tools for their users, such as Amazon's CloudWatch or Microsoft's Azure Monitor. In the context of our proposed architecture, system monitors are generally assumed to be dedicated tools built as part of the architecture implementation.

- *Third-Party Tools*
This last category serves as a catch-all for tools that do not fit cleanly into one of the identified categories. This may include custom-built scripts, offline data visualization and exploration tools, or other data mining and modeling tools. Examples here include Weka, a tool implementing many machine learning algorithms, and RapidMiner, a data mining and analytics tool.

**Data Access Endpoints** As noted, the variety of data tools and analysis needs make it impossible to definitively assign methods of data access to analysis tools. However, it is possible to identify cases where affordances and needs match well.

*TSV Files* A simple, flat, tabular file format is perhaps the most general and widely-supported means of data access possible. The comma-delimited version of such files (CSV) is supported by every major data processing software. Most support tab-delimited (TSV) files as well; we chose the TSV format because event and feature data structures contain some internal JSON-formatted elements. A tab delimiter ensures file parsers do not confuse the comma-separated JSON elements with the rest of the tabular data structure. The general-purpose nature and wide support for this file format format makes it a good match for general 3rd-party tools, as well as interactive notebook environments.

*File API* While TSV files may be easily shared and used locally, effective data sharing may be supported via an API for accessing datasets on a file server. Such an API could be used by a central repository website for dataset distribution. Accessing files from a server, rather than locally from the analyst's machine, may also be a good match for a notebook environment. Notebooks are often hosted in cloud-based environments, such as Google Colab or GitHub Codespaces. A simple API request that can obtain a specific dataset from any environment could maximize interoperability between cloud-based and locally-run notebooks. Certain types of dashboard are also well-served by a file API, specifically dashboards designed for summarizing a full dataset.

*Random Access API* A "random access API" allows users to request an arbitrary time range or set of IDs for data retrieval, rather than a fixed dataset as offered by a "File API." This is desirable for analyses that require data from a highly specific cohort or sub-population of players, such as a group from a specific gameplay event. This endpoint is a good match for dashboards designed for exploratory data analysis. Fixed datasets may be too limiting for such tools; instead, the ability to re-parameterize the choice of data on-the-fly is desirable.

*Real-Time API* This type of API provides access to data for users with active play sessions. The emphasis here is on low latency, allowing for evaluation of game data as it is generated. While this is the least general option we have listed, the implementation of such an API can unlock research that would not be feasible with any of the other data access methods described so far, such as studies of how teachers can use gameplay data to better facilitate classroom play sessions [29]. Real-time APIs are the best option for a system monitor application, allowing issues with the system to be detected as soon as they occur. They are also appropriate for certain data dashboard use-cases, particularly for dashboards meant for live usage concurrent with an event, such as a play-test.

# 4 Implementation

Having laid out a comprehensive description of a general architecture for repeatable, flexible, scalable processing of video game data, we now present an implementation of this architecture through a series of publicly-available, permissively-licensed software packages. We discuss the design decisions made to generate a specific implementation of the general architecture, and suggest alternate approaches or potential future improvements. Collectively, this discussion should serve to illustrate how the proposed architecture can be realized in a practical research environment.

## 4.1 Data Collection

The first block of the architecture is implemented in client packages `opengamedata-unity` and `opengamedata-js-log`, and logging package `opengamedata-logger`. The client packages implement the event schema proposed by Gagnon and Swanson [4] for Unity- and JavaScript-based games, and use simple configurations to direct their output to an instance of `opengamedata-logger`. Data is sent via standard HTTP POST requests. Request header parameters are used for any schema elements that are constant within a given gameplay session (e.g. identifier and versioning items), while data that varies per-event (game state, timestamps, etc.) is merged into a binary-encoded request body package. This allows for packaging of co-occurring events into a single request.

Conversely, `opengamedata-logger` decomposes the request body into multiple events, copying the request parameters into the corresponding elements of each event. We use a relational database system for raw event storage, and the packaging of events within requests is extended to allow multiple events to be packaged into a single database insertion. This minor implementation feature helps to manage potential server load issues by reducing the overall number of HTTP requests needed to log a given set of events.

Finally, we provide system monitoring via a web-sockets-based API, in the `opengamedata-monitor` package. This API serves a simple client web page for monitoring incoming data. Each event received by a `opengamedata-logger` instance is forwarded to an HTTP endpoint for the API, where the `opengamedata-monitor` instance parses and routes the events to its web clients based on per-game "rooms." Thus, incoming data for any game can be checked by researchers or system developers who need to ensure a particular game's logging is not failing.

## 4.2    Data Processing

A full implementation of the data processing step is contained in `opengamedata-core`. This implementation uses a request format that allows for users to specify either a date range or set of player/session IDs for processing, as well as a list of event detectors and feature extractors to be included in the output of the processing request. This allows users a great degree of control over the amount of data and complexity of processing. If a researcher is working with a particularly large-scale dataset, they can easily turn off extraction of any features they do not intend to use in their analysis, avoiding potentially long processing times.

**Event Manager and Detectors** In our implementation, an event detector defines an *event filter, update rule, trigger*, and *generator rule*. The event filter defines which game events are inspected by the detector. The manager passes any events that match the filter, one-by-one, to the update rule, which updates the detector's internal state. Following each update, the trigger checks for a condition in the detector state, and if the condition is met, "triggers" the generator rule, which produces a new event.

In the simplest case, a generator's update rule might contain hard-coded checks for patterns of event sequences. More complex detectors could use machine learning models trained to predict a human-coded label from sequences of event data. Thus, our implementation supports the broad set of use cases described by our proposed architecture.

**Feature Manager and Extractors** Like event detectors, our implementation of feature extractors use an *event filter, update rule*, and *generator rule*, which converts the current state into the single summary value. Unlike a detector, there is no need for a "trigger;" the feature manager simply invokes the generator rule when all events have been passed through the update rule.

In order to reduce the need for redundant calculations, our implementation also supports "sub-features." These are additional feature values generated by a single code module. Thus, a feature extractor module for an "average score" feature, which divides a total score by number of completed levels, could generate a "total score" sub-feature, avoiding redundant calculation by a standalone "total score" module.

Finally, our implementation supports a "second-order feature" class, as initial work towards the general "higher-order features" described in 3.2. These are feature extractors that define an additional *feature filter* and *feature update rule*, which function similarly to the event filter and update rule, but filter and update based on feature data.

As with the event detectors, our implementation supports arbitrarily complex calculation of feature values from event (and feature) data. Thus, our framework for feature engineering maintains flexibility and power, while ensuring analyses are reusable with future datasets that share the common event schema.

### 4.3    Data Access and Analysis

We have discussed the variety of data access and analysis approaches possible. Our implementation of the third block of the architecture provides packages for several data access services.

- The `opengamedata-core` package produces TSV output files by default. We automate the production of per-game, per-month datasets, including raw event, raw + calculated event, session feature, player feature, and population feature files. Thus, workflows for general 3rd-party tools and notebook environments are well-supported.
- The `opengamedata-api-files` package is a RESTful API for access to datasets stored on a file server. `OGDUtils` provides functionality for accessing data from the `opengamedata-api-files` API directly in any Python environment, such as a Jupyter Notebook.
- The `opengamedata-api-data` package implements a RESTful API for generalized requests for feature data. Users can request, per game, a custom set of features at the session, player, or population level, based on a set of IDs or a range of dates. The API server retrieves and extracts all feature data for the custom dataset using the `opengamedata-core` package, returning the data in a JSON-formatted web response.
- A general-purpose real-time API for data access remains a work-in-progress; the `opengamedata-monitor` package implements a sockets-based system monitoring tool as proof-of-concept for such an API. Future work on the API will allow a persistent instance of the monitor to build metrics and player models for select users as new events are generated live in a play-testing or classroom environment.

## 5    Case Studies

In order to illustrate the potential uses of Open Game Data we provide a few case studies in two categories, namely research using large datasets, and automated analysis designed for operation at large scales.

One of the promises of learning engineering is the ability to conduct large scale design experiments. This process was recently demonstrated in a four-condition experiment on the game Jo Wilder and the Capitol Case. This project utilized the existing game, making only low cost modifications to explore the effect of different game scripts on player engagement, enjoyment, and relatability with the game's protagonist with and nearly 12,000 game sessions [2,23].

In another recent experiment, researchers focused on understanding players strategies and approaches to a city-building game called *Lakeland*. In this study, data from 32,000 game sessions was analyzed using an unsupervised clustering method and visualized as radar plots to describe different types of player interactions [28].

Most recently, researchers utilized large datasets from 10 different games on Open Game Data to empirically validate their development of an interoperable ontology of game-based assessment metrics [8].

Another area that may benefit from our system is the automation of qualitative analysis. Utilizing a method previously developed for automated labeling of data from a cognitive tutor [21], researchers used game data from the game *Wake: Tales from the Aqualab* to train an automated detector for students who are experiencing "struggle" [14]. This was done by displaying segments of gameplay in text, effectively creating a textual narration of the players' actions and progression events. Researchers reviewed and labeled thousands of these game play text replays, providing a training set to a machine learning classifier. Once trained, the system can be deployed at arbitrarily large scale, and assess play sessions in real time.

## 6    Discussion and Future Work

Open Game Data is promising open science project in service of the educational game research community. The platform provides open source client-side code for integration into any game project, and a scalable architecture for data ingestion, real-time relay, and storage. A modular processing architecture supports the generation of post-hoc event identification, as well as feature engineering. Features can operate at different levels of aggregation, from a single play session up to a whole population. Additionally, these features can inform one another, so a session feature can be contextualized within a population, even with very large datasets. Finally, the data access components make data available via flat .tsv files as well as web APIs to integrate with extant and future tools.

While the project has shown promise to integrate with a number of games and support various forms of research, it has limitations across each component of the technical architecture and even more in the social infrastructure that will require significant additional investments and collaboration to resolve.

One of the fundamental challenges in games research is the significant cost of developing games that create the contexts, potential actions and data reporting required to conduct a specific experiment. One future direction for this project is to develop socio-legal-technological systems to broker the connections between researchers and the game studios that either own the game's licence or work within the game's licensing agreements. This will provide opportunities for existing games to be modified to support new research.

Similarly, additional infrastructure to support the automation of game modifications, or "remote configuration," is technically feasible and should be explored. If such infrastructure were developed, participating game studios could design their games to allow application of customizations at runtime without any modification to the game's compiled code. Establishing this capacity would allow for automation of experiments, where game owners have only to approve experiments before they are deployed.

Further work on data standards is also an area for development. Some preliminary work in this direction has been proposed by Gagnon et al. [5], but further work is needed to expand upon their proposed "ontologies" of event and feature collections. At each stage of coordination and standard development, new efficiencies are be gained for processes later in the data pipeline. The challenge will be developing these standards so they respect the flexibility of game design and do not add additional burden to implementation.

There are also many opportunities for reusable replay and annotation tools. Prior work (e.g. Rowe et al. [19]) have demonstrated the value of replay and labeling capability for learning research and game design. Work is underway to develop web-based tools to replay VR game sessions at high frame rates so that qualitative research can be conducted during or after a play session occurs. Given sufficient resources, a generalized client library could be produced that would create parity between events that are sent and events that would be required for replay and annotation to train detectors and other forms of models.

Another future technical direction focuses on the real time analysis of incoming game data. A first application of this capacity could be the creation of generalized tools for supporting classroom instruction with educational games, scaling the exploratory work of existing dashboard-based projects [29] and mixed reality interfaces for teachers [9]. The second application is for real-time augmentation of qualitative research efforts. This method, currently being explored by Hutt et al. [10] uses machine learning detectors to direct the attention of classroom researchers to previously-defined moments of interest so they can conduct observations and interviews at particular moments and synchronize those observations with game data. This is a promising new direction for human-machine pairing in educational research.

**Acknowledgment.** The authors would like to acknowledge Erik Harpstead for his recommendations and advice throughout the development of this project.

**Compliance with Ethical Standards**

**Disclosure of Interests.** The authors have no competing interests to declare that are relevant to the content of this article.

# References

1. El-Nasr, M., Drachen, A., Canossa, A.: Game Analytics: Maximizing the Value of Player Data. Springer (2013)
2. Gagnon, D.J., et al.: Exploring players' experience of humor and snark in a grade 3–6 history practices game. In: GLS 13.0 Conference Proceedings. Irving, CA (2022)
3. Gagnon, D.J., Ponto, K., Verbeke, M., Nathan, M., Kopp, K., Tredinnick, R.: Waddle: developing empathy for adélie penguins by direct embodiment in virtual reality. In: Joint International Conference on Serious Games, pp. 227–233. Springer (2023)

4. Gagnon, D.J., Swanson, L.: Open game data: a technical infrastructure for open science with educational games. In: Haahr, M., Rojas-Salazar, A., Göbel, S. (eds.) Serious Games, pp. 3–19. Springer Nature Switzerland, Cham (2023)

5. Gagnon, D.J., Swanson, L., Harpstead, E.: Defining an open data pipeline and standards for educational data mining and learning analytics with video game data. In: IEEE Conference on Games, in press (2024)

6. Gardner, J., Brooks, C., Andres, J.M., Baker, R.S.: MORF: a framework for predictive modeling and replication at scale with privacy-restricted MOOC data. In: 2018 IEEE International Conference on Big Data (Big Data), pp. 3235–3244 (2018). https://doi.org/10.1109/BigData.2018.8621874

7. Gee, J.P.: Learning and games. In: The Ecology of Games: Connecting Youth, Games, and Learning, pp. 21–40. The John D. and Catherine T. MacArthur Foundation Series on Digital Media and Learning (2007). http://www.mitpressjournals.org/doi/abs/10.1162/dmal.9780262693646.021

8. Gomez, M.J., Ruipérez-Valiente, J.A., Clemente, F.J.G.: Developing and validating interoperable ontology-driven game-based assessments. Expert Syst. Appl. **248**, 123370 (2024). https://doi.org/10.1016/j.eswa.2024.123370

9. Holstein, K., McLaren, B.M., Aleven, V.: Student learning benefits of a mixed-reality teacher awareness tool in AI-enhanced classrooms. In: Lecture Notes in Computer Science, vol. 10947, pp. 154–168. Springer International Publishing, Cham (2018). https://doi.org/10.1007/978-3-319-93843-1_12

10. Hutt, S., et al.: Quick red fox: an app supporting a new paradigm in qualitative research on AIED for STEM. In: Chapman & Hall/CRC Artificial Intelligence and Robotics Series, 1st edn. CRC Press, Boca Raton, FL (2023)

11. Ioannidis, J.P.A.: Why most published research findings are false. PLoS Med. **2**(8), e124 (2005). https://doi.org/10.1371/journal.pmed.0020124

12. Kim, Y.J., Almond, R.G., Shute, V.J.: Applying evidence-centered design for the development of game-based assessments in physics playground. Int. J. Test. **16**(2), 142–163 (2016). https://doi.org/10.1080/15305058.2015.1108322

13. Koedinger, K.R., Baker, R., Cunningham, K., Skogsholm, A., Leber, B., Stamper, J.: A Data Repository for the EDM Community: The PSLC DataShop, p. 21. CRC Press, Boca Raton, FL (2010)

14. Liu, X., et al.: Struggling to detect struggle in students playing a science exploration game. In: Companion Proceedings of the Annual Symposium on Computer-Human Interaction in Play, pp. 83–88. ACM, Stratford, ON, Canada (2023). https://doi.org/10.1145/3573382.3616080

15. Nielsen, M.: Reinventing discovery - the new era of networked. Science (2011). https://doi.org/10.1515/9781400839452

16. Nosek, B.A., et al.: Promoting an open research culture. Science **348**(6242), 1422–1425 (2015)

17. Nosek, B.A., Spies, J.R., Motyl, M.: Scientific utopia: II. Restructuring incentives and practices to promote truth over publishability. Perspect. Psychol. Sci. **7**(6), 615–631 (2012). https://doi.org/10.1177/1745691612459058

18. Pimentel, J.F., Murta, L., Braganholo, V., Freire, J.: A large-scale study about quality and reproducibility of Jupyter notebooks. In: 2019 IEEE/ACM 16th International Conference on Mining Software Repositories (MSR), pp. 507–517. IEEE (2019)

19. Rowe, E., et al.: Advancing research in game-based learning assessment: tools and methods for measuring implicit learning, pp. 99–123. IGI Global (2020). https://doi.org/10.4018/978-1-7998-1173-2.ch006

20. Ruiperez-Valient, J.A., Kim, Y.J., Baker, R.S., Martinez, P.A., Lin, G.C.: The affordances of multivariate Elo-based learner modeling in game-based assessment. IEEE Trans. Learn. Technol. 1–14 (2022). https://doi.org/10.1109/TLT.2022.3203912

21. Baker, R.S., de Carvalho, A.: Labeling student behavior faster and more precisely with text replays. In: Educational Data Mining, Montréal, Québec, Canada (2008)

22. Scianna, J., Gagnon, D., Knowles, B.: Counting the game: visualizing changes in play by incorporating game events. In: Ruis, A., Lee, S. (eds.) Advances in Quantitative Ethnography. ICQE 2021. Communications in Computer and Information Science, vol. 1312. Springer, Cham, Malibou, CA (2021). https://doi.org/10.1007/978-3-030-67788-6_15

23. Slater, S., Baker, R.S., Gagnon, D.J.: Changing students' perceptions of a history exploration game using different scripts. In: Proceedings of the 30th International Conference on Computers in Education. Kuala Lumpur, Malaysia (2022)

24. Slater, S., Bowers, A., Kai, S., Shute, V.: A typology of players in the game physics playground. In: Proceedings of the 2017 DiGRA International Conference, p. 12 (2017)

25. Steinkuehler, C., Duncan, S.: Scientific habits of mind in virtual worlds, pp 1–14 (2008)

26. Steinkuehler, C.A.: Massively multiplayer online video gaming as participation in a discourse. Mind Cult. Act. **13**(1), 38–52 (2006). https://doi.org/10.1207/s15327884mca1301_4

27. Stenerson, M.E., Salmon, A., Berland, M., Squire, K.: ADAGE: an open API for data collection in educational games. In: Proceedings of the First ACM SIGCHI Annual Symposium on Computer-Human Interaction in Play, pp. 437–438. ACM, Toronto, Ontario, Canada (2014). https://doi.org/10.1145/2658537.2661325

28. Swanson, L., et al.: Leveraging cluster analysis to understand educational game player styles and support design. In: GLS 13.0 Conference Proceedings (2022)

29. Swanson, L., Gagnon, D.J., Scianna, J.: A pilot study on teacher-facing real-time classroom game dashboards. East Lansing, MI (2022)

30. Willinsky, J.: The Access Principle: The Case for Open Access to Research and Scholarship. Digital Libraries and Electronic Publishing, MIT Press, Cambridge, MA (2006)

# Identifying When and Why Students Choose to Quit Jobs in a Science Exploration Game

Xiner Liu[1]($\boxtimes$) (iD), Stefan Slater[1] (iD), Luke Swanson[2] (iD), Shari J. Metcalf[3] (iD), David J. Gagnon[2] (iD), and Ryan S. Baker[1] (iD)

[1] University of Pennsylvania, Philadelphia, PA 19102, USA
xiner@upenn.edu
[2] University of Wisconsin, Madison, WI 53711, USA
[3] Harvard University, Cambridge, MA 02138, USA

**Abstract.** Students in open-ended educational games have a number of different pathways that they can select to work productively through a learning activity. Educators and system designers may want to know which of these pathways are most effective for engagement, learning, or other desirable outcomes. In this paper, we investigate which prior jobs and factors are associated with higher rates of student quitting behavior in an educational science exploration game. We use a series of Chi squared analyses to identify the jobs with the highest rates of quitting overall, and we calculate logistic regressions within specific jobs to determine the potential factors that lead to students quitting those jobs. Our analysis revealed that for 23 of the 40 jobs examined, having experience in at least one previous job significantly decreased the chances of students quitting the subsequent job, and that completing specific prior jobs reduces quit rates on specific later jobs. In our discussion, we describe the challenges associated with modeling quitting behavior, and how these analyses could be used to better optimize students' pathways through the game environment. Specially, guiding students through specific sequences of preliminary jobs before tackling more challenging jobs can improve their engagement and reduce dropout rates, thus optimizing their learning pathways.

**Keywords:** Educational games · Learning analytics · Player quitting

## 1 Introduction

Educational games represent useful and sophisticated tools for understanding how students learn in a wide range of educational contexts. Games have been used to improve or develop creativity [26], collaboration and problem-solving [29], communication [11], and interpersonal and decision-making skills [23]. They also have been used to assess spatial reasoning [15], computational thinking [27], and implicit science learning [28]. The complex nature of learners' potential interactions in educational games enables rich data collection and analysis of a complex range of behaviors and cognitive processes.

J. L. Plass and X. Ochoa (Eds.): JCSG 2024, LNCS 15259, pp. 56–69, 2025.
https://doi.org/10.1007/978-3-031-74138-8_5

The design of these game environments requires careful attention to detail for educational designers, to maintain an appropriate level of challenge for students that optimizes both learning and engagement [18]. Difficulty can be adjusted in several ways – either by modifications to the game's structure [25], or by runtime adaptations based on current player behavior and affect [8]. Providing learners with appropriate degrees of challenge is particularly complex within open-ended games, where students can move freely between levels, seeking out or avoiding tasks based on their own goals and motivations within the game. When the design is truly open, what can be done to ensure learners have been cognitively prepared for a particular challenge and have a reasonable chance of success?

In this paper we build models that predict student quitting of individual game challenges, towards enabling future versions of the game to make real-time estimates of how prepared a student is for different challenges within their open exploration. Specifically, we explore cases where a student quits their current game activity and switches to a different activity within the game, such as a different level [13, 31].

We explore these questions in the context of the science exploration game *Wake: Tales from the Aqualab*, where students can self-select the order in which they move through the game's challenges, referred to within the game as "jobs", and quit the current task to move to a different task. Our analyses explore the differential rates of quitting that students exhibit depending on the trajectory that student has taken through the game's jobs prior to that point, with the intuition that some activities may be too difficult if the student has not mastered the relevant skills in previous jobs. We construct both Chi-Squared analyses to identify potential problem jobs with high rates of job quitting, as well as logistic regressions to better understand the factors that contribute to a student's decision to quit specific jobs. The overall goal for this work is to identify productive and unproductive pathways that students can take within the game to minimize the disengaging experience of quitting a job. By identifying productive pathways, we can revise game design to nudge students towards these specific pathways during play.

## 2 Related Work

Educational games are increasingly recognized for their ability to engage students and improve learning outcomes through interactive experiences [3, 6, 20]. Research has shown their effectiveness in supporting learning across various contexts. For instance, [12] highlight the educational potential of games with rich storylines, which not only engage but also enhance learning by fostering curiosity within compelling contexts. Likewise, [14, 16] emphasize the importance of narratives and individualized feedback mechanisms in maintaining student interest and meeting individual learning needs. Further, studies by [1] demonstrate how strategic video gameplay can develop problem-solving skills, while [5] explores the motivational benefits of well-designed gamified elements, leaderboards, within business higher education.

Understanding why students quit games requires an in-depth analysis of the interplay between psychology, education, and game design. Reference [24] examine the impact of social support in games and propose that enhanced in-game support can reduce player frustration and quit rates. Reference [22] developed a model to differentiate productive and unproductive persistence in Mastering Math that enables real-time interventions to assist students at an early stage. Reference [30] explore how factors such as affective state and in-game progression influence learning outcomes in the game Physics Playground and found that frustration and engaged concentration indirectly affect learning outcomes through first affecting in-game performance.

Considerable research has also attempted to predict player quitting and struggles within games. Reference [7] modeled player retention in *Madden NFL 11* by using regression analysis on encoded gameplay patterns to predict the number of games played and identify key factors that influence player retention. Similarly, [32] used regression analysis to predict player churn in an MMO called *World of Warcraft* using features derived from demographic data, survey responses, and in-game activity data. Reference [2] utilized a hidden Markov model to find a plausible mechanism of gameplay that could predict player performance and quitting in the game *Axon*. Reference [13] used machine learning to develop models to identify student quitting in the game Physics Playground. Reference [9] evaluated the accuracy of common machine learning algorithms in predicting quitting within two science learning games: *Crystal Cave* and *Wave Combinator*. Additionally, [31] used decision trees to analyze whether players' activity would decrease from one month to the next based on their behavior in the first month in two popular commercial online games: *I Am Playr* and *Lyroke*.

In our previous efforts to understand players in *Wake* [17], we constructed a model of points in the game where expert coders identified that students were struggling, developing machine learning models using features derived from the game's interaction log data to predict hand-coded observations of struggle behaviors. However, the performance of these models was modest, achieving an area under the curve (AUC) of only 0.64. This level of performance is sufficient for describing trends of struggle in aggregate, across many students, but not sufficient for predictions of an individual student's experiences in the game. Instead, in this study, we investigate the factors that lead students to quit game jobs in *Wake* in order to understand if completing specific preliminary jobs can improve students' overall experience and reduce quit rates within later target jobs. The broader goal of this analysis is to distill actionable insights that can improve learner experiences in *Wake* and inform the process of designing more engaging and effective educational gaming experiences in general.

## 3  Method

*Wake: Tales from the Aqualab* is a science exploration game, developed for grade 6–9 science classrooms and for use on Chromebook and web browser-based devices. In *Wake*, students take on the role of a young marine biologist, using observations, experimentation, modeling, and scientific argumentation to learn more about four biomes and their respective ecological systems in the game (See Fig. 1). The game is implicitly structured into 54 jobs, each comprised of a set of specific tasks. We refer to these segments as jobs rather than levels, because each job represents a distinct assignment or mission, similar to project-based activities, rather than consecutive challenges or stages. In the game, students have freedom to select any available job, though some jobs are gated behind the completion of previous jobs, or that require ship and tool upgrades purchased in the shop. The primary reason for this design is to facilitate analysis of the effectiveness of different pathways on learning outcomes. This design decision is also supported by previous research findings [4]; allowing learners to take on a virtual role within a story, deciding what paths to follow within a narrative, supports engagement and immersion in meaningful learning experiences.

Once a job has been started, if a player decides to leave that job for another before successful completion, this is considered a "switch" event for the original job. If the player accepts a job but never completes it, this is treated as quitting the job in our analysis. In other words, a student may switch from the job several times while still completing it (i.e., not quitting).

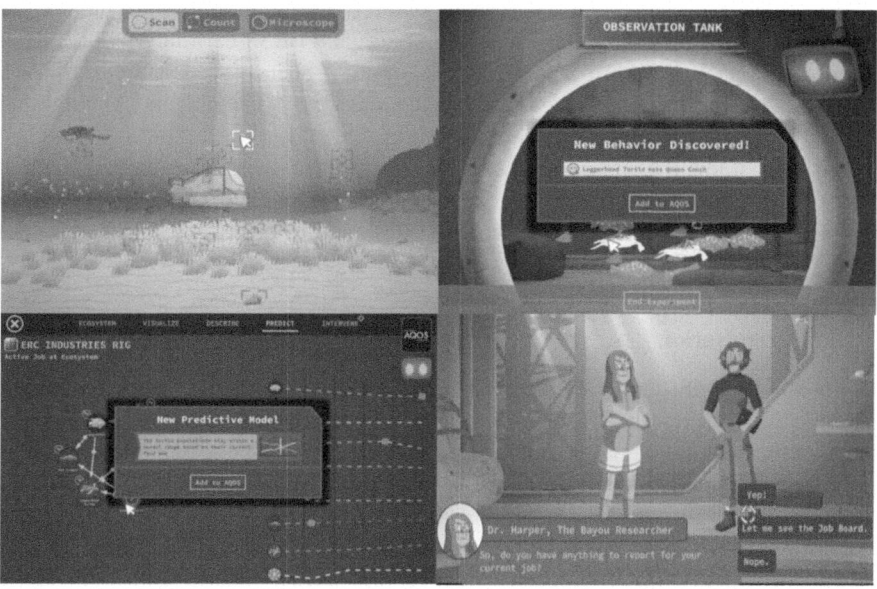

**Fig. 1.** Gameplay screenshot for Wake: collecting facts or evidence in one site (top left), conducting experiments in the observation tank (top right), modeling in the lab (bottom left), and completing an argument with the researcher to finish tasks (bottom right).

### 3.1  Data Collection

*Wake* uses the Open Game Data infrastructure for recording player interactions [10]. The opengamedata-unity package is integrated into the game, which allows it to connect with a cloud-based server that tracks and logs significant player activities during sessions. Each player is assigned a unique login, which tracks their patterns of play across multiple sessions, spanning multiple days. These recorded activities are collectively referred to as telemetry data. From a structural perspective, *Wake* transmits telemetry data using an event-based schema, influenced by the model suggested by [21]. It categorizes recorded events into three broad types: Player Actions, System Events, and Progression Events. Player Actions range from general navigation, such as moving to a designated research area, to more specific interactions like inputting species data in a modeling tool or choosing specific evidence during discussions. System Events capture moments like feedback on player choices or the appearance of characters guiding the player in new scenarios. Progression Events track milestones like the discovery of new facts or species, or the completion of tasks and jobs. *Wake* documents 33 different player actions, 12 system events, and 6 progression events, all of which are immediately uploaded to the Open Game Data server as they happen. Each event is detailed with metadata that includes the timing, sequence, player identification, and specifics about the event and the game's current state. These elements together provide a chronological account of all crucial interactions within a session, articulated in the game's specific language.

*Wake: Tales from the Aqualab* was made publicly available online in January 2023 via BrainPOP, a private educational media company, and PBS Learning Media, a public media distributor. As of April 30, 2024, the game has been played 128,488 times by 56,516 unique players. In the data we analyzed, there were 4,124 players. Among them, 79% completed the first three tutorial jobs, and 6.75% completed the final job. Game analytics suggest that the game is played primarily in formal learning contexts, with the majority of sessions taking place between 8 am and 3 pm local time on weekdays and excluding holidays. Jobs within the game are designed to take 5–15 min to complete individually.

## 3.2 Data Preparation

We segmented the chronologically organized log data into distinct job IDs, each representing a player's interaction history with a unique job until they decide to switch. Subsequently, the data is aggregated into a single row per job ID, which provides a summary of their engagement patterns and behaviors within that job. From this aggregation, several relevant features are derived to potentially capture nuances in student experience and performance for future analysis.

We begin by determining whether a student completed a job successfully or not, based on the presence or absence of a "complete_job" event in the log data (the alternative to successfully completing a job is quitting that job, unless the player quits the game entirely during that job and never resumes play).

Aggregated data also includes the number of jobs completed. In *Wake*, jobs typically center around a key question, like "What is causing the sea urchins to multiply so rapidly?" In each job, players must discover new insights about the ecosystem, formulate a hypothesis, and supply evidence to back it up. Players achieve these discoveries through direct observations at research locations, conducting experiments, and creating multiple scientific models. As players progress, the jobs introduce increasingly complex information and interdependencies within ecosystems. Consequently, the cumulative number of completed jobs can serve as a potential indicator of students' overall progress, engagement in the game, and possibly their mastery of fundamental concepts in the game.

The number of tasks completed is also calculated. In *Wake*, each job is further subdivided into smaller "tasks" to scaffold players. While certain tasks within jobs follow a specific sequence (e.g., scanning an organism before conducting an experiment with it), others can be completed in any order (e.g., scanning historical population data for a site and counting all current populations). Keeping track of the number of tasks completed provides a more fine-grained understanding of player progression. This information is particularly useful for tracking the progress of players who frequently switch jobs. Focusing solely on the total number of jobs completed might obscure noteworthy progress made by the student, as some players may have completed many tasks even if they haven't finished many jobs.

Acknowledging that students may not complete jobs in a single session, we also keep track of the number of usage sessions each student has engaged in so far. This feature allows us to distinguish between students who finish jobs in one session and those who require multiple sessions. These distinctions offer insights into students' task management strategies and their overall persistence in tackling complex challenges within the game environment.

We have also developed 4 supplementary features that cover the difficulty aspects of jobs that the students have previously completed and the extent of their visits to research stations within the game. The first three features quantify the average complexity of completed jobs. Based on a review of science learning trajectories for this grade band, we assigned each job a difficulty rating, ranging from 1 to 4, across three dimensions: argumentation, experimentation, and modeling [19]. Higher ratings denote greater difficulty. Given that students completing a series of easy tasks differ from those tackling more challenging ones, these features serve as indicators of students' proficiency within the game. The average argumentation difficulty, for instance, serves as a window into students' completion of complex reasoning tasks, while the average experimentation difficulty illuminates their proficiency in exploration and scientific inquiry skills. Similarly, the average modeling difficulty provides an indication of the student's ability to construct and comprehend complex systems across varied contexts. We choose to use average difficulty levels rather than maximum difficulty levels to reflect a student's performance across jobs; a student could complete a challenging job involving one skill while generally struggling with other skills. The fourth feature, the number of biomes visited, indicates a player's experience of different settings within the game, which may potentially influence their decision to quit jobs as well.

Following our feature development, we used two separate analytical approaches to determine how student quitting was associated with students' decisions to quit a job: a Chi-Square analysis to understand the impact of previous job completion, and a logistic regression analysis to investigate the role played by the other factors discussed in this section. In the next sections, we present our methods and results for each of these analyses.

### 3.3 Understanding the Impact of Previous Job Completion: Chi-Square Test

In order to investigate whether the previous jobs that a student completed are associated with their decision of whether or not to quit their target job without completing it, we conducted a Chi-square test of independence. This analysis allows for the assessment of the statistical significance of associations between categorical variables, which, in our analysis, consist of what jobs players completed before the target job they are on. In our analysis, we excluded (1) the first three tutorial jobs, which cannot be quit and are always played in the same order and (2) jobs with less than 30 successful job completion events (insufficient sample size), as well as jobs with fewer than 30 instances of quitting (insufficient evidence for quitting being a problem), which resulted in 40 total jobs in our dataset.

For each of the 40 jobs, we arranged the data into multiple contingency tables, with each table corresponding to a different previous job that students might have accepted (whether completed or not) before taking on the target job. Each table documents the frequency with which students either completed or did not complete (i.e., quit) the target job, in relation to their prior experiences—specifically, whether they have completed this previous job before attempting the target job.

A Chi-square is valid for these tests because these datasets satisfy all prerequisite conditions; there are no independence issues since each data point represents a distinct student, and there is a minimum expected count of 5 in at least 80% of the cells.

In our analysis, we also employed the Benjamini-Hochberg procedure (B&H), a statistical technique aimed at controlling the false discovery rate (FDR) when performing multiple comparisons. Because we conducted around 20–50 Chi-square tests for each target job analyzed, depending on the number of previous jobs students have played before their target job, our chances of any one of these tests being a false positive is relatively high. The B&H method allows us to manage this rate of false positives, by determining an adjusted significance threshold for our p-values. This technique orders the p-values in ascending sequence and compares them against adjusted critical values based on the total number of comparisons and the number of significant results thus far (i.e., adjusted alpha value). These adjusted values ensure that the expected ratio of erroneous rejections among all rejected null hypotheses does not exceed the FDR threshold of 0.05. Specifically, each p-value is evaluated against a progressively adjusted threshold: the lowest p value compared to 0.05 divided by the number of tests, the second lowest p value compared to 0.05 divided by the number of tests multiplied by 2, the third lowest p value compared to 0.05 divided by the number of tests multiplied by 3 and so on, down to 0.05 for the last p-value. A p-value that is below or equal to its respective critical value signifies statistical significance at the set FDR level, while a p-value above this threshold but less than twice the threshold suggests marginal significance at that level. The adjusted significance levels are calculated based on the number of previous jobs associated with each target job. For instance, if there are 20 previous jobs that students have played before a target job, then the adjustment calculated is based on 20 tests.

For each target job analyzed, we focus only on the top three previous jobs, selected based on their respective Chi-square statistics. These jobs are then included within subsequent logistic regression analysis. We only include the top three jobs in order to focus on the most impactful features in later efforts to nudge players to select better job sequences.

### 3.4   Chi-Square Results

Our Chi-square analysis revealed that for 23 out of 40 target jobs, at least one other job was associated with a significant difference in quit rate on the target, even after controlling for multiple comparisons. If we expand our significance threshold to marginal significance, this number increases to 29 jobs. This indicates that for the 40 target jobs analyzed, only 11 did not show any evidence of a relationship where completing prior jobs would decrease the quit rates of the target jobs.

For the regression analysis, we selected the top three jobs based on their Chi-square statistics from the Chi-square test. These jobs were included in the regression to assess whether completing these previous jobs significantly affects the likelihood of quitting the target job, while controlling for other variables. Our results showed that for 23 target jobs, experience in at least one previous job significantly reduced the likelihood of quitting that target job. For two additional 25 target jobs, at least one prior job was found to have a marginally significant effect on reducing the chances of quitting that target job.

Although there is a noticeable reduction in the number of target jobs significantly associated with prior jobs, this is expected as the regression analysis incorporates additional sources of variance that can explain quitting behavior. The findings suggest that while not all prior jobs strongly influence the outcomes of target jobs, a substantial number still demonstrate a potential impact.

Due to the extensive number of analysis results from our study, it is not feasible to list each individual result in this section; instead, we present findings from a Chi-square test and regression analysis on one specific target job with a notably high quit rate in the game: Hunting Lions in the station Coral Reef. Appendices of our full analysis are available on our project GitHub at https://github.com/pcla-code/Wake-Job-Progression. Hunting Lions requires players to conduct experiments on food web relationships for lionfish at a Coral Reef site, and then construct a predictive model of the future of that ecosystem if human hunters are allowed to hunt lionfish in that location. The job has the highest difficulty rating (5) across all three dimensions (argumentation, modeling, and experimentation) and involves 11 detailed tasks requiring players to collect 32 necessary facts.

Analysis of log data showed that out of the 631 students who accepted this job, 379 did not complete it, resulting in a quit rate of 60%. Through Chi-square tests and regression analysis, we explored the influence of completing prior jobs on the likelihood of quitting from the target job. Findings for the Chi-square test are detailed in Table 1.

The results highlighted that players who had completed the Reef Decision job, in the Bayou biome, were less likely to quit the target job, with a quit rate of 16.13%, compared to 42.27% among those who did not complete this job. This difference was statistically significant ($\chi^2(1, N = 631) = 26.392$, $p < 0.001$, adjusted $\alpha = 0.017$), which indicates a significant effect of prior job completion on player decisions to quit the target job after the correction.

Further examinations showed similar patterns for jobs Hide n Seek and Methanogen. Players who completed these jobs also demonstrated lower quit rates from the target job. The Chi-square statistics were significant for both jobs and remained significant after the correction (Hide n Seek: $\chi^2(1, N) = 14.414$, $p < 0.01$, adjusted $\alpha = 0.017$; Methanogen: $\chi^2(1, N) = 11.486$, $p < 0.01$, adjusted $\alpha = 0.017$). The result shows how previous job completions may significantly influence player retention at the target job.

**Table 1.** Statistical results from the Chi-square test on the effect of previous job experience on target job

| Target job | Prior job | Played before target job | # quit target job | # not quit target job | % quit target job | Chi-square statistic | p-value |
|---|---|---|---|---|---|---|---|
| (Coral) Hunting Lions | (Bayou) Reef Decision | Yes | 20 | 104 | 16.13% | 26.392 | < 0.001* |
| | | No | 153 | 209 | 42.27% | | |
| | (Bayou) Hide n Seek | Yes | 35 | 113 | 23.65% | 14.414 | < 0.001* |
| | | No | 148 | 204 | 42.05% | | |
| | (Bayou) Methanogen | Yes | 41 | 121 | 25.31% | 11.486 | < 0.001* |
| | | No | 142 | 202 | 41.28% | | |

* Significant after B&H correction

### 3.5 Assessing the Impact of Previous Job Completion and Other Factors: Regression Analysis

Following the initial analysis with the Chi-square test, we further explored other factors influencing players' decisions to quit the target jobs using logistics regressions. This statistical approach allowed us to incorporate a broader range of variables into our model. Through this analysis, we hope to understand how each factor, individually and collectively, affect the probability of a player quitting jobs.

The logistic regression model was constructed to predict the likelihood of a player deciding to quit jobs, based on the abovementioned 9 variables (from Sect. 3.2). The analysis provided coefficients (scaled as odds) for each predictor, which reflect their respective impacts on the probability of quitting jobs. A positive coefficient indicated an increase in the likelihood of quitting jobs as the value of the predictor increased, while a negative coefficient suggested the opposite. The significance of each coefficient was assessed to determine which factors had a statistically meaningful influence on job-quitting decisions of the target job.

We applied the B&H correction method to the p-values obtained from our regression analysis, following the same procedure previously used for the Chi-square tests. The adjusted significance level for each target job analyzed was calculated based on 27 (3 * 9) tests, where 9 represents the number of features included in each regression (excluding the constant term, as it does not constitute an independent test of interest like the other features), and 3 represents the three previous jobs selected from the Chi-square tests.

### 3.6 Regression Analysis Results

The logistic regression analysis examined the effect of various factors, beyond merely completing the selected prior jobs, on the probability of players quitting Hunting Lions.

Table 2 presents a consistent negative correlation between completing those earlier jobs and the likelihood of quitting from Hunting Lions. For example, players who completed Reef Decision had a coefficient of $-1.555$ ($p < 0.001$, adjusted $\alpha = 0.002$), which implies a 79% lower probability of quitting during the target job compared to those who did not complete it. Similarly, completion of Hide n Seek resulted in a $-1.382$ coefficient ($p < 0.001$, adjusted $\alpha = 0.002$), which suggests a 75% reduced probability of quitting the target job, and completion of Methanogen showed a $-1.274$ coefficient ($p < 0.001$, adjusted $\alpha = 0.002$), which translates to a 72% reduced likelihood in quitting. These results support the hypothesis that completing these jobs decreases the probability of quitting from Hunting Lions, which corroborates the Chi-square test results.

The p-value for the number of jobs completed with higher difficulty in argumentation and experimentation was not statistically significant. However, the completion of jobs with greater difficulty in modeling and experimentation showed a significant negative relationship with target job completion. Specifically, coefficients for modeling ranged from $-0.340$ to $-0.397$, which remained significant after adjustment ($p < 0.001$, adjusted $\alpha = 0.002$). This indicates that for each additional job a student completes with a modeling difficulty greater than 2, the likelihood of them quitting the target task decreases by approximately 29–33%.

Interestingly, the overall number of jobs completed showed a slight positive relationship (coefficients 0.120–0.131, with p-values around 0.02), which suggests that completing one additional job is associated with a modest increase in the probability of quitting the target job, by 13–14%. However, these findings did not retain significance following the correction for multiple comparisons (adjusted $\alpha$ ranging from 0.002 to 0.003). The time spent, the number of tasks completed, the number of biomes visited, and the number of times paused showed no significant association with the likelihood of job-quitting at the target job.

## 4   Discussion and Conclusions

This study explores the influence of prior job completions on the likelihood of quitting future target jobs in the educational game *Wake*. Additionally, we studied the influence of factors such as time spent on jobs and the difficulty level of completed jobs on the quitting of the target jobs. Target jobs were identified as any job within the game, excluding the first three introductory jobs and any job for which there was insufficient data (i.e., fewer than 30 players who completed it and 30 players who did not complete it), for a total of 40 target jobs.

The results show that students' decisions to quit from jobs in *Wake*, for more than 50% of the jobs analyzed, were influenced by whether they had played some specific previous jobs or not. Towards our goal of identifying productive and unproductive pathways for student learning in *Wake*, we have some evidence that specific sequences of jobs may be better for promoting student engagement than others.

In specific, the results from the Chi-square test demonstrated that completing the three prior jobs, Reef Decision, Hide-n-Seek, and Methanogen significantly reduced the likelihood of quitting the target job Hunting Lions. Logistic regression analysis showed that the impact of completing the three preceding jobs on quitting the target job was

**Table 2.** Statistical results from logistic regression analysis on the impact of previous job experience on target job (p-values are shown in parentheses)

Part 1:

| Target job | Prior job | Prior job completed | # of jobs completed with Arg. diff. > 2 | # of jobs completed with Mod. diff. > 2 | # of jobs completed with Exp. diff. > 2 |
|---|---|---|---|---|---|
| (Coral) Hunting Lions | (Bayou) Reef Decision | − 1.555 (< 0.001)* | 0.075 (0.440) | − 0.340 (< 0.001)* | − 0.239 (0.045) |
| | (Bayou) Hide n Seek | − 1.382 (< 0.001)* | 0.077 (0.426) | − 0.345 (< 0.001)* | − 0.233 (0.048) |
| | (Bayou) Methanogen | − 1.274 (< 0.001)* | 0.093 (0.333) | − 0.397 (< 0.001)* | − 0.181 (0.123) |

Part 2:

| Target job | Prior job | Time (min) | # of jobs completed | # of tasks completed | # of biome visited | # of time paused |
|---|---|---|---|---|---|---|
| (Coral) Hunting Lions | (Bayou) Reef Decision | 0.180 (0.237) | 0.131 (0.016) | − 0.012 (0.528) | − 0.164 (0.477) | 0.012 (0.648) |
| | (Bayou) Hide n Seek | 0.189 (0.218) | 0.129 (0.016) | − 0.011 (0.549) | − 0.156 (0.496) | 0.001 (0.749) |
| | (Bayou) Methanogen | 0.176 (0.224) | 0.120 (0.024) | − 0.012 (0.517) | − 0.107 (0.642) | 0.001 (0.667) |

* Significant after B&H correction

significant even after accounting for other factors. This finding could be attributed to several factors. Firstly, all three preceding levels have a difficulty rating of 4 for either experimentation or modeling, which indicates that these levels are still challenging but slightly less difficult than Hunting Lions. This allows players to develop and refine their skills at a manageable pace. Additionally, each of these levels helps players develop specific skills required for the more challenging target job. For example, Hide n Seek involves substantial tasks completed in the observation tank, Methanogen focuses on measuring rates and environmental effects, and Reef Decision emphasizes modeling and making predictions based on collected data. These skills are necessary for successfully completing the complex tasks in Hunting Lions. Lastly, players may become familiar with using various tools (e.g., Measurement Tank, Stress Tank, Flashlight) across these levels. This familiarity can reduce the cognitive load when encountering similar tools in Hunting Lions, which may make it easier for the players to focus on the tasks rather than figuring out how to use the tools.

Meanwhile, this finding also suggests that directing players through specific jobs before attempting the target job could potentially help reduce the rate of quitting. Specifically, for players finding the target job challenging, recommending a switch to any of these three previous jobs before retrying the target job might improve their gameplay experience and reduce quit rates and the experience of struggle with the target job.

The insights from logistic regression analysis highlight additional factors that play a role in the quitting of target jobs. One key observation is that completion of earlier jobs with a modeling difficulty rating greater than 2 is associated with lower probability of quitting of the target job. This suggests that facing and overcoming challenges in more complex modeling jobs can potentially improve player persistence at subsequent, potentially more difficult jobs. Moreover, it also suggests that designers should offer students extra scaffolding and support the first time they encounter a job with a modeling difficulty greater than 2. Providing support at this point can help students overcome the challenges and improve their ability to handle jobs of similar or greater difficulty in the future. This pattern is evident not only in the specific example presented but throughout the entire analysis.

Our findings indicate that not every target job has a prior job that, when completed, can reduce the target job's quit rate. However, many previous jobs do contribute positively to decreasing quit rates for the subsequent target jobs. This insight might be helpful for the game designers, as reducing the quit rate and easing struggles could potentially make the game more engaging and enjoyable for players. By strategically designing job sequences, and nudging players to more effective sequences, designers may improve the player experience and ultimately increase player retention and satisfaction.

However, there are limitations to our study. We used data collected from May to October 2023, a brief six-month period that may not fully capture the variability in player behavior influenced by factors like academic calendars, holiday seasons, or game updates. To develop a more nuanced understanding of what influences job completion and the propensity to quit later jobs in *Wake*, future research should aim to broaden the scope of data collection to include more varied player interactions over a longer period.

Additionally, our analysis might not fully capture the complex interactions between different factors. Important external factors, such as the age of the player, their previous gaming experience, or educational background, were not considered in our study. These elements could also play a role in a player's decision to quit jobs and their overall performance within the game.

Despite these limitations, our findings provide actionable recommendations for game designers. The effect of completing some prior jobs on maintaining persistence in subsequent target jobs highlights the benefit of strategically structuring game progression. In carefully designing the sequence of jobs to gradually improve player skills and confidence before introducing more significant challenges, game designers can potentially reduce player frustration and the likelihood of quitting and produce a more rewarding and educational gaming experience for players.

# References

1. Adachi, P.J., Willoughby, T.: More than just fun and games: the longitudinal relationships between strategic video games, self-reported problem solving skills, and academic grades. J. Youth Adolesc. **42**(7), 1041–1052 (2013)
2. Agarwal, T., Burghardt, K., Lerman, K.: On quitting: performance and practice in online game play. In: Proceedings of the International AAAI Conference on Web and Social Media, vol. 11, no. 1, pp. 452–455 (2017)
3. Backlund, P., Hendrix, M.: Educational games-are they worth the effort? A literature survey of the effectiveness of serious games. In: 2013 5th International Conference on Games and Virtual Worlds for Serious Applications (VS-GAMES), pp. 1–8. IEEE (2013)
4. Barab, S., Gresalfi, M., Ingram-Goble, A.: Transformational play: using games to position person, content, and context. Educ. Res. **39**, 525–536 (2011)
5. Ćwil, M.: Leaderboards—a motivational tool in the process of business education. In: Joint International Conference on Serious Games, JCSG 2020, pp. 193–203 (2020)
6. De Freitas, S.: Are games effective learning tools? A review of educational games. J. Educ. Technol. Soc. **21**(2), 74–84 (2018)
7. Debeauvais, T., Lopes, C.V., Yee, N., Ducheneaut, N.: Retention and progression: seven months in World of Warcraft. In: Proceedings of the 2014 Foundations of Digital Games Conference (2014)
8. Frommel, J., Schrader, C., Weber, M.: Towards emotion-based adaptive games: emotion recognition via input and performance features. In: Proceedings of the 2018 Annual Symposium on Computer-Human Interaction in Play, pp. 173–185 (2018)
9. Gagnon, D.J., Harpstead, E., Slater, S.: Comparison of off the shelf data mining methodologies in educational game analytics. In: The 12th International Conference on Educational Data Mining (Workshops), pp. 38–43 (2019)
10. Gagnon, D., Swanson, L.: Open game data: a technical infrastructure for open science with educational games. In: Joint International Conference on Serious Games, JCSG 2023. Lecture Notes in Computer Science, pp. 3–19 (2023)
11. Jansen, E., Söbke, H.: Communication skills in construction projects and promoting them through multiplayer online games. In: Joint International Conference on Serious Games, JCSG 2022, pp. 169–181 (2022)
12. Jemmali, C., Bunian, S., Mambretti, A., El-Nasr, M.S.: Educational game design: an empirical study of the effects of narrative. In: Proceedings of the 13th International Conference on the Foundations of Digital Games, pp. 1–10 (2018)
13. Karumbaiah, S., Baker, R.S., Shute, V.: Predicting quitting in students playing a learning game. In: Proceeding of the 11th International Educational Data Mining, pp. 167–176 (2018)
14. Kickmeier-Rust, M.D., Marte, B., Linek, S.B., Lalonde, T., Albert, D.: The effects of individualized feedback in digital educational games. In: Proceedings of the 2nd European Conference on Games Based Learning, pp. 227–236 (2008)
15. Kim, Y.J., Knowles, M.A., Scianna, J., Lin, G., Ruipérez-Valiente, J.A.: Learning analytics application to examine validity and generalizability of game-based assessment for spatial reasoning. Br. J. Educ. Technol. **54**(1), 355–372 (2023)
16. Lester, J.C., Rowe, J.P., Mott, B.W.: Narrative-centered learning environments: a story-centric approach to educational games. In: Emerging Technologies for the Classroom: A Learning Sciences Perspective, pp. 223–237 (2012)
17. Liu, X., et al.: Struggling to detect struggle in students playing a science exploration game. In: Companion Proceedings of the Annual Symposium on Computer-Human Interaction in Play, pp. 83–88 (2023)

18. Lomas, D., Patel, K., Forlizzi, J.L., Koedinger, K.R.: Optimizing challenge in an educational game using large-scale design experiments. In: Proceedings of the SIGCHI Conference on Human Factors in Computing Systems, pp. 89–98 (2013)
19. Metcalf, S.J., Sommi, A., Haddadin, S., Scianna, J., Gagnon, D.: Work-in-progress—game design informed by learning progressions for science practices. In: Proceeding of the 7th International Conference of the Immersive Learning Research Network (iLRN), pp. 1–3 (2021)
20. Noemí, P.M., Máximo, S.H.: Educational games for learning. Univers. J. Educ. Res. 2(3), 230–238 (2014)
21. Owen, V.E., Baker, R.S.: Fueling prediction of player decisions: foundations of feature engineering for optimized behavior modeling in serious games. Technol. Knowl. Learn. 25(2), 225–250 (2020)
22. Owen, V.E., et al.: Detecting wheel-spinning and productive persistence in educational games. In: Proceeding of the 12th International Educational Data Mining, pp. 378–383 (2019)
23. Pagel, M., Söbke, H., Bröker, T.: Using multiplayer online games for teaching soft skills in higher education. In: Joint International Conference on Serious Games, JCSG 2021, pp. 276–290 (2021)
24. Pusey, M., Wong, K.W., Rappa, N.A.: The effect of a more knowledgeable other on resilience while playing single-player puzzle video games. In: 28th International Conference on Computers in Education (ICCE) (2020)
25. Qin, H., Rau, P.L.P., Salvendy, G.: Effects of different scenarios of game difficulty on player immersion. Interact. Comput. 22(3), 230–239 (2010)
26. Rahimi, S., Shute, V.J.: The effects of video games on creativity. In: The Cambridge Handbook of Lifespan Development of Creativity, p. 368 (2021)
27. Rowe, E., et al.: Assessing implicit computational thinking in Zoombinis puzzle gameplay. Comput. Hum. Behav. 120, 106707 (2021)
28. Rowe, E., et al.: Assessing implicit science learning in digital games. Comput. Hum. Behav. 76, 617–630 (2017)
29. Sánchez, J., Olivares, R.: Problem solving and collaboration using mobile serious games. Comput. Educ. 57(3), 1943–1952 (2011)
30. Shute, V.J., et al.: Modeling how incoming knowledge, persistence, affective states, and in-game progress influence student learning from an educational game. Comput. Educ. 86, 224–235 (2015)
31. ten Broeke, N., Hofman, A., Kruis, J., de Mooij, S., van der Maas, H.: Predicting and reducing quitting in online learning (2022)
32. Weber, B., John, M., Mateas, M., Jhala, A.: Modeling player retention in Madden NFL 11. In: Proceedings of the AAAI Conference on Artificial Intelligence, vol. 25, no. 2, pp. 1701–1706 (2011)

# Integrating Data from Multiple Sources in Evaluation Studies of Educational Games: An Application of Cross-Classified Item Response Theory Modeling

Tianying Feng[(✉)] [iD] and Li Cai

UCLA/CRESST, Los Angeles, USA
tfeng0315@ucla.edu

**Abstract.** It is crucial to evaluate the purported instructional benefits of educational games while developing tools to integrate insights from the rich interactions they facilitate into reliable systems of measurement of learning. Existing game-based evaluation studies use statistical tools that rarely integrate information from different sources. These sources include traditional test items assessing skills or knowledge targeted by the game, fine-grained gameplay process data (moment-to-moment records of learners' game-based interactions), background surveys measuring attributes of the individuals or their contexts (e.g. schools), and information on game or game level design features. We present a new application of a type of psychometric model (cross-classified item response theory modeling) to analyze gameplay and assessment data collected from a large-scale game-based randomized controlled trial. This application (a) jointly models data collected from multiple sources, allowing for a more holistic evaluation of the game's instructional effect; (b) quantifies changes in individuals' educational outcomes; (c) relates changes to gameplay behaviors and patterns. The application can be extended to include individuals' background and game level design information (explanatory predictors) in model equations to answer substantive questions. We demonstrate the advantages of our application over three other approaches to analyzing gameplay and assessment data. We also note the implications for using game-based analytic results to inform learning and instruction.

**Keywords:** game-based evaluation · data integration · data analysis · cross-classified item response theory modeling

## 1 Introduction

In evaluation research of educational games, multiple sources of data are often collected. Such data include traditional test items assessing skills or knowledge targeted by the game, fine-grained process data (moment-to-moment records of individuals' game-based interactions), background surveys measuring individuals' attributes (e.g., age), and information on game or game level design

© The Author(s), under exclusive license to Springer Nature Switzerland AG 2025
J. L. Plass and X. Ochoa (Eds.): JCSG 2024, LNCS 15259, pp. 70–76, 2025.
https://doi.org/10.1007/978-3-031-74138-8_6

features that can impact the instructional effectiveness of the game. Existing research uses tools that cannot do one or more of the following: (a) include information from gameplay process data generated to explain assessment gains or their absence thereof; (b) quantify (direct) changes in individuals' performances; (c) accommodate explanatory variables to investigate how the changes relate to characteristics of the individuals (e.g., socio-economic status and age) and of the game levels (e.g., design features); and (d) account for the interaction between characteristics of the individuals and their contexts (e.g., schools).

Given these limitations, existing game-based evaluation studies, such as randomized controlled trials of learning games, prioritize analyzing improvements in assessment outcomes to show the game's effectiveness, with lesser or little attention given to what happened to learners in the intervention (game) itself. As a result, the estimation of the game's effect is based on only a subset of the collected information or separate analyses of which findings are not or cannot be integrated. The lack of integration also hampers the effort to validate and use gameplay as a diagnostic tool for addressing questions such as "How and why did learning, growth, or change (not) occur?".

We present a new application of a contemporary unified and flexible psychometric modeling framework, cross-classified item response theory (IRT) modeling, that integrates data from various sources. Using data collected from a multisite evaluation study of math learning games, we compare our application with three alternatives to show advantages.

## 2   Cross-Classified IRT Modeling

**Latent Variables.** IRT models use random variables, termed *latent variables*, to describe hard-to-measure complex or conceptual properties of a system, whose influences can be inferred through one or more observable variables. For example, while we do not have direct access to Student A's prior knowledge on fractions, we use a latent variable to represent this construct and posit that the student's prior knowledge manifests in their generating observable responses to assessment items on fractions.

**Traditional IRT.** Traditional IRT models specify how a person's dichotomous or polytomous response to each assessment item is affected by the person's latent variables and the item's properties. Assuming binary responses (1 or 0), an IRT model may be expressed by constraining or extending Eq. 1 [5].

$$P(y_{pi} = 1 \mid \theta_p, a_i, b_i, c_i) = c_i + (1 - c_i)F(a_i\theta_p + b_i), \tag{1}$$

where $\theta_p$ is a latent variable for Person $p$, $[a_i, b_i, c_i]$ are parameters describing properties of Item $i$, and $F(\cdot)$ is a cumulative distribution function. For example, $F(\cdot)$ can be logistic, where $a_i$ is the slope and $b_i$ is the intercept in the linear predictor. When used, $c_i$ is the lower asymptote capturing the probability of guessing correctly.

**Cross-Classified   IRT.** Equation 1   assumes   that   person's   observed responses are affected by their knowledge and skills and by item-specific properties, and these effects do not follow a strict hierarchy, or order of influence.

A cross-classified IRT model extends this by considering persons and items as separate sources of variation affecting observed responses. It treats an item-specific parameter, such as $b_i$ in Eq. 1, as a random variable, in addition to having one or more person-specific latent variables. Observed responses are simultaneously influenced—or cross-classified—by persons and items.[1] A similar argument can be made for gameplay responses, which are affected by characteristics of the players and features of the game levels. The general modeling framework of cross-classified IRT accommodates multivariate and multidimensional data, making it possible to jointly model assessment item data and gameplay metric or indicator data (see [2]).

## 3    Data Analyses

We compared our cross-classified IRT application to three alternatives, including (a) descriptive statistics and correlations, (b) multiple linear regression, and (c) structural equation modeling (SEM).[2] For (a)–(c), we used assessment sum scores and aggregated indicators derived from gameplay data. For (b), (c), and our proposed application, we created school dummy variables to account for the impact of school-level differences on student outcomes.

### 3.1    Data Source

The data include gameplay and pretest-posttest item response data collected from 1711 students in 24 schools participating in a multisite randomized controlled trial of math learning games [1]. Students were randomly assigned to the treatment ($n_{trt} = 873$) or control condition ($n_{ctrl} = 838$) at the classroom level within each school. The treatment group played four games about rational numbers. The control group played four games about solving equations. Both groups received the same amount of instructional time.

**Game of Interest**. The analyses used data from one treatment game, *Save Patch*, designed to target concepts of fraction addition. In each level, students are presented with a grid and rope pieces that have the length of one unit or fractions of a unit (e.g., halves) and prompted to use ropes with the correct lengths to guide the avatar to the target location.[3]

**Assessment of Fractions Knowledge**. The assessment data contain students' responses to 10 dichotomously scored items used for the pre- and post-assessments. The items target the meanings of the unit, denominator, numerator, and addition of fractions [1,6].

**Game-Based Indicators of Misconceptions About Fractions**. By *game-based indicators*, we refer to variables derived from the gameplay process,

---

[1] Other sources can be present and modeled, but we do not consider them in this paper.

[2] Another type of latent variable models.

[3] Details on the game and its user interface can be found here: https://cresst.org/games-simulations/save-patch/.

log, or clickstream data. The indicators capture different aspects of players' performance and progress within a game, including variants of time spent and counts of low-level events (e.g., number of times clicking a button), as well as markers of gameplay patterns reflective of strategies or (mis)conceptions.

The gameplay indicator data contain students' responses on nine binary indicators of misconceptions, derived using process data from 27 game levels [3,4]. One example of such indicators is "converting to wholes error." Its value is 1 when a student appears to regard the solution as a mixed number and tries to add a whole unit and a fractional unit without converting everything to have the same denominator. Its value is 0 when such patterns are not detected. For the paper, only data based on students' first submissions are used. The first submission window starts when each level begins and ends when a student clicks on the submit button and observes whether or not the submitted solution leads the game character to the target location.

### 3.2  Two Research Questions

All analyses address two research questions often asked in evaluation studies of learning games:

1. **Treatment effect of the game**: To what extent do students in the treatment group, who are assigned to play *Save Patch*, differ from students in the control group in their knowledge of fractions as measured by the pre- and post-assessments?
2. **Relationship between gameplay and assessments**: To what extent is students' game-based performance (e.g., misconception) related to their knowledge of fractions?

## 4  Summary of Results

Results from all four analyses showed similar patterns of findings. First, the game had a positive effect on promoting students' knowledge of fractions. The estimated treatment effects are shown in Table 1, where each effect size is a form of standardized estimate of the treatment effect (higher is better). Second, game-based misconception negatively related to assessment performance measured at a given time point, or assessment gains measured over time points.

**Table 1.** Effect size estimates from all four analyses.

| Approach | Effect size | Effect size is relative to |
|---|---|---|
| A | 0.18 | Pooled variance of observed posttest sum scores |
| B | 0.19 | Unit variance of observed posttest sum scores |
| C | 0.29 | Unit variance of posttest latent variable |
| Cross-classified IRT | 0.26 | Estimated variance of pre-to-post latent change variable |

Note that the effect sizes obtained via Approach A and Approach B did not consider any gameplay information. The effect size obtained via Approach C, while seemingly higher, was likely obtained at the risk of violating two key model assumptions.[4] Approaches A–C did not directly model changes in student performance. We would be one step closer to making claims about student learning if we could directly examine changes in performance, such as changes from pre- to post-assessments.

**Approach A: Descriptive statistics and correlational analysis.** The estimated effect of 0.18 was a Cohen's $d$ measure based on the difference in mean posttest sum scores between the two experimental groups and pooled posttest standard deviation. The mean number of misconceptions, calculated per player by dividing the total occurrences of misconceptions by the 27 unique game levels, negatively correlated with pretest ($\rho = -.46, p < .001$) and posttest sum scores ($\rho = -.47, p < .001$). Limitations of this approach included: (a) the treatment effect was gauged using only posttest sum scores, ignoring information from other sources such as pretest and gameplay; (b) data complexities, such as the nesting of students within schools, were not considered; (c) findings based on descriptive statistics and pairwise correlations could not be integrated.

**Approach B: Multiple linear regression,** The estimated effect of 0.19 ($SE = .04, p < .001$) was obtained by regressing students' posttest sum scores on their pretest sum scores, the treatment assignment indicator (*Treatment* = 1, *Control* = 0), and 23 school dummy variables that account for the impact of school-level differences on student outcomes. The model could not simultaneously estimate the game's effect and include gameplay data about fractions. This issue arose because estimating the effect required data from both treatment and control groups. However, when gameplay data were included, the model would drop data from the control group as a means to handle the missing gameplay data from the control group, which did not play the treatment game.

**Approach C: SEM.** Three latent variables were used: (a) Posttest (latent posttest performance), (b) Pretest (latent pretest performance), and (c) Gameplay (latent game-based non-positive behaviors, e.g., exhibiting misconceptions). The estimated effect of 0.29 ($SE = .01, p < .001$) was obtained by regressing Posttest on the treatment assignment indicator, alongside other model specifications detailed in [2]. Gameplay had a negative impact on Posttest ($\hat{\beta} = -3.33$, $SE = .51, p < .001$). Gameplay and Pretest were negatively correlated ($\hat{\phi} = -.20$, $SE = .03, p < .001$). In addition to two potential violations of model assumption[5], one major drawback of this approach was its use of aggregated data that overlooked the varying characteristics of game levels introduced by design.

---

[4] The assumptions are (a) normality of the observed variables and (b) no measurement errors for the pretest and posttest latent variables.

[5] See footnote 4.

**Cross-classified IRT modeling**. Five latent variables were used: (a) baseline performance measured at pretest, (b) pre-to-post latent change, (c) game-based misconception, (d) relative intercepts of the 10 assessment items, and (e) relative intercepts of the game levels. The estimated effect of 0.26 ($SE = .03, p < .05$) was obtained by regressing students' pre-to-post latent changes on the treatment assignment indicator, alongside other model specifications detailed in [2]. Students' latent game-based misconception was negatively correlated with their latent baseline performance as measured by the pretest ($\hat{\sigma} = -.64, SE = .07, p < .05$). Said differently, students with lower baseline performance or prior knowledge tended to exhibit more misconceptions during gameplay. Game-based misconception was also negatively correlated with the pre-to-post change ($\hat{\sigma} = -.15, p < .05$). That is, students who exhibited more misconceptions in their gameplay tended to experience a lesser degree of change from pretest to posttest.

**Advantages of Cross-Classified IRT Modeling**. While all analyses produced similar patterns of findings, our proposed application has several methodological advantages over the three alternatives. A major advantage is the ability to jointly analyze data from different sources, specifically data of gameplay and assessments. This integration allows us to (a) use more information and more accurately estimate the game's instructional effect, (b) directly estimate the game's effect on latent pretest-to-posttest changes, and (c) relate behaviors detected during gameplay to help explain the changes.

The application also makes use of students' responses to assessment items and in-game responses captured by indicators developed per game level. Unlike Approach C, it does not aggregate assessment and gameplay data, and thus we can model differences between or *variability* in how different items and game levels affect student performance. One computational benefit of modeling variability is the reduction in the number of parameters to be estimated. Our proposed approach may thus be more viable for studies with limited sample sizes while retaining all the aforementioned modeling capacities.

While not explored in this paper, researchers can explore additional hypotheses by regressing any of the latent variables on relevant explanatory predictors, such as students' background characteristics or design variables of game levels.

## 5 Discussion

We present a new application of cross-classified IRT modeling to integrate data from different sources collected in evaluation studies of educational games. We also compared our application to three popular alternatives and discussed the methodological advantages of our proposed approach over these methods.

Findings based on our application have three important implications for learning and instruction. First, information extracted from gameplay process data, such as indicators of misconceptions, can help surface students' prior knowledge and common conceptions (e.g., about adding fractions). Second, the presence of misconceptions during gameplay may hinder the extent to which students can make progress in their understanding. Third, these findings can serve as valuable inputs for instructional planning. For example, teachers may adjust subsequent instructions to address common conceptions and misconceptions identified during students' gameplay.

# References

1. Chung, G.K.W.K., Choi, K., Baker, E.L., Cai, L.: The effects of math video games on learning: a randomized evaluation study with innovative impact estimation techniques. CRESST Report 841, UCLA/CREEST (2014). http://files.eric.ed.gov/fulltext/ED555700.pdf
2. Feng, T., Cai, L.: Sensemaking of process data from evaluation studies of educational games: an application of cross-classified item response theory modeling. J. Educ. Meas. (2024). https://doi.org/10.1111/jedm.12396
3. Kerr, D.: Into the black box: using data mining of in-game actions to draw inferences from educational technology about students' math knowledge. Doctoral dissertation, University of California, Los Angeles (2014). https://escholarship.org/uc/item/54c4z14h
4. Kerr, D., Chung, G.K.W.K.: Identifying key features of student performance in educational video games and simulations through cluster analysis. J. Educ. Data Min. 4(1), 144–182 (2012)
5. Levy, R., Mislevy, R.J.: Bayesian Psychometric Modeling. CRC Press (2016)
6. Vendlinski, T.P., Delacruz, G.C., Buschang, R.E., Chung, G.K.W.K., Baker, E.L.: Developing high-quality assessments that align with instructional video games. CRESST Report 774, University of California, Los Angeles, National Center for Research on Evaluation, Standards, and Student Testing (CRESST) (2010). https://cresst.org/publications/cresst-publication-3145/

# Identifying Player Strategies Through Segmentation: An Interactive Process Visualization Approach

Zhaoqing Teng[1]([✉])[iD], Jonattan Holmes[1][iD], Francis Dominguez[1][iD], Johannes Pfau[2][iD], Mario Escarce Junior[1][iD], and Magy Seif El-Nasr[1][iD]

[1] University of California, Santa Cruz, CA 95064, USA
zhteng@ucsc.edu
[2] Utrecht University, Utrecht, CS 3584, The Netherlands

**Abstract.** Identifying learners' problem-solving strategies from telemetry data is a critical task for serious games. Traditional methods like sequence mining, text replays, and statistical analysis often necessitate labor-intensive manual iterations to configure data appropriately and typically focus only on predominant trends. To improve our understanding of learner behaviors, this paper introduces a novel interactive visualization system that leverages *player journeys*-node-edge graphs depicting trends in sequences of player actions. We also present *player segmentation*, a new approach aimed at revealing and representing strategies that might otherwise be ignored, filtered out, or dismissed as outliers. We evaluated the effectiveness of our system through a mixed-methods study with 12 participants from our target demographic (game analysts). The results show that segmentation significantly reduces the time needed to identify strategies, suggesting that categorizing data based on causal factors can offer analysts more intuitive and insightful explanations.

**Keywords:** visual analytics · learning analytics · visualization systems · segmentation · mixed-methods evaluation

## 1 Introduction

Understanding trends and variations in player problem-solving strategies is essential for analyzing behavior in both commercial and educational games, especially within serious games where engagement and learning outcomes heavily depend on the game design's ability to accommodate diverse strategies [7,8,17,23]. Telemetry data, which logs interactions between players and games, is commonly used to decipher these strategies through various methods such as sequence mining or text replays [5,18,21,27,32]. While sequence mining algorithms are adept at revealing dominant strategies and verifying design goals, they often neglect atypical players such as cheaters, skilled experts, or differently-abled individuals whose behaviors diverge from the norm [5,10,19]. On the other hand, the text replays approach, which labels learner behaviors through text

J. L. Plass and X. Ochoa (Eds.): JCSG 2024, LNCS 15259, pp. 77–90, 2025.
https://doi.org/10.1007/978-3-031-74138-8_7

annotations, demands considerable labor and struggles to scale when analyzing strategies across numerous players [3]. In contrast, interactive visualization techniques promise a more adaptable environment that can enable analysts to actively explore player strategies using a variety of visual representations, provided they are built upon comprehensive and flexible analysis tools [20,25,26].

Among multiple types of visual representations, statistical charts, and diagrams, provide aggregated information useful for understanding player strategies [33,34]. However, these visualizations lack the process information necessary for analyzing strategies from a temporal perspective. Otherwise, promising node-edge systems that incorporate this process information, e.g., Glyph and Playtracer, suffer from a lack of user-friendly interaction that could assist analysts in uncovering concealed strategies amidst cluttered visualizations [2,23]. Consequently, there is a discernible need for a system that enables analysts to actively explore process visualizations of player strategies and simultaneously segment players to discover strategies adopted by specific populations.

This paper builds on the interactive process visualization system INSPECT [29–31] to answer the research question **"Does segmenting players assist in uncovering player strategies, from common to less popular ones, more efficiently and effectively?"**

The segmentation feature implemented in the system entails metadata segmentation, categorizing players into subgroups based on attributes (like gender or expertise), and behavioral segmentation, which organizes players by their actions or transitions. Therefore, by dividing players into subgroups, strategies adopted by minority players become noticeable, which provides opportunities for analysts to understand learner behaviors from a more inclusive perspective and introduce more diversity into game design as well. This contribution is particularly interesting to serious games, as it promotes a deeper understanding of diverse player behaviors and strategies, enabling the creation of more inclusive and effective educational and training tools.

We conducted a mixed-methods study to evaluate whether interactive visual segmentation can boost the efficiency and understanding of game analysts. The insights gained from this enhanced analytical approach not only lead to tailored educational content and improved user engagement but also bolster the development of serious games. For example, game analysts were able to identify and analyze less common strategies more quickly, leading to faster iteration cycles in game design. Additionally, the system allowed analysts to discover unique behavioral patterns among subgroups, such as differences in problem-solving approaches between novice and expert players. By leveraging diverse player behaviors, our system informs the design of game elements that enhance learning outcomes, towards making serious games more effective and appealing to a broad audience.

## 2   Related Work

Sequence mining algorithms and text replays are widely utilized to uncover player patterns in recent game analytics research [1,3,27]. For instance, Kang et al. analyzed keyboard inputs and mouse movements to uncover repetitive patterns in *League of Legends*, focusing on the frequency of occurrence [15]. Wallner et al. utilized lag sequence analysis to identify infrequent but critical patterns [32], while Mathonat et al. combined sequence mining with supervised learning to predict *skillshot* strategies in *Rocket League* [21]. Furthermore, Baker and Carvalho employed the text replay approach to label student behaviors in interactive learning environments, using these labels to train classifiers [3]. Despite their success in pinpointing prevalent strategies, these methods often lack the flexibility needed to explore strategies employed by specific player groups, and the text replay method introduces substantial labeling efforts for researchers.

Visualization-based approaches provide analysts with intuitive graphical representations to explore player strategies [7,33]. Wallner and Kriglstein, for example, used star graphs to highlight strategy differences across variables like gender in tower-defense games, observing gameplay differences that affected scores [34]. Liu et al. employed line charts to reveal different tool use patterns by distinct student characteristics in a serious game environment named *Alien Rescue* [16]. Similarly, Miller and Crowcroft visualized avatar movement trajectories in *World of Warcraft* to analyze patterns in player-versus-player battleground strategies [22]. While these approaches offer insights into aggregated data, they often fall short in providing detailed process insights into individual player strategies and the sequential actions that define their gameplay.

In regards to process visualizations, which provide a sequential view of player strategies, Javvaji et al. employed the *Glyph* interactive node-edge visualization system to elucidate problem-solving strategies in puzzle games [14]. Andersen et al. advanced this approach using Classical Multidimensional Scaling (CMDS) to simplify game states into two-dimensional node-edge graphs, facilitating gameplay analysis [2]. Disco is another commercialized process mining tool that allows users to discover dominant process through the fuzzy mining algorithm, and visualize these processes [11]. Although these methods have proven effective in revealing underlying sequential strategies [12], these systems either lack the necessary interactivity, requiring analysts to manually prepare datasets, or overly emphasize on the discovery of dominant processes without enough support for analysts to explore according to their preference. This increases the workload and separates the analytical process, complicating collaborative efforts and detracting from the immediate benefits of intuitive visual exploration. In contrast, our previous or parallel work tackled interactive segmentation with respect to spatial movement strategies, proficiency analysis, and mental models in educational and entertainment games [20,25,30]. In this work, we aim to bridge the before mentioned gaps by implementing and evaluating an interactive segmentation tool in game process visualization, enhancing the mining of explainable player strategies.

## 3   Methodology

Our study utilized a dataset from the RPG VPAL (*Virtual Personality Assessment Lab*[9]), which is a publicly available mod of *Fallout: New Vegas*[24]. In this mod, players are required to complete various quests to advance the game narrative. The dataset includes data from 51 players and captures each action taken by these players as they completed quests within the game. From the total of 14 quests available in the dataset, we selected three foundational quests and one complex, advanced quest for analysis. This selection was strategically made to offer a manageable yet comprehensive analysis of both basic and intricate player strategies.

The initial analysis of the complete dataset revealed an overwhelming 1,214,905 different subsequences, identified using the *PrefixSpan* algorithm [13]. Subsequences are defined as sequences of player actions within a specific time-frame. To refine our focus and make the data more tractable for analysis, we applied the *everygram* algorithm to mine consecutive subsequences from the reduced dataset [4]. This approach resulted in a dataset containing 3830 unique player traces, referring to the recorded sequences of player interactions, providing a rich yet manageable dataset for exploring both prominent and hidden player strategies. Our methodology thus balances the complexity of the data with the feasibility of detailed analysis, setting the stage for both classical and segmentation-enhanced process visualizations in our controlled and intervention groups, respectively.

### 3.1   Visualization System

To foster an environment where participants can iteratively deploy segmentation and visualization freely, we developed the interactive process visualization system INSPECT based on the concept of the *player journey*. This node-edge graph accumulates and visualizes sequential player behaviors, enabling analysts to intuitively derive player strategies [30]. The system is designed to enhance interactivity, usability, and the practicality of aligning with the analyst's intentions. It includes foundational operators that reduce visual clutter, such as the ability to filter out less popular nodes and/or edges temporarily, zooming, highlighting, and relocating nodes. The nodes and edges are interactive, allowing analysts to click on them to view additional details, such as the number of players who showed the underlying behavior of a particular node or edge.

Figure 1 illustrates an example of a *player journey* graph produced by INSPECT for the entire set of 51 players, focusing on just the three basic quests while Fig. 2 depicts the behavioral pathways for the more advanced quest, *Rescue Mission*. For three basic quests, players complete the *Talk To Paul* quest firstly, and start the *Rat Problem* quest. Players either follow all steps to complete the *Rat Problem* and the *Understanding* quest or start the *Understanding* quest before progressing the *Rat Problem* quest. There are two strategies for the latter group of players: returning and completing the *Rat Problem* quest and completing the *Understanding* quest, or completing the *Understanding* quest without returning back to the *Rat Problem* quest. For the *Rescue Mission* quest, players either receive the *looking for silver* request or *found silver* after starting the quest, after which they follow the rest steps to complete the quest. More details of how players complete the basic and the advanced quest is shown in Table 1.

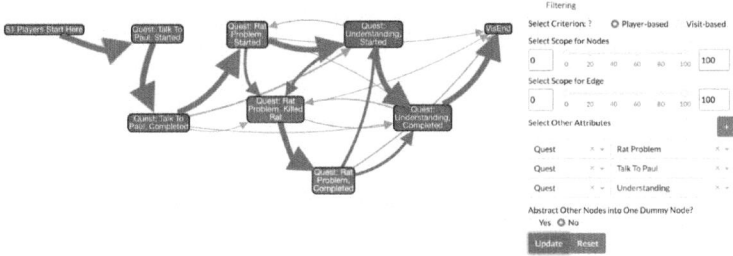

**Fig. 1.** The player journey mapping of three fundamental quests (*Talk to Paul, Rat Problem, Understanding*) for all players, displaying basic controls of data manipulation available to both groups. The red path highlights the most probable strategies, as detailed in Table 1.

For further analysis, this data could be segmented-exclusively by the intervention group in this study-into categories based on metadata, such as player experience levels (low and high), as shown in Figs. 3 and 4, or by behavioral segmentation, which differentiates player actions or transitions, such as between players who accepted multiple quests at once versus those who completed a quest before starting a new one, illustrated in Figs. 5 and 6.

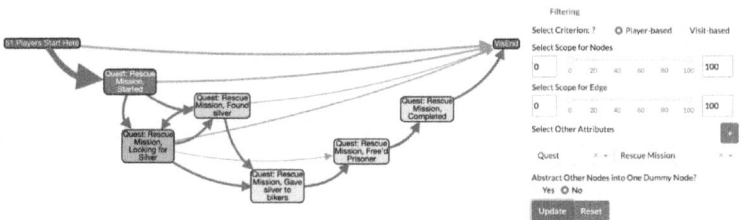

**Fig. 2.** The player journey mapping of the advanced quests (*Rescue Mission*) for all players, together with the basic controls of data manipulation available for both groups. The red path indicates the most probable strategies, as outlined in Table 1.

## 4   Evaluation

To address our research question—about whether segmenting players assists in uncovering both common and unpopular player strategies with more efficiency and efficacy—we conducted a mixed-methods study. This study assessed the efficacy and efficiency of detecting strategies, as well as the usability of the process, compared in-between two groups. The control group had access only to established process visualization techniques, such as filtering out infrequent behaviors,

**Table 1.** Most popular player strategies when accepting quests, advancing them or completing them (✓), as also depicted in the player journeys of all players of the dataset (cf. Figs. 1 and 2).

| Sequence |
| --- |
| *Talk To Paul → Talk To Paul ✓ → Rat Problem → Understanding → Rat Problem: Killed Rat → Rat Problem ✓ → Understanding ✓* |
| *Talk To Paul → Talk To Paul ✓ → Rat Problem → Rat Problem: Killed Rat → Rat Problem ✓ → Understanding → Understanding ✓* |
| *Talk To Paul → Talk To Paul ✓ → Rat Problem → Understanding → Understanding ✓* |
| *Rescue Mission → Found silver → Looking for Silver → Gave silver to bikers → Freed Prisoner → Rescue Mission ✓* |
| *Rescue Mission → Looking for Silver → Found silver → Gave silver to bikers → Freed Prisoner → Rescue Mission ✓* |

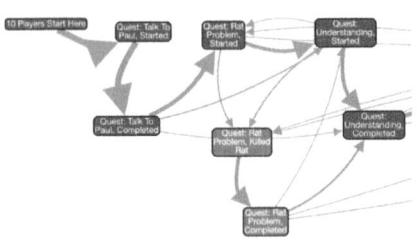

**Fig. 3.** Player journey map of VPAL quest data containing all players who have rated their expertise as 1 ("very inexperienced").

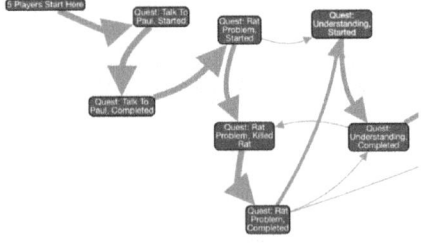

**Fig. 4.** Player journey map of VPAL quest data containing all players who have rated their expertise as 4 ("very experienced").

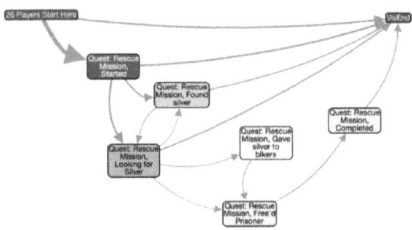

**Fig. 5.** Player journey map of players who had transmitted from the action 'Rat Problem, Started' to 'Understanding, Started'.

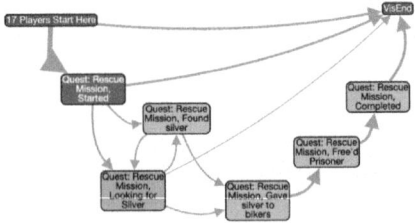

**Fig. 6.** Player journey map of players who had transmitted from the action 'Rat Problem, Started' to 'Rat Problem, Kill Rat'.

highlighting connections between nodes/edges. The intervention group, in contrast, was additionally provided with the two modes of metadata and behavioral segmentation. This setup allowed us to directly compare the effectiveness of analyzing original process visualization against enhanced player journeys supported by segmentation features.

### 4.1 Participants

To ensure the ecological validity of our evaluation, we specifically recruited participants with experience in data analysis software and libraries relevant to video game data processing. The study involved twelve participants ($n = 12$), with seven identifying as male and five as female. All participants were enrolled in PhD programs related to games and user experience research, games and media technology, or human-computer interaction, and demonstrated proficiency in using R or Python for analyzing player or user experience data. Participants' familiarity with R or Python is relevant as these skills are commonly used in data analysis, facilitating their understanding and interaction with the visualization tool presented and discussed in this study. Given their comparable experience levels and a balanced gender distribution, participants were randomly assigned to either the control group (G1) or the intervention group (G2). Notably, one participant from G2 who misunderstood the instructions and subsequently showed atypical results was excluded from further analysis to maintain data integrity.

### 4.2 Protocol

Participants in the control group (G1) utilized basic node-edge process visualization interactions such as filtering out less popular nodes and/or edges to simplify the visualization, and selecting nodes and edges to view statistical details about specific quests. The intervention group (G2) had access to additional features, including the segmentation capability to create and visualize *player journeys* for specific subgroups of players. The specific steps followed by both groups of participants were described in Table 2.

Participants could inquire about any aspect of the player journeys during the session, with support provided for uncertainties in generating the desired visualizations. Upon completing the tasks, a semi-structured post-study interview was conducted to assess their experience with the visualization system.

### 4.3 Measures

We measured how many strategies participants found from the visualization, with or without the support of segmentation features. Moreover, the time spent on analyzing the visualization for each participant was recorded after they understood the concept of player journeys, e.g., whether the nodes with deeper color were more visited compared to lighter ones. Additionally, the System Usability Scale (SUS) was employed to quickly gauge the perceived usability of INSPECT [6].

**Table 2.** The steps that G1 and G2 participants follow in the study.

| G1 participants | G2 participants |
|---|---|
| Participants watched a video introducing the fundamental concepts of *player journeys* | |
| They generated the player journey visualization for the provided dataset | |
| They used the filtering feature to retain only nodes (or edges) visited by more than 20% of players or to retain actions specific to selected quests | They were introduced to metadata segmentation based on players' self-reported game expertise, leading to the creation of two distinct player journey graph visualizations |
| | They experimented with behavioral segmentation across datasets, for instance, visualizing quest step sequences of the *Rescue Mission* for two sets of players who exhibited different behaviors within the basic quests (refer to Figs. 5 and 6) |
| They identified strategies (sequence patterns) for completing the basic quests (*Talk to Paul, Rat Problem*, and *Understanding*) | |
| Finally, they identified player strategies throughout the advanced quest (*Rescue Mission*) | |

## 5   Results

In the analysis of the three basic quests, all six participants in the control group (G1) successfully identified the third strategy listed in Table 1, while at least five participants recognized the first two strategies. Notably, one participant focused solely on the most dominant strategy, explaining that he believed his task was specifically to identify the most prevalent strategy.

For the advanced quest (*Rescue Mission*), five out of six G1 participants identified at least one of the strategies mentioned in Table 1. These participants observed that players typically began either by *looking for silver* or having already *found silver*, and then followed other steps in a sequential order. Furthermore, these participants identified additional strategies that involved players discontinuing their engagement with the quest, either by aborting the mission or exiting the game entirely, resulting in observed strategies such as:

- *Rescue Mission* → Abort
- *Rescue Mission* → Looking for Silver → Abort

However, only two participants noticed a less straightforward subsequence, which they interpreted as a potentially cunning method of completing the quest:

- *Rescue Mission* → Looking for silver → Freed Prisoner

This observation suggests an understanding of the quest's dynamics and player decisions, which may not be immediately apparent from the more common strategies.

Several participants in the control group (G1) experienced challenges due to the complexity of the visualization graph, which contained numerous edges. This complexity often led them to revisit different parts of the graph repeatedly during their analysis. Specifically, in the quest *Understanding*, participants expended considerable effort deciphering the incoming and outgoing edges and the volume of players interacting with these edges to understand player movements between the *Rat Problem* and *Understanding* quests. Participant P7 expressed confusion: "It's clear here in the 'Talk to Paul' quest, right? But between 'Understanding' and 'Rat Problem,' it gets confusing what players did; I need to go back and forth to figure it out." Additionally, unfamiliarity with the game's narrative and mechanics contributed to uncertainties about player strategies, as highlighted by P4: "It seems like people don't complete the 'Rat Problem' quest if they've missed it, possibly because they've already completed it, or maybe they just don't care."

In contrast, all five participants in the intervention group (G2) swiftly identified the third strategy listed in Table 1 using visualizations of less experienced players (cf. Fig. 3). Subsequently, four participants also noted the first and second strategies, guided by the prominent connection from the node *Rat Problem, Kill Rat* to *Rat Problem, Complete*. Among high-expertise players, all participants quickly recognized and declared the first strategy as dominant. An anomalous strategy was observed by one participant who noted an unusual transition from *Understanding, Complete* to *Rat Problem, Kill Rat*.

Furthermore, all G2 participants identified both strategies depicted in Fig. 6, which showed players initially *looking for silver* or having *found silver*, followed by subsequent actions. Similarly, four participants noted the absence of a link between *Rescue Mission, Found Silver* and *Rescue Mission, Gave Silver to Bikers*, indicating a singular strategy focus. Additionally, all participants observed an alternative path from *Rescue Mission, Looking for Silver* directly to *Rescue Mission, Freed Prisoner*, bypassing the expected *Rescue Mission, Gave Silver to Bikers* node, revealing an innovative approach to resolving the quest scenario.

**Table 3.** Statistical information about the time spent (in seconds) for discovering strategies, the total number of strategies found, and the $p$-value of the Welch's $t$-tests when comparing these metrics between groups.

| | Time spent for each strategy | | | Time spent on each visualization | | | Number of strategy found | | |
|---|---|---|---|---|---|---|---|---|---|
| | Mean | STD | $p$-value | Mean | STD | $p$-value | Mean | STD | $p$-value |
| G1 | 59.513 | 21.106 | 0.048 | 290.17 | 58.881 | 0.002 | 4.83 | 0.983 | 0.156 |
| G2 | 37.873 | 9.633 | | 154.4 | 39.908 | | 5.6 | 0.548 | |

To assess whether the introduced segmentation feature led to differences in efficiency (since the additional possibilities could increase the time spent in analysis, or conversely decrease the time necessary to come to an intuitive conclusion), we measured the time participants spent on revealing strategies. We report means, standard deviations, and $t$-tests (Welch's $t$-test) between both groups in Table 3 since the sample size of two groups are different. This reveals a significant difference in time spent per identified strategy ($G1 : 59.51$ seconds, $G2 : 37.87$ seconds, $p < 0.05$), and the total time they had to expend on each visualization ($G1 : 290.17$ seconds, $G2 : 154.4$ seconds, $p < 0.05$), while coming to the same conclusions (i.e., the number of detected strategies did not differ significantly) ($G1 : 4.83$ strategies, $G2 : 5.6$ strategies, $p > 0.05$).

According to the post-study interviews, participants in both groups expressed satisfaction with the implemented features of the process visualization system, demonstrating the enhancement of analytical depth and strategic insights. Within G1, participants emphasized the overall benefits in visualizing player progression, while some of the participants of G2 highlighted the segmentation feature's ability to facilitate comparisons between different types of players. Concerns were raised as well, by one participant in G1, about the complexity of the visualization with a large dataset, particularly regarding overlapping edges.

In terms of measured usability, SUS scores of the control group were significantly higher ($G1 : 84.79$) than within the intervention group ($G2 : 73.5$), which was to be expected when introducing a technically novel feature with which the target sample had no prior experience. Yet, the system achieved adequate above-median (68) performances, which indicates that participants did not experience major usability issues [28]. This is supported by positive qualitative feedback from most participants, as they stated that it was designed in an easy and understandable manner, and allowed them to explore the system satisfactorily. One participant (P11) mentioned that "I can understand graph traversal intuitively so I can think about like play strategy. Also, my knowledge of the game probably helps as well. So once I understand how these graphs work, it is pretty helpful." One participant (P3) revealed one disadvantage of this approach, which lies in the domain knowledge required to understand the segmentation idea, yet this only constitutes an initial hurdle: "Even though you have a basic tutorial and you also taught me to run through the tasks. If I actually work using these tools, I probably need to practice more times to be more familiar with each interface. This is not a reflection on the quality of your design, it is just based on the time. Just as with any new software, it takes some time initially to learn, but with continued use, proficiency follows". In summary, our study demonstrates that the use of player journeys allows analysts to uncover not only the most popular strategies but also other overlooked patterns, providing more inclusivity for understanding learner behavior.

## 6    Discussion

This paper addressed the challenge of identifying player behavior patterns within a potentially large pool of candidate strategies. Traditional approaches deployed algorithms or text replays, which failed to provide a flexible visual environment for active exploration. Moreover, algorithmic approaches or statistical analyses focus on popular or dominant strategies, neglecting less common patterns that are of significant interest for understanding learner behaviors. By utilizing interactive visualizations in the form of player journeys, we aimed to reveal player strategies in a more intuitive and explainable manner.

Our quantitative analysis demonstrates that the segmentation implementation effectively reduced the time required to analyze process visualization graphs. Segmented visualizations also improved the efficiency of strategy discovery, as evidenced by participants' ability to intuitively uncover underlying strategies. While the number of strategies found did not significantly differ between groups, this outcome may be attributed to the dataset primarily consisting of simple quests designed with fewer steps and variations to maintain low entry barriers. One participant (P1) highlighted this limitation, emphasizing the potential for more varied and complex quests to yield a greater diversity of strategies.

Overall, our system achieved a satisfying usability performance with above-median System Usability Scale (SUS) scores across both groups, indicating that the implemented features were perceived as suitable and purposeful for the target group of game analysts. Despite most participants lacking prior experience with interactive player journeys, our system provided an effective and efficient medium for transforming queries into informative process visualizations, thereby enhancing their understanding of player experiences.

In summary, our study demonstrates that the use of player journeys allows analysts to uncover not only the most popular strategies but also other overlooked patterns, providing analysts more inclusivity for understanding learner behavior. Moreover, segmentation of learners based on their metadata or behaviors has shown to increase the efficiency of strategy discovery, particularly when dividing them based on variables that may causally influence differences in strategies.

## 6.1   Limitations and Future Work

One of the limitations of our approach is the training required for analysts to fully understand the concepts of segmentation and player journeys. Analysts without prior data analysis knowledge may find it challenging to navigate the system and interpret the visualizations effectively. However, our intended target audience for such a system remains analysts in the domain of game data science within industry and academia, and we anticipate that initial usability obstacles will diminish with long-term usage and familiarity.

Moreover, the game used in our study is an RPG, not a serious game, which introduces some uncertainty about whether the approach would yield similar results in a serious game context. However, the focus on quest progression in the RPG mirrors problem-solving strategies typical of serious games, where players complete multiple tasks to finish a task (or reach a learning outcome). Therefore, the segmentation approach used in our study, which enhances the efficiency and effectiveness of strategy discovery, could provide valuable insights into exploring problem-solving strategies within serious games.

Our next step involves continuing the development of our system, incorporating iterative feedback from participants to enhance functionality and introduce new features. We aim to expand the application of the segmentation feature beyond quest-related behavior to include areas such as validating design goals and capturing human affective states. Additionally, within game user research, we plan to implement new features that will deepen analysts' understanding of player experiences.

## 7   Conclusion

In this paper, we presented an interactive visualization approach aimed at identifying player strategies, which can be extended to the context of serious games. Unlike traditional conventional algorithmic methods, our process visualization system empowers analysts to dynamically shape player journey illustrations. By leveraging this approach, analysts can detect both major and less popular strategy sequences, providing a comprehensive understanding of player behavior.

Our study demonstrated that custom segmentation based on behavioral patterns or metadata significantly accelerates the identification of strategies. This segmentation not only enhances the efficiency of strategy discovery but also provides a more intuitive representation of player behavior dynamics. Through the use of interactive visualizations, analysts can observe player's strategies, uncovering insights that may have been overlooked with conventional approaches.

The implications of our work extend beyond game analytics, offering insights into serious games and gamified applications. By understanding player strategies, developers and researchers can optimize game design, tailor interventions, and create more engaging and effective learning experiences. Moreover, our approach has the potential to contribute to various domains, including education, healthcare, and workforce training, where serious games play an important role in promoting learning, behavior change, and skill development.

In conclusion, our interactive visualization approach serves as a powerful tool for exploring player behavior. By enabling analysts to uncover hidden patterns and gain deeper insights into player strategies, this approach can be leveraged to enhance the development of more engaging and effective serious games. Ultimately, it enhances user experience and ensures the achievement of desired learning outcomes.

# References

1. Agrawal, R., Srikant, R.: Mining sequential patterns. In: Proceedings of the Eleventh International Conference on Data Engineering, pp. 3–14. IEEE (1995)
2. Andersen, E., Liu, Y.E., Apter, E., Boucher-Genesse, F., Popović, Z.: Gameplay analysis through state projection. In: Proceedings of the Fifth International Conference on the Foundations of Digital Games. pp. 1–8 (2010)
3. Baker, R., de Carvalho, A.: Labeling student behavior faster and more precisely with text replays. In: Educational Data Mining 2008 (2008)
4. Bird, S., Klein, E., Loper, E.: Natural Language Processing with Python: Analyzing Text with the Natural Language Toolkit. O'Reilly Media, Inc. (2009)
5. Bosc, G., Kaytoue, M., Raïssi, C., Boulicaut, J.F.: Strategic patterns discovery in rts-games for e-sport with sequential pattern mining. In: MLSA@ PKDD/ECML, pp. 11–20 (2013)
6. Brooke, J.: Sus: a "quick and dirty" usability. Usability Eval. Ind. **189**(3), 189–194 (1996)
7. Chaudy, Y., Connolly, T., Hainey, T.: Learning analytics in serious games: a review of the literature. In: European Conference in the Applications of Enabling Technologies 2014 (2014)
8. Desurvire, H., El-Nasr, M.S.: Methods for game user research: studying player behavior to enhance game design. IEEE Comput. Graphics Appl. **33**(4), 82–87 (2013)
9. El-Nasr, M.S., Nguyen, T.H.D., Canossa, A., Drachen, A.: Game Data Science. Oxford University Press, Oxford (2021)
10. Galli, L., Loiacono, D., Cardamone, L., Lanzi, P.L.: A cheating detection framework for unreal tournament iii: A machine learning approach. In: 2011 IEEE Conference on Computational Intelligence and Games (CIG'11). pp. 266–272. IEEE (2011)
11. Günther, C.W., Rozinat, A.: Disco: Discover your processes. In: Demonstration Track of the 10th International Conference on Business Process Management, BPM Demos 2012, pp. 40–44. CEUR-WS. org (2012)
12. Habibi, R., Maram, S.S., Pfau, J., Wei, J., Sisodiya, S.K., Kashani, A., Carstensdottir, E., Seif El-Nasr, M.: A data-driven design of ar alternate reality games to measure resilience. In: International Conference on Human-Computer Interaction, pp. 586–604. Springer, Berlin (2022)
13. Han, J., Pei, J., Mortazavi-Asl, B., Pinto, H., Chen, Q., Dayal, U., Hsu, M.: Prefixspan: Mining sequential patterns efficiently by prefix-projected pattern growth. In: Proceedings of the 17th International Conference on Data Engineering, pp. 215–224. IEEE (2001)
14. Javvaji, N., Harteveld, C., Seif El-Nasr, M.: Understanding player patterns by combining knowledge-based data abstraction with interactive visualization. In: Proceedings of the Annual Symposium on Computer-Human Interaction in Play, pp. 254–266 (2020)
15. Kang, S.J., Kim, Y.B., Kim, S.K.: Analyzing repetitive action in game based on sequence pattern matching. J. Real-Time Image Proc. **9**, 523–530 (2014)
16. Liu, M., Horton, L., Kang, J., Kimmons, R., Lee, J.: Using a ludic simulation to make learning of middle school space science fun. Int. J. Gaming Comput. Mediated Simul. (IJGCMS) **5**(1), 66–86 (2013)
17. Liu, M., Lee, J., Kang, J., Liu, S.: What we can learn from the data: a multiple-case study examining behavior patterns by students with different characteristics in using a serious game. Technol. Knowl. Learn. **21**, 33–57 (2016)

18. Low-Kam, C., Raïssi, C., Kaytoue, M., Pei, J.: Mining statistically significant sequential patterns. In: 2013 IEEE 13th International Conference on Data Mining, pp. 488–497. IEEE (2013)
19. Madden, D., Liu, Y., Yu, H., Sonbudak, M.F., Troiano, G.M., Harteveld, C.: "Why are you playing games? you are a girl!": exploring gender biases in esports. In: Proceedings of the 2021 CHI Conference on Human Factors in Computing Systems, pp. 1–15 (2021)
20. Maram, S.S., Pfau, J., Villareale, J., Teng, Z., Zhu, J., El-Nasr, M.S.: Mining player behavior patterns from domain-based spatial abstraction in games. In: 2023 IEEE Conference on Games (CoG), pp. 1–8. IEEE (2023)
21. Mathonat, R., Boulicaut, J.F., Kaytoue, M.: A behavioral pattern mining approach to model player skills in rocket league. In: 2020 IEEE Conference on Games (CoG), pp. 267–274. IEEE (2020)
22. Miller, J.L., Crowcroft, J.: Avatar movement in world of warcraft battlegrounds. In: 2009 8th Annual Workshop on Network and Systems Support for Games (NetGames), pp. 1–6. IEEE (2009)
23. Nguyen, T.H.D., El-Nasr, M.S., Canossa, A.: Glyph: Visualization tool for understanding problem solving strategies in puzzle games. In: Foundations of Digital Games (FDG) (2015)
24. Obsidian Entertainment, Bethesda Softworks: *Fallout: New Vegas*. [PS3 Xbox PC] (October 2010)
25. Pfau, J., Charan, M., Kleinman, E., Seif El-Nasr, M.: Damage optimization in video games: A player-driven co-creative approach. In: Proceedings of the CHI Conference on Human Factors in Computing Systems, pp. 1–16 (2024)
26. Pfau, J., Seif El-Nasr, M.: Player-driven game analytics: the case of guild wars 2. In: Proceedings of the 2023 CHI Conference on Human Factors in Computing Systems, pp. 1–14 (2023)
27. Sao Pedro, M., Baker, R.S., Montalvo, O., Nakama, A., Gobert, J.D.: Using text replay tagging to produce detectors of systematic experimentation behavior patterns. In: Educational Data Mining 2010 (2010)
28. Sauro, J.: Measuring usability with the system usability scale (SUS) (2011)
29. Teng, Z., Pfau, J., El-Nasr, M.S.: Visualization-based iterative segmentation to augment video game analytics. In: 2023 IEEE Conference on Games (CoG), pp. 1–2. IEEE (2023)
30. Teng, Z., Pfau, J., Maram, S.S., Seif El-Nasr, M.: Player segmentation with INSPECT: revealing systematic behavior differences within MMORPG and educational game case studies. In: Extended Abstracts of the 2022 Annual Symposium on Computer-Human Interaction in Play, pp. 87–92 (2022)
31. Teng, Z., Pfau, J., Maram, S.S., Seif El-Nasr, M.: Interactive player journeys: co-designing a process visualization system to video game analytics. In: Proceedings of the 19th International Conference on the Foundations of Digital Games, pp. 1–11 (2024)
32. Wallner, G.: Sequential analysis of player behavior. In: Proceedings of the 2015 Annual Symposium on Computer-Human Interaction in Play, pp. 349–358 (2015)
33. Wallner, G., Kriglstein, S.: Visualization-based analysis of gameplay data—a review of literature. Entertain. Comput. **4**(3), 143–155 (2013)
34. Wallner, G., Kriglstein, S.: Comparative Visualization of Player Behavior for Serious Game Analytics. Serious Games Analytics: Methodologies for Performance Measurement, Assessment, and Improvement, pp. 159–179 (2015)

# Serious Game Design

# Examining Student Responses to Game Layers in Cultural Geography: A Study About Game Spatiality in a Role-Playing Game Design

Lanxin Xue[1] , Eliza Pierce[2], Soren Larsen[3] , and Danielle Oprean[1(✉)]

[1] School of Information and Learning Technologies, College of Education and Human Development, University of Missouri, Columbia, MO, USA
opreand@missouri.edu
[2] Learning, Teaching, Curriculum, College of Education and Human Development, University of Missouri, Columbia, MO, USA
[3] Geography, College of Arts and Sciences, University of Missouri, Columbia, MO, USA

**Abstract.** This study examines the impact of the game space in *Stories of a Geo-Farmer*, a digital game prototype designed to enhance cultural geography in higher education. Employing the Cybermedia Model, we analyzed student perspectives on how various game design elements influence learner engagement across four layers: representational, mechanical, material, and player. Our qualitative analysis revealed that representational elements can enhance spatial learning and cultural recognition. At the same time, game mechanics can hinder student perceptions of learning due to complexity and lack of intuitiveness. Material issues such as technical robustness affected the gameplay experience, highlighting the need for improved game functionality. However, player interaction with the game's objectives led to positive learning outcomes, illustrating the game's potential as an effective educational tool. The findings suggest that carefully integrating educational content into game design can significantly enhance learning outcomes, particularly in cultural geography education. This study contributes to understanding serious games as versatile educational tools by underscoring the importance of spatial design as a means to maximize student perceptions towards pedagogical effectiveness.

**Keywords:** Geography Higher-Education · Cybermedia Model · Serious Game · Game Spatiality

## 1 Introduction

In recent years, the intersection of digital games and education has garnered increasing attention from academics and educators alike, particularly in the field of geography [1]. The immersive nature of digital games offers unique opportunities for engaging users in dynamic learning environments [2]. In geography higher education, there exists a need to engage space through not only landscapes and maps but also through connection with culture. Serious games offer a way for learners to engage in a space that may not be

J. L. Plass and X. Ochoa (Eds.): JCSG 2024, LNCS 15259, pp. 93–107, 2025.
https://doi.org/10.1007/978-3-031-74138-8_8

directly accessible while interacting with various cultural representations of those spaces [3]. *Stories of a GeoFarmer*, a two-dimensional Role-Playing Game (RPG) prototype we designed for an undergraduate geography course, leverages this potential by integrating educational content with engaging gameplay in an authentic context. The current story takes place in Malaysia, placing students into a digitized landscape meant to connect the concept of deforestation learned in the lecture with the cultural and environmental impact faced by rural farmers in the region. While the game does not focus on teaching Malaysian culture specifically. The goal of centering a chapter of the game in a real location encourages appreciation for the culture through direct interaction with problems and solutions documented in real-world case studies. These case studies highlight Malaysia's struggle with deforestation. Throughout the chapters of *Stories of a Geo-Farmer*, students can gain insight into how different cultures have addressed challenges such as deforestation by making decisions within the game, offering them a hands-on learning experience.

This study explores how *Stories of a GeoFarmer* uses different game elements to spatially engage the problem of deforestation through the perspective of a rural farmer. Through the lens of the Cybermedia Model, this study analyzes the impact of representational, mechanical, material, and player interaction layers within the game, offering insights into how each contributes to student perceptions of the learning experience. By examining the game's ability to connect players with complex geographical and cultural concepts, this research contributes to the broader discourse on the educational value of serious games [3].

## 2   Literature Review

Serious games offer novel ways to engage players in educational content from unique mechanics to vibrant and detailed environments. More specifically the use of serious games for geography higher education has grown as related fields like cultural heritage have embraced games to connect players with physical locations [4]. The in-situ nature of many of these games, which integrate geography and cultural topics, highlights the need to explore how students respond to the digital space within a game and how it contributes to their perception of knowledge creation through engagement.

### 2.1   Game-Based Learning

Game-based learning (GBL) integrates the motivational appeal of games with educational strategies to enhance learning outcomes. This approach leverages the intrinsic engagement of games to promote deeper interaction with educational content, facilitating both cognitive and emotional connections with the material. Tim Marsh's conceptualization of the serious games' continuum provides a useful framework for understanding the varying levels of gamification and their potential educational impacts [5].

Games designed purely for entertainment can be differentiated from those that incorporate substantive educational objectives, with a spectrum of hybrid models in between. These hybrids effectively blend gameplay with learning objectives, optimizing the balance between engagement and educational value. Narrative elements in games, as explored by Marsh et al., further enrich this engagement, linking storytelling with educational content to deepen learning and retention [6]. Narratives not only contextualize the learning material but also add an emotional dimension that enhances the educational experience, making complex concepts more accessible and memorable. Research by Abdul Jabbar and Felicia underscores the importance of specific game design features that drive engagement and learning in GBL environments [7]. Their systematic review identifies key design elements that significantly influence learner interaction, highlighting how these features can enhance both the cognitive and affective aspects of learning.

Furthermore, the broad review of educational technology by Tobias et al. supports the effectiveness of integrating gaming elements with curricular goals [8]. Their findings suggest that well-designed educational games not only improve cognitive skills but also positively affect attitudes towards learning, demonstrating the dual benefits of engagement and educational achievement.

## 2.2 Spatial Engagement

The game space offers several ways to embed information. This notion has historically been referred to as game spatiality [9]. As digital games grow more complex, enabling players to move through digital space, new opportunities to engage information become possible but also harder to classify. Games allow players to interact with the digital space which adds a layer of complexity to understanding the role of spatiality as a fundamental function of engagement. From an educational perspective, engagement is a complex construct, for the sake of clarity, we focus on engagement as a multidimensional response from students consisting of affective, behavioral, and cognitive responses [10]. We build on the notion from game spatiality literature that digital space can influence student responses of engagement.

From a geographic perspective, engaging a space generates an experience that derives from external stimulus [11]. Seeing and feeling the external world serves as a catalyst for emotion and cognition to develop. However, the development of emotion and cognition occurs through the lens of an individual's perception of the experience. People become involved in a space that allows them to actively participate and engage through affective, behavioral, and cognitive means [11]. The individual experience of a space can be influenced by various factors, inclusive of purposeful design, social function, and sensorial feelings [12]. This influence of space on the individual experience of the external world serves as a model for how we can view engagement with digital spaces [13].

In the digital space, be it a virtual environment or a game environment, players perceive audio-visual information as if it were an actual place. What occurs within this digital space then allows players to connect actions taken with the audio-visual information to become involved—spatial involvement [13]. Becoming involved in a digital space allows players to apply their perception of the experience of moving through space and thus respond through the different dimensions of engagement. The make-up of the game space could influence how players become involved within a space and engage with learning content. For example, in a text-based narrative game, players will be forced to develop the space cognitively through imagination, which is often influenced by individual experience. In a text-based narrative game, players may behave differently than in a three-dimensional game where a character avatar traverses a provided game environment. Building on the notion that players will respond to different game characteristics, game designers often intentionally shape how players can and should behave within a specific game space, similar to real-world architectural practice [14]. These fundamental differences in how digital spaces can be provided may depend on several game characteristics.

### 2.3  Cybermedia Model in Games

The Cybermedia Model for understanding game ontology focuses on defining games by key characteristics that make up a game's system. Addressing a persisting issue, even in today's literature of defining a game by characteristics [15], the model directly considered the differentiation between process and object. Such characteristics may include a game's rules, the players, or rewards. The purpose of this originating model was to clarify how we should look at and compare games. The original Cybermedia Model consisted of four characteristics: player, sign, mechanical system, and material medium [16]. A more recent review of the Cybermedia Model takes these four characteristics and introduces them as layers to the game: representational, mechanical, material, and player [17]. Isolating each layer of a game enables us a new perspective on understanding engagement with the game space – game spatiality. In particular, the layers provide an understanding of independent spatial objects impacting player experience which we can connect with intended learning outcomes. As layers, the Cybermedia Model enables a vertical structure that makes the organization of a game's objects more visible [17]. The layer structure starts with the player layer and descends next with the representational layer, mechanical layer, and then finally the material layer.

- The player layer focuses on the player's engagement with the game, analyzing how interactions influence their experiences and decision-making processes [16].
- The representational layer examines the game's content and aesthetics, including visuals, narrative, and audio elements that shape the player's immersion and understanding [16].
- The mechanical layer concerns the rules and functionality of the game, detailing the underlying mechanics that dictate gameplay dynamics [16].
- The material layer looks at the physical or digital format through which the game is accessed, considering how different technologies impact gameplay and user interaction [16].

## 3  Methodology

### 3.1  Research Question

Our research investigates how students respond to spatial game elements through player engagement within an educational context. Specifically, we aim to determine the student responsiveness towards spatial elements within different game layers including narrative, environmental storytelling, and task-based learning in connecting with geographical issues.

We hypothesize that the game's specialized elements, particularly its immersive narrative and task-oriented gameplay, enhance learner engagement through recognition of the game space. We anticipate that our findings will contribute valuable insights into the design of game space in educational games that integrate subject matter within each layer of a game's design.

## 3.2   Game Design

*Stories of a GeoFarmer*, a top-down RPG, is a prototype designed to enhance undergraduate geography education, specifically cultural geography. The game design was informed by James Paul Gee's principles for game-based learning, which emphasize the importance of identity, interactivity, and problem-solving in educational games [18]. By integrating these principles, the game facilitates engagement with the geographical and cultural contexts of Malaysia.

The game, developed using RPG Maker MV, offers a narrative-driven experience where players undertake the role of a farmer in various countries. As of the time of this manuscript, players can play as a farmer character in Malaysia, facing the geographic challenges of deforestation and environmental sustainability. The game environment is richly detailed with two-dimensional graphics, featuring rural landscapes with wood cabins, diverse vegetation, and interactive tasks that relate to course learning objectives [see 19 for more details]. Each task is designed to reveal the impacts of environmental choices from multiple perspectives, enhancing both empathy towards and understanding of the farmer's plight among players. Informed by several case studies, players can experience the real-life solutions attempted to resolve the growing issues of deforestation. In these experiences, players are actively forced to make increasingly difficult decisions and at times decisions that do not align with their perception of what is correct. The game environment encourages exploration as a reward for completing quest tasks where tools and new knowledge are gained.

Players interact via their two-dimensional character, an unnamed farmer who loses their farm and home in a bad storm. The narrative forces players to learn how to play the game (e.g., moving the character around and which buttons to press). The narrative starts the game experience and introduces other pertinent information to guide the player through future choices. Feedback within the game occurs through text-based responses from non-playable characters (NPCs), objective tracking located in the top right corner, and two meters in the top left corner (see Fig. 1). Previous research on the nature of scaffolded feedback in *Stories of a GeoFarmer* indicated the two meters: environmeter and populameter garnered the most attention from students in playing through the prototype [19]. As players progress through different actions, the meters fill or empty, indicating the disparity discovered in attempting real-life solutions that had succeeded in some areas but failed in others. The complexity of resolving the economic, geographic, and cultural challenges of the real-life situation presents an ill-structured problem [20]. The game environment allows for several types of interaction, all of which impact the meters, from cutting down trees to planting indigenous plants. The player's goal in the game is to help the farmer restore their farm and livelihood by participating in various events throughout the game. The challenge presented through the game's design illustrates the disparity faced by locals in regions such as the un-named village in Malaysia because of deforestation.

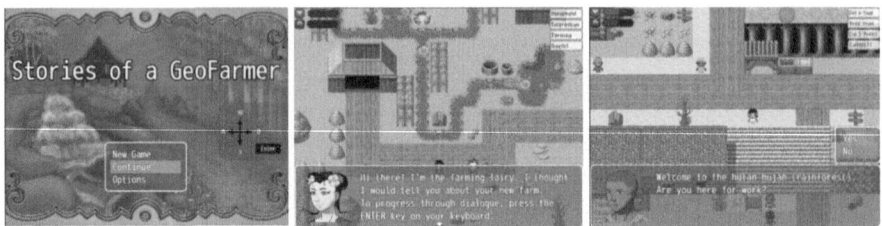

**Fig. 1.** Scenes from stories of a GeoFarmer

### 3.3  Participants

The study involved 68 undergraduate students from a geography course, divided across six sections, including one honors section and one online section. Participation in the study was optional, but all students in the course played the game which was introduced in the fifth week of a 16-week course. Students who chose to participate in the study could earn extra credit points.

### 3.4  Procedures

The game was introduced during a 50-min lab class session of an undergraduate Regions and Nations course at a mid-western university. The large lecture class consists of multiple sections offered both in-person and online. Before starting, students received the game's instructions and background information from a teaching assistant, ensuring that all participants were equally prepared. Consent to participate in the study was obtained through a post-game digital survey. The survey had approval from the Institutional Review Board (IRB) and was implemented through an ungraded survey in Canvas, the course's learning management system. Students were asked to submit a screenshot of where they ended the game prototype for reflection within the survey. If students completed the game, this final screenshot would be of the "score card" found on the farm the players were able to build during gameplay. During the session, the instructor and teaching assistant were able to assist with issues, technical and gameplay-based, as well as observe how students were able to interact with the game. Observations were broadly collected to protect the identities of students who elected to not participate in study portion of the gameplay session.

### 3.5  Data Collection

Data collection involved a two-part process tailored to capture a comprehensive understanding of player interactions and responses. The first part of the data collection was structured direct observation during gameplay, which primarily aimed to identify and document any unexpected problems that players encountered. Observers recorded instances where players faced challenges or disruptions that deviated from the anticipated game experience. This included technical glitches, interface issues, or any confusion with game mechanics that could impact the player's engagement and learning process.

Following the gameplay period, participants were asked to complete a post-game survey consisting of eight open-ended questions designed to elicit detailed reflections on their game experience. Questions such as "What were some of the most noticeable moments throughout your gameplay experience?" and "In what ways did any of the game elements (environment, people you interact with) improve or lessen the enjoyment of the game?" were included to delve deeper into the players' emotional and cognitive engagement with the game. Additional questions focused on players' likes and dislikes, providing space for specific reflections on key learning scaffolds like the environmeter and populameter scores. Responses to these surveys were intended to provide qualitative insights into the effectiveness of game elements in encouraging engagement and enhancing student opinions of educational outcomes.

## 3.6 Data Analysis

We conducted a qualitative thematic analysis [21] to understand the depth and complexity of player interactions with *Stories of a GeoFarmer* regarding their engagement with the game environment. Adopting the Collaborative Qualitative Analysis approach [22], two coders coded the data using four consensus meetings across one month. The data was coded in two rounds with the first round focusing on inductive codes and the second round focusing on refining the codes. A third independent researcher joined the final consensus meeting to assist with axial coding to align inductive codes into deductive themes—the game layers [23]. The initial inductive coding was crucial for uncovering patterns and insights that were grounded purely in the data, providing insights on the participants' experiences and perceptions. Following this, in the second round, we convened to discuss these emergent themes and began the process of refining and categorizing them. This collaborative effort led to the development of a dynamic codebook, which evolved as more data was analyzed and more themes were identified. This iterative refinement was key to ensuring that our thematic framework accurately represented the breadth and depth of the data. The final round involved further consolidation and refinement of these themes into a coherent set of categories. This stage of axial coding allowed us to define clear relationships between the main and sub-themes, finalizing the codebook.

Using the updated Cybermedia Model [18], which categorizes responses into four layers: representational, mechanical, material, and player, we axially aligned the refined inductive codes into each layer. We elected to use a consensus coding approach to improve trustworthiness of the codes and the axial alignment with the model while considering where student perceptions of learning connected with a part of the design. All data was analyzed using QualCoder, an open-source software analysis tool designed for handling complex qualitative data. Our analysis explored intricate patterns within the data, revealing how players interact with and perceive the game's educational content within the game space.

# 4  Results

Our study employed a qualitative approach to examine the impact of *Stories of a GeoFarmer* on student engagement with the game space and what the implications would be towards learning in a cultural educational context. The data gathered includes responses from a post-game survey completed by 68 undergraduate geography students. Observations were used in the contextualization of coding rather than to form codes directly.

## 4.1  Observations

During gameplay, students demonstrated significant interest and engagement, particularly when faced with tasks that involved critical thinking about environmental issues, such as deforestation. However, technical issues with the classroom internet disrupted one section's experience of the game, preventing students from completing the prototype. Another common observation across the course sections was the students' confusion in completing the first primary task of cutting down trees. One last observation was the amount of progress made by students during the class period and how much time was spent exploring the game world before attempting the objectives. Our observations also noted that students who encountered only a few technical issues during gameplay reported a smoother experience.

## 4.2  Qualitative Analysis of Thematic Coding

Our coding focused on aligning student responses into the Cybermedia Model to better understand how students responded to the game space as they learned about deforestation in Malaysia (Table 1).

**Representational Layer**. The representational layer, which included 134 codes, was pivotal in assessing how players perceive and interact with the game environment. Spatial learning emerged as a significant theme, with 15 mentions, indicating that players often saw the game's spatial arrangements as analogous to real-world settings, which heightened their perceived engagement and application of learning to real-life scenarios. An example of this was a player noting, "It led me to think how I would operate in real-life situations and scenarios." Landscape and environment, coded 61 times, highlighted the immersive experience provided by the game, with players appreciating the detailed depictions of the environment, as one remarked, "Transversing the area and looking at all the different plants and the environment around is the most noticeable." However, issues within the environment, noted 58 times, suggested that problems such as glitches or design flaws could detract from engagement.

**Mechanical Layer**. Comprising of 124 codes, the mechanical layer focused on gameplay mechanics and how they supported or hindered learning. Understanding meter actions, with 94 mentions, was a crucial aspect, showing that players recognized the impact of their actions within the game's ecological framework. For instance, a player expressed, "Planting the rubber trees caused the fall of my environmental score." The completion of quests (14 mentions) and additional learning elements (11 mentions) were

**Table 1.** Code book with code count results.

| Layer | Codes | Count | Description |
|---|---|---|---|
| Representational Layer (135) | Spatial Learning | 15 | This layer focused on how the game's design affects spatial awareness and immersion from content audio and visuals |
| | Landscape/environment | 62 | |
| | Issues with environment | 58 | |
| Mechanical Layer (127) | Understand meter/actions | 95 | This layer addresses the effectiveness of game mechanics |
| | Completing the quests | 14 | |
| | Learning | 12 | |
| | Not catching the game goal | 6 | |
| Material Layer (67) | Accessibility/usability | 13 | This layer reveals technical challenges affecting gameplay |
| | Issues within the game | 54 | |
| Player Layer (130) | Negative experience | 45 | This layer explores player experiences and values |
| | Positive experience | 26 | |
| | Personal value | 34 | |
| | Communication | 25 | |

also noted as enhancing engagement through clear goals and expanded knowledge. One player recalled, "I also found what I learned about rubber trees memorable because I'd never known what they were before." Challenges in grasping the game's objectives, however, were evident in five mentions, indicating potential areas for improving clarity and instructional design.

**Material Layer**. With 67 codes, the material layer focused on the game's accessibility and operational aspects. Thirteen codes addressed accessibility/usability issues, reflecting concerns over the interface and functionality across devices. These frustrations as articulated by a player stating, "I pressed escape and it said it did not understand my key so I had to restart." Other operational issues, such as bugs affecting gameplay progression, were highlighted, ultimately undermining student perceptions of engagement, and pointing to the need for technical refinement.

**Player Layer**. As the most emphasized layer, the player layer had 130 codes that captured direct player experiences and values. Negative experiences, coded 45 times, often related to gameplay elements pushing players too rigidly, diminishing the educational impact as one player noted, "It felt like the player was pushed by objectives more than the world or educational content." Conversely, positive experiences (26 codes) and personal value (34 codes) underscored moments of meaningful engagement and learning, with players finding personal relevance in the game scenarios, as illustrated by a player's experience, "I most notably remember accidentally setting fire to a large forest.....definitely not my intention!" Communication within the game (25 codes) also played a vital role in enhancing engagement, helping players to internalize and contextualize learning, as seen in interactions like, "By talking to the characters and hearing their unique perspectives, the player is able to reinforce concepts learned in class but also understand the effects of each decision being made."

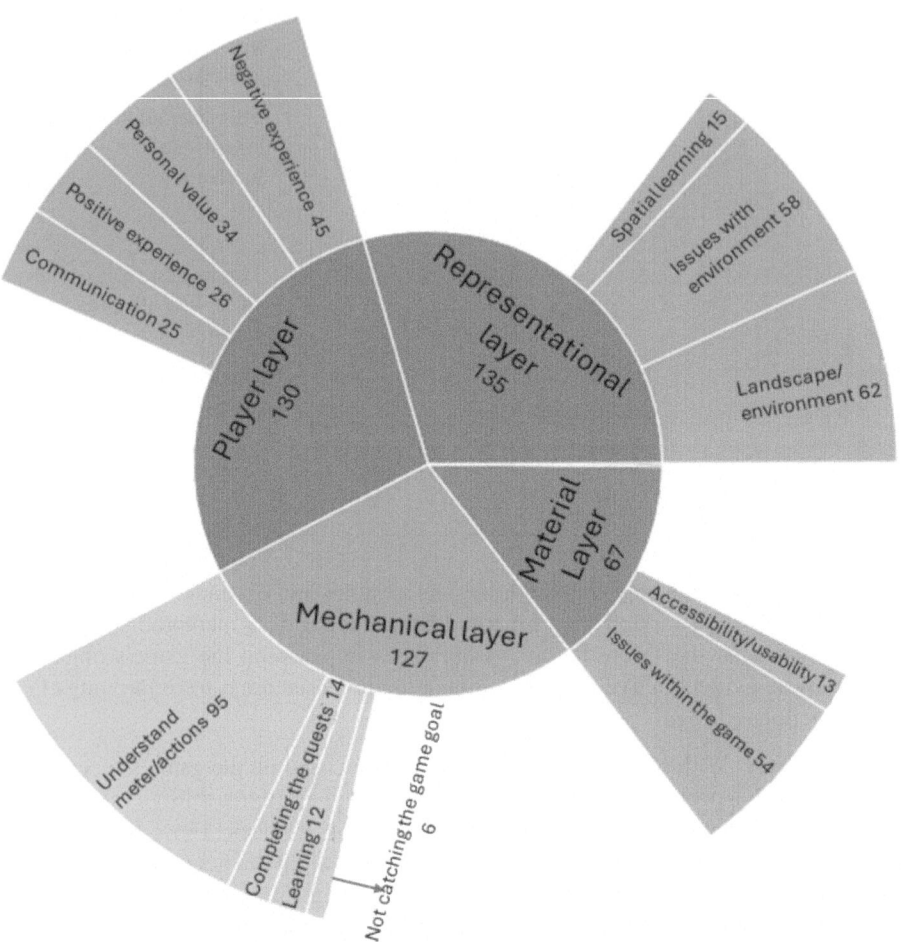

**Fig. 2.** Sunburst chart of code distribution across cybermedia model layers

In addition to our detailed analysis of the qualitative data, we visualized the distribution of codes across the four layers of the Cybermedia Model using a sunburst chart (see Fig. 2). This graphical representation underscores the relative frequency of themes within each layer. In the chart, each segment represents a specific layer with its associated codes, demonstrating the thematic focus and engagement level detected within that layer. The Representational Layer shows students focused on landscape/environment, indicating player immersion in the game setting. In contrast, the Mechanical Layer is concerned with understanding meter/actions, reflecting the players' engagement with the game mechanics and their understanding of how actions impact the game environment. The Player Layer, notably, shows positive and negative experiences, highlighting the game's emotional impacts. The Material Layer reflects technical and usability issues that players encountered, pointing to potential areas for improvement in game design.

The analysis of these codes reveals a nuanced view of how game design elements from each layer of the Cybermedia Model interact to impact learner engagement. While the representational and mechanical layers contributed positively to perceptions of engagement, issues highlighted in the material and player layers suggest areas for improvement. Overall, the predominance of codes related to positive experiences and effective learning mechanisms in comparison to those indicating problems suggests that the game did engage learners though not entirely through the game space. Furthermore, our codes indicate a need for refinement to minimize negative experiences and technical issues that may have been disruptive towards engagement.

## 5  Discussion

This section interprets the findings from *Stories of a GeoFarmer*, focusing on how the game's design across different layers influences student perceptions of engagement with the game space and cultural learning context. Each layer's impact is discussed for the relative impact on how we addressed our research questions.

### 5.1  Representational Layer

**Spatial Elements**. The game's utilization of visual and auditory elements did enhance spatial learning as indicated by student comments. This notion echoes Gagnon's findings that interactive environments promote spatial cognitive skills [24]. Players' feedback, such as "It gave me structure on where to start and in what path I should be heading," highlights the game's ability to use the environment to guide and shape engagement. Much as with actual architectural practice, environments can guide users through a space without issue when designed well. There were, however, times when the spatial elements were not well structured as another player indicated, "Because of the placement of some things and the design of the tongkat I had a really hard time figuring out where it was."

**Connected to Learning**. The immersive elements were viewed as capable of bridging abstract geographical concepts with tangible experiences, supporting Ash and Gallacher's perspective on the potential of video games as tools for cultural and geographical education [25]. For instance, a player's observation, "I think it was interesting to learn that some trees are not great for the environment," illustrates how well the game facilitates engagement with educational content.

**Cultural Relevance**. Our game's authentic representation of Malaysian rural life enriches the educational experience and contrasts sharply with the stereotypical portrayals critiqued by Šisler [26]. Such depth encourages players to appreciate and respect cultural diversity, highlighting the game's role in fostering cultural empathy.

## 5.2  Mechanical Layer

**Spatial Elements**. The design and function of the meter system illustrate the direct consequences of players' actions within the game environment, reflecting Gagnon's emphasis on the need for user-friendly mechanics that enhance learning outcomes [24]. Feedback like "it was interesting to see all of the different scenarios that can play out when companies are trying to make money off of ruining the environment," underscores the educational impact of integrating game mechanics with real-world ecological principles.

**Connected to Learning**. Aligning game mechanics with educational goals, as highlighted by feedback such as "Very confusing and I don't understand the learning aspect," suggests a need for improved clarity in game instructions and objectives. This aligns with literature advocating for game mechanics that enhance rather than obstruct learning [27].

**Cultural Relevance**. Incorporating local cultural elements within game mechanics not only deepens engagement but also enhances cultural understanding, resonating with Šisler's advocacy for culturally sensitive game design [26]. From a mechanics perspective, students related the most to the cultural interactions where they could associate conversation with NPCs to the local flora and fauna.

## 5.3  Material Layer

**Spatial Elements**. Technical stability is critical for maintaining engagement, as technical issues disrupt the learning flow and immersion, highlighted by players' frustrations with game functionality, "I pressed escape and it did not understand my key so I had to restart." This issue underscores the importance of robust game design noted in game studies literature [25].

**Connected to Learning**. Ensuring material robustness is essential, as supported by literature emphasizing the importance of accessibility and seamless interaction in educational games [27].

**Cultural Relevance**. The game's technical inclusivity ensures equitable educational opportunities, critical for a culturally diverse student body.

## 5.4  Player Layer

**Spatial Elements**. Navigational tasks within a culturally enriched environment enhance spatial learning and embed educational content effectively, as players like noting, "Cutting down the trees and running through the massive forest was memorable," reveal.

**Connected to Learning**. The direct link between engagement with game objectives and learning outcomes, as seen in players' feedback, supports theories advocating for active learning [24, 27].

**Cultural Relevance**. Integrating cultural elements into gameplay not only enhances geographical learning but also fosters deeper empathy and understanding of cultural diversity, aligning with the concept of games as mediums for comprehensive cultural education discussed in literature [26].

# 6 Limitations

This study's limitations include the absence of quantitative data and analysis, which might have provided a more robust validation of our findings. Additionally, our observations were broad and did not delve deeply into specific issues encountered by players, which could limit the understanding of particular design flaws or user experiences that impede learning. These limitations suggest areas for further research, particularly in enhancing data collection methods and analyzing observed data.

# 7 Conclusion

Our study employing the Cybermedia Model to analyze *Stories of a GeoFarmer* offers insights into how serious games can facilitate spatial engagement and connect players with cultural contexts. We examined various aspects of game design across representational, mechanical, material, and player layers, revealing their impact on learning and engagement. The Representational Layer showed that immersive environments enhance spatial learning and cultural immersion, underscoring the potential of digital games in geographical education. In the Mechanical Layer, findings indicated the need for more intuitive mechanics to align better with educational objectives. The Material Layer emphasized the importance of technical robustness for sustained immersion and learning continuity. The Player Layer demonstrated that engaging objectives significantly enhance learning outcomes and deepen cultural understanding. This research highlights the potential of serious gaming in education, particularly in promoting cultural awareness and geographical knowledge. Future efforts should aim to refine game design elements to maximize educational benefits.

**Acknowledgments.** We would like to thank our game developers, Blake Piper and Nannan Huang.

**Disclosure of Interests** The authors have no competing interests to declare that are relevant to the content of this article.

# References

1. Bereitschaft, B.: Commercial city building games as pedagogical tools: what have we learned? J. Geogr. High. Educ. **47**(2), 161–187 (2023). https://doi.org/10.1080/03098265.2021.200 7524
2. Gee, J.P.: What video games have to teach us about learning and literacy. Comput. Entertain. (CIE) **1**(1), 20 (2003)
3. Barab, S.A., Gresalfi, M., Ingram-Goble, A.: Transformational play: using games to position person, content, and context. Educ. Res. **39**(7), 525–536 (2010)
4. Stintzing, M., Pietsch, S., Wardenga, U.: How to teach "landscape" through games? In: Edler, D., Jenal, C., Kühne, O. (eds.) Modern Approaches to the Visualization of Landscapes, pp. 333–349. Springer Fachmedien Wiesbaden (2020). https://doi.org/10.1007/978-3-658-30956-5_19

5. Marsh, T.: Serious games continuum: between games for purpose and experiential environ-ments for purpose. Entertain. Comput. **2**(2), 61–68 (2011). https://doi.org/10.1016/j.entcom. 2010.12.004

6. Marsh, T., Nickole, L.Z., Klopfer, E., Xuejin, C., Osterweil, S., Haas, J.: Fun and learning: blending design and development dimensions in serious games through narrative and char-acters. In: Ma, M., Oikonomou, A., Jain, L.C. (eds.) Serious Games and Edutainment Appli-cations, pp. 273–288. Springer, Berlin (2011). https://doi.org/10.1007/978-1-4471-2161-9_14

7. Abdul Jabbar, A.I., Felicia, P.: Gameplay engagement and learning in game-based learning: a systematic review. Rev. Educ. Res. **85**(4), 740–779 (2015). https://doi.org/10.3102/003465 4315577210

8. Tobias, S., Fletcher, J.D., Wind, A.P.: Game-Based Learning. In: Spector, J., Merrill, M., Elen, J., Bishop, M. (eds.) Handbook of Research on Educational Communications and Tech-nology, pp. 485–503. Springer, New York, NY (2014). https://doi.org/10.1007/978-1-4614-3185-5_38

9. Günzel, S. (2008). The space-image: interactivity and spatiality of computer games. In: Günzel, S., Liebe, M., Mersch, D. (eds.) Proceedings of the Philosophy of Computer Games 2008, pp. 179–189. University Press. http://pub.ub.uni-potsdam.de/volltexte/2008/2456/

10. Ben-Eliyahu, A., Moore, D., Dorph, R., Schunn, C.D.: Investigating the multidimensionality of engagement: affective, behavioral, and cognitive engagement across science activities and contexts. Contemp. Educ. Psychol. **53**, 87–105 (2018). https://doi.org/10.1016/j.cedpsych. 2018.01.002

11. Tuan, Y.: Space and Place: The Perspective of Experience. University of Minnesota Press (2002)

12. Lefebvre, H.: The Production of Space (D. Nicholson-Smith, Trans.; 33. print). Blackwell Publishing (2013)

13. Calleja, G.: In-game: From Immersion to Incorporation. MIT Press, Cambridge (2011)

14. Totten, C.W.: An Architectural Approach to Level Design, 2nd edn. CRC Press, Taylor & Francis Group, Boca Raton (2019)

15. Elias, G.S., Garfield, R., Gutschera, K.R.: Characteristics of Games. MIT Press (2012)

16. Aarseth, E., Calleja, G.: The word game: The ontology of an undefinable object. In: 10th International Conference on the Foundations of Digital Games (2015). https://www.um.edu. mt/library/oar//handle/123456789/26620

17. Bakkerud, F.: The ontology of game spatiality. Game Stud. **23**(3) (2023). https://gamestudies. org/2303/articles/bakkerud

18. Gee, J.P.: What Video Games Have to Teach Us About Learning and Literacy. Second Edition: Revised and Updated Edition. Palgrave Macmillan, New York, NY (2007)

19. Oprean, D., Brown, D., McGorry, N., Pieper, B., Rankin, N., Larsen, S.: Exploring in-game scaffolds for higher-order learning in a case-based RPG learning game. Europ. Conf. Games Based Learn. **17**(1), 467–474 (2023). https://doi.org/10.34190/ecgbl.17.1.1590

20. Jonassen, D.H.: Instructional design models for well-structured and ill-structured problem-solving learning outcomes. Educ. Tech. Res. Dev. **45**(1), 65–94 (1997)

21. Braun, V., Clarke, V.: Using thematic analysis in psychology. Qual. Res. Psychol. **3**, 77–101 (2006)

22. Richards, K.A.R., Hemphill, M.A.: A practical guide to collaborative qualitative data analysis. J. Teach. Phys. Educ. **37**(2), 225–231 (2018). https://doi.org/10.1123/jtpe.2017-0084

23. Williams, M., Moser, T.: The art of coding and thematic exploration in qualitative research. Int. Manage. Rev. **15**(1), 45–55 (2019)

24. Gagnon, D.: Videogames and spatial skills: an exploratory study. ECTJ **33**, 263–275 (1985). https://doi.org/10.1007/BF02769363

25. Ash, J., Gallacher, L.A.: Cultural geography and videogames. Geogr. Compass **5**(6), 351–368 (2011). https://doi.org/10.1111/j.1749-8198.2011.00427.x
26. Šisler, V. (2008). Digital arabs: Representation in video games. Europ. J. Cultural Stud. **11**(2). https://doi.org/10.1177/1367549407088333
27. Subrahmanyam, K., Greenfield, P.M.: Effect of video game practice on spatial skills in girls and boys. J. Appl. Dev. Psychol. **15**(1), 13–32 (1994). https://doi.org/10.1016/0193-3973(94)90004-3

# Game-Based Learning Analytics: Insights from an Integrated Design Process

Maurice Boothe Jr.(✉)(iD), Madhumitha Gopalakrishnan(iD), Mischa Huynh,
Yanzhi Wang(iD), and Xavier Ochoa(iD)

New York University, New York, NY 10012, USA
mab1488@nyu.edu

**Abstract.** Game-Based Learning Analytics (GBLA) is a method of integrating Game-Based Learning and Learning Analytics to enhance the effectiveness of the learning process in educational games by providing actionable learning analytics information to players within the game environment. This paper presents initial insights from an integrated design process to achieve this goal. Through a series of interdisciplinary workshops culminating in a participant playtest session, this paper highlights the challenges and opportunities that arise from this integration. The findings point to the importance of early consideration of learning analytics in game design, the challenges of conceptualizing the differences between game feedback and learning feedback, and how learners interpret learning feedback within the context of the game. This work lays the groundwork for future research and development in the interaction between Game-Based Learning and Learning Analytics.

**Keywords:** feedback · game-based learning · learning analytics · GBLA

## 1 Introduction

The field of developmental psychology has long recognized play as an important tool to help children learn [24,25]. Games continue to gain increasing importance as a rich medium with the potential to facilitate and enhance students' learning [26]. Game design researchers have coined the term "serious" or "educational" games for games that are designed to help students acquire or practice a given knowledge or skill [19]. The development of games as learning environments has evolved into an active area of research called Game-Based Learning (GBL) [27]. This field of research has shown that serious games utilize successful game design principles to generate personalized, engaging, and deep learning experiences [13], and are seen to help students achieve better learning outcomes in comparison to conventional ways of learning [20,21].

On the other hand, the field of Learning Analytics (LA) involves the measurement, collection, analysis, and reporting of data about learners and their

J. L. Plass and X. Ochoa (Eds.): JCSG 2024, LNCS 15259, pp. 108–123, 2025.
https://doi.org/10.1007/978-3-031-74138-8_9

contexts, with the aim of understanding and optimizing learning and the environments in which it occurs [15, 31]. One important aspect of Learning Analytics that differentiates it from other avenues of Educational Research is its objective to present the results of the data analysis to the stakeholders, enabling them to reflect on these data and make informed decisions to improve their learning process. This is known in the Learning Analytics field as "closing the loop" [8].

There is a natural affinity between these two fields. As students play, their multi-level engagement with the game environment creates large amounts of detailed logs of their activity-rich data that can be analyzed by learning analytics systems to study how students learn through gameplay. The results of these analyses can then be used to improve the learning process fostered by the game. In alignment with the goal of Learning Analytics to "close the loop," analyses of educational game data have been presented to diverse stakeholders to inform and support their decisions. These stakeholders include researchers, instructional game designers, teachers, and students.

*Educational researchers* can use learning analytics to better understand diverse dimensions of the learning process. Their objective is to develop generalizable principles that could improve the design of educational games, such as the roles of emotion in learning [33], locus of control [17], student agency [14], or reflection behavior [4]. *Game designers* can use learning analytics to evaluate the current effectiveness of educational games and gain insights into how to improve their learning design. Their main objective is to enhance the learning process in specific games or their future iterations. For example, [14] propose the use of replay analytics to explore and evaluate the design of an open-ended educational game. *Instructors* use analytics extracted from the game to evaluate or assess the performance of students in a specific knowledge area or skill. Their objective is usually to measure the learner's progress and to guide interventions. For example, [16] used evidence-centered strategy to conduct stealth assessment in educational games. Providing learning analytics information to the final group of stakeholders, students, is of special interest. They are the only stakeholders who can directly use the results of the analysis to gain insights about their own learning during gameplay and use that information to self-regulate their learning behavior in real-time.

Unfortunately, there is a surprising lack of studies on how to provide learning analytics information to students about their learning experiences in educational games. Several recent surveys on the integration of Game-Based Learning and Learning Analytics [1, 6, 18, 19] reveal few examples of student-facing analytics. Out of the 151 works reviewed in these surveys, the great majority (about 90%) used game data to inform educational researchers, instructional game designers, or teachers, but not the students themselves. Across these surveys, only *four* studies specifically offered results back to students [7, 22, 28, 29]. Not only are there very few examples, but these examples do not leverage the affordances of the game environment to provide more natural feedback to learners. For instance, the four studies cited previously use a dashboard (or a dashboard-like visualization) to report the current learning status of a student [7, 22, 28, 29]. Both [22] and [7] use basic visualizations (colored circular graphs and tables) to show the percentage of learning quests completed by students, whereas [29] and [28] use line graphs to show students' progress over time. Given that access to analytics has been demonstrated to have a positive impact on learning self-regulation in other contexts [17], and that games are, by nature, excellent vehicles to deliver feedback [12], we would expect more educational games to include learning analytics information. Moreover, the lack of student-facing analytics is particularly problematic because, while playing educational games, students are the primary agents who can have an immediate and direct impact on their learning process, yet the necessary insight and feedback to reflect upon and modify their learning is often absent.

In this work, we aim to explore how student-facing learning analytics information can be deeply integrated into educational games. First, we conceptualize what Game-Based Learning Analytics is and how it could manifest (Sect. 2). Then, we describe an initial experience of integrating Game-Based Learning Analytics into the design of an educational game through a series of interdisciplinary workshops and the insights we gained from them (Sect. 3). Finally, we test a prototype of the resulting game to gain insights into how players react to the learning analytics feedback (Sect. 4). This paper will discuss three research questions that are addressed through subsequent the preceding phases of the project:

- RQ1: What is the effect of including learning analytics experts into the design process of an educational game?
- RQ2: What emerges from a design process integrating learning analytics into educational games?
- RQ3: How do participants react to learning analytics feedback during gameplay?

We conclude the paper with a discussion of the findings, the limitations of our approach, and directions for further research.

## 2  Game-Based Learning Analytics

To guide our understanding of the relationship between Game-Based Learning and Learning Analytics, the authors provide and elaborate a definition for "Game-Based Learning Analytics" by expanding upon the original definition of "learning analytics" presented in the introduction of this paper. [15,31]

*Game-Based Learning Analytics* can be defined as the use of educational games as (1) the source of learning traces that can be analyzed to evaluate the learning process of a learner-player and (2) the vehicle for providing those analytics in an embedded and contextualized way to the learner-player to help them take meaningful, self-regulated decisions to impact their learning process in the game. This definition implies four distinct aspects that should be considered in the design of Game-Based Learning Analytics: Collection, Analysis, Presentation, and Actionability.

**Collection** is the first aspect and consists of the capturing of "learning data", that is, action traces that are relevant to infer the learning status of the student. This aspect should be informed by the long tradition of "stealth" assessment [30] in educational games.

**Analysis** is the second aspect and refers to the automatic calculation and modeling of the student's learning needs based on their current status and the desired levels of mastery or proficiency. In this aspect, the main consideration is how those analyses will eventually support the player. While it may be convenient to provide insight about their progress with how far they have left to go or how many interactions they have navigated correctly, these analytics are rudimentary and serve of little benefit. Analytics should be relevant, informative, and useful to the player as it relates to navigating the learning experience. This is dependent on the contextual elements provided by the educational game such as the learning objective or what data are collected. Another consideration during this phase is to determine what methodologies should be utilized in order to acquire these insights, whether they be machine learning algorithms or more simple thresholds related to the collective data. This aspect is informed by the varied analytic methods developed and used in the creation of learning analytics tools [11].

**Presentation** is the third aspect and deals with how to present the learning data analysis to the player. In this aspect, it is important to note that presenting data and analysis to the player should be done in a way that does not undermine the playfulness and engagement offered by Game-Based Learning. Presenting a dashboard of learning analytics in the middle of a game experience would be inappropriate, because it assumes a level of data literacy on the player's behalf, and pulls them out of the immersive experience that the narrative game world was intending to provide. By distracting the learner from the game itself, we are then relying on the game to be effective in drawing the learner back into the immersive experience, a task that is already challenging and even more so when interrupted regularly. Ideally, the learning analytics would be provided to the player in a way that does not break immersion. While there is a large research body about how and when feedback should be presented [23], the specifics about how to better exploit game elements to communicate this feedback to players is an interesting research challenge.

**Actionability** is the fourth and final aspect of GBLA and is concerned with the ways in which we allow the player to respond and make decisions given the presented learning analytics. An important aspect of this phase is how we enable the player to take action given the feedback they have received. Many educational games provide feedback by restricting the player from advancing until they have demonstrated their proficiency to a level that satisfies the learning game system. However, this actually takes away the player agency to engage in self-regulated learning. If the player receives feedback that they may not be ready for the next level, they should be given opportunities to continue working on those skills, but they should also not be restricted to remain at the same level or advance to the next. By allowing the player to choose to advance, even if the learning game system infers that they're not ready, the player gains the responsibility for their progression. If they realize that further levels are too challenging, they should still receive the contextualized feedback about their process and also be able to return to lower level practice opportunities. The best way to implement this level of player agency in response to the learning analytic feedback provided is also an open research opportunity of GBLA.

Game-Based Learning Analytics leverages the principles and insights from the respective fields and explores how aspects of each can inform and enhance the other. In educational games with the objective of reaching learners with immediately actionable information to improve their learning process, the game itself should be designed to support the collection of relevant data as well as the presentation of analytics back to learners. Similarly, the type of analytics used and the methods of feedback should take into account the environment of the game. By leveraging the affordances and considerations of GBL and LA, we find ourselves in a different space of GBLA that is built upon the principles and affordances of those fields. This perspective offers a different approach for designing games and analytics and is found at the core of GBLA for this purpose. The next section explores a first attempt to an integrated design process.

## 3    Integrated Learning Analytics and Game Design Process

This explorative, qualitative research study employed a modified version of the design research approach [2,9] to explore the design processes that emerge from the integration of Learning Analytics and Game-Based Learning. We conducted a series of interdisciplinary workshops involving game designers, learning analytics experts, and subject matter experts to provide tangible insights into the process of designing educational games with integrated learning analytics. The resulting emergent themes would provide a basis for further research in our attempt to better understand how to better integrate GBL and LA.

This phase of our research explored two research questions:

- RQ1: What is the effect of including learning analytics experts into the design process of an educational game?
- RQ2: What emerges from a design process integrating learning analytics into educational games?

Apart from the GBLA aspects discussed in the previous section, the research team adopted two other principles to guide this process towards these research questions. The first principle was to place Learning Analytics as a core design pillar in the process. By introducing the intention of LA at the beginning of the process, leaning on it as a touchpoint throughout the process, and including LA experts as part of the design team, we can understand if its inclusion would ultimately improve the integration of LA into the educational game's design. The second principle adopted was to advocate for the player or learner, recognizing the potential consequences of their absence [32]. We wanted to ensure that the players were agents of their own learning decisions and avoid any potential harm that could arise by removing them from the process. This required the design team to not rely upon systems that would automatically adapt to the player's performance [5]. This also allowed us to better "close the loop" [8] by ensuring that the learner was an active participant in their learning process by responding to the feedback systems offered by the LA.

A number of other constraints were imposed on the design team including the design be a single-player game, use a common game engine (like Unity or Unreal Engine), be intended for adult learners, and be focused on chemical engineering processes. No learning objectives were preemptively selected in order to allow for the design team to pursue objectives of interest.

The design process consisted of three, two-hour long collaboration sessions and the design team consisted of six self-identified experts, two for each role of game designer (GD1 and GD2), subject matter expert (SME1 and SME2), and learning analytics expert (LAE1 and LAE2). The GDs had previously worked in industry as game designers and had taught college-level game design courses, the SMEs had degrees in chemical engineering and were currently employed as chemical engineers, and the LAEs were PhD candidates who published peer-reviewed publications on learning analytics. There were also two members of the research team present during the workshops: a facilitator and an observer. The workshop facilitator prepared, explained, and delivered the design activities and would also address participant questions while the workshop observer would make note of interactions that provided context to the design team's decisions. The workshops facilitated a combination divergent and convergent design process [3] and included stages of theory-building, creative exploration, brainstorming, prototyping, playtesting, selecting and refining ideas, and producing the deliverable. This deliverable was a collaborative document outlining the objectives, mechanics, and learning analytics implementation of the designed learning game.

## 3.1  Description of Activities

In the first session, the facilitator introduced the design team to the guiding principles and then allowed them to collaborate. The session primarily involved discourse on the basics of chemical engineering, led by the subject matter experts (SMEs), to provide the game designers (GDs) and learning analytics experts (LAEs) with a fundamental understanding of chemical processes. The GDs contributed significantly by deconstructing and re-framing these processes, while brainstorming possible game mechanics and player goals.

During the second and third sessions, discussions were largely dominated by the GDs and SME1, who shared a background in games. While many ideas were brainstormed, translating these ideas into a game with effective learning mechanics proved challenging. This challenge was rooted in the inherent tension between game mechanics, which are engaging and play-oriented, and learning mechanics, which are more structured and less flexible. This tension led to separate discussions among participants matching their roles, hindering progress. The LAEs emphasized the importance of integrating mechanics that promote metacognition, suggesting features like a "handbook" for players to record their findings. Despite concerns about player frustration from repeated failures, the team focused on balancing the game to navigate this potential issue.

The final design brief outlined a post-apocalyptic RPG adventure where players, as chemistry trainees, identified materials through experimentation to benefit their community. The design aimed to teach players how to determine the properties of elements and understand their characteristics. The game's objectives included creating a materials database, fostering scientific identity, and enhancing problem-solving skills. By integrating game and learning mechanics, the design team aimed to create an engaging and rewarding learning experience where players not only built a knowledge database but also developed a scientific identity while solving problems to ensure their community's survival.

## 3.2 Discussion

The observation of this integrated design process provided insights into our research questions. The discussion below offers considerations for those who wish to engage in or expand upon an integrated game-based learning-analytic process and address our first two research questions:

- RQ1: What is the effect of including learning analytics experts into the design process of an educational game?
- RQ2: What emerges from a design process integrating learning analytics into educational games?

**Inclusion of Learning Analytics Experts** Including LAEs as part of the design team ensured that LA became a core design pillar and would be considered throughout the game's design. Unfortunately, that conversation was largely limited to responding to the discussion of the GDs and SMEs and did not have a clear tangible output beyond ensuring that it was present during the design process. The impact of interdisciplinary literacy among experts was significant in the collaborative design process. SME1, with a background in games, facilitated discussions with GDs by sharing personal gaming experiences and commercial game examples, creating a shared understanding and language. This contrasted with the learning analytics experts (LAEs) and SME2, who lacked game literacy and struggled to participate in discussions, leading to SME1 and the GDs dominating conversations. The constraint that the product would be a digital game further limited the contributions of the LAEs and SME2 due to their unfamiliarity. However, the GDs displayed some familiarity with learning analytics, likely due to their experience in teaching. These observations suggest that having a design team with interdisciplinary literacy, such as subject matter experts who understand game design or LAEs familiar with the content area, would greatly benefit the collaborative process.

**Outcome of the Process** A number of interesting and insightful themes emerged from the observation of this integrated design process. First, introducing LA as a pillar into an already complex system is difficult. Integrating GBL with LA significantly increases the complexity of the design process. The design team needed to make choices that captured meaningful data for LA and developed in-game mechanisms for delivering feedback, leveraging the game's medium. The game design process, inherently focused on creating an engaging experience, often conflicted with the data-oriented and objective-focused suggestions from the LA experts. Despite including LAEs on the design team, LA remained underrepresented as their rigid recommendations struggled to adapt to changes in the game's design. This indicates that effective integration of LA and GBL requires substantial support, such as extended timelines, larger teams, or a smaller project scope, beyond what was initially anticipated. Additionally, integrating LA with GBL faces inherent tension. LA aims to operationalize and capture the entire learning process to infer long-term learning patterns, while games focus on immediate data that enhance player experience or progression. GBL may collect data on player learning but often fails to capture the learning process as it doesn't directly enhance the player experience. For instance, "stealth assessment" evaluates performance without providing actionable feedback based on the learning process [16]. Addressing this tension requires additional support, resources, and further research into design strategies. Although this tension seems unavoidable, as observed in this collaboration, targeted design research can help navigate it.

## 4    Playtesting a Game with Basic Game-Based Learning Analytics

In this phase, participants playtested a paper prototype of the educational game designed with basic learning analytics according to the specifications of the design team to evaluate participant reactions and interactions with the feedback mechanisms. This section presents our findings, providing insights into the effectiveness of the learning analytics feedback.

### 4.1    Research Design

This final stage of the project focused on evaluating participant reactions to learning analytics feedback within the context of a paper prototype of an educational game. This part of the study aims to address our third and final research question:

– RQ3: How do participants react to learning analytics feedback during gameplay?

We adopted a qualitative approach to observe and analyze player interactions with the game prototype. The evaluation of the learning game prototype began with an introduction to the study's purpose and consent collection, followed by a pre-interview to gather participants' prior experiences with educational games, familiarity with games, and knowledge of the learning content. Participants then engaged with the game prototype in a gameplay session, thinking aloud while researchers observed and took detailed notes on behaviors, reactions, and interactions. A researcher used a modified "Wizard of Oz" technique [10] to facilitate interactions with the paper prototype, including scripted prompts to emulate the game experience. Post-interviews captured participants' reflections on the gameplay and feedback mechanisms, providing in-depth insights into their perceptions and any changes in understanding or strategies. This process yielded rich qualitative data to inform the effective integration of learning analytics into game-based learning environments.

In total, 8 undergraduate students consented to playtest the game. All the participants were already familiar with games, having played mobile and computer games regularly. Similarly, a large number of participants were familiar with chemical engineering and had relatively similar levels of basic knowledge regarding material composition and chemical processes. Each playtest session was divided into three segments: pre-interview, playtest, and post-interview.

**Playtest Description** Each participant engaged with the paper prototype with the facilitation of a researcher while another researcher observed. The participant was initially presented the game board (pictured in Fig. 1) and four unlabeled substances. They were then read a short narrative of the game world and presented with the objective of the game. Each in-game day, they were presented with the option of visiting the laboratory or the library.

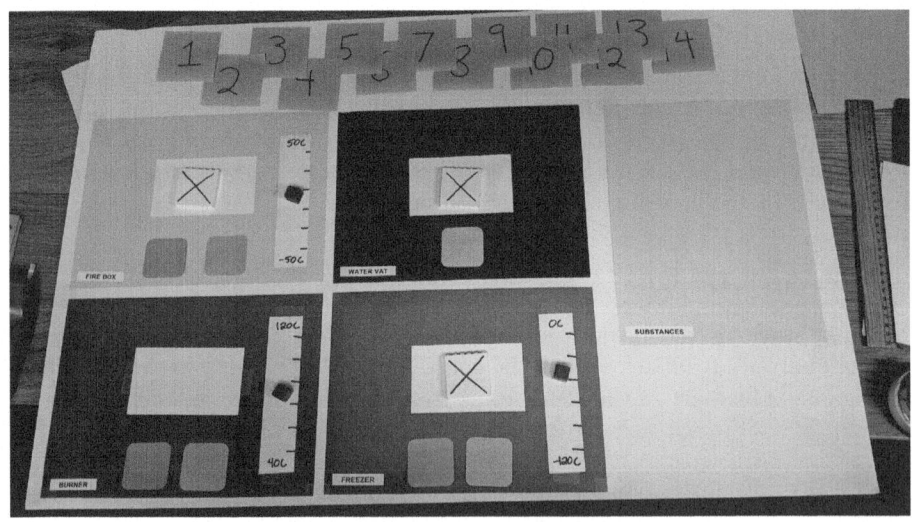

**Fig. 1.** Photo of the paper prototype

In the laboratory, the participant was permitted to "test" any of the materials they had by placing them into and operating the different machines. The facilitator would respond to each action with the result of the experiment. For example, if the participant placed Substance A into the freezer, changed the temperature to 0 °C, pressed set, then pressed run, the facilitator would indicate that the substance froze at that temperature. This process would continue until the player chose to end their day.

In the library, the participant was presented with a three short activities. First, the could choose one of the four machines available to hear a description of the machine and its use. Second, they would receive a random material for which all the information was solved that they could reference as they moved through the game. Last, they would receive the answer of a single property of one of the substances they were trying to solve.

At the end of Day 2 and Day 4, the participant would receive basic learning analytics feedback based upon the decisions they had taken. This feedback came in the form of a "mentor" sharing the information. An overview of these prompts can be found in Fig. 2. At the end of Day 5, the participant would make their final decision on matching the substances to materials and a short narrative conclusion was read based on the number of answers correct.

| Location Ratio | Feedback Prompt |
| --- | --- |
| Lab > Library (Day 2) | "You've spent most of your time in the laboratory, trying new things and making mistakes to learn about the properties of these materials. Remember that by spending time in the library, you can better understand the machines, learn about a new material, and discover a single property of one of your substances." |
| Lab > Library (Day 4) | "You have yet to spend a day in the library where you may learn about the machines, other materials, or learn a property of a substance. You have only one day left." |
| Library > Lab (Day 2) | "You've spent most of your time in the library, gaining the wisdom from those who came before you. Remember that by spending time in the laboratory, you can use the four machines to test for the different properties of each of your substances." |
| Library > Lab (Day 4) | "You have yet to spend a day in the laboratory, where you can use the machines to run experiments and infer the properties of your substances. You have only one day left." |
| Lab == Library | "You have evenly balanced your time between the laboratory and the library. Remember that your goal is to correctly match the materials requested from your community with three substances before the five days are up." |

**Fig. 2.** Overview of feedback prompts

**Data Collection** During the pre-interview, the participants were asked a series of questions that were coded and included in Fig. 3. The following topics were coded each in their respective ranges:

- familiarity with games (low, medium, high)
- frequency of playing games (low, medium, high)
- opinion of learning games (negative, neutral, positive)
- familiarity with content (not familiar, somewhat familiar, familiar)

| # | Familiarity with Games | Frequency of Playing Games | Opinion of Learning Games | Familiarity with Subject Matter | Relative Helpfulness of Learning | Feedback Reception |
|---|---|---|---|---|---|---|
| 1 | High | High | Positive | Familiar | More | Helpful |
| 2 | High | Medium | Positive | Somewhat familiar | More | Partially Helpful |
| 3 | High | High | Neutral | Somewhat familiar | More | Unhelpful |
| 4 | High | High | Positive | Not familiar | More | Unhelpful |
| 5 | High | High | Neutral | Familiar | Less | Helpful |
| 6 | High | Medium | Neutral | Somewhat familiar | More | Partially Helpful |
| 7 | High | Medium | Positive | Not familiar | More | Partially Helpful |
| 8 | High | Medium | Positive | Not familiar | More | Helpful |

| # | Actionability of Feedback - Day 1 | Actionability of Feedback - Day 2 | Order of Location *(book = library, beaker = laboratory)* | Score | Inferred Confidence for Final Answer |
|---|---|---|---|---|---|
| 1 | No | Somewhat | book > book > beaker > book > book | 3/3 | High |
| 2 | No | No | book > book > beaker > book > beaker | 3/3 | High |
| 3 | No | No | book > beaker > book > beaker > book | 2/3 | High |
| 4 | No | No | beaker > book > book > book > beaker | 3/3 | High |
| 5 | Yes | No | book > book > beaker > book > beaker | 3/3 | Low |
| 6 | Somewhat | Somewhat | beaker > book > book > beaker > book | 2/3 | Medium |
| 7 | Somewhat | Somewhat | book > beaker > book > beaker > beaker | 3/3 | High |
| 8 | Yes | Yes | book > beaker > book > beaker > book | 3/3 | Medium |

**Fig. 3.** Data table of participant observations

During the post-interview, the participants were asked another series of questions that were coded and included in Fig. 3. The following topics were coded each in their respective ranges:

- relative helpfulness of learning compared to other methods (less, same, more)
- reception to mentor feedback (unhelpful, somewhat helpful, helpful)
- actionability of feedback on day 2 (no, somewhat, yes)
- actionability of feedback on day 4 (no, somewhat, yes)

The research team also coded the sequence of locations visited by each participant between the library (book icon) or laboratory (beaker icon), their final score, and the researcher's "inferred confidence" in the participants' answers (low, medium, high).

## 4.2   Discussion

The observations of these playtest sessions and their accompanying interviews provide insights into our third research question:

- RQ3: How do participants react to learning analytics feedback during gameplay?

**Mentor Perceptions of Feedback** All eight (8) participants identified the feedback from their mentor as a recommendation for how they should modify their behavior. This is notable given that each of the feedback prompts, outlined in Fig. 2, only presented information about the actions taken by the player (e.g. "You've spent most of your time in the lab") or how the mechanics of the game work (e.g. "Remember that spending time in the library..."). These are intentionally not written as suggestions and yet were interpreted as such. This could be attributed to the narrative framing of the feedback as from your "mentor", the intonation of the facilitator reading the prompt, the participant expecting a recommendation and understanding it as such, or something else. Regardless, it was an interesting observation to find that all participants interpreted the feedback as guidance on what they should do and not simply information to be considered. This observation warrants further exploration, especially when compared to other systems of delivering feedback (e.g. learning dashboards).

**Timeliness of Feedback** Even though there wasn't a pattern in our coding, statements made by the participants suggested that the feedback presented earlier was used differently than the feedback later in the activity. Feedback provided to participants on Day 2 was still early in the game and participants were still becoming familiar. Feedback indicating they had spent an even amount of time in both locations was interpreted as a recommendation to continue to evenly balance between the two. Feedback provided on Day 4 was seen as a confirmation they were on the right "path" with a strategy that they had been using. This feedback was presented on the penultimate day of the game, and participants indicated that they would not change their strategy at this point as the game was nearly completed. This meant that even if there was insight to be drawn from the feedback, it was not actionable in the sense that they could or would do something with it.

# 5   Conclusion, Limitations, and Further Research

This paper highlights the insights gained from an interdisciplinary design process involving game designers, learning analytics experts, and subject matter experts. The collaborative workshops revealed the complexities and tensions between designing engaging game mechanics and effective learning analytics. Our findings underscore the importance of interdisciplinary literacy, the challenges of balancing game engagement with data-driven insights, and the need for timely, context-embedded feedback to learners. The playtesting phase further demonstrated that while players found real-time feedback useful, the timing of this feedback was crucial for its usefulness. These insights lay a foundation for future research aimed at optimizing the integration of Learning Analytics into educational games, ultimately fostering more effective and engaging learning environments.

Given the explorative nature of this work, there are some notable limitations that should be taken into account to understand and interpret our findings:

**Cognitive Load of Game Interface** The paper prototype (seen in Fig. 1) introduced cognitive load issues by overwhelming participants with information through numerous cards, physical "switches," and constant display of information, unlike a digital version where information could be managed with menus or tooltips. This excessive cognitive load may have impacted participants' ability to recall feedback and should be carefully considered in future work.

**Limited Design Time** The design team had a constrained timeframe to create the design brief, which may have affected the thoroughness and detail of the final design. This limited time for development and iteration could have resulted in missed opportunities for refining the integration of the learning analytic feedback, and addressing potential issues comprehensively. Future projects should allocate more time for the design phase to ensure a more robust and well-rounded outcome.

**Just One Design Team** A limitation of this study is that it involved only one design team. This singular perspective may not capture the diversity of approaches and insights that multiple teams could provide. Consequently, the findings and conclusions may be limited in their generalizability and applicability to different contexts or design environments. Future research should consider involving multiple design teams, as well as the participatory design contributions of potential players, to enhance the robustness and breadth of the results.

More than providing definitive conclusions, this work invites other researchers to study how learning analytics feedback can be integrated into new and existing educational games. This integration will help explore the theoretical opportunities that Game-Based Learning Analytics presents for enhancing self-regulation within educational games, potentially leading to better educational outcomes and more active learning experiences.

# References

1. Alonso-Fernández, C., Calvo-Morata, A., Freire, M., Martínez-Ortiz, I., Fernández-Manjón, B.: Applications of data science to game learning analytics data: a systematic literature review. Comput. Educ. **141**, 103612 (2019). https://doi.org/10.1016/j.compedu.2019.103612. Nov
2. Brown, A.L., Campione, J.C.: Guided discovery in a community of learners. In: McGilly, K. (ed.) Classroom Lessons: Integrating Cognitive Theory and Classroom Practice, pp. 229–272. MIT Press, Cambridge (1994)
3. Brown, T., Katz, B.: Change by Design: How Design Thinking Transforms Organizations and Inspires Innovation. Harper Business, New York (2009)
4. Carpenter, D., Cloude, E., Rowe, J., Azevedo, R., Lester, J.: Investigating student reflection during game-based learning in middle grades science. In: LAK21: 11th International Learning Analytics and Knowledge Conference. pp. 280–291. LAK21, Association for Computing Machinery, New York, NY, USA (Apr 2021). https://doi.org/10.1145/3448139.3448166
5. Chatti, M.A., Dyckhoff, A.L., Schroeder, U., Thüs, H.: A reference model for learning analytics. Int. J. Technol. Enhanced Learn. **4**(5–6), 318–331 (2013)
6. Chaudy, Y., Connolly, T., Hainey, T.: Learning analytics in serious games: a review of the literature. In: European Conference in the Applications of Enabling Technologies. Glasgow, Scotland (Nov 2014)
7. Chen, Z.H., Lee, S.Y.: Application-driven educational game to assist young children in learning English vocabulary. Educ. Technol. Soc. **21**(1), 70–81 (2018)
8. Clow, D.: The learning analytics cycle: closing the loop effectively. In: Proceedings of the 2nd International Conference on Learning Analytics and Knowledge, pp. 134–138. LAK '12, Association for Computing Machinery, New York, NY, USA (Apr 2012). https://doi.org/10.1145/2330601.2330636
9. Cobb, P.: Supporting the improvement of learning and teaching in social and institutional context. In: Carver, S., Klahr, D. (eds.) Cognition and Instruction: Twenty-Five Years of Progress, pp. 455–478. Lawrence Erlbaum Associates, Cambridge (2001)
10. Dahlbäck, N., Jönsson, A., Ahrenberg, L.: Wizard of Oz studies: why and how. In: Proceedings of the 1st International Conference on Intelligent User Interfaces, pp. 193–200 (1993)
11. Gašević, D., Merceron, A.: The Handbook of Learning Analytics. SoLAR, 2nd edn. (2022). https://doi.org/10.18608/hla22
12. Gee, J.P.: Learning by design: good video games as learning machines. E-Learn. Digital Media **2**(1), 5–16 (2005). https://doi.org/10.2304/elea.2005.2.1.5.
13. Gee, J.P.: Are video games good for learning? Nordic J. Digit. Lit. **1**(3), 172–183 (2006)
14. Harpstead, E., Richey, J.E., Nguyen, H., McLaren, B.M.: Exploring the subtleties of agency and indirect control in digital learning games. In: Proceedings of the 9th International Conference on Learning Analytics & Knowledge, pp. 121–129. LAK19, Association for Computing Machinery, New York, NY, USA (Mar 2019). https://doi.org/10.1145/3303772.3303797
15. Haythornthwaite, C., de Laat, M., Dawson, S.: Introduction to the special issue on learning analytics. Am. Behav. Sci. **57**(10), 1371–1379 (2013). https://doi.org/10.1177/0002764213498850

16. Ke, F., Shute, V.: Design of game-based stealth assessment and learning support. In: Loh, C.S., Sheng, Y., Ifenthaler, D. (eds.) Serious Games Analytics, pp. 301–318. Springer International Publishing, Cham, Switzerland (2015). https://doi.org/10.1007/978-3-319-05834-4_13

17. Kim, B., Rhim, J., Rho, J., Hwang, T., Lee, G., Gweon, G.: "I'll do it!": examining the relationship between locus of control and math game retention for preschoolers. In: Proceedings of the 8th International Conference on Learning Analytics and Knowledge, pp. 290–294. LAK '18, Association for Computing Machinery, New York, NY, USA (Mar 2018). https://doi.org/10.1145/3170358.3170368

18. Liu, M., Kang, J., Liu, S., Zou, W., Hodson, J.: Learning analytics as an assessment tool in serious games: A review of literature. In: Ma, M., Oikonomou, A. (eds.) Serious Games and Edutainment Applications, vol. 2, pp. 537–563. Springer International Publishing, Cham, Switzerland (2017). 10.1007/978-3-319-51645-5_24

19. Loh, C.S., Sheng, Y., Ifenthaler, D. (eds.): Serious Games Analytics: Methodologies for Performance Measurement, Assessment, and Improvement. Springer International Publishing, Cham (2015). https://doi.org/10.1007/978-3-319-05834-4

20. Mayer, R.E. (ed.) The Cambridge Handbook of Multimedia Learning. Cambridge Handbooks in Psychology, 2nd edn. Cambridge University Press, New York (2014)

21. Mayer, R.E.: Computer games in education. Annu. Rev. Psychol. **70**(1), 531–549 (2019). https://doi.org/10.1146/annurev-psych-010418-102744

22. Minović, M., Milovanović, M., Šošević, U., Conde González, M.Á.: Visualisation of student learning model in serious games. Comput. Hum. Behav. **47**, 98–107 (2015). https://doi.org/10.1016/j.chb.2014.09.005

23. Panadero, E., Lipnevich, A.A.: A review of feedback models and typologies: towards an integrative model of feedback elements. Educ. Res. Rev. **35**, 100416 (2022). https://doi.org/10.1016/j.edurev.2021.100416. Feb

24. Piaget, J.: The theory of stages in cognitive development. In: Green, D., Ford, M.P., Flamer, G.B. (eds.) Measurement and Piaget. McGraw-Hill, New York (1971)

25. Piaget, J.: Play, Dreams and Imitation in Childhood. Routledge, London (2013). https://doi.org/10.4324/9781315009698

26. Plass, J., O'Keefe, P., Homer, B., Case, J., Hayward, E., Stein, M., Perlin, K.: The impact of individual, competitive, and collaborative mathematics game play on learning, performance, and motivation. J. Educ. Psychol. **105**, 1050–1066 (2013). https://doi.org/10.1037/a0032688. Nov

27. Plass, J.L., Mayer, R.E., Homer, B.D.: Handbook of Game-Based Learning. MIT Press, Cambridge (2020)

28. Reese, D.D., Tabachnick, B.G., Kosko, R.E.: Video game learning dynamics: Actionable measures of multidimensional learning trajectories. Br. J. Edu. Technol. **46**(1), 98–122 (2015). https://doi.org/10.1111/BJET.12128. Jan

29. Seaton, J.X., Chang, M., Graf, S.: Integrating a learning analytics dashboard in an online educational game. In: Data Analytics Approaches in Educational Games and Gamification Systems, pp. 127–138. Springer, Singapore (2019). https://doi.org/10.1007/978-981-32-9335-9_7

30. Shute, V., Ventura, M.: Stealth Assessment: Measuring and Supporting Learning in Video Games, illustrated edition. MIT Press, Cambridge (2013)

31. Wise, A.F.: Designing pedagogical interventions to support student use of learning analytics. In: Proceedings of the Fourth International Conference on Learning Analytics and Knowledge, pp. 203–211 (2014)

32. Wise, A.F., Sarmiento, J.P., Boothe Jr., M.: Subversive learning analytics. In: LAK21: 11th International Learning Analytics and Knowledge Conference, pp.

639–645. ACM, Irvine CA USA (Apr 2021). https://doi.org/10.1145/3448139.3448210

33. Xu, Z., Woodruff, E.: Person-centered approach to explore learner's emotionality in learning within a 3D narrative game. In: Proceedings of the Seventh International Learning Analytics & Knowledge Conference. pp. 439–443. LAK '17, Association for Computing Machinery, New York, NY, USA (Mar 2017). https://doi.org/10.1145/3027385.3027432

# Crossing Valley: Development of a Serious Game to Measure Cognitive Flexibility in a Problem-Solving Context

W. L. Fu[1] (ID), N. L. Fischer[1] (ID), K. Kalaivanan[1], G. S. T. Ong[1], A. J. Oh[1], S. Tripathi[1], M. R. Ellefson[2], P. Seow[3], C. L. Teo[3(✉)], and D. Hung[4]

[1] Centre for Research and Development in Learning, Nanyang Technological University, Singapore, Singapore
[2] Faculty of Education, University of Cambridge, Cambridge, UK
mre33@cam.ac.uk
[3] Centre for Research in Pedagogy and Practice, National Institute of Education, Singapore, Singapore
chewlee.teo@nie.edu.sg
[4] Centre of Science of Learning in Education, National Institute of Education, Singapore, Singapore

**Abstract.** Cognitive flexibility (CF), the ability to swiftly shift between and adapt mental strategies to navigate novel situations, has been increasingly recognized as pivotal in classroom learning. Traditional behavioral measures tend to oversimplify the CF construct, mainly reducing it to set-shifting (i.e., attention switching within a task) or task-switching (i.e., alternating response between tasks) skills. However, recent literature has suggested that CF may encompass a wider range of abilities (e.g., adaptability to changes in the environment). To address this gap, we are adopting a unified framework that embraces a broader perspective and employs a serious game (SG) to assess CF within an educationally relevant, problem-solving context. By designing a serious game, we aim to provide a platform for an ecological assessment of CF skills within a problem-solving context. Our goal is to use game elements to enhance participant motivation, and to infuse educational relevance into assessments, thereby bridging the gap between psychological testing and real-world application.

**Keywords:** Cognitive Flexibility · Serious Game · Problem Solving · Cognitive Game

## 1 Introduction

Executive functions (EFs) are a set of abilities encompassing different behavioral and cognitive elements that play significant roles in learning and academic achievement [1]. In Miyake and colleagues' [2] seminal work that proposed the unity and diversity model of EFs, three core components were identified: updating, inhibition, and shifting.

These components interact dynamically to facilitate adaptive behavior in various contexts, underscoring the importance of these cognitive processes in everyday functioning and problem solving [3]. The "shifting" component of this model is believed to be subsumed within a broader construct called "cognitive flexibility" (CF), which refers to the ability to adaptively shift between different cognitive tasks or mental sets in response to changing environmental demands and encompasses a range of cognitive processes including task-switching, set shifting and efficient responding to error feedback [4]. Therefore, understanding CF requires recognizing its broader scope beyond the shifting skills originally identified by Miyake and colleagues [2].

## 2 Literature Review

CF has been studied in relation to various abilities and learning outcomes like reading ability [5–10], mathematical ability [11–14], science achievement in school [15], creativity [16, 17] and problem solving [18–20]. Additionally, some studies have highlighted the contribution of CF to classroom learning. Kwon and Lawson [21] found that the performance on the Wisconsin Card Sorting Test (WCST) significantly predicted scientific reasoning and concept learning in adolescents. Furthermore, Cragg and Gilmore [22] reviewed the impact of EFs on math proficiency, highlighting the crucial role of CF in learning new concepts and switching procedures (such as addition or subtraction) when solving mathematical problems.

The role of CF in learning seems to extend beyond a single subject matter. It can also be observed when students transition from one activity to another in the classroom, adjusting their focus and responses to meet the requirements of the new activity [23]. Therefore, accumulating evidence suggests that flexible thinking in problem solving allows the mind to adapt swiftly to the situation, making it a valuable skill when searching for solutions [20]. As a cognitive trait, CF relies on the collaboration of various mechanisms, including attention shifting, conflict monitoring, and perception. These mechanisms allow effective responses to specific environmental challenges, facilitating adaptive behavior and enabling problem-solving strategies to be expressed in novel ways [24].

Upon reviewing the literature, numerous studies have often equated CF with the shifting component of the three-factors Miyake and colleagues' [2] EF model, which might restrict a holistic understanding of the CF construct [24]. According to Ionescu [24], CF requires the interplay of multiple mechanisms in response to specific contextual demands (i.e., aligning task parameters with objectives). Therefore, this transition from a narrow to a broader perspective of CF forms the basis of this study.

A variety of tasks have been used to measure CF. Usually, these tasks require respondents to demonstrate switching skills by flexibly adapting to new rules. Some common measures are the Wisconsin Card Sorting Task (WCST; [25, 26]), the Trail Making Test (TMT; [27]), task-set switch (e.g. [28]) and probabilistic reversal learning (PRL; [29]) paradigms. From a psychometric standpoint, these neuropsychological tests have demonstrated construct (e.g., [30]) and external validity (e.g., [31]), and are widely used and validated in the field. However, some authors argue that these tasks are limited in ecological validity and may not reflect EFs capacity in naturalistic contexts [32–35]. For example, research has shown that the results of EF tests, including the WCST and TMT, account for only 18–37% of the variation in everyday activities [36, 37]. Therefore, a significant portion of the variance in functional outcomes remains unexplained by performance on these cognitive tasks [34]. This may happen due to a lack of unpredictable situations in conventional neuropsychological measures, which reflects real-life situations, making it challenging to ecologically evaluate CF [32, 38]. Hence, it is important to investigate CF skills employed in a problem-solving context, where situational demands change and prompt adaptation to the context.

With these considerations in mind, we believe that a measurement of CF that is ecologically valid and aligns with a unified framework is needed for studying the transfer of CF-related skills to classroom learning. Following this direction, together with recommendations from recent literature [33, 34], we have designed a serious game to increase the ecological validity of CF assessment.

Serious games (SG) show promise in the field of neuropsychological evaluation due to their computer-based nature, moving beyond the confined space of a laboratory [39]. The benefits include improved standardization of administration, more accurate timing of presentation and response latencies, and simplified administration [40]. SGs can also increase participants' motivation and engagement through entertaining game elements, potentially enhancing intrinsic motivation [33, 41, 42], since lack of effort is prevalent in cognitive assessments [41]. In addition, SGs provide opportunities to divert players' attention from the assessment, avoiding test anxiety, and in turn, authentically assessing an individual's ability [44]. Hence, the SG framework offers promising opportunities for assessing CF.

Previous efforts have been made to develop SGs that gamify CF assessments across various age groups, including older adults [45], primary school students [46], and university students [47]. However, these tasks mostly adopted a deterministic paradigm (e.g., a set-shifting task) and did not consider a broader range of CF-related abilities (e.g., adaptability to novel scenarios). Furthermore, they often overlook the educational context of CF assessment which is relevant since such assessment of cognitive skills in isolation contradicts real-world situations [34]. In addition, we recognize the importance of problem-solving skills not only for cognitive development but also for educational success. Therefore, we aim to develop a game inspired by an educational engineering problem-solving task (i.e., Straw Bridge Task; [48]) to measure CF in relation to classroom learning. By incorporating an educational layer into our game design, we aim to provide a more comprehensive assessment of CF that aligns with real-world educational contexts.

## 3   Game Design

We designed the "Crossing Valley" game to assess CF within a problem-solving context. Players are required to build bridges to meet different environmental requirements. Moving away from the perspective that views CF as synonymous with "set shifting", we instead conceptualize CF as a pool of abilities that enables us to change our cognitive strategies in response to fluctuating task demands [49]. Effective problem solving often involves exploring various potential solutions, and thus, transitioning between different solution strategies or options [12]. Hence, in our game, we implement situational changes that require players to switch strategies to obtain an optimal solution to the problem. Building upon the CF unified framework, as suggested by Ionescu [24] and Kupis & Uddin [4], Crossing Valley differs from conventional tests and other SGs that target purely set-shifting abilities as a way to measure CF.

An interdisciplinary team of researchers, educators, and a game developer was formed to take on the design task. The team employed an iterative design process in the design of "crossing valley", cycling through redesigns until achieving a satisfactory outcome [50]. This approach, as outlined by Braad and team [51], organizes stages including analysis, design, development, implementation, and evaluation. Engineering experts were consulted to provide feedback on bridge structure and mechanics, ensuring alignment with bridge-building elements. The game interface (see Fig. 1) was developed by a full-stack app developer using the Unity game engine for its physics features, cost-effectiveness, and multiplatform capabilities [52]. In consideration of player-centric design, the game was playtested by the team to gather feedback, which was then incorporated into the storyline and game mechanics. Multiple prototypes were tested to meet requirements, followed by an evaluation stage involving a pilot study. Future iterations will continue to integrate player feedback at all stages.

To decide for the game design features, we based our outline in the recommendations addressed by Wouters et al. [42]. According to these authors, SGs are believed to be interactive, governed by a set of defined rules and constraints, and aimed at achieving a clear goal typically set by a challenge. Malone [53] also noted that curiosity, fantasy, and challenge are the most important factors in an engaging game. Outlined as essential design elements [54, 55], we incorporated game elements such as narrative contexts, challenges, constraints, and feedback.

In this sense, to engage players, we created a storyline presented at the beginning of the game, in which participants were told that they have entered a fantasy land (called "Aurora Town") and that they needed to build bridges in order to help the town flourish. To start, we designed an introductory video explaining the game rules, different bridge designs, and possible strategies participants could adopt to solve the scenarios. This video aims to mitigate differences in prior knowledge among players, since the game's primary goal is to assess players' abilities in switching between different problem-solving strategies, rather than assessing their expertise on generating bridge designs. After the video, a tutorial round is included to help players understand the game mechanics and familiarize themselves with the environment. To reduce cognitive load, instructions are accessible in a tab on the top right corner of the screen throughout the game.

To solve the problem posed by the game (i.e., having a load crossing a bridge to reach Aurora Town), players must consider two dimensions: the gap's width and the load's weight. These dimensions will be manipulated across three difficulty levels. For example, players will build bridges across spans of 4 grids, 8 grids, and 14 grids, adapting their strategies to the different situational changes. Additionally, budget and time constraints will vary as players advance through the game levels. By manipulating these parameters, players must build bridges according to situational demands and switch strategies as needed. Further strategies will be discussed in the paper.

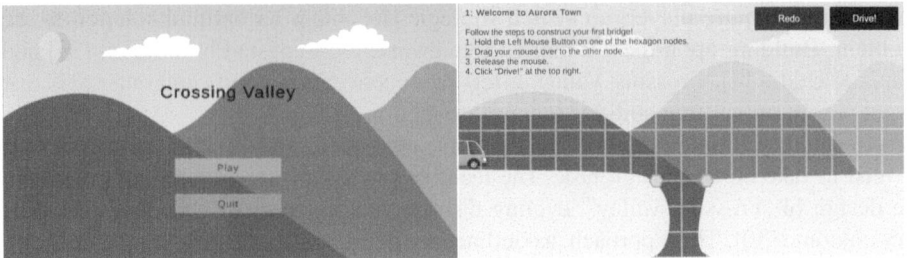

**Fig. 1.** Screenshots of the crossing valley interface

Finally, when finishing the bridge, players may test whether their solution works by selecting the "Drive" button. If the bridge is unstable, it will shake, providing feedback on their design. Stress points are highlighted as the vehicle crosses, indicating the distribution of stress. Observing the failures of the vehicle crossing the bridge can serve as feedback to students to learn and change their bridge-building strategies accordingly.

It is important to highlight that the Crossing Valley game does not solely focus on the ability of individuals to problem-solve. As it is designed to evoke participants' cognitive skills believed to be part of the CF construct (e.g., response switch, and adaptability to new situations), the ultimate goal of this game is to observe how flexible players behave when changing their strategies to tackle the challenges presented in the game. Having this goal in mind, we predict that players may manipulate three of the main bridge's features: (1) design, (2) shape, and (3) complexity (see Fig. 2). The features will be shown in the introductory video before the game starts, and players will be encouraged to explore different solutions when one fails. For instance, we will introduce the six bridge designs (i.e., beam, truss, arch, suspension, cantilever, and cable-stayed) commonly adopted in bridge construction [56]. By becoming aware of these possible features, when a solution fails, players may: (1) switch to a different bridge design (design change), (2) change the shape or symmetry of the bridge (shape change), or (3) add or remove items from the bridge (complexity change). We consider the manipulation of these features as changes in strategies adopted by the players to solve the scenario presented in the game. Therefore, we aim to observe whether players will switch or persist in using a certain strategy when their initial solution fails due to situational changes. Behaviors to be coded during the game are summarized in Table 1.

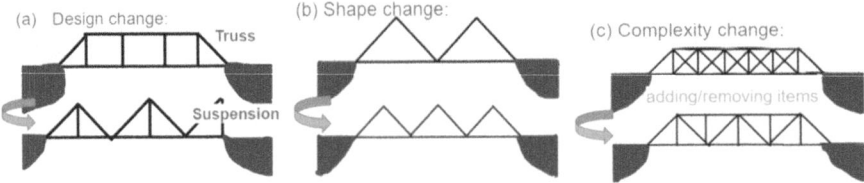

**Fig. 2.** Strategy change (**a** design change, **b** shape change, **c** complexity change)

**Table 1.** Conceptualization of CF in crossing valley.

| CF component | Definition | Measures |
|---|---|---|
| Strategy switch | Changing from a less to a more suitable strategy for the given problem | Strategy switch<br>Switching between different bridges':<br>(i) designs (as specified by [54])<br>(ii) shape (e.g., symmetrical vs asymmetrical bridge shapes)<br>(iii) complexity change (e.g., by adding or removing items) |
| Perseverative behavior | Continuing with the same response strategy following negative feedback or failure to inhibit a prepotent response | Perseverative error: Failure to shift after receiving negative feedback (e.g. bridge collapsing)<br>Efficient error: Shifting to a strategy that is less effective |

## 4   Future Work and Implications

There are two future plans: (i) a pilot study with a small group of students (e.g., N = 10) and focus group discussion for game refinement; (ii) a validation study in schools to understand how students' performance in the game is related to traditional CF tasks (e.g., WCST, PRL, TMT) and self-reported scales (e.g., Cognitive Flexibility Scale; [57]). In the validation study, we intend to employ tasks that measure other EFs (e.g., working memory and inhibition) for statistical modeling, and to account for the contribution of these additional cognitive skills in the participants' performance during our game.

The concept of bridge building was chosen for this game because it is a familiar structure in many cultures, ensuring that students from diverse backgrounds would likely have some familiarity with it. However, since the game is in English, students with limited proficiency may struggle with the rules in the introduction video. After the pilot study, we will assess the game completion times and may introduce a "Level 0" to help students learn the rules through hands-on experience.

With this game development effort, we believe there is an opportunity to bridge research and practice by translating the CF framework into problem solving within an educational context. By viewing the CF construct through a broader lens, this game aligns with the real-life manifestation of this cognitive ability unlike previous attempts to measure CF-related skills in isolation. We believe that the SG framework will allow for a more ecologically valid assessment of players' CF abilities, leveraging the entertaining aspects of games to enhance user motivation, while also transcending the laboratory environment. Additionally, Crossing Valley can be implemented without professional supervision, offering a resource-effective method of collecting behavioral data. Finally, our game may be beneficial for educators, as the use of SGs in the classroom has been found to support formal and informal learning [58] and foster the development of information and communication technology (ICT) literacy, critical thinking, and creativity skills, which are believed to be important abilities that cultivate learning throughout the lifespan [59].

**Acknowledgments.** This research is supported by the National Research Foundation, Prime Minister's Office, Singapore under its Campus for Research Excellence and Technological Enterprise Science of Learning (NRF-CREATE SoL) Programme with the funding administered by the Cambridge Centre for Advanced Research and Education in Singapore Ltd. (CARES) and housed at the Centre for Research and Development in Learning (CRADLE@NTU). The study funders did not and will not have any role in the study design, collection, management, analysis and interpretation of data, and writing of the manuscript.

**Disclosure of Interests** The authors have no competing interests to declare that are relevant to the content of this article.

# References

1. Baggetta, P., Alexander, P.A.: Conceptualization and operationalization of executive function. Mind Brain Educ. **10**(1), 10–33 (2016)
2. Miyake, A., Friedman, N.P., Emerson, M.J., Witzki, A.H., Howerter, A., Wager, T.D.: The unity and diversity of executive functions and their contributions to complex "frontal lobe" tasks: a latent variable analysis. Cogn. Psychol. **41**(1), 49–100 (2000)
3. Miyake, A., Friedman, N.P.: The nature and organization of individual differences in executive functions: four general conclusions. Curr. Direct. Psychol. Sci. J. Am. Psychol. Soc. **21**(1), 8–14 (2012). https://doi.org/10.1177/0963721411429458
4. Kupis, L.B., Uddin, L.Q.: Developmental neuroimaging of cognitive flexibility: Update and future directions. Annu. Rev. Develop. Psychol. **5**(1), 263–284 (2023). https://doi.org/10.1146/annurev-devpsych-120221-035310
5. Cartwright, K.B., Coppage, E.A., Lane, A.B., Singleton, T., Marshall, T.R., Bentivegna, C.: Cognitive flexibility deficits in children with specific reading comprehension difficulties. Contemp. Educ. Psychol. **50**, 33–44 (2017). https://doi.org/10.1016/j.cedpsych.2016.01.003
6. Johann, V., Könen, T., Karbach, J.: The unique contribution of working memory, inhibition, cognitive flexibility, and intelligence to reading comprehension and reading speed. Child Neuropsychol. **26**(3), 324–344 (2020). https://doi.org/10.1080/09297049.2019.1649381
7. van der Sluis, S., de Jong, P.F., van der Leij, A.: Executive functioning in children, and its relations with reasoning, reading, and arithmetic. Intelligence (Norwood) **35**(5), 427–449 (2007). https://doi.org/10.1016/j.intell.2006.09.001
8. Abreu, P.E.d., Abreu, N., Nikaedo, C.C., et al.: Executive functioning and reading achievement in school: a study of Brazilian children assessed by their teachers as "poor readers". Front. Psychol. **5**, 550 (2014). https://doi.org/10.3389/fpsyg.2014.00550
9. Cartwright, K.B., Marshall, T.R., Huemer, C.M., Payne, J.B.: Executive function in the classroom: cognitive flexibility supports reading fluency for typical readers and teacher-identified low-achieving readers. Res. Dev. Disabil. **88**, 42–52 (2019). https://doi.org/10.1016/j.ridd.2019.01.011
10. Colé, P., Duncan, L.G., Blaye, A.: Cognitive flexibility predicts early reading skills. Front. Psychol. **5**, 91936 (2014). https://doi.org/10.3389/fpsyg.2014.00565

11. Stad, F.E., Van Heijningen, C.J.M., Wiedl, K.H., Resing, W.C.M.: Predicting school achievement: differential effects of dynamic testing measures and cognitive flexibility for math performance. Learn. Individ. Differ. **67**, 117–125 (2018). https://doi.org/10.1016/j.lindif.2018.07.006

12. Yeniad, N., Malda, M., Mesman, J., van IJzendoorn, M. H., Pieper, S.: Shifting ability predicts math and reading performance in children: a meta-analytical study. Learn. Individ. Diff. **23**, 1–9 (2013) https://doi.org/10.1016/j.lindif.2012.10.004

13. Magalhães, S., Carneiro, L., Limpo, T., Filipe, M.: Executive functions predict literacy and mathematics achievements: the unique contribution of cognitive flexibility in grades 2, 4, and 6. Child Neuropsychol. **26**(7), 934–952 (2020). https://doi.org/10.1080/09297049.2020.1740188

14. Rahayuningsih, S.E., Sirajuddin, S., Nasrun, N.: Cognitive flexibility: exploring students' problem-solving in elementary school mathematics learning. J. Res. Adv. Math. Educ. **6**(1), 59–70 (2020)

15. Li, J., Zhao, Y., Zhou, S., Pu, Y., He, H., Zhao, M.: Set-shifting ability is specifically linked to high-school science and math achievement in Chinese adolescents. Psych J. **9**(3), 327–338 (2020)

16. Benedek, M., Franz, F., Heene, M., Neubauer, A.C.: Differential effects of cognitive inhibition and intelligence on creativity. Personal. Individ. Differ. **53**(4), 480–485 (2012). https://doi.org/10.1016/j.paid.2012.04.014

17. Pan, X., Yu, H.: Different effects of cognitive shifting and intelligence on creativity. J. Creat. Behav. **52**(3), 212–225 (2018). https://doi.org/10.1002/jocb.144

18. Cooper, R.P., Marsh, V.: Set-shifting as a component process of goal-directed problem-solving. Psychol. Res. **80**(2), 307–323 (2016). https://doi.org/10.1007/s00426-015-0652-2

19. Hacatrjana, L.: Flexibility to change the solution: an indicator of problem solving that predicted 9th grade students' academic achievement during distance learning, in parallel to reasoning abilities and parental education. J. Intell. **10**(1), 7 (2022). https://doi.org/10.3390/jintelligence10010007

20. Kalia, V., Fuesting, M., Cody, M.: Perseverance in solving Sudoku: role of grit and cognitive flexibility in problem solving. J. Cogn. Psychol. (Hove) **31**(3), 370–378 (2019). https://doi.org/10.1080/20445911.2019.1604527

21. Kwon, Y.-J., Lawson, A.E.: Linking brain growth with the development of scientific reasoning ability and conceptual change during adolescence. J. Res. Sci. Teach. **37**(1), 44–62 (2000)

22. Cragg, L., Gilmore, C.: Skills underlying mathematics: the role of executive function in the development of mathematics proficiency. Trends Neurosci. Educ. **3**, 63–68 (2014)

23. Vandenbroucke, L., Spilt, J., Verschueren, K., Piccinin, C., Baeyens, D.: The classroom as a developmental context for cognitive development: a meta-analysis on the importance of teacher-student interactions for children's executive functions. Rev. Educ. Res. **88**(1), 125–164 (2018). https://doi.org/10.3102/0034654317743200

24. Ionescu, T.: Exploring the nature of cognitive flexibility. New Ideas Psychol. **30**(2), 190–200 (2012). https://doi.org/10.1016/j.newideapsych.2011.11.001

25. Grant, D.A., Berg, E.: A behavioral analysis of degree of reinforcement and ease of shifting to new responses in a Weigl-type card-sorting problem. J. Exp. Psychol. **38**(4), 404–411 (1948). https://doi.org/10.1037/h0059831

26. Heaton, R.K., Chelune, G.J., Talley, J.L., Kay, G., Curtiss, G.: Wisconsin Card Sorting Test manual: Revised and expanded. Psychological Assessment Resources, Odessa, FL (1993)

27. Reitan, R.M.: Validity of the trail making test as an indicator of organic brain damage. Percept. Mot. Skills **8**, 271–276 (1958)

28. Kim, C., Johnson, N., Cilles, S., Gold, B.: Common and distinct mechanisms of cognitive flexibility in prefrontal cortex. J. Neurosci. **31**, 4771–4779 (2011). https://doi.org/10.1523/JNEUROSCI.5923-10.2011

29. Cools, R., Clark, L., Owen, A.M., Robbins, T.W.: Defining the neural mechanisms of probabilistic reversal learning using event-related functional magnetic resonance imaging. J. Neurosci. **22**(11), 4563–4567 (2002)

30. Sánchez-Cubillo, I., et al.: Construct validity of the trail making test: role of task-switching, working memory, inhibition/interference control, and visuomotor abilities. J. Int. Neuropsychol. Soc. **15**, 438–450 (2009)

31. Miranda, A.R., Franchetto Sierra, J., Martínez Roulet, A., Rivadero, L., Serra, S.V., Soria, E.A.: Age, education and gender effects on Wisconsin card sorting test: standardization, reliability and validity in healthy Argentinian adults. Aging Neuropsychol. Cogn. **27**(6), 807–825 (2020)

32. Han, K., Kim, I.Y., Kim, J.: Assessment of cognitive flexibility in real life using virtual reality: a comparison of healthy individuals and schizophrenia patients. Comput. Biol. Med. **42**(8), 841–847 (2012)

33. Lumsden, J., Edwards, E.A., Lawrence, N.S., Coyle, D., Munafo, M.R.: Gamification of cognitive assessment and cognitive training: a systematic review of applications and efficacy. JMIR Ser. Games **4**(2), e11 (2016)

34. Martínez-Pernía, D., Olavarría, L., Fernández-Manjón, B., Cabello, V., Henríquez, F., Robert, P., Alvarado, L., Barría, S., Antivilo, A., Velasquez, J., Cerda, M., Farías, G., Torralva, T., Ibáñez, A., Parra, M. A., Gilbert, S., Slachevsky, A.: The limitations and challenges in the assessment of executive dysfunction associated with real-world functioning: the opportunity of serious games. Applied Neuropsychology. Adult, ahead-of-prin t(ahead-of-print), 1–17 (2023) https://doi.org/10.1080/23279095.2023.2174438

35. Gobet, F., Sala, G.: Cognitive training: a field in search of a phenomenon. Perspect. Psychol. Sci. **18**(1), 125–141 (2023). https://doi.org/10.1177/17456916221091830

36. McAlister, C., Schmitter-Edgecombe, M., Lamb, R.: Examination of variables that may affect the relationship between cognition and functional status in individuals with mild cognitive impairment: a meta-analysis. Arch. Clin. Neuropsychol. **31**(2), 123–147 (2016). https://doi.org/10.1093/arclin/acv089

37. Chaytor, N., Schmitter-Edgecombe, M., Burr, R.: Improving the ecological validity of executive functioning assessment. Arch. Clin. Neuropsychol. **21**(3), 217–227 (2006). https://doi.org/10.1016/j.acn.2005.12.002

38. Smith, L.B.: Cognition as a dynamic system: principles from embodiment. Dev. Rev. **25**(3), 278–298 (2005). https://doi.org/10.1016/j.dr.2005.11.001

39. Adi, M.N., Roberts, D.J.: Using virtual environments to test the effects of lifelike architecture on people. In: Brooks, A.L., Brahnam, S., Jain, L.C. (eds.) Technologies of Inclusive Well-Being. SCI, vol. 536, pp. 261–285. Springer, Heidelberg (2014). https://doi.org/10.1007/978-3-642-45432-5_13

40. Valladares-Rodríguez, S., et al.: Trends on the application of serious games to neuropsychological evaluation: a scoping review. J. Biomed. Inform. **64**, 296–319 (2016)

41. Allen, K.R., Brändle, F., Botvinick, M., Fan, J., Gershman, S.J., Gopnik, . alison ., Griffiths, T.L., Hartshorne, J.K., Hauser, T.U., Ho, M.K., de Leeuw, J.R., Ma, W.J., Murayama, K., Nelson, J.D., van Opheusden, B., Pouncy, H.T., Rafner, J., Rahwan, I., Rutledge, R., Sherson, J., Simsek, O., Spiers, H., Summerfield, C., Thalmann, M., Vélez, N., Watrous, A., Tenenbaum, J., Schulz, E.: Using Games to Understand the Mind, osf.io/preprints/psyarxiv/hbsvj (2023)

42. Wouters, P., van Nimwegen, C., van Oostendorp, H., van der Spek, E.D.: A meta-analysis of the cognitive and motivational effects of serious games. J. Educ. Psychol. **105**(2), 249–265 (2013). https://doi.org/10.1037/a0031311

43. DeRight, J., Jorgensen, R.S.: I just want my research credit: frequency of suboptimal effort in a non-clinical healthy undergraduate sample. Clin. Neuropsychol. **29**(1), 101–117 (2015). https://doi.org/10.1080/13854046.2014.989267

44. Altomari, L., Altomari, N., Iazzolino, G.: Gamification and soft skills assessment in the development of a serious game: design and feasibility pilot study. JMIR Ser. Games **11** (2023)

45. Wang, P., Fang, Y., Qi, J.Y., Li, H.J.: FISHERMAN: A serious game for executive function assessment of older adults. Assessment **30**(5), 1499–1513 (2023)

46. Berg, V.: A game-based online tool to measure cognitive functions in students. Int. J. Serious Games **8**(1), 71–87 (2021)

47. Urakami, J., Hu, Y. Z., Chignell, M.: Monitoring cognitive performance with a serious game: A longitudinal case study on online cognitive assessment using serious games. In: Extended Abstracts of the 2021 CHI Conference on Human Factors in Computing Systems, pp. 1–7. Yokohama, Japan (2021) https://doi.org/10.1145/3411763.3443431

48. TeachEngineering: Straw Bridges (2022) https://www.teachengineering.org/activities/view/cub_brid_lesson01_activity2

49. Gonzalez, C.A., Figueroa, I.J., Bellows, B.G., Rhodes, D., Youmans, R.J.: A new behavioral measure of cognitive flexibility. Eng. Psychol. Cogn. Ergon. Understand Human Cogn 8019(1):297–306. Springer, Berlin Heidelberg. (2013) https://doi.org/10.1007/978-3-642-39360-0_33

50. Viudes-Carbonell, S.J., Gallego-Durán, F.J., Llorens-Largo, F., Molina-Carmona, R.: Towards an iterative design for serious games. Sustainability **13**(6), 3290 (2021)

51. Braad. E., Žavcer, G., Sandovar, A.: Processes and models for serious game design and development. In: Entertainment Computing and Serious Games, vol. 9970, pp. 92–118. Springer International Publishing AG (2016) https://doi.org/10.1007/978-3-319-46152-6_5

52. Cowan, B., Kapralos, B.: An overview of serious game engines and frameworks. In: Brooks, A. L., Brahnam, S., Kapralos, B., Jain, L.C. (eds.) Recent Advances in Technologies for Inclusive Well-Being, pp. 15–38. Springer International Publishing (2017) https://doi.org/10.1007/978-3-319-49879-9_2

53. Malone, T.W.: Toward a theory of intrinsically motivating instruction. Cogn. Sci. **5**(4), 333–369 (1981). https://doi.org/10.1207/s15516709cog0504_2

54. Ferreira-Brito, F., et al.: Game-based interventions for neuropsychological assessment, training and rehabilitation: which game-elements to use? A systematic review. J. Biomed. Inform. **98**, 103287 (2019). https://doi.org/10.1016/j.jbi.2019.103287

55. Gomez, M.J., Ruiperez-Valiente, J.A., Clemente, F.J.G.: A systematic literature review of game-based assessment studies: trends and challenges. IEEE Trans. Learn. Technol. **16**(4), 1–16 (2023). https://doi.org/10.1109/TLT.2022.3226661

56. DT Online: Common bridge types (2021). https://wiki.dtonline.org/index.php/Common_Bridge_Types

57. Martin, M.M., Rubin, R.B.: A new measure of cognitive flexibility. Psychol. Rep. **76**(2), 623–626 (1995). https://doi.org/10.2466/pr0.1995.76.2.623

58. Arnab, S., Berta, R., Earp, J., Freitas, S.D., Popescu, M.M., Romero, M., Stanescu, I.A., Usart, M: Framing the adoption of serious games in formal education. Electron. J. e-Learning **10**, 159–-71 (2012)

59. Romero, M., Usart, M., Ott, M.: Can serious games contribute to developing and sustaining 21st century skills? Games Culture **10**(2), 148–177 (2015). https://doi.org/10.1177/1555412014548919

# Serious Practices for Interactive Waste Sorting Mini-game

Qiming Sun$^{(\boxtimes)}$ (ID) and I-Han Hsiao (ID)

Santa Clara University, Santa Clara, CA 95053, USA
{qsun4,ihsiao}@scu.edu

**Abstract.** Effective waste management is crucial for sustainable living, but many individuals find it challenging to navigate the complexities of waste classification. This study presents a web-based serious game that utilizes interactive sorting quizzes, created by both users and AI, to promote environmental sustainability learning. The game incorporates AI-generated feedback, a carbon credit system, and user-generated content to engage and educate participants. Two user studies involving 48 university students were conducted to evaluate the game's effectiveness. The findings suggest that the game effectively promotes learning and improves participants' understanding of sustainable waste management practices. The results highlight the potential of serious games to encourage environmental education and sustainable behaviors, particularly when they incorporate user agency and community involvement. Using emerging technologies and engaging users, serious games can serve as valuable tools to promote sustainable practices and address environmental challenges.

**Keywords:** Environmental sustainability · Waste management · Interactive learning · Distributed practices

## 1 Introduction

Effective waste management is a fundamental component of sustainable living, yet many people find it challenging to navigate the complexities of waste classification, such as identifying recyclable materials and understanding the varying recycling guidelines across different regions. The complexity of the field and the lack of clarity and up-to-date learning resources often hinder proper waste sorting.

Researchers have explored the impact of gamification [5,21] and interactive learning approaches [10,11,14,22] to promote sustainable practices and raise awareness about waste management. These studies underscore the capacity of serious games to educate and inspire individuals to adopt environmentally conscious habits. In our work, we explore the feasibility of designing effective practices into a serious game for waste management learning. The goal is to introduce

J. L. Plass and X. Ochoa (Eds.): JCSG 2024, LNCS 15259, pp. 134–141, 2025.
https://doi.org/10.1007/978-3-031-74138-8_11

the well-researched learning science principle, and distributed practices [12,20], in the form of a lightweight mini-game, and promote sound waste management and sustainability awareness.

We design a web-based system that emulates the popular culture of social media applications (i.e. Instagram), to provide "endless" bite-size content feeds that fill with educational materials about waste management and environmental sustainability. The system supports social and AI content creation to enable user collaborations and content scalability. To investigate serious practices in waste sorting, we specifically engineer interfaces that support the waste sorting interaction and create a sizable collection of interactive waste sorting practices. Each sorting practice is like a mini quiz. A reward of virtual carbon credits is used to incentivize proper sorting practices. Such mechanism not only attempts to interpret the amount of carbon generated by the size, quantity, and types of waste, but also allows the estimation of other quantitative metrics (such as *mileage-travel-by-car* and *tree-days equivalent* to represent the amount of $CO_2$ sequestered by a mature tree per day) to understand the importance of proper waste management. Based on the virtual carbon credits, a ranked leaderboard is designed to recognize top community performers and positively motivate the appropriate waste sorting.

Two user studies were designed and conducted to examine the effects of the *seriousness* & *gamification* in practicing waste sorting. The first study required participants to complete all available system-generated quizzes, while the second study allowed participants to engage with the game at their own pace and create user-generated content. The findings suggest that both approaches effectively promote learning and improve participants' understanding of sustainable waste management practices. The second study resulted in higher objective ratings from participants regarding AI-generated assistance, explanations, and the carbon credit system.

## 2    Related Work

**Interactive Learning in Sustainability Education**. Gamification and interactive learning have emerged as powerful tools to educate and engage diverse audiences in sustainable practices. The effectiveness of gamification in promoting eco-friendly behaviors has been investigated in several studies, such as the EcoDrive mobile application, which encourages sustainable driving styles [21]. Educational games like ROBOTE [11], PEAR [22], and FoodFights [10] were developed to raise awareness about waste management and sustainability in various real-life scenarios. Immersive technologies, such as Augmented Reality (AR), were used to visualize the impact of waste [2] and guide individuals to the proper disposal of waste [17,18]. Some serious games have also been developed for learning waste sorting [8,9]. In this paper, our game features a web interface that is easier to access, and integrates the language model to provide real-time natural guidances to players.

**Distributed Practices**. Distributed practice, a learning strategy where practice sessions are spaced out over time, has been shown to enhance knowledge retention compared to massed practice [23]. This effect, also known as the spacing effect or lag effect, is believed to result from a memory advantage that occurs when learning materials are encountered on multiple occasions [16]. Distributed practice not only consolidates memory but also refines students' understanding by allowing time for forgetting between successive presentations [15]. Researchers have applied multiresolution analysis to extract practice patterns spaced by different periods, revealing a positive correlation between small-spaced practice and exam performance [4]. The impact of self-assessment and self-regulation on learning gains were also examined in an adaptive programming learning platform, highlighting the effectiveness of daily learning opportunities in introductory education [1].

## 3   Methodology

### 3.1   Interactive Sorting Practices/Quizzes with Adaptive Feedback

Our web-based game presented in this study features interactive sorting quizzes designed to support environmental sustainability learning (Fig. 1). The quizzes challenge users' knowledge of waste sorting by presenting a variety of waste objects that must be categorized correctly. Users can drag and drop each object onto the appropriate labels, such as landfill, compost, or recycle.

To generate interactive quizzes, 96 waste items were sourced from California's recycling guidelines [3] and the EPA's directions on universal waste programs [7]. The category labels assigned to these waste items serve as the "ground truth" for evaluating the correct solution to the quizzes. In particular, ground-truth information provides the context for the AI agent in shaping the feedback guidance, which is deliberately used to prevent the risk of any potential AI hallucination that could lead to misinformation. Note that the waste items are presented as words without any visual elements. In addition to AI-generated quizzes, our game allows users to create their own quizzes. This feature enables users to contribute to the learning experience by sharing their knowledge and real-life examples of waste sorting scenarios.

### 3.2   Sustainability Awareness Features

Upon completing each quiz, users receive immediate feedback on their performance, highlighting correctly sorted items and providing explanations for incorrect choices. The AI-generated feedback offers guidance and educational content to help users understand the reasoning behind proper waste-sorting decisions.

To further motivate users, the game incorporates a scoring system based on the concept of "carbon credits", which was initially introduced by the United Nations [19]. Adopting the EPA's national overview on waste and recycling [6], we estimate the environmental benefits from correctly processing a unit of waste

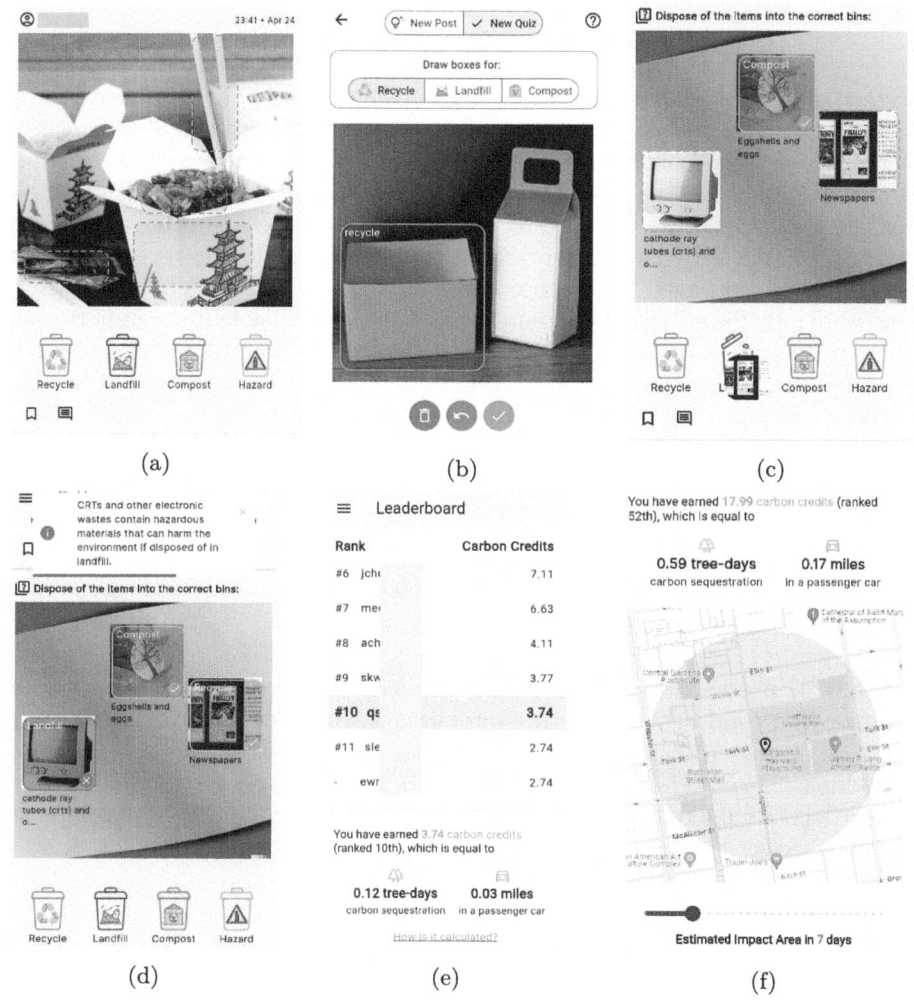

**Fig. 1.** The interactive waste-sorting quizzes: (a) A quiz created by a user; (b) The editor for creating a quiz; (c) An AI-generated quiz, to play with it, drag and drop a waste item onto a bin; (d) The AI-guidance when a user makes a mistake; (e) The leaderboard of carbon credits; (f) Based on users' feedback, an improved stainability awareness visualization is prototyped, to show the impacted area on map given the carbon saved.

item through recycling, landfill, and composting. These credits are converted into tangible metrics to enhance the user's understanding by utilizing the green algorithm [13], the virtual carbon credits are presented into *tree-days* and *travel mileage* (Fig. 1e), which represents the number of days a tree can offset the equivalent carbon emissions, and the emission produced by traveling certain miles in a car.

### 3.3   User Studies

We designed and conducted two user studies to evaluate the effectiveness of the interactive sorting practices for waste management learning. There were 27 and 21 participants in Study 1 and Study 2, respectively. Both studies were conducted over a period of 2 weeks, and participants were given access to the same set of 30 AI-generated quizzes. The only difference between these two studies was that the participants were tasked to practice all 30 of them in Study 1 without exposing to any user-generated practices and functionality. However, in Study 2, they were encouraged but were not obligated to use the system. Meanwhile, users were introduced to the quiz-authoring feature so they had the opportunity to create their own quizzes. Such setup allowed us to control the effect of AI-generated practices, examine users' reception and involvement in social content contribution, and simulate a more realistic scenario in using the system. Both studies included a pre-study and a post-study survey, including objective questions about their experiences and a knowledge test. The test includes 15 waste objects in daily life to assess participants' understanding of sustainable waste management practices before and after engaging with the game.

## 4   Evaluations and Results

In Study 1, participants completed an average of $104 \pm 26$ sorting attempts, resulting in a total of 2,900 sorting interactions. In Study 2, participants completed an average of $17 \pm 47$ sorting attempts, resulting in a total of 509 sorting interactions. The high standard deviation in Study 2 can be attributed to a student who completed all available quizzes, while the majority of participants completed fewer quizzes. Additionally, Study 2 participants created 26 quizzes using the provided authoring tool.

**Table 1.** Waste sorting accuracy analytics

|  | Winter 2024 | Spring 2024 |
|---|---|---|
|  | **Study 1** | **Study 2** |
| **Correctness** |  |  |
| Landfill | 0.67 | 0.67 |
| Recycle | 0.86 | 0.82 |
| Compost | 0.82 | 0.81 |
| Hazardous | 0.79 | 0.83 |
| Overall | 0.80 | 0.79 |

The overall correctness of sorting in both studies was similar, with 80% in study 1 and 79% in study 2 (Table 1). In both studies, participants demonstrated the lowest accuracy in sorting landfill items (67% in both studies). In contrast, recycle, compost, and hazardous categories all reached relatively high accuracy (from the high 70 s to mid-80 s) in both studies. It showcased the profound challenges of classifying waste items in the landfill category.

The pre-study knowledge test results were identical in both studies, with an average of 79% in scoring. After users practiced the sorting quizzes in the system, a significant improvement was found in Study 1 ($p < 0.01$), where participants achieved an average score of 87%. Although participants in Study 2 also found an increase in their post-knowledge (83%), the improvement was not significant. Such outcome may be attributed to the fact that Study 2 users completed fewer practices on average compared to Study 1. However, they contributed to the ecosystem of the game by creating their own practices, which add value to the learning experience and promote engagement within the community. Even though all sorting practices' accuracy was found to be coherent and comparable with Study 1. Overall, Study 1 illustrated an effective focused practices that resulted in high sorting accuracy and high knowledge gain, which is consistent with the findings of the distributed practice in the literature (see Sect. 2). Study 2, however, revealed a more realistic scenario where the users normally will not be conditioned to practice as hard and frequently as they do, but they can still thrive by interacting with the waste sorting practices in limited exercises.

## 5   Conclusions

This study presents a web-based serious game that utilizes interactive sorting quizzes to promote waste management practices. Two user studies were conducted to evaluate the effectiveness of the game. Participants in both studies demonstrated improvements in their knowledge of sustainable waste management practices, the focused serious practices indicated a significant post-knowledge gain. The findings highlight the potential of serious games and interactive learning approaches in promoting environmental education. By leveraging emerging technologies such as LLM and encouraging user-generated content, our game provides an engaging and informative learning experience for positive changes in sustainable behaviors. One limitation of the virtual carbon credit system was that it was only associated with waste sorting and not with other activities (i.e. quiz creation or sorting frequency). This might have discouraged highly motivated participants from creating more quizzes. Finally, based on users' feedback, we further improved the sustainability awareness visualization (Fig. 1f) to envision the amount of carbon saved will empower the *green travel* by car on a map, and a slider capability to enable simulating the impact and persistent sorting.

**Disclosure of Interests.** The authors have no competing interests to declare that are relevant to the content of this article.

# References

1. Alzaid, M., Hsiao, S.: Utilising problem-solving: from self-assessment to self regulating. New Rev. Hypermedia Multimed. **25**(3), 222–244 (2019)
2. Assor, A., Prouzeau, A., Dragicevic, P., Hachet, M.: Exploring augmented reality waste data representations for eco feedback. In: Extended Abstracts of the 2023 CHI Conference on Human Factors in Computing Systems, pp. 1–4 (2023)
3. California Environmental Protection Agency: Calrecycle. https://calrecycle.ca.gov/
4. Chung, C.Y., Hsiao, I.H.: From detail to context: modeling distributed practice intensity and timing by multiresolution signal analysis. International Educational Data Mining Society (2021)
5. Delnevo, G., Aguzzi, G., Letizi, S., Luffarelli, M., Petreti, A., Mirri, S.: Encouraging users in waste sorting using deep neural networks and gamification. In: Proceedings of the Conference on Information Technology for Social Good, pp. 230–235 (2021)
6. Environmental Protection Agency: National overview: facts and figures on materials, wastes and recycling. https://www.epa.gov/facts-and-figures-about-materials-waste-and-recycling/national-overview-facts-and-figures-materials
7. Environmental Protection Agency: State universal waste programs in the United States. https://www.epa.gov/hw/state-universal-waste-programs-united-states
8. Hoffmann, G., Pfeiffer, J.: Gameful learning for a more sustainable world: measuring the effect of design elements on long-term learning outcomes in correct waste sorting. Bus. Inf. Syst. Eng., 1–24 (2022)
9. Idrobo, M.L., Fernanda Saenz, M., Márceles, K., Chanchí, G.E., Vidal, M.I., Burbano, C.L.: Recycling: a serious game focused on the classification of waste. In: Telematics and Computing: 7th International Congress, WITCOM 2018, Mazatlán, Mexico, 5–9 Nov 2018, Proceedings, vol. 7, pp. 234–245. Springer (2018)
10. Jespersen, K.N., Odgaard, R., Julsgaard, K., Madsbøll, J.L., Lundbak, M.H., Niebuhr, M., Skovfoged, M.M., Löchtefeld, M.: Foodfighters-improving memory retention of food items through a mobile serious game. In: Extended Abstracts of the 2023 CHI Conference on Human Factors in Computing Systems, pp. 1–7 (2023)
11. Jiménez Barriga, N., Hernández Villalba, B.: Robote: interactive educational tool to teach basic education children to classify and collect waste in their school environment. In: Extended Abstracts of the 2023 CHI Conference on Human Factors in Computing Systems, pp. 1–8 (2023)
12. Karpicke, J.D., Aue, W.R.: The testing effect is alive and well with complex materials. Educ. Psychol. Rev. **27**, 317–326 (2015)
13. Lannelongue, L., Grealey, J., Inouye, M.: Green algorithms: quantifying the carbon footprint of computation. Adv. Sci. **8**(12), 2100707 (2021)
14. Robelia, B., Greenhow, C., Burton, L.: Adopting environmentally responsible behaviors: how learning within a social networking application motivated students to act for the environment. Environ. Educ. Res. **17**(4), 553–575 (2011)
15. Shimoni, R., Barrington, G., Wilde, R., Henwood, S.: Addressing the needs of diverse distributed students. Int. Rev. Res. Open Distrib. Learn. **14**(3), 134–157 (2013)
16. Sobel, H.S., Cepeda, N.J., Kapler, I.V.: Spacing effects in real-world classroom vocabulary learning. Appl. Cogn. Psychol. **25**(5), 763–767 (2011)
17. Sun, Q., Hsiao, I.H., Chien, S.Y.: Immersive educational recycling assistant (era): learning waste sorting in augmented reality. In: Conference Proceedings of the 9th

International Conference of the Immersive Learning Research Network. In Press (2023)

18. Sun, Q., Hsiao, I.H., Chien, S.Y.: Immersive educational technology for waste management learning: a study of waste detection and feedback delivery in augmented reality. In: International Conference on Human-Computer Interaction, pp. 509–515. Springer (2023)

19. United Nations: United nations carbon offset platform. https://unfccc.int/climate-action/united-nations-carbon-offset-platform

20. Van Gog, T., Sweller, J.: Not new, but nearly forgotten: the testing effect decreases or even disappears as the complexity of learning materials increases. Educ. Psychol. Rev. **27**, 247–264 (2015)

21. Vitiello, G., Cantone, A.A., Romano, M., Sebillo, M., Silvestri, S.: Can gamification make driving styles more sustainable? A real-world pilot study. In: Proceedings of the 2023 ACM Conference on Information Technology for Social Good, pp. 315–323 (2023)

22. Wang, K., Tekler, Z.D., Cheah, L., Herremans, D., Blessing, L.: Evaluating the effectiveness of an augmented reality game promoting environmental action. Sustainability **13**(24), 13912 (2021)

23. Zhang, L., Li, B., Zhang, Q., Hsiao, I.H.: Does a distributed practice strategy for multiple choice questions help novices learn programming? Int. J. Emerg. Technol. Learn. (iJET) **15**(18), 234–250 (2020)

# Kongruent - A Shader Language and Compiler for Efficient and Approachable GPU-Programming

Robert Konrad$^{(\boxtimes)}$ and Stefan Göbel

Serious Games Group, Technische Universität Darmstadt, Darmstadt, Germany
{robert.konrad,stefan_peter.goebel}@tu-darmstadt.de

**Abstract.** We introduce Kongruent, a new shader language and compiler, developed from scratch without any dependencies. Kongruent can cross-compile to all relevant system shader languages and bytecodes and provides significant advances in ease of use, compilation times, shader optimization and data-exchange between CPUs and GPUs. We provide an overview of the overall project and detail a collection of interesting features currently implemented in Kongruent. This includes its handling of data-buffers, data-exchange between shader stages, integration with regular programming languages and its compilation model. The compilation model in particular is discussed in detail as it is the basis that unlocks many of its other features.

**Keywords:** GPU-Programming · Shaders · Compilers · GLSL · HLSL · MSL · SPIR-V

## 1 Introduction

Most of today's computers contain two primary programmable chips or chip-segments - a CPU and a GPU. CPUs are the most foundational component of any computer and are supported by a big variety of high level languages. The Online Historical Encyclopaedia of Programming Languages'[1] list of 8945 programming languages can be considered as a rough lower bound estimate. CPUs run machine code and only a small number of different kinds of machine code was deployed. Each kind of machine code has a multitude of CPUs that support it. Graphics chips, commonly called GPUs since Nvidia popularized the term in 1999[2], are a more recent addition that has a complicated history in terms of programmability. Early graphics chips designed for triangle- or quad-rasterization based 3D graphics could not run any user-provided code and instead

---

[1] https://hopl.info.
[2] https://www.nvidia.com/object/IO_20020111_5424.html.

J. L. Plass and X. Ochoa (Eds.): JCSG 2024, LNCS 15259, pp. 142–154, 2025.
https://doi.org/10.1007/978-3-031-74138-8_12

simply rendered a provided list of primitives with pre-defined parameters. Over time more and more parts of the rendering-pipeline became programmable and in the late 2000s the ability to sidestep the rendering-pipeline alltogether and use the compute units of GPUs more directly was introduced [1,2]. GPUs also run a form of machine code but traditionally compatibility breaks even with new GPU models by the same vendor. It is therefore not practical for applications to bundle GPU machine code, instead they bundle bytecode or high level language code which is then compiled to the actual GPU machine code at runtime. The form in which GPU code has to be provided is dictated by the operating system that the code is to run on as it is the operating system's GPU driver system that is responsible for generating the final GPU machine code. This has made the creation of GPU languages more difficult if the language is to be used across platforms as it has to be possible to compile the language into other high level languages and into lower level bytecodes. As of now four relevant high level GPU languages (GLSL, HLSL, MSL and WGSL) and three bytecodes (DXIL, DXC and SPIR-V) are in common use. In addition to that OpenCL and CUDA are two options for running compute shaders that also provide their own programming languages. The list of GPU languages is very modest, with the SPIR-V registry listing 44 tools overall that can output SPIR-V as of May 2024[3] with not all of these tools being compilers and many of the compilers in the list not primarily being focused on GPU-programming. As we consider this list to be much smaller than it should be we introduce one more entry with Kongruent, a new high level shader language and compiler. With divergence being among the biggest performance challenges in modern GPU programming [3,4] we chose a name that reflects the opposite and imposes a neat abbreviation. The compiler can already output GLSL, HLSL, MSL, WGSL and SPIR-V and is therefore fully usable in practice across all platforms that are popular today. It advances the state of the art in several key areas such as compilation times and CPU/GPU data-exchange as detailed in the later sections of this paper.

## 2   Related Work

Shaders run on the primary execution units of a GPU. Those execution units were first unified with Ati/AMD's Xenos GPU in the Xbox 360 [5], shortly followed by the GeForce 8 series by Nvidia. Nowadays those units are not dissimilar to CPUs with the main differentiating factor being a much larger focus on parallelism which is however still achieved using concepts that also exist in CPUs. Like in multicore CPUs, GPUs use multiple execution cores. Higher end models are typically scaled up primarily by increasing the amount of those cores. SIMD instructions are the primary instruction form used in GPUs but usually a greater simd-width is used compared to CPUs - 32 or 64 is common instead of eight. A set of simd-data running on one core is commonly called a wave and a single simd-element is called a lane - though other naming conventions are also common. Simultaneous Multithreading (SMT, also called Hyperthreading by intel)

---

[3] https://github.com/KhronosGroup/SPIRV-Headers/commit/7d500c4d.

is used extensively with GPUs being able to hold large numbers of execution contexts on hold, ready to be switched in to hide memory latencies - which can be very important as graphics tend to be very memory intensive. Apart from the larger focus on parallelism the primary differentiator to CPUs are according to intel's conclusions in the Larrabee project the added texture sampling units and instructions [6].

While modern GPU execution units are similar in design to CPUs the programming model is different. Programs are written in terms of what happens to each data-element which allows compilers to easily transform programs into simd instructions. In the following we list the shader languages and bytecodes provided by today's operating systems and web browsers which all employ this design.

## 2.1    GLSL

GLSL (OpenGL Shading Language) is the shader language used by OpenGL, OpenGL ES and WebGL [7]. GLSL is closely based on C. GLSL has many different flavors and it is generally not possible to use a GLSL shader across all graphics APIs that support GLSL. A shader-compiler has to be able to output different flavors of GLSL for that reason. In practice a flavor of GLSL is also often used to target Vulkan via the glslang compiler that can compile GLSL (with some specific additions for Vulkan data-binding) to SPIR-V.

## 2.2    HLSL, DXIL and DXC

HLSL (High-Level Shader Language) is the shader language used by Microsoft for Direct3D from version 9 onwards [8,9]. It is based on C++, recently also introducing more recent C++ features like templates[4]. Microsoft provides HLSL compilers that output DXIL or DXBC bytecode which is then used by Direct3D graphics drivers. DXIL and DXC, the current bytecode and compiler, are based on LLVM and clang[5].

## 2.3    MSL

MSL (Metal Shading Language) is the shader language used by Apple for their Metal API [11]. It is interestingly also based on C++ instead of Swift - Apple's own C-like programming language.

## 2.4    WGSL

WGSL (WebGPU Shading Language) is the shader language used for WebGPU, the successor to WebGL [12]. It is not directly based on C or C++ but still very similar. Compared to other shader languages it adds as well as removes a few

---

[4] https://devblogs.microsoft.com/directx/announcing-hlsl-2021/.

[5] https://github.com/microsoft/DirectXShaderCompiler.

convenience features. Originally WGSL was supposed to be a textual form of SPIR-V as a compromise between the team at Apple that wanted to create a new shader language based on HLSL and all other teams that intended to use SPIR-V directly[6]. Over the standardization process WGSL became a relatively normal, textual shader-language.

## 2.5  SPIR-V

SPIR-V is an SSA bytecode used for Vulkan shaders [13]. Vulkan does not directly support high level language shaders but Khronos supports the development of GLSL and HLSL to SPIR-V compilers.

## 2.6  OpenCL and CUDA

OpenCL and CUDA are two languages and APIs solely focused on compute shaders [14]. Kongruent can not currently output OpenCL and CUDA as it focuses on language targets that can support the complete graphics pipeline, but their featuresets are nonetheless relevant.

More directly comparable to Kongruent are the various non-system shader compilers but only few of them try to introduce new features compared to the established system level compilers. A very widely used setup is a combination of glslang and SPIRVCross that is used to make GLSL work on most platforms. glslang is a compiler that compiles GLSL to SPIR-V bytecode while SPIRVCross is a compiler that compiles SPIR-V bytecode to GLSL, HLSL or MSL.

Slang is a language and compiler that adds on top of HLSL [15–17]. Its main features are however automatic differentiation and generics which is a different focus compared to Kongruent.

# 3  Serious Games and GPU Programming

GPU programming is fundamental for modern graphics programming which in turn makes it fundamental for most game programming, also when the end result is a Serious Game. But most games, especially most Serious Games, do not concern themselves much with the problems of GPU programming and let a pre-made game engine handle all of it. The most popular game engines, namely Unity and Unreal, are relatively well equipped to run their GPU code on a lot of platforms and provide the basic shader code needed out of the box.

But general game engines are primarily focused on the regular gaming market and do not necessarily have the needs of Serious Games in mind. Serious Games often target web browsers on outdated hardware to reach a target audience outside of the core gamer market with school computers being a prime example of that. Serious Games are also not necessarily distributed via traditional game distribution channels. This can make it tricky or impossible to use common game

---

[6] https://github.com/gpuweb/gpuweb/issues/570.

engines. Unreal discontinued browser support in 2019[7] and the Unity Runtime Fee introduced in 2023 might make it infeasible to use it for free or low cost products[8]. Using Unreal or Unity also makes it nearly impossible to implement games in unusual ways. A Serious Game about physics might for example benefit greatly from a dynamic voxel worls as seen in Teardown[9].

But GPU/Shader programming is a difficult topic for a lot of programmers, as it is not taught in regular programming courses with shaders often being treated as a black box, making modern graphics programming inaccessible for many. While fundamentally not very different from regular programming, GPU programming poses specific challenges but we argue that at least some of them exist mainly for historic reasons and can be overcome with new tools. Ultimately, we consider making shader programming more accessible and more portable as fundamental for making Serious Games development independent of regular game engines, which can unlock new markets and new game concepts.

In the project DeineStadt[10] that is developing a Serious Game for urban planning, Kongruent is used for prototyping large scale 3D geography data visualization for integration into the game. It provides a simple yet powerful and very fast environment for testing and optimizing parallel algorithms without the burdens of starting up a complete game engine.

## 4   The Kongruent Language and Compiler

Kongruent[11] is a compiler and GPU programming language. It generates code in the target shader language or bytecode in addition to C-files that can be integrated in the host program to automate various CPU/GPU data exchange scenarios. Kongruent is completely implemented in C without any dependencies, so it can easily be embedded into a game or application and provide runtime shader compilation as it is often necessary for game development tools or just debug versions of games. It can output GLSL, HLSL, MSL, SPIR-V and its own bytecode.

The generated C-files describe the shaders and provide CPU-versions of any accessible GPU-data with correct padding. It also outputs additional data when it is needed for specific graphics APIs to decide on what exact kinds of GPU objects it has to create. The generated C-code also contains everything needed to create the necessary vertex buffers when vertex data is not fetched manually.

### 4.1   Kongruent Bytecode

Kongruent is compiled into its own bytecode. This provides an option for distributing the shader source code in an obfuscated low level form that can be

---

[7] https://docs.unrealengine.com/4.26/en-US/SharingAndReleasing/HTML5/.
[8] https://unity.com/pricing-updates.
[9] https://teardowngame.com/.
[10] https://deinestadt.science.
[11] https://github.com/Kode/Kongruent.

used across platforms. Like SPIR-V or DXIL the bytecode is uses SSA form, making it well suited for compiler optimizations. After optimization are applied target source code or target bytecode is generated. For a regular compilation bytecode is only generated for functions while other data is accessed directly in the abstract syntax tree as using that in bytecode form would only slow down compilation without helping in any way.

Names are optionally kept in the bytecode-data so that generated source code more closely resembles the original code - but names can also be left out to obfuscate the resulting code more thoroughly and to save on space. Overall the bytecode is similar to SPIR-V but in detail sports many small differences to accomodate portability across graphics APIs and languages.

## 4.2 Program Structure

A Kongruent program (see Fig. 1) contains at least one pipeline struct, which defines a complete graphics or compute pipeline and optionally various rendering state. The compiler is invoked with parameters pointing to one or more directories containing .kong files. Each shader entry point results in a separate shader in the target language/bytecode being output. The entry points are infered from the pipeline structs. Vertex stages can optionally have input parameters which trigger the generation of vertex buffer creation data.

How data is passed in and out of shaders is inferred from the input and output parameters of the entry points. As usual later shader stages are compatible with earlier stages that provide more parameters than are used in the later stages but as the compiler is directly aware of all used shader combinations it can optimize the whole pipeline across the shader stages and provide automatic options for packing and unpacking data to optimize shader stage data-passing.

Unlike in other shader languages buffer, functions and other language constructs can be used by multiple shaders directly. Language constructs are generally referenced by name and each name can only exist once across all the .kong files passed to the compiler. This makes the compiler aware across shaders of the usage of the same data structures and functions. While the knowledge of multiple usage of functions is currently of little use as target languages do generally not allow calling functions in a global way, being aware of multiple usage of structures shared with the CPU can aid in data-exchange.

# 5 Compilation Models

## 5.1 The C Compilation Model

GPU programming languages are traditionally based on C or C++, likely for historical reasons as high performance 3D graphics applications like game engines are usually implemented in C or C++. C/C++ uses a very old-school compilation model [18].

Source files are compiled separately, forming so-called compilation or translation units. These units are in the end linked together using a program called a

```
struct vertex_in {
    pos: float3;
}

struct vertex_out {
    pos: float4;
}

fun pos(input: vertex_in): vertex_out {
    var output: vertex_out;
    output.pos = float4(input.pos.x, input.pos.y, 0.5, 1.0);
    return output;
}

fun pixel(input: vertex_out): float4 {
    var color: float4 = float4(1.0, 0.0, 0.0, 1.0);
    return color;
}

#[pipe]
struct pipeline {
    vertex = pos;
    fragment = pixel;
}
```

**Fig. 1.** Basic Kongruent sample

linker. To share code across compilation units, each unit has to see a declaration of the variable or function to share. By convention this is done using header files which are files containing code snippets which are copied into other files using a pre-compilation step that is run automatically before the regular compilation occurs (the so-called precompiler).

Header files tend to be the primary reason for long compilation times in C/C++ which can easily reach hours for a complete rebuild of a game engine, leading to widespread use of distributed compilation tools like Incredibuild[12] in the games industry. GPU programming emphasizes these problems. A linker does usually not exist and all code-sharing happens via header files. Each shader entry-point triggers a completely separate compilation.

Adding shader variants to that and a single header file can easily be parsed hundreds of times when a single game is compiled. This compilation model also prevents shader-compilers from applying any optimizations or convenience features across different shaders.

## 5.2   Shader Variants

Using conditional jumps on GPUs can be challenging for performance. GPUs apply two strategies for implementing them. A traditional jump is efficient but

---

[12] https://www.incredibuild.com.

can only be used when all lanes in a wave take the same route. For different routes within a single wave lanes are deactivated and activated as needed. In this situation the wave visits both branches of an if-else-construct and this is where performance is lost. To make the best of the situation shader compilers can output code that tries to do a proper jump and falls back to lane activation/deactivation when the lanes are not taking the same routes as seen in Fig. 2.

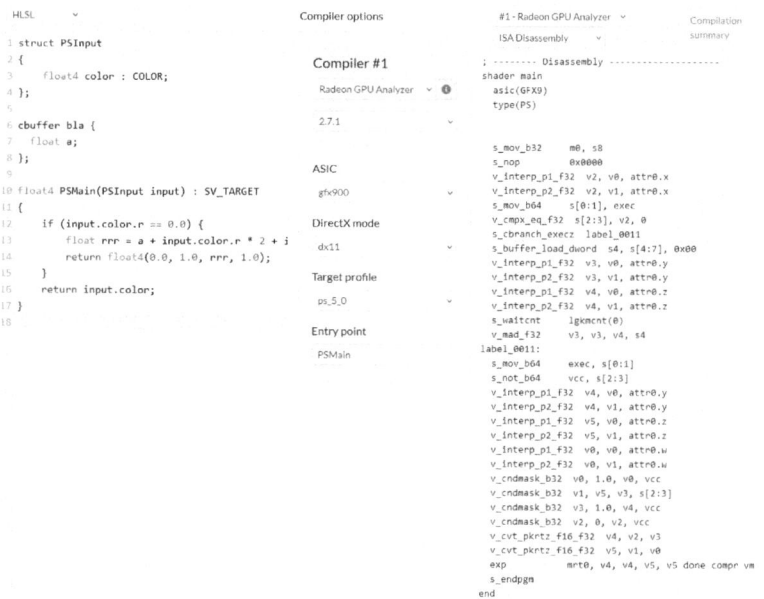

**Fig. 2.** A mix of a conditional branch and cndmask operations

Shader programming languages support hints that can be used to get the compiler to leave out the jump or the lane masking which can be used to improve performance slightly when the data is know to always be coherent or to mostly be incoherent inside of one wave.

But even when things are setup in a way that proper conditional jumps can generally be used they can cause another performance problem. Increased code complexity causes increased register usage which limits a GPU's ability to hold more shaders invocations ready for SMT-like execution. This number of shader contexts that can be held available for a given shader by the GPU is called occupancy [19] and maximizing this value is important in memory bound shaders to give the GPU more opportunities to do useful work while one shader invocation waits for memory reads or writes.

The performance problems caused by conditional jumps can partially be overcome using shader variants, meaning that various configurations of conditional jumps are precompiled into different shaders, moving the actual conditional jump to the CPU which dispatches the shader variants accordingly. Every single shader variant is in this case smaller than the original shader and when this removes particularly complex code paths, register usage is typically reduced, increasing occupancy for at least some of the shader variants.

Vulkan provides explicit support for shader variants using a feature called specialization constants that works on the generated bytecode but this is of little use in a cross-platform context. For other APIs code has to be compiled multiple times and code paths are typically switched using the C-like precompiler provided by other shader languages.

## 5.3  The Kongruent Compilation Model

Kongruent builds a model of all shaders that are included in a program. This is the usual approach taken by most of today's programming languages with the big exception being C and C++ and the various languages directly based on C or C++ - which includes GLSL, HLSL and MSL.

In Kongruent every piece of code is only parsed once, independently of the number of output shaders it ends up being used in. In the end when targeting source languages Kongruent outputs shader files that are optimized for compilation time - instead of using header files every generated shader file only contains exactly the code that is needed.

In an arbitrary example that uses a piece of code in a file that's used in 100 shaders of which only ten use that actual piece of code, the code is parsed 100 times with a traditional shader compiler but only 11 times (one time by Kongruent itself, ten times by the target shader compiler) when using Kongruent. Consequently the compilation-speedup has no upper bound but depends entirely on the intricacies of the shader source code.

Having a look at all shader files at once also allows Kongruent to get rid of manual resource indexing - it can directly see when the same data is used across different shaders in the same way this is done in regular programming languages, via its name. Buffer, texture and sampler indices are then assigned to make sure that data that is shared across shaders is not overridden. The indices also end up in the generated C-sources and can therefore be used automatically.

# 6  Data-Handling

## 6.1  Buffer Types

Kongruent generates C-code that can be integrated in the host applications. All data-structures that can be used across CPU and GPU are represented in that code. This automatically handles the different alignment rules required for the various buffer types of various graphics APIs. The concrete buffer types for the target platforms are selected based on modifiers and hints.

MSL only provides a single buffer type which can be marked to reside in constant, device, thread or threadgroup address spaces. As this maps relatively well to GPU feature sets [20] it was used as the basis for Kongruent's buffer modifiers. Additionally Kongruent supports a push-modifier, a priority-hint and an update-group hint.

**Constant buffers** are buffers that are read-only on the GPU. They are only written by the CPU and can therefore not change in between draw-calls, making them constant across shader invocations. The direct equivalent is severely restricted in size on several graphics APIs which can generally require workarounds or using a different buffer type. Kongruent's buffer type selection for HLSL and GLSL is aided by its complete view of all shaders.

In HLSL constant buffers are mapped to CBV buffers or SRV buffers depending on their size. The number of CBV buffers is also more restricted than the number of SRV buffers and therefore SRV buffers are used when the number of CBV buffers runs out. The priority hint (when provided) and the number of usages across all shaders are considered for the CBV/SRV split.

Similarly, in GLSL constant buffers are mapped to Uniform Buffer Objects or Buffer Textures. Using Buffer Textures is normally very different from using Uniform Buffer Objects as the texelFetch function has to be used to read memory but Kongruent handles these differences automatically.

Uniform buffers are used for the constant buffer implementations in WGSL and SPIR-V.

**Device buffers** are general read/write buffers. Graphics APIs usually support big sizes for read/write buffers in general so a more direct mapping is possible.

In GLSL device buffers are mapped to Shader Storage Buffer Objects, in HLSL they are mapped to UAV buffers. They are mapped to storage buffers in WGSL and SPIR-V.

**Push buffers** are the equivalent of root constants/push constants in Direct3D 12 and Vulkan - a small amount of memory that can be updated by the command processor and therefore requires no explicit synchronization across shader invocations. Metal and MSL implement this without a special buffer type so Kongruent simply outputs the buffer without modifiers in this case. WebGPU/WGSL as of now does not support an equivalent feature unfortunately.

## 6.2   Descriptor Sets and Root Signatures

Vulkan and HLSL provide a way to pack data set switching for more efficient shader data preparation via their descriptor layouts/descriptor sets and root signatures. Kongruent supports automatic creation of the necessary data structures

Root Signatures are embedded in the generated HLSL source so it can then be used directly, making runtime shader compilation more efficient. Descriptor layouts are also created automatically and provided by the C-interface. Data is split up into descriptor sets according to the update-group hint, making it basically equivalent to the layout set modifier in Vulkan-flavored GLSL.

### 6.3   Dynamic Pipeline Data

As already discussed, shader stage combinations are declared in the language itself. These declarations also contain all further data required to instantiate a compute or render pipeline. Where it is not appropriate to declare all elements of a pipeline statically, elements can be declared as *dynamic*. Dynamic pipeline-elements can then be changed at runtime.

This can lead to performance problems as internally multiple pipeline objects have to be created in Direct3D 12, Vulkan, Metal or WebGPU. Older graphics APIs are however less restrictive in this aspect and Vulkan recently gained the option to work without pipelines via the VK_EXT_shader_object extension[13].

### 6.4   Shader Stage Data Transfer

But minimizing data sizes that are passed between shader stages is an important performance optimization and a lot of difficult to maintain shader code is often dedicated to pack data that goes out of a shader stage and then unpack it when it comes into a shader stage.

Unlike in other shader languages shader stage combinations are declared in Kongruent directly. This allows data packing/unpacking to be optimized across shader stages, among other things like removing variables that are not used in a later stage.

Kongruent also provides automatic support for data-packing via a syntax similar to bit-fields in C as seen in Fig. 3.

```
struct data {
    position: float : 12;
    material: int : 4;
}
```

**Fig. 3.** A mix of a conditional branch and cndmask operations

This automatically creates packing and unpacking code as needed and also considers what data is actually used in the later shader stages.

## 7   Conclusion

Shader compilation is a field that still does not have a lot of contenders and the cost of entry for a practically useful project is relatively high as a lot of output options have to be provided for the different system APIs and shader

---

[13] https://registry.khronos.org/vulkan/specs/1.3-extensions.

languages. Kongruent is a new project that already provides various fundamental improvements beyond the current status quo.

The simple, dependency-less implementation of the compiler will hopefully also allow further developers to implement new features like language extensions and new optimization passes.

Not discussed in this paper is Kongruent's close relation with the cross-platform framework and API Kinc[14]. Developing both projects in tandem provides many opportunities to further simplify graphics programming. The Kinc-integration can also be used as a basis to develop a tighter integration with other graphics APIs. Kongruent is now also the primary GPU language in the Kinc project and community involvement will influence further development.

**Acknowledgments.** This research has partially been funded in the course of the research project DeineStadt (engl.: your town), where the proposed GPU programming concepts are used for the presentation of a 3D city model.

# References

1. Kirk, D.: NVIDIA CUDA software and GPU parallel computing architecture. In: ISMM, vol. 7, pp. 103–104
2. Ni, T.: Direct compute: bring GPU computing to the mainstream. In: GPU technology conference, vol. 2009 (2009)
3. Xiang, P., Yang, Y., Zhou, H.: Warp-level divergence in GPUs: characterization, impact, and mitigation. In: 2014 IEEE 20th International Symposium on High Performance Computer Architecture (HPCA), pp. 284–295. IEEE (2014)
4. Anantpur, J., Govindarajan, R.: Taming warp divergence. In: 2017 IEEE/ACM International Symposium on Code Generation and Optimization (CGO), pp. 50–60. IEEE (2017)
5. Moya, V., Gonzalez, C., Roca, J., Fernandez, A., Espasa, R.: Shader performance analysis on a modern GPU architecture. In: 38th Annual IEEE/ACM International Symposium on Microarchitecture (MICRO'05), 10 pp. IEEE (2005)
6. Seiler, L., Carmean, D., Sprangle, E., Forsyth, T., Abrash, M., Dubey, P., Hanrahan, P.: Larrabee: a many-core x86 architecture for visual computing. ACM Trans. Graph. (TOG) **27**(3), 1–15 (2008)
7. Rost, R.J., Licea-Kane, B., Ginsburg, D., Kessenich, J., Lichtenbelt, B., Malan, H., Weiblen, M.: OpenGL Shading Language. Pearson Education (2009)
8. St-Laurent, S.:. The Complete HLSL Reference. Paradoxal Press
9. Oneppo, M.:. Hlsl shader model 4.0. In: ACM SIGGRAPH 2007 Courses, pp. 112–152
10. Pop, S.: The SSA representation framework: semantics, analyses and GCC implementation. Doctoral dissertation, École Nationale Supérieure des Mines de Paris (2006)
11. Gebraad, L., Fichtner, A.: Seamless GPU acceleration for C++-based physics with the metal shading language on Apple's M series unified chips. Seismol. Soc. Am. **94**(3), 1670–1675 (2023)
12. Kenwright, B.: Introduction to the WebGPU API. In: ACM SIGGRAPH 2022 Courses, pp. 1–184 (2022)

---

[14] https://github.com/Kode/Kinc.

13. Kessenich, J., Ouriel, B., Krisch, R.: SPIR-V specification. Khronos. Group **3**, 17 (2018)
14. Munshi, A.: The OpenCL specification. In: 2009 IEEE Hot Chips 21 Symposium (HCS), pp. 1–314. IEEE (2009)
15. He, Y., Fatahalian, K., Foley, T.: Slang: language mechanisms for extensible real-time shading systems. ACM Trans. Graph. (TOG) **37**(4), 1–13 (2018)
16. He, Y.: Slang-a shader compilation system for extensible, real-time shading. Doctoral dissertation, Carnegie Mellon University (2021)
17. Bangaru, S.P., et al.: Slang. d: fast, modular and differentiable shader programming. ACM Trans. Graph. (TOG) **42**(6), 1–28 (2023)
18. International Organization for Standardization: ISO/IEC 9899:1999: programming languages-C (1999). https://www.iso.org/standard/29237.html
19. Mistry, P., Purnomo, B.: Profiling OpenCL kernels using wavefront occupancy with radeon GPU profiler. In: Proceedings of the International Workshop on OpenCL, pp. 1–2 (2019)
20. Barczak, J.: Let's close the buffer zoo (2016). Retrieved from http://www.joshbarczak.com/blog/?p=1260

# "Masters Against Food Waste" Providing Children with Strategies to Avoid Food Waste

Sandra Câmara Olim[1,2(✉)] [ID], Francisco Vasconcelos[3] [ID], Mara Dionisio[1,3] [ID], and Pedro Campos[1,3,4] [ID]

[1] ITI-LARSyS, Funchal, Portugal
sandra.olim@tecnico.ulisboa.pt
[2] Instituto Tecnico de Lisboa (IST), Lisboa, Portugal
[3] Universidade da Madeira, Funchal, Portugal
[4] Wow! Systems, Funchal, Portugal

**Abstract.** Addressing food waste is a critical concern for the sustainability of our environment. Various approaches have been utilized, such as campaigns to educate the general population to be more mindful and responsible. However, when targeting children, especially on school premises, there is a notable lack of engagement and effectiveness compared to their impact on other demographic groups. Serious games promote the development of social, cultural, and cognitive skills. Through game-play, children acquire content knowledge, enrich their experience, and become engaged with the learning information. Recognizing the opportunity of these tools, we created "Masters Against Food Waste" designed and developed to impart children with strategies to combat food waste. The results of a study with 22 students yielded positive results, highlighting the game's potential to raise awareness and prevent food waste effectively.

**Keywords:** Game Design · Serious Games · Food Waste and Children

## 1 Introduction

The implications of food waste extend significantly to the sustainability and economy of the global population, as the production of tons of food requires considerable resources [65].

Households are considered the largest group to produce food waste [28,42, 55]. Consumer's actions including cooking excessively large meals, purchasing excessive amounts of food, storing and neglecting to repurpose leftover food, are some of the factors that lead to household food waste [7,12]. While parents are responsible for these actions, children can have an important role to avoid food waste.

Children sustainable behaviour has received significant practical and scholarly interest [30]. The United Nations Sustainable Development Goals recognise children as drivers of change for a sustainable future [30,63].

J. L. Plass and X. Ochoa (Eds.): JCSG 2024, LNCS 15259, pp. 155–174, 2025.
https://doi.org/10.1007/978-3-031-74138-8_13

Current research also shows that younger consumers are more likely to engage in food waste reduction practices than their older counterparts [4, 29]. As stated by Vieira et al. secretary of agriculture and food of Portugal, food waste education starts in school among the new generation of future producers and consumers [65].

Some ongoing initiatives approach the food waste problem and try to raise awareness among children and their parents [14, 40, 58, 62, 66]. Nonetheless, there is a need for strategies to engage and motivate younger consumers and their families to enhance their food waste management practices [30, 38, 54].

In the local context of Madeira, the food bank is an entity that regularly organizes lectures and activities aimed at educating children on their role in combating food waste. However, they have observed that young children are difficult to engage using traditional approaches. Hence, this institution presented us with the challenge to find an engaging solution to raise awareness of food waste and deliver the best practices to avoid it.

Inspired by previous research that highlights the potential of using games as effective tools for shaping attitudes and behaviors regarding sustainability issues [60], and by leveraging the engaging nature of games, in this article we present "Masters Against Food Waste", a serious game designed and developed to target eight to twelve year old children to impart food storage management skills.

The game, used as an artifact to conduct research through design, aims to answer: How can we design engaging and effective serious games that provide children with strategies to reduce food waste?

We contribute to this area of research by:

– Describing the design and development of a food waste game for children, to be promoted by the local food bank, aiming to provide awareness about food waste through an entertainment medium.
– Presenting insights from our study, into the design of educational games as tools that can offer strategies for reducing food waste.

## 2   Related Work

### 2.1   Food Waste

Food waste denotes the percentage of edible food that remains unconsumed [57], encompassing edibles intended for human consumption that undergo degradation, discharge, or contamination [23]. Food waste is often associated with financial loss or to be morally wrong, leading to a belief that individuals are reluctant to generate unnecessary food waste due to feelings of guilt or economic concerns [1]. The Food Waste Index Report (FWIR) 2021 estimated that around the world in 2019, 931 million tonnes of food waste were generated across the household, food service and retail sectors, with a per capita average of 121 kg per year[1]. The UN Environment Program (UNEP) and FWIR of 2024, showcased that households were responsible for 631 million tonnes of waste[2]. In the European Union, households account for approximately 53% of the food wasted [59]. In this context, there is an urgent need for heightened efforts to explore novel interventions addressing food waste practices within households. Geffen et al. [64], describes behaviors linked to household food waste as:

- Planning by creating shopping lists, specifying the needed food items and quantities before heading to the supermarket. This has demonstrated positive effects in preventing the purchase of excess food, as indicated by precious research [50].
- Shopping impulsively can contribute to increased waste. In this context, some studies suggest that price-oriented individuals tend to produce more waste [51], while others indicate the opposite, recent research refuting the notion that price-oriented individuals waste more and instead considering them as generating less waste [33].
- Storing food items according to the temperature and light intensity is crucial for preserving the shelf life of food items, making them safe to consume [50]. Adopting proper storage practices can effectively minimize food waste and enhance the likelihood of safely consuming the stored items [18].
- The absence of accurate measurements during food preparation or overcooking is cited as a contributing factor to food waste[3].
- Consumption of leftovers is another practice that is related directly to food waste[4].

While the introduction of strategies towards educating households actions are critical on all the consumer's behaviours, in the scope of this article, we reinforce the proper storage of food items. Food storage management which encompass the selection of suitable storage conditions, organizing food items to prevent spoilage and contamination, and vigilantly monitoring inventory can contribute to the decrease of household food waste [50].

## 2.2 Serious Games

Games are a powerful tools for education as through games children acquire knowledge, enrich their experience, and are active participants in their learning process. Serious games are defined as games designed with a primary purpose beyond mere entertainment [9]. These games are powerful tools in the domain of education, since through game-play children acquire content knowledge, enrich their experience, and become engaged with the learning content [16,46].

These games can follow different learning approaches or **pedagogical methods**. Some use a constructivism approach whereas the player construct their

---

[1] https://wedocs.unep.org/handle/20.500.11822/45230.
[2] https://www.unep.org/resources/publication/food-waste-index-report-2024.
[3] https://eu-refresh.org/best-practice-assessment-consumer-level-food-waste.
[4] https://eu-refresh.org/quantified-consumer-insights-food-waste.

understanding through the experience, interaction and exploration of the content [67]. Within this approach, Situated Learning Theory (SLT) offers a perspective on learning that departed from a learning process embedded in the context and culture of the user [37]. Experiential learning theory also evolves around the concept that effective learning occurs through direct interactive experiences or "learning by doing" in this case "learning by playing" and through reflection of those actions [11]. Behaviorism focus on the use of reinforcement and punishment as a way to create a stimuli-response to a change in behaviour [24]. In this sense, extrinsic motivation (external reward or avoiding punishment) can be a component that promotes the learning and engagement of the player.

Various elements employed within serious games to enhance children's engagement include **gamification** features such as achievements, character/avatar customization, badges, progress bars, competitiveness, experience points, feedback mechanisms, and ubiquitous leaderboards and point systems. According to Hallifax et al. [25], other elements that should be considered are the different levels that the user can achieve, the narrative or story-plot of the game, challenges that need to be overcome, the social component (being able to work in pairs or groups), stage, and the time (finishing the game before time runs out) [26].

### 2.3   Serious Games and Food Waste

Past research highlights the potential of using games as effective tools for shaping attitudes and behaviors regarding sustainability issues [60]. This topic is a worldwide concern paralleled by a growing interest in Human Computer Interaction (HCI) to support more sustainable practices [47]. Many topics like recycling [10,31], energy consumption [60], and climate change [19] have been explored using this medium. In this sense, using games to change children's social behaviors has gained more attention over the last two decades [15,45].

For instance, "The Grumpy Bin" [3] is an app designed for student housing that uses a camera-equipped container to capture images of discarded food and notify household members who was the perpetrator. The Bin displays its "mood" via an e-ink display and speaker based on the amount of food waste, aiming to raise awareness about food waste among young adults. Inspired by this, other authors have integrated interactive social networking and technology to promote food waste awareness. Similarly, "FoodWise" [69] targets campus communities to reduce food waste. It features a data storytelling dashboard showing food waste data from university canteens and a mobile web app encouraging users to document their waste reduction efforts, rewarding active participants.

"FridgeCam" by Farr-Wharton et al. [17] employs visual cues, such as color coding, to inform users about the longevity of food items and the need for timely consumption. Their study showed that organizing products within the fridge enhances users' memory and awareness of their food inventory, thereby reducing food waste. Similarly, "FridgeSort" [41] is a game designed to highlight the impact of inadequate food storage on food waste using color coding to encourage grouping similar food types.

"FoodFighters" [32] is a game that encourages young adult players to interact with their food items (by taking pictures) and customize them into so-called Food Fighters, avatars that are used to battle other players, making them memorable for reuse.

"Face-the-Waste" [56] is a public installation aimed at enhancing food literacy and highlighting the consequences of food waste. It engages users with multiple-choice questionnaires, where incorrect answers result in the disposal of real food. This mechanism provokes strong emotional reactions and encourages more profound reflection on food waste issues. Similarly, Ganglbauer et al. [22] developed an app that uses a food waste diary to help users reflect on instances of household food waste and understand the underlying reasons for these occurrences.

While there has been an increase in serious games addressing food waste, only a few are specifically targeted at a younger audience.

"Ratatouille" [27] for the Nintendo DS provides a culinary chef experience, where players simulate the food-slicing process using touchscreen interactions and manage the cooking of multiple dishes simultaneously. In "Fridge Organizing" [13], players arrange food items on specific shelves by matching their colors to the corresponding shelf colors, requiring strategic placement. Similarly, "Fill up Fridge" [21] focuses on the efficient organization of food items on shelves.

These games provide valuable insights into gameplay mechanics for introducing food waste concepts to preteens. However, to our knowledge, studies have yet to be conducted to evaluate their efficacy in providing strategies and engaging children with food waste practices.

# 3   Masters Against Food Waste Game Design

"Masters Against Food Waste" is a serious game developed for mobile devices because of the widespread availability of such equipment to the majority of children. The use of this equipment also afforded the prospect of not only engaging children within a formal classroom setting, but also replaying the game in an informal educational context.

## 3.1   Initial Concept Design and Rationale

The design and development of the game went through several stages and iterations.

1. Proper Food Storage: How to organize the refrigerator/pantry to store food correctly, maintain its freshness, and prevent spoilage;
2. Leftover Management: Re-purposing leftovers into new dishes;
3. Meal Planning: Plan meals to avoid overbuying and ensure that all purchased ingredients are used efficiently.

However, in this article's scope, we describe our approach/study about educating children on storing food on the shelves to prolong its life effectively.

The pedagogical approach followed a constructivist methodology, allowing children to explore concepts related to food storage at their own pace through game mechanics [48]. This approach involved repetitive actions, such as selecting food items and organizing them in appropriate locations, with feedback for correct or incorrect choices. An avatar was used to create empathy with the users, offering guidance and feedback throughout the game. To enhance user engagement, we incorporated rewards such as points, experience levels, and customization options for the main character. Additionally, we implemented a situated learning approach [37], incorporating familiar food items (e.g., apples, peppers, cake, salmon, peaches, tomatoes, leftovers) and objects (e.g., refrigerator, pantry, freezer) that are part of the children's daily routines. This method aims to make the learning experience more relevant and memorable, facilitating the application of food waste strategies at home. The objective was to engage children through gameplay, enabling them to complete tasks such as correctly identifying storage locations for various food items. Through this interactive experience, children could reflect on these strategies, understand their importance in real-life contexts at home, and ultimately share the game and knowledge with friends and family.

### 3.2   Game Iterations

The game follows different development stages, which were tested and provided useful feedback towards our high fidelity prototype. In the following paragraphs, we provide a synthesis of the main findings of each iteration.

The initial **concept design** was inspired by existing works, including related research, games, and apps that address food waste. The game development utilized Figma[5], which enabled rapid prototyping. This facilitated the implementation and evaluation of game mechanics, providing a comprehensive understanding of how these elements contribute to the overarching objectives (see Fig. 1).

Feedback from participants (n = 5) indicated that the initial gameplay was clear and easy to follow; however, selecting the freezer or pantry was confusing, causing participants to revisit the tutorial for clarification. Most users appreciated the different game mechanics, mainly character customization, and requested more options. While participants understood the reward systems, such as coins collected at each task, they found the experience points system-acquired after storing food, preparing a meal, and having it tasted by the chef-difficult to grasp. Participants enjoyed using a character/animal to guide the tasks, with comments such as, "he is so cool, funny, and cute." Other feedback included a desire for a more realistic environment and the addition of storytelling elements.

A **paper prototype** was developed (see Fig. 2) to facilitate rapid adjustments to game features, economizing time and resources. This prototype primarily focused on identifying more engaging mechanics for storing food, struc-

---

[5] https://www.figma.com/.

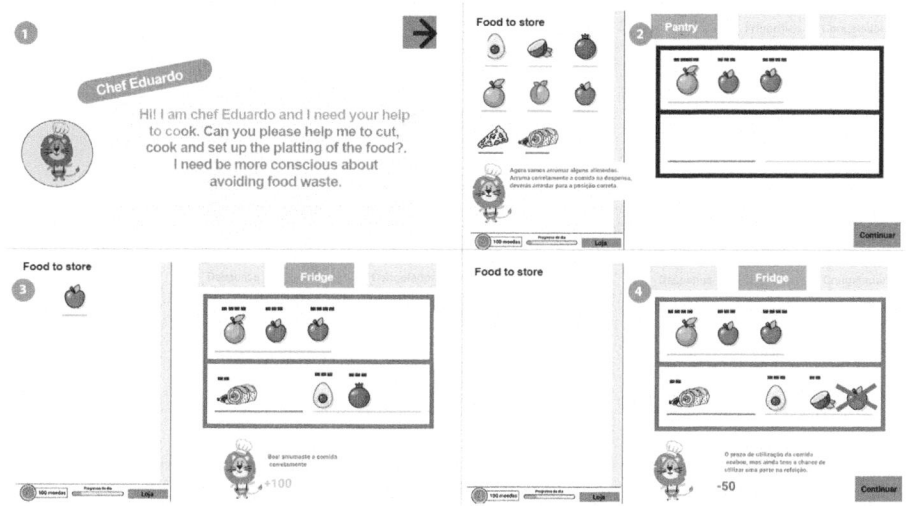

**Fig. 1.** Initial concept design using Figma - 1: Introduction to chef Edu; 2: Food items to be stored in the pantry; 3: Food items to be stored in the fridge; 4: Food item organized on the wrong location.

turing the environment according to learning objectives (e.g., a cooking area for leftover management), and assessing the necessary resources (assets needed for all interactions).

A **second Figma prototype** (see Fig. 3) was designed with a simple screenshot of the *Unreal Engine 5* food storage level. This prototype allowed us to envision the overall game environment, UI placement, and features. The development team also used it to define the progress toward the high-fidelity prototype.

### 3.3   High Fidelity Game Prototype

The game was developed using Unreal[6], and the creations of the different tridimensional and User Interface (UI) assets were developed using Autodesk Maya, Mudbox and Adobe Illustrator. Following the feedback from our previous iterations, we added more characters, storytelling and customization items.

The **game narrative** unfolds in a fictional city named Funimal, where monkeys face discrimination for aspiring to become chefs. As a first-person game, players step into the shoes of Edu, a young monkey apprentice who dreams of becoming a renowned chef. Edu is guided by Chef Olivia (second character) (see Fig. 4, number 2), a prestigious monkey chef who has recently opened her own restaurant called *Banastico*. Throughout the game, Chef Olivia helps and teaches the aspiring chef Edu to fulfill his dream while instilling a sense of consciousness and responsibility towards food waste.

---

[6] https://www.unrealengine.com/, May 2024.

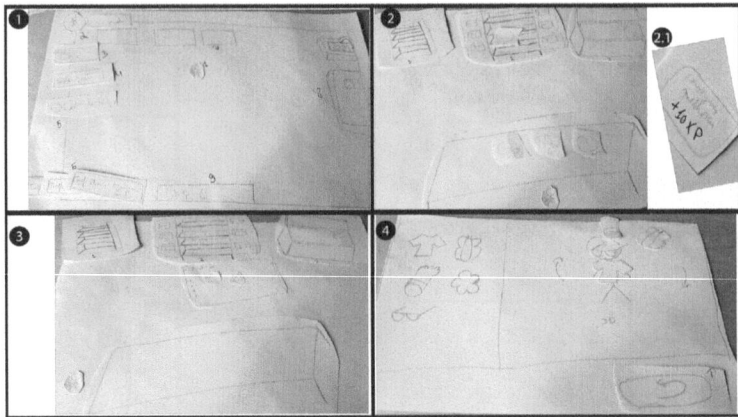

**Fig. 2.** Collection of scenarios from the paper prototype papers. 1 -Main hub/kitchen; 2 - Initial layout of the storing level; 2.1 Feedback for incorrect answer in the game; 3 - End of storing level with scores, based on stars (2/5) and feedback text; 4 - Initial concept for the character's customization.

 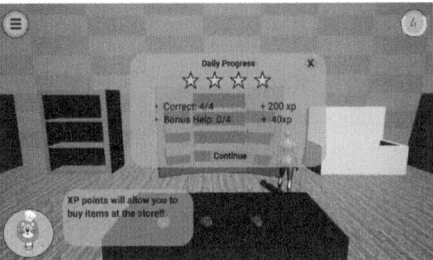

**Fig. 3.** Left: Storing mechanic concept. At the center, food is to be stored. The bar on the right displays the fridge zone where such items will be stored. The color represents the different types of food. Right: Screen showcasing the daily progress point system, and a message from the chef to guide the player

Monkeys were chosen as **characters** based on their behavioral paradigms, particularly their involvement in unique social situations, such as being perceived sometimes as clumsy animals and engaging in activities like grabbing, throwing, and sometimes stealing food in parks. Children often find these animals amusing and adorable, providing the possibility to foster emotional empathy and a desire to assist them, in this case, in accomplishing their objectives within the game. The age contrast between Edu and Chef Olivia is intentional, with Olivia symbolizing experience and authority due to her age. At the same time, Edu represents youth and inexperience, aligning with our target group of young players (see Fig. 4, number 3). In past studies, virtual coaches have shown positive effects in guiding and motivating children, especially in areas like exergames [20]. Moreover, when users establish a connection with a virtual character, their

motivation, and performance tend to rise [6]. According to Birk et al., the identification with a digital representation can increase intrinsic motivation, leading
to more enjoyment and invested effort [6], which is pertinent in the case of games
for learning or behavioral change.

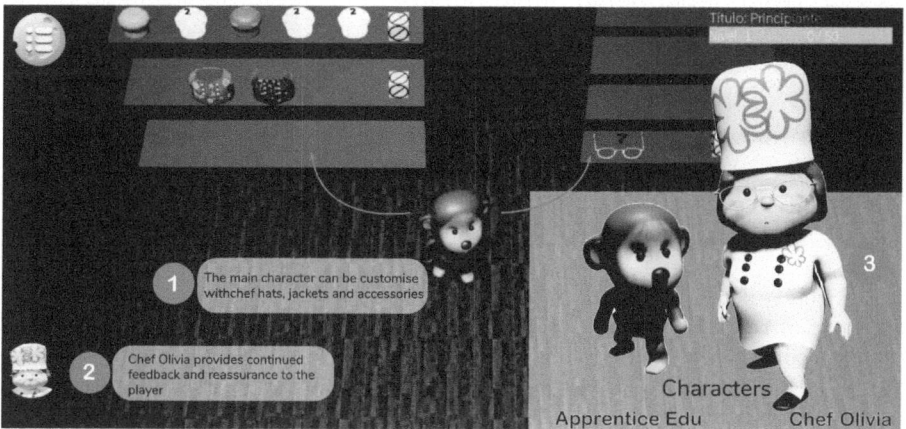

**Fig. 4.** Game characters and area dedicated to customization

The **gameplay mechanics** were divided into stages according to the learning
content and intended achievement. The game starts on a kitchen set, where
the user can explore different areas according to the handling of the food and
strategies to increase its life cycle/expectancy. The task of storing food items
(see Fig. 5) teaches the user how to organize the food correctly. The player selects
the food item that they pretend to store, then needs to point to the location by
clicking on the screen (fridge, pantry, or freezer) and afterward needs to target
the most appropriate shelf (according to the temperature) using an arrow that
moves up and down.

If the food is stored correctly, the player is rewarded by receiving forty experience points and a pop-up with a congratulatory message. The player also gathers
"badges" in the form of stars according to the points acquired (correct answers
as the first choice). Otherwise, only ten experience points are attributed. A feedback message on the screen also alerts the user towards the incorrect choice. The
player unlocks new customization options as the "level of experience" increases.
Also, if the player needs to go back to change their choices, they can click on a
button with an arrow leading to the previous screen.

Once this task is finished, the player can exchange the points/experience
gathered in an area dedicated to customizing the character (see Fig. 4). Players
can customize their character with various hats, jackets, and glasses based on
their current level. The more experience, the higher the level and more options
will be available to customize the character.

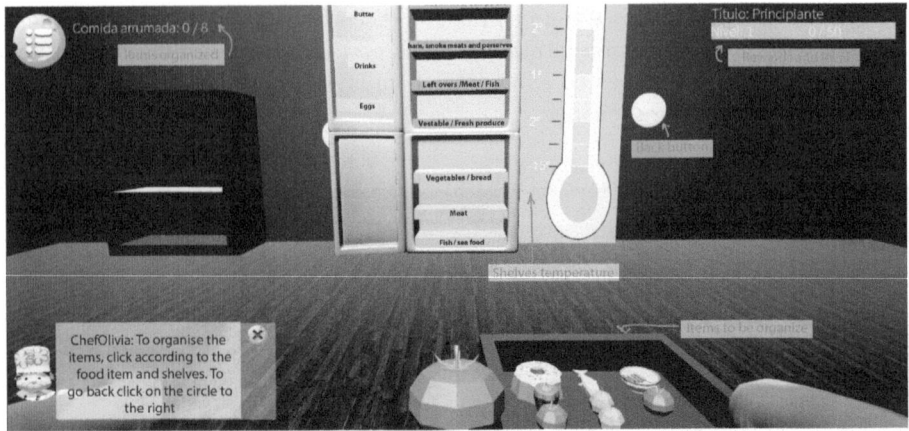

**Fig. 5.** Storage level - Food items need to be selected and organized (bottom-right) within one of the areas (pantry, fridge or freezer). Chef Olivia guides the player and provides feedback (bottom-left).

## 4   Evaluation

Our study used a mixed-method approach to gather quantitative and qualitative data. We gathered the participation of 22 students from a public school at "Escola Básica e Secundária Ângelo Augusto da Silva". The study was part of a school activity dedicated to the week of technologies, where a computer science teacher invited the researchers to showcase the game.

Days before the study, a consent form was sent to gather the children's parental/guardian permission (signature) to participate.

On the day of the study, the protocol implemented was the following: 1. Briefing of activity; 2. Pre-questionnaire - about previous knowledge on how to organize the food items leading to an increase in the life cycle of such food, and 3. Pre-test with images about storing food items (freezer, pantry or fridge) (see Fig. 6); 4. Interaction with the game. As players interacted with the game, three researchers took observational notes; 5. Post-test with images (same questions as pre-test but in random order), and usability questionnaire; 6. Group interviews with open questions.

In the case of the pre and post test using images, each correct answer got a score of "1" point, and a wrong answer "0" points, for a max score of "6" points, as the activity had these numbers of food elements to be organized in the pantry, fridge or freezer.

A questionnaire was also used to identify the existence of some usability issues: *Was Olivia, the Chef, helpful in understanding the gameplay? Were you able to use the back button? Could you understand the function of the arrow (to identify the selected shelf)? Did you find anything else that made the game difficult to use?* Please indicate: *The selection of the food items; Select the areas to store the food; Storing the food; Understanding the correct place to store the*

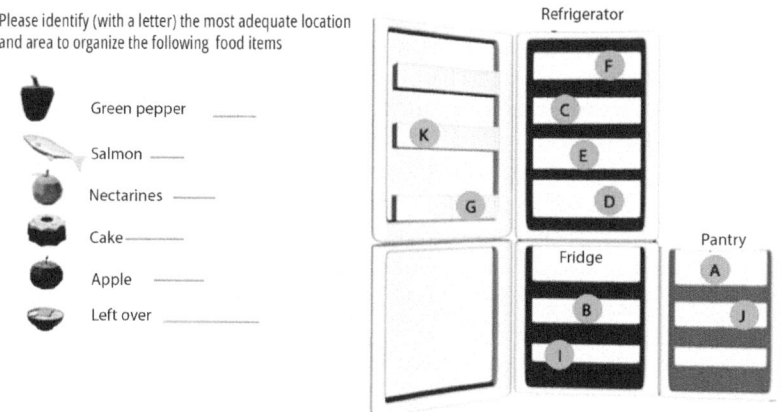

**Fig. 6.** Evaluation about the previous knowledge of how to organize a refrigerator or pantry. Participants had to respond using the letters that described the most adequate location and shelves

*food; Other.* This information was gathered using a Likert scale of 5 levels - "1" for totally disagree and "5" for totally agree. A smileymeter [34] (pictorial representation of emotions) complemented the Likert scale.

Finally, open questions were used to gather information to understand the effectiveness of some game mechanics: *What did you like the most about the game? Please indicate three things. What did you least enjoy? Please indicate three things. Do you think that you learned anything from the game? If yes, what?* And finally, *If you could, what would you change in the game?* Another two questions were added about the engagement of the participants: *Did you enjoy the game?* and *Would you recommend this game to your friends?*

The study took around 70 min, of which 30 were dedicated to the participant's interaction with the game.

For Data Analysis, we used the Statistical Package for Social Science (IBM - SPSS) to compare and measure the results of the data gathering (means, standard deviations) and a 2-tailed testing at $\alpha$ of 0.05.

## 5   Study Results

Our study involved 22 participants, predominantly male (n=17), with a smaller representation of females (n = 5). Most participants were eleven years old (n = 12), while the remaining were ten years old (n = 10). All participants were fifth-grade students. According to their teachers, these students were avid gamers, frequently engaging in mobile games during class intervals. Although 15 participants claimed to be aware of strategies to minimize food waste, their understanding was primarily limited to the Reduce, Reuse, and Recycle concepts.

Some participants specifically emphasized the importance of reuse to avoid food waste.

A Shapiro-Wilk test (p > 0.05) confirmed that the difference between pre-test and post-test scores was normally distributed, with skewness of 0.405 (SE = 0.913) and kurtosis of −0.017 (SE = 2.00). Consequently, we conducted a parametric analysis using a within-groups paired-sample t-test to evaluate the learning outcomes. The mean post-test score (M = 2.909, SD = 1.77) was significantly higher than the mean pre-test score (M = 1.77, SD = 1.23), indicating a mean increase of 1.136 (SD = 2.49) in learning scores. This difference was statistically significant, t(21) = 2.13, p = 0.04, with an effect size of r = 0.42, denoting a medium effect.

The game proved to be engaging, with 19 participants expressing their enjoyment, two participants not liking the game, and one participant being unsure. When asked about recommending the game to peers, 21 participants responded affirmatively, while one was ambivalent. The game's educational value was acknowledged by 21 participants, with 20 stating that they learned how to organize food avoiding waste. In contrast, one participant mentioned avoiding waste in general. Participants provided valuable feedback on the game's mechanics. They found the character Olivia helpful as a guide (M = 4.18, SD = 0.79) and understood the navigation tools, such as using the menu to go back (M = 4.23, SD = 0.90) and the arrow indicating areas for organizing food items (M = 4.18, SD = 0.90). However, the task of organizing food items was identified as challenging by 11 participants, followed by difficulties in recognizing the appropriate shelf (n = 8) and selecting food items (n = 3). One participant found character movement difficult initially.

While some participants suggested that no changes were needed within the game (n = 7), other suggested improvements like adding more customization items (n = 4), more levels (n = 4), improved graphics (n = 3), and enhanced storytelling elements (n = 2). Additional suggestions included adding multiplayer features, the ability to retry upon failure, and modifying the selection process from clicking on food items to clicking on shelves.

Observational data, collected through guidelines adapted from Devan Scheme [5] and semi-structured interviews, revealed initial confusion and frustration among three participants regarding game mechanics. Some participants did not understand how to play the game, this was demonstrated by the repeated clicking and expressions of doubt. Players, who were quicker in understanding the mechanics, provided assistance to those who did not by indicating the need to select the food item and then selecting the proper shelve to store the food.

G17 asked *"Where should I store the green bell pepper?"*, but afterward was able to understand, showing to be relieved, and commenting *"Ah!, I understand now, I have to store them on the shelves according to the temperature"*. Some ignored the Chef's instructions, relying on trial and error instead. Participant G22 commented: *"Ah! I did not even read anything, I just pressed on things"*. Also participant G5, G8, G22, G13, and G21 said that they only recurred to the text when stuck.

Frustration also arose from character customization settings needing to be saved between levels, leading to repeated complaints about lost items. Participant G16 replied, *"Why is the character back to how it was?"* participant G6 and G7 said, *"I do not like this, the character changed again and the clothing is gone!"* (referring to the jacket and hat which were part of the customization); G1 *"When I left this area the character changed!"*; participant G18 *"The game has a bug, the character's clothing is gone"*. However, despite the initial frustration with the character customisation, the participants enjoyed the game, with smiles and enthusiasm evident as they explored its features. They appreciated the gamification elements such as receiving stars based on performance and fostering a competitive spirit among peers.

Interviews highlighted that participants found the game educational, enhancing their understanding of proper food storage to prolong shelf life. All participants acknowledged enjoying the game and said they would recommend it to family and friends. They also commented on its usefulness and educational component, showing confidence in their acquired skills, with nineteen participants saying they learned how to organize the food items properly. Some comments were: *"I learned that by putting the food items in the right location, they will be good for a longer period"; "The game allowed me to learn the location of some food items"; "I learned how to organize the food properly."*

While most participants enjoyed the graphics, two preferred more realistic visuals. Participant G8 commented *"I wanted a more refined and a realistic approach"*, participants G4, G9, and G11 said *"We liked the graphics"*, and G18 said *"I liked them and think the graphics were spectacular."* Despite differing views on aesthetics, the overall feedback indicated that the game was engaging, with potential areas for improvement in user experience and functionality. Other comments: *" I like this pink jacket! ";" The monkey is naked!" then laughed; "The characters are cute!"; "I would not change anything!"; "You need to change the customization, we lost our level, and the character customization was not saved between levels"*.

## 6   Discussion

The quantitative results showed positive results on the participants' learning outcomes about selecting appropriate storage conditions and arranging food items to promote longevity and minimize food waste. We believe that the interaction with the game allows children to acquire this knowledge through reflection (allocation of the item according to factors like temperature), repetition, and engagement with the game's aesthetics and mechanics.

Using a constructivism approach to learning, the child can: 1. Explore the different food elements and use their previous knowledge of household storage handling; 2. Reflect on the best conditions towards its storage; and 3. Confirm their choices through trial and error. The repetitive actions allow them to verify and recall the new knowledge. These actions can also revert to the user's real context by transferring the information gathered through the game to real-life situations, as previous empirical research corroborates [39,49,61]. The learning topic becomes more relevant, leading to an increase in retention and recall of the content knowledge [52,53]. Before the interaction with the game, the participant's vision about avoiding food waste was generalized concepts gathered in the classes about the 3Rs. Afterward, they demonstrated confidence in food storage management skills as a strategy to prevent this issue.

However, we acknowledge that future studies to validate these results are needed due to the small sample group, the limited number of questions, and the lack of a week post-test to evaluate the participant's retention and recall of the information. Conversely, through the participant's qualitative feedback, we believe that incorporating everyday daily tasks like organizing food into a refrigerator, freezer, or pantry into game mechanics can aid in learning strategies to reduce food waste, as these actions can be transferable to household food storing management.

The game's fun factor was concluded from the user's interactions, observation notes, and answers about repeating the experience or recommending it to colleagues or friends. The narrative, which, while not implicit within the game, of helping a young Monkey to achieve his dream of becoming a chef, seemed to engage the children in finishing all the tasks. This finding is consistent with prior studies [25,44] that demonstrated the effectiveness of narratives in enhancing the meaningfulness of learning for students. Based on the reactions and comments, the characters and visuals seem appropriate to the age group. The projected age gap between the main character (representing the user with the desire to learn) and an older character (role model representing experience and knowledge) seemed to be a factor that impacted the players' performance. Previous research accounts for attributes of role models perceived by the player as being competent [43] and able to achieve success [8] as a factor in player performance and self-reported engagement. We can also observe a parallel between behaviorism theory and the use of external rewards within the game to stimulate interest in learning content [2]. The scores, experience points, positive feedback by the chef, and customization of the character reinforce the tasks well performed, motivating the players and raising their self-confidence. As cited previously, educational games that increase motivation through raising self-confidence and perceived self-efficacy and by affording more opportunities for reinforcement have been shown to have an impact on cognition, memory, attention, and motivation [68]. As such, from a ludology perspective, awareness of emotional responses by players is essential in developing and designing these types of games.

The results also indicated areas that can be iterated and refined to improve the game. Introducing a social component can enhance the experience by allowing the player to include other colleagues or players to assist in overcoming challenges. The players can benefit from peer or collaborative learning, whereas players can learn from each other. This was evident early in the game when some participants' interventions helped their colleagues to understand the gameplay. The game can also benefit by the introduction of competitiveness element among the groups/team of players to gain a ranking according to their performance, leading to camaraderie and social interaction among players and providing the opportunity for friendly rivalry, which has shown to increase engagement [35, 36].

Addressing the cited areas can further elevate the game's impact, ensuring a more immersive and comprehensive educational experience for children, fostering a greater understanding of food waste, and encouraging responsible behavior toward this issue.

## 7 Limitations and Future Work

Some limitations of our research are related to the coding, especially the malfunctioning of the character customization. This item was a significant issue because of the young age of the participants, where frustrations and negative experiences can bias their attitudes toward the subject. Luckily, while some participants were affected by this issue, their results were positive; nevertheless, consideration should be taken towards this potential problem in the future.

As we conducted the study in the context of a school, time restrictions and the availability of the teachers and students limited our research. Our data was gathered in one session, limiting the possibility of conducting a week-after study to analyze if the information can be recalled, with a relatively small sample group and using a short pre/post-test questionnaire. As such, further research is needed to validate our results. In the future, we also envision researching how "Masters Against Food Waste" can influence the behavior of parents and children within the household context. We hope that children can be more responsible and transfer their food storage management skills to their households, decreasing food waste.

## 8 Conclusion

This manuscript introduces a serious game designed to involve children in strategies to actively reduce food waste. Given the persistent issue of food waste in our society, especially in the context of households, it is essential to recognize that children play a pivotal role in shaping future solutions. Educating them about effective practices to combat food waste at home becomes critical. To address this need, we have developed a game prototype that utilizes game mechanics and gamification elements to ensure their interest and sustained engagement with strategies for organizing food items, thus avoiding food waste. The optimistic results of this study indicate that the game "Masters Against Food Waste" can gather children's interest and awareness about sustainability issues while educating them in a fun and engaging manner and providing us with feedback to continue iterating, refining, and improving the game.

**Acknowledgements.** We want to thank all the participants, including teachers and students that were part of this study. This research was funded by the Portuguese Recovery and Resilience Program (PRR), IAPMEI/ANI/FCT under Agenda C645022399-00000057 (eGamesLab), also supported by LARSyS-FCT Plurianual funding 2020–2023 (UIDB/50009/2020).

# References

1. Abeliotis, K., Lasaridi, K., Chroni, C.: Attitudes and behaviour of Greek households regarding food waste prevention. Waste Manage. Res. **32**(3), 237–240 (2014)
2. Ahmad, T.S., et al.: A review of learning theories for gamification elements in instructional games. In: Conference: Malaysian International Conference on Academic Strategies in English Language Teaching (MyCASELT). At: Sutera Harbour Resort, Kota Kinabalu Sabah (2019)
3. Altarriba, F., et al.: The grumpy bin: reducing food waste through playful social interactions. In: Proceedings of the 2017 ACM Conference Companion Publication on Designing Interactive Systems, pp. 90–94 (2017)
4. Attiq, S., et al.: Drivers of food waste reduction behaviour in the household context. In: Food Quality and Preference, vol. 94, p. 104300 (2021). ISSN 0950-3293. https://doi.org/10.1016/j.foodqual.2021.104300
5. Barendregt, W., Bekker, M.M.: Developing a coding scheme for detecting usability and fun problems in computer games for young children. Behav. Res. Methods **38**(3), 382–389 (2006)
6. Birk, M.V., et al.: Fostering intrinsic motivation through avatar identification in digital games. In: Proceedings of the 2016 CHI Conference on Human Factors in Computing Systems, pp. 2982–2995 (2016)
7. Boulet, M., Hoek, A.C., Raven, R.: Towards a multi-level framework of household food waste and consumer behaviour: untangling spaghetti soup. Appetite 156, 104856 (2021). ISSN 0195-6663. https://doi.org/10.1016/j.appet.2020.104856. https://www.sciencedirect.com/science/article/pii/S0195666320301537
8. Buunk, A.P., Peiró, J.M., Griffioen, C.: A positive role model may stimulate career-oriented behavior 1. J. Appl. Soc. Psychol. **37**(7), 1489–1500 (2007)
9. Calvo-Morata, A., et al.: Serious games to prevent and detect bullying and cyberbullying: a systematic serious games and literature review. Comput. Educ. 157, 103958 (2020)
10. Centieiro, P., Romão, T., Eduardo Dias, A.: Playing with the environment. In: Playful User Interfaces: Interfaces that Invite Social and Physical Interaction, pp. 47–69 (2014)
11. Cherry, K.: The experiential learning theory of David Kolb. In: Artikkeli. Viitattu (2020)
12. Cicatiello, C., et al.: The value of food waste: an exploratory study on retailing. J. Retail. Consum. Serv. **30**), 96–104 (2016. ISSN 0969-6989. https://doi.org/10.1016/j.jretconser.2016.01.004. https://www.sciencedirect.com/science/article/pii/S0969698916300078
13. CrazyLabs LTD: Fridge organizing. Game [Android]. Version 0.3.1.6 (2007). https://www.crazylabs.com/games/?page=1/
14. Unidos Contra o Desperdício: Livro Contra o Desperdicio - Receitas & Dicas Sustentáveis. In: Livro Contra o Desperd í cio (2020). https://livrocontraodesperdicio.pt/
15. Dias, M., Agante, L.: Can advergames boost children's healthier eating habits? A comparison between healthy and non-healthy food. J. Consum. Behav. **10**(3), 152–160 (2011)
16. Dwipayana, I.M., Sukajaya, I.N.: Delta's adventure: a constructivism-based serious game for the 1st grade of elementary school students on inequality concept. In: 2020 International Conference on Computer Engineering, Network, and Intelligent Multimedia (CENIM), pp. 127–131. IEEE (2020)

17. Farr-Wharton, G., Choi, J.H.-Z., Foth, M.: Technicolouring the fridge: reducing food waste through uses of colour-coding and cameras. In: Proceedings of the 13th International Conference on Mobile and Ubiquitous Multimedia, pp. 48–57 (2014)
18. Farr-Wharton, G., Foth, M., Choi, J.H.-Z.: Identifying factors that promote consumer behaviours causing expired domestic food waste. J. Consum. Behav. **13**(6), 393–402 (2014)
19. Galeote, D.F., Hamari, J.: Game-based climate change engagement: analyzing the potential of entertainment and serious games. In: Proceedings of the ACM on Human-Computer Interaction, vol. 5, pp. 1–21. CHI PLAY (2021)
20. Gago-Masague, S., Chen, T.M., Li, G.-P.: Promoting physical exercise through embodied trainers: a systematic literature review. In: The Digitization of Healthcare: New Challenges and Opportunities, pp. 293–322 (2017)
21. GameLord 3D: Fill Up Fridge Organizing Game. Game [Android]. Version 3.1 (2023). https://gamelord3d.com/
22. Ganglbauer, E., Fitzpatrick, G., Güldenpfennig, F.: Why and what did we throw out? Probing on reflection through the food waste diary. In: Proceedings of the 33rd Annual ACM Conference on Human Factors in Computing Systems, pp. 1105–1114 (2015)
23. Girotto, F., Alibardi, L., Cossu, R.: Food waste generation and industrial uses: a review. Waste Manage. **45**, 32–41 (2015). ISSN 0956-053X. https://doi.org/10.1016/j.wasman.2015.06.008. https://www.sciencedirect.com/science/article/pii/S0956053X15004201
24. Hadi, S., Setiyatna, H., Sutiyono, A.: Learning Behaviour Theory According to Ivan Pavlov, Thorndike, Skinner and Albert Bandura, vol. 1, pp. 175–184. Novateur Publications (2023)
25. Hallifax, S., et al.: From points to progression: a scoping review of game elements in gamification research with a content analysis of 280 research papers. In: Proceedings of the ACM on Human-Computer Interaction, vol. 7, pp. 748–768. CHI PLAY (2023)
26. Hanus, M.D., Fox, J.: Assessing the effects of gamification in the classroom: a longitudinal study on intrinsic motivation, social comparison, satisfaction, effort, and academic performance. Comput. Educ. **80**, 152–161 (2015). Accessed on: 24 Jan 2023. ISSN 03601315. https://doi.org/10.1016/j.compedu.2014.08.019. Visited on 24 Jan 2023
27. Heavy Iron Studios: Ratatouille. Game [Video Game -Nintendo DS] (2007). https://heavyiron.games/
28. Hebrok, M., Heidenstrøm, N.: Contextualising food waste prevention - decisive moments within everyday practices. J. Clean. Prod. **210**, 1435–1448 (2019). ISSN 0959-6526. https://doi.org/10.1016/j.jclepro.2018.11.141. https://www.sciencedirect.com/science/article/pii/S0959652618335443
29. Heidari, A., et al.: A theoretical framework for explaining the determinants of food waste reduction in residential households: a case study of Mashhad, Iran'. Environ. Sci. Pollut. Res. **27**(7), 6774–6784 (2020). ISSN 0944-1344, 1614-7499. https://doi.org/10.1007/s11356-019-06518-8. http://link.springer.com/10.1007/s11356-019-06518-8. Visited on 19 June 2023
30. Shaheen Hosany, A.R., Hosany, S., He, H.: Children sustainable behaviour: a review and research agenda. J. Bus. Res. **147**, 236–257 (2022)
31. de Jesús Luis González Ibánez, J., Wang, A.I.: Learning recycling from playing a kinect game. Int. J. Game-Based Learn. (IJGBL) **5**(3), 25–44 (2015)

32. Jespersen, K.N., et al.: Foodfighters-improving memory retention of food items through a mobile serious game. In: Extended Abstracts of the 2023 CHI Conference on Human Factors in Computing Systems, pp. 1–7 (2023)

33. Jörissen, J., Priefer, C., Bräutigam, K.-R.: Food waste generation at household level: results of a survey among employees of two European research centers in Italy and Germany. Sustainability **7**(3), 2695–2715 (2015)

34. Kano, A., Horton, M., Read, J.C.: Thumbs-up scale and frequency of use scale for use in self reporting of children's computer experience. In: Proceedings of the 6th Nordic Conference on Human-Computer Interaction Extending Boundaries - NordiCHI '10, p. 699. ACM Press, Reykjavik, Iceland (2010). Accessed on: 31 Dec 2022. ISBN 978-1-60558-934-3. https://doi.org/10.1145/1868914.1869008. http://portal.acm.org/citation.cfm?doid=1868914.1869008. Visited on 31 Dec 2022

35. Tomé Klock, A.C., et al.: Tailored gamification: a review of literature. Int. J. Hum.-Comput. Stud. **144**, 102495 (2020)

36. Kölln, K.: Maybe we don't need a new gamification framework after all. In: Extended Abstracts of the 2022 Annual Symposium on Computer-Human Interaction in Play, pp. 384–387 (2022)

37. Lave, J., Wenger, E.: Situated Learning: Legitimate Peripheral Participation. Cambridge University Press

38. Filho, W.L., et al.: Higher education and food waste: assessing current trends. Int. J. Sustain. Dev. World Ecol. **28**(5), 440–450 (2021)

39. Lieberman, G.A., Hoody, L.L.: Closing the achievement gap: using the environment as an integrating context for learning. Results of a Nationwide Study (1998)

40. Linhares, E., Correia, M.: Reduzir o desperdício alimentar: aprender e sensibilizar através de um jogo online Reduce food waste: learn and raise awareness through an online game. In: Reduzir o desperd í cio alimentar: aprender e sensibilizar atrav é s de um jogo online Reduce food waste: learn and raise awareness through an online game 11 (2019). Accessed on: 5 Sept 2022. ISSN 1645-4774. http://www.eduser.ipb.pt. Visited on 5 Sept 2022

41. Löchtefeld, M., et al.: FridgeSort-improving fridge sorting behaviour to reduce food waste through a mobile serious game. In: Proceedings of the 22nd International Conference on Mobile and Ubiquitous Multimedia, pp. 420–427 (2023)

42. Lucifero, N.: Food loss and waste in the EU law between sustainability of well-being and the implications on food system and on environment. Agric. Agric. Sci. Procedia **8**, 282–289 (2016)

43. Marx, D.M., Stapel, D.A., Muller, D.: We can do it: the interplay of construal orientation and social comparisons under threat. J. Pers. Soc. Psychol. **88**(3), 432 (2005)

44. McQuiggan, S.W., et al.: Story-based learning: the impact of narrative on learning experiences and outcomes. In: Intelligent Tutoring Systems: 9th International Conference, ITS 2008, Montreal, Canada, 23–27 June 2008, Proceedings, vol. 9, pp. 530–539. Springer (2008)

45. Nunes, E.P.S., et al.: Mobile serious game proposal for environmental awareness of children. In: 2016 IEEE Frontiers in Education Conference (FIE), pp. 1–8 (2016). https://doi.org/10.1109/FIE.2016.7757353

46. Panagiotopoulou, L., et al.: Design of a serious game for children to raise awareness on plastic pollution and promoting pro-environmental behaviors. J. Comput. Inf. Sci. Eng. **21**(6) (2021)

47. Pierce, J., et al.: Introduction to the special issue on practice-oriented approaches to sustainable HCI (2013)

48. Polin, L.G.: A constructivist perspective on games in education. In: Constructivist Education in an Age of Accountability, pp. 163–188 (2018)
49. Potvin, P., Hasni, A., Sy, O.: Using inquiry-based interventions to improve secondary students' interest in science and technology. Eur. J. Sci. Math. Educa. **5**(3), 262–270 (2017)
50. Quested, T.E., et al.: Spaghetti soup: the complex world of food waste behaviours. Resour. Conserv. Recycl. **79**, 43–51 (2013)
51. Roodhuyzen, D.M.A., et al.: Putting together the puzzle of consumer food waste: towards an integral perspective. Trends Food Sci. Technol. **68**, 37–50 (2017)
52. Sadler, T.D.: Situated learning in science education: socio-scientific issues as contexts for practice. Stud. Sci. Educ. **45**(1), 1–42 (2009)
53. Keith Salyer, B., Thyfault, A.: Developing Situational Learning Events: A Practical Merger of Real-Life Events with Content Instruction (2003)
54. dos Santos, A.D., Strada, F., Bottino, A.: Approaching sustainability learning via digital serious games. IEEE Trans. Learn. Technol. **12**(3), 303–320 (2018)
55. Schanes, K., Dobernig, K., Gözet, B.: Food waste matters-a systematic review of household food waste practices and their policy implications. J. Clean. Prod. **182**, 978–991 (2018)
56. Sinclear, D., et al.: Face-the-waste-learning about food waste through a serious game. In: Proceedings of the 20th International Conference on Mobile and Ubiquitous Multimedia, pp. 67–72 (2021)
57. Smith, T.A., Landry, C.E.: Household food waste and inefficiencies in food production. Am. J. Agric. Econ. **103**(1), 4–21 (2021). ISSN 0002-9092, 1467-8276. https://doi.org/10.1111/ajae.12145
58. Sofia, M., Correia, M.: Sensibilizar para o desperdí cio alimentar: impacto de um jogo online em alunos do 1°. CEB. Accessed on: 5 Sept 2022
59. Stenmarck, Â., et al.: Estimates of European Food Waste Levels. IVL Swedish Environmental Research Institute (2016)
60. Tragazikis, P., Meimaris, M.: Engaging kids with the concept of sustainability using a commercial video game-a case study. Trans. Edutainment **III**, 1–12 (2009)
61. Trigwell, K., Prosser, M.: Improving the quality of student learning: the influence of learning context and student approaches to learning on learning outcomes. High. Educ. **22**(3), 251–266 (1991)
62. Trindade., B.: Desperdício Zero à Mesa com o Pingo Doce (Costa, M., ed.), pp. 10–19 (2020)
63. ESD UNESCO: Global action programme on education for sustainable development information folder (2015)
64. Van Geffen, L., van Herpen, E., van Trijp, H.: Household Food waste—how to avoid it? An integrative review. In: Food Waste Management: Solving the Wicked Problem, pp. 27–55 (2020)
65. Vieira, L.: Combate ao desperdí cio alimentar come ç a entre os alunos das escolas - XXI Governo - Rep ú blica Portuguesa (2017). Accessed on: 9 March 2022. https://www.portugal.gov.pt/pt/gc21/comunicacao/noticia?i=20170519-seaa-desperdicio-alimentar. Visited on 9 March 2022
66. Vieira, L.: Combate ao desperdício alimentar começa entre os alunos das escolas - XXI Governo - República Portuguesa (2017). Accessed on: 9 March 2022. https://www.portugal.gov.pt/pt/gc21/comunicacao/noticia?i=20170519-seaa-desperdicio-alimentar. Visited on 9 March 2022
67. Waite-Stupiansky, S.: Jean Piaget's constructivist theory of learning. In: Theories of Early Childhood Education. Routledge, pp. 3–18 (2022)

68. Wilkinson, P.: Affective educational games: utilizing emotions in game-based learning. In: 2013 5th International Conference on Games and Virtual Worlds for Serious Applications (VS-GAMES), pp. 1–8. IEEE (2013)
69. Yu, Y., et al.: FoodWise: food waste reduction and behavior change on campus with data visualization and gamification. In: Proceedings of the 6th ACM SIGCAS/SIGCHI Conference on Computing and Sustainable Societies, pp. 76–83 (2023)

# Impact Studies

# Understanding Player Experience in Museum-Based Learning Games: A Mixed-Methods Analysis

Simon Morard[1]($\boxtimes$) (iD), Elsa Paukovics[2] (iD), and Eric Sanchez[1] (iD)

[1] University of Geneva, 7 Route de Drize, 1227 Carouge, Switzerland
simon.morard@unige.ch
[2] University of Sherbrooke, 150 Pl. Charles-Le Moyne, Longueuil, QC J4K 0A8, Canada

**Abstract.** The main objective of this paper is to report on the impact of a game-based museum school visit on player experience while solving complex problems about food production. We used a mixed-methods approach, combining quantitative analysis of digital traces with qualitative case studies to assess how players engage with the mixed reality game AL2049. The data includes digital traces from 174 games and video recordings collected via on-board cameras. Our results reveal clusters characterizing attitudes towards complexity, identifying four categories of players: Explorers, Rushers, Strategists, and Inactive. Through case studies of these categories, using a dedicated model, we identified the dimensions that characterize their subjective experiences. This model highlights player experiences across four main dimensions: actions, information processing, knowledge, and emotions. Our results highlight the tension that can arise in game-based learning between the way the game is designed and the way it is played. They also underscore the value of using mixed methods to analyze the player's experience.

**Keywords:** Game-Based-Learning · Player Experience · Museum · Mixed-Methods · Case Study · Gameplay · Complexity

## 1 Introduction

Attracting visitors to museums often requires unique, captivating experiences. Advanced technologies transform how people interact with exhibitions and collections. Mixed reality has transformed both entertainment and interactive learning, especially in museums aiming for active participation [1]. While museums are vital for preserving cultural heritage, they must adapt to meet diverse audience expectations. Gamification and mixed reality offer a promising way to enhance museum experiences by blending entertainment, education, and immersive storytelling. Digital game-based learning in museums should boost visitors' motivation and engagement through immersive gameplay and captivating environments, while also promoting reflective exploration and hypothesis testing [2–6]. Mixed reality technologies and game-based learning present new opportunities for museums to enhance engagement and educational offerings, though research on its effectiveness is still evolving [1].

© The Author(s), under exclusive license to Springer Nature Switzerland AG 2025
J. L. Plass and X. Ochoa (Eds.): JCSG 2024, LNCS 15259, pp. 177–195, 2025.
https://doi.org/10.1007/978-3-031-74138-8_14

From a methodological perspective, evaluating and analyzing player experiences remains a challenge. Play is a complex phenomenon to study, there are tensions between the way the game is designed and the way it is played. Due to this complexity, mixed methods approaches are beneficial if we are interested in the players, the game, and the moments when they come together to play [7].

We conducted empirical research in a food museum. We created AL2049, a mixed reality learning game tailored for middle schoolers aged 12 to 15 during school visits. This game introduces students to the complex and intricate connections between humans, the resources used to produce and consume food, and their environment. It challenges them with open-ended, complex socio-environmental issues that encourage curiosity, critical thinking, and independent decision-making. The gameplay should help players to grasp the complexity of the food production system and its upcoming challenges. We designed the game as an ill-structured problem with no single solution. This approach highlights how outcomes can be enhanced through a deeper understanding of this system [8, 9]. As Grenier [10] we consider playing in a museum as "the phase in which a visitor is assimilating and mastering skills through practice and problem-solving" Nevertheless, how players, especially teenagers, engage with the problem to be solved and their ability to manage and manipulate complexity is important to improve game design. To do this, we proceeded in two steps. From digital traces of interactions, we identified different player profiles in response to the impact of food production (i.e. health, well-being, feeded population). In the second step, we conducted case studies for each group. Using video recordings from on-board cameras, we identified the characteristics of the players' teams based on indicators of their actions in the game, their processing of information and interaction with the game master, their verbalization of strategies, hypotheses for solving the complex problem, and emotions experienced. This two-step approach, inspired from mixed-methods, aims to gain a more comprehensive view of the players' learning experiences and their attitudes towards the complex challenges of the game AL2049 in the museum. Our investigation should not only probe the methodological efficacy of mixed-methods but also refines our understanding of how gameplay is actualized by the player.

## 2   AL2049 to Grasp Food Production Complexity

The game AL2049[1] is designed to incorporate knowledge about the complexities of the food system, as well as broader skills central to the curriculum for secondary schools of Switzerland [8, 9]. Food production is a subject addressed in a variety of school subjects: geography (agricultural production), natural sciences (ecosystems and climate changes and nutritional education). Beyond disciplinary knowledge, the core focus is on a systemic understanding of the food system, essential for grasping environmental and social challenges related to food production [11]. A systemic approach considers various actors, phenomena, spaces, and their interactions, emphasizing that a system is complex

---

[1] Although designed for museum play, a web version is available for teachers to replay in the classroom (available in English, French and German): https://www.alimentarium.org/sites/def ault/files/games/AL2049/index.html.

with multiple interconnected elements—political, economic, social, cultural, or natural—without necessarily being complicated [8, 9]. A collaborative team of researchers, game designers, teachers, and museum professionals developed AL2049. The game starts with a game master introduction. The primary task is to feed 30 visitors imprisoned for 10 years in the museum. Players use a tablet-based simulator to experiment with different strategies of food production to feed the population. The game interface features a map of the museum, displaying various rooms across two floors (see Fig. 1).

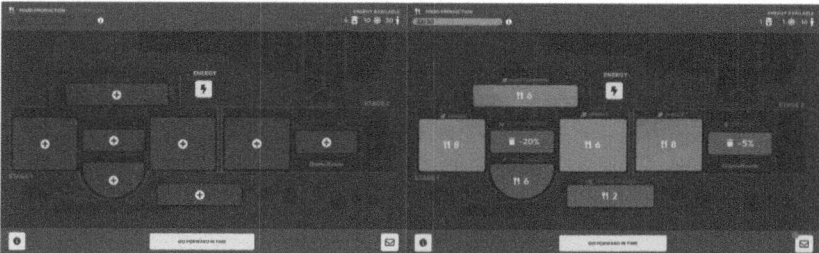

**Fig. 1.** Major game interface once the players unlocked each space of the museum, and after allocations of various food production units. © Digital Kingdom

In the initial phase of the game, players are required to unlock the museum rooms. To achieve this, they must enter each museum room and scan it. This stage is based on exploring the museum and is supported by mixed reality technology.

**Fig. 2.** Players unlock a room using mixed reality and object recognition. The same room with cattle & sheep breeding allocated in AL2049. © Digital Kingdom

Once a room is unlocked, the core mechanic involves assigning specific food production to it. Players allocate units such as production (crop cultivation, animal breeding), processing (transforming plants or animals), consumption (markets or restaurants), and research (agronomic laboratory). The room is then illustrated based on the assigned area (i.e. cattle and sheep breeding, Fig. 2). Each unit consumes energy, sourced from human labor, renewable or fossil energy. The resources are limited.

The game also features processing units and consumption places to reduce food losses, which start at 35% but can be minimized to 5%. Each function in the food system is interdependent. For example, crop cultivation is needed to raise pigs or poultry as they provide feed, but this reduces the amount of food for humans. Conversely, animal farms boost crop yields with manure as fertilizer. These interactions are not explained to the player, who only sees changes in food production values. Additionally, the agronomic science laboratory offers bonuses and increases the amount of reliable advice from the newsfeed [8, 9]. The newsfeed, an important game feature, is significant for critical thinking, knowledge, and media literacy. It randomly presents news (e.g., about corn, climate change, GMOs) that may be reliable or erroneous. Players must decide whether to trust this information and revise their strategy. To our knowledge, this approach is both unique and innovative, as it is rare to find games in academic literature that not only focus on critical thinking but also apply it in a contextualized manner [6].

After setting up the rooms, players can see the outcomes of their choices 10 years later. The interface displays the number of survivors, which is determined by the food produced and the proportion of food loss. Additionally, new criteria, "*health*" and "*well-being*" are introduced. Players are informed that "*health*" is influenced by nutritional variety, pollution, and greenhouse gas emissions, while "*well-being*" depends on pleasure and workload. In the second phase, players can revisit and modify their choices, now considering health and well-being. The challenge relies on balancing well-being, health, and the number of survivors. These gauges cannot be all filled, requiring players to make compromises. This design simplifies the complexity of the food system, reflecting the interdependencies among the three parameters. This phase introduces more open-ended gameplay, allowing players to refine their strategies based on their values and choices, adding complexity to the objective of feeding the population [8, 9].

After finishing the game, players engage in a debriefing led by the game master to discuss their strategies and decisions. This moment unpacks the game's metaphor, linking the simulated museum environment to the global food system, akin to how a closed system represents the planet [8, 9]. This educational phase transforms gameplay into a reflective learning experience, where learners analyze their choices to apply the insights gained in broader contexts [12].

The previous paragraphs detail how the game is intended to be played. However, literature on player experiences alerts us that players might interact with systems in unexpected yet playful ways [13]. Therefore, we pose the following preliminary research question: *How will players experience complexity and engage with the game?* The next chapter will allow us to operationalize this question into two specific research inquiries.

## 3   Assessment and Analysis of the Player Experience

### 3.1   From Gameplay to Player Experience

Gameplay experiences encompass the player's sensations, thoughts, feelings, actions, and meaning-making processes. These experiences emerge from the dynamic interaction between the game and the player, who actively shape their experiences based on desires, expectations, and prior encounters. The context significantly influences how gameplay is perceived, with the same activity potentially being enjoyable or unappealing depending on the social setting. This highlights the importance of social context in shaping gameplay experiences [14–16]. The distinctive nature of gaming experiences significantly contributes to the widespread success of digital games. Learning games or game-based-learning aim to leverage this captivation to boost engagement, with the ultimate goal of enhancing the learning and acquisition of specific knowledge or skills [17]. Thus, understanding the structure of player experience is crucial for effectively targeting the mechanisms that generate such experiences. In precise terms, "player experience" is a more fitting descriptor than "game experience" since it is the individual player who undergoes these unique experiences. It is important to differentiate between "player experience," which is a transient and dynamic state, and "player types", which refer to more stable, static traits [16].

## 3.2  Mixed-Methods to Assess Player Experience

Research on gameplay and player experience is now still in its infancy [15, 16]. However, considering the interactive essence of games and that there is no game without a player, understanding games fully necessitates an exploration of the act of playing and the player's experience [6, 17–19]. Games User Research is an evolving field that combines Human-Computer Interaction and Game Development research [20, 21]. It focuses on understanding player experience, defined as "the individual, personal experience held by the player during and immediately after playing the game" [22], to design games that meet players' expectations and provide actionable insights for game designers across various domains, including serious games and game-based learning [23–25].

To analyze and evaluate player experiences, academics employ a variety of tools, such as, playability heuristics [26, 27], game analytics [28], play-testing protocols [29] and biometrics [21]. In recent years, there has been a notable increase in the use of advanced data mining techniques to scrutinize player data [30, 31] as well as self-reports through questionnaires, and several instruments exist for inquiring into players' subjective experiences [32–34] However, some of these scales still await scientific validation [25, 35, 36].

Despite advancements in connected technologies, algorithms, and players' behavior, there is a need to combine objective behavioral player data with subjective or qualitative observation [25]. According to Lieberoth and Roepstorff [7] games remain a tricky phenomena to study as they exist both as practices and artifacts. A restricted portion of the available data will be noticed by designers and researchers who only use a single method, be it surveys, brain scans, questionnaires, ethnography, or another method when observing a game. A mixed methods approach is necessary to study the link between players and games [7]. By employing mixed methods, we facilitate a dialogue among various types of findings related to the same subject [37, 38]. However, without integrating these data, findings from different sources may end up as parallel strands of information, akin to separate research projects coincidentally targeting the same topic [7].

Mixed-methods to analyze game-based-learning in museum contexts are quite rare [39]. Rubino et al. [40] conduct mixed-methods research to assess the *Gossip at Palace*[2], a serious game dedicated to impart historical knowledge and enhance visitor enjoyment

---

[2] The game, created for an Italian historical residence, uses narrative and game mechanics to engage teenagers with its 18th-century history, encouraging exploration and aiding their interpretation of the museum's content [40].

in museums. The findings showed the game successfully engaged users and delivered cultural content. However, the qualitative aspect mainly analyzed the game's strengths and weaknesses, without deeply exploring the factors affecting users' learning experiences during gameplay.

Recently, frameworks have been developed to monitor player experience, as well as their learning [13, 16, 41, 42]. These frameworks typically focus on supporting successful design, which aims to achieve the game's (usually pedagogical) goals by concentrating on interrelated elements [43] and categories such as pedagogy, play, and simulational fidelity [13, 44]. According to Madsen [45], the literature review highlighted a significant gap in methods, frameworks, and theories specific to gamification within the museum context. Among the sparse literature, only one publication by Nicholson [46] discusses strategies for creating meaningful gamification in participatory museums and proposes initial ideas for a framework.

Our main concern will be to develop and use a specific framework for museums [46], and others academics in the game-based-learning field [13, 16, 41, 42] to assess player experience with a focus on actions, information processing, knowledge and emotion that emerge between the players and the intended gameplay of AL2049.

### 3.3  Player Experience Model

Games differ from other media like books or movies due to their unpredictable outcomes driven by player decisions [47, 48]. Although gamified systems, such as playful museum visits, aim to engage users, success is not guaranteed. If players feel coerced or restricted, their intrinsic motivation can diminish, negatively impacting their gaming and learning experiences [13, 49]. Nicholson's framework [46]' focuses on using game design elements to help users find personal meaning in non-game contexts. Unlike traditional gamification that relies on external rewards (Badges, Levels, Achievements, Points), meaningful gamification fosters intrinsic motivation through engaging, user-relevant play [13, 46].

Game design frameworks commonly prioritize pedagogical objectives, yet solely concentrating on design overlooks player behavior deviations during gameplay [13, 50]. Hence, comprehending the player experience, which centers on the player's role and interaction within the game, becomes crucial and is typically examined both during and after gameplay. Player behavior encompasses the full spectrum of game-related actions and interactions [22]. While this experience is subjective and multifaceted, players' behaviors are amenable to analysis [6].

Our framework relies on the idea that players shape their own playful experience and interpret the game mechanics, tasks, universe and challenge set to them by the game designer. Since the player cannot always be forced to follow the predetermined path designed and scripted by the game designer [13], they actualize and interpret the gameplay, making it their own interpretation. The model can be used as a proper lens, to monitor players' action that goes beyond learning, such as: ignoring specific information, horsing around, adopting unwanted or unhelpful behaviors for the resolution of the game, or interpreting game elements differently [13]. Such behaviors, termed "process" in our model, can impact and influence both the player experience and the learning experience. They emerge in the dynamic interaction between the game and the player

[15, 16]. The model aims to identify the potential for actualizing gameplay (the script, expected reflections, and behaviors anticipated by the game designer) and to study player behaviors that either meet or do not meet the conditions necessary for achieving the learning objectives. While our specific focus is on the complexity of the food production system, the model is designed to evaluate any type of learning objective (Fig. 3).

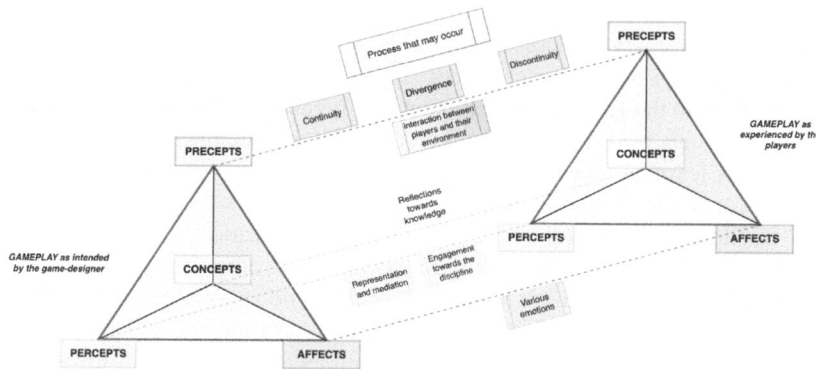

**Fig. 3.** The player experience model, inspired by the frictions between design and play [13]

Given that player experience is a complex and multimodal phenomenon, we characterize it using four dimensions that are both interactive and dynamic. The central dimension is *concepts* consisting of knowledge and reflexions expected from the players. Game-based learning should offer a structured, immersive problem-solving experience that facilitates the development and transfer of knowledge and ways of knowing to other situations, while also focusing on practicing existing skills, preparing for future learning, and acquiring learning and innovation skills [51]. We consider both knowledge acquisition, often specific to a domain, than personal epistemology (way of knowing) [4, 52] as the finalities of a playful learning experience. This dimension manifest themself through problem-solving during gameplay, the processes (what players do) may be: learning new information, developing a new concept, connecting with prior knowledge, connecting with intention, being uncertain about specific information, comment the game [13], formulate strategies or hypotheses, express their value or opinion, make compromises, question specific knowledge.

The second dimension of our model entitled *precepts* is composed of the tasks, missions and activities performed by the player, his actions which are interpretations of the game mechanics [53], challenge [16] and conflict to be solved framed by a set of rules [54]. Player's action can either follow a form of continuity, divergence or discontinuity [13].

*Continuity* occurs when players act as the game intended in the design. Players focus on the presented information, examine elements with clear goals, wander without clear direction, achieve intended goals, act on goals before processing information, over-interact or consider feedback from the game. Some actions (i.e. aimless exploration or premature goal-directed action) may lead to discontinuity. *Discontinuity* happens when events or player behavior hinder the proper progression of the gameplay. Players may encounter various obstacles, such as using ineffective methods, accidental success, anticipating failure, ignoring information, or refusing to engage due to moral dilemmas. Additionally, physical discomfort, lack of guidance, and technical failures can hinder their progress in the game [13]. *Divergence* occurs when player behaviors deviate from the intended game path but do not constitute discontinuity, it can be considered as a new departure, a new meaning is given to the player experience. Players may exhibit behaviors that diverge from game objectives, such as ignoring the goal, failing on purpose, engaging in seemingly aimless actions or attempting to achieve unprompted goals like interacting with non-interactive elements. Additionally, they might make humorous comments unrelated to the game's topic or intentionally fail to provoke desired emotions or fulfill personal goals [13]. Both discontinuity and divergence may impact the learning experience, as learners may not necessarily engage with the intended knowledge, issues, and concepts. Our model aims to anticipate such processes, which manifest in the players' freedom, their playful attitudes, and their actualization of the gameplay.

The third dimension, *percepts*, compose the game world, narrative, and all information useful for executing the game. This game world should support players' reflective thinking [2]. An adequate combination of visual and sound elements will contribute to the aestheticism of a game, which can trigger emotions and engagement towards the topic [53]. Players will evaluate the game environment based on the following criteria: game's mechanics, user interface, characters, audiovisual aesthetics and characters [13].

Inspired by the research on the interrelation between emotions and epistemology [55–57] we add the *affects* dimension to the model. It relates to the plurality of emotions that we can feel in a game, with a focus on the so-called epistemic emotions which are related to the cognitive process. They are provoked by cognitive incongruity produced by unexpected information that contradicts prior knowledge or personal beliefs [55]. These emotions can be indicators of learning performance [55, 56]. Feeling confusion may be correlated with better performance and is a precursor to deeper learning [56], whereas emotions such as frustration or boredom may be associated with poorer learning. The main epistemic emotions are: surprise, curiosity, confusion, anxiety, frustration, joy and boredom [55]. Other emotions can occur in a learning game, but the emotions listed are specific to complex problem-solving (i.e. food production in AL2049).

Now that we have seen the value of using a mixed-method approach and the multimodal aspects of the player experience, we apply this theoretical framework to our research object, the game AL2049. To further explore our initial question: How will players experience complexity and engage with the game? We will formulate the following research questions: How do players explore the complexity of food production in relation to the different game parameters (well-being, health, population)? (quantitative - digital data analysis). How does the model, used as a lens, enable the interpretation of players' actions, emotions, and reflections when they solve a complex problem related to food production? (qualitative case study).

# 4   Research Methods (Mixed Method)

Our approach is a mixed-method, as we first analyze different groups of players using statistical analysis, i.e. game analytics [28]. Following this, the second phase involves three case studies, using thematic analysis to explore multiple dimensions of the player experience.

## 4.1   Collected Data

Between September 2022 and July 2023, 174 game sessions were played by groups of 2–4 students aged 12 to 15. Each session lasted about 60 min, including instructions, the two game phases, and debriefing, led by one or two museum mediators. Digital traces from player actions on tablets were recorded and stored in JSON format, then exported to CSV for analysis. During gameplay, actions affected the number of survivors (variable 1 "survivors"), their health status (variable 2 "health"), and well-being (variable 3 "WellBeing"). Each action recorded included these timestamped variables values (see Table 1).

**Table 1.** Survivor, health and well-being scores linked to player actions

| Action number | Action type | Survivors score | Health score | WellBeing score | Timestamp |
|---|---|---|---|---|---|
| 1 | Plant wheat | 23/30 | 4/6 | 3/6 | 20230620T10:38:01 |
| 2 | Add restaurant | 23/30 | 4/6 | 6/6 | 20230620T10:38:57 |
| 3 | Use 2 fossil fuels | 22/30 | 3/6 | 6/6 | 20230620T10:39:15 |

The data preprocessing involved normalizing variable values, filling missing values with the last observed value, and capping the "foodProduction" variable at 30 to prevent outliers. For each game, the three variables (number of survivors, health status, well-being) were combined by timestamp to capture the game's state at each moment. The games were segmented into units called "actions," each corresponding to a timestamp and representing the combination of the three variable values at that moment. This structuring enabled detailed analysis of player interactions and the impact of their actions on the studied variables.

In September 2022, alongside collecting digital traces, two experimental sessions were conducted with researchers and class teachers. Some students, divided into groups and equipped with shoulder-mounted GoPro cameras, generated about 720 min of video and audio recordings. They were instructed to stay together for comprehensive audio and visual capture. These videos provide data on players' behaviors and attitudes, reflections, comments, hypotheses on food production solutions, statements on moral values related to feeding the population, and group dynamics, collaboration, and interaction—all within a museum context.

## 4.2  Digital Traces Analysis

The analysis of the prepared digital traces was conducted in four steps using a Python environment. First, a descriptive analysis of all played sessions was performed, calculating maximum, minimum, mean, median, and standard deviation values, with results presented using box plots. Next, cluster analyses were carried out using k-means clustering (with silhouette, elbow, and t-SNE tests) to distinguish different game states based on health, survivors, and well-being values for each action. Four clusters were chosen, and their means and standard deviations were calculated. The third step involved creating chronograms (i.e. Diachronic representations) to visualize the sequence of average clusters in each session, using a color code for easy interpretation. Finally, four different types of sessions were identified, characterizing four main groups of players. Representative chronograms for these groups illustrate the various strategies and interactions observed in the game. The detailed methodology and analysis of digital learning traces are described in a separate article [58], which addresses specific research questions.

## 4.3  Thematic Analysis

Observations, based on the on-board video data, allow us to study the interactions between the players and the game [48]. We consider the interactions with the environment, including museography, other players, and present adults (such as teachers, researchers or cultural mediators). Each detailed dimensions of the model are considered as specific indicators, to attract our attention on specific players' behavior, action, affects or reflections towards knowledge or strategies to adopt. This inductive and interpretative approach [59] should allow us to confront our model to players' attitudes and to obtain a better understanding of the player's actualization of AL2049 gameplay.

# 5  Results

## 5.1  Step 1: Game State Clusters and Player Type Hypotheses

On average, the game sessions consisted of 88.4 actions performed by the players (standard deviation 54.1), with a median of 74.5 actions. Cluster analyses were performed on the digital traces generated during the 174 game sessions. The mean values and standard deviations for each cluster are as follows (Table 2).

In terms of gameplay and score combinations, the clusters represent the following game states: Cluster 0 (pink): Maximum number of survivors, but lowest health and well-being. Cluster 1 (orange): Many survivors, very good health, and very good well-being, but none of the three scores at their maximum. Cluster 2 (light blue): Maximum number of survivors, very good health, but lowest well-being. Cluster 3 (dark blue): Few survivors, lowest health, and moderate well-being. The chronograms below illustrate the sequence of these clusters, representing the progression of game states through the health, survival, and well-being scores for each action performed by the players. The first chronogram (see. Figure 4) shows the sequence of clusters in session 51 throughout the actions performed. During this session, players performed a total of 125 actions, resulting in 125 changes in the combined survival, health, and well-being scores. The

**Table 2.** Mean values and standard deviations

| Cluster | Food production mean | Food production std | Health mean | Health std | WellBeing mean | WellBeing std |
|---------|---------------------|---------------------|-------------|------------|----------------|---------------|
| 0 | 0.915070 | 0.117449 | 0.161032 | 0.082942 | 0.146149 | 0.080984 |
| 1 | 0.750670 | 0.139131 | 0.416812 | 0.176473 | 0.553662 | 0.124660 |
| 2 | 0.914790 | 0.110223 | 0.601218 | 0.150371 | 0.183531 | 0.111937 |
| 3 | 0.348597 | 0.171453 | 0.145765 | 0.092018 | 0.401547 | 0.233898 |

diagram shows that all clusters appear in the session, indicating that players explored different score combinations. Between actions 78 and 100, players navigate between clusters 3, 1, 2, and 0, frequently returning to cluster 1, indicating a search for balance between the three variable scores.

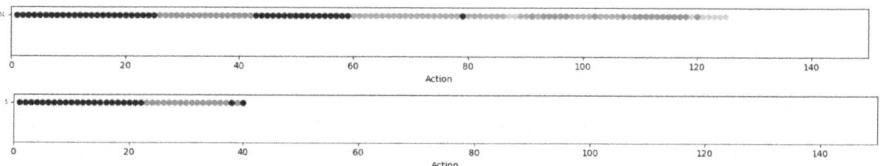

**Fig. 4.** Illustration of chronograms for sessions 51 (The Explorers) and 5 (The Inactive).

The second chronogram shows the sequence of clusters in Session 5 throughout the actions performed. In this session, players performed 40 actions, resulting in 40 changes in the combined survival, health, and well-being scores. Only two clusters appear: cluster 3 (few survivors, lowest health, and moderate well-being) at the session's start, and cluster 0 (maximum number of survivors at the expense of other scores). Players did not explore all combinations and were relatively inactive, with only 40 actions, well below the average of 88.4 actions per session.

From analyzing the 174 diagrams, four playing styles (groups) were identified. Group 1, The group Explorers, consists of curious players who aim to explore as much as possible and as quickly as possible. Group 2, The Rushers, includes players who progress quickly in the game but remain focused on the same objectives without exploring all possibilities. Group 3, The Strategists, comprises thoughtful players who take time to think before acting and explore complexity by testing different combinations. Finally, Group 4, The Inactive, consists of players who are not fully engaged in the game or explore its possibilities minimally.

## 5.2  Step 2: Case Study

The second step of our research involves identifying characteristics, based on the model (see 3.3) and video data, for three distinct groups: Session #51: Explorers, Session #105 (The Rushers), Session #5 (Inactive). During the experiments using GoPro cameras, none of the groups belonged to the *Strategists*.

**Players of Session #51** consist of 1 female student and 2 male students. The girl was, most of the time, holding the tablet and one of the boys had the GoPro on his shoulder. As the gamemaster introduces the game and gives explanations on how to use the game interface, as well as the main objective (i.e. Feeding 30 persons), the two boys sometimes joke about the situation (divergence). They begin exploring the museum as expected by the design (continuity). However, one player quickly drew the group's attention to a museum screen that was not part of the elements to be scanned, marking the first form of discontinuity. According to our indicators, this discontinuity may be due to poor game guidance (the map does not allow players to navigate independently) or, more likely in this case, the museum environment competes with the expected and required actions of the players. According to the video, players understood the zone unlocking mechanic well, but space allocation led to poorly reasoned discussions. For instance, when the girl asked if they wanted insects, one boy responded: "*Well, yes, because look, I'm an insect,*" while clinging to a museum exhibit. The museum exploration is repeatedly interrupted by discontinuities, particularly by the two boys who frequently approach and manipulate various museum exhibits. The collective gaming experience then takes a different turn, with the girl having to allocate the zones alone while her peers are primarily occupied with making jokes (divergence). Acts of mediation by the teachers or researchers present, asking the players to stay together, had very little success. The discontinuity becomes generalized for all three players when the girl is also tempted to use a sound exhibit in the museum, which is not part of the game. She sets the tablet aside for a few minutes. However, these moments of discontinuity are not always disconnected from the game (*percepts*) or the learning objectives (*concept*), as the players sometimes comment on the display items, suggesting ideas for space allocation. From an epistemological perspective, the player once asked an adult present if what they had done so far was "*right or not.*" This, according to our indicators, may indicate a dualistic view of reality and a low tolerance for uncertainty. As the game progresses, the student holding the tablet, who has been diligent from the start, begins to argue more effectively for the allocation of spaces. For example, she knows that polyculture will produce less food, and she explains this to her peers during the space allocation (*concepts*). In terms of *affects,* the emotions that seem to be felt include confusion: "*But guys, I don't understand, where are we supposed to go? I don't know?*" (related to lack of guidance - *discontinuity*) and frustration when, at the end of phase 1, they manage to feed only 29 out of 30 people (tasks - *precepts*).

The second phase of the game takes on a completely different dynamic. After learning about the state of the population, the three players sit down and remain grouped around the tablet for over 25 min. All the players then seem concerned about the state of the game, and numerous hypotheses are proposed to solve the problems. Initially, their discussions aim to simplify the complexity of the situation: "*It's simple, we'll put them in the natural world... In nature, they will find food and do whatever they want. We won't keep them inside* (the museum)". In the same vein, one player suggests improving health by setting up multiple laboratories "*to get medicine*". However, they can only set up one lab, and it does not affect health. This type of player-perceived information diverges from what the game designer had anticipated (percepts). Quickly, moral stances emerge, as one player suggests increasing well-being, to which another player responds, "*health is the most important*". It is interesting to observe that the girl wants to increase all the parameters, while the boys suggest focusing on just one. As she allocates fish, she points out that, "*if health increases, well-being decreases*" which seems to demonstrate some understanding of the systemicity (*concept*). One of the boys then argues that this is due to "*racism against the fish*" without considering the effects of fossil fuel used for fish farming (*concept*). As frustration seems to resurface due to the difficulty of increasing all the parameters, one student suggests letting them die (divergence, failing on purpose), a temporary strategy that would nonetheless increase well-being and health of the survivors. The teacher's intervention, after they had been autonomous until then, puts them on the track of reducing the workload by prioritizing fossil or renewable energy, a strategy they had not yet considered. As the game master announces the end of the game and calls for the debriefing, the players observe their results and repeatedly say, "*in reality, it's good*" demonstrating a form of satisfaction and joy (*affects*).

**Players of Session #105 (Rushers)** consist of three teenage girls. After receiving instructions from the game master, they begin exploring the museum. One quickly tries an interactive element, but her team-mates call her back. This player is repeatedly distracted by the museum's scenography, to the detriment of the game (discontinuity). They interact frequently without formulating strategies, moving aimlessly (concept). The first zone is assigned randomly after a brief discussion while one player uses a touchscreen kiosk. Starting from the second scanned zone, one player takes the lead. Instead of helping, one says, "*come on, let's look through the binoculars and mess around.*" Such aimless actions fall under divergence. Similarly, another suggests imitating the animals and humans on a screen. Though playful, their attitude isn't focused on solving the game (divergence). The game master's numerous interventions don't change anything. At the end of the first phase, having fed 20 people, they consult to achieve a better score (*Percepts - continuity*). Their choices are based on personal preferences: "*Put some cereal, we need cornflakes in the morning.*" As the game master gathers them, noticeable frustration arises because they didn't manage to feed everyone (*affects*). A technical error occurred when advancing in time (discontinuity). However, they were able to resume without losing their progress. The second phase starts and they manage to feed 30 people quickly, without sharing strategies together. The group then moved to a large interactive touchscreen table featuring skill-based games. Two of the three players used the table for several minutes, leaving the third player to modify the game alone (was already the case in the first phase). After interacting with various museum elements, all three players pursue their own imitation game, which diverged significantly from the intended expected behavior. An intervention by one of the researchers redirected the activity after nearly 15 min of divergence. Through this interaction, the players realized that the barrels shown in the game represented fossil fuels, not water. They also hadn't understood the significance of human energy (i.e., the 30 people). This posed a major problem for understanding the interdependencies of the food system and the resulting complexity (*Concepts*). The game representations (*Percepts*) were not identified as they should have been. In this phase, they focus on feeding as many people as possible, paying little attention to well-being and health. This is evident in the chronograms and can be explained by the videos showing low collective engagement and a poor understanding of the game's resources (i.e., the energies). The gameplay failed to prompt reflections on their knowledge or values regarding the food production system, nor did it help them explore its complexity (*Concepts*).

**Players of *Session #5 (Inactive)*** are also three teenage girls. As the game starts, immediately after the game master's explanations, one player declares, "*Did you understand? I don't know what we have to do.*" After scanning the first room, they exchange comments: "*What do we want to put here?... In a corridor?... We can't put animals in a corridor, can we?*" They do not seem to grasp the second degree or possess the level of abstraction intended by the game design (*Percepts*), which involves transforming spaces into food production units (*Precepts*). They then ask a researcher for help, who tells them they must first unlock all the rooms (whereas it is preferable to scan and immediately assign a function to each room). A little later, the game master gives them the same advice: "I suggest unlocking everything." As a result of these recommendations, the players ultimately use very few of the other game mechanics (such as space allocation) during this first phase, which is evident in the chronogram. The mixed reality technology seems to have hindered their playful experience (discontinuity). They then sit in a quiet area of the museum, ensuring that each of them can see the tablet. Each space allocation results from a lengthy discussion among them. They question each other, check for consensus, and take the time to read the functionalities of the spaces. Sometimes, their reasoning for assigning zones is based on the physical constraints of the museum (e.g., placing plants where there are windows), which does not align with the game design's expectations. The videos clearly show that they engage in discussion and collaboration before each "click" on the tablet, which likely explains their low number of traces and exploration of clusters. They add an unforeseen difficulty to the game by considering the physical characteristics of the museum rooms: "*If we put plants there, it looks bigger.*" Additionally, when allocating energy, they mistake the oil barrel for water. This over-consumption of energy seems to cause confusion (*Affects*). As a result, they finish the first phase having taken very few actions (exploring only one cluster of complexity) and having fed only 6 people.

At the beginning of phase 2, they formulate their first hypotheses to improve the situation based on arguments that do not consider complexity or interdependencies: "*We'll put the restaurant here, it's much nicer*" or "*We need to put things with water, otherwise we won't have enough to drink.*" This mistaken representation of water leads them down a wrong path in terms of understanding complexity (*Concepts*) and represents a form of divergence. The confusion persists into the second phase (with water). Their primary concern is to feed the 30 people, and the constant but unintentional allocation of fossil energy (which they believe to be water) leads them to a solution where well-being and health do not improve. This keeps them constrained within the same cluster (i.e., pink, low health and well-being). As they consult the newsfeed, they read a recommendation about GMOs (which is actually fake news). They then remove all vegetables to improve health. This immediate reaction demonstrates a certain credulity regarding information in a game (*Concepts*). They maintained a slow and deliberate style of play, with numerous discussions before assigning spaces. They explored the complexity in terms of only one parameter: energy, with an incorrect understanding of its meaning. They did not attempt strategies to modify other parameters, such as workload or food diversity. As they gather for the debriefing, they compare their results with other groups and declare, "*Well, for us it's a disaster.*"

Watching the videos allows us to better understand their gaming experience. The low number of traces in the first part may be related to the recommendations of the adults present and some technical errors that slowed their progress. Although categorized by the traces as "inactive," their behavior in the museum was genuinely focused on solving the game. Unlike the other two groups studied, they were not easily distracted by the museum's exhibits. Furthermore, their collaboration was remarkable, as space allocation was always preceded by discussion and consensus within the group. It was a misinterpretation of the game's information (*Percepts*) that seems to have constrained their exploration of complexity.

## 6   Discussion and Conclusion

The analysis of player experience in game-based-learning seems to require a multifaceted approach to capture the complexity of interactions and outcomes [7]. Our results allow us to discuss the use of mixed-methods. The chronograms provide an overall view of how the game can be played and how the complexity parameters are utilized (or not) by the players to solve the assigned problem. The data obtained from the on-board cameras capture the decisions and strategies that motivated the players during their visit. We observe that their reasoning for space allocation is not always based on group consensus and is sometimes superficial. The game environment (i.e., the museum, its scenography, and its interactive elements) tends to compete with the gameplay and the various tasks and actions assigned to the player. Discontinuity thus becomes the norm, especially in the exploration phase of the museum but it does not always pose a risk to the learning objectives. Divergence, on the other hand, is more problematic. It can be caused by a desire to simplify the rules, a misunderstanding of the game, or the freedom that players allow themselves. It is difficult to eliminate the latter (freedom), as it is an integral part of the act of playing. Nonetheless, we see that we oscillate between constraining and persuading the player to engage in solving the complex problem and allowing freedom and interpretation of the game, its gameplay, its rules, and its representations. This effectively translates the tension, identified in previous studies [6, 13], between the potential game experience desired by the game designer, which should facilitate achieving the set learning objectives, and the subjective player's experience, which is instantiated and actualized by the player, and sometimes unpredictable. Our model, tested during this study, aims to capture the subjectivity of the player's experience across four main dimensions: actions, information processing, knowledge, and emotions. We identify potential improvements for this model as an analytical tool, particularly concerning group dynamics (how to handle group splits and their effects on the collective) and the impact of context (considering the environment and context of play). We may have underestimated, during the game design phase, the potential interpretations of the gameplay of AL2049 and the rich environment in which it is deployed. As a future perspective, the model could benefit and evolve from new case studies (9 recorded sessions not analyzed here). From a pragmatic perspective on the orchestration of the game by the museum, our study allows us to formulate recommendations on the instructions given to players (regarding the allocation of fossil energies) and to suggest evolving the game's aesthetics and interfaces from a game design perspective.

**Acknowledgments.** This research was funded by the Swiss National Sciences Foundation (SNSF 100019_185474), as well as a close partnership with teachers from compulsory schools, the game design studio Digital Kingdom.

**Disclosure of Interests.** The authors have no competing interests to declare that are relevant to the content of this article.

# References

1. Tongpaeng, Y., Nobnop, R., Wongwan, N., Homla, P., Intawong, K., Puritat, K.: Comparison of gamified and non-gamified mixed reality in enhancing museum visitor engagement, motivation, and learning outcome. J. Herit. Tourism, 1–30 (2024). https://doi.org/10.1080/1743873X.2024.2351852
2. Kiili, K.: Digital game-based learning: towards an experiential gaming model. Internet High. Educ. **8**(1), 13–24 (2005). https://doi.org/10.1016/j.iheduc.2004.12.001
3. Davallon, J., Gottesdiener, H., Vilatte, J.-C.: A quoi peuvent donc servir les recherches sur les visiteurs. Cult. Musées **8**(1), 161–172 (2006). https://doi.org/10.3406/pumus.2006.1411
4. Hofer, B., Sinatra, G.: Epistemology, metacognition, and self-regulation: musings on an emerging field. Metacogn. Learn. **5**, 113–120 (2010). https://doi.org/10.1007/s11409-009-9051-7
5. Bonnat, C., Oliveira, G., Sanchez, E.: "Geome", un juego para comprender el Antropoceno durante las visitas escolares a un museo. Enseñanza de las Ciencias de la Tierra **28**(1), Article 1 (2020)
6. Morard, S., Sanchez, E., Bonnat, C.: Museum games and personal epistemology: a study on students' critical thinking with a mixed reality game. Int. J. Serious Games **10**(4), Article 4 (2023). https://doi.org/10.17083/ijsg.v10i4.695
7. Lieberoth, A., Roepstorff, A.: Mixed methods in game research: playing on strengths and countering weaknesses. In: Game Research Methods, pp. 271–289. ETC Press (2015)
8. Morard, S., Sanchez, E., Oliveira, G., Godinot, N.: AL2049, a Playful Museum's Visit to Grasp the Issues of Complexity (2023)
9. Oliveira, G., Godinot, N., Sanchez, E., Bonnat, C., Morard, S., Dall'Aglio, S.: Game Design for a Museum Visit: Insights into the Co-design of AL2049, a Game About Food Systems, pp. 22–31 (2022). https://doi.org/10.1007/978-3-031-22124-8_3
10. Grenier, R.S.: All work and no play makes for a dull museum visitor. New Direct. Adult Continuing Educ. **2010**(127), 77–85 (2010). https://doi.org/10.1002/ace.383
11. Ericksen, P.J.: Conceptualizing food systems for global environmental change research. Glob. Environ. Chang. **18**(1), 234–245 (2008). https://doi.org/10.1016/j.gloenvcha.2007.09.002
12. Sanchez, E., Plumettaz-Sieber, M.: Teaching and learning with escape games from debriefing to institutionalization of knowledge. In: 7th International Conference, GALA 2018, Palermo, Italy, 5–7 Dec 2018, Proceedings, pp. 242–253 (2019). https://doi.org/10.1007/978-3-030-11548-7_23

13. Fernández Galeote, D., Diamant, M., Volkovs, K., Zeko, C., Thibault, M., Legaki, N.-Z., Hamari, J.: Understanding the game-based learning experience: a framework of frictions between design and play. In: Proceedings of the 17th International Conference on the Foundations of Digital Games, pp. 1–4 (2022). https://doi.org/10.1145/3555858.3555933
14. Blythe, M., Hassenzahl, M.: The semantics of fun: differentiating enjoyable experiences. In: Blythe, M. A., Overbeeke, K., Monk, A.F., Wright, P.C. (eds.) Funology: From Usability to Enjoyment, pp. 91–100. Springer, Netherlands (2004). https://doi.org/10.1007/1-4020-2967-5_9
15. Ermi, L., Mäyrä, F.: Fundamental components of the gameplay experience: analysing immersion. In: DiGRA Conference (2005)
16. Mäyrä, F., Ermi, L.: Fundamental Components of the Gameplay Experience (2011)
17. Abdul Jabbar, A.I., Felicia, P.: Gameplay engagement and learning in game-based learning: a systematic review. Rev. Educ. Res. **85**(4), 740–779 (2015). https://doi.org/10.3102/0034654315577210
18. Genvo, S.: Caractériser l'expérience du jeu à son ère numérique: Pour une étude du "play design". Le Jeu Vidéo : Expériences et Pratiques Sociales Multidimensionnelles (2008). https://hal-unilim.archives-ouvertes.fr/hal-00653194
19. Genvo, S.: Penser les phénomènes de ludicisation à partir de Jacques Henriot. Sciences Du Jeu, 1 (2013)
20. Drachen, A., El-Nasr, M.S., Canossa, A.: Game analytics – the basics: maximizing the value of player data. Game Anal., 13–40 (2013). https://doi.org/10.1007/978-1-4471-4769-5_2
21. Nacke, L.E., Bateman, C., Mandryk, R.L.: BrainHex: A neurobiological gamer typology survey. Entertainment Comput. **5**(1), 55–62 (2014). https://doi.org/10.1016/j.entcom.2013.06.002
22. Wiemeyer, J., Nacke, L., Moser, C., 'Floyd' Mueller, F.: (2016). Player experience. In: Dörner, R., Göbel, S., Effelsberg, W., Wiemeyer, J. (eds.) Serious Games: Foundations, Concepts and Practice (pp. 243–271). Springer International Publishing. https://doi.org/10.1007/978-3-319-40612-1_9
23. Arnab, S., et al.: Mapping learning and game mechanics for serious games analysis. Br. J. Edu. Technol. **46**(2), 391–411 (2015). https://doi.org/10.1111/bjet.12113
24. Connolly, T.M., Boyle, E.A., MacArthur, E., Hainey, T., Boyle, J.M.: A systematic literature review of empirical evidence on computer games and serious games. Comput. Educ. **59**(2), 661–686 (2012). https://doi.org/10.1016/j.compedu.2012.03.004
25. Abeele, V.V., Spiel, K., Nacke, L., Johnson, D., Gerling, K.: Development and validation of the player experience inventory: a scale to measure player experiences at the level of functional and psychosocial consequences. Int. J. Hum. Comput. Stud. **135**, 102370 (2020). https://doi.org/10.1016/j.ijhcs.2019.102370
26. Desurvire, H., Wiberg, C.: Game usability heuristics (PLAY) for evaluating and designing better games: the next iteration. In Ozok, A.A., Zaphiris, P. (eds.) Online Communities and Social Computing, pp. 557–566). Springer (2009). https://doi.org/10.1007/978-3-642-02774-1_60
27. Korhonen, H., Koivisto, E.M.I.: Playability heuristics for mobile games. In: Proceedings of the 8th Conference on Human-Computer Interaction with Mobile Devices and Services, pp. 9–16 (2006). https://doi.org/10.1145/1152215.1152218
28. Seif El-Nasr, M., Drachen, A., Canossa, A. (eds.): Game Analytics: Maximizing the Value of Player Data. Springer (2013). https://doi.org/10.1007/978-1-4471-4769-5
29. Medlock, M., Wixon, D.R., Terrano, M., Romero, R.L.: Using the RITE method to improve products; a definition and a case study (2007). https://www.semanticscholar.org/paper/Using-the-RITE-method-to-improve-products%3B-a-and-a-Medlock-Wixon/5340ef8a91900840263a4036b0433a389b7097b2

30. Bauckhage, C., Drachen, A., Sifa, R.: Clustering game behavior data. IEEE Trans. Comput. Intell. AI Games **7**(3), 266–278 (2015). https://doi.org/10.1109/TCIAIG.2014.2376982

31. Drachen, A., Canossa, A.: Towards gameplay analysis via gameplay metrics. In: Proceedings of the 13th International MindTrek Conference: Everyday Life in the Ubiquitous Era, pp. 202–209 (2009). https://doi.org/10.1145/1621841.1621878

32. Brockmyer, J.H., Fox, C.M., Curtiss, K.A., McBroom, E., Burkhart, K.M., Pidruzny, J.N.: The development of the game engagement questionnaire: a measure of engagement in video game-playing. J. Exp. Soc. Psychol. **45**(4), 624–634 (2009). https://doi.org/10.1016/j.jesp.2009.02.016

33. Cheng, M.-T., She, H.-C., Annetta, L.A.: Game immersion experience: its hierarchical structure and impact on game-based science learning. J. Comput. Assist. Learn. **31**(3), 232–253 (2015). https://doi.org/10.1111/jcal.12066

34. Poels, K., de Kort, Y., Ijsselsteijn, W.: "It is always a lot of fun!": Exploring dimensions of digital game experience using focus group methodology. In: Proceedings of the 2007 Conference on Future Play, pp. 83–89 (2007). https://doi.org/10.1145/1328202.1328218

35. Johnson, D., Gardner, M.J., Perry, R.: Validation of two game experience scales: the player experience of need satisfaction (PENS) and game experience questionnaire (GEQ). Int. J. Hum. Comput. Stud. **118**, 38–46 (2018). https://doi.org/10.1016/j.ijhcs.2018.05.003

36. Law, E.L.-C., Brühlmann, F., Mekler, E.D.: Systematic review and validation of the game experience questionnaire (GEQ)—implications for citation and reporting practice. In: Proceedings of the 2018 Annual Symposium on Computer-Human Interaction in Play, pp. 257–270 (2018). https://doi.org/10.1145/3242671.3242683

37. Johnson, R.B., Onwuegbuzie, A.J., Turner, L.A.: Toward a definition of mixed methods research. J. Mixed Methods Res. **1**(2), 112–133 (2007). https://doi.org/10.1177/1558689806298224

38. Fielding, N.G.: Triangulation and mixed methods designs: data integration with new research technologies. J. Mixed Methods Res. **6**(2), 124–136 (2012). https://doi.org/10.1177/1558689812437101

39. Kara, N.: A mixed-methods study of cultural heritage learning through playing a serious game. Int. J. Hum.-Comput. Inter. **40**(6), 1397–1408 (2024). https://doi.org/10.1080/10447318.2022.2125627

40. Rubino, I., Barberis, C., Xhembulla, J., Malnati, G.: Integrating a location-based mobile game in the museum visit: evaluating visitors' behaviour and learning. J. Comput. Cult. Herit. **8**(3), 15:1–15:18. https://doi.org/10.1145/2724723

41. Carvalho, M.B., et al.: An activity theory-based model for serious games analysis and conceptual design. Comput. Educ. **87**, 166–181 (2015). https://doi.org/10.1016/j.compedu.2015.03.023

42. Aranguren, R.V., Rodriguez, P.P., Vela, F.L.G., Arango-López, J.: Model for pervasive social play experiences. In Agredo-Delgado, V., Ruiz, P.H., Villalba-Condori, K.O. (eds.) Human-Computer Interaction, pp. 171–180. Springer International Publishing (2020). https://doi.org/10.1007/978-3-030-66919-5_18

43. Annetta, L.A.: The "I's" have it: a framework for serious educational game design. Rev. Gen. Psychol. **14**(2), 105–113 (2010). https://doi.org/10.1037/a0018985

44. Rooney, P.: A theoretical framework for serious game design: exploring pedagogy, play and fidelity and their implications for the design process. Int. J. Game-Based Learn. (IJGBL) **2**(4), 41–60 (2012)

45. Madsen, K.M.: The gamified museum: a critical literature review and discussion of gamification in museums. In: Gamescope: The Potential for Gamification in Digital and Analogue Places (2020). https://vbn.aau.dk/en/publications/the-gamified-museum-a-critical-literature-review-and-discussion-o

46. Nicholson, S.: Strategies for Meaningful Gamification: Concepts behind Transformative Play and Participatory Museums (2012)
47. Hunicke, R., Leblanc, M., Zubek, R.: MDA: a formal approach to game design and game research. In: AAAI Workshop—Technical Report, 1 (2004)
48. Ribbens, W., Poels, Y.: Researching player experiences through the use of different qualitative methods. In: Breaking New Ground: Innovation in Games, Play, Practice and Theory—Proceedings of DiGRA 2009 (2009)
49. Koivisto, J., Hamari, J.: The rise of motivational information systems: a review of gamification research. Int. J. Inf. Manage. **45**, 191–210 (2019). https://doi.org/10.1016/j.ijinfomgt.2018.10.013
50. Pereira de Aguiar, M., Winn, B., Cezarotto, M., Battaiola, A.L., Varella Gomes, P.: Educational Digital Games: A Theoretical Framework About Design Models, Learning Theories and User Experience (Marcus, A., Wang, W. eds.), vol. 10918, pp. 165–184. Springer International Publishing (2018). https://doi.org/10.1007/978-3-319-91797-9_13
51. Shaffer, D.W., Gee, J.P.: Shaffer D. W.: Before every child is left behind: how epistemic games can solve the coming crisis in education. WCER Working Paper No. 2005-7. http://archive.org/details/ERIC_ED497010
52. Hofer, B.K., Pintrich, P.R.: The development of epistemological theories: beliefs about knowledge and knowing and their relation to learning. Rev. Educ. Res. **67**(1), 88–140 (1997). https://doi.org/10.2307/1170620
53. Suovuo, T., Skult, N., Joelsson, T., Skult, P., Ravyse, W., Smed, J.: The Game Experience Model (GEM), pp. 183–205 (2020). https://doi.org/10.1007/978-3-030-37643-7_8
54. Smed, J., Hakonen, H.: Algorithms and Networking for Computer Games, 2nd edn. Wiley (2017)
55. D'Mello, S., Lehman, B., Pekrun, R., Graesser, A.: Confusion can be beneficial for learning. Learn. Instr. **29**, 153–170 (2014). https://doi.org/10.1016/j.learninstruc.2012.05.003
56. Pekrun, R., Stephens, E.J.: Academic emotions. In: APA Educational Psychology Handbook, Vol 2: Individual Differences and Cultural and Contextual Factors, pp. 3–31. American Psychological Association (2012). https://doi.org/10.1037/13274-001
57. Marshall, M., Brown, J.: Emotional reactions to achievement outcomes: is it really best to expect the worst? Cogn. Emot. **20**(1), 43–63 (2006). https://doi.org/10.1080/02699930500215116
58. Paukovics, E., Morard, S., Rioja, K., Sanchez, E.: Clustering Player Behaviors to Reveal Complexity Exploration Patterns in an Educational Museum Game, submitted for publication
59. Nowell, L.S., Norris, J.M., White, D.E., Moules, N.J.: Thematic analysis: striving to meet the trustworthiness criteria. Int J Qual Methods **16**(1), 1609406917733847 (2017). https://doi.org/10.1177/1609406917733847

# Tracing Emerging Complexity of Scientific Reasoning Actions During Game-Based Learning

Daryn Dever[1]([✉]) [iD], Megan Wiedbusch[2] [iD], and Roger Azevedo[2] [iD]

[1] University of Florida, Gainesville, FL 32611, USA
ddever@ufl.edu
[2] University of Central Florida, Orlando, FL 32816, USA

**Abstract.** Scientific reasoning is a critical foundational skill learners need to practice and know for increased science learning outcomes. Game-based learning environments (GBLEs) provide learners a platform for developing and practicing scientific reasoning skills but little is known about how learners should engage in scientific reasoning during game-based learning. As such, this paper aimed to understand if and how learners engaged in effective scientific reasoning activities during learning with a GBLE. This paper used analytical techniques from Complex Systems Theory to quantify learners' scientific reasoning actions during game-based learning. High-school students ($N = 170$) played Crystal Island, a microbiology GBLE requiring learners to engage in scientific reasoning to successfully identify an illness infecting residents of a virtual island. Categorical auto-Recurrence Quantification Analysis was run on participants' log files as they deployed scientific reasoning actions. This analysis revealed several metrics of complexity, including recurrence rate which is the proportion of repetitive to novel scientific reasoning actions. Results found that as time progressed, recurrence rates decreased. Successful learners (i.e., those who solved the mystery) demonstrated less repetition in their scientific reasoning activities where their recurrence rates decreased at a slower rate over time than learners who were unsuccessful in solving the mystery. Findings provide implications for adaptively scaffolding learners' emerging complexities in their scientific reasoning processes during game-based learning to increase learners' GBLE success.

**Keywords:** Scientific Reasoning · Complexity · Game-based Learning · Log-file Data

## 1 Introduction

Scientific reasoning is a foundational skill required for increased science knowledge and problem solving as learners engage in information gathering, hypothesis generation, and hypothesis testing and adjustment throughout a learning task [1]. With the COVID-19 pandemic, scientific reasoning has become an increasingly critical skill for high school students as they are faced with persisting challenges such as sorting misinformation in media [2], overcoming existing misconceptions related to microbiology

© The Author(s), under exclusive license to Springer Nature Switzerland AG 2025
J. L. Plass and X. Ochoa (Eds.): JCSG 2024, LNCS 15259, pp. 196–210, 2025.
https://doi.org/10.1007/978-3-031-74138-8_15

[3], and increasing their science knowledge [4]. To assist learners in achieving better science outcomes, game-based learning environments (GBLEs) have served as a valuable tool, integrating playful learning with gamification to maintain interest and engagement during learning about difficult topics in science (e.g., microbiology; [5–8]). However, while several studies have examined how learners engage in scientific reasoning during game-based learning [9–12], little is known about the extent to which learners' complexity of dynamically deploying scientific reasoning actions relates to their learning outcomes, such as learners' increased domain knowledge or their successful use of scientific reasoning within the game to achieve the objectives of the GBLE. As such, the goal of this paper is to quantify high school learners' emerging complexity of scientific reasoning actions during game-based learning and understand how this emerging complexity relates to students' increased domain knowledge and success in engaging in accurate scientific reasoning. By evaluating how learners dynamically engage in scientific reasoning actions through a complexity science lens, we can: (1) extend theoretical frameworks of game-based learning [13]; (2) establish guidelines for how scientific reasoning should be deployed by learners in terms of functional versus dysfunctional scientific reasoning behavior (i.e., overall use of scientific reasoning actions); and (3) provide implications for the design of adaptive scaffolds embedded within GBLEs to support and foster learners' use of scientific reasoning actions and therefore increase domain knowledge and accuracy in scientific reasoning to successfully achieve science game objectives.

## 2  Scientific Reasoning

Science education has been centered on the foundational development of scientific reasoning and argumentation skills across all educational levels [14–16]. Consequently, this has encouraged more active and learner-centered instruction such as inquiry learning [17–19]. These approaches require learners to take on the role of a scientist to develop, apply, and practice scientific reasoning skills while engaging in self-regulated learning [16, 20–22]. Scientific reasoning has been conceptualized through multiple theoretical lenses, defining the processes as problem-solving [23, 24], a cycle of discovery [25, 26], and a collection of epistemic activities [27]. Across these various conceptualizations, all definitions mention sets of skills, related domain-specific and domain-general knowledge, and a cycle of stages to create and adapt one's knowledge construction during complex learning [26]. Given the complicated nature of many of these skills (e.g., drawing conclusions, evaluating evidence) and activities (e.g., problem identification, evidence generation), it is of no surprise that research has consistently found learners continuously run into difficulties with scientific reasoning [28, 29]. Students who are effective self-regulators, however, can actively monitor and regulate their cognitive, affective, metacognitive, and motivational processes during these activities to improve learning outcomes [30, 31]. Self-regulation is particularly crucial for determining which scientific reasoning techniques to employ and when to do so [21]. As such, various support tools and scaffolds embedded within learning environments have been developed to help foster self-regulation during scientific reasoning [21, 32].

## 2.1 Scientific Reasoning During Game-Based Learning

GBLEs have an established history as effective tools for increasing learners' scientific reasoning abilities [11, 12, 33]. This is due to the highly interactive and engaging nature of GBLEs as learners are able to directly engage in actions that correspond to the scientific reasoning process such as gathering information using instructional materials [34] and generating hypotheses that can then be tested to achieve game objectives [23]. Several GBLEs have been extensively researched to understand how these environments encourage and support learners as they complete game objectives by learning and enacting scientific reasoning processes. Casanoves et al. [35] examined how learners' conceptual understanding of genetics was enhanced using a GBLE environment named *Recal* as they embodied the role of detective to solve a criminal case. Another GBLE named *Operation ARA* has been shown to increase learners' critical thinking and scientific reasoning as learners engage in interactive dialogs with non-player characters [36].

In addition to the aforementioned GBLEs and relevant to this study, *Crystal Island* is a GBLE that requires learners to engage in scientific reasoning where learners must engage in several actions, such as reading texts, talking with non-player characters, hypothesizing and testing which food items hold a certain disease, in order to identify a mysterious illness plaguing researchers on a virtual island [6, 37]. Several studies have examined how learners engaged in scientific reasoning with Crystal Island. Taub et al. [38] used sequential pattern mining and differential sequence mining to examine undergraduate learners' efficiency of game completion success. This study found differences in how learners engaged in metacognitive monitoring while enacting scientific reasoning actions where learners who were more efficient in completing the game demonstrated lower frequencies of engaging in sequences of transitioning across hypothesis generation and testing actions. Another study by Cloude et al. [11] used multimodal data to identify when learners were, or were not, engaging in actions that were related to scientific reasoning within Crystal Island. Results from this study found that eye gaze behaviors and prior knowledge about microbiology were predictive of learners' time engaging in information gathering behaviors where learners with lower prior knowledge spent more time gathering information from the environment than learners with higher prior knowledge. Similar to Cloude et al. [11], Dever et al. [39] also used eye tracking data to examine how learners engaged in scientific reasoning actions over time with Crystal Island. Results found that as time on task progressed, learners' dwell times on information gathering actions decreased where lower dwell times on these actions were significantly correlated with lower learning gains.

From all studies, there is extensive literature on examining how learners engage in scientific reasoning during learning with GBLEs, specifically within Crystal Island. However, while research has examined the dynamics of emotions and cognitive processes during game-based learning (e.g., [6, 40]), few studies have examined the extent to which learners' scientific reasoning actions demonstrate emergent indices of complexity and related this to learners' achievement of learning outcomes to quantify the functionality of learners' scientific reasoning processes.

# 3   Complex Systems Theory

Complexity science encompasses multiple concepts, methods, and theories to examine complex systems [41]. Complex Systems Theory (CST) is the study of how components within a system interact with each other from which system behaviors arise [42]. A complex system is characterized by self-organization, interaction dominance, and emergence where the behavior of a system is not dictated by a single controller, rather it is the exponential and multiplicative relationship between component interactions that elicit system-level behavior [43–45]. Concepts within CST define how system-level behavior should demonstrate a healthy, functional system. Far-from-equilibrium, also known as edge of chaos, is a concept in which the health of a system is defined as its ability to fluctuate between stable and unstable states. For example, a functional system demonstrates an ability to maintain a balance of stable and unstable patterns of behavior whereas a dysfunctional system demonstrates behavior with too much stability or instability [46, 47].

CST is not just a theoretical, abstract understanding of a system, rather it is also the computational measurement of system behaviors that provide quantitative indices of system complexity, and therefore evidence of functional and dysfunctional systems. For this paper, we use these quantitative indices as measured by auto-Recurrence Quantification Analysis (aRQA; [48]) and compare them between groups of learners who engaged in successful scientific reasoning (i.e., successfully solved the mystery by identifying the correct illness) and those who did not (i.e., did not successfully identify the correct illness) during learning with Crystal Island to identify the extent to which learners' scientific reasoning demonstrated healthy, functional systems and how this changed as they progressed through the game.

## 3.1   CST in GBLE Literature

While most GBLEs are considered complex systems in and of themselves [49–51], few studies have used CST to ground their work on the learning processes that are deployed within GBLEs [6, 52, 53]. For example, Dever et al. [6] examined how learners deployed self-regulated learning strategies to interact with several types of instructional materials during gameplay using aRQA and grouped learners based off of the metrics output from this analysis. This was then related to learning outcomes which showed that learners who were scaffolded via restricted agency and had greater recurrence in their interactions with instructional materials had the greatest learning gains. Another study by Kumar et al. [53] examined how learners within an immersive multiplayer game, City Settlers, collaborated with each other as a method for quantifying learners' understanding of complex systems and the interaction between system components. However, the use of complexity science to examine learning processes during game-based learning remains largely unexplored. As such, this study progresses the field's understanding of how games for education can be used to better support learners' functional learning processes.

# 4   Current Study

The goal of this paper is to quantify the degree to which learners' engagement with scientific reasoning actions exemplify functional system behaviors and how this changes over time within a single session of learning with a game-based learning environment as well as how this differs between learners who are either successful or unsuccessful in achieving the game objective (i.e., identify an illness infecting researchers on a virtual island). This goal aims to address a gap in our current understanding of *how* learners should be engaging in scientific reasoning throughout learning to provide actionable implications and contributions for implementing scaffolds that assist learners in acquiring scientific reasoning skills. Within this paper, we identify learners' complex system as scientific reasoning where system behaviors represent the culmination and use of several scientific reasoning actions. To address the goal of this paper, we answer three research questions: (1) To what extent do learners' indices of complexity in their scientific reasoning actions relate to their learning outcomes?; (2) How does the emergence of recurrent scientific reasoning actions account for the variation of emerging complexity within and between learners?; and (3) To what extent is the emergence of recurrent scientific reasoning actions related to learning outcomes?

Because scientific reasoning processes have not been examined through a complex systems theory lens, we pull from other works on learning and complexity to situate our hypotheses. We hypothesize that learners who demonstrate higher recurrence rates will demonstrate lower learning outcomes than learners who have lower recurrence rates [6, 54]. We do not hypothesize a directional relationship between the learning outcomes and learners' emerging complexity in scientific reasoning actions. However, from far-from-equilibrium concepts, we hypothesize that learners who have greater learning outcomes will demonstrate greater functional system behaviors in terms of their balance between novel and repetitive scientific reasoning actions [46, 47].

# 5   Methodology

## 5.1   Participants

High school students ($N = 170$) from a North American public school system participated in this study during normal school hours. Participants' ages ranged from 14 to 18 ($M = 15.6$, $SD = 0.98$) with 50 identifying as Female, 119 as Male, and 1 as other. Originally, 181 students were recruited for this study, however participants were removed due to incomplete data or issues during data collection.

## 5.2   Experimental Procedure

Upon arrival to the classroom, participants provided signed informed parental consent forms in exchange for login information unique to each individual student. Participants were then directed to their computer stations and asked to navigate to a website which hosts the game, Crystal Island (see Crystal Island section). Upon logging in, participants were asked to complete several pre-task questionnaires including one on demographics and a 17-item multiple-choice quiz on microbiology knowledge. When the pre-task questionnaires were complete, the game automatically started. Participants were given 60 min to complete the game by providing the correct solution to the game objectives. Participants who did not complete the game after 60 min were asked to go directly to the post-task questionnaires without completing the game. The post-task questionnaires included a 17-item multiple-choice microbiology quiz that was similar to, not identical, to the quiz administered pre-task. Upon completion of the post-task questionnaires, participants were thanked for their time and told to wait for their teacher's dismissal.

### 5.3 Crystal Island

Crystal Island [6, 12, 37] is a game-based learning environment that promotes microbiology domain knowledge. During this game, participants are given two goals: (1) learn as much as they can about microbiology; and (2) complete the objective. The objective of the game is to identify a mysterious illness that is infecting researchers on a virtual island including its transmission source and treatment. To achieve these goals, participants can engage in several actions that allow them to gather information about the possible illnesses and the symptomology of infected virtual researchers, generate hypotheses about the illness, and test hypotheses. These actions include reading books and research articles, viewing posters, talking with non-player characters, testing emerging understanding of microbiology by completing concept matrices, gathering food items that could be the transmission source, scanning food items for specific diseases, and using the diagnostic worksheet to synthesize information provided by the environment.

### 5.4 Coding and Scoring

**Learning Outcomes**. Two learning outcomes were identified within this study. The first, learning gains, uses participants' pre- and post-test knowledge scores on microbiology to calculate the differences between these scores while accounting for prior knowledge [55]. Learning gains was interpreted as the degree to which participants learned about microbiology with crystal island. This metric was examined within Research Question 1. The second learning outcome was identified as game success, examined throughout all Research Questions. This was a binary code in which participants either successfully completed Crystal Island by identifying the correct illness affecting island inhabitants ($N = 72$) or did not successfully complete the game ($N = 98$). We used participants' game success as a grouping variable to be able to understand the differences in participants' complexity metrics depending on if the participant successfully completed the game or did not successfully complete the game.

**Scientific Reasoning Actions**. The order in which participants edited the worksheet, submitted the worksheet, opened books, research articles, and posters, started dialogue with an NPC, scanned food items for diseases, and completed concept matrices were identified using log files as participants played Crystal Island. These are identified as scientific reasoning actions as all actions participants could enact contribute to participants' information gathering, hypothesis generation, and hypothesis testing [23].

**Indices of Complexity**. These indices were estimated using categorical auto-recurrence Quantification Analysis (aRQA; [48]) which outputted several metrics to identify the degree of complexity a system demonstrates. The three indices of complexity were identified as entropy, trapping time, and recurrence rate. Entropy indicates the extent to which a system is predictable where a greater entropy score indicates a system demonstrates less predictable and more complex behaviors. Trapping time estimates the lengths of laminar structures within the aRQA matrix where greater laminarity indicates greater signal constancy, i.e., more stable behaviors. Finally, recurrence rate is a measure of the ratio of recurrent to novel behaviors where the greater the recurrence rate, the greater system repetition.

# 6 Results

## 6.1 Research Question 1: To What Extent Do Learners' Indices of Complexity in Their Scientific Reasoning Actions Relate to Their Learning Outcomes?

First, we wanted to understand if learning gains significantly differed between learners who were successful in solving Crystal Island and those who were unsuccessful. A t-test revealed no significant differences in learning gains between learners who were successful in solving the mystery ($N = 98$; $M = 0.08$, $SD = 0.32$) and those who were unsuccessful ($N = 72$; $M = 0.04$, $SD = 0.38$; $t(164.2) = 0.82$, $p > .05$).

We then wanted to know if learning gains were related to the various indices of complexity. Pearson's correlations revealed no significant relationship between learning gains and indices of complexity, including recurrence rate, entropy, and trapping time. In relation to the learning outcome of game success, a t-test was conducted for each of the three indices of complexity to identify the differences between those who were successful and those who were unsuccessful in solving the mystery. While analyses revealed no significant differences in entropy and trapping time ($p > 0.05$), participants who successfully solved the mystery had lower recurrence rates ($M = 18.8$, $SD = 1.95$) than those who were unsuccessful ($M = 21.8$, $SD = 4.24$; $t(144.6) = -6.27$, $p < 0.01$). This indicates that participants who are less successful in solving the mystery demonstrate greater repetition in their scientific reasoning actions.

## 6.2 Research Question 2: How Does the Emergence of Recurrent Scientific Reasoning Actions Account for the Variation of Emerging Complexity Within and Between Learners?

Two-level multilevel quadratic growth models analyzed our hierarchically structured data with observations (i.e., level 1; $N = 13371$) nested within individual learners (i.e., level 2; $N = 170$) where each learner had approximately 62.5 observations on average (Range: 10–158). An unconditional means model (Model 1) was estimated first, producing an intraclass correlation (ICC) coefficient of 0.51. ICC is a metric of the degree of variation within and between groups (i.e., learners; [56]). In the current study, 51% of the variation in the cumulative recurrence rate is between learners, with 49% of variation in recurrence rate within learners. The high ICC within this model validates our use of a multilevel modelling approach, avoiding Type 1 errors [56]. To examine the extent to which increasing time intervals (i.e., iterations) accounts for the variation in the grouping structure, an unconditional growth model (Model 2) was estimated and compared to Model 1.

Model 2 includes the iteration of aRQA recalculation as a level-1 predictor of learners' recurrence rate (see Eq. 1). According to this model, the average recurrence rate of participants' initial calculation, i.e., after they enacted 10 scientific reasoning actions, is 34.4 ($t(199.1) = 92.5$, $p < 0.001$) and decreases by approximately 0.30 for every unit increase in iteration (i.e., recalculation of recurrence rate after every additional action; $t(13226.03) = -51.0$, $p < 0.001$). This model produced an ICC coefficient of 0.64, indicating that the degree of variation between learners is better explained by including iteration as a level-1 predictor of cumulative recurrence rate. A chi-square test was conducted to compare Models 1 and 2 which found that Model 2 (AIC $= 72384$, BIC $= 72422$, $D = 72374$) was significantly better than Model 1 (AIC $= 81181$, BIC $= 81204$, $D = 81175$; $X^2(2) = 8801.4$, $p < 0.001$), indicated by lower AIC and BIC scores in Model 2. From these models, we can see that as participants engaged in increasingly more scientific reasoning actions, cumulative recurrence rates decreased.

$$\text{Model 2} : Y_{ti} = \pi_{0i} + \pi_{1i}(Iteration) + \pi_{2i}(Iteration)^2 + e_{ti} \tag{1}$$

$$\pi_{0i} = \beta_{00} + r_0$$
$$\pi_{1i} = \beta_{10}$$
$$\pi_{2i} = \beta_{20}$$

### 6.3 Research Question 3: To What Extent is the Emergence of Recurrent Scientific Reasoning Actions Related to Learning Outcomes?

Three additional models were calculated to include the maximum number of iterations for each participant, their learning gains, and success in solving the mystery. While learning gains (Model 3) and the number of iterations (Model 4), nor their cross-effects with level-1 predictors, were not significant predictors of participants' cumulative recurrence rate, there was a significant effect of learners' success in solving the mystery on cumulative recurrence rate (Model 5), following the relationships identified in Research Question 1. Specifically, participants who successfully completed the mystery had significantly lower recurrence rates during the first iteration ($M = 36.1$, $SD = 7.13$) than participants who did not complete the game ($M = 36.8$, $SD = 12.66$; $t(172.0) = -2.78$, $p = .01$). To examine the extent to which participants who were successful in solving the mystery demonstrated emergence of recurrence rate in their scientific reasoning actions differently than participants who were unsuccessful, cross-level interaction effects were examined between iteration and success predictors (Model 6, final model; see Eq. 2).

$$\text{Model 6} : Y_{ti} = \pi_{0i} + \pi_{1i}(Iteration) + \pi_{2i}(Iteration)^2 + e_{ti} \tag{2}$$

$$\pi_{0i} = \beta_{00} + r_0$$

$$\pi_{1i} = \beta_{10}$$
$$\pi_{2i} = \beta_{20} + \beta_{21}(Success)$$

While the main effect of success became insignificant (i.e., the differences in the recurrence rate at the initial iteration of the estimation became negligible), this model found that as iteration increased, cumulative recurrence rates decreased at a slower rate for participants who were successful in solving the mystery than learners who were not successful ($t(13247.5) = -9.80, p < 0.01$; see Fig. 1).

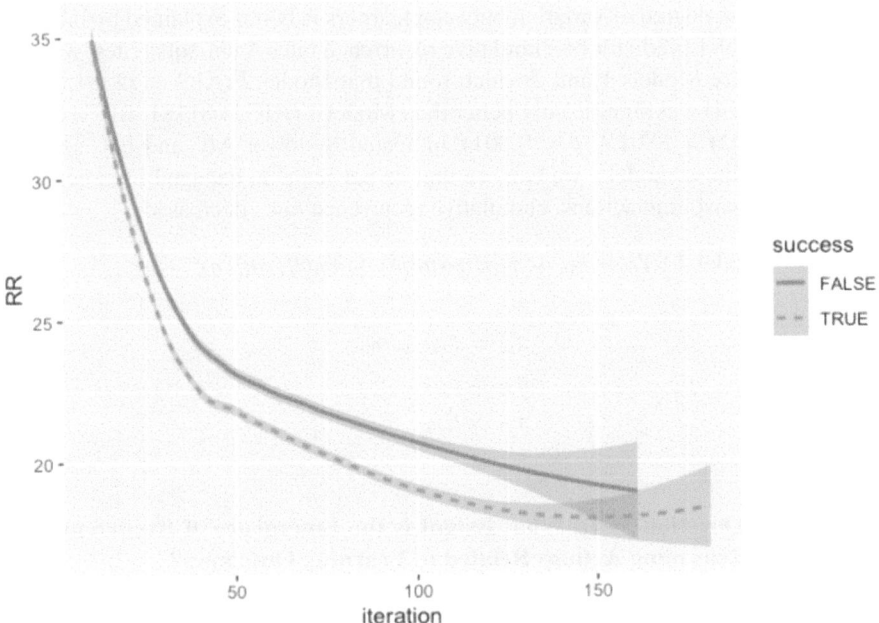

**Fig. 1.** Graph depicting participants' cumulative recurrence rate over time between groups of participants who were successful and unsuccessful in completing the game.

## 7 Discussion

The goal of this paper was to quantify the extent to which learners' use of scientific reasoning actions during game-based learning demonstrated emerging complexity and how this related to learning outcomes in terms of increased domain knowledge and learners' success in using accurate scientific reasoning skills to achieve the science GBLE objectives. The first research question asked to what extent learners' indices of complexity (i.e., recurrence rate, entropy, laminarity) were related to learning outcomes. Results showed that while learners who were successful in completing the game did not significantly differ in their learning gains compared to learners who were not successful and learning gains were not correlated to any indices of complexity, learners who successfully completed the game demonstrated lower overall recurrence rates than learners who were unsuccessful. In other words, learners who were able to accurately use scientific reasoning skills to complete the game demonstrated lower repetition of scientific reasoning actions throughout gameplay. This means that learners who demonstrate fewer repetitive scientific reasoning actions have a greater self-regulatory ability in mitigating the number of times they engage in repetitious behaviors, producing better learning outcomes. This partially confirms our hypothesis and follows prior studies [6, 54] in which a more functional system, denoted by game success, demonstrates lower recurrence or repetition of scientific reasoning actions. This may be attributed to learners' understanding of how to engage in scientific reasoning as well as confidence in engaging with the different actions within the game environment. Future studies should capture learners' scientific reasoning abilities as well as learners' confidence in engaging in scientific reasoning prior to them engaging with a GBLE that requires learners to deploy these abilities.

The second research question examined how cumulative recurrence rates changed over time and the extent to which the differences in the change of rates is attributed to individual-level characteristics rather than variability within learners. Results showed that the majority of variation in the cumulative recurrence rate is between learners, demonstrating a need to account for individual-level characteristics that significantly affect how learners engage in a balance of repetitious and novel scientific reasoning actions. Further, results showed that generally as learners engage in increasingly more actions, cumulative recurrence rate decreases over time. This was expected as time on game progresses, increasingly more actions were available to learners and more non-repetitious actions executed sequentially were required to complete the game (e.g., scan food item, open worksheet to report scan results, talk with a non-player character to submit the final diagnosis to end the game). In other words, at the beginning of learners' time in game, there are fewer opportunities for learners to engage in scientific reasoning actions where these opportunities become more available as they explored the environment.

The third research question added individual-level characteristics of learning outcomes to see how learning gains and success in completing the game explained the variability in learners' rate of change in cumulative recurrence rates. Similar to the findings in the first research question, learning gains was not a significant factor in accounting for the variability between and within learners' recurrence rates. However, learners who were successful in completing the game demonstrated a slower decrease in their cumulative recurrence rates. This result is interpreted as learners who were unsuccessful in accurately using scientific reasoning skills to complete the game objective demonstrated a rapid, dramatic shift in the repetition of scientific reasoning actions. As such, we conclude that *functional scientific reasoning characterizes a slower, controlled approach to individual learners' recurrence rate means rather than a rapid shift from repetitive to novel patterns of scientific reasoning actions.*

The results from the second and third research questions follow the far-from-equilibrium concept in which functional systems are characterized by a balance between novel and repetitive system behavior (i.e., collection of actions), confirming our hypotheses. The results from this paper extend the far-from-equilibrium concept to include time as an essential component of how a system demonstrates functional behavior. Specifically, not only is it the overall balance between novel and repetitive actions that characterize a functional system but the rapidity in which the system establishes this equilibrium.

## 8   Conclusion and Future Directions

Complex system theory (CST) emerges as a powerful and versatile framework for studying scientific reasoning within GBLEs, providing advantages across theoretical, empirical, methodological, and analytical dimensions. Its theoretical strength is its ability to capture dynamic learning systems' intricate interactions and feedback loops. Game-based learning environments are inherently complex, featuring multiple components and emergent properties that can best be captured within the assumptions of CST. Complex system theory offers a holistic perspective, allowing researchers to grasp the interconnectedness of various elements influencing scientific reasoning and, therefore, extend traditional approaches that focus on static measures and fail to integrate the dynamics of learner-system interactions during complex learning.

Empirically, complex system theory facilitates examining non-linear relationships and the emergence of patterns within learners' interactions. It accommodates the unpredictable nature of game-based learning, enabling the exploration of how diverse factors, processes, and mechanisms contribute to the development of scientific reasoning skills over time. Methodologically, the framework accommodates the dynamic nature of game-based learning environments, emphasizing the importance of longitudinal studies to capture evolving complexities while generating new indices that significantly augment our understanding of the dynamics of GBLEs. This aligns well with scientific reasoning skill acquisition's gradual and cumulative nature.

Analytically, complex system theory offers sophisticated tools to model and interpret intricate relationships within the learning system. It enables researchers to identify critical leverage points for instructional interventions, optimizing the design of game-based learning experiences. Lastly, complex system theory enhances our understanding of scientific reasoning in game-based learning environments, fostering a more nuanced and comprehensive approach to educational research and practice.

In terms of future directions, generative AI holds immense potential in transforming self-regulated learning, particularly in game-based learning, by tracing learners' emerging complexity of scientific reasoning actions. GBLEs provide a dynamic platform where students can engage in authentic, problem-solving scenarios, fostering the development of critical thinking and scientific reasoning skills. Generative AI can play a pivotal role by continuously monitoring and analyzing learners' interactions within these digital systems. For example, by employing advanced algorithms, generative AI can decipher the intricate patterns of students' scientific reasoning as they navigate through challenges and make decisions within the game. This real-time analysis allows for a comprehensive understanding of the learners' cognitive and metacognitive processes and identifies areas of strength and weakness based on emerging complexity indices. Subsequently, the AI can generate personalized recommendations or pedagogical interventions tailored to individual learners, such as when to prompt learners to attempt novel behaviors and explain why it is an opportune time to attempt novel behaviors, depending on a myriad of trace data and behaviors that may be indicative to self-efficacy in using scientific reasoning actions. These recommendations may include targeted feedback, additional learning resources, or adaptive challenges to scaffold the development of scientific reasoning skills.

Moreover, generative AI can adapt to the evolving complexity of learners' cognitive abilities and metacognitive skills, ensuring that instructional interventions are timely and aligned with the learners' progression. This adaptability enhances the efficiency of self-regulated learning, as learners receive targeted support precisely when needed. Ultimately, the integration of generative AI in GBLEs empowers learners to take control of their educational pathways in open-ended learning environments, fostering a more personalized and effective approach to developing scientific reasoning skills.

**Acknowledgments.** This study was supported by funding from the National Science Foundation (DUE#1761178 and DRL#1661202) and the Social Sciences and Humanities Research Council of Canada (SSHRC 895–2011–1006). The authors would like to thank members of the SMART Lab at UCF and the IntelliMEDIA Group at North Carolina State University for their contributions.

**Disclosure of Interests**  The authors have no competing interests to declare that are relevant to the content of this article.

# References

1. Van Vo, D., Csapó, B.: Exploring inductive reasoning, scientific reasoning and science motivation, and their role in predicting STEM achievement across grade levels. Int. J. Sci. Math. Educ. **21**, 1–24 (2023)
2. Hossain, T., Iv, R. L. L., Ugarte, A., Matsubara, Y., Young, S., Singh, S.: COVIDLies: detecting COVID-19 misinformation on social media. In: Verspoor, K., Cohen, K.B., Conway, M., de Bruijn, B., Dredze, M., Mihalcea, R., Wallace, B. (eds.) 1st Workshop on NLP for COVID-19 (PART 2) at EMNLP 2020, Association for Computational Linguistics, Online (2020)
3. Reyna, V.F., Edelson, S.M., Broniatowski, D.A.: Misconceptions, misinformation, and moving forward in theories of COVID-19 risky behaviors. J. Appl. Res. Mem. Cogn. **10**, 537–541 (2021)
4. Perillat, L., Baigrie, B.S.: COVID-19 and the generation of novel scientific knowledge: evidence-based decisions and data sharing. J. Eval. Clin. Pract. **27**(3), 708–715 (2021)
5. Chen, Y.C., Lu, Y.L., Lien, C.J.: Learning environments with different levels of technological engagement: a comparison of game-based, video-based, and traditional instruction on students' learning. Interact. Learn. Environ. **29**, 1363–1379 (2021)
6. Dever, D.A., Amon, M.J., Vrzakova, H., Wiedbusch, M.D., Cloude, E.B., Azevedo, R.: Capturing sequences of learners self-regulatory interactions with instructional material during game-based learning using auto-recurrence quantification analysis. Front. Psychol. **13**, 813677 (2022)
7. Lester, J.C., Spires, H.A., Nietfeld, J.L., Minogue, J., Mott, B.W., Lobene, E.V.: Designing game-based learning environments for elementary science education: a narrative-centered learning perspective. Inf. Sci. **264**, 4–18 (2014)

8. Nietfeld, J.L.: Predicting transfer from a game-based learning environment. Comput. Educ. **146**, 103780 (2020)

9. Carpenter, D., Cloude, E., Rowe, J., Azevedo, R., Lester, J.: Investigating student reflection during game-based learning in middle grades science. In: Scheffel, M., Dowell, N., Joksimovic, S., Siemens, G. (eds.) Proceedings of the 11th International Learning Analytics and Knowledge Conference, pp. 280–291. ACM, New York, NY (2021)

10. Cheng, M.T., Huang, W.Y., Hsu, M.E.: Does emotion matter? An investigation into the relationship between emotions and science learning outcomes in a game-based learning environment. Br. J. Edu. Technol. **51**, 2233–2251 (2020)

11. Cloude, E.B., Dever, D.A., Wiedbusch, M.D., Azevedo, R.: Quantifying scientific thinking using multichannel data with Crystal Island: Implications for individualized game-learning analytics. Front. Educ. **5** (2020). https://doi.org/10.3389/feduc.2020.572546

12. Taub, M., Sawyer, R., Lester, J., Azevedo, R.: The impact of contextualized emotions on self-regulated learning and scientific reasoning during learning with a game-based learning environment. Int. J. Artif. Intell. Educ. **30**, 97–120 (2020)

13. Plass, J.L., Homer, B.D., Mayer, R.E., Kinzer, C.K.: Theoretical Foundations of Game-Based and Playful Learning. The MIT Press, Cambridge, MA (2019)

14. Engelmann, K., Neuhaus, B.J., Fischer, F.: Fostering scientific reasoning in education—meta-analytic evidence from intervention studies. Educ. Res. Eval. **22**, 333–349 (2016)

15. National Research Council: Next Generation Science Standards: for States, by States. The National Academies Press (2013)

16. Organisation for Economic Co-operation and Development (OECD): Trends Shaping Education 2022. OECD Publishing, Paris (2022). https://doi.org/10.1787/6ae8771a-en

17. de Jong, T.: Moving towards engaged learning in STEM domains; there is no simple answer, but clearly a road ahead. J. Comput. Assist. Learn. **35**, 153–167 (2019). https://doi.org/10.1111/jcal.12337

18. Freeman, S., et al.: Active learning increases student performance in science, engineering, and mathematics. Psychol. Cogn. Sci. **111**(23), 8410–8415 (2014). https://doi.org/10.1073/pnas.1319030111

19. Kober, N.: Reaching Students: What Research Says About Effective Instruction in Undergraduate Science and Engineering. The National Academies Press, National Academies (2015)

20. Greene, J.A., Anderson, J.L., O'Malley, C.E., Lobczowksi, N.G.: Fostering self-regulated science inquiry in physical sciences. In: DiBenedetto, M.K. (ed.) Connecting Self-regulated Learning and Performance with Instruction Across High School Content Areas, pp. 163–183. Springer International Publishing (2015). https://doi.org/10.1007/978-3-319-90928-8_6

21. Omarchevska, Y., Lachner, A., Richter, J., Scheiter, K.: It takes two to tango: how scientific reasoning and self-regulation processes impact argumentation quality. J. Learn. Sci. **31**, 237–277 (2022)

22. Wallace, C.S., Coffey, D.J.: Investigating elementary preservice teachers designs for integrated science/literacy instruction highlighting similar cognitive processes. J. Sci. Teacher Educ. **30**, 507–527 (2019)

23. Klahr, D., Dunbar, K.: Dual space search during scientific reasoning. Cogn. Sci. **12**, 1–48 (1988)

24. Zimmerman, C.: The development of scientific thinking skills in elementary and middle school. Dev. Rev. **27**(2), 172–223 (2007). https://doi.org/10.1016/j.dr.2006.12.001

25. De Groof, J., Donche, V., Van Petegem, P.: Onderzoekend Leren Stimuleren: Effecten, Maatregelen en Principes [Stimulating Learning by Inquiry: Effects, Measures and Principles]. Leuven, Belgium: Acco (2012)

26. Janssen, E., Depaepe, F., Claes, E., Elen, J.: Fostering students scientific reasoning skills in secondary education: an intervention study. Int. J. Sci., Math. Technol. Learn. **26**, 1–19 (2019). https://doi.org/10.18848/2327-7971/CGP/v26i01/1-19

27. Fischer, F., Kollar, I., Ufer, S., Sodian, B., Hussmann, H., Pekrun, R., et al.: Scientific reasoning and argumentation: advancing an interdisciplinary research agenda in education. Front. Learn. Res. **2**(3), 28–45 (2014)

28. Van Mil, M.H.W., Postma, P.A., Boerwinkel, D.J., Klaassen, K., Waarlo, A.J.: Molecular mechanistic reasoning: toward bridging the gap between the molecular and cellular levels in life science education. Sci. Educ. **100**, 517–585 (2016). https://doi.org/10.1002/sce.21215

29. Woolley, J.S., et al.: Undergraduate students demonstrate common false scientific reasoning strategies. Thinking Skills Creativity **27**, 101–113 (2018). https://doi.org/10.1016/j.tsc.2017.12.004

30. Andersen, C., Garcia-Mila, M.: Scientific reasoning during inquiry: teaching for metacognition. In: Taber, K.S., Alpan, B. (eds.) Science Education: New Directions in Mathematics and Science Education, pp. 105–117. Brill (2017). https://doi.org/10.1007/978-94-6300-749-8_8

31. Dent, A.L., Koenka, A.C.: The relation between self-regulated learning and academic achievement across childhood and adolescence: a meta-analysis. Educ. Psychol. Rev. **28**, 425–474 (2016). https://doi.org/10.1007/s10648-015-9320-8

32. Manlove, S., Lazonder, A.W., de Jong, T.: Trends and issues of regulative support use during inquiry learning: patterns from three studies. Comput. Hum. Behav. **25**, 795–803 (2009). https://doi.org/10.1016/J.CHB.2008.07.010

33. Shute, V.J., Ke, F., Almond, R.G., Rahimi, S., Smith, G., Lu, X.: How to increase learning while not decreasing the fun in educational games. In: Feldman, R. (ed.) Learning Science: Theory, Research, and Practice, pp. 327–357. McGraw Hill, New York, NY (2019)

34. Dever, D.A., Azevedo, R., Cloude, E.B., Wiedbusch, M.: The impact of autonomy and types of informational text presentations in game-based environments on learning: converging multi-channel processes data and learning outcomes. Int. J. Artif. Intell. Educ. **30**, 581–615 (2020)

35. Casanoves, M., Sole-Llussa, A., Haro, J., Gericke, N., Valls, C.: Assessment of the ability of game-based science learning to enhance genetic understanding. Res. Sci. Technol. Educ. **41**(4), 1496–1518 (2023)

36. Halpern, D.F., Millis, K., Graesser, A.C., Butler, H., Forsyth, C., Cai, Z.: Operation ARA: a computerized learning game that teaches critical thinking and scientific reasoning. Thinking Skills Creativity **7**, 93–100 (2012)

37. Rowe, J.P., Shores, L.R., Mott, B.W., Lester, J.C.: Integrating learning, problem solving, and engagement in narrative-centered learning environments. Int. J. Artif. Intell. Educ. **21**, 115–133 (2011). https://doi.org/10.3233/JAI-2011-019

38. Taub, M., Azevedo, R., Bradbury, A.E., Millar, G.C., Lester, J.: Using sequence mining to reveal the efficiency in scientific reasoning during STEM learning with a game-based learning environment. Learn. Instr. **54**, 93–103 (2018)

39. Dever, D.A., Banzon, A.M., Ballellos, N.A.M., Azevedo, R. (2021). Capturing learners interactions with multimedia science content over time during game-based learning. In: de Vries, E., Hod, Y., Ahn, J. (eds.) Proceedings of the 1st Annual conference of the International Society of the Learning Sciences (ISLS), pp. 195–202. ISLS, Online (2021)

40. Cloude, E.B., Dever, D.A., Hahs-Vaughn, D.L., Emerson, A.J., Azevedo, R., Lester, J.: Affective dynamics and cognition during game-based learning. IEEE Trans. Affect. Comput. **13**, 1705–1717 (2022)

41. Favela, L.H., Amon, M.J.: Reframing cognitive science as a complexity science. Cogn. Sci. **47**, e13280 (2023)

42. Mitchell, M.: Complexity: A Guided Tour. Oxford University Press, New York, NY (2009)

43. Francescotti, R.M.: Emergence. Erkenntnis **67**, 47–63 (2007)

44. Kelso, J.A.S.: Dynamic Patterns: The Self-organization of Brain and Behavior. MIT Press, Cambridge, MA (1995)
45. Strogatz, S.H.: Nonlinear Dynamics and Chaos: With Applications to Physics, Biology, Chemistry, and Engineering, 2nd edn. CRC Press, New York, NY, New York (2015)
46. Larsson, J., Dahlin, B.: Educating far from equilibrium: chaos philosophy and the quest for complexity in education. Complicity: Int. J. Complex. Educ. **9**(2) (2012)
47. Prigogine, I., Stengers, I.: Order Out of Chaos: Man's New Dialogue with Nature. Flamingo, London (1985)
48. Webber, C.L., Jr., Zbilut, J.P.: Recurrence quantification analysis of nonlinear dynamical systems. Tutorials Contemp. Nonlinear Methods Behav. Sci. **94**, 26–94 (2005)
49. Gibson, D., Jakl, P.: Theoretical considerations for game-based e-learning analytics. Gamification Educ. Bus. 403–416 (2015)
50. Kim, Y.J., Pavlov, O.: Game-based structural debriefing: how can teachers design game-based curricula for systems thinking? Inf. Learn. Sci. **120**(9/10), 567–588 (2019)
51. Storey, B., Butler, J.: Complexity thinking in PE: game-centered approaches, games as complex adaptive systems, and ecological values. Phys. Educ. Sport Pedagog. **18**(2), 133–149 (2013)
52. Dever, D.A., Azevedo, R.: Scaffolding self-regulated learning in game-based learning environments based on complex systems theory. In: Rodrigo, M.M., Matsuda, N., Cristea, A.I., Dimitrova, V. (eds.) International Conference on Artificial Intelligence in Education, LNCS, vol. 13356, pp. 41–46. Springer International Publishing, Cham (2022)
53. Kumar, V., Tissenbaum, M.B., Kim, T.: Procedural collaboration in educational games: Supporting complex system understandings in immersive whole class simulations. Commun. Stud. **72**(6), 994–1016 (2021)
54. Dever, D.A., Sonnenfeld, N.A., Wiedbusch, M.D., Schmorrow, G., Amon, M.J., Azevedo, R.: A complex systems approach to analyzing pedagogical agents scaffolding of self-regulated learning within an intelligent tutoring system. Metacogn. Learn. **18**, 659–691 (2023). https://doi.org/10.1007/s11409-023-09346-x
55. Marx, J.D., Cummings, K.: Normalized change. Am. J. Phys. **75**, 87–91 (2007). https://doi.org/10.1119/1.2372468
56. Musca, S.C., Kamiejski, R., Nugier, A., Méot, A., Er-Rafiy, A., Brauer, M.: Data with hierarchical structure: impact of intraclass correlation and sample size on type-I error. Front. Psychol. **2**, 74 (2011)

# Sky Dash: Evaluating the Effects of a Serious Low-Threshold Mobile Game on Learning Efficacy and User Experience in a Repetitive Learning Task

Benjamin Schnitzer[1]([✉]) [iD], Polona Caserman[2] [iD], and Oliver Korn[1] [iD]

[1] Affective and Cognitive Institute, Offenburg University, Offenburg, Germany
benjamin.schnitzer@hs-offenburg.de
[2] Serious Games Research Group, Technical University of Darmstadt, Darmstadt, Germany

**Abstract.** Training and further education are crucial for efficiency and safety in large companies. However, learning special vocabulary about dangerous goods, occupational safety, or internal codes can be tedious due to the need for repetition. Combining learning with the intrinsic motivation and fun of playing digital games, a concept known as serious games, is gaining traction with recent advancements in the gaming industry. Particularly mobile games have become popular due to their accessibility. Despite evidence of the benefits of serious games, the potentials of low-threshold mobile games in vocational training are still underexplored. In this work, we present the results of a study (n = 79) investigating the potentials of a serious low-threshold mobile game called "Sky Dash" to enhance the experience of a repetitive learning task in the context of a large company in ground logistics. We used a between-subjects design with employees working in the baggage handling at an international airport. The findings underline the users' appreciation of interactive gamified learning in comparison to non-gamified passive learning. Although participants learning with the non-gamified method performed significantly better than those using the gamified method, it is another major finding that knowledge gain among participants learning with the game was still significant between pre-, post-, and memory tests, and they reported significantly more fun.

**Keywords:** Serious games · Mobile games · Large companies · Training · Learning effectiveness · User experience

## 1 Introduction

Training and further education are essential measures in large companies, e.g., in the logistics sector, to make workflows and processes efficient and safe. However, learning descriptions for dangerous goods, measures for occupational safety and

J. L. Plass and X. Ochoa (Eds.): JCSG 2024, LNCS 15259, pp. 211–227, 2025.
https://doi.org/10.1007/978-3-031-74138-8_16

fire protection, or special knowledge such as internal codes can be boring and monotonous, as it is usually only possible with sufficient repetition. Playing is associated with joy and fun, making the idea of combining learning and playing obvious. Games' intrinsic motivation, or autotelic activity, means people engage for the sake of the activity itself [1]. In fact, the idea to leverage this motivating character to convey information and achieve goals beyond entertainment, known as serious games, is not a new concept. However, recent developments in the game industry have made serious games development even easier and more priceworthy, making them a promising approach in education. The global video game industry is a billion-dollar market. In 2022, the worldwide gaming market revenue was estimated at $347 billion, with mobile gaming generating $248 billion [2]. Thereby, the players come from all demographics and age groups. For example, by 2024, the number of US gamers is expected to surpass 200 million. Mobile games had the largest US audience, with about 163 million users [2]. With widespread mobile devices and connectivity, mobile gaming is the easiest entry into gaming. This is reflected in the popularity of casual mobile games with enduring hits like'Candy Crush', released in 2012 [2].

Evolving technologies like Virtual Reality and Head-Mounted Displays are becoming ubiquitous, offering immersive gaming and learning experiences. However, developing these applications and acquiring the hardware is costly, particularly because the hardware often cannot be used by multiple people at once [3]. Moreover, mobile games can be played nearly everywhere, traditional gaming hardware and immersive technologies generally need a static setup. While there is evidence in the literature regarding the positive effects of serious games and simulations [4] and the potentials of gamified processes in vocational contexts [5], surprisingly the potentials of low-threshold mobile games are fairly unexplored. Regarding their popularity, the latter particularly appear to be a promising opportunity for large companies to make repetitive training processes more entertaining and fun. Given the outlined gap, this work investigated the potentials of serious low-threshold mobile games for large companies by examining the following research questions:

**RQ1:** How effective is a serious low-threshold mobile game for learning technical terminologies?

**RQ2:** What are the effects of a serious low-threshold mobile game for learning technical terminologies on the user experience?

We define serious low-threshold mobile games as digital games for mobile devices (smartphones or tablets) that offer low entry barriers due to their accessibility and with a learning objective that is an integral part of the game itself. In this way, they also enable learning on the go. To investigate these questions, we developed a serious mobile game called "Sky Dash" in cooperation with a large logistics company and as part of the baggage handler training program at one of the world's largest international airports. The special knowledge that baggage handlers have to learn includes the so-called 3-Letter-Codes, which consist of three letters and are associated with a specific international airport. While some codes, such as BER for Berlin, are simple and obvious, there are others, such as YYZ for Toronto, that do not follow any logic. Thus, they simply have to be learned by heart. We conducted a user study with 79 employees by comparing our interactive gamified learning method with a passive non-gamified method and to evaluate the following hypothesis regarding learning efficacy:

**H1.1:** A serious low-threshold mobile game is an effective learning method for learning repetitive technical terminologies.

Regarding user experience, the following hypotheses are investigated:

**H2.1:** A serious low-threshold mobile game has a positive effect on fun.
**H2.2:** It has an intensifying effect on loss of time.
**H2.3:** It has a positive effect on focus.
**H2.4:** It has a positive effect on perceived feedback.
**H2.5:** It has a positive effect on self-efficacy.
**H2.6:** It has a positive effect on flow.
**H2.7:** It has a positive effect on the overall user experience.

## 2   Related Work

In a review by Wouters et al. [6], investigating 28 studies with empirical data regarding the effectiveness of serious games compared to other learning approaches, the authors conclude that serious games generally improve the acquisition of knowledge and cognitive skills. A meta analysis over 39 studies, again by Wouters et al. [7] shows that serious games were more effective in terms of learning and retention but are not more motivating than conventional instruction methods. These findings contradict the results of a systematic review by Connolly et al. [8] with 129 papers reporting empirical evidence on the effects of computer games and serious games. The authors reported a range of positive perceptual, cognitive, behavioral, affective and motivational impacts and outcomes [8]. In an updated review by Boyle et al. [9], the authors reported the most frequently occurring outcome reported for games for learning was knowledge acquisition, while entertainment games addressed a broader range of affective, behavior change, perceptual and cognitive and physiological outcomes.

More recent research by Barz et al. [10] revealed a significant medium effect for overall learning and cognitive learning outcomes as well as a small effect for affective-motivational learning outcomes. Another review by Hung et al. [11] highlights the positive effects of digital game-based language learning on affective or psychological states, closely followed by language acquisition. Regarding the huge popularity of mobile games, to the best of our knowledge, there is little empirical evidence about their effects. To conclude, the majority of research has shown that serious games are effective, e.g. in the area of health education [12], or to improve the reading performance of children with disorders [13]. Gamified solutions were even found to be beneficial for mitigating social isolation and loneliness [14]. Although there is empirical evidence for the impacts of serious games on vocabulary and content learning [15], the effects of serious mobile games on content requiring repetition, such as vocabulary training, remain relatively unexplored.

A notable example of successful vocabulary training is the game "Vocabicar", which won the German Award for Computer Games "Best Serious Game" in 2018 [16]. In "Vocabicar", players search for letters and words as a miniature vehicle in an oversized classroom. This approach motivates the repetitive task of classic memorization while maintaining a modular structure. Additionally, it is available as a mobile application, providing a low-threshold solution accessible to a large audience without the need for expensive or high-maintenance hardware. While literature has investigated the effects of simulations and Virtual Reality on learning in vocational contexts [17,18], the effects of low-threshold serious games like Vocabicar for learning repetitive content such as descriptions for dangerous goods, measures for occupational safety and fire protection, or special knowledge like internal codes remain unexplored.

At the same time, there is indication for gamification, the use of elements from game design to improve user experience and user engagement in non-game contexts, to be a promising method to increase engagement and motivation among employees [19]. Recently, Caserman et al. investigated intergenerational disparities in the acceptance of gamification in large companies. Interestingly, "minigames" introducing the facts about a company, such as the true-or-false minigame or Vocabicar, were generally appreciated by the participants, but most accepted by Generation Z. Moreover, Generation Z, now entering the labor market, also believes that such a game can be successfully used to integrate new employees into a company [5]. The potential shown and the lack of empirical evidence for the use of mobile games encouraged us to conduct the following study.

## 3    Methods

To investigate the stated hypotheses we conducted a user study (n = 79) using a between-subjects design with two groups. We developed an interactive application for mobile devices in the Unity engine as a gamified method (in the following called group $B_{gamified}$) to learn the 3-Letter-Codes and compared it to a passive non-gamified learning method (in the following called group $A_{non\text{-}gamified}$) by watching a standardized video. The aim of the serious mobile game "Sky Dash" is to hit the correct one of three 3-Letter-Codes with an aircraft. The 3-Letter-Codes appear randomly ordered on the horizon and fly towards the player (Fig. 1). The aircraft is controlled either by changing position and rotation of the mobile device or by a small UI joystick in the right corner of the screen. In the following, we first describe the essential elements of the game and subsequently describe applied measures as well as the overall procedure.

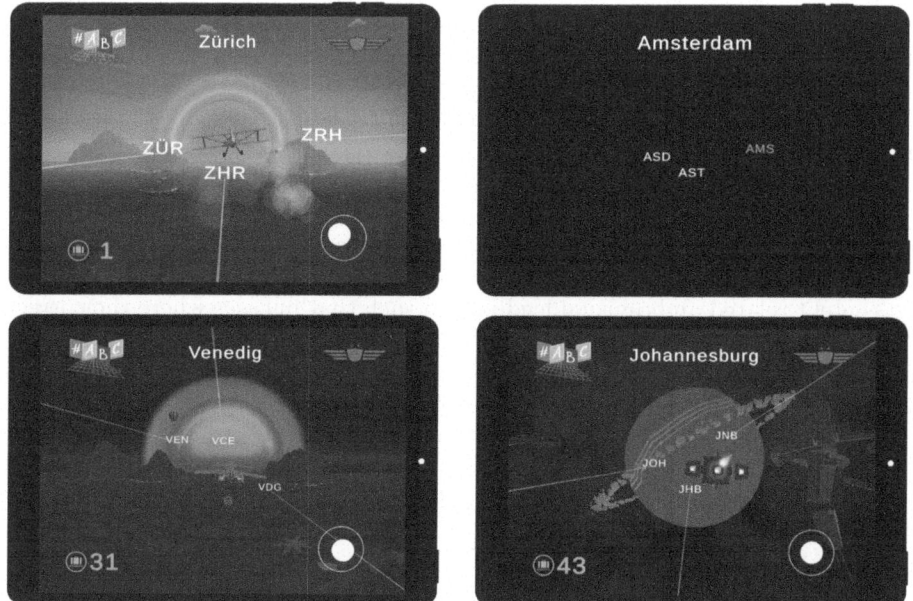

**Fig. 1.** Top left: level 1 of "Sky Dash" group $B_{\text{gamified}}$. Top right: excerpt of the video of group $A_{\text{non-gamified}}$. Bottom left and right: level progression with different machines and level designs group $B_{\text{gamified}}$.

## 3.1    Characterizing Goal

Following the definition of serious games by [20], we focused on incorporating attractive and effective elements, embedding the characterizing goal into game-play, and ensuring that learning tasks are integrated within game elements. On the more general level of competence domains [21] and following the classification by [22], the game trains several cognitive and perceptual competences, stress control and endurance, as well as sensory-motor competences such as reaction time. In the context of literacy training, the latter is closely related to rapid automatized naming and the ability to identify and process familiar symbol sequences as quickly as possible. This ability is critical in the daily work of baggage handlers. Regarding game design and to create a joyful experience, we used the following game elements and mechanics.

## 3.2    Game Elements and Mechanics

Similar to vocabulary learning, repetition is a critical factor for learning the 3-Letter-Codes. We consciously chose an endless runner as a game type which includes repetitive elements and simultaneously challenges the players' reaction time. To instantiate a triplet of 3-Letter-Codes consisting of one correct code and two wrong codes, the game references a list of shortcuts in a .json file. The structure of this list is shown in the Appendix. To ensure comparability with the non-gamified learning group, the sequence of codes was not randomized. The algorithm iterates linearly through the list of 3-Letter-Codes to instantiate the triplets at runtime and starts again with the first triplet as soon as the last of the list has been reached.

The characterizing dynamic of an endless runner is pure progression. It is thus essential to present this progression in terms of visual feedback and dedicated mechanics such as varying challenge and competition. For "Sky Dash", feedback is mainly achieved with the help of two components: points represented by a score and content related audio-visual feedback in such that in cases where the correct 3-Letter-Code is hit, the score increases, auditive feedback is given (cheering and applause), and a green thumbs-up pictogram is displayed. Conversely, in cases where a wrong 3-Letter-Code is hit, the score decreases, auditive feedback is given (a long spoken "no" implying a poor performance), and a red thumbs-down pictogram is displayed. Additionally, the missed correct 3-Letter-Code is marked in green and the game runs in slow-motion for the next two seconds. This was done to ensure that the direct feedback is noticed and can lead to knowledge gain in the next cycle.

Moreover, the score influences the level which influences the appearance of the player's aircraft in turn. Higher scores lead to different flying machines such as helicopters or spacecraft (Fig. 1). Additionally, the appearance of the surrounding environment is influenced by the score, e.g. the spacecraft is flying through space. A higher level also leads to increased difficulty in terms of speed of the approaching 3-Letter-Codes. Finally, a badge in the upper right corner of the screen visualizes the overall medium-term progress. While lower scores (e.g., < 20 points) lead to a bronze badge, medium scores (e.g., > 30 points) lead to a silver badge, and highscores (e.g., > 100 points) lead to a gold badge (Fig. 1).

### 3.3    Participants

We recruited 79 people from a large international airport with more than 80,000 employees in Germany. Since baggage handling departments in ground logistics are dominated by men, there were 78 male and only one female participant. All participants were between 18 and 60 years old. Since the company could not predict which participants would attend the individual evaluation sessions, participants were assigned to one of the two groups on an alternating, quasi-randomised basis on the day of the assessment. All subjects were recently hired and had just started a ground logistics training program at the time of the evaluation. Thus they had no prior knowledge of the 3-Letter-Codes. The company enabled the subjects to participate during working hours, which is why all participants received remuneration in the form of their wages. As the authors have learned from the company, the training program also includes language courses as many employees have a migration background and thus have low language skills, too. It was therefore necessary to (1) make the information presented in the game as clear as possible and only show essential text information, and (2) not to overwhelm the participants with the overall evaluation in terms of long questionnaires. The applied measures are described in the next section.

## 3.4 Measures

We employed both, objective assessments with the help of simple metrics and subjective assessments as self-reported questionnaires. To assess the general learning efficacy we employed a pre-test, post-test, and a memory test measuring the number of correct answers. Similar to the game, participants had to choose an option in a multiple choice test evaluating the knowledge of 23 predefined 3-Letter-Codes. Hence, a maximum of 23 correct choices was possible.

To assess the overall user experience, we created a questionnaire consisting of seven items on a Likert-Scale from 1 (strongly disagree) to 5 (strongly agree) which was additionally asked as part of the post-test assessment. Two items were adapted from the established Game Experience Questionnaire [23]. The other four items were created for ease of use considering [1, 24–26]. Table 1 shows the seven items.

**Table 1.** Items 1–7 used in the post-test questionnaire. Items 4, 5 and 7 are independent indicators for focus, feedback and loss of time. Items 4–7 are part of the flow construct. All items 1–7 form the overall user experience score

| No. | Item | Construct | References |
|---|---|---|---|
| 1 | The learning exercise was fun | Joy/UX | [23] |
| 2 | I know the 3-Letter-Codes | Knowledge/Self-Efficacy/UX | [26] |
| 3 | I think that I will be able to solve this task well in the future | Future Knowledge/Self-Efficacy/UX | [26] |
| 4 | I was fully concentrating on the task (game) | Focus/Flow/UX | [23, 25] |
| 5 | I was aware of the progress I was making | Feedback/Flow/UX | [23, 24] |
| 6 | I was challenged, but I could handle the challenge well | Challenge/Flow/UX | [1, 23, 24] |
| 7 | I thought about how long the task (game) would take | Loss of Time/Flow/UX | [24, 25] |

Individual scores for user experience, self-efficacy, and flow are computed as simple means of the corresponding items. Moreover, to better understand the employees' opinions and to get some qualitative feedback, we conducted two short focus group discussions with 3 participants each from groups $A_{\text{non-gamified}}$ and $B_{\text{gamified}}$ after the post-test. We asked questions like why they liked or disliked the learning method or what could have been done differently. These discussions were recorded.

## 3.5 Procedure

The study took place between July 2023 and April 2024 in training classrooms of the airport company and consisted of two sessions. Before the start, we explained the purpose and procedure of the study with the help of a standardized written text and assured the confidentiality of data which was only used in anonymized form. We employed a between-subjects design with two groups. While group $A_{\text{non-gamified}}$ learned the 3-Letter-Codes with a non-gamified method, group $B_{\text{gamified}}$ learned the codes by playing "Sky Dash" as the gamified training method. To standardize the non-gamified learning method and to ensure a temporal alignment with exposure times of the game, group $A_{\text{non-gamified}}$ learned the 3-Letter-Codes by watching a pre-rendered video. Similar to the game, the actual destination was shown on the top, while three 3-Letter-Codes appeared randomly positioned in the distance and approached the screen. The correct 3-Letter-Code was marked in green. However, no additional information was shown on the black screen and no auditive feedback was given. Figure 6 in the appendix shows extracts of the video.

In summary, the independent variable is the gamification level categorized by a non-gamfied and a gamified learning method. The dependent variables are learning efficacy (immediate and medium-term effect) and game experience consisting of the subcategories joy, self-efficacy, focus, flow, feedback, and loss of time. The characterizing differences regarding gamification level thus are (1) the degree of interactivity and proactive decisions combined with sensory-motor activity. And (2), the degree of visualized progression and feedback.

After subjects had given their written consent, the pre-test was conducted on a tablet device. Participants had a maximum of 10 min to complete this test before starting the actual training phase. While group $A_{\text{non-gamified}}$ immediately started to watch the training video on the mobile device, group $B_{\text{gamified}}$ were given a 3 min pre-training phase to familiarize with the game and its controls. In this phase the game was referencing a shortcut list with 3-Letter-Codes differing from the list of the following 10 min training phase. After the training phase, subjects were asked to conduct the post-test. Finally, participants came in for a second session 24 h after the post-test to conduct the memory test. Figure 2 shows the overall procedure of study.

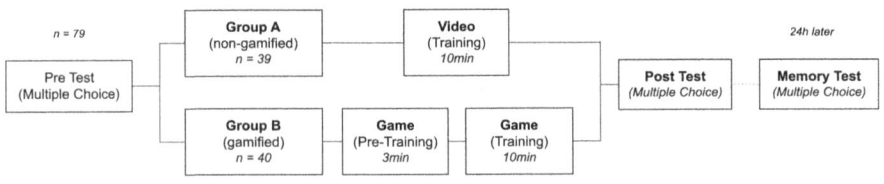

**Fig. 2.** Overall study design.

## 4  Results

In this section, we first describe the results on learning efficacy by comparing the results of the pre-, post-, and memory tests. Then we report the results of the questionnaire. Results of Shapiro-Wilk tests indicated non-normally distributed data for both the number of correct 3-Letter-Codes and the answers of the questionnaire. Therefore, we used non-parametric Friedman tests and pairwise Wilcoxon post-hoc tests including Bonferroni correction to evaluate possible differences between pre-, post-, and memory tests and Mann-Whitney-U tests to evaluate possible differences between the two learning groups regarding game experience and knowledge gain. Furthermore, we calculated the effect sizes for the paired Wilcoxon post-hoc and Mann-Whitney-U tests using Cohen's r, with a value of $> 0.1$ representing a small, $> 0.3$ a moderate, and $> 0.5$ a large effect size [27] and calculated as Z statistic divided by the square root of the sample size (N) $(Z/\sqrt{N})$. Additionally, we calculated means per person for self-efficacy, flow, and the overall user experience, as well as a knowledge gain score as the subtraction of post-test and memory test results minus the pre-test result. Two persons from group $A_{\text{non-gamified}}$ and four persons from group $B_{\text{gamified}}$ were excluded from the analyses as they did not take part in the memory test. Thus, we ended up with group sizes of $A_{\text{non-gamified}}$ (n = 37) and $B_{\text{gamified}}$ (n = 36).

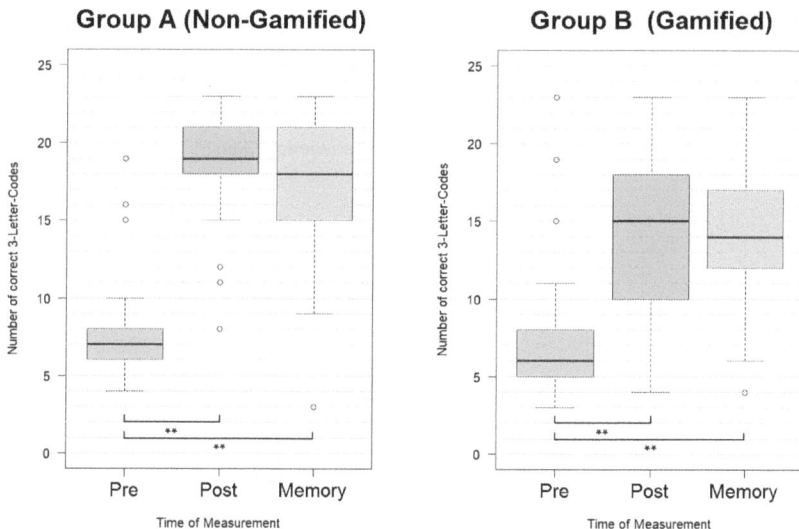

**Fig. 3.** On the left: results for pre-, post-, and memory test of group $A_{\text{non-gamified}}$. On the right: results for pre-, post-, and memory test of group $B_{\text{gamified}}$.

### 4.1  Learning Efficacy

A Friedman test for group $A_{\text{non-gamified}}$ yielded a significant difference regarding learning efficacy ($\chi^2$ (2) = 56.30, p < 0.001). Paired Wilcoxon post-hoc tests confirmed a significant increase of correctly chosen 3-Letter-Codes between the pre-test and the post-test (Z = −5.31 , p < 0.001). A large effect size (r = 0.88) was observed for this comparison. Likewise, a paired Wilcoxon post-hoc test confirmed a significant difference between pre-test and memory test (Z = −5.26 , p < 0.001). Likewise, a large effect size (r = 0.88) was observed for this comparison. The difference between post-test and memory test was insignificant. Figure 3 shows the results for pre-, post-, and memory tests of group $A_{\text{non-gamified}}$.

However, while standard deviation and interquartile range for pre- and post-test are constant, results for the memory test are clearly more scattered (Fig. 3).

A Friedman test for group $B_{gamified}$ yielded a significant difference regarding learning efficacy ($\chi^2$ (2) = 50.28, p < 0.001). Paired Wilcoxon post-hoc tests confirmed a significant increase of correctly chosen 3-Letter-Codes between the pre-test and the post-test (Z = −5.14 , p < 0.001) with a large effect size (r = 0.87). Likewise, a paired Wilcoxon post-hoc test confirmed a significant difference between pre-test and memory test (Z = −5.10 , p < 0.001) with a large effect size (r = 0.87). The difference between post-test and memory test was insignificant. Figure 3 shows the results for pre-, post-, and memory tests of group $B_{gamified}$. Interestingly, while the difference between post-test and memory test was insignificant, results for the memory test were less scattered than for the post-test indicated by differences for standard deviations and interquartile ranges (Fig. 3).

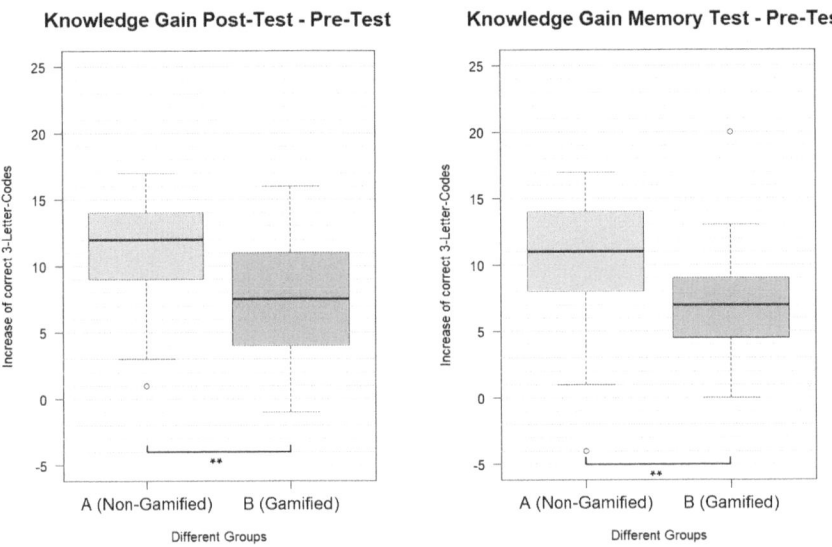

**Fig. 4.** On the left: results for knowledge gain between pre- and post-test for group $A_{non\text{-}gamified}$ and group $B_{gamified}$. On the right: results for knowledge gain between pre- and memory test for group $A_{non\text{-}gamified}$ and group $B_{gamified}$.

With regard to knowledge gain, Mann-Whitney-U tests revealed significant differences between group $A_{non\text{-}gamified}$ and group $B_{gamified}$ for both comparisons between pre- and post test (W = 982, p < 0.001) and pre- and memory test (W = 964, p < 0.001). Large effect sizes (r > 0.55) were observed for both comparisons. Figure 4 shows the results for knowledge gain between pre- and post-tests as well as pre- and memory tests of groups $A_{non\text{-}gamified}$ and $B_{gamified}$.

## 4.2   User Experience

Regarding experienced fun, a Mann-Whitney-U test revealed a significant difference between group $A_{\text{non-gamified}}$ and group $B_{\text{gamified}}$ (W = 581.5, p = 0.01). A moderate effect size (r = 0.41) was observed for this comparison. Mann-Whitney U tests for items 2, 3, 4, 5, 6 and 7 did not reveal any significant differences between the groups. Likewise, Mann-Whitney-U tests for self-efficacy, flow, and the overall user experience were insignificant. Figure 5 shows the results for all items as well as for self-efficacy, flow, and user experience scores.

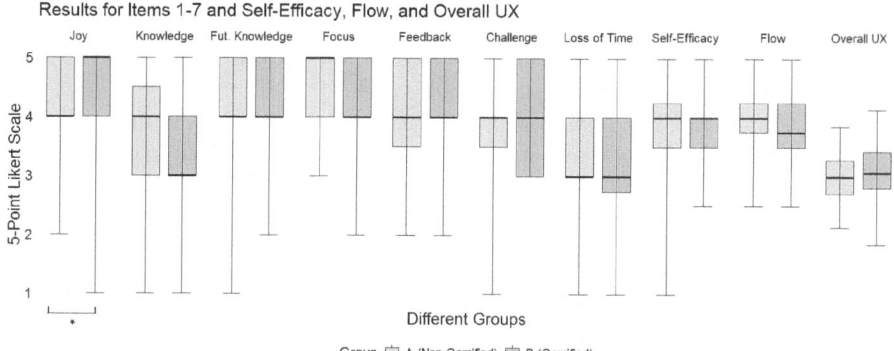

**Fig. 5.** Results for items 1–7, self-efficacy, flow, and overall user experience of group $A_{\text{non-gamified}}$ and $B_{\text{gamified}}$.

## 5   Discussion

In this section, we first discuss the results of the pre-, post-, and memory tests as well as the results of the questionnaire. To underline some findings, we will use excerpts of the semi-structured focus group discussions.

### 5.1   Learning Efficacy

The results imply the general effectiveness of both methods, the non-gamified and passive approach by watching a video and simply learning by playing the game "Sky Dash" which allows for active decision making and interaction and provides feedback on one's own progress. Participants of both groups significantly improved their knowledge of the 3-Letter-Codes between pre- and post-test. Considering the forgetting curve by Ebbinghaus [28] and the proven assumption that people forget 70% of what they have learned after 24 h [29], the results also imply the effectiveness for learning retention. Participants of both groups performed significantly better in the memory test compared to the pre-test.

Regarding RQ1 ("How effective is a serious low-threshold mobile game for learning technical terminologies by heart?"), we argue for the acceptance of the corresponding H1.1 ("A serious low-threshold mobile game is an effective learning method for learning repetitive technical terminologies by heart."). This is an important finding, as it shows that repetitive learning processes and the memorization of technical terminologies can be interactively designed and mapped through the game type of an endless runner and that good learning success can be achieved at the same time. Due to the modular design and structure of the game, completely different vocabulary is also conceivable as content, opening up new possibilities to gamify repetitive learning. These are often encountered in large companies, e.g., in learning abbreviations of dangerous goods, special policies, and standard specifications. Generally, these findings align with previous research showing the learning effectiveness of serious games [4,8,12] and gamified digital learning interventions [10].

At the same time, the results show that the non-gamified learning approach was significantly more effective than the game "Sky Dash". Participants of group $A_{non-gamified}$ showed a significantly higher knowledge gain compared to group $B_{gamified}$. A possible explanation is the amount of information provided by the game which consequently leads to an increased cognitive load. While participants of group $A_{non-gamified}$ could solely focus on the relation between airport name and the correct 3-Letter-Code, participants of group $B_{gamified}$ had to process sensory-motor data: controlling the aircraft, making a decision to hit the correct target, as well as cognitive stimuli such as feedback on a chosen 3-Letter-Code. It is worth mentioning that the experimenters realized that some participants were struggling with controlling the game. For example, despite an explanation and a pre-training phase to adapt to the controls, one subject was constantly trying to touch the correct letter code instead of navigating the aircraft towards it. It seems obvious that such difficulties lead to a reduced focus on the actual goal of learning the letter codes, which in turn can be a possible explanation for the lower knowledge increase of group $B_{gamified}$.

Although there are no statistically significant differences between post- and memory tests, the changes in dispersion between the latter in both groups are worth mentioning. Interestingly, while group $B_{gamified}$ shows a concentration of knowledge, the opposite can be observed for group $A_{non-gamified}$. These changes should be further investigated in future work on possible long-term effects of active learning through games.

### 5.2   User Experience

Both groups were mostly aligned regarding overall user experience, flow, self-efficacy, focus, and loss of time. Regarding RQ2 ("What are the effects of a serious low-threshold mobile game for learning technical terminologies on the user experience?") and the corresponding hypotheses H2.2 ("A serious low-threshold mobile game has an intensifying effect on loss of time."), H2.3 ("It has a positive effect on focus"), H2.4 ("It has a positive effect on perceived feedback"), H2.5 ("It has a positive effect on self-efficacy."), H2.6 ("It has a positive effect on flow"), and H2.7 ("It has a positive effect on the overall user experience"), we can not accept the stated hypotheses. Consequently, one could reason that there are no positive effects on the user experience. However, participants of group $B_{\text{gamified}}$ enjoyed the learning significantly more than group $A_{\text{non-gamified}}$. Hence, we argue for accepting H2.1 ("A serious low-threshold mobile game has a positive effect on fun."). This is an important finding due to its relevance and the positive effects of fun and enjoyment on motivation and endurance [30], furthermore it contradicts previous findings [7].

The qualitative feedback from the focus group discussions stresses this latter result and questions the results of group $A_{\text{non-gamified}}$ regarding the other items at the same time; for example, one participant from group $B_{\text{gamified}}$ asked whether he "could also play the game at home on his cell phone." The fact that employees use the low-threshold offer on a mobile device such as a smartphone, for example on the way home on the bus or train, would of course be the ideal case and emphasizes the potential of such a low-threshold mobile game. Another participant from group $B_{\text{gamified}}$ emphasized that the game was "fun and entertaining". At the same time, one participant from group $A_{\text{non-gamified}}$ suggested perhaps adding music to the learning video so that "it wouldn't be so boring". Another participant from the group $A_{\text{non-gamified}}$ suggested to "maybe use different colors for the different airports, so Berlin is black and Barcelona is red." This desire for clearer visualization and differentiation could be a sign of fatigue caused by the monotonous presentation of learning content in the non-gamified video method. On the other hand, another participant from group $A_{\text{non-gamified}}$ thought that the video is "a good learning method" and he would "remember them even in two hours." Considering the higher knowledge gain achieved in group $A_{\text{non-gamified}}$, this could be an indication of self-efficacy that was influenced by one's own knowledge acquisition. It is therefore conceivable that the non-gamified learning method, which is more effective but also much more monotonous, leads to greater self-efficacy with regard to one's own knowledge, but in the long term does not have a motivating character in terms of fun.

# 6   Conclusion

In this work, we presented the results of a study investigating the potentials of a serious low-threshold mobile game to enhance the experience of a repetitive learning process in the context of a large company in ground logistics. The findings of the study with 79 employees working in the baggage handling at an international airport underline the effectiveness of the game "Sky Dash" as an interactive gamified learning method in comparison to a non-gamified passive learning method watching a video. As described in the Related Work section, while the potentials of gamification in large companies have been shown in literature [5,19], the potentials of digital interventions like serious mobile games are still fairly unexplored. Exposure time and repetition can be critical factors for learning processes of special knowledge such as abbreviations for dangerous goods or standard specifications. At the same time, classic learning can be tedious. Since game development can be a cost-intensive process and some applications and hardware components are still not accessible for a broad audience (e.g. Head-Mounted-Displays), low-threshold solutions such as mobile games may bridge a gap here. Both learning methods were effective for short term memorization as well as for learning retention, although participants who learned with the passive and non-gamified method performed significantly better in the post- and memory test. At the same time, participants playing the game experienced significantly more fun than participants watching the video. The results therefore underline the potential of low-threshold mobile games to effectively automate repetitive and tedious learning processes while being joyful and motivating at the same time. Finally, this work might contribute to further research efforts regarding gamification through serious games in vocational contexts.

**Acknowledgments.** As part of the project #ABCforJobs, this work was funded by the Federal Ministry of Education and Research of Germany in the frame of the National Decade for Literacy 2016–2026 under the funding code W1505AAOG. All responsibility for the content of this publication is assumed by the authors.

# Appendix

**Listing 16.1.** Each entry consists of two strings (a name and the corresponding shortcut) and an additional boolean defining the correct answer. Three consecutive entries result in a logically related triplet.

```
{
    "shortcuts": [
        {
            "name": "Amsterdam",
            "shortcut": "AST",
            "label": false
        },
        {
            "name": "Amsterdam",
            "shortcut": "ASD",
            "label": false
        },
        {
            "name": "Amsterdam",
            "shortcut": "AMS",
            "label": true
        },
        ...
    ]
}
```

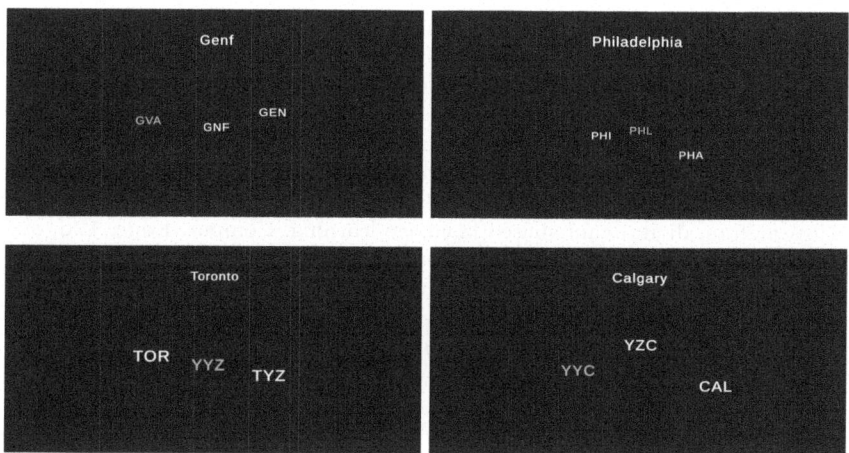

**Fig. 6.** Excerpt of the video presented to group $A_{\text{non-gamified}}$

# References

1. Csikszentmihalyi, M.: Flow: The Psychology of Optimal Experience. Harper & Row, New York (1990)
2. Clement, J.: Video Game Industry—Statistics & Facts. https://www.statista.com/topics/868/video-games/#topicOverview (2024)
3. Korn, O., Zallio, M., Schnitzer, B.: Young skeptics: exploring the perceptions of virtual worlds and the metaverse in generations Y and Z. Front. Virtual Real. **5**, 1330358 (2024). https://doi.org/10.3389/frvir.2024.1330358
4. Boyle, E.A., Hainey, T., Connolly, T.M., Gray, G., Earp, J., Ott, M., Lim, T., Ninaus, M., Ribeiro, C., Pereira, J.: An update to the systematic literature review of empirical evidence of the impacts and outcomes of computer games and serious games. Comput. Educ. **94**, 178–192 (2016). https://doi.org/10.1016/j.compedu.2015.11.003
5. Caserman, P., Baumgartner, K.A., Göbel, S., Korn, O.: A best practice for gamification in large companies: an extensive study focusing inter-generational acceptance. Multimed. Tools Appl. (2023). https://doi.org/10.1007/s11042-023-16877-7
6. Wouters, P., Van Der Spek, E.D., Van Oostendorp, H.: Current practices in serious game research: a review from a learning outcomes perspective. In: Connolly, T., Stansfield, M., und Boyle, L. (hrsg.) Games-Based Learning Advancements for Multi-Sensory Human Computer Interfaces, pp. 232–250. IGI Global (2009)
7. Wouters, P., Van Nimwegen, C., Van Oostendorp, H., Van Der Spek, E.D.: A meta-analysis of the cognitive and motivational effects of serious games. J. Educ. Psychol. **105**, 249–265 (2013). https://doi.org/10.1037/a0031311
8. Connolly, T.M., Boyle, E.A., MacArthur, E., Hainey, T., Boyle, J.M.: A systematic literature review of empirical evidence on computer games and serious games. Comput. Educ. **59**, 661–686 (2012). https://doi.org/10.1016/j.compedu.2012.03.004
9. Boyle, E.A., et al.: An update to the systematic literature review of empirical evidence of the impacts and outcomes of computer games and serious games. Comput.

226     B. Schnitzer et al.

Educ. **94**, 178–192 (2016). https://doi.org/10.1016/j.compedu.2015.11.003. ISSN 0360-13

10. Barz, N., Benick, M., Dörrenbächer-Ulrich, L., Perels, F.: The effect of digital game-based learning interventions on cognitive, metacognitive, and affective-motivational learning outcomes in school: a meta-analysis. Rev. Educ. Res. **94**, 193–227 (2024). https://doi.org/10.3102/00346543231167795

11. Hung, H.-T., Yang, J.C., Hwang, G.-J., Chu, H.-C., Wang, C.-C.: A scoping review of research on digital game-based language learning. Comput. Educ. **126**, 89–104 (2018). https://doi.org/10.1016/j.compedu.2018.07.001

12. Bartolome, N.A., Zorrilla, A.M., Zapirain, B.G.: Can game-based therapies be trusted? Is game-based education effective? A systematic review of the Serious Games for health and education. In: 2011 16th International Conference on Computer Games (CGAMES), pp. 275–282. IEEE, Louisville, KY, USA (2011)

13. Görgen, R., Huemer, S., Schulte-Körne, G., Moll, K.: Evaluation of a digital game-based reading training for German children with reading disorder. Comput. Educ. **150**, 103834 (2020). https://doi.org/10.1016/j.compedu.2020.103834

14. Bordini, R.A., Korn, O.: Strengthening invisible ties: decreasing loneliness indices of university students through a gamified mobile app. In: Proceedings of the 2022 ACM Conference on Information Technology for Social Good, pp. 424–430. ACM, Limassol Cyprus (2022)

15. Chen, H.J.H., Hsu, H.L.: The impact of a serious game on vocabulary and content learning. Comput. Assist. Lang. Learn. **33**(7), 811–832 (2019). https://doi.org/10.1080/09588221.2019.1593197

16. Westermann Digital GmbH: Vocabicar. https://vocabicar.de/ (2024)

17. Navarro-Parra, S.L., Chiappe, A.: Simulated learning environments as an interdisciplinary option for vocational training: a systematic review. Simul. Gaming. **55**, 135–158 (2024). https://doi.org/10.1177/10468781231221904

18. Jensen, L., Konradsen, F.: A review of the use of virtual reality head-mounted displays in education and training. Educ. Inf. Technol. **23**, 1515–1529 (2018). https://doi.org/10.1007/s10639-017-9676-0

19. Korn, O.: Gamification in industrial production: an overview, best practices, and design recommendations. In: Röcker, C., Büttner, S. (hrsg.) Human-Technology Interaction, pp. 251–270. Springer International Publishing, Cham (2023)

20. Caserman, P., et al.: Quality criteria for serious games: serious part, game part, and balance. JMIR Serious Games. **8**, e19037 (2020). https://doi.org/10.2196/19037

21. Dörner, R., Effelsberg, W., Göbel, S., Wiemeyer, J. (hrsg): Serious Games: Foundations, Concepts and Practice. Springer International Publishing: Imprint: Springer, Cham (2016)

22. Bredl, K., Bösche, W. (hrsg): Serious Games and Virtual Worlds in Education, Professional Development, and Healthcare: IGI Global (2013)

23. IJsselsteijn, W.A., de Kort, Y.A.W., Poels, K.: The Game Experience Questionnaire. https://pure.tue.nl/ws/files/21666907/Game_Experience_Questionnaire_English.pdf (2013)

24. Law, E.L.-C., Brühlmann, F., Mekler, E.D.: Systematic review and validation of the game experience questionnaire (GEQ)—implications for citation and reporting practice. In: Proceedings of the 2018 Annual Symposium on Computer-Human Interaction in Play, pp. 257–270. ACM, Melbourne VIC Australia (2018)

25. Rheinberg, F.: Die Flow-Kurzskala (FKS) übersetzt in verschiedene Sprachen The Flow-Short-Scale (FSS) Translated into Various Languages. http://rgdoi.net/10.13140/RG.2.1.4417.2243 (2015)

26. Schwarzer, R., Jerusalem, M.: General Self-Efficacy Scale. http://doi.apa.org/getdoi.cfm?doi=10.1037/t00393-000 (2012)
27. Cohen, J.: Statistical Power Analysis for the Behavioral Sciences. Routledge (2013)
28. Ebbinghaus, H.: Urmanuskript "Ueber das Gedächtniss" 1880. Passavia Universitätsverlag, Passau (1983)
29. Murre, J.M.J., Dros, J.: Replication and analysis of ebbinghaus forgetting curve. PLOS ONE. **10**, e0120644 (2015). https://doi.org/10.1371/journal.pone.0120644
30. Wiemeyer, J., Nacke, L., Moser, C., 'Floyd' Mueller, F.: Player experience. In: Dörner, R., Göbel, S., Effelsberg, W., Wiemeyer, J. (hrsg.) Serious Games, pp. 243–271. Springer International Publishing, Cham (2016)

# Collaborative Knowledge Development: An Exploration of Knowledge Space Theory in Multiplayer Learning Games

Lauren Yannick Pflüger[ID], Wolfgang Friedrich Brabänder[ID], Sabrina Vogt[ID], and Stefan Göbel[(✉)][ID]

Serious Games Research Group, Technical University of Darmstadt, 64289 Darmstadt, Germany
stefan_peter.goebel@tu-darmstadt.de
https://www.etit.tu-darmstadt.de/serious-games/willkommen_sg/index.de.jsp

**Abstract.** Collaborative learning has been shown to enhance the motivation and enjoyment of learners. However, when trying to utilize these advantages in collaborative educational games, the game has to effectively keep track of the learners' states of knowledge and adapt the game accordingly. This includes only confronting players with tasks appropriate for their capabilities to avoid frustration or boredom and promote engagement. This requires the consideration of multiple learners' skills and respecting their potentially varying learning paces. In this paper, a concept is developed for updating the learners' knowledge states after completing a task and dynamically selecting the next appropriate level based on these states. This concept leverages the Competence-based Knowledge Space Theory (CbKST) to represent the learner's state of knowledge. The developed concept is implemented into a collaborative learning game, which is subsequently evaluated through a user study. The results of the evaluation indicate that the concept successfully enhanced player motivation and enjoyment within the collaborative learning game. However, it is important to note that these findings are limited in significance and require further research to fully determine the impact of the proposed approach on the players' motivation and enjoyment.

**Keywords:** Educational · Serious games · Adaptive · Multiplayer · Knowledgespaces

## 1 Motivation

When implementing the characterizing goal of serious games [3]—for example learning—there will most likely be some sort of sequence in which you have to learn certain things. However, a problem arises when this sequence is implemented statically. Every person has a different knowledge and skill base resulting in them potentially being overstrained or not challenged enough when given tasks of equal difficulty. The competence-based knowledge space, explained in more

J. L. Plass and X. Ochoa (Eds.): JCSG 2024, LNCS 15259, pp. 228–243, 2025.
https://doi.org/10.1007/978-3-031-74138-8_17

detail in Sect. 2.1, can be used to resolve this issue since it stores the current knowledge state of a learner and the next skills that can be learned with this knowledge [5].

## 2  Related Work

### 2.1  Competence-Based Knowledge Space Theory

Educational games can be used for teaching school subjects while utilizing the advantages of video games. However, to effectively teach the game requires the student's current state of knowledge at each stage of the game. This is necessary for the game to make informed decisions about which concept/skill to introduce next, ensuring that students are neither overstrained nor underchallanged. This is where the Knowledge Space Theory (KST) comes into play with its ability to store many millions of possible knowledge states, thus enabling a more personalized and adaptive learning experience.

An extension of the KST is the Competence-based Knowledge Space Theory (CbKST), which focuses on learning objects and skills or competencies. This will be used in the concept of this paper.

To represent a subject in the form of a competence-based knowledge space, the subject has to be broken down into skills and competencies, which will be brought in a logical order by defining the prerequisites between them [6].

These skills and competencies are called items and when visualizing a competence-based knowledge space as a skill graph, as shown in Fig. 1, the items on the left side are prerequisites for those on the right, e.g. a learner can only learn $c$ when $a$ and $b$ are already mastered. Additionally, the outer fringe is defined as all items that can currently be learned, meaning all prerequisites are mastered. The empty item $\varnothing$ represents no skill and thus is always mastered. This item is the prerequisite for items with no prerequisites and can be used as a starting point for traversal algorithms [2,7,13].

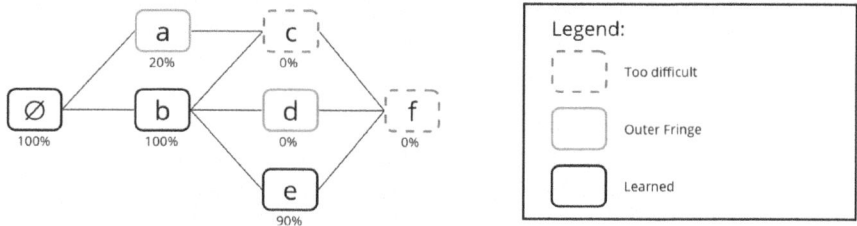

**Fig. 1.** This is an example of a skill graph modeled as a Hasse diagram.

## 2.2    Learning in Groups

Typically there are three ways of interaction among students regarding learning. They can either compete against each other, work on their own, or they can work together. In the modern world, competition seems to be valued more than cooperation. Cooperative learning, characterized by positive goal interdependence, requires the group to accept their common goal [8, 10].

Cooperative learning involves five elements: positive interdependence, face-to-face promotive interaction, individual accountability, interpersonal and small-group skills, and group processing. These elements are structured by the teacher, who also monitors each group member's work and learning progress [10].

When students learn in groups while utilizing these elements, they learn how to resolve conflicts and differences in a friendly manner. Furthermore, group learning promotes critical thinking skills and makes learning more fun and engaging compared to competitive or individualistic learning environments [8].

Collaborative learning, similar to cooperative learning, also requires the five elements of cooperation. However, it focuses more on the students being responsible for their actions, with the teacher available for consultation or help. In a collaborative learning environment, students share authority and distribute roles and tasks among themselves. Collaborative learning can lead to a more profound understanding compared to individual or competitive learning [9].

## 2.3    Learner Engagement

Romero shows in her paper "Learner Engagement in the Use of Individual and Collaborative Serious Games" multiple factors for increasing the learner's engagement in the use of serious games. She defines the learners' engagement as the learners' behavior in the learning activity. For multiplayer relationships, the paper considers positive interdependence for intragroup and competition for intergroup dynamics. The positive interdependence influences the learners' engagement by leading the players to find solutions for the given problems together as a group and helping each other. When using competition to influence the learners' engagement, players have to solve problems while competing with other players, making it more challenging and competitive. Both approaches can be combined to achieve intragroup cooperation and intergroup competition. The author states that the most important factor of motivation and engagement in multiplayer serious games is intragroup cooperation and the sense of belonging as one. This suggests that a multiplayer serious game can be more engaging for the player if it is implemented properly [11].

## 3    Concept

As outlined in the related work section, when implemented correctly, multiplayer educational games can utilize the advantages of learning in groups (Sect. 2.2), which are increased learning motivation and productivity as well as other social advantages like improved communication. However, the development of such a game poses multiple challenges, combining challenges of educational single-player games, (multiplayer) games for entertainment, and collaborative learning.

Moreover, when creating a collaborative educational game, it is important to keep track of the learner's knowledge at playtime. This can then be used by the game to make decisions and adapt accordingly to their states of knowledge. Different from single-player games, multiplayer games have to make sure that a learner is not left behind to keep the motivation high. When one learner learns faster or possesses more knowledge than their team partner, there is a risk of boredom for the quicker learner or potential frustration and loss of motivation for the less knowledgeable one, due to being overstrained.

This section contains the concept of this paper for using the CbKST in multiplayer collaborative level-based learning games, to represent the learners' states of knowledge. This consists of an algorithm, evaluating the next skill to be taught, taking into account the learners' states of knowledge and their potential knowledge gap. Furthermore, the special requirements for implementing this algorithm into a collaborative learning game are outlined. This approach is based upon the state of the art research and in particular on the learner model from Wendel [13].

## 3.1   Requirements and Assumptions

The concept is developed for multiplayer collaborative level-based learning games with a team of two players. Furthermore, this paper focuses on level-based puzzle games with the purpose of teaching some sort of subject. These subjects should have clear dependencies like programming or math, so that they can be divided into skills for the knowledge space. Puzzle games require the players to solve puzzles, which can help to improve cognitive skills e.g. problem-solving skills. A popular example of puzzle games is the Portal series where the player progresses from level to level while solving puzzles, with Portal 2 even having the option to solve these with a friend [1].

For collaborative learning to be successful, communication is crucial. Therefore players need to be able to somehow communicate with each other. Since this concept offers no communication tool, it is assumed that players have some sort of communication. This may involve leveraging existing online platforms such as Discord, Zoom, and Skype or engaging in a face-to-face interaction while playing the game.

Furthermore, this concept assumes that the players are motivated to play the game and learn new concepts as long as they are provided with appropriately difficult tasks. In addition to that, they have to know the basic collaborative principles and need to be willing to help each other. Moreover, different from other concepts, this concept assumes that learners won't forget things they already learned and the Knowledgespace never contains knowledge that the learner doesn't know.

## 3.2   System Overview

In general, an educational game needs to keep track of the learner's state of knowledge to adapt the game accordingly. This can be achieved by using the CbKST presented in Sect. 2.1.

When the next appropriate skill to be taught is selected based on the knowledge states of the players, there might be no skills appropriate for both players. This problem can occur when players start at different states of knowledge, which can increase this problem, but also when they start with a similar knowledge state but learn at different paces. The learning pace is even more challenging to predict than the starting knowledge and can vary even for one person regarding different topics, thus this problem has to be taken into account when developing collaborative educational games.

For the concept of this paper, the adaptations made in the game are limited to the selection of the next item and level based on the current state of knowledge of each player after they finish a level. The selection algorithm tackles the problem of leaving a learner behind in combination with the requirements formulated for the levels in the game.

**Multiplayer Level Selection Algorithm** The KST only provides a mathematical framework for storing a player's state of knowledge. This state has to be modified and used in some way so the game can actually use this information. This subsection will cover the detailed concept for updating the skill graph, introduced in Sect. 2.1, which stores the current state of knowledge for each player. Furthermore, this information will be utilized in an algorithm for selecting the next appropriate level in a collaborative level-based learning game for two players.

*Definition of the KS* The skill graph consists of different items $i$ representing the skills to be taught. As presented in the definition of the CbKST, each item in the skill graph has a probability of how likely the player $p$ can solve a level/task/puzzle $l$ associated with this item. In other words, the probability shows how experienced the player is concerning the item. For the mathematical definitions, this is defined as $EXP_{p,i} \in [0,1]$, since every player has a different experience value concerning each item.

Every item, with the empty item being an exception, contains multiple levels, teaching these skills. These levels are either categorized as mandatory, deepening, or special and can either be finished or unfinished. In addition to that, each level requires a predefined experience gain ($EXP\_Gain_l \in [0,1]$) representing how much a player can learn in the item when the level is finished optimally. Mandatory levels are designed to teach the basics in both subject concepts of the item and new game mechanics. Deepening levels don't introduce new concepts but deepen the knowledge of the players with equally difficult tasks for both players. Special levels are designed similarly to the deepening levels but expect one player to have already mastered the item. These levels need to be designed so that the better player can support the other player to also master the skill.

*Initialization of the KS* As defined in Sect. 2.1, the empty item is always learned and therefore every player has the value 1 for the empty item. Every other item starts with the value 0, meaning the player has no knowledge about the skill yet. However, this still allows players that have more knowledge to play the game, since they will just progress faster. But with everyone starting from the beginning it is ensured that every player gets to know the game mechanics. In addition to that, all levels are initially unfinished. Figure 2 shows the initial knowledge state of the players.

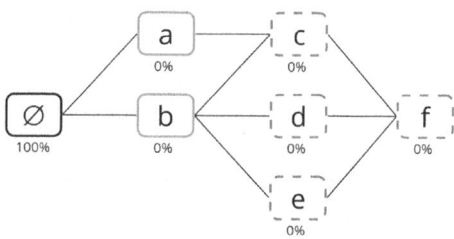

**Fig. 2.** This is the skill graph modeled as a Hasse diagram, visualizing the initial state of knowledge each player has. (The legend is the same as in the definition in Fig. 1)

*Updating the KS* Updating the skill graph happens independently from other players and is done after a level is completed. Since this concept is mainly developed for puzzle games, the adaptation and thus the evaluation and updating of the KS is only required for the selection of the next level/puzzle. This is different from other games, which need optimization and adaptation once per second.

After finishing a level, the experience for each player regarding the current item (the item which the level that was finished is associated with) needs to be updated accordingly to the newly gained experience. To achieve this, the game needs to know how efficiently each player solved their task in the level. This number can vary for each player and shows how much of the maximum experience value, possible for the level, they gain ($e_p \in [0, 1]$).

For the calculation of the new experience value of an item, the old experience value is required and defined as $EXP\_Old_{p,i} \in [0, 1]$. The old experience value is always updated before the next calculation is done ($EXP\_Old_{p,i} = EXP_{p,i}$). The new experience value of a level is calculated as shown below in Eq. 1:

$$EXP_{p,i} = \min\{EXP\_Old_{p,i} + (e_p \cdot EXP\_Gain_l), 1\} \qquad (1)$$

Afterwards, the percentage of the item is updated accordingly and the level which was finished is marked as such. This concept ignores failure by letting the players play the level until they succeed. The number of tries can be considered when calculating the efficiency value.

Normally in the CbKST, an item is marked as mastered, when the experience of this item exceeds a certain threshold (e.g. 80%), but this concept requires all mandatory levels of this item to be finished as well. This ensures that the players at least played all mandatory levels of an item and thus should have learned all game mechanics needed for the next items. Furthermore, our concept assumes, that a learned competence will never decline and thus the experience value of an item can only be increased.

Important to note is, that each level should only be evaluated once. Otherwise, players could gain more experience than intended per level and thus master an item by just replaying one level multiple times. And since the puzzle in the level won't change, the players would only need to repeat the solution from before without learning anything.

*Selecting the Appropriate Item Set* For the selection of the set of appropriate items, it is necessary to define the two players, the concept is developed for. Thus in the following the two players will be referred to as Player A and Player B. Furthermore, the outer fringe of a player ($OUTER_p$) is of great importance.

When selecting the set of appropriate items ($SAI$), two different scenarios have to be considered. The first one is that both players have a similar state of knowledge and thus items that are appropriate to learn for both of them are available. The other case would be that one player is more knowledgeable than the other and thus no item is appropriate to learn for both.

First of all the outer fringes of both players will be checked for items and if they are both empty, both players mastered everything the game offers and thus the game is finished and there is no appropriate item and level left. If the game is not finished yet, the present scenario has to be figured out. For this, the interception of the outer fringes of the players will be determined ($SAI = OUTER_A \cap OUTER_B$). Afterwards, the interception will be checked for items.

The first scenario is present when the interception of the outer fringes contains items because then there are items that are appropriate for both players, since the outer fringe of a player contains per definition all items they should learn next based on the current state of knowledge. In this case, the interception is the set of appropriate items and thus the selection of the appropriate items is finished. However, if the interception contains no items, there are no items that are appropriate to learn for both players, since one player is more knowledgeable (e.g. Player A) than the other and thus the second scenario is present.

Now the algorithm will choose an item from the outer fringe of the less knowledgeable player (e.g. Player B), thus enabling him/her to catch up. But since the outer fringe of Player B is not necessarily learned completely by Player A, even though he/she is more knowledgeable, the learned items from Player A need to be taken into account. To identify which player is more knowledgeable, the number of mastered items of each player is determined ($m(p) \in \mathbb{N}_0$). The player with more mastered items is considered to be more knowledgeable. If they have the same amount of mastered items, one player is picked at random to be more knowledgeable.

The set of appropriate items is now determined by the interception of the outer fringe of the less knowledgeable player and the set of all learned items ($LEARNED_p$) of the more knowledgeable player. In addition to the set of appropriate items, the algorithm retains data regarding the difference in knowledge between the players. This information is important for the selection of the level covered in the next part.

$$SAI = \begin{cases} OUTER_A \cap LEARNED_B, & \text{if } m(a) \leq m(b) \\ LEARNED_A \cap OUTER_B, & \text{otherwise} \end{cases} \tag{2}$$

The set of all learned items can be exchanged with the inner fringe. However, the inner fringe can be more difficult to calculate or to keep track of. Furthermore, the inner fringe limits the starting knowledge states of the players, which is no problem for the concept of this paper but if the concept would be extended this needs to be considered.

The selection of the appropriate items ensures that the players will always either learn new items together or one player will help the other understand an item until he/she masters it and they can continue learning new items together.

An example on how the knowledge spaces of the players are updated and which items are appropriate is shown on page 236.

For the next part, the algorithm will choose a level from all appropriate items. This requires a set of appropriate items, evaluated in this part, and for the second scenario, the player who has already mastered the selected items. *Selecting the Level* From the set of appropriate items, an item will be selected. The selection of the item can be done based on information, for example, the algorithm could try to let the players master items that are closest to mastery first or the other way around for an equal progression of the items, or like in this paper it will just be selected randomly.

After picking an item, the next level to be played has to be selected. For this only levels that are associated with the appropriate items and marked as unfinished will be considered since replaying a level that doesn't change is most likely not fun and only of limited learning progress because the solution to the puzzle is already known to the players.

For the selection of the level the current scenario from the previous part is required. If the first scenario is present, meaning both players learn something new, the first levels to be played are the mandatory levels. The order in which they are played should be given by the game since they also teach game mechanics. When all the mandatory levels are played, the deepening levels are considered next. They can be picked, similar to the selection of the item from the appropriate item set, either randomly or by taking the progress of the item into account. The game implementing the concept for this paper will not have many levels, making a complicated selection unnecessary, and thus a random selection will be used. Otherwise, it could be useful to define a difficulty for each level and select levels based on it in combination with the item's progress. When all deepening levels are finished, but the players still haven't mastered this item, the game either didn't provide enough levels or levels of low quality. In this case, all the deepening levels will be marked as unfinished and the players have to replay these levels.

When the second scenario is present, since one player has to catch up, the selection of the level inside of the selected item will be a bit different. Due to the fact that one player has already mastered the item, the mandatory levels were already played. Now a level from the special set of levels will be selected similar to the deepening levels. These levels are designed for two players with different states of knowledge for the selected item.

*Example Item Selection* The players start at the initial state, represented by Fig. 2. Since the players' outer fringes are the same, a random item is chosen and from that either mandatory or deepening levels. In this example, Player A is a faster learner and thus masters items *a* and *b* before Player B. The players' knowledge states can be seen in Fig. 3. Since now no item is appropriate for both players, an appropriate item from the less knowledgeable player (Player B) will be chosen, e.g., item *b*. Now the players play special levels from this item until they reach the knowledge spaces shown in Fig. 4, where they now have appropriate items for both players again.

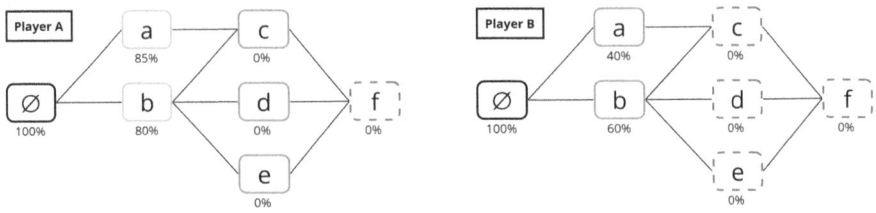

**Fig. 3.** The skill graphs, visualizing the knowledge states of the players after Player A mastered items *a* and *b*.

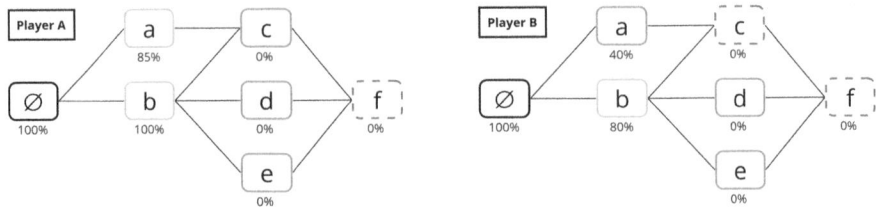

**Fig. 4.** The skill graphs, visualizing the knowledge states of the players after Player B caught up regarding the item *b*.

**Implementing the Concept** When developing a collaborative multiplayer puzzle learning game that utilizes the level selection algorithm and thus the KS presented in the subsection above, the game has to meet some requirements. These requirements will be covered in this subsection.

The modularity of the game is an important aspect when implementing the algorithm, which means that the levels have to be mostly independent of each other. This comes from the fact that the order, in which levels are played, is not predictable, since levels are picked based on the state of knowledge and thus even can be skipped. The prerequisites only provide limited structure by defining which items had to be mastered to get to the current item.

When implementing a story, one has to consider that levels are not played in a predefined order and some levels can even be skipped. This only leaves the mandatory levels to be used for story elements and even they are not played in a strict order.

Similar to the story, when game mechanics are introduced as a part of a level, the limited knowledge of what levels the players already played has to be taken into account. The game mechanics could also be taught by providing level-independent help whenever a mechanic is seen for the first time by the players. However, with this generic way of teaching game mechanics, players could be over-strained due to the lack of a tutorial.

The number of mandatory levels should be limited to one or two per item, since too many of these would hinder a fast progression of a knowledgeable or fast learner. Deepening and special levels should contain the most number of levels since a slow learner needs them to practice the newly taught skill.

As required by the algorithm, for each level, an experience gain needs to be defined. This represents the maximum amount of progress a player can make in the item when finishing the level optimally and needs to be balanced carefully. Additionally, to evaluate how efficiently the players succeeded and thus how much experience they gained, the game needs knowledge about how much each player contributed to the collaborative success of the level. To define these experience-gain values for each level, a simulation was used to evaluate different combinations of these. Afterwards, the best combination for supporting both fast and slow learners was chosen.

To evaluate the concept, a collaborative level-based learning game for two players was developed. A screenshot from the game can be seen in Fig. 5. This game fulfills all requirements of the concept and is a programming learning game where players have to drag and drop code snippets to interact with drones which are used to solve puzzles.

# 4 Evaluation

## 4.1 Goals and Methodology

The concept, developed in Sect. 3, focuses on utilizing the Competence-based Knowledge Space Theory in a collaborative level-based learning game, as the

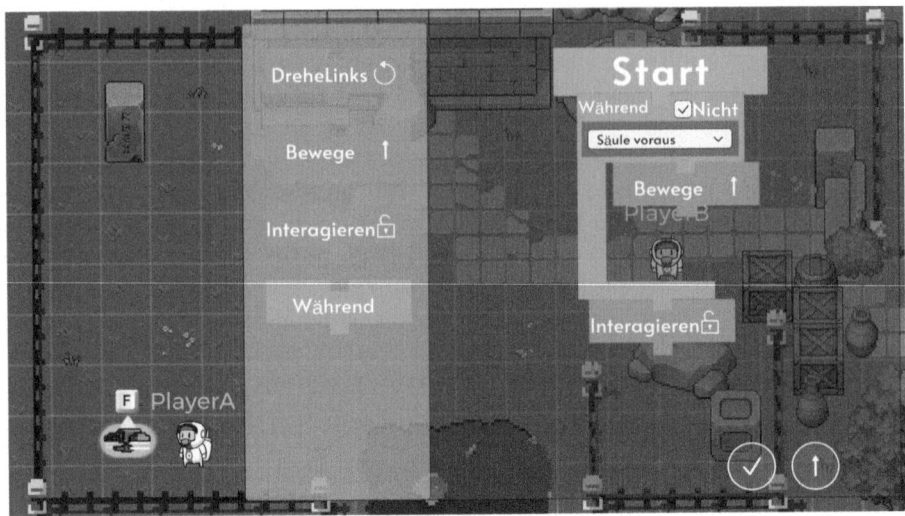

**Fig. 5.** A screenshot showing the game implementing the concept. This game was developed by Timo Holst, Lauren Pflüger, Sebastian Jilge, Jakob Speitkamp, and Robert Alles. The game is currently only available in German.

representation of the current knowledge each player has while playing to select the next appropriate level the players can play.

The goals of this evaluation are derived from the intentions behind the creation of the concept. Thus the first goal of this evaluation is to evaluate whether the concept helps the players to maintain their level of motivation while playing the game and prevents any player from being left behind. Since the concept was developed for multiplayer games, it is also relevant to evaluate if the multiplayer aspect of the game helped to raise engagement for the game and if players had more fun while playing because of it.

To achieve these goals, a user study is conducted where participants answer a pre- and post-game questionnaire with a 30-minute break where the participants play the game. While they play the game, a spectator notes relevant information about the communication of the players and their type of gameplay. Furthermore, the game automatically logs the played levels and their efficiency values.

## 4.2 Evaluation Setup

The questions and statements from the pre- and post-game questionnaires can be found in Table 1. Both questionnaires feature questions and statements that are either directly derived from or inspired by those found in Yavuz Samur's [12] questionnaires. Access to the questionnaire was given through a web-based survey and the communication between players was established via online voice chat. The game itself was played in a web browser.

Since both the game and concept were designed for two players, participants had to form groups of two. They were encouraged to team up with a friend or family member to enhance focus on gameplay and teamwork, rather than having to establish new interpersonal relationships.

After completing the Self-Assessment part of the questionnaire, participants engaged in playing the game for 30 min, followed by the post-game questionnaire segment. To observe gameplay and automatically collect relevant data, such as levels played and how efficiently they were solved, We joined their lobby using a spectator account. After the 30-minute gameplay session, participants were given the option to either resume the questionnaire or continue playing. However, only the initial 30 min will be taken into account for the evaluation to ensure comparability. The post-game part of the questionnaire evaluated the motivation, enjoyment, perceived difficulty, and teamwork experience during gameplay.

A total of twelve participants, divided into six groups, took part in this user study. Although they had the option to discuss questions with their team partner, each participant completed the questionnaire independently. Participants encountered the game for the first time at the beginning of the gameplay session.

**Table 1.** This table contains all questions and statements from the pre- and post-game questionnaires. These are translated from German to English.

| Nr. | Question |
| --- | --- |
| A1 | How old are you? |
| A2 | What is your gender? |
| A3 | How often to you play video games? |
| A4 | How long do you play video games per day? |
| A5 | On what device/s do you play video games? |
| A6 | I am interested in computer science and coding |
| A7 | I can code |
| A8 | I am good at maths |
| A9 | Mathematical and logical thinking is fun to me |
| A10 | Coding is fun |
| B1 | I always knew what the goal of the game was |
| B2 | I had fun while playing the game |
| B3 | I was motivated to play the game |
| B4 | Some puzzles were too difficult /unintelligible |
| B5 | Some puzzles were too easy /boring |
| B6 | If I played the game again, I would solve the puzzles faster |
| B7 | I got along well with my team partner |
| B8 | It helped me to solve the puzzles in pairs |
| B9 | I had more motivation because I was not playing alone |

### 4.3   Evaluation Results

The first section of the Post-Game Questionnaire aims to gauge participants' experiences during the gameplay session. The statements in this section were evaluated using a 4-point Likert scale. The scale ranged from "strongly agree" (4) to "strongly disagree" (1). Intentionally, a neutral opinion—which would correspond to a score of 2.50—was not provided as an option to enforce a tendency.

Almost all participants consistently knew what the goal of the game was, as reflected in the average Likert score of 3.33 for the corresponding statement. Furthermore, every participant reported enjoyment while playing the game (average Likert score 3.92) and expressed confidence in their ability to solve puzzles faster upon replaying the game (average Likert score 3.83). The motivation for playing the game was rated similarly, with an average Likert score of 3.75. However, statements assessing whether some levels were perceived as too difficult /unintelligible or others as too easy /boring, received the lowest scores, both averaging 3.08 on the Likert scale (note: for the calculation of these two statements, the scale was reversed).

Afterwards, statements regarding teamwork during the gameplay session revealed that every participant got along with their team partner greatly, reflected in an average Likert score of 3.92. Additionally, collaborative problem-solving was helpful for all groups (average Likert score of 3.42) and helped to raise motivation (average Likert score of 3.75).

Half of the participants reported an increased interest in computer science compared to pre-game, while the other half stated no change. Notably, the change of interest was independent of the participant's initial interest in computer science/coding or their coding skills, which were part of the Pre-Game Questionnaire.

### 4.4   Analysis of the Results

As reported in the Post-Game Questionnaire, participants stayed highly motivated and had much fun while playing the game. However, it remains rather unclear if it was due to the implemented concept or the inherent fun of the game. A follow-up study with a control group playing the game in a predefined order could provide a comparative analysis. Even though all participants reported a high level of motivation and enjoyment, some perceived certain levels as a bit too difficult and others as a bit too easy.

Teamwork played a significant role in enhancing motivation and supporting problem-solving, as reported by the participants. Lastly, half of the participants reported an increased interest in computer science or coding after playing the game, indicating a motivational shift towards these areas.

### 4.5   Discussion

Our concept of using an asymmetric level design in collaborative learning games, which is based on the idea that the game designer creates different levels of challenge or reward for different learners or groups of learners, fosters a peer-tutoring process. During this process, learners exchange knowledge and skills, give feedback, and support each other to enhance the learning experience. The evaluation indicates that our concept can provide several benefits for the learners, such as improving their motivation, interest, and even learning/play time and that it can also avoid some potential drawbacks of collaborative learning games, such as preventing the learners from feeling overwhelmed, discouraged, left behind, bored, frustrated, under-challenged or developing negative attitudes or behaviors towards each other.

We approached this challenge by building upon the learner model from Wendel [13], utilizing the CbKST to represent a learner's state of knowledge. The developed concept provides an algorithm for updating the learners' knowledge spaces after completing a level and selecting the next appropriate level based on the knowledge spaces of two players. Furthermore, different types of levels were introduced to address the problem of team partners having different learning paces.

Although this concept has been demonstrated in a programming educational game, it is independent of the learning domain and can be applied to various types of collaborative learning games, it is intended as a general and flexible framework that can be applied to various types of collaborative learning games, and it can be adapted to the specific needs and preferences of the learners and the game designer.

As shown in other works like He et al. [4], the potential for learning in groups (or pairs in our case) exceeds the lone learner's potential. Therefore, extending the Competence-based Knowledge Space Theory to encompass multiplayer learning games is a significant contribution. This expansion not only enhances our understanding of the dynamics of group learning but also provides a robust theoretical framework for designing more effective multiplayer learning environments.

## 5 Conclusion

### 5.1 Summary

This paper presents an approach for using the Competence-based Knowledge Space Theory (CbKST) in collaborative level-based learning games to represent a learner's state of knowledge and choose the next appropriate level based on two learners' current knowledge states. The concept addresses the problem of having learners with different learning paces, introducing three types of levels: mandatory, deepening, and special. An algorithm has been developed to update the players' knowledge spaces after completing a level and select the next appropriate level based on them. The implementation of the concept requires the game to evaluate the players' puzzle solutions separately and after each level, as well as the integration of the different types of levels.

The concept was implemented into a game which was then evaluated, by conducting a user study, during which participants played the game while being observed. Additionally, participants completed both Pre- and Post-Game Questionnaires to provide further insights.

The participants of the user study reported a high level of motivation and enjoyment during the gameplay session, which was also perceived during their observation. However, due to a rather small number of participants, the significance of this evaluation is limited and it remains unclear whether the concept helped to raise motivation and enjoyment or if the game itself was motivating and fun to play. Additionally, as anticipated before the study and further affirmed by it, an important part of educational games' effectiveness lies in level design and the balancing of parameters and thresholds. This can be seen in the developed concept regarding the experience gain values per level and the threshold for mastering an item. These values were chosen rather arbitrarily and were polished using the simulation, without taking the actual level difficulty into account. Furthermore, the levels developed were only tested by a computer scientist and thus were not optimized for the target audience. The game implementing the presented concept is currently available in German on itch.io: https://ag-serious-games-tu-da.itch.io/code-commanders.

## 5.2  Future Work

To further evaluate the developed concept, more studies should be conducted. These should encompass more participants and control groups. Additionally, as derived from the evaluation of the concept, participants should engage in longer and/or multiple gameplay sessions to increase the progress they can make, thus utilizing the potential of the concept more exhaustively. This is especially necessary when dealing with larger knowledge spaces since otherwise they won't be used to their full extent. However, when playing over a timespan of multiple weeks/months, the concept should consider the possibility of players partially losing previously acquired knowledge. Furthermore, there is potential for expanding the concept to be used in collaborative teams consisting of more than two players.

**Acknowledgments.** This invested research has been partially funded in the course of the zQSL project "3DVirtualCampus4GamifiedOnlineTeaching" to improve the quality of study conditions and teaching at the Technical University of Darmstadt and the research project "Pflegeschätze" (engl.: Care-Treasures, grant no. 16SV9231), funded by the German Ministry for Education and Science. **Disclosure of Interests** The authors have no competing interests to declare that are relevant to the content of this article.

## References

1. Puzzle video game (2023) https://en.wikipedia.org/w/index.php?title=Puzzle_video_game&oldid=1189830049. Page Version ID: 1189830049
2. Brabänder, W.F., Göbel, S.: Bridging the gap: knowledge spaces and storylines in serious games. In: Joint International Conference on Serious Games, pp. 111–123. Springer, Heidelberg (2023)

3. Dörner, R., Göbel, S., Effelsberg, W., Wiemeyer, J.: Serious Games. Springer (2016)
4. He, T., Minervini, M.S., Puranam, P.: How groups differ from individuals in learning from experience: evidence from a contest platform. Organization Science **0**(0), null (0). https://doi.org/10.1287/orsc.2021.15239
5. Heller, J., Steiner, C., Hockemeyer, C., Albert, D.: Competence-based knowledge structures for personalised learning. Int. J. E-learning **5**(1), 75–88 (2006)
6. Kickmeier-Rust, M.D., Albert, D.: Supporting formative assessment and appraisal by smart, competence-based, probabilistic systems. In: International Conference on the Future of Education (2013)
7. Kickmeier-Rust, M.D., Albert, D.: Using Hasse diagrams for competence-oriented learning analytics. In: International Workshop on Human-Computer Interaction and Knowledge Discovery in Complex, Unstructured, Big Data, pp. 59–64. Springer, Heidelberg (2013)
8. Laal, M., Ghodsi, S.M.: Benefits of collaborative learning. Proc. Soc. Behav. Sci. **31**, 486–490 (2012)
9. Laal, M., Laal, M.: Collaborative learning: what is it? Proc. Soc. Behav. Sci. **31**, 491–495 (2012)
10. Roger, T., Johnson, D.W.: An overview of cooperative learning. In: Creativity and collaborative learning, pp. 1–21 (1994)
11. Romero, M.: Learner engagement in the use of individual and collaborative serious games. In: Increasing Student Engagement and Retention using Immersive Interfaces: Virtual Worlds, Gaming, and Simulation, pp. 15–34. Emerald Group Publishing Limited (2012)
12. Samur, Y.: Measuring Engagement Effects of Educational Games and Virtual Manipulatives on Mathematics (2012)
13. Wendel, V.: Collaborative Game-based Learning-Automatized Adaptation Mechanics for Game-based Collaborative Learning using Game Mastering Concepts. Ph.D. thesis, Dissertation, Darmstadt, Technische Universität Darmstadt (2015)

# Extended Realities

# Playful Locative Interaction in Museums and Exhibitions with Immersive Augmented Reality

Yu Liu$^{(\boxtimes)}$ (iD), Manuel Feller, and Ulrike Spierling (iD)

Hochschule RheinMain, Wiesbaden, Germany
{yu.liu,ulrike.spierling}@hs-rm.de,
Manuel.Feller@student.hs-rm.de

**Abstract.** Head-mounted augmented reality (AR) technology enhances the museum experience by immersing visitors in heritage content. Location-based applications attract online audiences to physical sites, which is also crucial for the dissemination of cultural heritage. This study develops and evaluates specific interaction design patterns to address typical challenges of physical navigation and interaction with AR in a museum, focusing on usability and the enhancement of visitor enjoyment through adding game elements. By prototyping and testing in both simulated and real-world museum environments, the research confirms that these patterns can enhance playfulness. The findings advocate for tailored interaction patterns that enhance usability and engagement, supporting the wider adoption of AR in cultural heritage domains.

**Keywords:** Interaction design pattern · Head-mounted display · Augmented reality · Usability · Playful experience · Location-based interaction · Cultural heritage

## 1 Introduction

The distinctive feature of head-mounted augmented reality (AR) technology lies in its ability to create the illusion through glasses that actually invisible things are seemingly located in the immediate physical environment as digital information. Applied within museum exhibitions, this technology holds the potential to attract visitors from online to onsite environments [9,19]. Several museums have already started employing AR technology to enhance enjoyment and improve the visitor experience, aiming to bolster their impact on cultural heritage dissemination and increase visitor engagement [18,38]. However, given that AR technology with head-mounted displays (HMD) incorporates innovative interaction technologies, such as eye and hand tracking found in devices like the HoloLens 2, it remains relatively novel to many end-users and application developers [24]. This novelty still shows gaps in research regarding the broad application of

J. L. Plass and X. Ochoa (Eds.): JCSG 2024, LNCS 15259, pp. 247–262, 2025.
https://doi.org/10.1007/978-3-031-74138-8_18

HMD-based AR in museums, especially in terms of user-friendliness, organizational feasibility and application possibilities. Within the EU-funded international research project LoGaCulture [30], location-based gaming experiences at diverse cultural heritage sites are being developed and explored, including the use of immersive digital technology. The aim of our current research presented here is to take further steps in creating playful interactions in prototypes, to test them and analyze their usability and potential for enjoyment of the technology in an exhibition.

As Shneiderman [34] has argued, once functionality and usability issues have been addressed in a design, it is essential to incorporate additional elements that enhance the user's enjoyment and entertainment. This approach is particularly relevant in the exhibition and museum sector, where providing delightful and engaging experiences can increase visitor participation and encourage more interaction with cultural heritage content. As it can also be assumed that head-mounted displays place greater demands on museums in terms of organizing the flow of visitors than a bring-your-own-device solution, there is a requirement that this must be worthwhile. Our research therefore focuses not only on the usability of interactions in HMD-based AR applications, but also on how to increase the expected feelings of immersion and the motivation and enjoyment of the interaction.

Interaction design patterns, commonly used to address usability issues, have been extensively applied in research related to the field of Human-Computer Interaction [5,11,37]. This study began by developing prototypes based on existing museum exhibitions, for which various interactions were designed according to the visitor flow and subsequently iterated and optimized. Through systematic testing and enhancement of these designs, we propose interaction design patterns that support the development of engaging applications using head-mounted AR technology. To determine the effectiveness and generalizability of these patterns and their ability to create site-specific, enjoyable visitor experiences, we redesigned several user interfaces based on these patterns and conducted usability and play value evaluations of the experiences. We present two sub-studies with these evaluations based on a research-through-design method.

After presenting related research, we first describe our design and prototypes and generalize interaction patterns for HMD-based AR applications within exhibition and museum spaces. Finally, we report on the evaluation of the prototypes.

## 2    Related Work

In the 1990s, Gamma et al. [12] extended Alexander's [1] theoretical framework to computer science, presenting a seminal collection of design patterns for object-oriented software development. This initiative marked the beginning of pattern language theory's application in software development, particularly influencing interaction design and usability studies.

While projects from Battistoni et al. [2] and MacWilliams et al. [27] have examined the user experience and engagement of AR applications through a pattern-based approach, research on applying these patterns specifically in the cultural heritage domain remains limited. Existing studies, such as those by Börsting et al. [6] and Lee et al. [21], have investigated general interactions within AR applications using pattern approaches but did not focus on museum and exhibition contexts.

Current research predominantly targets technological advancements to support interactions within AR applications. Studies from Hunsucker et al. [17], Li et al. [23] and Okanovic et al. [29] have ventured into novel interactions and usability enhancements, yet these have not been extensively developed or evaluated within exhibition environments. While research from Brondi et al. [7] and Shin et al. [33] has been conducted in exhibition settings, the interaction designs were generally based on the system's inherent capabilities rather than through a deliberate pattern-based approach.

Chung et al. [8] and Rzayev et al. [32] have introduced innovative interaction designs for navigational purposes; however, these have largely focused on enhancing the user experience without a thorough evaluation of usability. Moreover, while certain projects from Hammady et al. [15] and Spierling and Kampa [36] have utilized hand-held displays (HHDs) to evaluate novel sensor-based interactions and usability within exhibitions, there is a notable absence of similar studies using head-mounted displays.

One study by Hammady et al. [16] aligns closely with our research direction, focusing on the usability of the entire visitor experience. However, there remains a research gap in using pattern language methodologies to specifically support interaction design for HMD-based AR applications in the cultural heritage sector.

Furthermore, although Berland et al. [3] and Ntalla [28] have explored the potential of playful experiences to enhance visitor engagement at museums and exhibitions, there is a lack of studies evaluating interaction design patterns that could facilitate the creation of location-based playful experiences using HMD-based AR applications in the cultural heritage field. Additionally, while the integration of game mechanics and the creation of engaging interactions for exhibitions have been explored by Haahr [13,14], no projects have yet explicitly utilized interaction patterns to develop location-based interactions, nor has there been research into how these patterns could be applied to create 'playful' experiences with HMD-based AR in museum and exhibition settings.

Game mechanics and game patterns are terms that are often used to improve playfulness, such as Karavolos et al. [20] explores the integration of mission objectives directly into the procedural generation of game levels, using generative grammar to create more cohesive and mission-specific environments in games. They discussed key-lock mechanics to demonstrate how these elements can strategically structure procedural level generation, ensuring gameplay progression aligns with the narrative and objectives of the game. Previously, Clanton [10] discussed the user interface of a game and suggested that the lock-and-key mechanic can offer hints, tools and obstacles to a certain extent. This mechanic can motivate players to explore more content and fits particularly well with puzzles.

# 3  Interaction Patterns in Cultural Heritage Sites

In order to design playful interactions with HMDs in a museum, we look into game design patterns that would also fit well with typical interaction patterns in cultural heritage sites. In a previous project, we analyzed that museum visitors act in one of two possible modes at the highest level of abstraction: Either they adopt an interaction pattern for navigation to find exhibits or other points of interest (PoI), or they use exploration patterns when viewing or enjoying an exhibit [26]. We developed a set of initial interaction prototypes for navigation and exploration patterns with HMD-based AR at a natural science museum [31]. On this basis, we formulate a general structure for describing interaction patterns in order to develop further patterns with a variety of new styles. Each of these patterns should include design knowledge, evaluated usability findings, a description of how it can be used and when it is recommended, and a prototype interactive example for illustration and implementation support. Towards this end, we present two new prototypes with similar interaction patterns, but different design ideas for interaction styles.

## 3.1  Interaction Patterns Geared Towards Immersive Augmented Reality

Based on the two modes of the museum visit, we divide the experience of HMD-based AR content at dedicated locations in the museum into the following sub-patterns.

- Orientate and/or guide visitors to exhibits for which AR content has been prepared.
- Encourage visitors to trigger digital content automatically when they come close to certain objects or move in certain ways.
- Facilitate visitors to consciously activate digital content at PoIs in a controlled manner.
- Help visitors navigate through presentations and narratives according to their preferences.
- Enable physical and spatial interactions that fit the specifics of a particular exhibit. This may also require special designs that are not readily reusable.

According to these steps, in previous research we implemented interactive prototypes tailored to an exhibition of animal bones in a natural history museum. It contained the following patterns performed with a HoloLens 2: Be guided by a flying AR avatar into a remote showroom; orientate oneself by seeing AR-based indicators as big virtual circles on the floor; trigger content automatically when stepping into these virtual circles; trigger content with targeted hand gestures via an air-tap menu; control the voice narrator through air menus and gestures; and watch specially produced animations.

Following the established design principles by Gamma et al. [12], and considering the specific usage characteristics of head-mounted AR devices in museums and exhibitions along with the results from usability testing, we formulated a specialized interaction pattern structure for head-mounted augmented reality devices.

In the following, we focus on two essential user goals within this framework, namely "Orientation/Guiding visitors to AR PoIs" and "Activating digital AR content at PoI". These are addressed by three distinct interaction patterns (depicted with examples in Fig. 1): Piloting a visitor towards a PoI, visually indicating PoI locations, and a way to trigger an AR presentation. Within this AR presentation, further interaction possibilities are offered by air menus that can be operated using hand gestures. The previously implemented immersive experience was evaluated with encouraging results [35], which is the groundwork for our further development presented here, now with the goal to include game elements and make interactions more playful.

**Fig. 1.** Orientation and content activation. Left and middle: Piloting visitors to PoIs with an avatar and indicating PoI with a circle on the ground. Right: Activating AR content by stepping into the circle, with feedback sound.

### 3.2   Towards Playful Interaction Patterns

The three more general patterns illustrated by the examples in Fig. 1 have further been extended with variations. Game interaction patterns have been revisited, mainly to explore their usefulness for gamification in a museum in connection with immersive AR. In particular, we explored an "unlocking" mechanics for getting access to information, replacing the "activation" action (above by stepping into the indicator on the ground). At the same time, we want to enhance the feelings of immersion and presence in the space of the museum, which we address by the means of navigating.

Two designed variations have been implemented as prototypes and later evaluated with users concerning their usability and for playfulness. Both prototypes were developed using Unity3D and tested using MS HoloLens 2.

**Variation 1.** Based on the three selected interaction patterns, our design included the following features, see Fig. 2:

- Guiding to PoI: We placed virtual arrows at each turn along a path to guide visitors to an exhibition area. We used premises at our University for testing the overall usability first. Auditory feedback was provided at each turn, and upon arrival, a visualized "home" element notified visitors that they had reached their destination.
- Activating further exploration: Once visitors reached the specially set up exhibition area, they were informed by a virtual signpost about which exhibits could be explored and how to activate them. To add a game element, we employed a spatial key and lock mechanic that mimicked the everyday action of unlocking a gate with a padlock with a key. Users needed to find the color-matching virtual key, grab it with an appropriate gesture and use it (apply and turn it like a real key) with the padlock to activate the exhibit's exploration features.

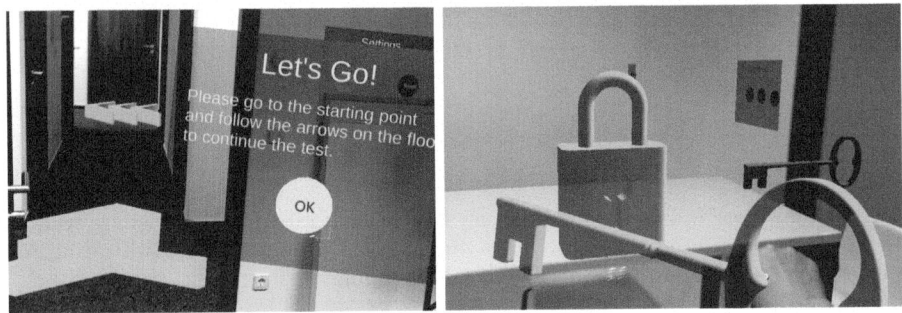

**Fig. 2.** Prototype (Variation 1) for the usability evaluation. Left: Guiding visitors to PoIs with directional arrows on the ground. Right: Opening AR padlock with a matching AR key to activate the exhibit exploration function.

After successfully testing the implemented functionality and usability of these interactions with the first prototype at our university premises, we have adapted the design so that it specifically addresses the thematic needs of the Natural History Museum. As before, it should resemble the game mechanics of "unlocking". With the example of eliciting narrations about the orca whale on display, we replaced the key with a prey fish to which a virtual orca can react. We then developed the second prototype to better understand if these interaction patterns could also work as playful experience in the real museum.

**Variation 2.** The second design was also based on the same three selected interaction patterns. In addition, we wanted to add immersive features by including abstract sounds during interaction. It included the following features, see Fig. 3:

- Guiding to PoI: A forward-facing, progressive animation of overlapping small rings that simulate virtual raindrops with tinkling noises during the process leads visitors to the exhibition area. Each bend on the path contains an atmospheric text, and the background noise of tinkling drops shall enhance immersion and enjoyment.
- Activating further exploration: On reaching the exhibition area, visitors are presented with a virtual fish that they need to "grab" (by hand gesture, supported by the HoloLens tracking) and show towards a virtual orca to activate the exhibit's exploration feature. While visitors hold the fish and move it around, animated visualised echo waves emanate from the orca's head in the direction of the fish. The whale's orientation also constantly adapts to the position of the fish, producing clicking echolocation sounds. This movement is intended to encourage users to play with the virtual object and also to experience orca behaviour in an abstract way. Placing the fish near the orca's head ends the feeding and thus "unlocks" further content.

The prototypes aimed to explore in which way immersive augmented reality could facilitate interactive and engaging museum experiences through intuitive and playful interaction designs.

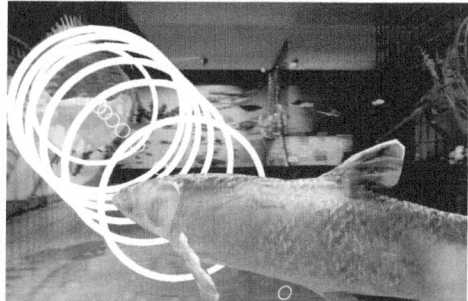

**Fig. 3.** Prototype (Variation 2) for playful experience at the museum. Left: Guiding visitors to the PoI with raindrop circles flowing away on the ground. Right: Feeding orca with an AR fish to activate the exhibit exploration function.

### 3.3  Pattern Abstraction

All variations mentioned above, the one from a previous project and the two newer playful ones, follow the same interaction patterns at an abstract level. The patterns combine characteristics of patterns from museum visits, user interface patterns and game patterns. They can be summarized in the following structure.

**Interaction Pattern: Interactive Exhibition Navigation.** This interaction pattern aims to guide visitors to the point of interest:

– **Name:** "Interactive Exhibition Navigation"
– **Problem:** Visitors in spaces such as museums or exhibitions that include (at first invisible) AR content often struggle to navigate efficiently to such points of interest, potentially missing key exhibits or information.
– **Context:** This pattern is applicable in environments where visitors explore rooms with multiple points of interest in museums, galleries or trade fairs, only a selection of which are equipped with AR content.
– **Use When:** Use at the starting point of visitors' exploration, or when there are PoI remaining, or when visitors wish to revisit certain exhibits. Preferably use if the target PoI is not within sight of the current position.
– **Solution:**
  • PoI Selection Interface: An interface that allows visitors to select specific points of interest for personalized navigation.
  • Navigation Control Interface: Enable the tour function to be started, stopped, paused and resumed at will.
  • Visual Cues: Display directional visual cues that augment the physical world and represent the path to the PoI.
  • Auditory Feedback: Use auditory cues as interaction feedback on (partial) goals achieved or to provide information about exhibits.
– **Examples, Variations:**
  • Visual cues: Flying avatar guide with sparkling tail to follow (see Fig. 1 left)
  • Visual cues: Arrows at the next visible corner (see Fig. 2 left)
  • Visual cues: Growing trail of abstract raindrops (see Fig. 3 left)

**Interaction Pattern: Indicating for Triggering.** The objective of this interaction pattern is to indicate visitors the locations of target exhibits, providing them with an affordance for action (Indicating and Triggering/Unlocking are here combined to save space.)

– **Name:** "Indicating for Triggering Content"
– **Problem:** Without an obvious hint, visitors may not be aware of hidden AR content and may not know how to activate it.
– **Context:** In an exhibition area with numerous exhibits, only selected exhibits are equipped with AR content. Visitors need clear affordances and assistance for activation.
– **Use When:** To be used when visitors enter a room with exhibits that are within sight. Used to give an overview of a room.
– **Solution:**
  • Visual Indicators: Use distinct visual elements with consistent style attributes during a walkthrough (e.g. icons, titles, 3D objects) near or at exhibits to signal that content is available.
  • Activation Mechanism: Implement a virtual trigger that visitors can recognize and use to activate the digital content.
  • Feedback Cues: Upon activation, offer immediate visual and/or auditory feedback to confirm.

- **Examples, Variations:**
  - Indicators as big circles on the ground marking an active area, activation by stepping into the circle (see Fig. 1 right)
  - Indicators that display 3D objects to literally unlock content (see Fig. 2 right)
  - Thematic indicator, e.g. as a prey animal that can be fed to activate the orca, including motivating explanation and playful interaction (see Fig. 3 right)

# 4    Evaluation of Usability and Playful Experience

The evaluation of the proposed interaction patterns was conducted in two phases. We first tested the gamified version 1 in the simulated exhibition on the university premises in order to evaluate the usability, especially with regard to effectiveness and functionality. After verifying this, we built the second variation for testing it with visitors at a natural history museum. In this phase, the interactions created with the interaction patterns should be evaluated to determine the extent to which they provide a playful experience for visitors to the HMD-based AR applications. We used observations and structured questionnaires for our research.

## 4.1    Evaluation

For testing the Variation 1, we recruited 21 students with a background in media design but no experience with AR applications, considering them as our target users. Given their expertise, we anticipated they could provide comprehensive and effective feedback on the interactions. Employing the evaluation method proposed by Liu et al. [25], we used quantitative measures, supplemented with observation sheets and the think-aloud method. We primarily recorded the number of interaction failures and the issues raised by participants, focusing on tracking their progress and completion of the interactions. After the testing, participants were invited to an interview to discuss their overall perceptions and suggestions.

The test of the second variant was carried out directly in the museum exhibition, close to the orca skeleton on display. We recruited 18 museum visitors aged between 16 and 67 on site. While we approached the first few ourselves, we received further enquiries from interested parties during the day. The evaluation should cover two main criteria: playful experience and usability. We utilized a playful experience questionnaire adapted from Boberg et al. [4], see Table 1, and a usability evaluation questionnaire derived from Lewis [22]. Both questionnaires employed a 5-point Likert scale, where 1 represented strongly disagree and 5 represented strongly agree. We hypothesized that the interaction would not only provide adequate usability but also substantial entertainment value.

## 4.2   Test Result

**Variation 1.** The test with "following arrows" and "unlocking with keys" interactions revealed that all 21 participants were able to complete the "following arrow" interaction without additional support, although three participants initially missed the guiding arrows on the ground and required 2 to 3 attempts to initiate the guidance correctly. In the "unlocking with key" interaction, where participants had to match the color of a key with a lock to activate an exhibit's exploration features, all participants completed the task. However, only six managed to do so on their first attempt without extra help. Ten participants needed more than two attempts, and the remainder succeeded with additional guidance to find the appropriate key and lock.

Furthermore, the interview results from participants highlighted the need for providing basic knowledge about using head-mounted AR devices to first-time users. This included instructions on how to wear the device and ensuring that hand gestures were performed within the sensor's detectable range. Participants' verbal feedback also indicated that pre-informing them about the purpose of the interactions and what to expect could reduce the psychological burden associated with learning new interaction techniques.

**Variation 2.** Upon completing the test of "following raindrop circles" and "feeding orca with fish" interactions, we gathered 15 valid responses in total. We applied quantitative measurement for the questionnaire results and analyzed the data by calculating the mean and mode for each question, see Table 1. The mode represents the majority response to each question, while the mean provides an overall assessment of responses, which helped to refine the mode results.

Overall, the quantitative results of the test aligned with our initial expectations: With sufficient usability of these two interactions, participants enjoyed the interaction process and encountered playful experiences in various categories. During the "following raindrop circle" interaction, participants reported a positive learning experience in the "Challenge" category, with the mode for these questions consistently above 4. In the "Control" category, the mode ranged from 3 to 5. Although the mean for the statement "I felt powerful" was below 3, the guidance interaction did not intend to evoke a sense of power, and the novelty of the interface and interaction modes could understandably overwhelm first-time users. In the "Relaxation and Sensation" category, the mode was above 4 for all questions, with the mean exceeding 3 only for "I felt relieved from stress" and "I felt pleased by its aesthetics." The categories "Discovery, Exploration, and Humor" received very positive evaluations, see Fig. 4, with all mode values at 5 and mean values above 4. The only lower scores were in the "Captivation" category for the questions "I forgot about my surroundings" and "I lost track of time and space," with both mode and mean values below 3. This is reasonable considering that participants could not completely disregard their surroundings or other visitors, especially in a crowded environment, while following the virtual raindrop trails.

**Table 1.** Playful experience questionnaire

| Category | Items | Follow circles | | Feed orca | |
|---|---|---|---|---|---|
| | | Mode | Mean | Mode | Mean |
| Captivation | I forgot about my surroundings | 2 | 2.5 | 4 | 3.2 |
| | I felt completely absorbed | 4 | 3.2 | 5 | 3.6 |
| | I lost track of time and space | 2 | 2.5 | 3 | 2.8 |
| Challenge | It stimulated me to learn new things | 4 | 4.3 | 5 | 4.3 |
| | It was a true learning experience | 5 | 3.9 | 5 | 3.9 |
| | I enjoyed learning new things | 5 | 4.3 | 5 | 4.1 |
| Control | I had the capability to influence | 5 | 3.8 | 4 | 3.9 |
| | I felt powerful | 3 | 2.7 | 2 | 2.7 |
| | I enjoyed being in control | 3 | 3.3 | 2 | 3.1 |
| Discovery | I enjoyed discovering new things | 5 | 4.5 | 5 | 4.4 |
| | I enjoyed finding useful new ways of using it | 5 | 4.5 | 5 | 4.3 |
| | I enjoyed finding something unexpected | 5 | 4.7 | 5 | 4.3 |
| Exploration | I felt curious | 5 | 4.8 | 5 | 4.5 |
| | I enjoyed experimenting | 5 | 4.8 | 5 | 4.5 |
| | I enjoyed trying out new things | 5 | 4.7 | 5 | 4.5 |
| Humor | It made me laugh | 5 | 3.9 | 5 | 4 |
| | I had fun | 5 | 4.5 | 5 | 4.7 |
| | I experienced funny situations | 3 | 3.8 | 5 | 3.8 |
| Relaxation | I felt relaxed | 4 | 4 | 4 | 4.2 |
| | I enjoyed passing time with it | 5 | 4.5 | 5 | 4.5 |
| | I felt relieved from stress | 4 | 3.8 | 4 | 3.9 |
| Sensation | I felt pleased by its aesthetics | 4 | 3.8 | 4 | 4 |
| | I enjoyed the visuals | 5 | 4.1 | 4 | 4.3 |
| | I felt pleased by the quality of it | 4 | 3.6 | 4 | 3.7 |

In the "feeding orca with fish" interaction task, where participants fed a fish to an orca to activate the exploration feature, the assessment categories mirrored those of the first interaction. The "Discovery, Exploration, and Humor" category again scored the highest, see Fig. 4, with a mode of 5 and mean values above 4. The "Relaxation and Sensation" categories followed, with mode values between 4 and 5 and mean values around 4. The "Captivation" and "Challenge" categories had mode values ranging from 3 to 5, and mean values between 3 and 4.5. Unlike the first interaction, the "Control" category questions "I felt powerful" and "I enjoyed" during the second interaction had a mode of 2 and mean around 3, largely attributable to the users' initial unfamiliarity with the device and the need for a period of adjustment to the new interaction style.

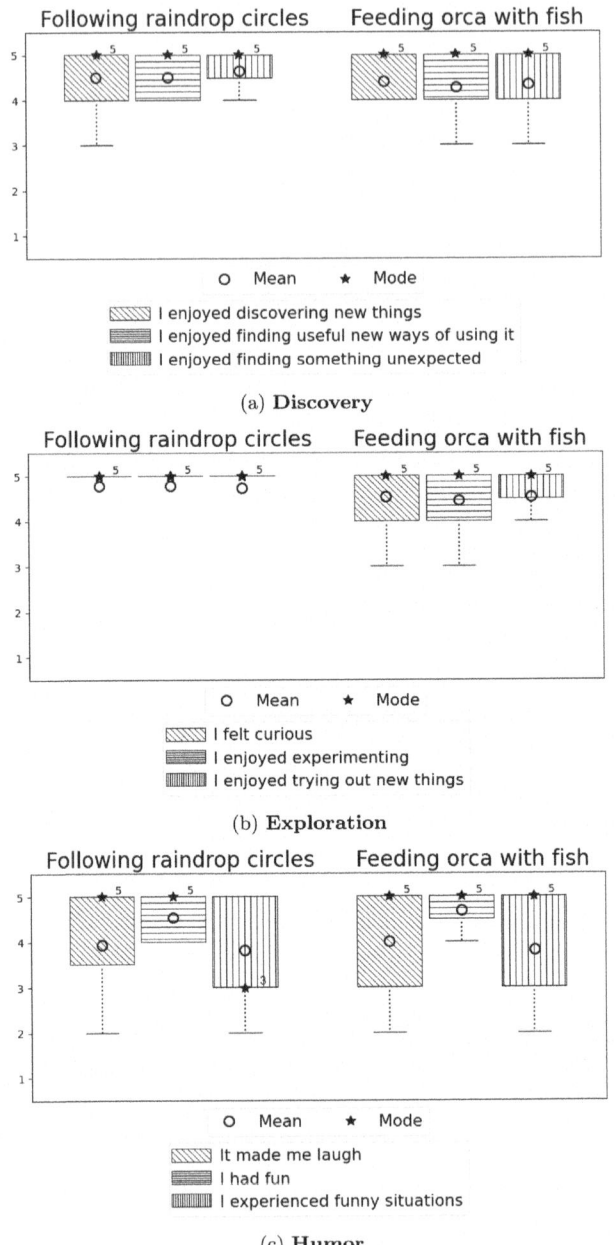

**Fig. 4.** Comparison of Mean and Mode value: Playful experiences with (a) Discovery, (b) Exploration and (c) Humor categories in "following raindrop circles" and "feeding orca with fish" interactions.

# 5  Discussion

The test with the interactions 'follow the arrows' and 'unlock with the key' showed that the designed solution was able to form appropriate expectations for the interaction. The results of the second prototype showed that the interactions designed with these patterns were not only effective, but also had a high entertainment value. These results from both tests confirmed the effectiveness of the interaction patterns.

Participants were able to successfully complete both interaction tasks. In the lock-opening interaction, which involved more steps and required participants to compare colors, some participants enjoyed the fact that they deliberately tried out the wrong keys to open the locks. While the "key and lock" game mechanic added more entertainment value to the interaction, providing participants with clear instructions was crucial. For example, although participants were supposed to insert the key into the lock, some initially looked for a virtual door rather than the lock. Additionally, some participants attempted to turn the key in the lock as they would in real life after insertion. Thus, the extent to which an interaction mimics real-life actions can affect its entertainment value.

The results also suggested that the application of game mechanics in interactions should be paired with appropriate exhibits. Our test, conducted in a simulated exhibition without a specific door, caused some confusion among participants when they received a key, but this mechanic might provide clearer usability and entertainment in a more playful exhibition, such as one themed around games or toys. Compared to the simpler guide interaction using arrows, the key and lock interaction was more entertaining but also increased the complexity of the interaction. Therefore, when designing interaction patterns with game elements, it is necessary to consider additional game attributes in the structure, including how to start the game and explanations for winning.

The test in the museum showed that the interaction of feeding fish to an orca was slightly more enjoyable than following the raindrop circle guidance. Participants were able to successfully follow the raindrop circles on the ground to reach the exhibition area. Although simple directional arrows in the first prototype had already successfully guided users to the exhibition area, in the second prototype, we employed a more enjoyable visual interface and added the sound of rain, enhancing the positive experience while following the path. In the interaction of feeding fish to an orca, all participants completed the task, which was designed to effectively activate the exploration features of the exhibit upon reaching the point of interest. Unlike the interactions in the first prototype, this interface was directly designed based on the characteristics of the exhibit: orcas use ultrasonic waves emitted from their heads to locate prey. Thus, this interaction ensured functionality while also incorporating knowledge about orca hunting, thereby providing better entertainment both visually and operationally.

## 6   Conclusion

This study explored the application of head-mounted AR technology in museum exhibitions, demonstrating that interaction patterns including knowledge from game patterns can enhance both usability and enjoyment. Through systematic testing of two prototypes, the study confirmed their effectiveness. The first prototype, tested in a simulated environment, highlighted the importance of clear instructions in game-like interactions, such as the "key and lock" mechanic, which, while engaging, revealed complexities in user interaction that may need simplification for optimal enjoyment. The second prototype, focused on creating a playful experience for museum visitors, provided insights into how AR can be used to enhance educational content through gamified elements that are both enjoyable and informative.

The results indicate that AR technology, when combined with playful interaction design, can transform the museum experience by making it more interactive and enjoyable. The study underscores the necessity of aligning interactive elements with the physical and thematic aspects of exhibits. Moving forward, the generalized description of interactions can guide the development of AR applications based on a dedicated pattern language. We expect further that by making interaction patterns available in authoring software, AR developers can be supported in creating engaging interactive applications. Hence, this research leads to a foundational framework for further innovation in the integration of AR technology within the cultural heritage sector.

Finally, it should be noted that the effectiveness of the interaction patterns may vary depending on the type of AR technology employed. Our research focuses on head-mounted augmented reality, which provides an immersive experience. Conversely, augmented reality on mobile devices (HHD) offers a more accessible and cost-effective alternative. There is an opportunity to further enhance the development of AR by exploring playful interaction patterns that are effective across both HHDs and HMDs.

**Acknowledgments.** This work has been funded (in part) by the European Commission under grant agreement LoGaCulture (101094036).

## References

1. Alexander, C.: A Pattern Language: Towns, Buildings, Construction. Oxford University Press (1977)
2. Battistoni, P., Di Gregorio, M., Romano, M., Sebillo, M., Vitiello, G., Brancaccio, A.: Interaction design patterns for augmented reality fitting rooms. Sensors **22**(3), 982 (2022)
3. Berland, M., de Royston, M.M., Lyons, L., Kumar, V., Hansen, D., Hooper, P., Lindgren, R., Planey, J., Quigley, K., Thompson, W., et al.: Reframing playful participation in museums: identity, collaboration, inclusion, and joy (2020)
4. Boberg, M., Karapanos, E., Holopainen, J., Lucero, A.: Plexq: towards a playful experiences questionnaire. In: Proceedings of the 2015 Annual Symposium on Computer-Human Interaction in Play, pp. 381–391 (2015)

5. Borchers, J.O.: A pattern approach to interaction design. In: Proceedings of the 3rd Conference on Designing Interactive Systems: Processes, Practices, Methods, and Techniques, pp. 369–378 (2000)
6. Börsting, I., Fischer, B., Gruhn, V.: Ar scribble: evaluating design patterns for augmented reality user interfaces. In: Augmented Reality, Virtual Reality, and Computer Graphics: 8th International Conference, AVR 2021, Virtual Event, 7–10 Sept 2021, Proceedings 8, pp. 169–177. Springer (2021)
7. Brondi, R., Carrozzino, M., Lorenzini, C., Tecchia, F.: Using mixed reality and natural interaction in cultural heritage applications. Informatica **40**(3) (2016)
8. Chung, H.L., Chin, K.Y., Wang, C.S.: Development of a head-mounted mixed reality museum navigation system. In: 2021 IEEE 4th International Conference on Knowledge Innovation and Invention (ICKII), pp. 111–114. IEEE (2021)
9. Chung, N., Han, H., Joun, Y.: Tourists' intention to visit a destination: the role of augmented reality (AR) application for a heritage site. Comput. Hum. Behav. **50**, 588–599 (2015)
10. Clanton, C.: An interpreted demonstration of computer game design. In: CHI 98 Conference Summary on Human Factors in Computing Systems, pp. 1–2 (1998)
11. Dearden, A., Finlay, J.: Pattern languages in HCI: a critical review. Hum.-Comput. Interact. **21**(1), 49–102 (2006)
12. Gamma, E., Helm, R., Johnson, R., Vlissides, J.: Design patterns. In: Elements of Reusable Object-Oriented Software. Addison-Wesley (1995)
13. Haahr, M.: Creating location-based augmented-reality games for cultural heritage. In: Alcañiz, M., Göbel, S., Ma, M., Fradinho Oliveira, M., Baalsrud Hauge, J., Marsh, T. (eds.) JCSG 2017. LNCS, vol. 10622, pp. 313–318. Springer, Cham (2017). https://doi.org/10.1007/978-3-319-70111-0_29
14. Haahr, M.: Reconciling immersion and presence: locative game mechanics and narrative techniques for cultural heritage. Virtual Creativity **8**(1), 23–37 (2018)
15. Hammady, R., Ma, M., Powell, A.: User experience of markerless augmented reality applications in cultural heritage museums: 'MuseumEye' as a case study. In: Augmented Reality, Virtual Reality, and Computer Graphics: 5th International Conference, AVR 2018, Otranto, Italy, 24–27 June 2018, Proceedings, Part II 5, pp. 349–369. Springer (2018)
16. Hammady, R., Ma, M., Strathern, C., Mohamad, M.: Design and development of a spatial mixed reality touring guide to the Egyptian museum. Multim. Tools Appl. **79**(5), 3465–3494 (2020)
17. Hunsucker, A.J., Baumgartner, E., McClinton, K.: Evaluating an AR-based museum experience. Interactions **25**(4), 66–68 (2018)
18. Jung, T., tom Dieck, M.C., Lee, H., Chung, N.: Effects of virtual reality and augmented reality on visitor experiences in museum. In: Information and Communication Technologies in Tourism 2016: Proceedings of the International Conference in Bilbao, Spain, 2–5 Feb 2016, pp. 621–635. Springer (2016)
19. Jung, T., et al.: Value of augmented reality to enhance the visitor experience: a case study of Manchester Jewish museum. E-Rev. Tourism Res. **7** (2016)
20. Karavolos, D., Bouwer, A., Bidarra, R.: Mixed-initiative design of game levels: integrating mission and space into level generation. FDG **2015**, 8 (2015)
21. Lee, B., Sedlmair, M., Schmalstieg, D.: Design patterns for situated visualization in augmented reality. IEEE Trans. Vis. Comput. Graph. (2023)
22. Lewis, J.R.: IBM computer usability satisfaction questionnaires: psychometric evaluation and instructions for use. Int. J. Hum.-Comput. Interact. **7**(1), 57–78 (1995)

23. Li, Y., Ch'ng, E., Cai, S., See, S.: Multiuser interaction with hybrid VR and AR for cultural heritage objects. In: 2018 3rd Digital Heritage International Congress (DigitalHERITAGE) Held Jointly with 2018 24th International Conference on Virtual Systems & Multimedia (VSMM 2018), pp. 1–8. IEEE (2018)

24. Liu, Y.: Human-computer interaction patterns for head-mounted-device-based augmented reality in the exhibition domain. In: Doctoral Consortium ACM International Conference, pp. 21–26 (2022)

25. Liu, Y., Bitter, J.L., Spierling, U.: Evaluating interaction challenges of head-mounted device-based augmented reality applications for first-time users at museums and exhibitions. In: International Conference on Human-Computer Interaction, pp. 150–163. Springer (2023)

26. Liu, Y., Spierling, U., Rau, L., Dörner, R.: Handheld versus head-mounted AR interaction patterns for museums or guided tours. In: International Conference on Intelligent Technologies for Interactive Entertainment, pp. 229–242. Springer (2020)

27. MacWilliams, A., Reicher, T., Klinker, G., Bruegge, B.: Design patterns for augmented reality systems. In: Proceedings of the International Workshop Exploring the Design and Engineering of Mixed Reality Systems (MIXER), Funchal, Madeira, CEUR Workshop Proceedings (2004)

28. Ntalla, I.: Play and manifestations of playfulness in interactive and immersive museum spaces. Cult., Theory Critique **62**(3), 266–286 (2021)

29. Okanovic, V., Ivkovic-Kihic, I., Boskovic, D., Mijatovic, B., Prazina, I., Skaljo, E., Rizvic, S.: Interaction in extended reality applications for cultural heritage. Appl. Sci. **12**(3), 1241 (2022)

30. Project, L.: Logaculture: locative games for cultural heritage (2024). https://logaculture.eu/. Accessed: 2024-07-18

31. Rau, L., Liu, Y., Bitter, J.L., Spierling, U., Dörner, R.: Supporting the creation of non-linear everyday AR experiences in exhibitions and museums: an authoring process based on self-contained building blocks. Front. Virtual Reality, p. 113 (2022)

32. Rzayev, R., Karaman, G., Henze, N., Schwind, V.: Fostering virtual guide in exhibitions. In: Proceedings of the 21st International Conference on Human-Computer Interaction with Mobile Devices and Services, pp. 1–6 (2019)

33. Shin, C., Oh, S., Jeong, H.: Extended reality platform for metaverse exhibition. J. Web Eng. **22**(7), 1055–1073 (2023)

34. Shneiderman, B.: Designing for fun: how can we design user interfaces to be more fun? Interactions **11**(5), 48–50 (2004)

35. Spierling, U., Bitter, J.L., Liu, Y., Müller, T.: Chances and limitations of immersive augmented reality for game-based learning in museums. In: European Conference on Games Based Learning, vol. 17, pp. 643–650 (2023)

36. Spierling, U., Kampa, A.: An extensible system and its design constraints for location-based serious games with augmented reality. In: Alcañiz, M., Göbel, S., Ma, M., Fradinho Oliveira, M., Baalsrud Hauge, J., Marsh, T. (eds.) JCSG 2017. LNCS, vol. 10622, pp. 60–72. Springer, Cham (2017). https://doi.org/10.1007/978-3-319-70111-0_6

37. Wilde, A.G., Bruegger, P., Hirsbrunner, B.: An overview of human-computer interaction patterns in pervasive systems. In: 2010 International Conference on User Science and Engineering (i-USEr), pp. 145–150. IEEE (2010)

38. Wu, C.H., Lin, Y.F., Peng, K.L., Liu, C.H.: Augmented reality marketing to enhance museum visit intentions. J. Hosp. Tour. Technol. **14**(4), 658–674 (2023)

# Assessing the Impact of Haptic Feedback on Stress and Performance in Virtual Reality-Based Police Training

Polona Caserman[1]($\boxtimes$)(iD), Robert Konrad[1], Dennis Purdack[2](iD),
Thorsten Göbel[2], Pascal Tonecker[3], André Kecke[2], and Stefan Göbel[1](iD)

[1] Serious Games Research Group, Technical University of Darmstadt, Darmstadt 64283, Germany
{polona.caserman,robert.konrad,stefan_peter.goebel}@tu-darmstadt.de
[2] Hesse University of Applied Sciences for Public Management and Security, Mühlheim am Main 63165, Germany
{dennis.purdack,thorsten.goebel,andre.kecke}@hoems.hessen.de
[3] Crytek GmbH, Frankfurt am Main 60386, Germany
pascalt@crytek.com
https://www.etit.tu-darmstadt.de/serious-games,
https://hoems.hessen.de,
https://www.crytek.com

**Abstract.** Police forces frequently face a variety of critical situations in their daily routines, where tactical errors can result in severe consequences. To improve the training of police officers it is important to train various scenarios as often as possible. However, traditional training methods, relying on operational trainers to observe and identify tactical errors, restrict the number of sessions due to trainer availability. Towards this end, we developed a virtual reality (VR)-based police training simulation that analyzes trainees' tactical decisions and body postures in real time. Using full-body motion capture suits with haptic feedback, we provide tactile stimulation to alert trainees and warn them when they are about to make a severe tactical error. This paper presents results on the effectiveness of haptic feedback using crossover repeated-measures design (training without vs. with haptics in counterbalanced order) involving pairs of police recruits to assess psychological (i.e., stress, anxiety, mental effort) and physiological stress responses (i.e., heart rate and heart rate variability), as well as training performance. Results reveal a significant increase in perceived anxiety during training with haptic feedback ($p = 0.01$), albeit physiological responses are comparable in both conditions. Findings further show that haptic feedback significantly improves trainees' performance in terms of secured areas ($p = 0.03$). These results could be particularly valuable for police operational trainer considering the adoption of VR-based training with haptic feedback to enhance training. Future research should explore long-term effects and strategies of using haptic feedback to improve stress resilience in VR training environments.

© The Author(s), under exclusive license to Springer Nature Switzerland AG 2025
J. L. Plass and X. Ochoa (Eds.): JCSG 2024, LNCS 15259, pp. 263–280, 2025.
https://doi.org/10.1007/978-3-031-74138-8_19

**Keywords:** Virtual Reality · Simulation · Haptic Feedback · Police
Training · Stress

# 1   Introduction

Police officers often encounter hazardous and potentially life-threatening scenarios, such as when entering and searching apartments. Traditional training
methods involve police officers engaging in scenarios while an operational trainer
observes and identifies tactical errors. However, this approach has some disadvantages, as operational trainers must monitor multiple trainees simultaneously,
making it challenging to detect all tactical errors. Additionally, training sessions
are constrained by the availability of trainers, limiting the frequency of training sessions. Moreover, traditional training involving multiple actors and various
(dangerous) equipment entails significant effort and high costs [24]. With modern technology, particularly virtual reality (VR), some of these challenges can be
addressed. VR environments can enhance traditional training by providing additional scenarios and supporting operational trainers, thus offering police agencies
new opportunities to advance their training. Practical guidelines emphasize the
main strengths of VR-based training to simulate dangerous scenarios realisti-
cally, enable more frequent training, and facilitate post-training performance
analysis [8,25,37]. However, they also point out potential weaknesses, including
economic considerations and technical limitations.

Previous research has shown that most immersive VR experiences predominantly rely on audiovisual stimuli and often do not include other sensory cues,
which could significantly enhance the VR experience [23]. Little research has
been conducted to incorporate additional sensory feedback, e.g., tactile stimuli
(e.g., using weapons and other equipment or receiving haptic feedback from virtual obstacles [18,37]) and olfactory stimuli (e.g., implementing smells [7]). When
incorporating haptic feedback, simple vibration might not be sufficient [23] and
should therefore be adapted to the application domain. To address this challenge, we developed a VR-based simulation for police officers, integrating haptic
feedback in addition to the audio-visual stimuli. Towards this end, we utilize
full-body motion capture suits with haptic feedback enabling real-time recognition of trainees' movements. The key innovation of our VR simulation is the
assessment of trainees' tactical decisions and body postures, providing immediate tactile feedback on specific body parts. Thereby minor posture deviations
trigger subtle electrical impulses aimed at correcting the body posture, while
more significant errors lead to stronger feedback.

The goal of our study is to investigate the effects of haptic feedback in a
VR-based training environment on stress, anxiety, mental effort, and training
performance. In a crossover repeated-measures design, participants paired up
to enter and search apartments, either without or with haptic feedback. Our
findings reveal a significant increase in perceived anxiety during training sessions
with haptic feedback, supported by the analysis of vital signs. These results show
promising implications for police forces considering the integration of VR-based

training with haptic feedback. Future research should explore the longitudinal effects of such training methods to determine their effectiveness in reducing tactical errors over time.

## 2 Related Work

### 2.1 VR-Based Training and Simulations

Due to recent advances in VR technology, many immersive serious games and simulation-based training environments were developed, e.g., for firefighters [7], paramedics [10,24], surgeons [34], military [1,22], and police [14,18]. These simulations represent a specific category of serious games, as they integrate a learning or training task into the interactive experience [6]. VR-based simulations are often provided to train specific action sequences that are not always possible in the real world because they are either too risky, too complicated, or too expensive and can therefore be used to support or supplement training. Safe VR-based training environments allow trainees to make mistakes without serious consequences and to gain experiences that help to avoid wrong decisions and mistakes in the future [19]. Virtual training further enables real-time dashboards and after-action reviews, making it possible to dynamically adjust training protocols based on immediate feedback from trainees' performance, thereby tailoring the stress level to their needs [26]. The advantages of VR training to safely train in high-risk situations and guidelines for effective police training within VR have been determined by [8,12,37].

### 2.2 Stress Response in VR-Based Training

An interesting research area explores the use of VR in the training of military personnel to enhance resilience in war zones and prevent the occurrence of mental health problems [1,13,30,31]. According to the review by Pallavicini et al. [29], VR is a promising technology for stress resilience training to reduce perceived stress levels and negative affect in military personnel. In contrast to stress resilience training, further research focused on exploring the impact of different audio-visual stress cues on the trainees' stress levels [9,28,37]. Furthermore, Uhl et al. [36] investigated the effects of multi-sensory stimuli, such as pain and heat, to elicit more authentic threat responses in high-risk situations.

Regarding vital signs, the work of McAllister et al. [22] revealed a significant increase in salivary and subjective stress markers during active shooter training within VR. Furthermore, Martaindale et al. [20] found that VR-based training scenarios can elicit a similar stress response (as identified through saliva samples) in police officers as in traditional training with real persons. Moreover, Kleygrewe et al. [18] investigated the effects of adding pain stimulus on training responses (heart rate, stress, and mental effort) and sense of presence during training in immersive VR and using a 2D simulator (cave-similar system, consisting of five canvases). Their results showed that during the training without pain stimuli,

VR provoked significantly higher levels of perceived stress compared to the 2D simulator. During the training with pain stimuli, the 2D simulator provoked a higher level of perceived stress.

## 3  Materials and Methods

### 3.1  VR Simulation

The VR Simulation, initially presented in [2], with a trailer available online[1], comprises three main components:

**Configuration tool** enables operational trainers to easily create training environments by either modifying existing room layouts or creating new layouts from scratch. Additionally, as shown in Fig. 1, the training environments can be equipped with furniture from the assets library through a simple drag-and-drop interface.

**Fig. 1.** Configuration tool

**VR environment** can subsequently be utilized for training sessions involving multiple users. The objective is for police officers to enter and search an apartment while ensuring sufficient cover. A central training goal is to secure the entire apartment without exposing themselves to danger by turning their backs to unsecured areas. For this purpose, an algorithm has been developed to identify hazardous areas where NPCs are spawned to alert trainees when they lack cover. Unsecured areas are represented by a gray color, which turn red when a dangerous situation arises (see Fig. 2). These areas are not visible during the training but can be reviewed afterwards using the after-action

---

[1] KITE Trailer: https://youtu.be/bBk8St5bOD8, last accessed on May 13, 2024.

review tool. When an area is seen by a trainee, it becomes secured (transparent). A secured area can also transform to unsecured if it is outside the users' field of view and adjacent to an unsecured area. This transition simulates the movements of a potential attacker who may hide in an unsecured area and then move into a previously secured area. The speed of these transformations, akin to the attackers' movement speed, can be adjusted according to the desired difficulty level of the training.

**Fig. 2.** Dangerous areas, represented by red cubes, indicating zones lacking protection.

**After-action review tool** enables a debriefing of the training. During the training, motion capture data, haptic feedback, and vital signs for all trainees are recorded together with AI data, to replay the training sequence. During the review, the training session can be viewed from both a first-person and a top-down perspective. Additionally, AI decisions, particularly the areas (gray and red cubes) are now visible. This function plays an essential role in understanding tactical errors made and being able to learn from them.

## 3.2  Hardware

We use the integrated systems of the Teslasuit[2], which encompass motion capture, haptics, and biometric systems:

**Motion capture system** utilizes 14 sensors to track trainees' movements. These sensors are attached to the limbs (three on each arm and three on each leg) and back (two), enabling the reconstruction of full-body avatars within the VR environment, so that the trainees can interact with each other through body gestures. Additionally, the motion capture system is also used to verify the correctness of the trainees' body postures, ensuring they maintain proper posture, particularly ensuring their arms and legs are not visible from unsecured or dangerous areas (see Fig. 3).

(a) Narrow posture                    (b) Outstretched arms

**Fig. 3.** Correct (left) and wrong (right) posture of the arms, according to police curriculum

**Haptic system** employs electrical muscle stimulation (EMS) and transcutaneous electrical nerve stimulation (TENS) on the arms, legs, abdomen, and back. By adjusting the intensity, frequency, and duration of haptic feedback, trainees can experience a range of tactile sensations, enhancing immersion and realism during VR training. "Soft" haptic feedback (i.e., slight tingling sensations) is provided when the trainee's postures are incorrect, while "hard" haptic feedback (i.e., painful stimuli) is given at the end of the simulation when a severe tactical error occurs.

**Biometrics system** monitors trainees' heart activity using a photoplethysmography (PPG) sensor located on the shoulder. This optical technique

---

[2] Teslasuit: https://teslasuit.io, last accessed on May 7, 2024.

detects volumetric changes in blood flow in peripheral circulation, measuring the trainee's pulse and calculating various heart rate variability metrics. Thus, the biometric system enables the detection of stress levels, allowing the training to be adapted for individual learners and offering personalized experiences. This includes the ability to provide stimuli to increase stress levels and observe trainee responses, as well as to reduce stimuli to decrease stress levels.

The simulation was developed using the CryEngine[3] game engine. To facilitate multiplayer functionality, we employed two HTC Vive Pro Eye[4] headsets and four base stations to ensure coverage of an area measuring approximately $7 \times 10\,\mathrm{m}$.

## 3.3 Participants and Experimental Design

To evaluate the impact of haptic feedback on stress and performance within a VR-based training simulation, a crossover repeated-measures design was used, with each pair undergoing two training sessions - one with haptic feedback and one without. To ensure comparability and prevent participants from anticipating the training scenarios beforehand, two training apartments with comparable difficulty levels were created. The order of feedback conditions (with vs. without haptic feedback) and the assignment of apartments (A or B, as depicted in Fig. 4) were counterbalanced, resulting in four possible sequences.

(a) Apartment A                    (b) Apartment B

**Fig. 4.** Apartment layouts used in the study

---

[3] CryEngine: https://www.cryengine.com, last accessed on May 7, 2024.
[4] HTC Vive Pro Eye: https://www.vive.com/us/product/vive-pro-eye/overview/, last accessed on May 7, 2024.

Participants consisted of current university students in their sixth semester, who provided written informed consent. Each participant completed a health history questionnaire to ascertain their suitability for participation, ensuring they were free from acute medical conditions such as cardiovascular diseases, blood clotting disorders, neurological diseases (e.g., epilepsy), oncological diseases, skin lesions (e.g., dermatitis or skin infections), and balance disorders. Additionally, participants were required to be free from implants or metal prostheses (including pacemakers, insulin pumps, and other implantable electronic devices). Female participants also confirmed non-pregnancy (or lack of knowledge thereof).

### 3.4   Data Collection and Analysis

We employed both subjective and objective assessments.

**Psychological Measures:** To assess subjective stress levels, participants completed a shortened version of the Spielberger State-Trait Anxiety Inventory (STAI) twice during the study: once immediately after experiencing the condition with haptic feedback and once immediately after experiencing the condition without haptic feedback. The original STAI comprises 40 items commonly used to measure trait and state anxiety. The shorter version utilized in our study consists of six items, focusing solely on state anxiety, including following statements "I feel calm", "tense", "upset", "relaxed", "content", and "worried." The validity and reliability of the short scale has been previously shown in [21,35]. All items were rated on a scale from 1 to 4 ("not at all" to "very much so"). The order of the six items was randomized across participants. After reversing the responses for "calm", "relaxed", and "content", the final score was calculated by summing all scores, resulting in a minimum value of 6 and a maximum value of 24.

In addition to evaluating state anxiety, we employed an adapted version of the Visual Analogue Scale (VAS) to assess perceived stress and mental effort. The validity of the original VAS, used to assess anxiety, has been shown in [11] and has also been validated for stress assessment [17]. Participants were instructed to indicate their level of stress or mental effort experienced during the experiment on an unmarked, continuous scale ranging from "not at all" to "extremely", allowing participants to provide a single score between 1 and 100.

**Physiological Measures:** In addition to subjective measures, we assessed heart rate and heart rate variability as objective indicators of anxiety state and stress levels. For this purpose, we utilized the PPG sensor integrated into the suit (see Sect. 3.2) to capture vital parameters. Heart rate variability is a widely utilized physiological measure for detecting arousal and mental stress [3,33]. We recorded the mean of R-R intervals (mean RR), the standard deviation of NN intervals (SDNN), the square root of the mean squared difference of successive RR intervals (RMSSD), and the ratio of low- to high-frequency power (LF/HF) during the training sessions. Due to imperfect skin contact for some participants, the collected data occasionally contained only zero values. Thus, for the analysis, the heart rate and heart rate variability data were adjusted as follows: values outside the realistic heart rate or heart rate variability range (i.e., zero values) were removed, and data points with confidence levels at or below 25% were filtered out.

**Training Performance:** Performance assessment involved measuring the percentage of the total secured area and the maximum secured area. The total secured area represents the portion secured at the time of severe tactical errors and NPC spawning, while the maximum secured area reflects the highest extent of the secured area. Note that the secured area at the end of the simulation can be smaller than the maximum secured area, as areas can become unsecured after initially being secured (see Sect. 3.1).

## 3.5 Study Procedure

Before the start of the experiment, participants were briefed about the purpose of the study and assured that all data will be used confidentially and in anonymized form. They were informed of their right to withdraw from the experiment at any point, without providing a reason. Approval for the study was obtained from the local ethics committee of the Technical University of Darmstadt (EK 23/2024).

Subsequently, participants were directed to a separate room where they put on the motion-capture suit. For optimal haptic feedback, male participants were instructed to wear only underpants, while female participants could retain their bra or a top. The suit was then properly fastened with assistance from the experimenter to ensure a snug fit, enhancing motion capture and haptic experience. Participants individually calibrated the haptic feedback by gradually adjusting the power until they experienced a tingling sensation, then increasing it further until it reached their maximum comfort threshold without causing excessive pain.

Following suit calibration, participants put on the HTC Vive Head-Mounted Display (HMD) and adjusted it for a sharp sight. Motion capture calibration was performed while participants were standing in an I-pose, ensuring accurate avatar representation. This process was repeated until a minimal visible offset was achieved when participants clapped their hands. In the virtual environment, participants viewed their virtual bodies from a first-person perspective and could see their partner. Because the VR lab was larger than the virtual environment (approx. 10 x 7 m), trainees could physically move through the entire virtual apartment without interruption.

Afterwards participants experienced two conditions (with vs. without haptic feedback) in a counterbalanced order to minimize order effects. It's important to note that participants wore the suit in both conditions, including the condition without haptic feedback, to control for variance in ratings. Additionally, the layout of the apartment to be entered and searched differed between the first and second training sessions. Each experimental session lasted approximately one hour. The experimental procedure is detailed in Fig. 5.

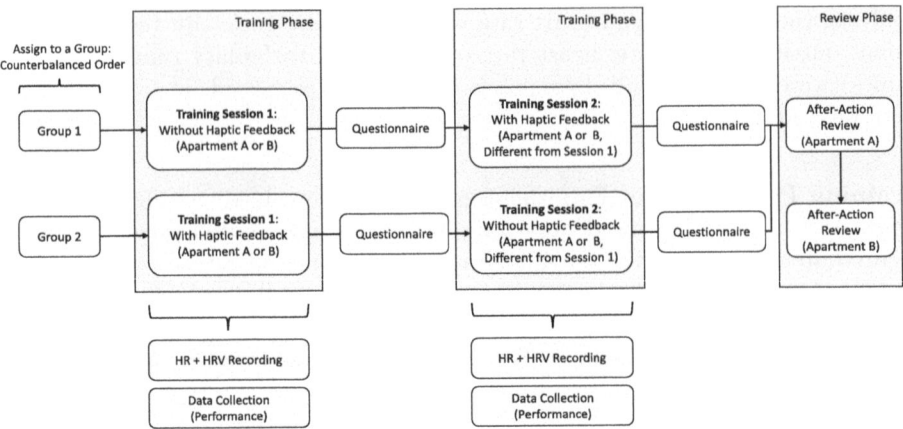

**Fig. 5.** Study procedure followed during the experiment, detailing training sessions, data recording, and after-action review.

In the condition with haptic feedback, trainees with incorrect posture received slight feedback ("soft" haptic feedback) at corresponding body parts to prompt correction, while those lacking protection additionally felt haptic feedback on the entire body ("hard" haptic feedback). Successful completion of apartment searches was indicated by a sound effect, whereas severe tactical errors triggered the spawning of an NPC accompanied by a distinct sound effect. Throughout the sessions, the experimenter remained uninvolved. Heart rate and heart rate variability were recorded continuously using the PPG sensor. Furthermore, at the end of each training phase, we collected performance data.

Upon completion of the first training phase, participants removed the HMD and filled out questionnaires (as outlined in Sect. 3.4) before transitioning to the next training phase. Immediately after both scenarios were completed, trainees received an after-action review of their training performance. After the conclusion of the experiment, the suit underwent disinfection and cleaning to prepare for subsequent participants.

## 4    Results

According to the Kolmogorov-Smirnov test, the data did not follow a normal distribution. Therefore, we used the Wilcoxon signed rank test to evaluate the statistical significance among the two conditions (without vs. with haptic feedback), considering p-values of $< 0.05$ as statistically significant. For each condition, we calculated the median (MED) and interquartile ranges (IQR) and further plotted box plots. Furthermore, we calculated the effect size using Hedges' g, taking the sample size into account [32], with a value of 0.2 representing a small, 0.5 a medium, and 0.8 a large effect size [4]. All statistical analyses were performed using MATLAB.

### 4.1   Participants

Forty undergraduate police students (19 females, 21 males) aged 20 to 30 years (mean age: $23.45 \pm 2.61$ years), completed both training sessions. Due to technical problems, questionnaire data from two participants could not be collected. Thus, the questionnaire response analysis included data from 38 participants (18 females, 20 males). Additionally, despite multiple attempts to calibrate and ensure the PPG sensor's connectivity, valid data for 12 participants were not obtained. Given time constraints, we prioritized proceeding with the training sessions and obtaining results regarding the training performance and subjective responses. Consequently, biometric system analysis was conducted with data from 28 participants (15 females, 13 males).

Despite concerns about cybersickness in VR experiences, no participant reported symptoms of cybersickness after the experiment, and no participant dropped out during the experiment.

### 4.2   Stress Responses

As shown in Fig. 6, participants (n = 38) reported higher scores for anxiety, perceived stress, and mental effort in the condition with haptic feedback compared to the condition without haptic feedback. A one-tailed Wilcoxon test revealed a significant difference only for anxiety ($p = 0.01$, $z = -2.35$) with an effect size of $g = -0.35$.

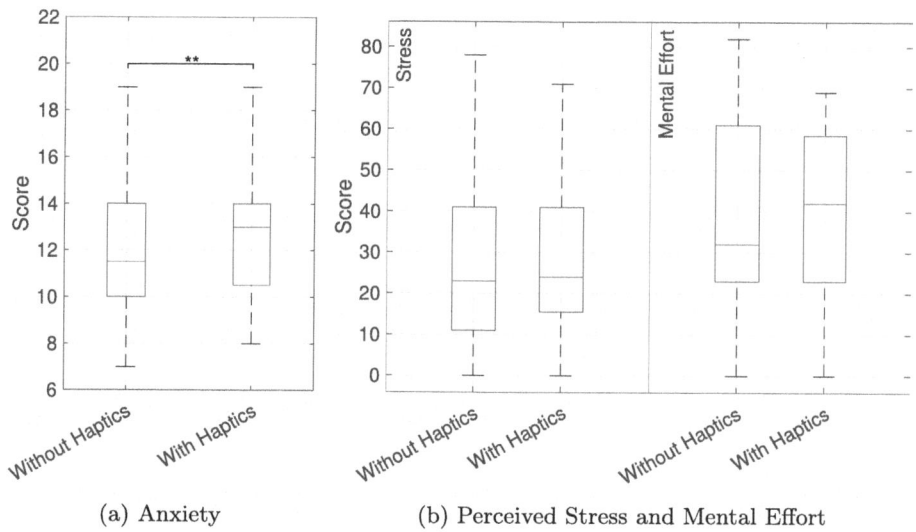

(a) Anxiety                    (b) Perceived Stress and Mental Effort

**Fig. 6.** Subjective ratings during training without and with haptic feedback. Statistical significance between conditions is denoted by asterisks (** for $p < 0.01$).

Regarding the physical training responses (n = 28), as shown in Fig. 7, the results show that HR and LF/HF ratio were higher, while mean RR, SDNN, and

RMSSD were lower during training with haptic feedback compared to training without haptic feedback. However, no statistically significant differences were found between the two conditions.

### 4.3  Training Performance

To assess the impact of haptic feedback on training outcomes, we measured both the total secured area and the maximum secured area achieved by participants at the end of the simulation. Since the training was conducted in pairs, we gathered data from 20 pairs. After identifying and removing outliers, specifically pairs that significantly underperformed as indicated by boxplots, we retained 17 data points for analysis.

The outcomes of the training performance are presented in Fig. 8. The results from the one-tailed Wilcoxon test show that the total covered area during training with haptic feedback was significantly higher compared to training without haptic feedback ($p = 0.03$, $z = -1.89$) with an effect size of $g = -0.41$. Similarly, the maximum covered area during training with haptic feedback was significantly higher compared to training without haptic feedback ($p = 0.03$, $z = -1.89$) with an effect size of $g = -0.48$.

Further findings show that in the condition without haptic feedback, only one pair successfully secured the entire apartment, whereas in the condition with haptic feedback, three pairs were able to secure the entire apartment.

## 5  Discussion

The results indicate that participants experienced higher stress levels during the condition with haptic feedback, as evident by the subjective results. Notably, anxiety ratings were significantly higher after training with haptic feedback (see Fig. 6). Although physical responses (see Fig. 7) also suggested increased stress levels-such as decreased mean RR, SDNN, RMSSD, and increased LF/HF ratio as previously identified in [3, 15, 27]-these were not statistically significant. Provoking higher stress during training also aligns with the curriculum for decision-making and acting under stress and in high-risk situations [16], where researchers propose to add pain stimuli to VR training for immediate feedback on performance and to increase perceived stress levels. Increasing the stress level in training is essential to prepare officers for the actual stress that they will experience on the job; however, it is also important to adapt the training scenario to the optimal stress level [5, 8].

Participants provided additional feedback, highlighting moments inducing stress, anxiety, or mental strain. Some participants mentioned being confused or uncertain when receiving "soft" haptic feedback. "Soft" haptic feedback, particularly slight tingling sensations on arms and legs, was triggered when the trainees had incorrect postures, e.g., outstretched arms visible from unsecured areas. Most trainees also pretended to hold a gun, affecting their posture by outstretching their arms instead of keeping their hands close to their bodies, as

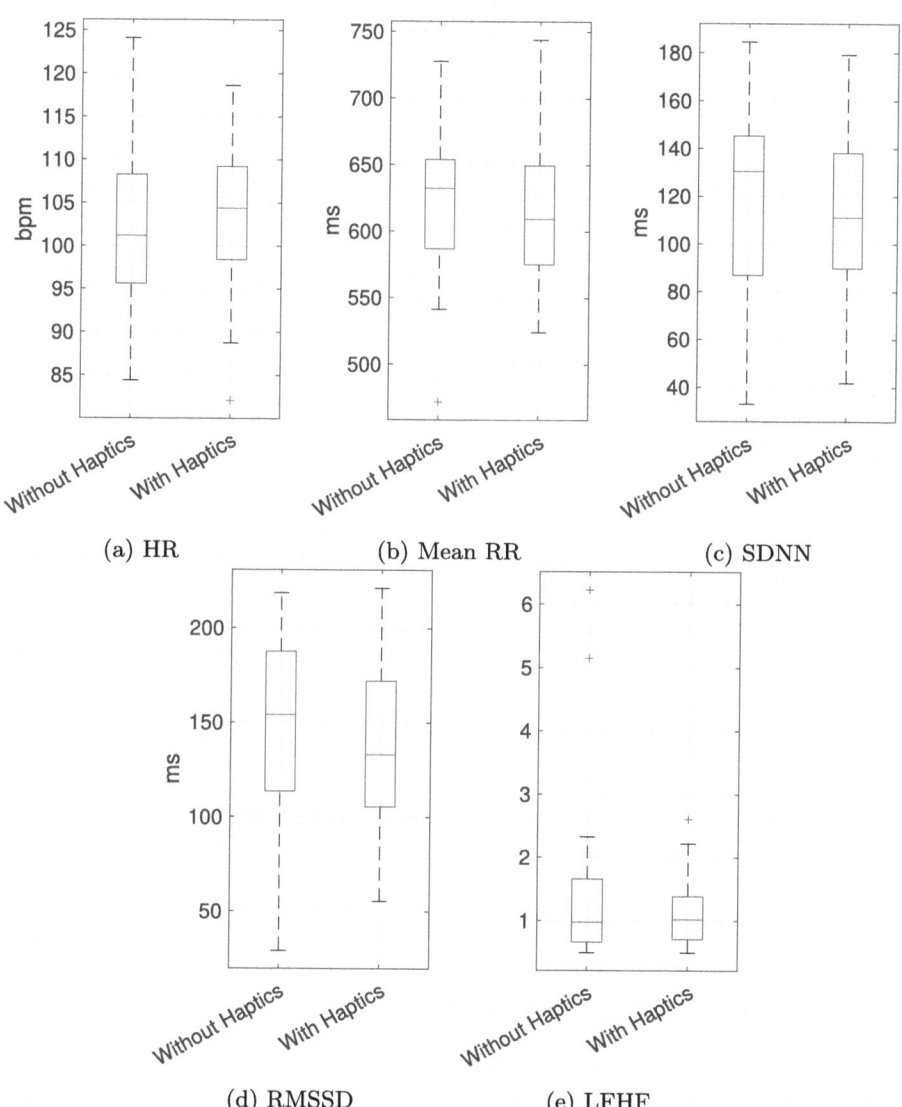

**Fig. 7.** Physical training responses during training without and with haptic feedback.

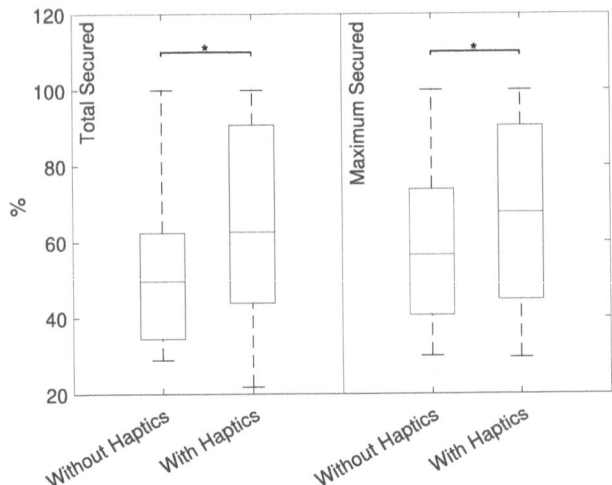

**Fig. 8.** Training performance for training without and with haptic feedback. Statistical significance between conditions is denoted by asterisks (* for $p < 0.05$).

recommended in the police curriculum (see Fig. 3). Hutter et al. [12] suggest that learning should be self-regulated, allowing trainees to choose when and where they receive feedback. In our VR simulation, the intensity of haptic feedback can be adjusted, ranging from a tingling sensation to painful stimuli. The confusion about the "soft" haptic feedback, especially during incorrect postures, might come from trainees' unfamiliarity with the system and the overwhelming number of new stimuli. Specifically, we did not explain when participants would receive haptic feedback, believing it should be intuitive. Another reason for confusion with "soft" haptic feedback could be caused by inaccurate motion capture. Despite individual avatar calibration minimizing tracking offset, the sensors integrated in the suit may have shifted over time, causing the avatars to misalign with the trainees' movements.

Overall, participants secured a significantly larger area when haptic feedback was provided (see Fig. 8). This suggests that particularly "soft" haptic feedback during the training itself is helpful, as it alerts trainees when they are about to make a mistake, making them pay more attention. However, some participants mentioned that the absence of haptic feedback increases their confidence, leading them to believe they had not made mistakes. Specifically, they were not told whether the current training phase included haptic feedback or not. This sometimes resulted in participants in the no-haptic feedback condition to proceed faster and, thus, securing a larger area, contrary to the intended outcome. After training within both VR conditions, there was enough time to replay both trainings using the after-action review tool. Thereby the participants were able to reflect their training on their own, without experiment supervisors intervening. All participants intuitively understood where the tactical error was made. The possibility to review the training itself was also identified as crucial by [8,12,37].

Participants also noted that the appearance of the opponent and the associated sound effects increased stress levels. As mentioned in Sect. 4.3, only 3 out of 17 pairs were able to secure the entire apartment successfully. The remaining 14 pairs were not able to secure the entire apartment, resulting in one trainee (for each pair) receiving "hard" haptic feedback on the whole body, which could cause pain. We believe the stress response rather comes from the haptic feedback than the visual appearance of the NPC. The current simulation uses an alien-like NPC to counteract biases, but in future we could also feature NPCs resembling children, elderly persons, neurodivergent individuals, or animals. More importantly, different aural feedback, particular screams or barking as well as other sound effects could in introduced to further make training more immersive. As already identified in previous work, virtual training provides an opportunity to easily adjust training scenarios by including vulnerable populations that otherwise cannot be easily included in traditional training [14, 25].

Other aspects causing stress, as mentioned by participants, include discovering a double room layout. Mostly, one of the trainees stayed in the doorstep and paid attention to the corridor, while the other trainee entered the room and reported the findings. Participants also mentioned stress from opposite doors, large apartment sizes, and challenges encountered while cutting open angles.

## 6  Conclusion

In this study, we present results on the impact of haptic feedback on perceived stress and training performance. We implemented haptic feedback in a VR-based training simulation to alert trainees of incorrect postures, such as outstretched arms visible from unsecured areas where a potential opponent could be hidden and prepared to attack. Haptic feedback is also used to indicate severe tactical errors. This implementation of haptic feedback aims to help trainees improve their performance. Psychological measures indicate that state anxiety significantly increases when haptic feedback is provided. Although not significant, these results are further supported by physiological measures such as heart rate and heart rate variability. Additional findings confirm that haptic feedback enhances trainees' performance, enabling them to cover a significantly larger area when searching apartments. We hope these results will help operational trainers or special units in improving their training methods by incorporating VR technology, including motion capture suits with haptic feedback.

**Acknowledgments.** This study was initially conducted by TU Darmstadt (grant number: 13N15547) in cooperation with Hesse University of Applied Sciences for Public Management and Security (grant number: 13N15546) and Crytek GmbH (grant number: 13N15548) in the course of the research project KITE, under the *Research for Civil Security* program funded by the German Federal Ministry of Education and Research. The research results on motion reconstruction are being adapted and further developed to be used for education purposes and form the foundation for the interdisciplinary project The Analyst (project number: FR-253/2023), funded by the *Stiftung Innovation in der Hochschullehre*.

**Conflict of Interest**. The authors have no competing interests to declare that are relevant to the content of this article.

# References

1. Buckwalter, J.G., Rizzo, A., John, B., Newman, B., Williams, J., Parsons, T.: STRIVE: stress resilience in virtual environments. In: 2012 IEEE Virtual Reality Workshops (VRW), pp. 173–174 (2012). https://doi.org/10.1109/VR.2012.6180936
2. Caserman, P., Müller, P.N., Göbel, T., Tonecker, P., Yildirim, S., Kecke, A., Purdack, D., Göbel, S.: Virtual reality simulator for police training with AI-supported cover detection. In: Haahr, M., Rojas-Salazar, A., Göbel, S. (eds.) Joint Conference on Serious Games, JCSG, pp. 181–193. Springer Nature Switzerland, Cham (2023).https://doi.org/10.1007/978-3-031-44751-8_13
3. Castaldo, R., Melillo, P., Bracale, U., Caserta, M., Triassi, M., Pecchia, L.: Acute mental stress assessment via short term HRV analysis in healthy adults: a systematic review with meta-analysis. Biomed. Signal Process. Control **18**, 370–377 (2015). https://doi.org/10.1016/j.bspc.2015.02.012
4. Cohen, J.: Statistical Power Analysis for the Behavioral Sciences. Academic Press (1977)
5. Di Nota, P.M., Huhta, J.M.: Complex motor learning and police training: applied, cognitive, and clinical perspectives. Front. Psychol. **10** (2019). https://doi.org/10.3389/fpsyg.2019.01797
6. Dörner, R., Göbel, S., Effelsberg, W., Wiemeyer, J.: Serious Games: Foundations. Concepts and Practice. Springer (2016). https://doi.org/10.1007/978-3-319-40612-1
7. Eller, C., Bittner, T., Dombois, M., Rüppel, U.: Collaborative immersive planning and training scenarios in VR. In: Smith, I.F.C., Domer, B. (eds.) Advanced Computing Strategies for Engineering, pp. 164–185. Springer International Publishing, Cham (2018)
8. Giessing, L.: The potential of virtual reality for police training under stress: a SWOT analysis. In: Interventions, Training, and Technologies for Improved Police Well-Being and Performance, pp. 102–124. IGI Global (2021). https://doi.org/10.4018/978-1-7998-6820-0.ch006
9. Giessing, L., Frenkel, M.O., Zinner, C., Rummel, J., Nieuwenhuys, A., Kasperk, C., Brune, M., Engel, F.A., Plessner, H.: Effects of coping-related traits and psychophysiological stress responses on police recruits' shooting behavior in reality-based scenarios. Front. Psychol. **10**, 1523 (2019). https://doi.org/10.3389/fpsyg.2019.01523
10. Gutiérrez-Fernández, A., Fernández-Llamas, C., Vázquez-Casares, A.M., Mauriz, E., Riego-del Castillo, V., John, N.W.: Immersive haptic simulation for training nurses in emergency medical procedures. Vis. Comput., pp. 1–11 (2024). https://doi.org/10.1007/s00371-023-03227-9
11. Houtman, I., Bakker, F.: The anxiety thermometer: a validation study. J. Pers. Assess. **53**(3), 575–582 (1989). https://doi.org/10.1207/s15327752jpa5303_14
12. Hutter, R.I., Renden, P.G., Kok, M., Oudejans, R., Koedijk, M., Kleygrewe, L.: Criteria for the high quality training of police officers. In: Police Conflict Management, Volume II: Training and Education, pp. 7–32. Springer International Publishing, Cham (2023). https://doi.org/10.1007/978-3-031-41100-7_2
13. John, B.S., Oliva, L.S., Buckwalter, J.G., Kwok, D., Rizzo, A., et al.: Self-reported differences in personality, emotion control, and presence between pre-military and non-military groups in a pilot study using the stress resilience in virtual environments (STRIVE) system. In: Medicine Meets Virtual Reality 21, pp. 182–184. IOS Press (2014). https://doi.org/10.3233/978-1-61499-375-9-182

14. Kent, J.A., Hughes, C.E.: Law enforcement training using simulation for locally customized encounters. Front. Virtual Reality **3**, 960146 (2022). https://doi.org/10.3389/frvir.2022.960146

15. Kim, H.G., Cheon, E.J., Bai, D.S., Lee, Y.H., Koo, B.H.: Stress and heart rate variability: a meta-analysis and review of the literature. Psychiatry Invest. **15**(3), 235–245 (2018). https://doi.org/10.30773/pi.2017.08.17

16. Kleygrewe, L., Koedijk, M., Oudejans, R., Hutter, V., Schäfer, A., Maetzing, O.: D7.5 SHOTPROS Final Training Curriculum for DMA-SR (2022). https://shotpros.eu/wp-content/uploads/2023/01/D7.5-SHOTPROS-Final-Training-Curriculum-for-DMA-SR_v1.0.pdf. Accessed 22 May 2024

17. Lesage, F.X., Berjot, S., Deschamps, F.: Clinical stress assessment using a visual analogue scale. Occup. Med. **62**(8), 600–605 (2012). https://doi.org/10.1093/occmed/kqs140

18. Lisanne Kleygrewe, R.I.V.H., Oudejans, R.R.D.: No pain, no gain? The effects of adding a pain stimulus in virtual training for police officers. Ergonomics **66**(10), 1608–1621 (2023). https://doi.org/10.1080/00140139.2022.2157496

19. Lukosch, H., van Ruijven, T., Verbraeck, A.: The participatory design of a simulation training game. In: Proceedings of the 2012 Winter Simulation Conference (WSC), pp. 1–11 (2012). https://doi.org/10.1109/WSC.2012.6465218

20. Martaindale, M.H., Sandel, W.L., Duron, A., McAllister, M.J.: Can a virtual reality training scenario elicit similar stress response as a realistic scenario-based training scenario? Police Q. **27**(1), 109–129 (2024). https://doi.org/10.1177/10986111231182729

21. Marteau, T.M., Bekker, H.: The development of a six-item short-form of the state scale of the Spielberger state-trait anxiety inventory (STAI). Br. J. Clin. Psychol. **31**(3), 301–306 (1992). https://doi.org/10.1111/j.2044-8260.1992.tb00997.x

22. McAllister, M.J., Martaindale, M.H., Gonzalez, A.E., Case, M.J.: Virtual reality based active shooter training drill increases salivary and subjective markers of stress. Yale J. Biol. Med. **95**(1), 105–113 (2022)

23. Melo, M., Gonçalves, G., Monteiro, P., Coelho, H., Vasconcelos-Raposo, J., Bessa, M.: Do multisensory stimuli benefit the virtual reality experience? A systematic review. IEEE Trans. Visual Comput. Graphics **28**(2), 1428–1442 (2022). https://doi.org/10.1109/TVCG.2020.3010088

24. Mills, B., Dykstra, P., Hansen, S., Miles, A., Rankin, T., Hopper, L., Brook, L., Bartlett, D.: Virtual reality triage training can provide comparable simulation efficacy for paramedicine students compared to live simulation-based scenarios. Prehospital Emerg. Care **24**(4), 525–536 (2020). https://doi.org/10.1080/10903127.2019.1676345

25. Murtinger, M., Jaspaert, E., Schrom-Feiertag, H., Egger-Lampl, S.: CBRNe training in virtual environments: SWOT analysis & practical guidelines. Int. J. Saf. Secur. Eng. **11**(4), 295–303 (2021). https://doi.org/10.18280/ijsse.110402

26. Murtinger, M., Uhl, J., Schrom-Feiertag, H., Nguyen, Q., Harthum, B., Tscheligi, M.: Assist the VR trainer—real-time dashboard and after-action review for police VR training. In: 2022 IEEE International Conference on Metrology for Extended Reality, Artificial Intelligence and Neural Engineering (MetroXRAINE), pp. 69–74 (2022). https://doi.org/10.1109/MetroXRAINE54828.2022.9967532

27. Narciso, D., Melo, M., Rodrigues, S., Cunha, J.P.S., Bessa, M.: Impact of different stimuli on user stress during a virtual firefighting training exercise. In: 2020 IEEE 20th International Conference on Bioinformatics and Bioengineering (BIBE), pp. 813–818 (2020). https://doi.org/10.1109/BIBE50027.2020.00138

28. Nguyen, Q., Jaspaert, E., Murtinger, M., Schrom-Feiertag, H., Egger-Lampl, S., Tscheligi, M.: Stress out: translating real-world stressors into audio-visual stress cues in VR for police training. In: Human-Computer Interaction–INTERACT 2021: 18th IFIP TC 13 International Conference, Bari, Italy, August 30–September 3, 2021, Proceedings, Part II 18, pp. 551–561. Springer (2021). https://doi.org/10.1007/978-3-030-85616-8_32

29. Pallavicini, F., Argenton, L., Toniazzi, N., Aceti, L., Mantovani, F.: Virtual reality applications for stress management training in the military. Aerosp. Med. Hum. Perform. **87**(12), 1021–1030 (2016). https://doi.org/10.3357/AMHP.4596.2016

30. Rizzo, A., Buckwalter, J.G., John, B., Newman, B., Parsons, T., Kenny, P., Williams, J.: STRIVE: stress resilience in virtual environments: a pre-deployment VR system for training emotional coping skills and assessing chronic and acute stress responses. In: Medicine Meets Virtual Reality 19, pp. 379–385. IOS Press (2012). https://doi.org/10.3233/978-1-61499-022-2-379

31. Rizzo, A., John, B., Newman, B., Williams, J., Hartholt, A., Lethin, C., Buckwalter, J.G.: Virtual reality as a tool for delivering PTSD exposure therapy and stress resilience training. Mil. Behav. Health **1**(1), 52–58 (2013). https://doi.org/10.1080/21635781.2012.721064

32. Rosnow, R.L., Rosenthal, R.: Effect sizes for experimenting psychologists. Can. J. Exp. Psychol./Rev. can. psychol. expérimentale **57**(3), 221–237 (2003)

33. Shaffer, F., Ginsberg, J.P.: An overview of heart rate variability metrics and norms. Front. Public Health **5** (2017). https://doi.org/10.3389/fpubh.2017.00258

34. Shewaga, R., Uribe-Quevedo, A., Kapralos, B., Lee, K., Alam, F.: A serious game for anesthesia-based crisis resource management training. Comput. Entertain. **16**(2) (2018). https://doi.org/10.1145/3180660

35. Tluczek, A., Henriques, J.B., Brown, R.L.: Support for the reliability and validity of a six-item state anxiety scale derived from the state-trait anxiety inventory. J. Nurs. Meas. **17**(1), 19–28 (2009). https://doi.org/10.1891/1061-3749.17.1.19

36. Uhl, J.C., Murtinger, M., Zechner, O., Tscheligi, M.: Threat assessment in police vr training: Multi-sensory cues for situation awareness. In: 2022 IEEE International Conference on Metrology for Extended Reality, Artificial Intelligence and Neural Engineering (MetroXRAINE). pp. 432–437 (2022).https://doi.org/10.1109/MetroXRAINE54828.2022.9967692

37. Zechner, O., Kleygrewe, L., Jaspaert, E., Schrom-Feiertag, H., Hutter, R.I.V., Tscheligi, M.: Enhancing operational police training in high stress situations with virtual reality: experiences, tools and guidelines. Multimodal Technol. Interact. **7**(2) (2023). https://doi.org/10.3390/mti7020014

# Against Isolation in the Museum: Playful Co-presence with Immersive Augmented Reality

Jessica Laura Bitter$^{(\boxtimes)}$ (iD) and Ulrike Spierling (iD)

Hochschule RheinMain, Wiesbaden, Germany
{jessicalaura.bitter,ulrike.spierling}@hs-rm.de

**Abstract.** Immersive augmented reality with head-mounted displays is increasingly being researched for museums and cultural heritage sites. However, the isolating nature of the devices is at odds with the usual group sizes of visitors. This paper firstly provides a systematic literature review of the field of co-presence as a quality of experience in immersive AR. Based on these findings, a collaborative prototype is built using a research-through-design approach. We then report on a preliminary evaluation study (n = 20) to assess the effect of the prototype on communication between participants. We conclude that there are still few solutions for delivering collaborative and playful immersive AR experiences in museums, but early indications suggest that it is promising.

**Keywords:** Collaborative Augmented Reality · Head-Mounted Device · Multi-User Applications · Social Presence · Co-Presence

## 1 Introduction

Augmented Reality (AR) in cultural heritage (CH) has garnered significant attention in recent years, particularly in the realm of single-user gaming experiences. With the proliferation of Head-Mounted Displays (HMDs), research in AR has expanded to explore new frontiers of immersive interaction. However, while single-user AR applications offer engaging experiences, they often lead to a sense of isolation in museums, while people are often visiting in groups.

In this study, we aim to investigate the landscape of co-located playful collaboration in CH, focusing on synchronous and asynchronous interactions of visitors in exhibitions and museums, facilitated by HMD-based AR. Our research questions are threefold: (1) Which synchronous and asynchronous co-located playful collaboration applications for HMD AR exist in museums? (2) What parameters can be used to describe these collaborations? (3) How does our prototype following these parameters influence communication between visitors?

To address our first research question, we conduct a literature review to identify existing multi-user AR applications in cultural heritage settings, aiming to gain insights into their game structures and interaction dynamics. From

J. L. Plass and X. Ochoa (Eds.): JCSG 2024, LNCS 15259, pp. 281–297, 2025.
https://doi.org/10.1007/978-3-031-74138-8_20

this review, we deduce parameters that characterize these collaborative experiences, which form the basis for answering our second research question. Leveraging design science research principles, we use these parameters to inform the development of a prototype aimed at enhancing communication among museum visitors, which we then evaluate formatively.

While our primary focus is on HMD-based AR, we recognize the importance of considering other AR modalities such as mobile AR and Spatial AR (SAR), which may also play a significant role in cultural heritage settings. Therefore, we will incorporate insights from studies on these modalities to inform our understanding of game design for multi-user AR experiences in cultural heritage contexts.

## 2   Co-presence in Cultural Heritage AR Games

### 2.1   Definition of Co-presence

Presence, as coined by Slater [39], is defined as the "feeling of being there". When feeling present in a mediated environment, people behave in it and with it as if in the real world. Immersion, on the other hand (according to Slater), describes properties of the used technology, and is therefore closely connected to its properties such as field of view, performance etc.

Co-presence as an experience is a subset of feelings of presence and encompasses a complex interplay of personal presence and the sensation of sharing the same space with other participants [9]. In collaborative AR games, the sense of co-presence is heightened by the perceived possibilities for interaction and the presence of other individuals, as well as the sense of object-presence, which refers to the subjective experience of an object's existence within the user's environment [21, 41].

Another subset of presence is social presence, meaning the feeling of interacting with another person or character, with them being virtual or not physically there [30]. Other factors such as telepresence (the sense of being present although being in a remote location), spatial presence (the sense of being in the same physical space) [28, 30] or engagement (there being three different ways to engage in a collaborative AR experience according to Sereno et al. [38]: viewing, interacting/exploring and sharing/creating) can also influence a collaborative AR experience. Depending on the use case, other concepts such as trust may also be important to consider [34].

Given the focus on cultural heritage, we will exclude telepresence, as the goal is to enhance the experience of the physical exhibits on-site, rather than experiencing a digital twin. We extend social presence to co-located scenarios, as we want to lift the isolation occurring in single-user HMD-based AR applications.

### 2.2   Dimensions of Co-presence

Co-presence in collaborative AR experiences exists along two axes: time and space. Time-wise, the experience can be synchronous or asynchronous, and users can be co-located or remotely connected [13,34]. Synchronous means a real-time synchronization between the users, whereas asynchronous describes the existence of a time-delay. When users are remote, it means that they are not in the same physical space while collaborating, while co-located describes them being in the same physical space.

There are also different forms of symmetry that can be introduced into a collaborative experience, concerning roles, technology, information, awareness of others and the environment, interdependence, and timing [31,38]. Aside from that, interactions between the users can influence the feeling of co-presence. Generally, interactions can be divided into the active interactions between users, and the passive ones collected by the used devices [17]. Active interactions consist of observating and discussing, manipulating and moving, and annotating virtual objects. Broadcasting awareness cues indicating the users' location or orientation also belong to the active interactions [13]. Awareness cues consist by a large part of eye gaze directions that can be augmented or shared through rays or points [35]. These cues can help reducing cognitive load during a collaboration. Passive interactions consist of information that can be gathered without active input by the user, such as time spent at one location.

### 2.3  AR Games in Cultural Heritage

In this work, the term cultural heritage is used to describe places where people can experience art, natural sciences or history in an exhibition or museum. To develop AR games for CH, knowledge about the visitor behavior is helpful. According to Falk [12], there are five different visitor types : explorer, facilitator, experience seeker, professional/hobbyist and recharger. The types are based on the personal context of the visitor, meaning their prior knowledge, experience and interest; their physical context meaning the exhibition, programs etc. in the museum; and the socio-cultural context, describing the group interactions during the museum visit, and the visitor's cultural experiences and values. On the other side, Bartle [1] defined types: achievers, killers, socializers and explorers. These types can be positioned in a coordinate system that ranges from players to world on the x-axis, and from acting to interacting on the y-axis. In a museum, one can argue that we want to kindle interest in the world, meaning the exhibition, and interaction with it. This makes explorers in both models a suitable target group for AR games in the cultural heritage sector.

## 3  Related Work

Collaboration in Augmented Reality (AR) is a vibrant research area with applications ranging from gaming to industrial support. Despite its potential, the use of AR for collaborative experiences in exhibitions remains underexplored. This section reviews relevant literature overviews, focusing on general AR collaboration and the specific needs of cultural heritage exhibitions.

Several surveys and reviews provide a broad overview of collaborative AR, though they do not focus specifically on exhibitions. One study investigated the impact of virtual interactions, system feedback, and co-presence on social presence in single-user AR games, emphasizing the significance of these factors in designing collaborative AR experiences, though it did not directly address exhibitions [27].

Another investigation into computer-supported collaborative work (CSCW) analyzed the symmetry of roles and technology in collaborative AR. Here, Sereno et al. [38] highlight a notable gap in the literature concerning synchronous, co-located experiences. Expanding on the theme of social presence, Osmers et al. [30] look into AR-supported cooperative work scenarios where an expert supports another worker, either co-located or remotely. They provide valuable insights into the effects of social presence, particularly in remote collaboration contexts, without differentiating between symmetrical and asymmetrical collaboration.

A comprehensive review of design principles for collaborative AR applications focused on remote collaboration between AR-VR and PC-based applications. It was noted that although a third of the reviewed studies involved co-located AR-AR scenarios, the guidelines provided were general rather than specific to cultural heritage exhibitions. This work identified essential collaborative needs such as awareness of others' attention and activities, coordination of instructions, privacy, and manipulation of virtual objects within a shared environment [36]. Further analysis of AR and VR collaboration along time and space axes revealed a lack of material on asynchronous, on-site collaboration. The review predominantly covered older applications, with a focus on mobile and CSCW. The mentioned synchronous on-site mixed reality (MR) setups are older than 10 years, thus not fully addressing the contemporary needs of cultural heritage exhibitions, especially with head-mounted displays [34]. In a study including CSCW in co-located settings, Feng et al. [13] found few results relevant to museums.

Specific reviews on collaborative AR in cultural heritage are sparse. In an overview of AR applications in museums, Bekele et al. [3] categorized experiences based on display types such as tabletop, spatial AR, and head-mounted displays (HMDs). While collaboration was identified as one important interaction interface, most described experiences were single-user. In another study, the use of AR/VR to enhance engagement among young visitors in educational environments like museums was explored, highlighting the pedagogical potential of AR/VR, though it focused more on learning platforms than on recent co-located AR applications in museums [37].

A review of specifically HMD-based collaborative AR applications confirmed that only a few were focused on cultural heritage. Interactions such as annotation and cooperative object manipulation were discussed, aiming to reduce cognitive workload and enhance perceptual awareness. However, only a small subset of these applications involved co-located users in cultural heritage settings [4]. Another review of extended reality in archaeology revealed that few papers considered collaboration, and even fewer were visitor-focused, pointing to a trend toward single-user applications in archaeology and a gap in understanding collaborative experiences for museum visitors [11].

Syed et al. [42] provided a comprehensive overview of AR displays, authoring systems, and tracking techniques, including collaboration. Although the review distinguished between synchronous and asynchronous remote collaboration, it did not do so regarding co-located scenarios. They present diverse device configurations, i.e. how many users are watching at how many devices simultaneously. This focuses on mobile collaborative AR and is not applicable to HMD-based AR applications.

As these surveys show, there are only a few works on co-located multi-user AR experiences or games that fall into the area of cultural heritage. In Sect. 4, we will supplement this list with our own literature review. Guidelines can help to close the gap between the isolation experienced by visitors wearing HMDs and the usual group constellations of visitors in a museum.

## 4  Literature Study

### 4.1  Study Design

To find works specifying in AR experiences in cultural heritage, we conducted a systematic literature review. We followed the PRISMA method to ensure a thorough and transparent selection process [32]. Our search string was designed to capture studies related to augmented reality (AR), collaboration, co-presence, and co-located experiences within museum or exhibition contexts:

*("augmented reality" OR "AR" OR "mixed reality") AND ("collaboration" OR "co-presence") AND ("co-located" OR "onsite") AND ("museum" OR "exhibition")*

The review covered publications from 2014 to 2024 and included only papers, short papers and book chapters to maintain focus and relevance. We searched databases that include works in extended reality (XR), gaming, and human-computer interaction (HCI). To refine our results, we applied specific inclusion and exclusion criteria, which are detailed in Table 1. This methodical approach ensured that our review was comprehensive and targeted, capturing the most relevant and recent advancements in the field.

As stated in Sect. 1, we target HMD-based AR games. However, during the screening process, we realized that there is little work in this specific area, so we expanded our research to all forms of AR experiences to gather more data.

### 4.2  Multi-user AR in Cultural Heritage

Our systematic literature review yielded 15 relevant papers, providing an overview of existing research on multi-user AR games in museum settings. Among these, only a few utilized HMDs, as detailed in Table 2. A notable gap in the literature is the lack of detailed descriptions regarding challenges such

**Table 1.** Inclusion and exclusion criteria for the literature review.

---

*Inclusion criteria*

1. The paper has one of the terms specified in the search string in title, abstract, keywords or body
2. The paper describes an experience with AR
3. The described experience can be classified as multi-user
4. The described experience can be classified as co-present (see Sect. 2)
5. The described experience can be classified as co-located (symmetry of space)
6. The paper describes a (serious) game or playful experience
7. The paper is located in cultural heritage

---

*Exclusion criteria*

1. The paper does not describe an experience with AR
2. The described experience cannot be classified as multi-user
3. The described experience cannot be classified as co-present (see Sect. 2)
4. The described experience cannot be classified as co-located (symmetry of space)
5. The paper does not describe a (serious) game or playful experience
6. The paper is not located in cultural heritage

---

as ownership and turn-taking in multi-user AR environments. Additionally, the technical aspects of synchronization in these collaborative experiences are rarely addressed. This indicates a significant area for further research to enhance the understanding and implementation of multi-user AR applications in cultural heritage contexts. We categorized the findings by year, symmetry of time, group size, type and number and symmetry of devices, symmetry of roles, type of tasks and type of interactions. The categories symmetry of time, devices and roles are based on our findings in Sect. 2. The type of tasks specifies whether each participant has a fixed assigned task or whether the tasks can be distributed freely and flexibly.

## 5   Parameters of Multi-user AR in Cultural Heritage

Our literature study highlights several critical considerations for creating a multi-user AR playful experience. First, synchronization of virtual objects in real-time or within a short time span is essential to maintain coherence and consistency across users' perspectives. Handling different perspectives, both visually and interactively, ensures that each participant can engage with the AR environment meaningfully. Role management is another important factor. Developers must decide whether roles and tasks should be predefined or open for all participants to ensure smooth collaboration. Enabling different interactions tailored to the specific needs and capabilities of each user enhances the overall experience. Additionally, it is crucial for the experience master to have the ability to alter parameters during runtime, allowing for dynamic adjustments and the accommodation of unforeseen challenges or opportunities. These considerations

**Table 2.** Papers found in the field of cultural heritage.

| Reference | Authors | Year | Time | Group | Device | # Devices | Roles | Tasks | Interactions |
|---|---|---|---|---|---|---|---|---|---|
| [2] | Bekele, M.K. et al. | 2021 | Synchronous | Dyad | HMD | Each person | Visitor-visitor | Open | navigate, hand gestures, speech |
| [8] | Blanco-Fernández, Y. et al. | 2014 | Synchronous | Multi | smartphone | Each person | Guide-visitor | Fixed | Navigate, fight |
| [10] | Ch'ng, E. et al. | 2023 | Synchronous | Six | Smartphone | Each person | Visitor-visitor | Open | Manipulate object, leave marker |
| [14] | Franz, J. et al. | 2019 | Synchronous | Dyad | Smartphone | Each person | Visitor-visitor | Fixed | Observe, manipulate |
| [15] | Grammatikopoulou, A., Grammalidis, N. | 2023 | Asynchronous | Multi | Smartphone | Each person | Guide-visitor | Open | Annotate |
| [16] | Hine, P. et al. | 2022 | Synchronous | Multi | Smartphone, tangible | One per group | Visitor-visitor | Open | Reveal, select |
| [19] | Kasomoulis, A. et al. | 2016 | Synchronous | Four | Projection | Each person | Visitor-visitor | Fixed | Place mobile phones |
| [20] | Kim, M., Lee, J.Y. | 2015 | Synchronous | Multi | Screen, smartphone | One per group, each person | Visitor-visitor | Open | Observe, annotate |
| [22] | Krzywinska, T. et al. | 2020 | Synchronous | Four | HMD, tangible | each person | Visitor-visitor | Open | morse, navigate |
| [24] | Lee, Y.J. et al. | 2019 | Synchronous | Multi | Screen, projection | One per group | Visitor-visitor | Open | Observe |
| [26] | Lourenço, P. et al. | 2023 | Asynchronous | Multi | mobile | Each person | Visitor-visitor | Open | Annotate |
| [29] | Oh, S. et al. | 2017 | Synchronous | Dyad | HMD | Each person | Visitor-visitor | Open | Shoot, walk |
| [29] | Oh, S. et al. | 2017 | Synchronous | Dyad | HMD, PC | Distributed | Visitor-visitor | Fixed | shoot, walk, observe |
| [33] | Perry, S. et al. | 2019 | Synchronous | Dyad | Tablet | Each person | Visitor-visitor | Open | Navigate, personalise, swap and leave objects |
| [43] | Yule, D. et al. | 2015 | Synchronous | Multi | Mobile | One per group | Visitor-visitor | Open | Navigate, talk |

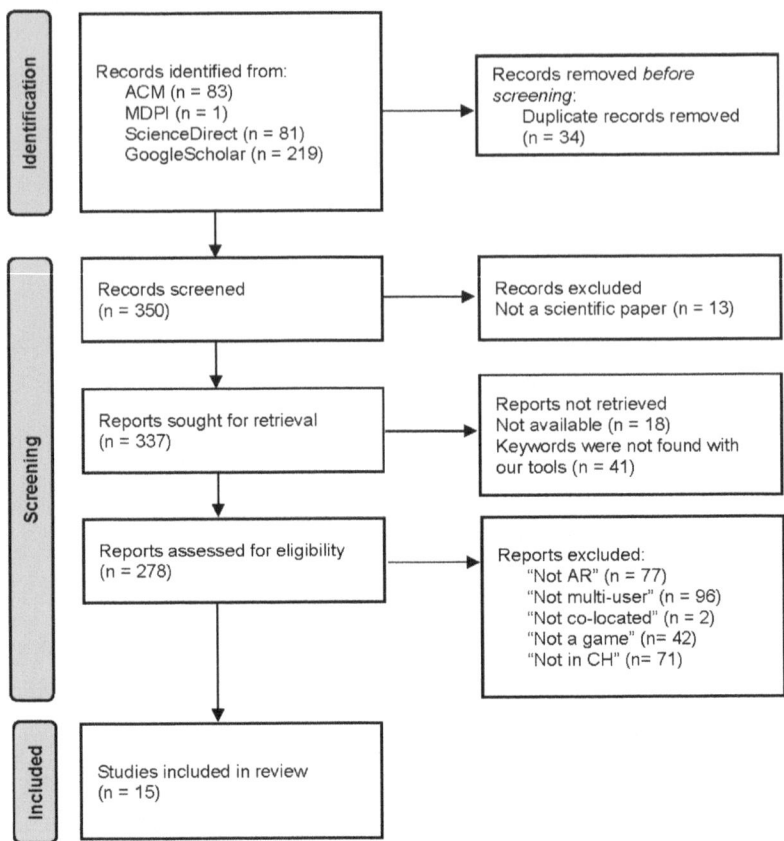

**Fig. 1.** Process of selecting, screening and reviewing the papers. Some exclusion categories may occur more than once.

are fundamental to developing effective and engaging multi-user AR experiences in cultural heritage and other contexts.

We take into account that users need to be aware of others' attention and activities, previous actions, need to coordinate attention and instructions, manipulate virtual objects and share the same environment [36]. In addition, individual users should be able to view content depending on their personal needs and interests [18]. Therefore, we propose a set of parameters to describe any multi-user AR application as described in Table 3.

## 6    Application of the Parameters to a Prototype

Following design science research [23], we developed an immersive AR prototype using two HoloLens 2 devices with the goal of creating a mini-game that fosters

**Table 3.** Framework to describe immersive AR games in cultural heritage.

| Parameter | Properties |
| --- | --- |
| Ownership | Describes which users are able to manipulate a virtual object. Ownership can be fixed, transferrable or requestable. |
| Attributes | Define which attributes of a virtual object should be synchronized (non-exhaustive list).<br>• Position<br>• Orientation<br>• Scale<br>• Properties (color, texture, etc.)<br>• Animations |
| Lifetime | Defines whether a virtual object is synchronized during the whole session. Does the synchronization start/stop at a certain point? Which conditions determine that? |
| Visibility | Determines whether a virtual object is visible for every user or specific to a viewpoint. |
| Instancing | Determines if a virtual object appears to be the same for every user or if users manipulate their own instances of it. |
| Mutability | Defines if a parameters' property can be changed during runtime. |

communication and shared learning experiences within a group. Drawing inspiration from a previous project where we implemented a static labelling system for whale skeletons in a natural history museum [40] (see Fig. 3), we designed a game where two participants collaboratively match Latin names to corresponding bones (see Fig. 2). The future learning effect in the museum should be to demonstrate homology between vertebrates, such as the relationship between a whale and a human. Although the current prototype for our university was designed with a mannequin instead of real animal skeletons, the basic experience remained intact.

In our prototype, no specific roles were enforced, allowing participants to freely engage with the game by either actively participating or observing. The setup included a shared list of labels, a virtual skeleton overlaid on the physical mannequin, and feedback mechanisms such as text and sound to indicate the correctness of matched labels. Interaction involved grabbing a virtual label and placing it on the appropriate virtual bone atop the mannequin.

Key parameters of our prototype, as described in Sect. 5, included transferable ownership of labels, real-time synchronization of the position, orientation, and scale of labels, ensuring they appeared identical and correctly positioned for both users throughout the session. Additionally, labels were synchronized during the entire session, and their parameters were not mutable at runtime.

## 7    Evaluation

### 7.1    Evaluation Design

In a next step, we wanted to evaluate our prototype to gain knowledge about our identified parameters and feedback on design. We employed a mixed-methods

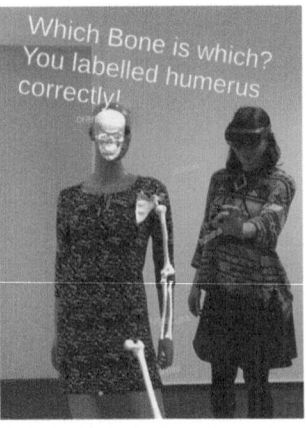

**Fig. 2.** Prototype, left: two users grabbing the same label. Right: Set-up with a real mannequin and virtual bones on which pre-made labels are to be placed.

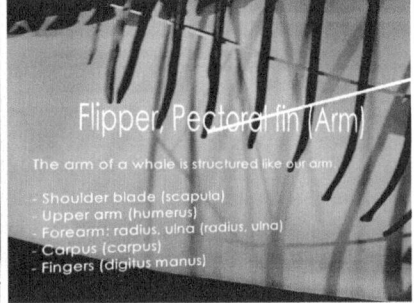

**Fig. 3.** Target situation: expansion of our previous immersive prototype in the museum to include gamified interaction.

approach consisting of a questionnaire and an observation sheet. The primary instrument was the Networked Minds Questionnaire [5], recognized for its validity and frequent use in assessing co-presence [30]. This questionnaire was translated into German and supplemented with a validated user experience questionnaire, the System Usability Scale, an open question, and demographic queries. The observation sheet was developed based on previous evaluations of immersive AR experiences [6,7,25]. It consisted of three sections: First asking about the initial emotion the user displayed after putting on the HoloLens, then an assessment during the experiment, and finally a section to quickly account for technical difficulties that arose. The section about the experiment consisted of an item for communication, interaction, walking around, cooperation vs. competition and a set of emotions like happiness, surprise and confusion.

The Networked Minds Questionnaire, originally designed for telepresence and remote social presence assessments [5] (see Table 4), was chosen for its validated effectiveness and applicability to our study. Ch'ng et al. successfully used this questionnaire in a co-located setting similar to ours [10,30]. By incorporating this tool, we aimed not only to leverage its established reliability but also to evaluate its relevance and effectiveness in assessing co-presence in co-located AR scenarios.

**Table 4.** Scales of the NetworkedMind Questionnaire

| Scale | Subscales |
|---|---|
| Co-presence | Isolation and aloneness, Mutual awareness, Attentional allocation |
| Psychological involvement | Empathy, mutual understanding |
| Behavioral engagement | Behavioral interdependence, mutual assistance, Dependent action |

Hypotheses that guided our evaluation:

- H1: Participants collaborate (communicate and interact) despite having the freedom of not doing so.
- H2: There is a connection between the awareness of the presence of others and communication.
- H3: There is a connection between the awareness of the presence of others and collaboration.

The evaluation took place in a designated room at our university where the mannequin setup was located. We recruited 20 participants, grouped into dyads, consisting of 2 males, 17 females, and one participant who did not specify their gender. The majority of participants were students aged between 18 and 35.

## 7.2   Results

In the following, we present our evaluation results. To address Hypothesis 1 (H1), we analyzed data from the observation sheet, which revealed that most participants engaged in substantial communication (19 out of 20) (see Table 7), whereas fewer participants exhibited high levels of physical interaction (7 out of 20). Communication was defined as verbal exchanges between participants, while interaction involved physical contact, such as handing each other labels or simultaneously grabbing the same label. All dyads were observed to collaborate rather than compete, with most opting to work together and communicate verbally. During the testing, we realized that it was difficult to discern the emotions of the participants. Therefore, we do not report on the emotion items from the observation sheet.

**Table 5.** Descriptive Statistics of the Networked Mind Questionnaire. 1= strongly agree, 2 = agree, 3 = neutral, 4 = disagree, 5 = strongly disagree. Negatively posed questions have been inverted for better readability, so that 1 represents the positive at all times.

|  | Mean | Std. deviation |
|---|---|---|
| Isolation and Aloneness | 1.800 | 1.044 |
| Mutual Awareness | 1.867 | 0.529 |
| Attentional Allocation | 1.897 | 0.596 |
| Empathy | 2.125 | 0.585 |
| Mutual Understanding | 1.992 | 0.579 |
| Behavioral Interdependence | 1.758 | 0.704 |
| Mutual Assistance | 1.913 | 0.736 |
| Dependent Action | 1.875 | 1.011 |

To address Hypothesis 2 (H2), we compared perceived communication with the scale of co-presence using a Spearman correlation test (see Table 6). The results indicated a small correlation ($\rho = 0.098$) between the perceived presence of others and communication, though this was not statistically significant (p = 0.681). Similarly, for Hypothesis 3 (H3), we compared perceived communication with the scale of co-presence and found a small correlation ($\rho = 0.184$) between the perceived presence of others and collaboration, which also lacked statistical significance (p = 0.438).

**Table 6.** Spearman's Correlations for H2 and H3.

|  | Spearman's rho | p |
|---|---|---|
| Mutual awareness - Communication | −0.098 | 0.681 |
| Mutual awareness - Collaboration | −0.184 | 0.438 |

Additionally, observations revealed that participants did not move around the mannequin (see Table 7), even though the virtual scapula bone was positioned at the back. This behavior can be attributed to the occlusion setting, which made bones visible from the front, minimizing the need for movement. However, some participants did bend down to reach lower parts, such as the knuckle of the foot. This implies that the affordance for moving around was not high enough yet. Our finding is consistent with our previous research [6,7], where participants similarly avoided movement despite being encouraged to navigate around in the three-dimensional exhibit. After analyzing the results from the Networked Minds questionnaire, we identified several areas for potential adjustment to better suit our use case. Items related to pretending to pay attention to others appeared to confuse participants and seemed less relevant to our context. Additionally, the repeated questions concerning feelings of aloneness, while pertinent in telepresence scenarios, are less applicable in a physically co-located setting.

Thus, we suggest reducing the emphasis on this aspect. Conversely, we found that elements such as empathy, mutual assistance, and interdependent action were highly relevant and should be retained to effectively evaluate co-presence and collaboration in an AR application.

**Table 7.** Descriptive Statistics of the Observation Sheet

|  | Communication | Interaction | Collaboration | Walking around |
|---|---|---|---|---|
| Mean | 1.300 | 2.650 | 1.000 | 3.300 |
| Std. deviation | 0.571 | 0.671 | 0.000 | 0.979 |

Concerning the System Usability Scale, it can be reported that participants were positive about the idea of using such a system in the museum (see Table 8). The results were in general quite positive. The most remarkable result is that the participants agreed with the statement: "I would need the support of a technical person to be able to use this system". Not surprisingly, this suggests that it is difficult to install HMDs in a museum unsupervised.

**Table 8.** Results of system usability scale. 1 = strongly agree, 2 = agree, 3 = neutral, 4 = disagree, 5 = strongly disagree.

|  | Valid | Missing | Mean | Std. deviation |
|---|---|---|---|---|
| **Positively posed questions** | | | | |
| I think that I would like to use this system during a museum visit | 19 | 1 | 1.895 | 1.049 |
| I thought the system was easy to use | 19 | 1 | 2.316 | 0.749 |
| I found the various functions in this system were well integrated | 19 | 1 | 1.895 | 0.567 |
| I would imagine that most people would learn to use this system very quickly | 19 | 1 | 2.105 | 0.875 |
| I felt very confident using the system | 19 | 1 | 2.053 | 1.026 |
| I think that such an AR multi-user application would offer added value during a museum visit | 19 | 1 | 1.421 | 0.607 |
| **Negatively posed questions** | | | | |
| I found the system unnecessarily complex | 18 | 2 | 4.167 | 0.924 |
| I think that I would need the support of a technical person to be able to use this system | 19 | 1 | 2.842 | 0.958 |
| I thought there was too much inconsistency in this system | 19 | 1 | 3.632 | 0.895 |
| I found the system very cumbersome to use. | 19 | 1 | 3.895 | 0.658 |
| I needed to learn a lot of things before I could get going with this system | 19 | 1 | 4.158 | 0.898 |

The answers from our open question support these findings. Overall, people were happy during the experiment. Participants wrote "It was fun" (four times) and "exciting" (three times). They also stated that it was helpful to be able to work in a group: "It was an advantage as we were able to advise each other on which Latin name belonged to which bone. As my partner had difficulty grasping the words, I helped her and was responsible for grasping and attaching the words." On the other hand, some participants noted that it was not really necessary to collaborate: "However, matching the words can be done on your own, so the experience doesn't necessarily have to be multi-user" (three times). These remarks could be attributed to the openness of the roles, everybody could do everything or nothing as they chose. Participants attributed the experience with "I felt safe" or "I felt comfortable". The group experience was described as "more like working alongside each other than with each other", but also as "it was fun to solve a task together and to see and hear the same thing" and "It was good to exchange ideas with the partner and to work together".

## 7.3   Limitations

Our evaluation faced several limitations that should be considered when interpreting the results. Firstly, we did not collect information on how well group members knew each other, e.g. whether they were friends, which could influence their communication and interaction dynamics. Secondly, the questionnaire was translated into German, which might have introduced subtle biases or misinterpretations. Additionally, our participant pool consisted mainly of students, which limits the generalizability of our findings to broader demographics, such as age and gender. The small sample size further restricts the robustness and statistical power of our conclusions. Moreover, the testing environment was a university setting rather than an actual museum, which might have impacted the authenticity of the experience. However, our primary focus was on the socializing effect of the AR application, with exploring its use in a museum context as a subsequent step. Future work should compare this application, where labels are synchronized, with a version where labels are not synchronized, requiring both participants to label the bones simultaneously. This comparison will help us understand the impact of synchronization on communication and collaboration.

## 8   Conclusion

In this paper, we focused on reducing the isolation of single-user AR users in cultural heritage by researching multi-user games in immersive AR. To address this, we formulated three research questions 1. To answer the first one, we conducted a comprehensive literature review, which yielded 15 results in the context of co-located experiences. Based on these findings, we deduced five parameters to answer our second objective: Ownership, attributes, lifetime, visibility, instancing and mutability. This is a first step towards a framework to describe any multi-user experience or game in immersive AR in cultural heritage. To answer our third research question, we built a first quiz-like prototype of labelling vertebrate bones using the introduced parameters, enabling communication and interaction of multiple users. This experience was then basis of an evaluation using the Networked Minds Questionnaire. The results show that our prototype effectively enhanced communication and was enjoyable for the participants. Our experiment points toward the parameters providing a structured guideline for designing multi-user games in immersive AR.

Moving forward, we plan to develop additional applications using these parameters to further validate their utility. Moreover, the works identified in our literature review could be explicitly described using these parameters for a more detailed analysis. Future research will also involve comparing our current open-scenario app with a version featuring fixed roles and assigned tasks to examine how structured roles impact communication and collaboration. Our next evaluation will be conducted in an actual museum setting with a larger participant pool to obtain more statistically significant insights. This approach will help us better understand the dynamics of multi-user AR experiences in cultural heritage environments and refine our framework and applications accordingly.

**Acknowledgments.** We would like to thank Leonie Ferdinand for her support throughout the evaluation preparation and conduction. This work has been funded (in part) by the European Commission under grant agreement LoGaCulture (101094036).

**Disclosure of Interests.** The authors have no competing interests to declare that are relevant to the content of this article.

# References

1. Bartle, R.: Hearts, clubs, diamonds, spades: players who suit muds. J. MUD Res. **1** (1996)
2. Bekele, M.K., Champion, E., McMeekin, D.A., Rahaman, H.: The influence of collaborative and multi-modal mixed reality: cultural learning in virtual heritage. Multimodal Technol. Interaction **5**(12) (2021). https://doi.org/10.3390/mti5120079, https://www.mdpi.com/2414-4088/5/12/79
3. Bekele, M.K., Pierdicca, R., Frontoni, E., Malinverni, E.S., Gain, J.: A survey of augmented, virtual, and mixed reality for cultural heritage. Journal on Computing and Cultural Heritage (JOCCH) **11**(2), 1–36 (2018)
4. de Belen, R.A.J., Nguyen, H., Filonik, D., Favero, D.D., Bednarz, T.: A systematic review of the current state of collaborative mixed reality technologies: 2013–2018. AIMS Electron. Electr. Eng. **3**(2), 181–223 (2019). https://doi.org/10.3934/ElectrEng.2019.2.181
5. Biocca, F., Harms, C., Gregg, J.: The networked minds measure of social presence: Pilot test of the factor structure and concurrent validity. In: 4th Annual International Workshop on Presence, Philadelphia, PA. pp. 1–9 (2001)
6. Bitter, J.L., Kräuter, N., Spierling, U.: As if they were here: The impact of volumetric video on presence in immersive augmented reality storytelling. In: International Conference on Interactive Digital Storytelling. pp. 425–441. Springer (2023)
7. Bitter, J.L., Senk, G., Spierling, U.: Effects of volumetric video capture on interactive storytelling in immersive augmented reality: a short film experiment. In: Proceedings of the 2023 7th International Conference on Virtual and Augmented Reality Simulations, pp. 45–51 (2023)
8. Blanco-Fernández, Y., López-Nores, M., Pazos-Arias, J.J., Gil-Solla, A., Ramos-Cabrer, M., García-Duque, J.: Reenact: A step forward in immersive learning about human history by augmented reality, role playing and social networking. Expert Syst. Appl. **41**(10), 4811–4828 (2014). https://doi.org/10.1016/j.eswa.2014.02.018
9. Casanueva, J., Blake, E.H.: Presence and co-presence in collaborative virtual environments (2000). https://api.semanticscholar.org/CorpusID:2317845
10. Ch'ng, E., Cai, S., Feng, P., Cheng, D.: Social augmented reality: Communicating via cultural heritage. J. Comput. Cult. Herit. **16**(2) (2023). https://doi.org/10.1145/3582266
11. De Bonis, M., Nguyen, H., Bourdot, P.: A literature review of user studies in extended reality applications for archaeology. In: 2022 IEEE International Symposium on Mixed and Augmented Reality (ISMAR). pp. 92–101. IEEE (2022)

12. Falk, J.: Identity and the Museum Visitor Experience. Routledge, New York (2009). https://doi.org/10.4324/9781315427058
13. Feng, S., He, W., Zhang, X., Billinghurst, M., Wang, S.: A comprehensive survey on AR-enabled local collaboration. Virtual Reality **27**(4), 2941–2966 (2023)
14. Franz, J., Alnusayri, M., Malloch, J., Reilly, D.: A comparative evaluation of techniques for sharing AR experiences in museums. In: Proceedings of the ACM on Human-Computer Interaction **3**(CSCW), pp. 1–20 (2019)
15. Grammatikopoulou, A., Grammalidis, N.: Artful–an AR social self-guided tour app for cultural learning in museum settings. Information **14**(3) (2023). https://doi.org/10.3390/info14030158
16. Hine, P., Tadesse Mamo, L., Pares, N.: AR magic lantern: Group-based co-located augmentation based on the world-as-support AR paradigm. In: Extended Abstracts of the 2022 CHI Conference on Human Factors in Computing Systems. CHI EA'22, Association for Computing Machinery, New York, NY, USA (2022). https://doi.org/10.1145/3491101.3519918
17. Irlitti, A., Smith, R.T., Von Itzstein, S., Billinghurst, M., Thomas, B.H.: Challenges for asynchronous collaboration in augmented reality. In: 2016 IEEE International Symposium on Mixed and Augmented Reality (ISMAR-Adjunct). pp. 31–35. IEEE (2016)
18. Jacob, J., Nóbrega, R.: Collaborative augmented reality for cultural heritage, tourist sites and museums: sharing visitors' experiences and interactions. In: Augmented Reality in Tourism, Museums and Heritage: A New Technology to Inform and Entertain, pp. 27–47. Springer (2021)
19. Kasomoulis, A., Vayanou, M., Katifori, A., Ioannidis, Y.: Magicholo: A collaborative 3d experience in the museum. In: Proceedings of the 20th Pan-Hellenic Conference on Informatics. PCI'16. Association for Computing Machinery, New York, NY, USA (2016). https://doi.org/10.1145/3003733.3003813
20. Kim, M., Lee, J.Y.: Interactive lens through smartphones for supporting level-of-detailed views in a public display. J. Computat. Des. Eng. **2**(2), 73–78 (2015)
21. Klatt, J., Broeke, S.T., von der Pütten, A.M.R., Schütz, A.C., Vervoort, J., McCall, R., Krämer, N.C., Wetzel, R., Blum, L., Oppermann, L.: Let's do the time warp again: subjective and behavioral presence measurement and interactivity in the collaborative augmented reality game timewarp (2011). https://api.semanticscholar.org/CorpusID:182466
22. Krzywinska, T., Phillips, T., Parker, A., Scott, M.J.: From immersion's bleeding edge to the augmented telegrapher: a method for creating mixed reality games for museum and heritage contexts. J. Comput. Cult. Herit. **13**(4) (2020). https://doi.org/10.1145/3414832
23. Kuechler, W., Vaishnavi, V.: Theory development in design science research: anatomy of a research project. In: Baskerville, R., Vaishnavi, V. (eds.) Proceedings of the Third International Conference on Design Science Research in Information Systems and Technology (2008). https://doi.org/10.1201/b18448-8
24. Lee, Y.Y., Lee, J.H., Ahmed, B., Son, M.G., Lee, K.H.: A new projection-based exhibition system for a museum. J. Comput. Cultural Heritage (JOCCH) **12**(2), 1–17 (2019)
25. Liu, Y., Bitter, J.L., Spierling, U.: Evaluating interaction challenges of head-mounted device-based augmented reality applications for first-time users at museums and exhibitions. In: International Conference on Human-Computer Interaction. pp. 150–163. Springer (2023)
26. Lourenço, P., Correia, N., Rodrigues, A.: Augmenting local and remote cultural visits with mixed reality (2023)
27. Marto, A., Gonçalves, A.: Augmented reality games and presence: a systematic review. J. Imaging **8**(4) (2022). https://doi.org/10.3390/jimaging8040091

28. Marto, A., Gonçalves, A.: A scope of presence-related feelings in AR studies. Virtual Reality **28**(1) (2024). https://doi.org/10.1007/s10055-023-00908-7
29. Oh, S., So, H.J., Gaydos, M.: Hybrid augmented reality for participatory learning: the hidden efficacy of multi-user game-based simulation. IEEE Trans. Learn. Technol. **11**(1), 115–127 (2018). https://doi.org/10.1109/TLT.2017.2750673
30. Osmers, N., Prilla, M., Blunk, O., George Brown, G., Janßen, M., Kahrl, N.: The role of social presence for cooperation in augmented reality on head mounted devices. In: Kitamura, Y., Quigley, A., Isbister, K., Igarashi, T., Bjørn, P., Drucker, S. (eds.) Proceedings of the 2021 CHI Conference on Human Factors in Computing Systems. pp. 1–17. ACM, New York, NY, USA (2021). https://doi.org/10.1145/3411764.3445633
31. Ouverson, K.M., Gilbert, S.B.: A composite framework of co-located asymmetric virtual reality. Proc. ACM Human-Comput. Interact. **5**(CSCW1), 1–20 (2021)
32. Page, M.J., McKenzie, J.E., Bossuyt, P.M., Boutron, I., Hoffmann, T.C., Mulrow, C.D., et al.: The Prisma 2020 statement: an updated guideline for reporting systematic reviews. BMJ **372** (2021). https://doi.org/10.1136/bmj.n71
33. Perry, S., Roussou, M., Mirashrafi, S., Katifori, A., Mckinney, S.: Shared Digital Experiences Supporting Collaborative Meaning-Making at Heritage Sites, pp. 143–156 (12 2019)
34. Pidel, C., Ackermann, P.: Collaboration in virtual and augmented reality: a systematic overview. In: International Conference on Augmented and Virtual Reality (2020)
35. Plopski, A., Hirzle, T., Norouzi, N., Qian, L., Bruder, G., Langlotz, T.: The eye in extended reality: a survey on gaze interaction and eye tracking in head-worn extended reality. ACM Comput. Surveys (CSUR) **55**(3), 1–39 (2022)
36. Radu, I., Joy, T., Bowman, Y., Bott, I., Schneider, B.: A survey of needs and features for augmented reality collaborations in collocated spaces. Proc. ACM Human-Comput. Interact. **5**(CSCW1), 1–21 (2021)
37. Scavarelli, A., Arya, A., Teather, R.J.: Virtual reality and augmented reality in social learning spaces: a literature review. Virtual Reality **25**(1), 257–277 (2021)
38. Sereno, M., Wang, X., Besançon, L., Mcguffin, M.J., Isenberg, T.: Collaborative work in augmented reality: a survey. IEEE Trans. Visual Comput. Graphics **28**(6), 2530–2549 (2020)
39. Slater, M., Linakis, V., Usoh, M., Kooper, R.: Immersion, presence and performance in virtual environments: an experiment with tri-dimensional chess. In: Proceedings of the ACM Symposium on Virtual Reality Software and Technology, pp. 163–172 (1996)
40. Spierling, U., Bitter, J.L., Liu, Y., Müller, T.: Chances and limitations of immersive augmented reality for game-based learning in museums. In: European Conference on Games Based Learning. vol. 17, pp. 643–650 (2023)
41. Stevens, B., Jerrams-Smith, J., Heathcote, D., Callear, D.: Putting the virtual into reality: assessing object-presence with projection-augmented models. Presence: Teleoperators Virtual Environ. **11**, 79–92 (2002). https://api.semanticscholar.org/CorpusID:7163825
42. Syed, T.A., Siddiqui, M.S., Abdullah, H.B., Jan, S., Namoun, A., Alzahrani, A., et al.: In-depth review of augmented reality: Tracking technologies, development tools, ar displays, collaborative AR, and security concerns. Sensors **23**(1), 146 (2023)
43. Yule, D.H., MacKay, B., Reilly, D.F.: Operation citadel: Exploring the role of docents in mixed reality. In: Proceedings of the 2015 Annual Symposium on Computer-Human Interaction in Play (2015). https://api.semanticscholar.org/CorpusID:17871206

# Exploring Emotional Design Features
# for Virtual Reality Games

Yuli Shao[1] ⓘ, Yuqi Hang[1] ⓘ, Fabian Froehlich[1] ⓘ, Bruce D. Homer[2] ⓘ,
and Jan L. Plass[1(✉)] ⓘ

[1] New York University, New York, NY 10012, USA
jan.plass@nyu.edu
[2] The Graduate Center, City University of New York, New York, NY 10016, USA

**Abstract.** Recognizing the importance of emotion for learning in general, and for VR games in particular, we investigated three emotional design features, including two visual features (background lighting and particle effects) and an interaction feature (available actions). Our findings revealed the affective quality of these three design features, showing that particle effects and actions significantly increase positive emotion, while dark background lighting induces slightly negative emotions. Action, however, also increased the perceived level of cognitive load. Only action had an effect on perceived presence, whereas background lighting and particle effects did not. We discuss the implication of our findings for the design of VR games for learning.

**Keywords:** Virtual Reality · Emotion · Design · Game

## 1 Introduction

With the increasing use of digital games for learning purposes, learning experience designers are faced with the question of how games should be designed to best facilitate learning while providing a playful, enjoyable experience. For this reason, the field has investigated the cognitive, motivational, affective, and socio-cultural factors that underlie the design of effective Games for learning [1]. While cognition, motivation, and socio-cultural factors have been extensively investigated, the effect of emotion on learning, and the question of how to induce emotions that are conducive to learning, have received less attention. This is especially problematic as recent findings in affective neuroscience have shown that regions in the brain implicated in emotion processing also process cognition, and regions implicated in processing cognitive information also process emotion [2]. This suggests that the mechanisms of cognition and emotion are not fundamentally different [3]. It also suggests a reciprocal relationship of emotion and cognition such that our emotional state affects how we process information, and, in turn, that information we process can affect our emotional state [4].

The deliberate use of specific design features to induce emotions that are conducive to learning has been described as the emotional design principle [4, 5]. Emotional design has shown its effectiveness in enhancing learning, in games and beyond, but most of

J. L. Plass and X. Ochoa (Eds.): JCSG 2024, LNCS 15259, pp. 298–312, 2025.
https://doi.org/10.1007/978-3-031-74138-8_21

the related research has been conducted using screen-based media. We are interested in extending this work to immersive virtual reality games.

Technologies such as immersive virtual reality (VR) are being increasingly used to design learning experiences. Research has found that VR can provide effective learning experiences that outperform traditional media [6] by taking advantage of its specific affordances, including the ability to induce emotions. We are especially interested in the use of playful VR due to its strong potential for emotion induction, which is much stronger than that of 2D environments [7]. We will next define emotions for the context of this research, situate our work in the context of the Integrative Model of Emotional Foundations of Game-Based Learning, and describe different haptic, auditory, and visual design factors for emotional design for games.

## 2   Emotions in Game-Based Learning

### 2.1   What Are Emotions?

To explore the role of emotions in game-based learning (GBL), it is important to first define emotions. The Circumplex Model of Affect refers to Russell's [8] conceptualization of emotions, presenting a framework where emotions are categorized based on two dimensions, valence and arousal, see Fig. 1. Valence distinguishes emotions as either positive or negative, while arousal categorizes them as either activating or deactivating.

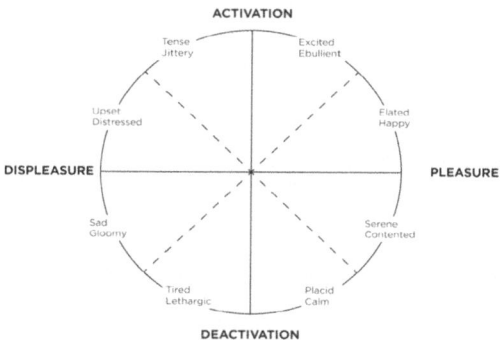

**Fig. 1.**  The circumplex model of affect

Contrary to thinking of emotions as discrete, this model allows for a fluid understanding of emotions, where some may align in both dimensions, such as joy and excitement, which are both positive and activating. Others may share similarities in one dimension, like boredom and relaxation, both characterized by their deactivating nature. Conversely, emotions can also diverge in both dimensions, exemplified by delight (activating and positive) and sadness (deactivating and negative). This understanding of the complexities of emotions is especially important in the context of game design.

## 2.2   An Integrated Framework of Emotions in GBL

The Integrative Model of Emotional Foundations of Game-Based Learning (EmoGBL model) proposed by Loderer and colleagues [9] positions emotions at the center of learning experience and illustrates how emotions can enhance learning outcomes in GBL environments (see Fig. 2). Game design elements like visual aesthetics, musical score, narrative, and game mechanics can induce emotions in learners through processes such as emotional transmission and appraisal [10]. We are interested in the affective quality of these design elements, that is, in their ability to induce an emotional response in individuals [8]. Learners' emotions, including achievement, topic, social, aesthetic, and technology-related emotions, significantly impact motivation, cognitive resources, memory processes, problem-solving strategies, and self-regulation. Consequently, these emotional experiences shape cognitive, emotional, and motivational learning outcomes. Therefore, understanding the emotional dynamics in GBL, and the affective quality of design features that influence these dynamics, can provide important insights that can help guide design choices that lead to more engaging, motivating, and effective learning experiences.

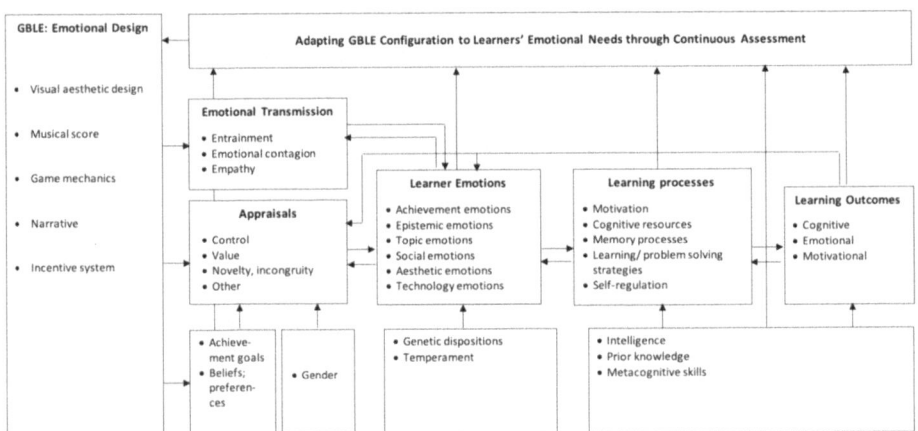

**Fig. 2.** Integrative model of emotional foundations of game-based learning

## 2.3   Affective Quality of Design Features

If we want to deliberately design learning experiences to enhance outcomes through the use of emotion, then we need to understand how different design features affect the learners' emotional state, i.e., we need to understand the affective quality of design elements. A wide variety of design features in visual, auditory, and haptic modalities have been shown to be effective in inducing emotions, but most of the related studies have been conducted with 2D materials.

For example, for auditory design features, melodic directionality, mode, and harmonies have the potential to elicit negative and positive emotions in listeners, while tempo and rhythm have the potential to mediate arousal levels [11]. Haptic design features have the potential to induce emotions due to their impact on the sense of presence [12]. Presence as a subjective quality relates to the technology's ability to evoke affection in the user through haptic stimuli. In combination with immersive VR technology, some studies have highlighted the importance of haptic cues and their impact on emotional and affective states [13].

While our research agenda spans visual, auditory, and haptic design features in VR, this study will report on the results of a study on visual features. The affective quality of specific visual design features, such as color, shape, and anthropomorphism, has been established using multimedia learning materials [14, 15]. Um et al. [15] found that specific color combinations (bright, warm, and saturated colors) and visual shapes (anthropomorphic round shapes) were successful in inducing positive emotions in learners and thus enhanced learning outcomes, whereas neutral emotional design using monochromatic grayscale with rectangular shapes did not have such an effect. A similar effect of anthropomorphism on emotions was found in other research [16, 17]. In addition to color, shape, and anthropomorphism, Plass and colleagues [18] reported a strong effect of game characters' facial expressions and dimensionality on emotions, especially during immersive 3D gameplay. The emotional design of visual features has predominantly been examined in non-immersive learning environments, such as computer-based learning lessons [15], games for learning [19, 20], and video lessons [21, 22]. The current study adds to this literature by investigating the well-known visual design features and their effects on emotion within an immersive VR environment.

## 2.4  The Current Study

In the present study, we focused on two visual design features for immersive VR: background lighting and particle effects. Background lighting has a high potential to influence the overall atmosphere of an environment and trigger emotional responses in people situated in it [23]. We hypothesize that different lighting conditions, such as warm versus cool tones or bright versus dim settings, will have varied effects on learners' emotions. The use of particle effects is a key design feature in game design that elevates the overall pleasantness of an experience by enhancing gameplay responsiveness and amplifying player interactions [24]. Thus, the presence of particle effects in a VR environment is believed to be more emotionally arousing than an environment without them.

Since interactivity is another essential affordance of VR, we investigated, in addition to the visual design factors, whether different levels of actions in VR would lead to different emotional experiences, comparing a condition where participants just observed the environment to one where they could move objects.

Our research sought to answer the questions: What is the affective quality of specific design features in immersive VR? Specifically, we focused on three design features: background lighting (dark and cool vs. bright and warm), particle effects (particles present vs. no particles), and action (the ability to move objects vs. no action).

# 3  Method

## 3.1  Research Design

This study comprised two 2 × 2 factorial designs for which all factors were within-subject, resulting in a total of eight treatment stimuli. The treatments were blocked by the two visual factors, meaning the designs were background lighting × action and particle effect × action. The treatments were sequenced as follows: the lighting block, which included observing in dark lighting, moving in dark lighting, observing in bright lighting, and moving in bright lighting, and the particle effect block, which included observing with particle effects, moving with particle effects, observing without particle effects, and moving without particle effects. Half of the participants started with the lighting block, and the other half with the particle effect block.

## 3.2  Participants

This study involved 40 participants (20 females, 1 non-binary), with a mean age of 24 years (SD = 5.5), ranging from 14 to 37 years. All participants reported having no neurological or psychological disorders and having normal or corrected-to-normal vision. The languages most frequently spoken at home by the participants included English (25 participants), Chinese (10 participants), and Spanish (1 participant). The educational backgrounds of the participants were as follows: 20 were in graduate school, 12 were undergraduate students, 6 were in 12th grade high school, and 2 were in 9th grade. Participants' reported ethnicities included Asian (42.5%), South Asian (2.5%), White/Caucasian (20%), Hispanic/Latino (7.5%), Black or African American (7.5%), and multiple or other ethnicities (20%). Regarding prior VR experiences, 34 participants had used VR before. Of these, 29 reported using VR only a few times ever, and 5 reported using it less than once a week. Additionally, 25 out of these 34 participants had used VR for less than two years. Each participant received a $15 Amazon gift card as remuneration for participating in the experiment. The study received ethical approval from the ethics committees of New York University and the New York Department of Education, and informed consent or assent was obtained from all participants prior to their participation in the experiments.

## 3.3  Materials

The VR materials comprised eight treatments that differed in background lighting, particle effects, and enabled actions, see Fig. 3a, b. In conditions where no actions were enabled, each participant watched three different animal cell organelles (left side) moving to the cell membrane (right side), one at a time, for a total of 18 s. In conditions where actions of manipulating objects were enabled, participants used the controller to drag the organelles into the cell membrane. Participants could also use the joystick to rotate the organelles or bring them farther or closer. There was no time limit for these conditions. In the bright lighting conditions, the background of the simulation was brightly lit, while in the dark lighting conditions, the background was dimly lit. The warm color tone in the bright lighting and the cool color tone in the dark lighting were chosen to enhance the perception of brightness levels. In the conditions in which particle effects were present, there were colored orbs or dots that sparkled around each organelle while it moved into the cell. The color of the particles was consistent with the organelles' colors. In the no-particle conditions, there were no such particle effects around organelles. All treatments were followed by a neutral induction composed of a green park scene, viewed for 15 s. The VR materials were developed in Unity software and were delivered to participants via Meta Quest 2.

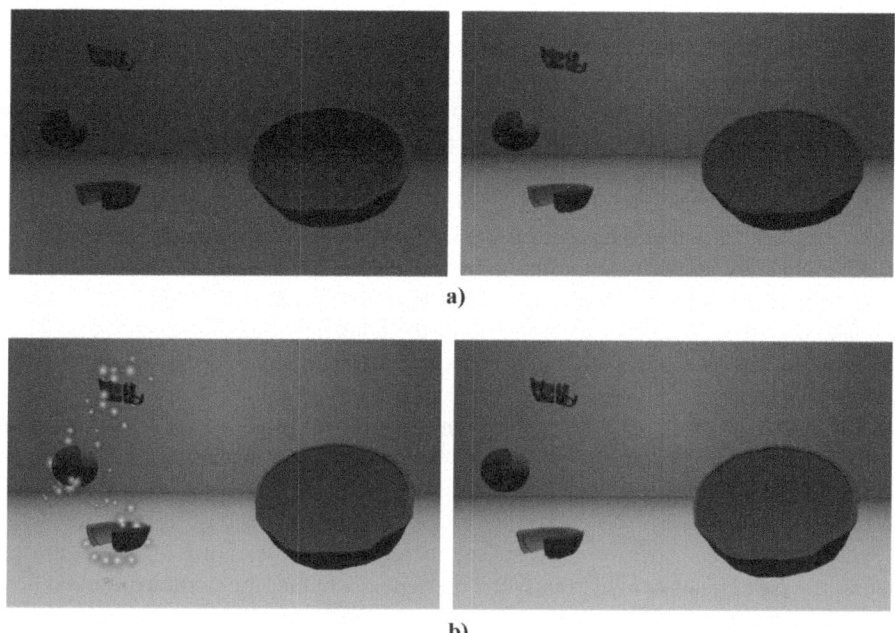

**Fig. 3. a** Background lighting – left image shows the Dark/Cool condition, right image the Bright/Warm condition. Note that the dark background condition appears darker than in VR, where it still allowed participants to discern individual organelles. **b** Particle effects – left image shows the condition with particle effects, right image shows the condition without particle effects.

## 3.4 Measures

Measures employed in this study included scales for state variables such as emotion, presence, and mental effort, as well as for demographics and a trait variable, immersion tendency. A post-treatment survey elicited participants' responses to the environment.

*Emotion–SAM.* SAM is a non-verbal pictorial assessment technique that uses a series of abstract graphic characters, horizontally arranged according to a 5-point Likert scale, to measure emotion valence and arousal [25].

*Emotion–PANAS-VR.* The PANAS-VR is a Positive and Negative Affect Schedule specifically created for research in VR, and comprises 10 items from the PANAS-X that are most relevant to emotions and physical feelings experienced in VR [26]. These items include enthusiastic, scared, joyful, afraid, delighted, frightened, excited, nervous, attentive and distressed. Participants were asked to rate to what extent they have felt that specific emotion during the past VR experience using a 5-point Likert scale, ranging from "very slightly or not at all" to "extremely."

*Presence–IPQ Subscale.* The *Spatial Presence* subscale from Igroup Presence Questionnaire [27, 28] measures the sense of being physically present in the virtual environment. This subscale consists of 5 questions, including, for example, whether the participant felt the virtual world surrounded them. Participants responded on a 7-point Likert scale with anchors ranging from "fully disagree" to "fully agree."

*Mental Effort.* Perceived Mental Effort Scale [29], modified specifically for VR environments, was applied to measure how much mental effort the participant invested in the VR environment using a 7-point Likert scale with terms ranging from "very low mental effort" to "very high mental effort."

*Demographics.* Demographic information included the month and year of birth, gender, primary and other languages used, current grade level, ethnicity, and previous VR experience, including whether the individual has used VR before, devices used for VR, frequency and length of VR usage, and VR applications once used.

*Immersion Tendency.* This scale measures the tendency to be immersed in a virtual environment like movies or TV through several questions, including easiness of becoming deeply involved, mental alertness at the present time, physical fitness, the ability to block out external distractions when being involved, the degree of involvement in watching or playing sports, the easiness of being disturbed on tasks, the easiness of being excited or fearful, personal problem dwelling, and easiness of time perception loss [30].

*Post VR Experience Survey.* This survey included multiple choice questions asking whether the participant enjoyed this VR experience, whether the participant liked how the VR environment looked, whether it was easy to interact with objects, and whether they would like to use a VR environment like this at school to learn something such as cell biology. Open-ended questions asked what the VR experience they just had was like, whether there were any visual effects in the VR the participant particularly enjoyed or not enjoyed, and anything else the participant would like to share.

### 3.5 Procedure

Before their visit, participants were screened for their suitability to be in a VR study using the manufacturer's recommendations. Parental permission was obtained for participants under 18 prior to their visit. On the day of the study, participants were screened again to ensure that their present health and physical conditions did not prevent them from being in VR. After passing the screening, researchers informed the participants about the study objectives and process. Adult participants signed consent forms, and participants under 18 signed assent forms.

Once the consent or assent was obtained, participants were randomly assigned to one of the two treatment sequences. Before entering the VR environment, participants completed the Demographic survey and the Immersion Tendency questionnaire on tablets. During the VR experiment, participants were given instructions to complete the eight treatment tasks in VR and responded to survey measures after each task. Survey measures consisted of affect measures, including SAM and PANAS-VR, the Spatial Presence subscale from IPQ, and the Perceived Mental Effort scale. The total time in VR was about 20 to 30 min.

After completing the VR portion of the experiment, participants responded to the Post-VR Experience survey on tablets. A brief interview was conducted to allow participants to elaborate on their VR experience, which concluded the study visit. At the end of the study, participants were debriefed and thanked.

## 4  Results

Our general analytic strategy to determine the effects of the different design factors was to conduct separate $2 \times 2$ repeated measures ANOVAs for each of the two visual design features (background lighting and particle effects) by type of action (observe vs. move) for each of the dependent variables. The data met normality and homogeneity of variance assumptions. Our analyses focused on the four outcome emotion measures: positive affect (PANAS-VR), negative affect (PANAS-VR), emotional arousal (SAM), and emotional valence (SAM), the presence measure (IPQ), and the mental effort scale. The results from these analyses are presented in the following sections by design factor. The means of these measures with their standard deviations are shown in Table 1.

### 4.1  Background Lighting

*Emotion.* The analysis revealed no significant main effect for background lighting on positive affect, $F(1, 39) = 0.21$, $p = 0.64$, $\eta_p^2 = 0.01$, but we found a significant main effect for lighting on emotional valence, $F(1, 38) = 5.12$, $p = 0.03$, $\eta_p^2 = 0.12$. Bright lighting conditions were associated with more positive valence compared to dark lighting conditions. There was also a significant main effect of background lighting on negative affect, $F(1, 39) = 8.27$, $p < 0.01$, $\eta_p^2 = 0.18$. Participants reported higher negative affect under dark and cool lighting conditions compared to bright and warm lighting conditions. The analysis indicated no significant main effect for background lighting on emotional arousal, $F(1, 39) = 0.50$, $p = 0.48$, $\eta_p^2 = 0.01$.

*Presence.* There was no main effect of background lighting on presence, $F(1, 37) = 0.01$, $p = 0.90$, $\eta_p^2 = 0.00$.

*Cognitive Load.* There was a marginal trend for participants to report greater mental effort in dark/cool background color conditions compared to bright/warm lighting, $F(1, 39) = 3.59$, $p = 0.065$, $\eta_p^2 = 0.08$.

For all analyses, no interaction effects were found.

These results suggest that background lighting significantly affects negative affect and emotional valence. Specifically, dark and cool lighting tends to induce negative affect, while bright and warm lighting is associated with a more positive emotional valence and with slightly lower levels of cognitive load. However, background lighting does not significantly impact positive affect, emotional arousal, and presence.

**Table 1.** Means and standard deviations of measures

| Condition | Positive affect | | Negative affect | | Arousal | | Valence | | Presence | | Mental effort | |
|---|---|---|---|---|---|---|---|---|---|---|---|---|
| | M | SD | M | SD | M | SD | M | SD | M | SD | M | SD |
| Dark × Observe | 12.03 | 4.54 | 5.93 | 2.14 | 2.45 | 0.99 | 3.10 | 0.79 | 1.68 | 2.66 | 3.68 | 1.54 |
| Dark × move | 13.45 | 4.54 | 5.73 | 1.62 | 2.73 | 0.88 | 3.56 | 0.68 | 3.34 | 2.66 | 4.20 | 1.34 |
| Bright × Observe | 12.38 | 4.54 | 5.48 | 1.63 | 2.55 | 0.93 | 3.54 | 0.76 | 2.00 | 3.07 | 3.60 | 1.32 |
| Bright × Move | 13.45 | 5.28 | 5.65 | 1.63 | 2.75 | 0.98 | 3.59 | 0.82 | 3.11 | 3.40 | 3.80 | 1.47 |
| No particles × Observe | 11.13 | 4.18 | 5.43 | 0.87 | 2.18 | 0.82 | 3.25 | 0.67 | 1.21 | 3.39 | 3.21 | 1.38 |
| No particles × Move | 11.88 | 4.77 | 5.43 | 0.75 | 2.67 | 1.03 | 3.35 | 0.77 | 2.50 | 3.92 | 3.82 | 1.60 |
| Particles × Observe | 12.45 | 4.92 | 5.55 | 1.47 | 2.64 | 1.06 | 3.35 | 0.83 | 1.08 | 3.59 | 3.38 | 1.62 |
| Particles × Move | 13.55 | 5.18 | 5.53 | 1.01 | 3.05 | 1.00 | 3.45 | 0.90 | 2.68 | 4.22 | 3.85 | 1.44 |

## 4.2 Particle Effects

*Emotion.* The analysis revealed a significant main effects for particle effects on positive affect, $F(1, 39) = 6.12, p = 0.02, \eta_p^2 = 0.14$. Participants reported higher positive affect in the presence of particle effects compared to when there were no particle effects (Fig. 4). In addition, a significant main effect for particle effects was found on emotional arousal, $F(1, 38) = 10.50, p < 0.01, \eta_p^2 = 0.22$. Participants experienced higher emotional arousal when particle effects were present in VR tasks compared to when they were absent. No significant main effects of particle effects were found on negative affect, $F(1, 39) = 0.87, p = 0.36, \eta_p^2 = 0.02$, and emotional valence, $F(1, 39) = 1.03, p = 0.32, \eta_p^2 = 0.03$.

*Presence.* There was no main effect of particle effects on action, $F(1, 37) = .01, p = 0.95, \eta_p^2 = 0.00$.

*Cognitive Load.* There was no main effect of particle effects on mental effort, $F(1, 38) = 0.83, p = 0.37, \eta_p^2 = 0.02$.

For all analyses, no interaction effects were found.

These results suggest that the presence of particle effects significantly increases positive affect and emotional arousal while having no significant impact on negative affect or emotional valence, presence, and cognitive load.

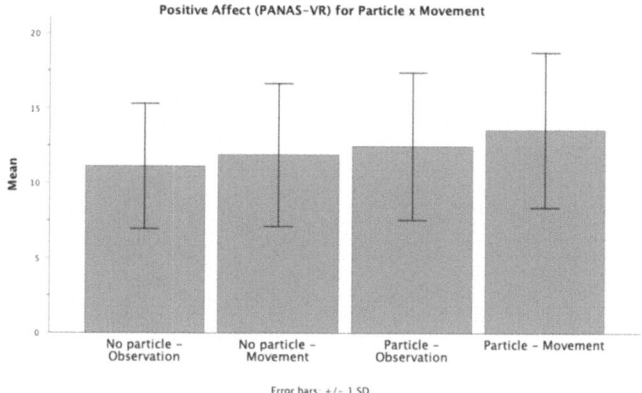

**Fig. 4.** Positive affect (PANAS-VR) for particle by action conditions. Main effects found for particle effects and action factors.

### 4.3 Action

*Emotion.* The analysis revealed a main effect for action on positive affect in both the background lighting conditions, $F(1, 39) = 8.67, p < 0.01, \eta_p^2 = 0.18$, and in the particle effect conditions, $F(1, 39) = 8.88, p < 0.01, \eta_p^2 = 0.19$. Participants reported higher positive affect in conditions where they could manipulate organelles compared to passive observation tasks in VR. There was no significant main effect for action on negative affect in both the background lighting and in the particle effect conditions. In addition, we found a main effect for action on emotional arousal for both the background lighting conditions, $F(1, 39) = 8.81, p < 0.01, \eta_p^2 = 0.18$, and the particle effect conditions (Fig. 5), $F(1, 38) = 24.07, p < 0.01, \eta_p^2 = 0.39$. Participants reported higher emotional arousal when they engaged in active manipulation VR tasks compared to passive observation tasks. There was also a significant main effect for action on emotional valence in the lighting conditions, $F(1, 38) = 2.56, p < 0.01, \eta_p^2 = 0.17$. Conditions allowing to move organelles were associated with higher positive valence compared to passive observation conditions.

No significant interaction effects were found between background lighting and activity level or between particle effects and activity level for reported emotions. Only one significant interaction effect was found between lighting and action on emotional valence, $F(1, 38) = 4.5, p = 0.04, \eta_p^2 = 0.11$. Observing in bright lighting had a more positive valence than observing in dark lighting.

*Presence.* In both analyses, there were significant main effects for action level on presence. In the background lighting conditions, participants reported greater experienced presence in the condition where they could move objects than in the no-action condition, $F(1, 37) = 24.24, p < 0.001, \eta_p^2 = 0.40$. Similarly, in the particle conditions, there was a main effect of action, with participants reporting greater presence when action was enabled than in the no-action condition, $F(1, 37) = 12.13, p = 0.01, \eta_p^2 = 0.25$.

*Cognitive Load.* In both analyses, there were significant main effects for action level on mental effort. In the background lighting conditions, participants reported greater

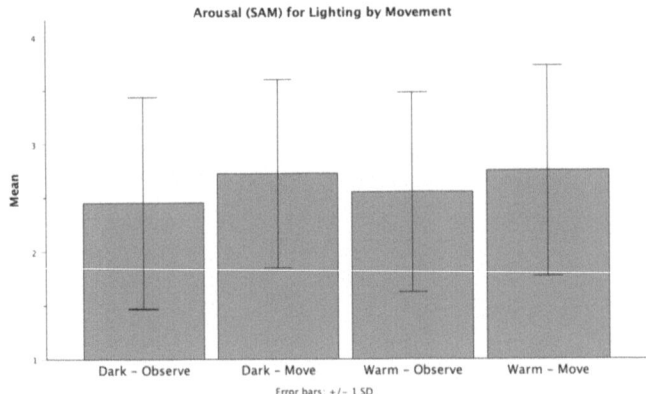

**Fig. 5.** Emotional arousal (SAM) for background lighting by action conditions. Main effect found for action factor.

mental effort in the condition with actions enabled than in the no-action condition, $F(1, 39) = 11.1, p = 0.002, \eta_p^2 = 0.22$. Similarly, in the particle conditions, there was a main effect of action, with participants reporting greater mental effort when they needed to move objects than in the observation-only condition, $F(1, 38) = 8.65, p = 0.006, \eta_p^2 = 0.185$.

These results indicated that being able to move or manipulate objects in virtual reality significantly enhanced participants' positive affect, emotional valence, emotional arousal, and sense of presence, but increased mental effort at the same time when compared to no actions. Furthermore, the significant interaction between background lighting and activity level on emotional valence highlights the nuanced impact of these combined factors on participants' emotional experiences.

## 5    Discussion and Conclusion

### 5.1    Discussion

The goal of the current study was to investigate the affective quality of three design features in immersive VR, namely background lighting, particle effects, and ability to manipulate objects. Results are in line with our predictions that all three design features were successful in inducing emotions, but they do so to different degrees. This research adds to the EmoGBL model by providing more insights into one of the distal antecedents of learner emotions, emotional design [9].

The affective quality of background lighting and particle effects we found confirmed the critical role of visual aesthetic design in shaping learners' emotional experiences. Background lighting was found to significantly affect emotional valence and negative affect, with bright/warm lighting conditions enhancing positive emotional responses and dark/cool lighting conditions inducing negative affect. This finding extends previous research that examined primarily visual aspects of specific objects such as color, shape, and dimensionality of game characters [18] by targeting the ambient atmospheres of the overall environment, which is less explored. The presence of particle effects had a notable impact on positive affect and emotional arousal. Participants experienced higher positive affect and arousal when particle effects were present, supporting the notion that dynamic visual elements can enhance the immersive and engaging qualities of VR environments [24]. The observed differences in lighting and particle effects' affective quality also point to the necessity of integrating various visual design elements to create emotionally engaging and effective VR learning environments, highlighting the potential interplay between environmental and object-specific features and between static and dynamic elements. Interestingly, the reported mental effort invested was lower under bright and warm background lighting conditions than under dark and cool conditions and was not affected by adding particle effects.

Furthermore, we found that being able to move or manipulate objects in VR significantly enhanced positive affect, emotional arousal, emotional valence, and perceived presence compared to conditions with no actions enabled. Interestingly, the reported mental effort investment was reported higher in conditions with interactions compared to no interactions. These findings align with the EmoGBL model's emphasis on game mechanics involving interactivity and control in the emotional design of GBL environments. Although we did not compare other media to VR in this research, the selection of this design feature was based on the unique affordances of VR. Future research should continue to explore design features that are unique to each media form and how design features can be adapted when applied to different media forms.

## 5.2  Implications

The findings reported have important theoretical and practical implications. On the theoretical side, we expanded our understanding of the use of design elements to induce emotions conducive to learning in VR environments. These findings are significant for the extension of the Integrative Model of Emotional Foundations of Game-Based Learning into virtual reality.

On the practical side, our findings provide important guidance for the designers of VR games that will allow them to design emotional experiences that can enhance learning outcomes. It is significant to know, for example, that background color and particle effects can be used to induce positive emotions, and that the addition of particles did not affect the perceived cognitive load. Our work also shows that it is important to align emotional design with media affordances. Within learning experience design, media affordances define the distinct capabilities of each medium that may facilitate learning. In the realm of immersive VR, affordances include interactivity and the sensation of presence, perception of spatial object relations, manipulation of 3D objects, and emotional design facilitated by visual, auditory, and haptic cues.

## 5.3  Limitations and Future Work

There are several limitations to this study. First, we investigated only a limited number of design factors, primarily focusing on the effects of visual design features on eliciting participants' emotions. Additionally, the combination of color tone and lighting conditions might have confounded the results, as we could not isolate the effects of brightness from color tone. Future research should aim to decompose the effects of these design factors to better understand their distinct impacts. We plan to continue to replicate this research using different visual features such as the interplay between background and object colors and audio features such as ambient sound to contribute to a more comprehensive understanding of emotional design space in GBL with VR. Second, as the main goal of our study is to explore the affective quality of design features, that is, whether specific features induce emotions, we did not incorporate a learning context into the environment in the current study, which allowed us to better isolate the effect of emotional design. Since emotions are closely intertwined with cognitive processes [5], future research is planned that will, based on the results of this work, examine emotional design in a more complex context. Finally, participant demographics were somewhat skewed with more than half of participants being graduate school students (50%) and English speakers (62.5%) and having previous experience of using VR (85%). However, the participants were diverse in terms of their primary language, educational background, and ethnicity. Future research should aim for a more balanced demographic to ensure the generalizability of findings.

## 5.4  Conclusion

Our study investigated the effect of two visual design features as well as of an interaction feature (available actions) on learners' emotions, sense of presence, and cognitive load. It represents the first step in a research agenda to investigate how to design VR environments, including VR games, to be effective for learning. Future studies will investigate additional design factors and apply findings to the study of learning outcomes on VR games.

# References

1. Plass, J.L., Mayer, R.E., Homer, B.D. (eds.): Handbook of Game-Based Learning. MIT Press, Cambridge (2020)
2. Pessoa, L.: On the relationship between emotion and cognition. Nat. Rev. Neurosci. **9**, 148–158 (2008). https://doi.org/10.1038/nrn2317
3. LeDoux, J.E., Brown, R.: A higher-order theory of emotional consciousness. Proc. Natl. Acad. Sci. **114**(10), E2016–E2025 (2017)
4. Plass, J.L., Hovey, C.: The emotional design principle in multimedia learning. In: Plass, J.L., Mayer, R.E., Homer, B.D. (eds.) Handbook of Game-Based Learning, pp. 111–152. MIT Press, Cambridge (2022)
5. Plass, J.L., Kaplan, U.: Emotional design in digital media for learning. In Tettegah, S.Y., Gartmeier, M. (eds.), Emotions, Technology, Design, and Learning, pp. 131–161. Academic Press (2016). https://doi.org/10.1016/B978-0-12-801856-9.00007-4
6. Froehlich, F., Hovey, C., Reza, S., Plass, J.L.: Beyond slideshows–investigating the impact of immersive virtual reality on science learning. In: IEEE Conference on Virtual Reality and 3D User Interfaces (VR), pp. 1–2. IEEE, Orlando (2024). https://doi.org/10.1109/VR58804.2024.00113
7. Hovey, C., Pawar. S., Plass, J.L.: Exploring the emotional effect of immersive virtual reality versus 2D screen-based game characters. In: Paper presented at the Annual Meeting of the American Educational Research Association, New York (2018)

8. Russell, J.A.: Core affect and the psychological construction of emotion. Psychol. Rev. **110**(1), 145–172 (2003). https://doi.org/10.1037/0033-295X.110.1.145

9. Loderer, K., Pekrun, R., Plass, J.: Emotional Foundations of game-based learning. In: Plass, J.L., Mayer, R.E., Homer, B.D. (eds.) Handbook of Game-Based Learning, pp. 111–152. MIT Press, Cambridge (2020)

10. Pekrun, R.: The control-value theory of achievement emotions: assumptions, corollaries, and implications for educational research and practice. Educ. Psychol. Rev. **18**(4), 315–341 (2006). https://doi.org/10.1007/s10648-006-9029-9

11. Olsen, A.F., Roginska, A., Plass, J.L.: Multilayered affect-audio research system for virtual reality learning environments. In: Audio Engineering Society Conference: 2022 AES International Conference on Audio for Virtual and Augmented Reality. Audio Engineering Society (2022)

12. Froehlich, F., Plass, J.L.: Can't touch this? Why vibrotactile feedback in educational VR matters. In: IEEE Conference on Virtual Reality and 3D User Interfaces (VR), pp. 1–2. IEEE, Orlando (2024). https://doi.org/10.1109/VRW62533.2024.00174

13. Venkatesan, R.K., Banakou, D., Slater, M.M.M.: Haptic feedback in a virtual crowd scenario improves the emotional response. Front. Virtual Reality **4**, 1242587 (2023). https://doi.org/10.3389/frvir.2023.1242587

14. Mayer, R.E., Estrella, G.: Benefits of emotional design in multimedia instruction. Learn. Instr. **33**, 12–18 (2014). https://doi.org/10.1016/j.learninstruc.2014.02.004

15. Um, E., Plass, J.L., Hayward, E.O., Homer, B.D.: Emotional design in multimedia learning. J. Educ. Psychol. **104**(2), 485–498 (2012). https://doi.org/10.1037/a0026609

16. Le, Y., Liu, J., Deng, C., Dai, D.Y.: Heart rate variability reflects the effects of emotional design principle on mental effort in multimedia learning. Comput. Hum. Behav. **89**, 40–47 (2018). https://doi.org/10.1016/j.chb.2018.07.037

17. Shangguan, C., Wang, Z., Gong, S., Guo, Y., Xu, S.: More attractive or more interactive? The effects of multi-leveled emotional design on middle school students' multimedia learning. Front. Psychol. **10**, 3065 (2020). https://doi.org/10.3389/fpsyg.2019.03065

18. Plass, J.L., et al.: Emotional design for digital games for learning: The effect of expression, color, shape, and dimensionality on the affective quality of game characters. Learn. Instr. **70**, 101194 (2020). https://doi.org/10.1016/j.learninstruc.2019.01.005

19. Homer, B.D., Plass, J.L., Rose, M.C., MacNamara, A.P., Pawar, S., Ober, T.M.: Activating adolescents' "hot" executive functions in a digital game to train cognitive skills: The effects of age and prior abilities. Cogn. Dev. **49**, 20–32 (2019). https://doi.org/10.1016/j.cogdev.2018.11.005

20. Javora, O., Hannemann, T., Stárková, T., Volná, K., Brom, C.: Children like it more but don't learn more: effects of esthetic visual design in educational games. Br. J. Edu. Technol. **50**(4), 1942–1960 (2019). https://doi.org/10.1111/bjet.12701

21. Chiu, T.K.F., Jong, M.S., Mok, I.A.C.: Does learner expertise matter when designing emotional multimedia for learners of primary school mathematics? Educ. Tech. Res. Dev. **68**(5), 2305–2320 (2020). https://doi.org/10.1007/s11423-020-09775-4

22. Wang, X., Mayer, R.E., Han, M., Zhang, L.: Two Emotional design features are more effective than one in multimedia learning. J. Educ. Comput. Res. **60**(8), 1991–2014 (2023). https://doi.org/10.1177/07356331221090845

23. Riva, G., et al.: Affective interactions using virtual reality: The link between presence and emotions. Cyberpsychol. Behav. **10**(1), 45–56 (2007)

24. Zhou, H., Forbes, A.G.: Data feel: exploring visual effects in video games to support sensemaking tasks. In: 2022 IEEE 7th Workshop on Visualization for the Digital Humanities (VIS4DH), pp. 6–12. IEEE, New Orleans (2022). https://doi.org/10.1109/VIS4DH57440.2022.00007

25. Bradley, M.M., Lang, P.J.: Measuring emotion: the self-assessment manikin and the semantic differential. J. Behav. Ther. Exp. Psychiatry **25**(1), 49–59 (1994)
26. Watson, D., Clark, L.A.: The PANAS-X: manual for the positive and negative affect schedule-expanded form (1994)
27. Igroup Presence Questionnaire (IPQ) Overview. https://www.igroup.org/pq/ipq/index.php. Last accessed 08 May 2024
28. Schubert, T.W., Friedmann, F., Regenbrecht, H.T.: Decomposing the sense of presence: Factor analytic insights. In: 2nd International Workshop on Presence (1999)
29. Paas, F.G.: Training strategies for attaining transfer of problem-solving skill in statistics: a cognitive-load approach. J. Educ. Psychol. **84**(4), 429–434 (1992)
30. Witmer, B.G., Singer, M.J.: Measuring presence in virtual environments: a presence questionnaire. Presence **7**(3), 225–240 (1998)

# Healthcare and Wellbeing

# Game On: Towards Long-Term Motivation in Exergames for Cardio Training

Lena-Marie Munderich$^{(\boxtimes)}$ and Stefan Göbel

Serious Games Research Group, Technical University of Darmstadt, Darmstadt, Germany
lena-marie.munderich@stud.tu-darmstadt.de,
stefan_peter.goebel@tu-darmstadt.de

**Abstract.** The advancement and integration of Serious Games significantly impact various industries, including medicine, pharmaceuticals, fitness and wellness, and insurance. Many popular exergames, such as Pokémon Go and BeatSaber, are known for enhancing motivation and making physical activity more accessible. However, they cannot replace traditional sports. While some exergames lack the personalization needed to accurately challenge and support the player, more fitness-oriented approaches often lack the necessary gameplay elements to sustain long-term motivation in their players. This paper aims to analyze how long-term motivational game elements based on different player types affect the game experience and the quality of cardio training in personalized exergames. Emphasis was placed on increasing personalization by expanding gameplay and implementing intelligent world generation based on players' physical conditions. An ergometer-based serious game designed to improve physical activity and long-term motivation was developed and qualitatively tested in two experiments. These experiments were conducted at different stages of development to adjust the game according to initial results. The first study involved 12 participants, while 20 participants joined the second one. The experiments investigated and quantified the quality of game experience and cardio training. The results showed clear improvements in both: game experience and the quality of cardio training. However, they also demonstrated that simple personalization based on heart rate and BMI alone cannot fully accommodate the diverse physiques of all players.

**Keywords:** Exergames · Cardio Training · Ergometer · Player Motivation · Personalization · Game Experience · Health Effects

## 1 Introduction

The World Health Organization recommends that adults engage in at least 150 minutes of moderate physical activity per week [1]. Global estimates indicate

© The Author(s), under exclusive license to Springer Nature Switzerland AG 2025
J. L. Plass and X. Ochoa (Eds.): JCSG 2024, LNCS 15259, pp. 315–329, 2025.
https://doi.org/10.1007/978-3-031-74138-8_22

that 25% of adults and 81% of adolescents do not meet this guideline [2]. Moreover, with economic and transportation development in various countries, levels of inactivity may rise to 70% [2]. This underscores the critical importance of integrating digital technologies into our healthcare system to relieve, motivate, and support people [3].

Exergames are one innovative way to increase motivation and make sports more accessible. However, in the context of health, it is not only important to motivate the player for a short period but to find sustainable solutions that enhance long-term physical activity and motivation.

The increase and sustainability of long-term motivation in games is a complex topic that involves creating a suitable game with adequate difficulty personalized for the individual player [4]. To challenge the player in the context of exergames means on the one hand to challenge the player suitably to their physical strength and on the other hand to make the game experience fitting to their expectations and enjoyment. Exergames have successfully used heart rate control to adjust difficulty and tailor the experience to the player's condition in real-time [5]. Additionally, health games are exploring different gamer types to understand their needs and adjust gameplay accordingly to enhance motivational effects [6].

In this paper, we combine personalization, real-time adaptation to the player and player-type-oriented gameplay to establish the foundation for a long-term motivating serious game for cardio training. We aim to deeply explore the quality of the player's game experience while maintaining a sustainable physical challenge. To achieve this, we personalize the physically challenging gameplay of Letterbird and analyze different player types to provide diverse gameplay elements, thereby increasing intrinsic motivation for a broad range of players.

## 2    Related Work

There have been various approaches and studies on different ergometer-based cardio training games.

The ergometer-based cardio training exergame approach we are continuing and expanding on is based on the project *ErgoActive* from 2010 [7]. In a Feasibility Study in 2015 [8] it was concluded that 15 out of 16 participants reached the intended individual heart rate for cardio training and the motivational effect was confirmed.

The *Cateye Gamebike* was introduced in 2002. The Gamebike functions as an alternative to a traditional controller for the PlayStation 2 [9]. In 2011, Kraft et al. [10] demonstrated that the Gamebike achieved the most efficient physical activity results compared to other exergames. They conducted a study with 37 participants that investigated heart rate, perceived exertion, and recovery heart rate while playing with the GameBike, Dance Dance Revolution, or while using the traditional cycle ergometer while watching television. The Gamebike showed significantly higher heart rates and perceived exertion and their results indicated that the Gamebike was as effective as traditional training.

A more recent study by Westmattelmann et al. [11] examined *Zwift*, an ergometer-based mixed reality sports platform specifically designed to enable players to participate in real-world sports through a virtual space. The study explored the influence of different power outputs and analyzed the data of the 2020 Virtual Tour de France, which showed how power output was the most powerful predictor in success while also visualizing a performance-result gap. In 2021, Westmattelmann et al. [12] further contextualized how Zwift can be classified as a valuable and effective complement to traditional road training. They conducted interviews with a mixed group of 22 users and non-users of Zwift, using qualitative content analysis based on the multi-level framework of technology acceptance and use.

Another exergame developed for the ergometer is Greedy Rabbit. In 2017, Pasco et al. not only observed the effectiveness of the exergame but also investigated the player's situational interest and motivation [13]. They conducted a study with 163 students which result's showed that physical effectiveness was slightly lower, as participants showed higher degrees of sendetary behaviour and 5% less moderate-to-vigorous physical activity, whereas they showed better results in interest, attention, enjoyment, novelty and challenge.

While these studies showcase the potential of ergometer-based exergames to raise and support physical activity levels, there has not been sufficient research on combining physical effectiveness, personalization, and motivation with a focus on the player's game experience and gameplay elements.

The goal of this paper is to qualitatively observe the direct effects of expanding gameplay elements, implementing intelligent world generation, and closely personalizing the experience for the player on effectiveness and appeal of a cardio training serious game. This is achieved through the results of two experiments conducted at different stages of the serious game's development.

## 3   Designing a Personalized Cardio-Training Serious Game

Our approach to designing an ergometer-based cardio training serious game, with development starting in April 2023, was based on prototypical games created since 2010 [7,8].

In these versions, players controlled a pigeon by varying their pedaling speed on the ergometer, while the pedaling resistance was adapted based on the player's heart rate (HR). The goal was to collect letters and dodge enemies.

In our iteration of Letterbird, we adapted and expanded upon this core gameplay. The game was implemented using Unity Game Engine [14]. We used the ErgofitCycle 457 MED ergometer and measured the players' heart rate (HR) with the Polar H10 Heart Rate Sensor System [15].

Figure 1 shows the game setup with the player controlling the game with the ergometer and it being displayed on a monitor in front of them. Figure 2 shows the bidirectional communication system that lies behind Letterbird. Player Data is gathered in a Data Bank to calculate personalized difficulty adjustments. While playing the player's heart rate and ergometer speed data is sent to them

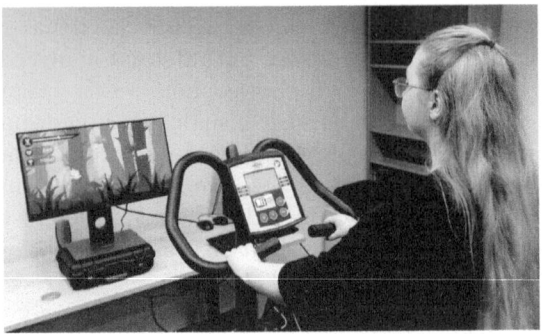

**Fig. 1.** Player playing Letterbird with the ergometer

game, the game calculates necessary difficulty for the player and adjusts gameplay as well as ergometer pedaling resistance. The game also saves the player's heart rate data for after game analyses.

# Letterbird

**Fig. 2.** System Structure behind Letterbird

## 3.1  Serious Part: Effective Cardio Training

For effective cardio training, the difficulty was adjusted through the pedaling resistance according to the player's condition. To efficiently increase the intensity of training over a ten-minute period of training we followed the calculation system visualized in Table 1. This resistance calculation has also been based on the prototypical game design and adjusted by the maximum HR calculation seen in Table 2 [8]. The adjusted calculation is used when a player's Body Mass Index (BMI) is larger than 29.9 and their physical activity level (PAL) does not indicate an inaccuracy of the BMI [1,16].

**Table 1.** Calculation on pedaling resistances depending on time, player HR, BMI, PAL and weight.

| Load Level | Time (min) | resistance (watt) |
|---|---|---|
| Load Level 1 | 0:00 - 1:59 | $L_1 = PlayerWeight$ $L_1$ *(adjusted)* $= 0.5 *$ Player Weight |
| Load Level 2 | 2:00 - 3:59 | $L_2 = 2 * PlayerWeight$ $L_2$ *(adjusted)* $=$ Player Weight |
| Calculated Target Load | 4:00 - 4:59 | $L = ((\frac{Heartrate_{intended} - HR_2}{HR_2 - HR_1}) * (L_2 - L_1) + L_2) * 0.9$ |
| Automatic Load Control | 5:00 - 10:00 | $HR_{current} < 0.7 * HR_{max} -> L = L + 10$ $HR_{current} > 0.8 * HR_{max} -> L = L - 10$ |

**Table 2.** Calculation used to determine maximum player heart rate [17,18]

| Maximum Heart Rate | |
|---|---|
| Men | Women |
| $HR_{max} = 208 - 0.7 * age$ | $HR_{max} = 206 - 0.88 * age$ |

## 3.2 Game Part: Appealing Gameplay

Humans have diverse sources of intrinsic motivation, and players have different reasons for playing games and staying motivated. To make the gameplay of Letterbird motivational from a long-term perspective, we analyzed different types of players. We specifically looked at the widely known Bartle Player Model and translated these insights of diverse expectations into appropriate gameplay elements [19,20].

According to Bartle, there are four player types: Achievers, Explorers, Socializers, and Killers.

- The achiever type enjoys reaching every goal and overcoming every obstacle the game world presents.
- The explorer type wants to interact with their surroundings and discover every aspect of the game, including hidden secrets and easter eggs.
- The socializer type likes to interact with other players and non-playable characters (NPCs), enjoying social interactions, and building relationships.
- The killer type, similar to the Socializer, focuses on interaction but is highly competitive and seeks to win over opponents, enjoying challenges and proving their skills.

## 3.3 Integrated Approach: Combining Serious and Game Part

In order to combine fun and physical activity, Letterbird was designed with the intent of integrating both the Serious and the Game Part as described in Sects. 3.1 and 3.2.

**Personalized Difficulty and Adapting World Generation** We adapted the pedaling resistance calculation into our gameplay and to further improve the personalization of the game introduced intelligent world-generation. Before, the generation of letters and enemies was randomized. In our development process, we adjusted the system to accurately demand pedaling speeds according to the player's HR. This means the player was required to pedal higher speeds when they were not challenged enough and lower speeds when they were starting to feel over-exerted, as shown in Fig. 3. To enforce this spawning locations of both, letters and enemies were mapped to fixed areas of the game, while still allowing random generation within these areas to not make the game feel static.

**Fig. 3.** Letterbird Stage *Blackmire*, showcasing dynamic world generation.

**Implementing Fitting Gameplay Elements for Player Types and Characterizing Goal** To accommodate the earlier analyzed four player types, the gameplay was substantially expanded. Collectibles, which are items that can randomly spawn during a playthrough, were added. This addition not only gives Explorers more aspects of the game to discover but also provides Achievers with a attainable goal-to find the entire collection.

The world map of Letterbird was also greatly expanded. Instead of a single location, there are now three different playable levels, a shop, and a home, as shown in Fig. 4. In addition to this, some hidden easter eggs were implemented.

The shop introduces new buyable items that alter the gameplay, such as shields or speed boosts that benefit the player. The currency for this shop is earned by completing gameplay with a certain rating, enhancing the experience for Achievers.

The shop is led by an NPC with whom players can interact, catering to Socializers. Additionally, there is interaction with the playable pigeon character in the home stage of the world.

High scores, already introduced in earlier versions [7,8], are typically well-suited to motivate Killers and thus were carried over into the development of our serious game as well.

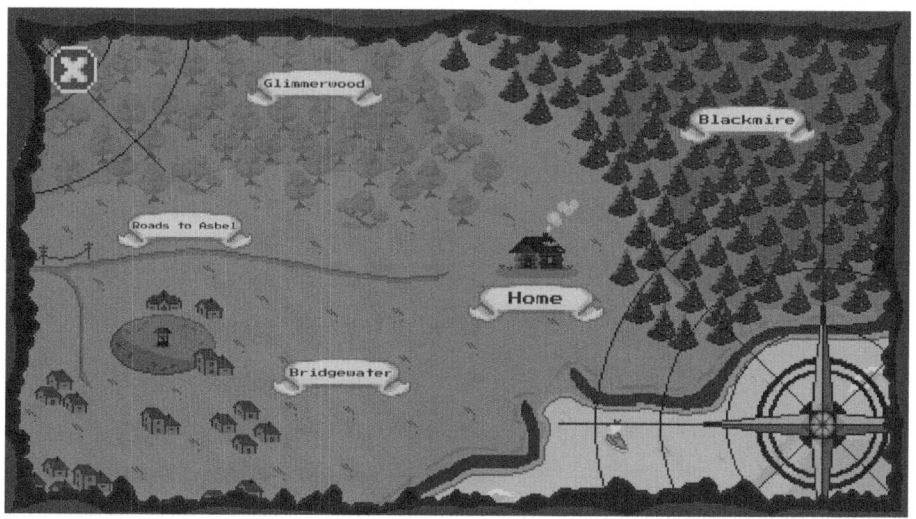

**Fig. 4.** The World Map of Letterbird in it's second stage of development.

## 4  Experiments

To evaluate the appeal and effectiveness of our game, we carried out two identically structured experiments at different stages of development. A variety of different measures to quantify physical activity and individual perception of game experience were incorporated, as seen in Table 3.

**Table 3.** Metrics to evaluate game attractivity and effectiveness

| Overview over the metrics to evaluate Letterbird | |
| --- | --- |
| Evaluating attractivity | Evaluating effectiveness |
| IGEQ | Borg Scale(physical exertion) |
| PGEQ | Borg Scale(cognitive exertion) |
| | Heart Rate |

### 4.1  Measuring Player Performance and Game Experience

We determined the effectiveness of Letterbird based on the player's physical activity. To measure this, we recorded the player's HR and used the original Borg Scale by Gunnar Borg to assess both physical and cognitive exertion [21,22]. The attractiveness of Letterbird was gauged by the player's subjective perception. To quantify this perception, we incorporated the In-Game Experience Questionnaire and the Post-Game Experience Questionnaire into our experiments [23].

The first experiment was conducted midway through the game's development to identify important aspects that needed adjustment to enhance player satisfaction. Table 4 presents the demographic background of the twelve players, aged between 21 and 27 years, who participated in this experiment. Participants were recruited through advertisements placed at the university, targeting students and faculty.

**Table 4.** The demographic background of the participant group of both experiments

| Demographic description of the Participants | | |
|---|---|---|
| Experiment | 1 | 2 |
| Number of overall participants | 12 | 20 |
| Number of female participants | 4 | 14 |
| Number of male participants | 8 | 6 |
| Average age (years) | 24.08 | 25.30 |
| Age standard deviation | 1.49 | 2.87 |

The second experiment enabled us to compare the results before and after making adjustments, demonstrating the applicability of our system and providing insights into potential future research areas. Table 4 presents the demographic background of the twenty players, aged between 22 and 33 years, who participated in this experiment.

### 4.2   Procedure of the Experiments

Both experiments followed the same structure. They started by gathering demographic information about the players and adjusting the game parameters to match their anthropometric measurements. Participants then set the HR sensor and adjusted the ergometer saddle height to fit their physique. After a brief introduction on the controls and a demonstration of the game, each participant played Letterbird for ten minutes while their heart rate was recorded.

Following the gameplay, participants completed a questionnaire that included the In-Game Experience Questionnaire (IGEQ), Post-Game Experience Questionnaire (PGEQ), seen in Table 5, and Borg scales for physical and cognitive exertion. They were also given the opportunity to provide individual feedback. In the second experiment, the questionnaire was expanded with three additional questions, seen in Table 7 based on findings from the first experiment.

## 5   Results and Discussion

This chapter presents the findings and discusses the results of the two experiments. As the results of Experiment 5.1 influenced the further development progress and thus Experiment 5.3, they will be regarded in chronological order.

**Table 5.** Questionnaire according to GEQ [21]

| Game Experience Questionnaire | | | |
| --- | --- | --- | --- |
| **IGEQ** | | **PGEQ** | |
| 1.1 - I was interested in the games story | | 2.1 - I felt revived | |
| 1.2 - I felt successful | | 2.2 - I felt bad | |
| 1.3 - I felt bored | | 2.3 - I found it hard to get back to reality | |
| 1.4 - I found it impressive | | 2.4 - I felt guilty | |
| 1.5 - I forgot everything around me | | 2.5 - It felt like a victory | |
| 1.6 - I felt frustrated | | 2.6 - I found it was a waste of time | |
| 1.7 - I found it tiresome | | 2.7 - I felt energised | |
| 1.8 - I felt irritable | | 2.8 - I felt satisfied | |
| 1.9 - I felt skillful | | 2.9 - I felt disoriented | |
| 1.10 - I felt completly absorbed | | 2.10 - I felt exhausted | |
| 1.11 - I felt confident | | 2.11 - I felt I could have done more useful things | |
| 1.12 - I felt challenged | | 2.12 - I felt powerful | |
| 1.13 - I had to put a lot of effort into it | | 2.13 - I felt weary | |
| 1.14 - I felt good | | 2.14 - I felt regret | |
| | | 2.15 - I felt ashamed | |
| | | 2.16 - I felt proud | |
| | | 2.17 - I had a sense that I had returned from a journey | |
| Category | Statements | Category | Statements |
| Competence | 1.2 and 1.9 | Positive Experience | 2.1, 2.5, 2.7, 2.8, 2.12 and 2.16 |
| Sensory and Imaginative Immersion | 1.1 and 1.2 | Negative Experience | 2.2, 2.4, 2.6, 2.11, 2.14 and 2.15 |
| Flow | 1.5 and 1.10 | Tiredness | 2.10 and 2.13 |
| Tension | 1.6 and 1.8 | Returning to Reality | 2.3, 2.9 and 2.17 |
| Challenge | 1.12 and 1.13 | | |
| Negative Affect | 1.3 and 1.7 | | |
| Positive Affect | 1.11 and 1.14 | | |

## 5.1   Experiment 1

As player performance and game experience are assessed using different metrics, they will be presented separately.

**Player Performance** Fig. 5 visualizes the differences between the measured heart rates and the players' target heart rates. It shows the averages for all players, highlighting the deviation rather than the raw heart rate values, which could not be easily contextualized. The heart rate measurements in Experiment 5.1 indicate promising results for the effectiveness of Letterbird, with the average player's heart rate being close to the target. However, at this stage of development, the game appears to overexert the players, as the average heart rate tends to be higher than desired. Observations of players engaging with Letterbird revealed rapid changes in pedaling speed, which is not ideal for a cardio training serious game. The Borg scale ratings, with an average of 14.5 and an interquartile range of 3, shown in Table 6, also demonstrated a significant level of exertion, suggesting that players would struggle to maintain this level of activity over a longer period.

**Game Experience** The results of the questionnaire from Experiment 5.1 were mixed. As shown in Fig. 6, participants felt quite challenged by the game but did not feel very competent. While the positive affect, which measured how good the players felt overall, received a high score, the negative affect, which measured boredom and how tiring the game was, also scored quite high. Although it can be

**Table 6.** Average Scoring and Interquartil-Range (IQR) of player's rating physical and cognitive exertion in both experiments.

| Results - Borg Scale | | | | | | | |
|---|---|---|---|---|---|---|---|
| Experiment 5.1 | | | | Experiment 5.3 | | | |
| physical exertion | | cognitive exertion | | physical exertion | | cognitive exertion | |
| mean | IQR | mean | IQR | mean | IQR | mean | IQR |
| 14.5 | 3 | 9.875 | 3.5 | 12.775 | 3 | 9.525 | 3.5 |

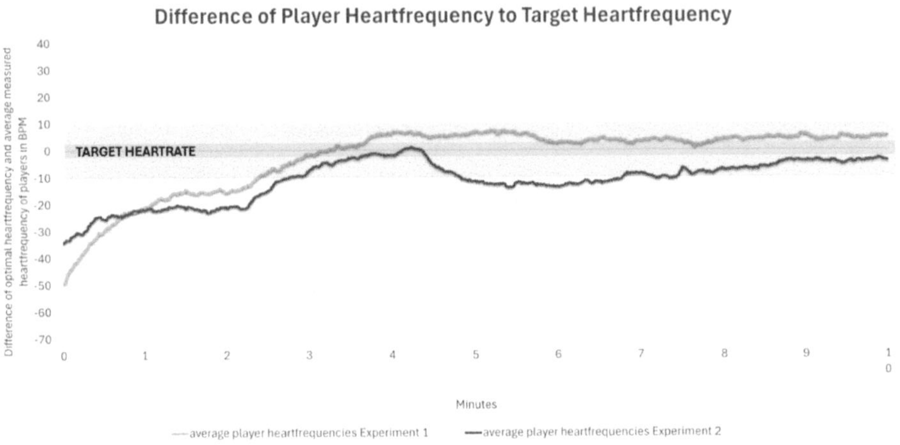

**Fig. 5.** Overview over the average player heartfrequencies in Experiment 5.1 and 5.3

argued that a cardio-training game is inherently tiring, it should not be boring. The high average value in tension, which reflects frustration and irritation, suggests that these specific negative emotions stem not from the physical activity itself, but from other aspects of the game design. The exhaustion resulting from physical activity is more accurately reflected in the high tiredness level shown in Fig. 7.

## 5.2    Adjustments

The results of player performance and game experience in Experiment 5.1 highlighted design flaws that needed correction for Experiment 5.3. In close consultation with the twelve participants of the first experiment, we discovered that players did not feel fully in control of the pigeon character they were playing. Additionally, they were widely frustrated by the randomized spawning of letters and enemies, which forced rapid changes in speed. Based on this feedback, we shifted our development focus to optimizing control sensitivity and establishing intelligent world generation.

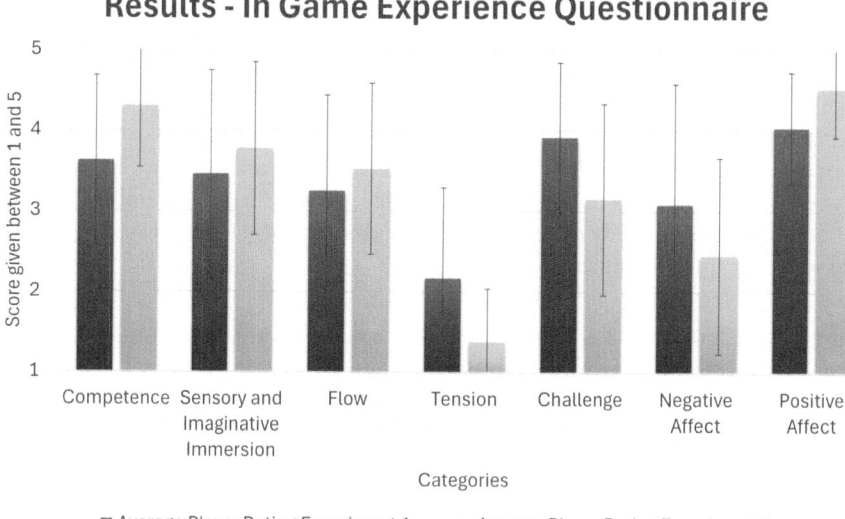

**Fig. 6.** Category results of the IGEQ

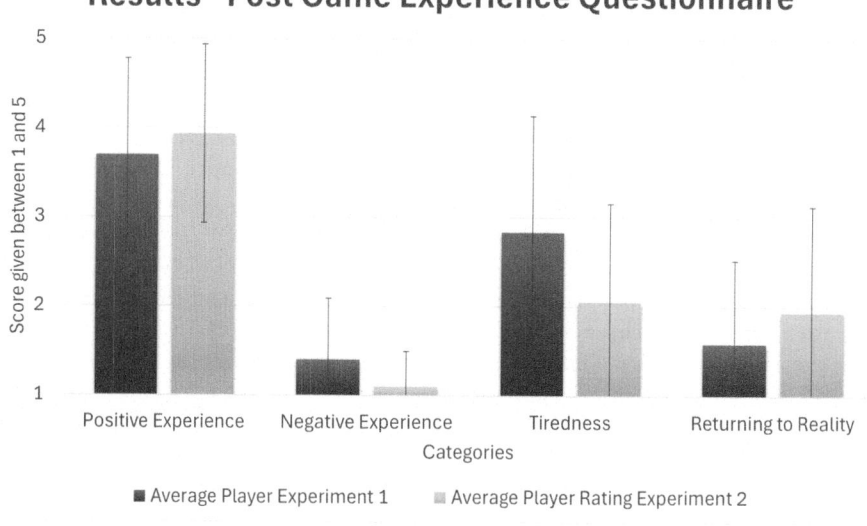

**Fig. 7.** Category results of the PGEQ

This new approach aimed to reduce frustration and optimize the required speed according to the player's current heart rate. Another issue we aimed to address in our adjustments was the players' experience of boredom during the mere 10 minutes of gameplay. Since our goal with Letterbird was to create a foundation for a long-term, appealing game that encourages physical activity in a sustainable manner, providing a high-quality gameplay experience is crucial. Therefore, we analyzed different player types using Bartle's taxonomy to understand the diverse needs of players. Based on this analysis, we introduced a variety of new gameplay elements to Letterbird, as detailed in Chapter 3. To test the effectiveness of our adjustments, we added four questions, shown in Table 7, to the existing questionnaire.

**Table 7.** Results, standard deviation (SD) and inquartil-range of additional questions to quantify the effectiveness of the adjustments after Experiment 5.1

| Results - Additional Questions | | | |
|---|---|---|---|
| Question | Average Score | IQR | SD |
| The adjustment time for the pigeon influenced the game massively | 2.65 | 2 | 0.99 |
| I felt frustrated by how enemies and letters came towards me | 1.3 | 1 | 0.57 |
| I felt how the game adjusted to me | 3.85 | 1 | 0.75 |
| I would be willing to play Letterbird again | 4.45 | 1 | 1.05 |

### 5.3 Experiment 2

Similar to Experiment 5.1, the results of this Experiment will be presented separately for player performance and game experience. The outcomes of the three additional questions, which are based on the adjustments, will be included in the discussion of the game experience.

**Player Performance** The heart rate measurements in Experiment 5.3, shown in Fig. 5, indicate an improvement in the over-exertion observed in Experiment 5.1. However, they also reveal that some players fell significantly below the target heart rate within the five to seven-minute mark. It is also to be noted that the rapid changes in pedaling speed were no longer observable and most players showed a consistent variation in speed. The player's exertion also slowly returned to the target HR over the course of the gameplay. While the initial increase in heart rate up to the three to four-minute mark is expected, the subsequent under-exertion highlights the need for further improvement in personalization to better challenge those participants who are not being adequately engaged. This is also reflected in the Borg scale results shown in Table 6. With an average score of 12.775, it indicates that the game is about two levels easier to play. The interquartile range (IQR) shows that the variation in perceived exertion remains consistent.

**Game Experience** Observing the results of the IGEQ, PGEQ, and the additional questions, shown in Figs. 6, 7, and Table 7, we see a significant improvement in the quality of the game experience. Notable increases in competence and positive affect indicate that players felt more in control. However, the average score of 2.65 on how much the adjustment times influence the game suggests there is still room for improvement.

The significantly lower scores in tension, negative affect, and negative experience demonstrate that participants experienced less frustration and boredom during gameplay. The results of our additional questions confirm that these changes resulted from our adjustments: players did not feel frustrated with the world generation, they noticed the adjustments made for them, and most would play Letterbird again. The average score of 3.85 on how players perceived the game's adjustments, along with the significant decrease in challenge seen in Fig. 6, further supports the observed under-exertion.

# 6 Limitations

Our experiments exclusively included young adults with an academic background. Therefore, our results may not generalize to children, adults over 33, or individuals from different backgrounds. Additionally, the limited number of subjects (12 and 20) prevents precise quantitative claims. Lastly, the short-term nature of our experiments does not allow for quantitative assertions on long-term effects.

# 7 Conclusion

We have elaborated a concept and a prototypical implementation for a cardio training exergame focusing on appeal and effectiveness. Evaluation studies in the form of two experiments have shown how the game experience has significantly increased through an increase of personalization and adaptation to the player. The significant reduction in frustration and boredom observed in the second experiment, combined with the addition of long-term gameplay elements that provide variety in each training session, has great potential for enhancing long-term motivation. The evaluation of heart rate data displayed how these changes decreased the intensity of training over the five to seven-minute period, recovering again after. The results of our experiments successfully demonstrate the importance of incorporating the player's perception of the game experience and its effects on motivation, rather than focusing solely on physical effectiveness and motivational patterns, in the development of a cardio training serious game. Thus, providing a qualitative statement to address the research gap identified in Chap. 2.

This data implies how the higher degree of personalization regulated the cardio training part of the game, as player's had shown a tendency of over-exertion in Experiment 5.1. Adjusting the gameplay to encourage a steadier pedaling speed, rather than rapid changes, helped create a more sustainable form of cardio training. However, this adjustment also led to some players not feeling sufficiently challenged during parts of the gameplay, although their exertion gradually returned to the target heart rate over time. This highlights the diverse needs of players in the context of sports.

Further comprehensive evaluation studies are required to show the effects of expanding the range of difficulty in Letterbird and how it would influence the perception of challenge and physical activity for individuals who are not adequately engaged with the current version, e.g. by adding tailored training plans. Future statistical tests to evaluate the reduction in stress and the perception may provide deeper insights into the game's effectiveness. Additionally, recognizing that Letterbird's game experience improved through the investigation of Bartle's Player Model, there may be further potential in exploring other existing player type models. A long-term study across a larger number of participants with a variety of backgrounds would be required to determine the statistical relevance of the effectiveness of long-term motivational gameplay elements, in order to transition from qualitative observations to quantitative conclusions.

**Acknowledgements.** This research has been investigated in the course of strategic research of the Serious Games group at TU Darmstadt in the field of personalized Games for Health. The presented work builds the ground for further research in that field, among others in will be considered in the Unite! seed fund initiative "Games for Health" towards an international, interdisciplinary Erasmus Mundus Joint Master program.

**Disclosure of Interests.** The authors have no competing interests to declare that are relevant to the content of this article.

# References

1. World Health Organization.: Physical Activity Level. https://www.who.int/initiatives/behealthy/physical-activity. Last Accessed 20 May 2024
2. World Health Organization.: Physical Activity. https://www.who.int/health-topics/physical-activity. Last Accessed 20 May 2024
3. Health Trend Map by zukunftsInstitut.: https://www.zukunftsinstitut.de/zukunftsthemen/gesundheitstrends-health-trend-map. Last Accessed 15 May 2024
4. Pfau, J., Smeddinck, J.D., Malaka, R.: Enemy within: long-term motivation effects of deep player behavior models for dynamic difficulty adjustment. In: Proceedings of the 2020 CHI Conference on Human Factors in Computing Systems (CHI '20). Association for Computing Machinery, New York, NY, USA, 1-10 (2020). https://doi.org/10.1145/3313831.3376423
5. Ketelhut, S., Röglin, L., Kircher, E., Martin-Niedecken, A.L., Ketelhut, R., Hottenrott, K., Ketelhut, K.: The new way to exercise? Evaluating an innovative heart-rate-controlled exergame. Int. J. Sport. Med. **43**(01), 77–82 (2021). (Georg Thieme Verlag KG)
6. Orji, R., Mandryk, R.L., Vassileva, J., Gerling, K.M.: Tailoring persuasive health games to gamer type. In: Proceedings of the SIGCHI Conference on Human Factors in Computing Systems (CHI '13). Association for Computing Machinery, New York, NY, USA, pp. 2467–2476 (2013). https://doi.org/10.1145/2470654.2481341

7. Göbel, S., Hardy, S., Wendel, V., Mehm, F., and Steinmetz, R.: Serious games for health: personalized exergames. In: Proceedings of the 18th ACM International Conference on Multimedia, pp. 1663–1666 (2010)
8. Hoffmann, K., Sportwiss, D., Hardy, S., Wiemeyer, J., Göbel, S.: Personalized adaptive control of training load in cardio-exergames-a feasibility study. Games Health J. 4(6), 470–479 (2015). https://doi.org/10.1089/g4h.2014.0073
9. GAMEBIKE Controller Operation Manual.: https://cateye.com/images/manual/GB_Controller_Ev1.pdf. Last Accessed 20 May 2024
10. Kraft, J.A., Russell, W.D., Bowman, T.A., Selsor, C.W., III., Foster, G.D.: Heart rate and perceived exertion during self-selected intensities for exergaming compared to traditional exercise in college-age participants. J. Strength Cond. Res. 25(6), 1736–1742 (2011). https://doi.org/10.1519/JSC.0b013e3181e06f13. PMID: 21386720
11. Westmattelmann, D., Stoffers, B., Sprenger, M., Grotenhermen, J.-G., Schewe, G.: The performance-result gap in mixed-reality cycling - evidence from the virtual Tour de France 2020 on Zwift. Front. Physiol. 13, 868902 (2022). https://doi.org/10.3389/fphys.2022.868902
12. Westmattelmann, D., Grotenhermen, J.G., Stoffers, B., Schewe, G.: Exploring the adoption of mixed-reality sport platforms: a qualitative study on ZWIFT. In: European Conference on Information Systems (2021)
13. Pasco, D., Roure, C., Kermarrec, G., Pope, Z., Gao, Z.: The effects of a bike active video game on players' physical activity and motivation. J. Sport Health Sci. 6(1), 25–32 (2017). https://doi.org/10.1016/j.jshs.2016.11.007.Epub 2016 Nov 24. PMID: 30356595; PMCID: PMC6188934
14. Unity Engine.: https://unity.com. Last Accessed 20 May 2024
15. Polar H10 Heart Rate Sensor System.: White Paper. https://www.polar.com/sites/default/files/static/science/white-papers/polar-h10-heart-rate-sensor-white-paper.pdf. Last Accessed 15 May 2024
16. World Health Organization.: A healthy lifestyle—WHO recommendations. https://www.who.int/europe/news-room/fact-sheets/item/a-healthy-lifestyle---who-recommendations. Last Accessed 20 May 2024
17. Tanaka, H., Monahan, K.D., Seals, D.R.: Age-predicted maximal heart rate revisited. J. Am. Coll.E Cardiol. 37(1) 153–156 (2001). https://doi.org/10.1016/S0735-1097(00)01054-8
18. Gulati, M., Shaw, L.J., Thisted, R.A., Black, H.R., Bairey Merz, C.N., Arnsdorf, M.F.: The St. James Women Take Heart Project: Heart Rate Response to Exercise Stress Testing in Asymptomatic Women. https://doi.org/10.1161/CIRCULATIONAHA.110.939249
19. Bartle, R.: Hearts, Clubs, Diamonds, Spades: Players Who Suit MUDS (1996). https://mud.co.uk/richard/hcds.htm. Last Accessed 20 May 2024
20. Dörner, R., Göbel, S., Effelsberg, W., Wiemeyer, J.: Serious games: foundations, concepts and practice (2016). https://doi.org/10.1007/978-3-319-40612-1
21. Borg, G.: Borg's perceived exertion and pain scales. Human Kinetics (1998)
22. Hutchinson, M.J., Kouwijzer, I., de Groot, S., Goosey-Tolfrey, V.L.: Comparison of two Borg exertion scales for monitoring exercise intensity in able-bodied participants, and those with paraplegia and tetraplegia. Spinal Cord 59, 1162–1169 (2021). https://doi.org/10.1038/s41393-021-00642-4
23. IJsselsteijn, W.A., De Kort, Y.A., Poels, K.: The Game Experience Questionnaire. Technische Universiteit Eindhoven (2013)

# Including Non-autistic Peers in Games Designed for Autistic Socialization

Yiqi Xiao[✉] [iD]

University of Illinois Urbana-Champaign, Champaign, IL 61802, USA
yiqix3@illinois.edu

**Abstract.** Through a review of current game practices, the author highlights concerns regarding the safety of public social games and the singular medical approach to serious game design for autism. The paper identifies a disconnect between the needs of autistic children and the existing solutions. To fill this gap, a neurodiversity approach to serious game design is proposed. This approach aims to address the social needs of autistic children, enabling them to interact with their neurotypical peers directly, confidently, and safely.

**Keywords:** Autistic Children · Neurodiversity · Social Skills · Educational Game

## 1 Introduction

### 1.1 Digital Spaces as Alternative Social Environments

Digital games present an important opportunity to support the growing number of autistic children in connecting them to their peers. According to the Centers for Disease Control and Prevention (CDC), the prevalence of autism among 8-year-old children in the United States is 1 in 36 in 2023, a significant increase from 1 in 150 in 2000 [1]. While youth generally enjoy the digital world, Paulus et al. [2] found that autistic boys aged four to seventeen play 85 min of video games per day, significantly more than their non-autistic peers. Simpson et al. [3] and Eversole et al. [4] highlighted that digital gaming is one of the most preferred at-home activities for autistic children from both the children's and parents' perspectives.

Ghanouni et al. [5] noted that autistic children often struggle with using language and recognizing social cues, such as picking up on jokes, maintaining eye contact during conversations, or understanding others' feelings through facial expressions or tone of voice [6]. This leads to reduced or atypical interactions between autistic children and their neurotypical peers, which may result in low self-esteem and a high risk of social isolation [7] and bullying at school [8]. To distance themselves from real-world challenges, autistic children often seek respite from the virtual world. Ringland [9] suggests that digital spaces provide an alternative where they can connect with peers, gain confidence, and forge a sense of community. In these digital environments, they can experience interactions and social connections that may be limited in the physical world due to being perceived as "disabled" and socially isolated.

© The Author(s), under exclusive license to Springer Nature Switzerland AG 2025
J. L. Plass and X. Ochoa (Eds.): JCSG 2024, LNCS 15259, pp. 330–337, 2025.
https://doi.org/10.1007/978-3-031-74138-8_23

## 1.2  Safety Concerns About Public Social Games

It is important to note that the existence of cyberbullying—the use of technology to harass, threaten, embarrass, or target another person [10]—makes autistic children's experiences in the virtual world remain concerning. According to the Annapolis Police Department, nearly 42% of kids have been bullied online and almost one in four have had it happen more than once [11]. Evidence shows that autistic children face significantly more online safety risks compared to their peers [12]. Digital environments created for public entertainment are not inherently designed for neurodiverse communication and cannot safeguard their wellbeing in social setting with non-autistic individuals.

# 2  Limitations in the Existing Serious Game Practice

## 2.1  Serious Games for Autism Exclude Non-autistic Children

Learning that public social games may not safely facilitate social interactions between autistic children and their non-autistic peers, it is natural to turn our attention to the field of serious games. While there are indeed many creative practices aimed at addressing the social challenges of autistic children [13–15], these games offer a singular approach to addressing the social challenges faced by autistic children—attempting to fix them. In the existing games, the activities typically involve fostering language speaking [16], recognizing facial expressions [18], maintaining eye contact [17], and learning appropriate actions or language to use in daily scenarios [19]. All the activities are designed based on social norms, training autistic children to behave more likely to their neurotypical peers.

Take TeachTown [19], a computer-assisted program that teaches young autistic children social and academic skills through games for example. The program transforms numerous social scenarios into engaging animations, helping players understand social norms and expectations in situations such as participating in group discussions or initiating conversations with peers. Following the animations, an interactive activity involves students completing a test on the social rules they have just learned. Games like Teach-Town do a good job of making the process of behavior change more bearable and joyful for children by engaging in visuals and interactions. However, at the core of those games, they convey a message to the children: "Your condition is an impairment."

Currently, the vast majority of these social games are designed only for autistic children to use. Among the approximately 60 serious games for autism that are reviewed in three review papers [13–15], there are about 44 games that aim to address the social challenges, and 0 of them intended to include both autistic children and their non-autistic peers to play together. While such games reduce safety concerns arising from autistic children's interactions with their neurotypical peers, they also potentially exacerbate social isolation and reinforce societal prejudices against autistic children.

## 2.2  The Medical Approach to Serious Game Design

The above approach aligns with the long-standing medical perspective on "treating" autistic children. DSM-5-TR, an international guideline for diagnosing mental health disorders, characterizes autism, or ASD, as a neurodevelopmental disorder [20]. Interventions for autism have traditionally been based on this medical model, aiming to "order the disorder" by providing various training and therapies to improve social and language skills so that they can meet public social standards [21, 22]. Though this approach has been proven effective in improving skills in many areas, it has been widely debated in recent years. Extensive evidence suggests that it can lead to feelings of self-repression, self-deprecation [23], lack of autonomy [24], and thwarted belongingness [25] when autistic individuals feel that they cannot meet expectations or are forced to behave in ways that do not align with their natural tendencies.

Influenced by the medical model, serious game designers typically associate the autism community with a need for extra education. Games designed based on this singular perspective may show effectiveness in measurable behaviors—children learn skills and knowledge after playing the game —but could potentially cause harm on a less observable psychological level. Unlike the extensive research on the harm caused by therapies, there is currently limited research on the negative impacts of therapy-based games on children. This may result from the fact that, among all treatments implying "your condition is an impairment," games are already the most enjoyable parts.

In summary, neither public social games that allow free interactions nor serious games designed solely for autistic children to practice social skills can provide a virtual environment for social interactions between autistic and non-autistic children while ensuring the well-being of autistic children.

## 3   A New Approach to Social Game Design

### 3.1   The Neurodiversity Approach to Autism

A major misconception is that only autistic children need to connect to their peers. Jones [26] examined the contributors to friendship satisfaction and found that the most important factors are self-disclosure, trust, and companionship enjoyment. Another study, involving 2555 autism experts from 43 countries in 10 disciplines, identified individuals with autism as having a strong sense of morality, trustworthiness, loyalty, and kindness, indicating that autistic individuals have much to contribute to friendships [27]. It would be a loss if neurotypical children missed the opportunity to have such a reliable friend due to a lack of opportunity to connect and get to know them.

While the strengths of autistic children are not often highlighted and emphasized in the medical model, the neurodiversity approach, a relatively new approach, highlights the importance of recognizing the value of neurodivergent individuals in society. Instead of viewing autism as a disorder, disability, or impairment, this approach sees it as a natural variation of neurotypes [28]. People of different neurotypes need to respect and accept each other's unique mental conditions to support one another. The neurodiversity approach, as emphasized by Singer [29] and Chapman [30] is not a fixed, singular framework but rather a call for ongoing discussion and evolution of the idea. Compared to the medical approach, the discussion of the neurodiversity approach is limited, especially in game design. It is crucial to raise awareness of neurodiversity among practitioners who can make an impact in the autistic community by addressing why we need to change, and demonstrating how we could make a change. The goal of the rest of this paper is to establish such neurodiversity principles to serious game design that address the social needs of autistic children while ensure their wellbeing.

### 3.2 Three Fundamental Principles

This paper proposes three fundamental principles that can guide the design of games supporting neurodiverse socialization: inclusiveness, affirmation, and safety.

- Inclusiveness [39] requires involving all parties in the expected social interactions within the game, aligning with the idea of equity emphasized in the neurodiversity approach. This means that the game's audience should not be limited to only autistic children.
- Affirmation [40], or "neuro-affirming," ensures that the activities in the game allow players to feel comfortable and confident in expressing their neuro-identity. This usually means that game tasks are not designed to highlight the challenges of autistic children.
- Safety here refers only to avoiding the risks brought by interactions between autistic children and their neurotypical peers due to differences in social behavior caused by different neurotypes. This requires both a well-designed internal game mechanisms and an enhanced external supervision.

### 3.3 Case Study I: Inclusive, Safe, But Not Affirming

Sturm et al. [31] documented an innovative participatory design process of a hybrid game aimed at promoting complex emotion recognition and collaboration between autistic individuals and their peers. Players first assemble pieces of facial expressions in a digital puzzle independently and then communicate in person to agree on the appropriate emotion on the face of the body. This project design recognizes the necessity of connecting autistic children with non-autistic children and successfully creates a collaborative activity. It is "inclusive". Although the concept and measurement of safety are not mentioned in the article, the process can be considered "safe" because the experiment was conducted with a very small number of participants and under the supervision of researchers. However, the goal of the activity, "agree on the appropriate emotion," continues to encourage autistic children to modify their social behavior to align with societal expectations. Therefore, although not discussed in the paper, this process might bring stress and discomfort and still follows the medical approach. Besides making the games "inclusive," it is also crucial to ensure that the game activities are "affirming," where autistic children can feel comfortable and confident being themselves.

### 3.4 Case Study II: Affirming, Safe, But Not Inclusive

Battocchi et al. [32] presented the development and evaluation of a collaborative puzzle game for autistic children that is considered "affirming" because it focuses on connecting children through a collaborative experience rather than merely teaching social skills or language. The game employs a tabletop interface and an interaction rule that requires both players to simultaneously touch and drag puzzle pieces. It was tested separately on groups of autistic and non-autistic children, with results demonstrating its effectiveness in promoting social interactions, evidenced by a noticeable increase in simultaneous movements. Therefore, although the game primarily fosters collaboration, it is within the autistic community and thus not considered "inclusive." The process is deemed "safe" because it does not involve interactions between autistic and non-autistic children. Although it does not align with the principle of inclusiveness, it offers valuable insights into designing games for neurodiverse connections. Collaborative activities, such as accomplishing tasks together or creating something jointly, can be highly beneficial as they create more opportunities for communication. Interactions that do not rely on language, such as using body movements or images, reduce communication barriers and allow children with different language abilities to participate confidently.

### 3.5   Case Study III: Affirming, Safe, and Partially Inclusive

Possibly due to the inherent difficulty in creating a game that is inclusive, affirming, and safe, no perfect example embodies this idea that has been found. However, Autcraft [38] offers valuable insights into how developers can make a game affirming while maintaining a degree of inclusiveness for safety purposes.

Minecraft is a popular game among adults and children worldwide, including those with autism. It provides an open world with a lot of freedom for players to choose their activities, such as collaboratively building a city, playing survival games, or simply exploring while chatting [33]. This setting is "affirming" as it offers so much freedom which gives the players much control of what they do in the game. However, this flexibility can lead to rampant cyberbullying. People often enter young players' worlds and destroy their structures, sometimes causing distress by trapping them with lava. Numerous videos of such incidents exist on YouTube [34, 35]. Stuart Duncan [36], an autistic Minecraft player, noted "kids with autism would go onto public servers to play Minecraft and they would just be bullied" in the conversation with the Bridge.

Although Minecraft is not specifically designed for autistic individuals or other neurodiverse people and is thus not inherently a safe environment for them, Duncan saw an opportunity. He explained, "I've often heard it said that people with autism gravitate towards it because all the rules of the world are set and predictable." Building on Minecraft, he developed a server called Autcraft that offers limited access to autistic individuals, their families and friends. In Autcraft, autistic young people can freely and confidently interact with others who share similar experiences or understand the autistic community. To ensure this safe environment, Duncan also appointed parents as admins, who can mute people, temporarily jail them in the game, or ban players for serious rule violations.

As of December 2023, Autcraft has over 17,000 players [37], demonstrating the effectiveness of these measures. In Autcraft, Stuart limited access to non-autistic individuals who are family or friends of autistic individuals to ensure safe interactions and also used strict supervision over the server. However, there are not the only ways to handle it. We could also implement game mechanisms that restrict certain forms of social behavior among players, such as the function of public or private speech, while directing their attention to other well-designed forms of interaction. The example of Autcraft is a call for game designers to pay attention to the long-ignored but significant needs of the autistic community for safe and affirming social interactions with their peers.

## 4 Discussion

Although this paper has been emphasizing the limitations and potential harm brought by serious games developed to teach autistic children social skills, it is not intended to deny the advancements and improvements that gamification practices have achieved in medical treatment, nor their effectiveness in providing practical solutions for autistic children and their parents. Instead of criticizing any specific game, this paper challenges the current singular approach of serious games in addressing the complex life challenges of autistic children and seeks to enrich existing knowledge and practices.

This preliminary framework has two major limitations. Firstly, due to a scarcity of relevant work, there is a lack of empirical data or pilot studies to support its claims about the effectiveness of neurodiversity principles in game design. Secondly, it is challenging to implement all three principles in one game. In highly inclusive environments, the level of social safety may decrease, which can cause children to feel uncomfortable even if the activities within the game are designed to be affirming. Although previous sections have provided some actionable insights, more methods need to be discussed to better balance these three principles.

## 5 Conclusion

By reviewing current practices in the digital game area and referring to extensive research on autistic children, this paper highlights a disconnect between autistic children's need to safely and confidently socialize with their peers in the digital world and the existing solutions. To fill this gap, the author advises serious game designers to shift their focus from "teaching autistic children social skills" to "facilitating neurodiverse social interactions" with three main principles: inclusiveness, affirmation, and safety. This preliminary work intends to spark ongoing discussions in further developing these guidelines and enrich the existing knowledge and practices. The neurodiversity approach in serious game design is like an open door; a path will only be forged when more people pass through it.

**Acknowledgments.** The author would like to thank Boyang Wu and Katryna Starks for their valuable assistance in refining the language and improving the clarity of this paper.

## References

1. Centers for Disease Control and Prevention: CDC releases new data on autism prevalence in the US. https://www.cdc.gov/media/releases/2023/p0323-autism.html. Last accessed 2024/05/22

2. Paulus, F.W., Sander, C.S., Nitze, M., Kramatschek-Pfahler, A.R., Voran, A., von Gontard, A.: Gaming disorder and computer-mediated communication in children and adolescents with autism spectrum disorder. Z. Kinder Jugendpsychiatr. Psychother. **48**(2), 113–122 (2020). https://doi.org/10.1024/1422-4917/a000674

3. Simpson, K., Keen, D., Adams, D., Alston-Knox, C., Roberts, J.: Participation of children on the autism spectrum in home, school, and community. Child: Care, Health Dev. **44**(1), 99–107 (2018). https://doi.org/10.1111/cch.12483

4. Eversole, M., et al.: Leisure activity enjoyment of children with autism spectrum disorders. J. Autism Dev. Disord. **46**(1), 10–20 (2016). https://doi.org/10.1007/s10803-015-2529-z

5. Ghanouni, P., Jarus, T., Zwicker, J.G., Lucyshyn, J., Chauhan, S., Moir, C.: Perceived barriers and existing challenges in participation of children with autism spectrum disorders: 'he did not understand and no one else seemed to understand him.' J. Autism Dev. Disord. **49**(8), 3136–3145 (2019). https://doi.org/10.1007/s10803-019-04036-7

6. Aherne, D.: The Pocket Guide to Neurodiversity. Jessica Kingsley Publishers (2023)

7. Bauminger, N., Kasari, C.: Loneliness and friendship in high-functioning children with autism. Child Dev. **71**(2), 447–456 (2000). https://doi.org/10.1111/1467-8624.00156

8. Humphrey, N., Symes, W.: Perceptions of social support and experience of bullying among pupils with autistic spectrum disorders in mainstream secondary schools. Eur. J. Spec. Needs Educ. **25**, 77–91 (2010). https://doi.org/10.1080/08856250903450855

9. Ringland, K.E.: A place to play: the (Dis)Abled embodied experience for autistic children in online spaces. In: Proceedings of the 2019 CHI Conference on Human Factors in Computing Systems (CHI 2019), pp. 1–12. ACM, New York (2019). https://doi.org/10.1145/3290605.3300518

10. Nemours KidsHealth: What is cyberbullying? https://kidshealth.org/en/teens/cyberbullying.html. Last accessed 2024/05/22

11. City of Annapolis: Facts about cyberbullying. https://www.annapolis.gov/908/Facts-About-Cyberbullying. Last accessed 2024/05/22

12. Macmillan, K., Berg, T., Just, M., Stewart, M.E.: Are autistic children more vulnerable online? Relating autism to online safety, child wellbeing and parental risk management. In: Proceedings of the 2020 ACM International Conference on Interaction Design and Children (IDC '20), pp. 1–10. ACM, New York (2020). https://doi.org/10.1145/3419249.3420160

13. Kellidou, M., Andreadis, D., Antoniou, P.: A review of digital games for children with autism spectrum disorders (ASD). Adv. Neurodevelopmental Disord. **4**, 63–70 (2020). https://doi.org/10.1145/3439231.3439270

14. Carneiro, T., Carvalho, A., Frota, S., Filipe, M.G.: Serious games for developing social skills in children and adolescents with autism spectrum disorder: a systematic review. Healthcare **12**(508), (2024) https://doi.org/10.3390/healthcare12050508

15. Atherton, G., Cross, L.: The use of analog and digital games for autism interventions. Front. Psychol. **12**, 669734 (2021). https://doi.org/10.3389/fpsyg.2021.669734

16. Murdock, L.C., Ganz, J., Crittendon, J.: Use of an iPad play story to increase play dialogue of preschoolers with autism spectrum disorders. J. Autism Dev. Disord. **43**(9), 2174–2189 (2013). https://doi.org/10.1007/s10803-013-1770-6

17. Youtube: Ted's Ice Cream Adventures-WhizKid Games. https://www.youtube.com/watch?v=Had5Tmy0xYw. Last accessed 2024/05/22

18. Youtube: Robbie the Robot Gameplay. https://www.youtube.com/watch?v=BHBKGSui64I. Last accessed 2024/05/22

19. TeachTown Social Skills. TeachTown. Available: https://web.teachtown.com/solutions/teachtown-social-skills/. Last accessed 2024/05/22

20. American Psychiatric Association: Diagnostic and Statistical Manual of Mental Disorders. 5th edn. American Psychiatric Association, Arlington, VA (2013)

21. Sharma, S., Gonda, X., Tarazi, F.: Autism spectrum disorder: classification, diagnosis and therapy. Pharmacol. Ther. **190**, 91–104 (2018)
22. Vismara, L., Rogers, S.: Behavioral treatments in autism spectrum disorder: what do we know? Annu. Rev. Clin. Psychol. **6**, 447–468 (2010)
23. McGill, O., Robinson, A.: 'Recalling hidden harms': autistic experiences of childhood applied behavioural analysis (ABA). Adv. Autism **7**(4), Article 4 (2021)
24. Freitas, B.G.: Questioning normativity: exploring the experiences of autistic adults who have undergone applied behavioural analysis (ABA). M.S. thesis, Toronto Metropolitan University, Toronto, Canada (2020)
25. Cassidy, S.A., Gould, K., Townsend, E., Pelton, M., Robertson, A.E., Rodgers, J.: Is camouflaging autistic traits associated with suicidal thoughts and behaviours? Expanding the interpersonal psychological theory of suicide in an undergraduate student sample. J. Autism Dev. Disord. **50**(10), 3638–3648 (2020)
26. Jones, D.: Friendship satisfaction and gender: an examination of sex differences in contributors to friendship satisfaction. J. Soc. Pers. Relat. **8**, 167–185 (1991)
27. de Schipper, E., Mahdi, S., de Vries, P., et al.: Functioning and disability in autism spectrum disorder: a worldwide survey of experts. Autism Res. **9**(9), 959–969 (2016)
28. Dwyer, P.: The neurodiversity approach(es): what are they and what do they mean for researchers? Hum. Dev. **66**, 73–92 (2022)
29. Singer, J.: What does NeuroDiversity mean? NeuroDiversity 2.0. https://neurodiversity2.blogspot.com/p/what.html. Last accessed 2024/05/28
30. Chapman, R.: Defining neurodiversity for research and practice. In: Roqvist, H.B., Chown, N., Stenning, A. (eds.) Neurodiversity Studies: A New Critical Paradigm, pp. 218–220. Routledge (2020)
31. Sturm, D., Kholodovsky, M., Arab, R., Smith, D.S., Asanov, P., Gillespie-Lynch, K.: Participatory design of a hybrid Kinect game to promote collaboration between autistic players and their peers. Int. J. Hum.-Comput. Interact. **35**(8), 706–723 (2019)
32. Battocchi, A., Pianesi, F., Tomasini, D., Zancanaro, M., Esposito, G., Venuti, P., Ben Sasson, A., Gal, E., Weiss, P.L.: Collaborative puzzle game: a tabletop interactive game for fostering collaboration in children with autism spectrum disorders (ASD). In: Proceedings of the ACM International Conference on Interactive Tabletops and Surfaces, pp. 197–204 (2009)
33. Microsoft: Minecraft for Windows. Available: https://www.microsoft.com/en-ms/p/minecraft-for-windows/9nblggh2jhxj?activetab=pivot:overviewtab. Last accessed, 2024/05/22
34. Youtube: Trolling the angriest kid ever on Minecraft. https://www.youtube.com/watch?v=Kw9ZGZqSpyU. Last accessed, 2024/05/22
35. Youtube: Trolling a little kid in Minecraft. https://www.youtube.com/watch?v=G_CpPYSNkt8. Last accessed, 2024/05/22
36. ACAMH: Minecraft and young people with autism. https://www.acamh.org/blog/minecraft-young-people-autism/. Last accessed 2024/05/22
37. Wikipedia: Autcraft. https://en.wikipedia.org/wiki/Autcraft. Last accessed 2024/05/22
38. Autcraft: Home. Available at: https://www.autcraft.com/. Last accessed 2024/07/20
39. Cambridge Dictionary: Inclusiveness. Available at: https://dictionary.cambridge.org/us/dictionary/english/inclusiveness. Last accessed 2024/07/20
40. Dallman, A.R., Williams, K.L., Villa, L.: Neurodiversity-affirming practices are a moral imperative for occupational therapy. Open J. Occupat. Ther. **10**, 1–9 (2022). https://doi.org/10.15453/2168-6408.1937

# Developing Gamified Learning for Healthcare Professionals Through University Partnerships

Stephanie Nicely[1]([✉]) [ID], Jacy Richardson[2] [ID], and Tod Emma[2]

[1] Organizational Development and Learning Department, East Tennessee Children's Hospital, Knoxville, TN, USA
sanicely@etch.com
[2] Digital Media, East Tennessee State University, Johnson City, TN, USA
{richardsoje1,emma}@etsu.edu

**Abstract.** This paper presents an in-depth analysis of the collaborative game design process between the East Tennessee Children's Hospital and East Tennessee State University teams. Through a comprehensive examination, we look into the methodologies utilized, challenges encountered, and best practices established in fostering interdisciplinary collaboration. Emphasizing the crucial role of effective communication, proficient project management, and proactive stakeholder engagement, our study highlights the significance of these factors in driving successful outcomes. By analyzing recent game builds and key insights extracted from this collaborative project, our research offers valuable guidance for practitioners seeking to navigate similar interdisciplinary projects across multiple organizations.

**Keywords:** First Keyword · Second Keyword · Third Keyword

## 1  Introduction

In recent years gamified learning has witnessed a surge in popularity among medical professionals as an effective method for continuous education and skill development [10]. When comparing games and gamification, it can be noted that while games are primarily recreational, gamification serves a different purpose: facilitating learning, habit change, or system reorganization, the key distinction lies in whether the game itself is the ultimate goal or merely a tool for achieving other objectives. Despite the difference, both concepts incorporate challenges, rewards, rules, and a framework for engagement [8]. Thus, utilizing gamification in e-learning has proven effective across all educational levels, facilitating learning in diverse subjects such as foreign languages, entrepreneurship, and general communication skills [3].

The aim of this collaboration is to turn serious games into vital educational tools in healthcare training, offering immersive and interactive environments for medical professionals to build their skills, knowledge, and preparedness, especially in high risk, low volume scenarios, while simultaneously offering a constructionist environment [6] to Digital Media and Computer Science students. The partnership we've built allows for interdisciplinary collaboration, providing unique opportunities for college students in our community while fostering innovation in pediatric healthcare. It's a powerful illustration of major institutions looking within their own community for growth and support; providing the hospital customized pediatric learning content in VR (virtual reality), computer games, and other technology previously unexplored, as well as giving the university students real-world project experience whose deliverables are for a cause they know has a direct impact on children's lives. Here we analyze this collaborative game design process between the East Tennessee Children's Hospital and East Tennessee State University Digital Media teams, focusing on methodologies, challenges, and best practices for interdisciplinary collaboration while highlighting the importance of effective communication, project management, and stakeholder engagement in achieving successful outcomes.

## 2   Collaboration Details

### 2.1   Background and Current Status

The collaboration between East Tennessee State University Digital Media and East Tennessee Children's Hospital commenced in 2020, initiated by the Organizational Development and Learning (ODL) department's quest for innovative community partnerships. Since its inception, this collaboration has produced significant outcomes, including the development of two virtual reality simulations, each comprising four phases, along with the creation of a computer game. Currently, another computer game is in production, with the recent completion of its first semester of production. Production for this will continue in the fall, which will be the first time the class is offered during a fall semester; many of the students enrolled in this past spring's class are enrolled to take it again due to how impactful it has been for them. This testament to the transformative power of hands-on, experiential learning speaks volumes about the success of the collaboration and its ability to inspire and empower students to excel in their academic and professional endeavors.

A Professional Development Internship program is offered by East Tennessee Children's Hospital's ODL department in collaboration with ETSU, maintaining a minimum of two interns, and at current, funding two graduate assistants who stay for the duration of the project, instead of a single semester like other undergraduate students. The hospital provides project management mentorship along with leadership training within the hospital, networking opportunities, and potential for scholarships.

### 2.2   Future Plans

Hospital staff plans to continue the evaluation on educational impact of the gamified training simulations. Ideally, in addition to knowledge transfer for hospital staff, practice changes will be able to be observed as a result of increased critical thinking, e.g. Lesser wait times in an emergency department setting, and easier access to practicing high risk - low volume scenarios. The collaboration can continue to explore new concepts and ideas for developing immersive educational games. This could involve creating additional simulations or expanding existing games to cover a broader range of topics relevant to healthcare professionals and students. We aim to create serious games for all branches of the hospital, not only clinical staff, as it requires a synchronized effort of every department to achieve organizational excellence.

Additionally, as this is a partnership still in early years, the need for constant research and evaluation remains paramount. It is vital to assess the effectiveness of the games developed through the collaboration. This research will include the impact of the games on learning outcomes, skill acquisition, and retention, providing valuable insights for future game development and educational initiatives.

## 3  Program Components

### 3.1  Recruiting Needed Skill Sets

The Digital Media program at East Tennessee State University consists of four different concentrations that students can pursue: Game Design, Visualization, Visual Effects, and Animation. In the past, a production course focused on creating games and simulations for East Tennessee Children's hospital has been taught in the Spring and will be switching to Fall and Spring in the future. The production course operates on a collaborative model, where students are recruited to form teams based on their skills and interests. Teams consist of animators, programmers, modelers, lighting artists, concept artists, as well as the production interns who are also team leads. Team leads, who are often experienced students that have previously contributed to the project, play a pivotal role in the recruitment process. They review portfolios submitted by prospective team members, assessing not only technical proficiency but also the alignment of skills with the specific needs of the semester's production focus. For example, if we are going to kick off a new project, we would need to be sure we have concept artists on board as they are pivotal in sharing game design and flow ideas with clients. In contrast, if the project is coming to a close, depending on the work breakdown structure and scheduling, it is very likely the team would want to have more programmers and animators for bug fixes and last minute changes. This ensures that each team comprises a diverse mix of talent, drawing from various concentrations within the Digital Media program, as well as from the Computer Science department. The class is actively sought out by students with many retaking the class.

The second part of the recruitment process is the consideration of the team in of itself. There are few professional environments where one will not be a part of a working team in some form or fashion [5]. A functional team depends on everyone's ability to provide an accountable work ethic. As such, in choosing new team members, not only are individual skills and qualifications assessed, but also their compatibility with the existing team dynamic. Compatibility encompasses technical proficiency as well as interpersonal skills, communication abilities, and a willingness to collaborate and support fellow team members. Each individual contributes to the collective success of the team.

### 3.2  Scheduled Class Time

The class meets two to three times a week and is overseen by graduate students with a professor of record for grading purposes. It is arranged as a four credit hour class within the Digital Media major of the College of Business and Technology. This course is structured to mimic the operations of a professional game studio, incorporating daily check-ins, feedback reviews, and time audits. The student gives input on their ability to complete the task within the specified timeframe, fostering self-auditing of the time required to accomplish various tasks. Upon completion of a task, the student uploads files to an online drive and notifies other team members to ensure its successful implementation. Team leads have documents for students to refer to on properly exporting files and setting up software to make importation into Unreal Engine more stream-lined. They also provide style guides to ensure a cohesive art style among all artists.

It's set up which includes in person time as well as work required outside of the class, that is being monitored through various methods, is akin to a hybrid position in the professional world. While there is more research to be done on the best practice and specific elements of a hybrid classroom, the evidence does point towards students having increased flexibility and personal space for their work [4]. It differs from a traditional class and homework setting in that the entire class is always connected through various online methods such as Discord, Google Drive, and email.

### 3.3 Community Partners

Due to the nature of the class and its collaboration with an external entity, it follows the guidelines and goals of the ETSU's latest quality enhancement plan (QEP), Go Beyond the Classroom [1]. According to ETSU, "Community-engaged learning is the integration of academic coursework and intentional community partnerships that fosters student reflection and application of classroom learning." The production class is a designated Community Engaged Learning course. With this designation, the class has been awarded a grant which funded new VR headsets and various other pieces of technology that positively impacted efficiency and quality.

As a result of early success of the projects, our student leadership team grew to consist of two graduate assistants funded by East Tennessee Children's Hospital and two internships, also managed by ETCH. The productions are led by faculty from Digital Media and Computer Science, and a staff person at ETCH who is a Project Management Specialist in the Organizational Development and Learning Department. The mission of the ODL department is, "ODL works to progressively sustain the function and ongoing growth of East Tennessee Children's Hospital through our most important asset…our staff." The unique and constant cooperation between the hospital and university ensures that upper level stakeholders on both ends have a direct line to project statuses and updates. It also demonstrates what partnerships within regional communities can accomplish while providing services that directly impact children's lives ranging from infants to university students.

## 4   Methods

### 4.1   Project Management

Due to the inherent characteristics of traditional semester scheduling within the university, two types of management must be employed when coordinating student-led projects. The first is hyper-local, working within a single semester through a series of sprints and a student specific work breakdown structure. While defining activities is always essential for breaking down work packages and creating a foundation for various processes of project management [7], it is also the basis for classroom tasks. The second arm of the management comes from the hospital in terms of upper level project management. This side is responsible for controlling the scope of the project in its entirety, spanning across several semesters and regardless of class sizes, student participation, professor changes, etc.

For task management and project tracking, an Excel sheet is used as the central tool to organize tasks based on several factors like priority as well other attributes such as level of detail, texture needs, and UV mapping. Priority is a key aspect that helps students determine which tasks require immediate attention and which can be tackled later. By assigning priorities, students can focus their efforts on the most critical aspects of the project, ensuring that deadlines are met and goals are achieved in a timely manner. Other attributes such as the level of detail required, texture needs, and UV mapping specifications are also considered and documented within the Excel sheet. These attributes provide important context for each task, helping students understand the specific requirements and expectations associated with their work. For example, detailing to the level needed for a particular asset ensures that students allocate sufficient time and resources to achieve the desired outcome. Similarly, specifying texture needs and UV mapping requirements helps students plan and execute the technical aspects of their projects effectively, ensuring that final deliverables meet quality standards while also remaining optimized for a game engine (Fig. 1).

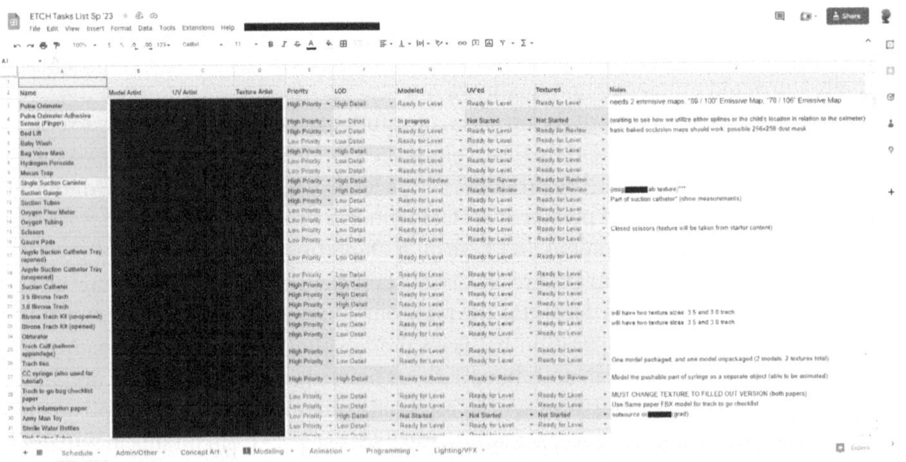

**Fig. 1.** Image of in-class Excel matrix utilized for student tasks

At the other end of the collaboration the staff member at ETCH manages the project via the interns and graduate assistants through meetings, project management software (such as Microsoft Projects, Teamwork, Jira, etc.) and continually working to develop the management skill sets of the student producers. In addition to the professional development of the students, all of the formal project management documents come from this side including the project charter, scope, and stakeholder registries. The overarching milestones are also controlled by the hospital staff person in parallel with ongoing iterations of other or past projects. The usage of popular project management software gives the students another opportunity of exposure to potential workplace tools. The interns and graduate assistants have dual responsibilities in the way that they must ensure day to day tasks are being accounted for, but also provide input on scope and schedule creation for the life of the project. This situation awards them a more comprehensive understanding of the process as well as collaborative decision making opportunities, while maximizing efficiency for the project as a whole.

This two-fold management serves as a checks and balances system for the project in addition to providing exposure to multiple facets and methodologies of project management. Students still require the structure the framework of the development class provides them, but also are afforded the freedom to develop as they might for external clients.

### 4.2 Stakeholder Engagement

When facilitating a collaboration between large institutions, stakeholder management is an important component to keep in consideration at all times. There are not only the hospital, client stakeholders, but also those invested in the learning outcomes and well being of the students at the university. Making sure both are satisfied with the deliverables, as well as the process, involves continuous meetings, emails, and demos so that there is an open line for negotiation and communication on any change requests that may come through. This falls outside of the (graduate) student responsibilities and lies with the professor of record and department head at ETSU. The latter have the professional capacity to attend meetings and delegate ensuing action items. The ETCH staff person is the point of contact for hospital and university stakeholders alike, also relaying communications received through various professional facets. This is not to say the interns or graduate students will not interact with major stakeholders at all; on the contrary, we have found it highly beneficial for the demos to be presented by the students. They get presentation experience and valuable networking opportunities while the stakeholders are able to see the collaboration's full merit with projects built for a cause and students reaping professional benefits.

Overall, it can be easy to be consumed by tasks, scheduling, and active development when building games in this fashion, but keeping stakeholders engaged with the deliverables and process is just as vital. Without their continued support or approval, the framework collapses.

## 5  Game Development and Implementation

Each game is built with customization and accuracy in mind. Meaning, the hospital's room, procedures, policies, even lighting are all taken into consideration with the mindset that the students learn through doing and aim to stretch the limitations of their current portfolios. For each of these completed projects, the team created every 3D model, material, and the lighting based off the physical elements in the hospital. Hundreds of images were taken for reference by team leads as part of the research portion of the projects. Having the students take charge of what they deem is needed allows for growing pains in terms of time management and attention to detail. When modeling assets in 3D, multiple angles of things as innocuous as an outlet must be taken. Every asset was created by a student, all the code created by a student, and all of the environmental art was created by a student. The only exception was some of the more recent character models. With the acceptance of a recent grant, the decision was made to purchase a small package of assets like characters, to help keep the project on track for completion within a short timeframe. The content and medical accuracy was created by the hospital through several content meetings where storyboards are reviewed and rechecked.

## 5.1  Crash Cart Computer Game

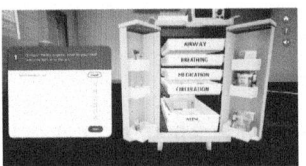  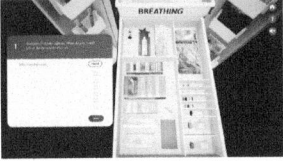

**Fig. 2.** The image trio consists of images of a question within the Crash Cart computer game

The first training game completed was the Crash Cart. The physical crash cart is used in code-blue situations at the hospital and it is critical for nurses and medical professionals to know exactly where each item is located. The game itself was fairly straightforward in design, but provided an interactive element previously unutilized in elearning at the hospital. The player can open and close doors and drawers of the cart to find items needed to answer questions. (See Fig. 2) It can be implemented in skills days, orientation of new clinical staff, competency checks, as well as learner-initiated self play. This computer game helps prepare them and they receive printable results at the end of the game. It was built using Unreal Engine 4 with minimal student-staff interaction and packaged for the hospital to run on specialized computers in their Discovery Innovation and Simulation Center. Custom models imported into Unreal were created in Autodesk Maya.

## 5.2  De-Escalation Virtual Reality Training Supplement

Following Crash Cart, a different digital media team created De-Escalation scenarios 1–4. This was the first production in virtual reality for ETSU Digital Media and ETCH. The game was used as supplemental practice for training given by the Crisis Prevention Institute, whose main goal is to teach clinical staff how to safely and effectively respond to individuals whose behavior is escalating [4]. There are four different scenarios within the game that take a staff member through an increasingly confrontational situation. The game is designed to pause at certain points and proceed after the correct action is chosen from a multiple choice question within the game. With virtual reality being relatively unexplored by ETSU Digital Media students, the coding process became unexplored territory for the programmers, creating a variety of technical hurdles. It was also built using Unreal Engine 4 and originally formatted for the Rift S headset before transitioning to the Quest 2 and 3. A significant amount of attention to detail was invested to ensure the game's environment (Fig. 3) was realistic. Even though it was a virtual reality experience, the immersive elements were minimal, leaving room for change in the game design for the next project. Opportunities were identified with the amount of on screen text a player had to read as well as the lack of movement within the virtual space. It was, however, a good first VR project as it was not overwhelmingly difficult to understand the purpose or flow of the game.

**Fig. 3.**  Screenshot of De-Escalation VR in game environment

### 5.3  Trach and Vent Virtual Reality Supplemental Practice

In Fall of 2022, after a successful VR game release, the ETSU team began pre-production on a VR Trach & Vent simulation. ETSU worked closely with content writers at ETCH to build storyboards (see Fig. 4) as well as game flow. The project was completed in Spring of 2024 and will go into regular training of new nurses as well as current clinical staff.

Building off of the feedback from the first VR build, this game was tasked with being significantly more immersive. As such, more intricate usage of the controllers was needed, creating a different tangent of issues due to inexperienced players. A tutorial was added to aid in this, taking players through simple actions with items they would be using in play, e.g. a syringe. After the tutorial, there are four phases which consist of hospital room readiness, tracheostomy changes and troubleshooting, as well as tracheostomy to-go bag training. The project was built using Unreal Engine 5 in order to utilize the new lighting systems available in that release. Custom 3D models were created in Autodesk Maya and textured using a mix of Adobe Photoshop and Substance Painter (Figs. 5 and

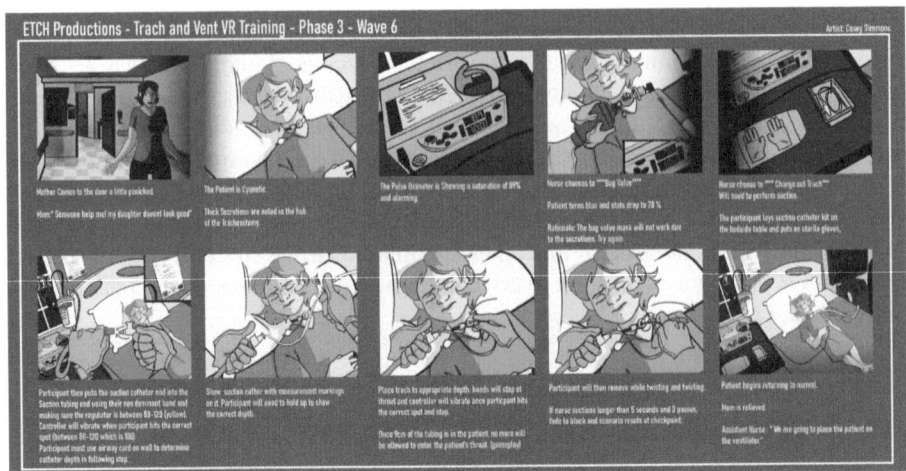

**Fig. 4.** The image showcases the storyboards created by students for the Trach and Vent production.

6). Character models were purchased from an external source to serve as the child and mother, but were animated in-house by the students.

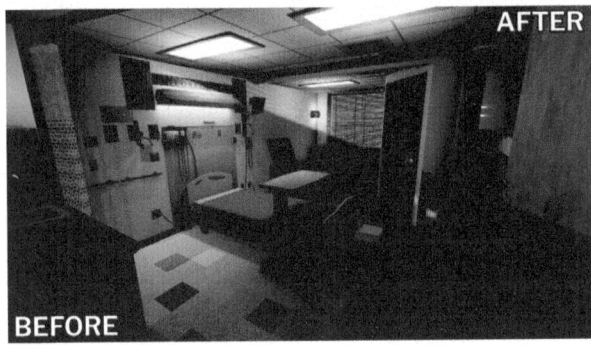

**Fig. 5.** The image showcases the lighting before and after utilizing Unreal Engine 5.

### 5.4   Builds in Progress

The team is currently immersed in the production of another innovative computer game, aiming to build critical thinking skills within high-risk scenarios prevalent in emergency department triage and differential diagnosis cases. The implemented core features encompass functionality for tracking score, main UI elements including progress bars, tab elements, main menu, and dialogue bubbles, interactive/clickable items within the environment, hitboxes/collision detection for individual components on the child model, a working camera-swap system for close-ups of different items/child model, implementation of a new toon shader compatible with Unreal Engine 4, and the ability to read-in

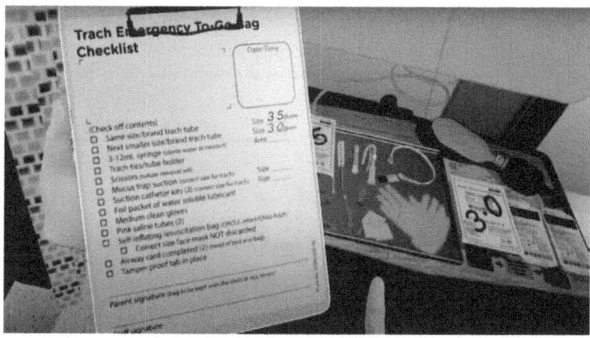

**Fig. 6.** The image shows a still from a section of gameplay within the trach to-go bag phase.

case study information through text files. We are creating this as a web based game with the goal of reaching as many staff members as possible through the hospital's LMS (learning management system), which does not support Unreal Engine at this time. The project is being built in Unreal Engine 4, as that release provides support to export as an HTML5 project.

For this game, there is a big push to move away from the hyper-realistic styles from VR and create something more stylized. This strategic change aims to heighten the learning process with an element of enjoyment, effectively distinguishing the game from conventional computer modules and producing a more engaging learning experience. While maintaining medical accuracy, the team wants to encourage fun and create an obvious difference between traditional computer modules and learning games.

## 6  Analysis and Evaluation

### 6.1  Computer Game

The Crash Cart computer game was the starting point and litmus test for how the hospital would react to a different style of learning. The results were overall positive in terms of reception by staff and learning outcomes. Figure 7 illustrates the marked increase in certain areas related to accuracy within the crash cart compared to tests without it.

### 6.2  Virtual Reality Games

For both, De-Escalation and the first two phases of Trach & Vent, quality and confidence surveys were conducted pre and post play. As the Trach and Vent VR game is still in production, the survey results are on-going. Here we look at the most recent analysis of the De-Escalation VR training. When reviewing the culmination of survey responses over an eight month period, we had a goal to ascertain two main feedback pieces. The first, if the training in question altered the confidence of the learner concerning the target skill. Second, if the player's opinion of virtual reality being used in an educational setting changed post play. These anonymous surveys were performed immediately before and after gameplay. When organizing the data, four hypotheses were formulated:

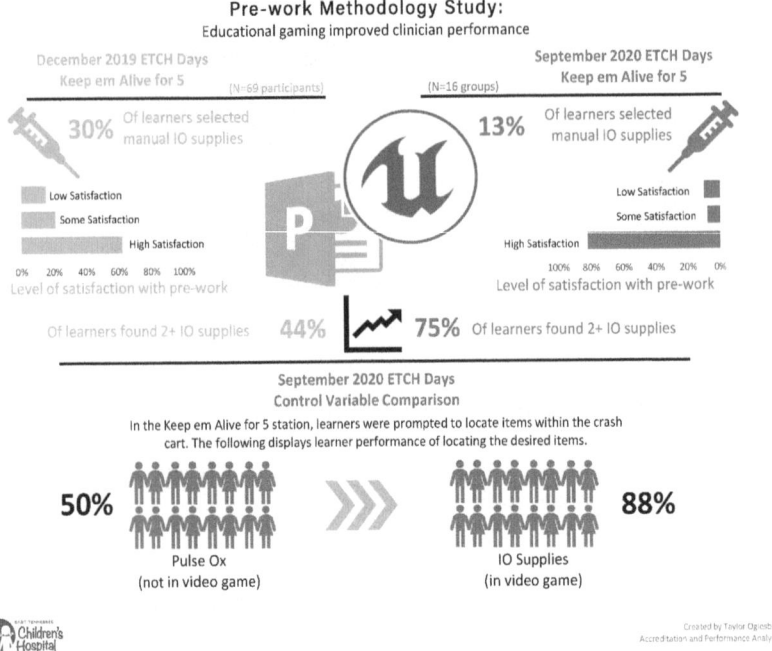

**Fig. 7.** The infographic highlights the increase in success for testers after playing computer based Crash Cart game.

Ho1: There is no improvement between Pre and Post Categories in Confrontational Capabilities.

Ha1: There is statistically significant growth in Confrontational Capabilities after Completion of Training.

Ho2: There is no improvement between Pre and Post Categories in Belief of VR Effective Tool.

Ha2: There is statistically significant growth in Belief of VR as an Effective Tool after Completion of Training (Fig. 8).

We were able to reject the null hypothesis for both areas in question, Confrontational Capabilities and Belief in VR as an Effective Tool for Training. There is evidence of statistically significant growth in both:

|  | P-Value |
| --- | --- |
| T Test Confrontational | 2.38773E-08 |
| T Test VR Effectiveness | 0.005147317 |

The analysis shed light on participants' evolving attitudes towards virtual reality as an educational tool. While some participants initially expressed skepticism or uncertainty

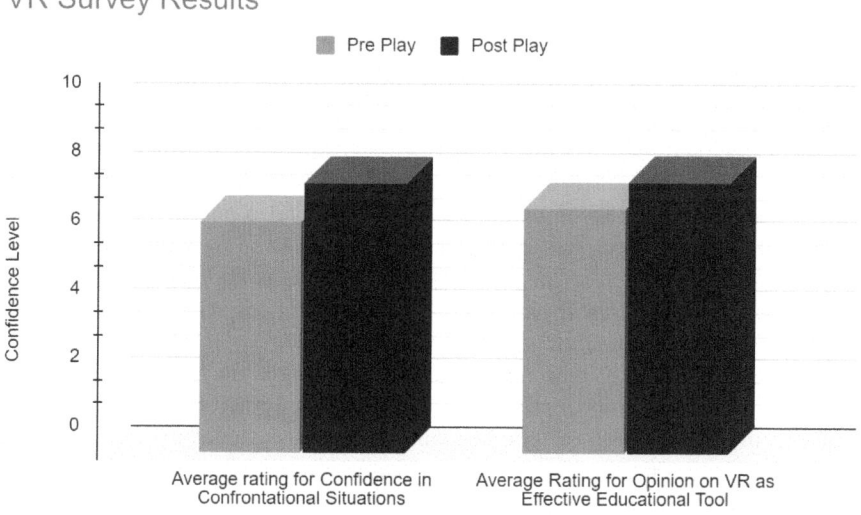

**Fig. 8.** Chart illustrating positive trends for survey results, n = 149.

about the effectiveness of VR for training purposes, a significant proportion reported a shift in their opinions following their VR experience. Many participants acknowledged the value of virtual reality in simulating real-world scenarios and providing hands-on, experiential learning opportunities that traditional training methods have potential to lack. With this training, specifically, each learner gets the opportunity to have these difficult conversations and interactions as if they were there; the game effectively taking the place of multiple additional instructors or facilitators. Often data-driven decision making is aligned with primary and secondary education. However, data-driven decision making has become an essential component of educational practice across all levels, including adult learning [2]. It necessitates that institutions with rigorous continued education practices stay in line with feedback from their learning population.

The affirmation of these positive trends not only validated the effectiveness of our collaboration but also served to bolster the confidence of participating students. It underscores the transformative potential of VR technology in enhancing training outcomes and reshaping perceptions of educational methodologies With tangible evidence of success, students and administration alike, were further motivated to continue the collaborative efforts. By leveraging immersive VR experiences, healthcare professionals can not only build essential skills and competencies but also embrace innovative approaches to learning that encourage engagement, confidence, and continuous professional development.

# 7 Challenges and Mitigating Responses

## 7.1 Unique Dynamics of Healthcare

In healthcare, bridging the gap between content authors and developers remains a significant hurdle, particularly due to the specialized nature of medical knowledge. Unlike more generalized fields, healthcare necessitates a deep understanding of intricate medical processes, terminology, and regulatory frameworks; all of which can be organization-specific. This demands meticulous attention to detail and a nuanced approach when translating medical concepts into applicable games. Allotting for appropriate amounts of time when discussing complex (medical) processes is paramount, as well as making sure there are multiple examples, displays, and references available for the student developers. It is vital in ensuring accuracy as well as efficiency in the final deliverable.

Another consideration is that many things in healthcare, much like technology, can be iterative. Policies and procedures are updated as new discoveries and patient safety statistics are made. This component is key when designing a game interface. One should be wary of including policy content or ever-evolving medical equipment unless they have a solid change-management plan with a team to support it when the inevitable need for edits arise.

## 7.2 The Student-Led Difference

In addition to navigating the intricacies of healthcare projects, developing a deliverable with a student-led team diverges notably from a professional operation in many ways. In an academic environment, students are given work, challenges, or tasks intentionally made for specific pedagogical motivations, or they are made to deal with scenarios reflective of real-world work and public life. In both instances, the utilization of tools aims to prompt learners to effectively respond to these challenges [9]. For many of the students, this is the first "external" client they have worked with, meaning, they are working on a project that goes beyond a grade in a class. Learning proper communication and project tracking becomes critical in their production toolkit. The students are faced with self-auditing the time it will take to complete each of their tasks and assessing if it is appropriate within the provided time frame. Essentially, the dynamic of a student-led team often entails a blend of enthusiasm and inexperience, fostering an environment primed for experimentation and innovation, but potentially lacking in practical know-how.

While professors and experts within the university are relied upon for verifying deliverables, this collaboration is designed to be duplicitous in its value so that students also learn while creating something for medical professionals. Thus, a lack of refinement should be expected during the semester and agile methods heavily relied upon. We also recognize that with a student-led team, time constraints may vary as well, with students often balancing coursework and extracurricular commitments alongside project work, contrasting with the professional's dedicated focus on task completion within defined timelines. These productions operate within ETSU's fall and spring semester which is roughly 15–16 weeks for each. Outside of the semester, some students will complete pre-production tasks such as storyboarding but as they are not enrolled in a class, there is no way to enforce the completion of the tasks.

One similarity between student-led teams and the professional world, however, is the need to choose your project leads, in our case graduate assistants, well. Interviews for deducing their experience, project management skills or potential thereof, and projected integration into the current team are key for congruency and success when you have projects that start and stop over multiple semesters.

## 7.3 Non-Gaming Stakeholders

A challenge faced on the opposite end of the project, with the end users, continues to be developing for different demographics in gameplay. The nurses and medical professionals span a broad range in age and level of familiarity with playing video games. Some users have never played games or used a VR headset. This creates an educational gap and learning curve for the player, possibly leading to frustration with the game itself, effectively making the game unusable. Multiple on-site testing sessions with clear feedback are essential in creating a product in line with the organization's culture and target learning audience. These on-site testing days not only aid in assessing the usability of the target learning population, but also work to address the challenges with "buy in." With the lack of familiarity and hesitation of implementing new technology that needs to be periodically updated, some think new ways of learning are more hassle and too much of an expenditure when compared with traditional learning ways. The opportunity for skeptics to test these games in a relaxed setting offers familiarity with the products and extra tutorial if needed.

Lastly, technical and logistical hurdles remain and will vary by institution. IT security settings and allowances for updates on web-based games, new VR headsets being approved in the budget on either side, and staffing infrastructure to grow an innovative program such as this will be a constant balance to navigate, requiring concise communication and transparency between the organizations for future plans.

## 8    Conclusion

Through trial and error of more than 3 serious games designed for healthcare, we have been able to piece together best practices for fostering a united team, managing conflicts, and maximizing creativity within interdisciplinary teams. Our examination of the collaborative game design process between the East Tennessee Children's Hospital and East Tennessee State University teams has shed light on the intricate dynamics, methodologies, and challenges inherent in interdisciplinary collaboration within the area of healthcare education. Through an analysis of recent projects, we have highlighted the pivotal role of effective communication, proficient project management, and proactive stakeholder engagement in driving successful outcomes. The positive trends observed not only validate the efficacy of our collaboration but also serve as a testament to the transformative impact of leveraging gamified learning tools in healthcare training. Despite the challenges encountered, including bridging the gap between content authors and developers, navigating the dynamics of student-led teams, and addressing the diverse demographics of end-users, our study underscores the resilience and innovation fostered through interdisciplinary collaboration. Along the same vein, by prioritizing collaboration, innovation, and continuous improvement, we can further advance the field of healthcare education and empower healthcare professionals with the knowledge and skills needed to deliver high-quality care in an ever-evolving healthcare landscape.

In terms of best practices for a student-led collaboration, it must be noted that engaging in collaborative projects with institutions like East Tennessee Children's Hospital provides invaluable opportunities for digital media students to apply their skills and knowledge in real-world contexts. Through these projects, students gain hands-on experience in developing serious games for healthcare education, allowing them to hone their technical abilities while making meaningful contributions to the healthcare industry. Open and concise communication are paramount, along with the ability to manage expectations through an agile workflow due to the inherent volatility of student schedules and work performance. In turn, however, giving students the opportunity, they see the direct application of their work in addressing critical issues within the pediatric healthcare sector. This sense of purpose can greatly enhance students' motivation and enthusiasm for their studies, driving them to produce high-quality work and strive for excellence in their endeavors. Ideally we are cultivating adaptability that equips students with the resilience and flexibility needed to navigate evolving project requirements and industry trends. In the fast-paced world of digital media and/or healthcare, the ability to adapt to changing circumstances and embrace new technologies is essential for staying competitive and relevant.

Moving forward, continued investment in communication, adaptability, and strategic planning will be critical in overcoming technical and logistical hurdles and ensuring the sustained success of similar collaborative initiatives in healthcare education, as well as the growth of digital media students, innovative solutions, and community partnerships.

# References

1. https://www.crisisprevention.com/blog/health-care/what-is-cpi-training-for-nurses/
2. https://www.etsu.edu/community-engagement/go_beyond_the_classroom-qep.php
3. Antonaci, A., Dagnino, F.M., Ott, M., Bellotti, F., Berta, R., De Gloria, A., et al.: A gamified collaborative course in entrepreneurship: focus on objectives and tools. Comput. Human Behav. **51**, 1276–1283 (2015). https://doi.org/10.1016/j.chb.2014.11.082
4. Hall, S., Villareal, D.: The hybrid advantage: graduate student perspectives of hybrid education courses. Int. J. Teach. Learn. High. Educ. V27 N1, **27**(1), 69–80 (2015). http://files.eric.ed.gov/fulltext/EJ1069791.pdf
5. Mandinach, E.B.: A perfect time for data use: using data-driven decision making to inform practice. Educ. Psychol. **47**(2), 71–85 (2012). https://doi.org/10.1080/00461520.2012.667064
6. Papert, S., Idit H.: Situating constructionism. Constructionism **36**(2), 1–11 (1991)
7. Project Management Institute: A Guide to the Project Management Body of Knowledge (PMBOK® guide), 6th edn (2017)
8. Sánchez Prieto, G.A., Martín Rodrigo, M.J., Rua, V.A.: Competitive debate as innovation in gamification and training for adult learners: a conceptual analysis. Front. Psychol. **15**(12), 666871 (2021). https://doi.org/10.3389/fpsyg.2021.666871.PMID:34975605;PMCID:PMC8715097

9. Wu, B., Wang, A.I.: A guideline for game development-based learning: a literature review. Int. J. Comput. Games Technol. **2012**, Article ID 103710, 20 (2012). https://doi.org/10.1155/2012/103710

10. van Gaalen, A.E., Brouwer, J., Schönrock-Adema, J., Bouwkamp-Timmer, T., Jaarsma, A.D.C., Georgiadis, J.R.: Gamification of health professions education: a systematic review. Adv. Health Sci. Educ. Theory Pract. **26**(2), 683–711 (2021). https://doi.org/10.1007/s10459-020-10000-3. (Epub 2020 Oct 31. PMID: 33128662; PMCID: PMC8041684)

# Applications

# Transforming Museum Experiences with Virtual Reality

Yuning Gao[1]([⊠]) [iD] and Daniel Foulen[2] [iD]

[1] New York University, New York, NY 11201, USA
yg3049@nyu.edu
[2] Hunter College, City University of New York, New York, NY 10065, USA
Daniel.Foulen47@myhunter.cuny.edu

**Abstract.** This study explores the paradigm-shifting impact of Virtual Reality (VR) on museum experience design, using the banjo's rich history as a case study to explore these benefits, especially in regards to understanding and empathizing with African-American culture throughout time. This VR museum's design model not only enhances visitor engagement through interactive 3D models, videos, and virtual explorations, but also transcends the limitations of physical space, making the museum experience accessible to a global audience, so long as they have access to a VR headset. Our findings indicate that the educational quality of the VR museum matches-and in some aspects surpasses-that of traditional museums by providing immersive, interactive learning environments where visitors can deeply engage with the cultural and historical narratives of the banjo. Additionally, VR facilitates the easy customization and updating of exhibits, allowing for content that remains current and relevant. Most importantly, the VR setting offers a sensitive platform for presenting emotionally charged content, such as the banjo's connections to slavery and African American history, fostering a deeper cultural connection and understanding. This study demonstrates that VR technology can significantly transform museum experiences, making them more inclusive, educational, and emotionally engaging, thus redefining the standard museum design paradigm. While VR headsets are not yet widely accessible due to socioeconomic factors, addressing this challenge is beyond the scope of this paper.

**Keywords:** Virtual Reality · Museum Education · Social Awareness · Culture Engagement · Game for Learning

## 1 Introduction

### 1.1 Technology Background

As digital technologies transform our interactions with cultural heritage, Virtual Reality (VR) stands out for its potential to revolutionize traditional museum experiences. According to V-Must, VR museums should deliver "personalized, immersive, interactive experiences [2]," making historical and cultural artifacts accessible from anywhere in the world. This paper presents the VR banjo museum, a pioneering project designed to not only educate but deeply engage users with the banjo's storied past-a quintessentially American instrument with profound ties to African American history. By leveraging VR, this museum transcends geographical limitations, inviting global audiences to explore the banjo's evolution and cultural significance through interactive 3D models, videos, and virtual explorations. This approach not only broadens access [3] but also enhances the educational impact by providing an immersive learning environment where history is both seen and experienced [4].

The VR banjo museum we developed serves as a virtual experience to showcase the quintessential American instrument: the banjo. The genesis of this immersive VR experience took root when Kristina Gaddy [1] briefly told the banjo's history during a small concert at The Metropolitan Museum of Art (The MET)'s Musical Instruments Galleries. As an instrument born from the hands of enslaved individuals in the New World, Gaddy [1] asserted that the history of the banjo is a profound reflection of African American history, as detailed in her book "Well of Souls." In the foreword of this book, the iconic musician Rhiannon Giddens mentioned that she possessed no prior knowledge of banjo history when she started to learn to play it. This sentiment resonates deeply with numerous musicians. Driven by our deep respect and curiosity for the banjo and its historical significance, we took the approach to create an educational experience, aiming to inspire a broader audience to enjoy the rich history.

## 1.2  Potential Challenges

Creating a virtual reality museum presents several challenges, including handling multimedia in virtual environments, adapting to VR headsets, learning to use controllers, and navigating the virtual space. Managing intense emotional content is also crucial. Ensuring user comfort with the technology and immersive experience is essential.

As VR has been shown to enhance engagement and learning outcomes in educational settings [5,6]. We aim to inspire the curiosity in visitors about VR technology, banjos, and VR museums. Research by Doz and colleagues [7] shows that VR technology can enhance curiosity and learning. User tests and interviews indicate strong interest in these topics. We hope to attract further interest in banjo's origins and its historical significance, particularly in its connection to American slavery and the Black community. This topic may appeal to those interested in music history, cultural studies, and social justice issues.

Exploring the resilience and creativity of the Black musicians who developed the banjo can inspire and educate visitors with the stories of cultural heritage and artistic expression overcoming oppression. Exhibitions outside the core collection offer non-guided experiences and emotional respite to avoid emotionally overwhelming the audience with too much all at once, featuring recent media content and fun facts to entertain and educate visitors [8].

Engaging with the banjo's history can empower the Black community by highlighting their ancestors' contributions to American music and the importance of preserving cultural heritage. This empowerment extends to other racial groups with similar histories, encouraging engagement and learning from the experience [9,10].

### 1.3  Ideate Concept

*Immersive Environment:* Based on Parong and Mayer's [13] research, learning performance improves in multimedia learning environments. This theory encouraged the utilization of VR technology to create a three-dimensional, immersive environment that simulates the space and medium of a real museum, complete with signs, multimedia exhibition, and interactive features. We took advantage of the virtual reality space and curated image, text, 3D model, audio and motion elements in the virtual reality museum(see Fig. 1), to create an immersive learning environment in the virtual space. We had to modify the elements multiple times for smooth navigation and avoid cognitive overload(see Fig. 2).

**Fig. 1.** Elements label in VR museum floor plan.

*Accessibility:* Providing access to the virtual museum across different VR platforms and devices, ensuring compatibility with various hardware setups to reach a wide audience. The Accessibility Virtual Reality YouTube channel helped a lot with the practical design process and software attachments. Benefited from using an open sourced platform Spatial, We can slowly proceed to add accessibility attachments in our VR museum.

*Social Significance:* Use multimedia content to demonstrate the various usage of banjos in the immersive environment. Utilize interactive features to enhance the engagement. From 3D model websites and official museum websites, we gathered banjo models from different years in history, and curated them around the virtual space based on the relative location and time. The combination of scanning and using existing 3D models is to ensure the accuracy, at the same time reducing cost and time for developing the VR museum.

*Emotional Value:* Offering educational resources, guided explorations, and object-based learning to enhance visitors' understanding of the museum's content and facilitate meaningful learning experiences. The figures following (see

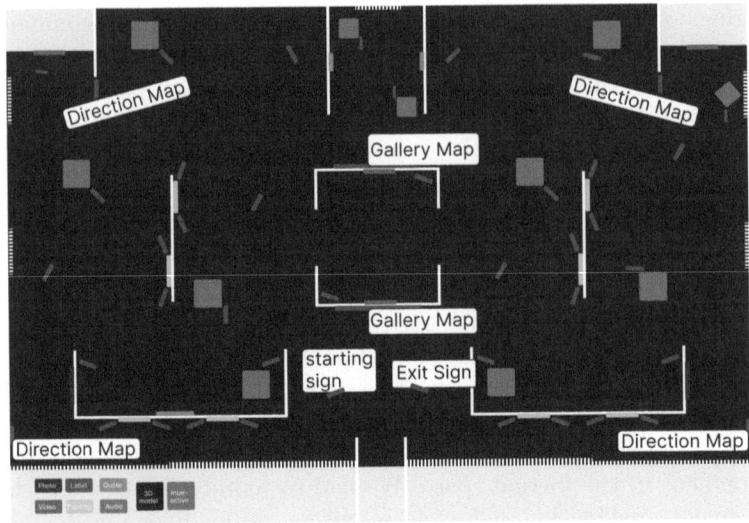

**Fig. 2.** VR museum floor plan with elements distribution.

Fig. 3) showing the guided experience, the time region, and the locations we planned for visitors to explore.

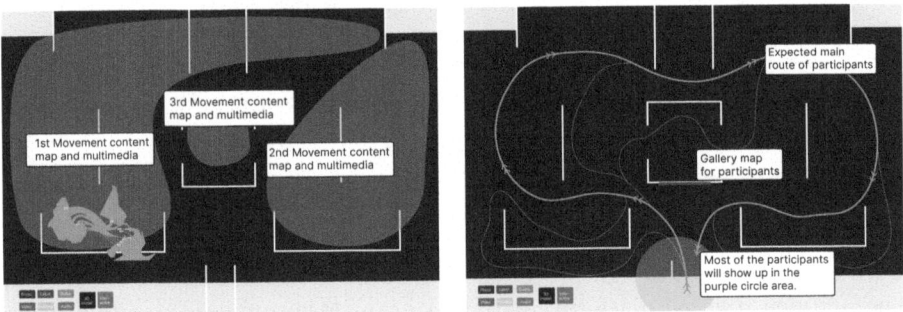

**Fig. 3.** VR museum floor map with content distribution and movement guidance.

## 2    Literature Review

Museums have long been informal learning institutions, showcasing artifacts to preserve culture and contribute to historical knowledge [17]. Traditionally, museums use spacious buildings to house exhibits, accompanied by text-based notes. To enhance visitor engagement, museums have started incorporating audio and video elements and adopting digitization to offer virtual content accessible through websites.

The advancement of virtual reality (VR) technology has transformed museums, enhancing both experiences and digital engagement. VR headsets immerse users in multimedia environments, offering a more engaging way to convey messages [18]. The COVID-19 pandemic accelerated the adoption of VR, allowing museums to provide remote, interactive educational experiences that complement traditional offerings. This research examines case studies and research papers on three VR museum experiences, including our personal experiences, to uncover the benefits, limitations, and objectives of VR in museums.

On the Morning You Wake (to the End of the World): This VR documentary, about the threat of nuclear weapons, was emotionally impactful. It used immersive storytelling and expert consultations to convey its message. Jan et al. [16] found that VR experiences offered higher enjoyment and learning outcomes compared to 2-D tablet experiences, suggesting that VR's immersion and interactivity enhance user engagement and learning.

Vintage Telecommunication Exhibition in 1960s Malaysia: Cheong et al. [17] explored the acceptance and usability of VR museums among young adults in Malaysia. Using high-resolution interfaces and interactive elements, the VR museum allowed users to navigate and interact with exhibits. The study found high usability and positive learning outcomes, though it acknowledged the need for a more diverse participant group.

E-Trouria App Based on Etruscan Museum in Rome: Poce et al. [14] developed a VR app using digital storytelling and reflective questioning to create personalized experiences. The VR museum focused on the female figure during the Etruscan age. Participants reported emotional engagement and positive experiences, though the soundtrack needed improvement.

These studies demonstrate VR's transformative potential in museums, enhancing engagement and learning. However, even with convincing potential of VR in education [19], these papers also highlight a gap in addressing accessibility for people with special needs. Future research should focus on inclusivity to fully leverage VRs benefits for enriching museum experiences.

## 3   Design Solution

Keeping in line with the paradigms brought in by new media, we hypothesize that incorporating multimedia elements such as sound, images, and videos can significantly enhance the public's understanding of musical instruments. With these concepts in mind, we started the task of assembling 3D models of various instruments (see Fig. 4). We positioned descriptive screenshots adjacent to the models and embedded videos behind them, effectively crafting information capsules for each instrument. This layout not only ensures effective information delivery, but also reduces the cognitive burden for visitors. As our project progressed, we saw the potential to arrange the 3D models based on their geographical origins across the globe, tracing their developmental journey. Leveraging the strengths of VR technology, we seamlessly integrated maps onto the virtual floor, marking the chronological placement of the 3D models. This setup empowers visitors to follow the trajectory, comprehending the instruments' evolution and transitions. By interweaving paintings containing musical instrument elements and juxtaposing videos and text, we created a gallery of musical instruments with specially curated related information, designed to provide participants the option to engage with the experience either through VR goggles or a web interface.

**Fig. 4.** VR museum multimedia display.

Upon clicking the shareable link, users undergo an initial process to select avatars, complete platform-provided training, and subsequently embark on their exploration of the VR museum. The notes are closely displayed next to the 3D models, alongside with images on virtual walls that enrich understanding. Through videos and text-based content, users gain profound insights into banjo history, sound, and playing techniques. The textual descriptions further illuminate the instrument's historical narrative.

The inclusion of paintings (see Fig. 5) featuring banjo elements stands as a highlight for much of the audience. This fixture offers users the opportunity to interact with historical evidence, immersing themselves in authentic settings that provide context and depicts the banjo's origins and evolution over time, with the diverse range of banjo players and distinct techniques among each becoming apparent. While some methods might have faded from contemporary musical practice, these paintings serve as enduring records of historical moments, reforming the broken links between our past and our present. This comprehensive approach accommodates diverse learning preferences and engagement modes, whether users opt for immersive VR goggles or a web-based experience. At its core, our VR banjo museum serves as a faithful digital recreation of the instrument's journey throughout history, from conception to modern usage, all presented on a culturally-sensitive and appreciative platform.

**Fig. 5.** Paintings featuring banjo elements.

### 3.1 Learner Characteristics

To gain deeper insight into our potential users, we adopted Falk's [15] classification of museum visitor types from his book "The Museum Experience Revisited". The Contextual Model of Learning (see Fig. 6) combines three parts of the museum learning experience into one diagram, highlighting their interaction and connection. To cater to visitors with different purposes, we utilized activity theory as a framework and created three personas, each focusing on different aspects of the learning model [11]. We categorized the personas into three groups: Experience Explorer, Musician (topic professional), and Activity Facilitator. By developing these personas, we can tailor the virtual reality museum experience to meet the diverse needs and preferences of different visitor types. This approach ensures that the museum educates, engages, and inspires a broad audience, making the history and cultural significance of the banjo, accessible and enjoyable for all. To create realistic personas, we conducted in-person interviews, sent out surveys, and collected notes from informal conversations. This information helped generate three distinct personas, each with their own mission and purpose for visiting a museum (Fig. 7).

For Musicians, we aim to attract them with a banjo-focused experience and music. Inspired by an Indian musician's story, we interviewed 5 to 6 musicians after their performances. we asked about their life stories with their instruments, what they seek in a museum visit, and what essential details should be included in a virtual reality environment. The musicians expressed interest and passion for the virtual reality museum and shared preferences for musical instrument-related museum experiences.

The museum lover persona combines insights from museum professionals and enthusiasts we encountered in person and through webinars. During the Museum Education course, we consulted with museum educators interested in our VR

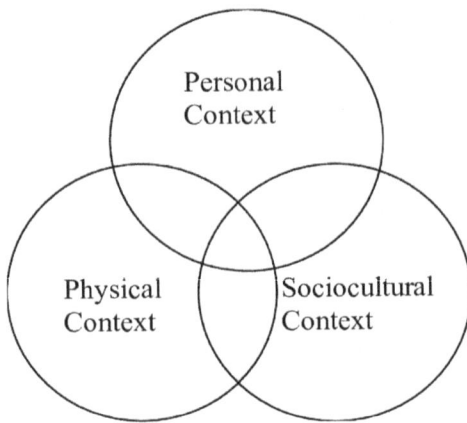

**Fig. 6.** The contextual model of learning.

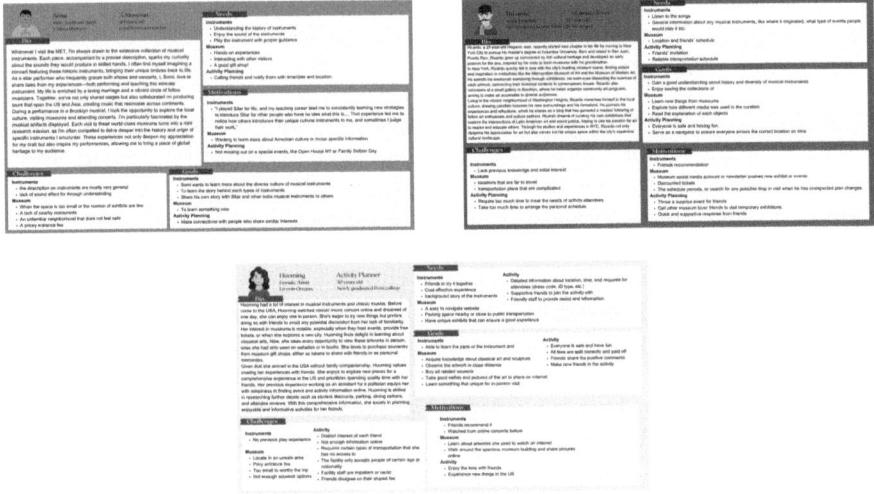

**Fig. 7.** Three personas for subject matter expert (upper left), museum enthusiastic (upper right), and activity facilitator (bottom middle).

project. Their ideal museum experiences and expectations were categorized and analyzed to find common themes.

Event Facilitators focus on socio-cultural expectations. Falk [15] noted that individuals' cultural backgrounds significantly influence their museum experience. we gathered insights from close friends who are passionate about seeking new events and planning trips. While most of our friends were female international students or employees, their feedback helped shape the persona. To ensure a more diverse perspective, we plan to extend interviews to community or school activity organizers.

By developing these personas, we aim to create a virtual reality museum experience that is engaging, educational, and tailored to the diverse needs of its visitors.

## 4  User Testing

### 4.1  Testing Research Plan

To better understand and serve the participants, we conducted user testing to evaluate the acceptance of the VR technology and the effectiveness of the VR museum in helping participants gain knowledge of banjo history. we utilized the thinking-aloud protocol and user interviews to gather feedback from New York University students and community members.

*Tasks:*

1. Create your own avatar in Spatial [20].
2. Find the content for New York, 1736.
3. Tell me what you learned from the current virtual reality experience.

*User Feedback:* Participants found the avatar creation process engaging and navigated the virtual space with ease. They expressed interest and empathy towards the banjos history, with some suggesting the addition of background music and vocal explanations to enhance the experience.

### 4.2  Design Iteration

With the valuable feedback from participants and subject matter experts, we improved the project for better user experience. By display interactive 3D models in the virtual space, we expect the participants can better focus on the historical content while interact with the models. We also modified the design style to ensure clear signage for a smooth experience flow, alongside with a self-paced vocal guide.

## 5  Conclusion

The VR banjo museum project successfully demonstrates the potential of virtual reality to revolutionize the museum experience by providing an immersive, engaging, and educational platform. Through the integration of 3D models, paintings, videos, and enriched informational content, the VR museum offers a comprehensive exploration of the banjo's historical and cultural significance. The project addresses several challenges present in traditional museum settings, such as the separation between exhibits and descriptions and the cognitive load on visitors. By leveraging the capabilities of VR technology, the museum creates an environment that allows for open exploration and deeper understanding of the banjo's evolution and impact.

The development process highlighted the importance of user-centered design, drawing on the needs and preferences of different visitor personas to create a meaningful and accessible experience. The inclusion of musician interviews, detailed historical narratives, and interactive elements ensures that visitors can connect with the content on multiple levels. Additionally, the project underscores the importance of continuous updates and the application of educational theories to enhance visitor engagement and learning.

Overall, the VR banjo museum exemplifies how virtual reality can be harnessed to preserve and share cultural heritage in innovative ways. It offers a promising model for future VR museum projects, demonstrating the potential to provide enriching, informative, and emotionally resonant experiences for diverse audiences. As technology continues to evolve, further research and development will undoubtedly expand the possibilities for VR in the museum sector, paving the way for even more transformative educational experiences.

# References

1. Gaddy, K.: Well of Souls. Uncovering the Benjo's Hidden History. W.W, Norton and Company (2022)
2. Pujol, L., Lorente, A.: The Virtual Museum: A Quest for the Standard Definition. Proceedings of the 40th Annual Conference of Computer Applications and Quantitative Methods in Archaeology (CAA), pp. 40–48 (2013)
3. Tsita, C., Satratzemi, M., Pedefoudas, A., Georgiadis, C., Zampeti, M., Papavergou, E., Tsiara, S., Sismanidou, E., Kyriakidis, P., Kehagias, D., Tzovaras, D.: A virtual reality museum to reinforce the interpretation of contemporary art and increase the educational value of user experience. Heritage **6**(5), 4134–4172 (2023). https://doi.org/10.3390/heritage6050218
4. Han, D.I.D., Weber, J., Bastiaansen, M., Mitas, O., Lub, X.: Virtual and Augmented Reality Technologies to Enhance the Visitor Experience in Cultural Tourism. Augmented Reality and Virtual Reality. Progress in IS. Springer, Cham (2019). https://doi.org/10.1007/978-3-030-06246-0_9
5. Elmqaddem, N.: Augmented reality and virtual reality in education. Myth or reality?. Ecole des Sciences de l'information (ESI), **14**(3), 234–242 (2019). https://doi.org/10.3991/ijet.v14i03.9289
6. McGovern, E., Moreira, G., Luna-Nevarez, C.: An application of virtual reality in education: Can this technology enhance the quality of students' learning experience?. J. Edu. Bus. **95**(7), 490–496 (2019). https://doi.org/10.1080/08832323.2019.1703096
7. Doz, D., Krahncan, M., Jenko, M., Vukovic, M.: Factors influencing educators' curiosity to learn about VR technologies in education. Association of Education Communications and Technology—TechTrends, **68**, 547–558 (2024). https://doi.org/10.1007/s11528-024-00961-2
8. Chang, C.: Being inspired by media content: psychological processes leading to inspiration. Media Psychol. **26**(1), 72–87 (2023). https://doi.org/10.1080/15213269.2022.2097927
9. Bheekie, A., van Huyssteen, M.: Be mindful of your discomfort: an approach to contextualized learning. Int. J. Res. Serv.-Learn. Commun. Engagement **3**(1) (2015)

10. Lave, J., Wenger, E.: Situated Learning: Legitimate Peripheral Participation. Cambridge University Press, New York, NY (1991)
11. Schmidt, M., Tawfik, A.A.: Activity theory as a lens for developing and applying personas and scenarios in learning experience design. J. Appl. Instr. Des. **11**(1) (2022). https://doi.org/10.59668/354.5904
12. Norman, D.: The Design of Everyday Things. Basic Books (2013)
13. Parong, J., Mayer, R.E.: Learning science in immersive virtual reality. J. Educ. Psychol. **110**(6), 785–797 (2018). https://doi.org/10.1037/edu0000241
14. Poce, A., Caccamo, A., Amenduni, F., Re, M., DeMedio, C., Valente, M.: A virtual reality Etruscan museum exhibition—preliminary results of the participants' experience. In: European Distance and E-Learning Network (EDEN) Conference Proceedings, no. 1, pp. 40–49 (2020). https://doi.org/10.38069/edenconf-2020-rw-0005
15. Falk, J., Dierking, L.: The Museum Experience Revisited. Routledge (2013). https://doi.org/10.4324/9781315417851
16. Plass, J., Homer, B., Ternasky-Holland, M., Budd, E.: Deepening Engagement and Learning Impact through Virtual Reality Activations. Case Study Project: On the Morning You Wake (to the End of the World). Games for Change (2023)
17. Cheong, S., Lim, Eunice, M. Sang Y., Joanne, T., Y. H., Permadi, D., Mahadzir, M., Jabbar, E.: Designing the future of museum exhibition: a user acceptance study of immersive VR museum. In: Advances in Social Science, Education and Humanities Research, pp. 102–112 (2023). https://doi.org/10.2991/978-2-38476-138-8_10
18. Lepouras, G., Katifori, A., Vassilakis, C., Charitos, D.: Real exhibitions in a virtual museum. Virtual Real. **7**(2), 120–128 (2004). https://doi.org/10.1007/s10055-004-0121-5
19. Pirker, J., Dengel, A.: The potential of 360° virtual reality videos and real VR for education—a literature review. IEEE Comput. Graph. Appl. **41**(4), 76–89 (2021). https://doi.org/10.1109/mcg.2021.3067999
20. Spatial Homepage: https://www.spatial.io/. Last accessed 2024/05/10

# Bridging Generations: The Impact of Digital Fluency on User Performance in a VR Learning Application

Erik Sindonen[✉], Markku Luotonen, and Harri Hahkala

Metropolia University of Applied Sciences, Myllypurontie 1, 00920 Helsinki, Finland
erik.sindonen@metropolia.fi

**Abstract.** This preliminary study explores performance differences between users of various ages within a VR environment during the user testing phase of a VR training application. The app developers observed that individuals under 18 years of age were significantly more comfortable and efficient with the VR environment, completing tasks more quickly than older users. This observation supports the widely discussed skills gap between "digital natives" and older generations.

**Keywords:** Virtual Reality · Digital Fluency · Generational Differences · Educational Technology · VR Simulation · AI Assistants · HVAC Training

## 1 Introduction

This paper examines the impact of generational differences in digital fluency on the effectiveness of Virtual Reality (VR) simulations in educational contexts. The term "digital natives" was first introduced by Prensky [1] and has evolved to describe generations who have grown up with digital technology. This study examines the latest cohort of these digital natives, who differ significantly in their technological fluency from those who were young during the internet's early proliferation [1]. Originating from a series of user tests of a VR application developed for HVAC systems maintenance training, this study delves deeper into the nuances of how different age groups interact with and benefit from VR technology [2].

Initial observations highlighted a significant disparity in how comfortably and efficiently users from different age groups could navigate and complete tasks within the VR environment. Notably, individuals under 18 years old demonstrated a remarkable ease and efficiency compared to their older counterparts, suggesting a generational gap in digital fluency that could be influenced by early exposure to technology such as the widespread availability of affordable tablets in the early 2010s.

These preliminary findings suggest that VR educational tools might need to be adapted to better meet the diverse needs of users across different age groups. This paper proposes that understanding these differences is crucial for developing more effective educational technologies and can inform the design of future VR applications to enhance learning outcomes. Therefore, the research expands to explore the comparative efficacy

© The Author(s), under exclusive license to Springer Nature Switzerland AG 2025
J. L. Plass and X. Ochoa (Eds.): JCSG 2024, LNCS 15259, pp. 368–374, 2025.
https://doi.org/10.1007/978-3-031-74138-8_26

of VR simulations against traditional learning methods and the potential role of AI assistants in enhancing the VR learning experience [3].

We invite researchers and practitioners interested in the practical application of VR in education to explore the VR simulation [4], available for download, to gain firsthand experience of these innovations and their implications for educational practice.

## 2  Methodology

Our methodology utilized both quantitative and qualitative analyses to examine the effects of age on performance in VR simulations across three distinct age groups: under 18, 18–35, and over 35. We leveraged an integrated data logging mechanism within the simulation to capture detailed metrics such as task completion times and other performance indicators. These were analyzed to evaluate engagement and efficiency across different stages of the simulation.

### 2.1  Measurement and Assessment Tools

To qualitatively assess the cognitive functions and behavioral responses of participants during VR interactions, we conducted direct observations, noting various behavioral responses relevant to their performance in the VR environment. Researchers meticulously documented these observations, capturing patterns such as confidence, hesitation, thoroughness, or carelessness in task execution. Our behavioral assessment strategy was informed by established psychological assessment principles as described by Malcolm Gladwell in "Blink: The Power of Thinking Without Thinking" [5] which provided a robust framework for understanding and interpreting rapid, intuitive judgments and decisions. The VR simulation stages were carefully chosen to provoke varied behavioral reactions, enabling a comprehensive analysis of participant behavior. This method allows for a nuanced exploration of how different age groups interact with VR technology.

### 2.2  Participant Segmentation

Participants were divided into groups of experienced and inexperienced users within each age category, ensuring a balanced representation and controlling for previous exposure to VR technology. This segmentation was vital in isolating the effects of age from prior VR experience.

### 2.3  Data Analysis Techniques

The collected data was aggregated and displayed in tables and graphs, highlighting significant differences in performance across age groups. These visual aids provided clear insights into the generational impact on VR learning efficiency.

### 2.4  Ethical Considerations

Strict ethical standards were maintained throughout the study. Informed consent was obtained from all participants, with additional care taken to protect the privacy and confidentiality of the data, especially for minors.

### 2.5  Limitations and Future Research

Although the initial study involved a small sample size of 30 participants (10 per age group), the results are indicative and call for further investigation with a larger cohort to validate these preliminary findings. This study lays the groundwork for more comprehensive research in the future.

## 3  Part I: Generational Differences in Reaction to Digital Content

The youngest participants, under 18, navigated the VR tasks with remarkable efficiency, completing them in an average of 5 min. This performance starkly contrasts with the older groups, where completion times ranged from 15 to 17 min. These differences are not solely a matter of speed but also reflect varying levels of comfort and adaptability with VR technology as noted by the researchers.

Notably, challenges were observed among older participants with the control scheme, specifically designed for intuitive interaction. The scheme includes a first trigger for various types of grasps, a second trigger for UI interaction, and a joystick for spatial navigation. Despite its deliberate simplicity aimed at minimizing the learning curve, significant variation in interaction ease across age groups was evident. Participants in the middle age category showed efficient adaptation to this control system, effectively utilizing the designated triggers and joystick for navigation and interaction within the simulation without encountering operational difficulties.

Furthermore, a noteworthy observation among the youngest participants was their sophisticated manipulation of interactive elements within the VR environment. This group demonstrated an adeptness at physically engaging with the simulation in a manner that included literally juggling objects—tossing them into the air with one hand and catching them with the other. Such interactions were facilitated by the simulation's accurate physics settings, including gravity effects on objects, highlighting the participants' ability to leverage these dynamics creatively. This behavior not only reflects a high degree of comfort and skill in navigating the VR space but also emphasizes the simulation's capability to support complex, physics-based interactions.

## 4  Analysis and Discussion

The analysis of data collected from the VR simulations reveals distinct generational differences in engagement with VR technology, underscoring the necessity for educational VR content to be adaptable across a broad spectrum of digital proficiency. These findings challenge the conventional novice-to-advanced progression often assumed in VR design, proposing instead a spectrum of interaction complexity that can more effectively engage diverse user groups.

However, this study's recruitment strategy, while ensuring a wide age range, might introduce a sampling bias. Participants were drawn from distinct environments—vocational schools, universities, and public exhibitions—which could influence the digital experiences and interaction patterns observed. This recruitment diversity is acknowledged as a potential limitation that could affect the generalizability of the findings. It is crucial for future research to consider a more standardized participant source to mitigate such biases and validate the observed patterns across more uniform cohorts.

Despite these limitations, the initial findings provide a valuable foundation for further investigation. They indicate significant potential for VR as a transformative educational tool, provided that content development can be aligned with the varied capabilities and expectations of different age groups. This study lays the groundwork for future research to explore these aspects more comprehensively, aiming to enhance the effectiveness of VR learning environments and maximize their educational impact.

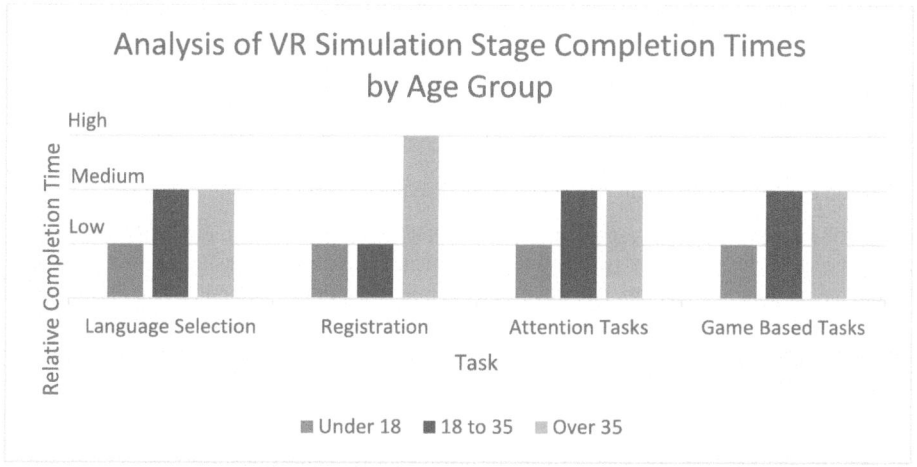

**Fig. 1.** Comparative analysis of key stage completion times in VR simulation by age group. This table shows the relative time it takes for participants from different age categories to complete specific gaming stages, classified as "high", "medium", and "low". Lower times indicate higher performance.

### 4.1 Analysis of the "Language Selection" in the Context of Spatial Navigation

**Relative Completion Time** (Fig. 1). The "Language Selection" analysis showed that participants under 18 completed the task faster than those aged 18–35 and over 35.

**Engagement Level** (Fig. 2). In assessing adaptation in the 3D space at the "Language Selection" stage, the under-18 group exhibited a high level of engagement. The 18–35 age group's adaptation was rated as medium, whereas the over-35 group was rated as low. Despite similar task completion speeds between the 18–35 and over-35 age groups, the quality of adaptation varied: participants aged 18–35 experienced no issues with control and demonstrated confidence in using the controllers but took more time to immerse in the 3D space atmosphere. Conversely, the over-35 group faced difficulties in control and using the controllers, reflecting in a low level of adaptation.

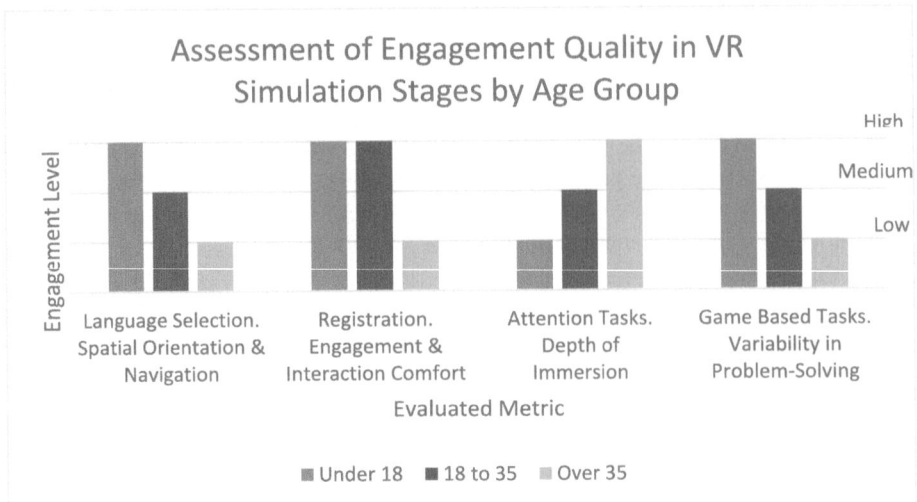

**Fig. 2.** Assessment of user engagement aspects in VR simulations by age group. This table analyzes and compares the level of participant engagement across four key aspects: Spatial orientation and navigation, engagement and interaction comfort, depth of immersion, and variability in problem-solving. Each aspect is rated on a three-level scale: "high", "medium", and "low". The ratings are based on qualitative analysis of participants' actions and behaviors, as documented by researchers during the VR simulation tasks.

### 4.2 Analysis of "Registration" in the Context of Interaction Comfort

**Relative Completion Time** (Fig. 1). At the "Registration" stage, the under-18 and 18–35 groups completed tasks quickly, while the over-35 group was slower.

**Engagement Level** (Fig. 2). Analyzing UI interaction at the "Registration" stage reveals a similar pattern: participants under 18 and those aged 18 to 35 exhibited a high level of UI interaction, while the over-35 group faced difficulties. High scores from younger groups show their ease with the VR interface; lower scores from older groups suggest difficulties in using it.

### 4.3 Analysis of "Attention Tasks" Considering Immersion Depth

**Relative Completion Time** (Fig. 1). In the "Attention Tasks" stage, under-18s showed high speeds, while the 18 to 35 and over-35 groups displayed medium speeds.

**Engagement Level** (Fig. 2). Analyzing the depth of immersion in the VR environment at this stage, significant differences between the groups were revealed: participants under 18 demonstrated a low level of immersion, the 18 to 35 age group showed a medium level, and the over-35 group exhibited a high level. These variations in immersion depth can be explained by different strategies adopted by:

*The under-18 group* tried multiple rapid attempts due to difficulties in guessing the correct answer initially.

*The 18 to 35 age group* sought to solve the tasks without resorting to guessing. However, it appeared that the presence of distracting factors in the VR environment may have contributed to errors.

*The over-35 group* approached task solutions very meticulously, examining the readings of meters and electronic logs in the simulation and providing correct answers It looks like this approach reflects a high depth of immersion and attention to detail.

### 4.4  Analysis of "Game-Based Tasks" and Problem-Solving Variability

**Relative Completion Time** (Fig. 1). At the "Game-Based Tasks" stage, participants under 18 exhibited high performance in terms of completion speed, while both the 18 to 35 and over-35 age groups showed medium results.

**Engagement Level** (Fig. 2). Analyzing the variety of approaches to problem-solving at this stage, the following observations were made:

*The under-18 group* exhibited a high level, employing flexible strategies, including testing the game's physics robustness and attempting to circumvent limitations. This indicates high adaptability and creativity in their problem-solving approaches.

*The 18 to 35 age group* displayed a medium level, with stable task completion but facing challenges at certain stages, suggesting a less flexible use of VR environment capabilities. For example, while they could navigate through tasks, they occasionally struggled to apply unconventional solutions that could solve challenges efficiently.

*The over-35 group* showed a low level of problem-solving diversity, encountering difficulties in control and interaction with the controllers, which significantly limited their ability to experiment and explore alternative strategies.

## 5  Conclusion

Our findings emphasize the need for continuous innovation in educational technology, beyond VR. As young learners adept at navigating digital environments, educational tools must evolve to match their skills and expectations. Failure to do so could decrease engagement. It's vital that educational strategies not only keep up with but also anticipate and influence future learning preferences.

The degree of digital literacy is critically important for stimulating innovation and creativity in education, essential tools for students to effectively overcome future challenges. This is also influenced by the so-called "digital landscapes" and the structure of interactions in social media, as well as the diversity in digital technologies. This perspective draws upon the works of Jennifer Sparrow, who highlights the evolving job market [6], and the research by Emily Weinstein and Carrie James, exploring the digital experiences of today's youth [7].

**Disclosure of Interests.** The authors have no competing interests to declare that are relevant to the content of this article.

# References

1. Prensky, M.: Digital natives, digital immigrants part 1. On the Horiz. **9**(5), 1–6 (2001)
2. Sindonen, E.: Development of VR Simulation for HVAC Training. https://www.theseus.fi/han
   dle/10024/818066?show=ful
3. Sindonen, E.: VR Simulation with AI Assistant—View the Video Presentation at: https://youtu.
   be/DCQ3_y3NzwI
4. Sindonen, E.: VR Simulation for HVAC Training: Demo Version [Software]. Meta Quest
   3 platform (2024). Available at: https://drive.google.com/drive/folders/154pyBOs9bUxUWg
   EvQVL-d2R-mweyiBDH
5. Gladwell, M.: Blink: The Power of Thinking Without Thinking. Little, Brown and Company,
   New York (2005)
6. Sparrow, J.: Digital Fluency: Preparing Students to Create Big, Bold Problems (Monday, March
   12, 2018 Emerging Technologies and Trends)
7. Weinstein, E., James, C.: The Complex World of Teens and Screens (Harvard ED CAST 5,
   September 2022)

# Kafka or Not? Concept for an AI-Supported Multi-touch Tabletop Game for Literature Classes

Jessica Kathmann[1]([⊠]) [iD], Peter Gerjets[1,2] [iD], and Birgit Brucker[1] [iD]

[1] Leibniz-Institut für Wissensmedien, 72076 Tübingen, Germany
j.kathmann@iwm-tuebingen.de
[2] University of Tübingen, 72074 Tübingen, Germany

**Abstract.** One key to understanding literature in literature classes and beyond is to investigate the author's writing style, which is often rather unexciting for many pupils when taught with classic teaching methods. Consequently, the educational game "Kafka or Not?", which is currently under development, is proposed, a game that enriches literary education through competitive and collaborative gameplay on a multi-touch tabletop. In this turn-based game, both players impersonate authors such as Franz Kafka and use paragraphs written by these authors as identifiers to navigate interconnected rooms, much like literary fingerprints. The game leverages the ability of AI to analyze writing styles and generate altered paragraphs that differ in stylistic characteristics. "Kafka or Not?" revolves around analyzing given paragraphs and comparing them to each other and an original prequel, "betting" on which of the paragraphs is the "real" identifier to navigate through the rooms. In each turn, the roles are swapped, i.e. one player is the impersonator in one turn and in the next turn they are the guard, challenging the other impersonator and themselves. The game's educational content, developed in collaboration with German didactics experts and the German Literature Archive, will provide the basis for a research program on how to use game-based approaches to foster motivation, curiosity and learning outcomes in literature classes.

**Keywords:** Serious Game · Multi-touch Table · GPT · Game-based Learning · Literature · Large Language Model

## 1 Introduction

### 1.1 Learning with Games

Even in an increasingly digital society, where text production and analysis are more and more outsourced to large language models such as GPT (Open AI, 2024), literary skills seem to remain an important asset. However, many students dislike reading and working with literary texts in their leisure time (Clark et al., 2023) and in the classroom (Ainley et al., 2002). Analyzing an author's writing style is an important approach (Berenike-Herrmann et al., 2015), yet it is difficult to arouse student's interest in content that is perceived as disconnected from their own experiences and interests (Schraw, 1997; Cantrell et al., 2017).

J. L. Plass and X. Ochoa (Eds.): JCSG 2024, LNCS 15259, pp. 375–383, 2025.
https://doi.org/10.1007/978-3-031-74138-8_27

Therefore, it is worth trying to make the content more appealing for the target group and to bridge the supposed gap between the literary content and the interests and consumption habits of the learners. As one of the most popular hobbies of young people is gaming (Feierabend et al., 2022; Feierabend et al., 2023; Gottfried & Sidoti, 2024), the integration of learning material into a game seems close at hand.

By now, many games deal with literary works or at least the universes in which their stories take place, e.g. Playing Kafka (Charles Games, 2024), Metamorphosis (Ovid Works, 2020), Hogwarts Legacy (Avalanche Software, 2023), or Ken Follet's The Pillars of the Earth (Daedalic Entertainment, 2017, 2018), but none deals explicitly with the writing style of an author. The authors of this paper are not aware of any such game in the field of serious games either. Thus, such games could at best be thematized as pop-cultural interpretations of a literary work and enriched pedagogically, but they don't teach anything about specific textual qualities. The proposed game "Kafka or Not?", which is being developed as a research object for a doctoral thesis, is intended to fill this content gap.

Many game features are expected to have positive effects on a wide range of outcomes, Greipl et al. (2020) count among others possible body involvement (e.g. implementation of movement elements), possible adaptivity (individualized feedback, scaffolding) and a secure setting for trial and error ("graceful failure"). While motivation (Delacruz, 2012; Przybylski et al., 2010; Ryan et al., 2006), interest (Plass et al., 2013; Plass et al., 2015), and learning outcomes (Boyle et al., 2016; Clark et al., 2016; Ninaus et al., 2017; Shin et al., 2012; Wouters et al., 2013) are frequently studied and discussed, the findings present a complex picture, with some studies finding null results (Greipl et al., 2020; Wouters et al., 2013).

One reason for this might be the often-lacking connection between learning content and game mechanics (Bogost, 2016; Thoma et al., 2024). Games constantly formulate messages through their rules, often referred to as procedural rhetoric (Bogost, 2010; Bogost, 2016; King, 2010). A concept closely related to this idea that games can teach players either explicitly or implicitly is known as intrinsic integration (Ke, 2016). It involves weaving learning content directly into game mechanics, which has been linked to positive educational outcomes across various domains (Ke, 2016; Thoma et al., 2024). Hence, "Kafka or Not" should include in its core game loop the analysis of text fragments regarding stylistic characteristics and provide useful information for text analysis as a reward, to achieve the closest possible integration of game mechanics and learning content.

Furthermore, many educational games are single-player experiences, while research suggests that playing in a group may be correlated with better outcomes (Wouters et al., 2013). Playing in a group offers several advantages, including the possibility of direct exchange about the game's tasks and learning content (Antle et al., 2011). Therefore, it is reasonable to design a game that can also be played in groups to take advantage of these positive effects.

## 1.2 Competition and Collaboration

The interplay between competition and collaboration has been an issue discussed in the context of commercial games (Koster, 2013) and has been investigated regarding its role in influencing learning outcomes, with significant heterogeneity across studies: A meta-analysis by Chen and colleagues (2020) suggested that competition fosters learning in several domain subjects, i.e. language learning, math, and science. Sailer and colleagues (2017) found that competition satisfies competence need and increases perceived task meaningfulness in participants, using leader boards among other things.

Interestingly, a study researching competition in an educational mathematics game that can be played in teams of two found an interaction effect: Data suggested that competition may detrimentally impact learners with below-average prior knowledge on domain knowledge gains, while learners with above-average prior knowledge seemed to benefit (ter Vrugte et al., 2015). The researchers note that results must be interpreted cautiously due to small sample sizes. Still, the results should be kept in mind when researching competitive elements in a collaborative educational game and vice versa.

Regarding collaboration, Wouters and colleagues (2013) found in their meta-analysis that group work, especially in dyads, enhances learning through serious games. However, due to insufficient descriptions regarding guidelines or instructions for collaboration in the studies reviewed, the authors were unable to explain the mechanisms behind the effect found. It should also be noted that there is research that contradicts these findings, such as Plass et al.'s (2013) study, which found that collaboration in a mathematics game decreased learning while competition increased learning.

This may support the argument of Greipl and colleagues (2020), "that the balance and interdependency of the competitive and collaborative elements seems the key aspect of game design" (p. 18). "Kafka or Not?" seeks to integrate both competition and collaboration, aiming to optimize educational outcomes through research.

### 1.3 Multi Touch Tabletops

One medium that is well suited for play in a group setting is the multi-touch tabletop (MTT). MTTs are touch displays of various sizes that are mounted horizontally and can be used by multiple people at the same time due to their ability to process multiple touch inputs simultaneously. The advantages of MTTs are particularly evident when the players are positioned around the table, as the necessary information can be presented selectively by rotating it appropriately. Mentally rotating the texts would be difficult and time-consuming (Müller et al., 2023) and, depending on the table and font size, not legible anyway. At the same time, there is enough space for multiple players to stand on the same side of the table, see the same information, and interact with it collaboratively (Rick et al., 2009).

Playing a game on an MTT comes with some advantages over traditional analog games, especially in schools and museums. The components of traditional tabletop games can be easily lost or damaged, while MTT games do not require such components and can also be operated by people with limited dexterity (Pereira et al., 2019), which is an advantage in terms of accessibility.

So far, there is only limited research on educational games on MTTs. The existing literature however shows an exetensive scope of subjects addressed by these games, encompassing areas such as STEM education (Heinemann et al., 2020; Hsiao et al., 2014; van Veen et al., 2009), environmental sustainability (Antle et al., 2011), and medical training (Anders et al., 2023). Target groups are also diverse and range from stroke rehabilitation patients (Pereira et al., 2019) and museum visitors (Antle et al., 2011) to children and adolescents (Van Veen et al., 2009). To the authors' knowledge, there is no MTT game that deals with the writing style of authors. Here we want to take a new approach and make use of the rapidly developing technology of large language models such as GPT (OpenAI, 2024).

### 1.4  Learning About Writing Styles Using AI Imitations

Recent advances in AI development have shown how well large language models (LLMs) are capable of analyzing and imitating different writing styles (Gunser et al., 2021; Gunser et al., 2022; Köbis & Mossink, 2021). On the one hand, this is crucial when it comes to fake news and other forms of AI-based deception that pose a potential risk to democracies (Kreps & Kriner, 2023).

On the other hand, however, these capabilities of AI could also be important for providing students with playful ways to explore the stylistic qualities of texts in educational contexts. This can not only lead to a deeper engagement with the learning content, but also equip learners with skills that are becoming increasingly important in the digital world, such as co-creating texts with AI (Luther et al., 2024). If supported by pedagogy in the classroom, playful experimentation and exploration can also encourage players to critically examine the potential and risks of LLMs.

For the use case of high school classrooms, we define writing style in terms of word choice, sentence structure, and the mood conveyed by the texts. This seems to be closest to what is taught in schools and is consistent with how GPT-4o describes writing style when it comes to the works of Franz Kafka (see below).

So far, the use of LLMs in digital games has mainly been aimed at enabling natural language interactions with NPCs, e.g. NVIDIA ACE (NVIDIA, 2024), or at creating a new dimension of text adventures (Yao et al., 2020). To the authors' knowledge, there have been no attempts to use the ability of LLMs to analyze and mimic writing styles to create learning material for digital games. The planned game "Kafka or Not?" aims to exploit this ability of LLMs and combine it with the advantages of MTTs to provide an engaging gaming experience.

## 2  Project

### 2.1  Game Description

The project "Kafka or Not?" aims to develop a multi-touch table serious game that provides collaborative and competitive elements, where learning the intended learning content is crucial to make progress in the game, thus providing an intrinsic integration (Ke, 2016) of learning material and game mechanics to foster curiosity and learning. This is done while leveraging the ability of GPT models to analyze literature and recognize patterns: The game aims to provide a better understanding of an author's writing style, suitable for literature classes or museum education.

In a multi-stage process, a customized GPT-4o (Open AI, 2024) was used to identify features of Franz Kafka's writing style, which will be evaluated by experts from the

German Literature Archive and German didactics experts regarding their accuracy and usefulness. Examples of writing style characteristics are simple and precise language, atmosphere of oppression, surrealism. At the time of writing, the final number of characteristics has not yet been determined. The learning objective is to be able to recognize and assign these stylistic features in texts.

The game will be playable by a minimum of two people and will allow for group play. Players assume the role of a famous author, currently Franz Kafka, and must navigate through a series of interconnected rooms by convincing a guard of their authenticity using paragraphs as identifiers, much like a literary fingerprint. The interconnected rooms are viewed from a top-down perspective. In this turn-based game, players start at opposite ends of the table, each aiming to reach the other side to win the game. When one player (the "impersonator") tries to enter a room, the other player becomes the guard who guards the door. On the guard's side of the screen, two independent paragraphs from Franz Kafka's works appear and the guard can choose one to present to the other player.

The "impersonator" must now prove his identity as Kafka by providing the guard with a continuation of the paragraph selected by the guard. To do this, both the guard and the player who wants to enter the room are presented with two possible continuations, one being the original and one being slightly altered by the AI in at least one of the style characteristics. For example, one rendition may not have the oppressive atmosphere element, while the original Kafka rendition does. At this point, neither player knows which is the original continuation.

This means that both players must analyze the continuations: Which one seems to fit better with the first paragraph provided by the guard? How do the two continuations differ? To help with this task, some style characteristics appear as movable cards on the screen and the players must drag them to the paragraph(s) they think they fit. There are two buttons for each style characteristic, making it possible to apply one style characteristic to both paragraphs. Players know that the AI-imitation lacks at least one of the style characteristics, so this can help them make the right choice. At the beginning of the game, only a few style features are provided, briefly described in a drop-down menu on each button, to make the task easier and to let the players learn them gradually.

When both players have matched the style characteristics to the paragraphs and decided which one might be the original, the correct solution is displayed. Both players receive rewards for correct answers (regarding style characteristics and paragraph), the rewards being new information, e.g. a more detailed description of a style characteristic or an example. This should make the learning content valuable and therefore rewarding, and encourage and motivate players for the next move - this hypothesis needs to be tested by research. The new information is then added to the corresponding drop-down menu to be accessible in later turns. In addition, if the "impersonator" makes the right choice, they are allowed to enter the room and move one step closer to the other side - and thus to victory. If not, they will have to try again next time. After that, the turn is over and the roles are swapped, so the former guard becomes the new "impersonator" trying to enter a room, and the former "impersonator" becomes the new guard.

Many variations are possible and might be worth researching, e.g. a version where the guard and the "impersonator" use one set of paragraph alternatives together, so they can see each other's decisions, maybe even play cooperatively? What would a fully cooperative variant of the game look like and how would it affect motivation and learning outcomes? Another variation would be to use the original competitive game idea and just have two groups play it instead of two people, encouraging discussion about the decisions – however, it would be difficult to ensure that the groups cannot hear each other's discussions.

## 2.2 Methods

Since we plan to have a customized GPT-4o (Open AI, 2024) generate sequels that include or omit certain writing style characteristics, it seems reasonable to have the GPT analyze Kafka's writing style and identify writing style characteristics. This will be achieved in a four-step process:

1. Letting GPT define a certain number of characteristics of Franz Kafka's writing style for a certain number of times.
2. Having GPT work out a procedure for defining the "final" characteristics based on the characteristics generated in step 1.
3. Converting the proposed procedure into a prompt for determining the final characteristics.
4. Letting GPT determine the final characteristics using the created prompt.

The final characteristics, the exact number of which has yet to be determined, will be evaluated for accuracy and usefulness by experts from the German Literature Archive and experts in German didactics.

Then, the GPT model will be asked to find paragraphs in Kafka's works where the defined writing characteristics are prominent. The corresponding preceding paragraph will then be selected by the guard as the "starting paragraph" and the paragraph selected by GPT as the original continuation, on the basis of which a second, AI-modified paragraph will later be created. GPT will be asked to rate which stylistic characteristics are present in the original continuation, and then will be prompted to modify it so that one or more of the features are missing. GPT's ratings of the features and the modified paragraphs will then be evaluated by experts from the aforementioned institutions to ensure accuracy, quality and fit with the BOLIVE model, which aims to systematize literacy skills and is currently gradually being introduced into the school system in parts of Germany (Boelmann & König, 2022). Apart from the ratings, it is planned to automate the above process as much as possible using Open AIs Assistant API to get a machine-readable file for the game software. It is planned to do research on the impact of the game on learning outcomes, motivation, and curiosity among participants.

## References

Ainley, M., Hillman, K., Hidi, S.: Gender and interest processes in response to literary texts: Situational and individual interest. Learn. Instr. **12**(4), 411–428 (2002). https://doi.org/10.1016/S0959-4752(01)00008-1

Anders, S., et al.: Adventure Legal Medicine: A free online serious game for supplementary use in undergraduate medical education. Int. J. Legal Med. **137**(2), 545–549 (2023). https://doi.org/10.1007/s00414-023-02946-x

Antle, A.N., Tanenbaum, T., Bevans, A., Seaborn, K., Wang, S.: Balancing act: enabling public engagement with sustainability issues through a multi-touch tabletop collaborative game. In: Campos, P., Graham, N., Jorge, J., Nunes, N., Palanque, P., Winckler M. (eds.), Human-Computer Interaction—INTERACT 2011. Lecture Notes in Computer Science, vol. 6947. Springer (2011). https://doi.org/10.1007/978-3-642-23771-3_16

Berenike Herrmann, J., van Dalen-Oskam, K., Schöch, C.: Revisiting style, a key concept in literary studies. J. Literary Theory **9**(1), 25–52 (2015). https://doi.org/10.1515/jlt-2015-0003

Boelmann, J.M., König, L.: Literarische Kompetenz messen, literarische Bildung fördern: das BOLIVE-Modell, vol. 5. wbv Media GmbH & Company KG (2022)

Bogost, I.: Persuasive Games: The Expressive Power of Videogames. MIT Press

Bogost, I.: Play anything: The pleasure of limits, the uses of boredom, and the secret of games. Basic Books (2016)

Boyle, E.A., et al.: An update to the systematic literature review of empirical evidence of the impacts and outcomes of computer games and serious games. Comput. Educ. **94**, 178–192 (2016). https://doi.org/10.1016/j.compedu.2015.11.003

Cantrell, S.C., Pennington, J., Rintamaa, M., Osborne, M., Parker, C., Rudd, M.: Supplemental literacy instruction in high school: what students say matters for reading engagement. Read. Writ. Q. **33**(1), 54–70 (2016). https://doi.org/10.1080/10573569.2015.1081838

Clark, C., Picton, I., Galway, M.: Children and Young People's Reading in 2023. National Literacy Trust, London (2023). https://literacytrust.org.uk/research-services/research-reports/children-and-young-peoples-reading-in-2023

Clark, D.B., Tanner-Smith, E.E., Killingsworth, S.S.: Digital games, design, and learning: a systematic review and meta-analysis. Rev. Educ. Res. **86**(1), 79–122 (2016). https://doi.org/10.3102/0034654315582065

Delacruz, G.C.: Impact of incentives on the use of feedback in educational videogames. CRESST Report 813. National Center for Research on Evaluation, Standards, and Student Testing (2012). http://files.eric.ed.gov/fulltext/ED530477.pdf

Feierabend, S., Rathgeb, T., Kheredmand, H., Glöckler, S.: JIM 2023. Jugend, Information, Medien, Basisuntersuchung zum Medienumgang 12- bis 19-Jähriger in Deutschland. Medienpädagogischer Forschungsverbund Südwest (2023). https://www.mpfs.de/fileadmin/files/Studien/JIM/2022/JIM_2023_web_final_kor.pdf

Feierabend, S., Rathgeb, T., Kheredmand, H., Glöckler, S.: KIM 2022. Jugend, Information, Medien, Basisuntersuchung zum Medienumgang 6- bis 13- Jähriger. Medienpädagogischer Forschungsverbund Südwest (2022).. https://www.mpfs.de/fileadmin/files/Studien/KIM/2022/KIM-Studie2022_website_final.pdf

Gunser, V.E., Gottschling, S., Brucker, B., Richter, S., Gerjets, P.: Can users distinguish narrative texts written by an artificial intelligence writing tool from purely human text? In Stephanidis, C., Antona, M., Ntoa, S. (eds.) HCI International 2021 - Posters. HCII 2021. Communications in Computer and Information Science: Vol. 1419, pp. 520–527. Springer. https://doi.org/10.1007/978-3-030-78635-9_67

Gunser, V.E., Gottschling, S., Brucker, B., Richter, S., Çakir, D., & Gerjets, P. The pure poet: how good is the subjective credibility and stylistic quality of literary short texts written with an artificial intelligence tool as compared to texts written by human authors? In: Culbertson, J., Perfors, A., Rabagliati, H., Ramenzoni, V. (eds.) Proceedings of the 44th Annual Meeting of the Cognitive Science Society, vol. 44, pp. 1744–1750. Cognitive Science Society (2022). https://escholarship.org/uc/item/1wx3983m

Gottfried, J., Sidoti, O.: Teens and Video Games Today. Pew Research Center (2024). https://www.pewresearch.org/wp-content/uploads/sites/20/2024/05/PI_2024.05.09_Video-Games_REPORT.pdf

Greipl, S., Moeller, K., Ninaus, M.: Potential and limits of game-based learning. Int. J. Technol. Enhanced Learn. **12**(4), 363–389 (2020). https://doi.org/10.1504/ijtel.2020.110047

Heinemann, B., Ehlenz, M., Schroeder, P.D.U.: Eye-tracking in educational multi-touch games: design-based (interaction) research and great visions. In: ACM Symposium on Eye Tracking Research and Applications, pp. 1–5. (2020). https://dl.acm.org/doi/10.1145/3379156.3391838

Hogwarts Legacy [Video game]. Avalanche Software (2023)

Hsiao, H.S., Chang, C.S., Lin, C.Y., Chang, C.C., Chen, J.C.: The influence of collaborative learning games within different devices on student's learning performance and behaviours. Austr. J. Educ. Technol. **30**(6) (2014). https://doi.org/10.14742/ajet.347

Ke, F.: Designing and integrating purposeful learning in game play: A systematic review. Educ. Technol. Res. Dev. **64**, 219–244 (2016). 10.1007

Ken Follet's The Pillars of the Earth [Video game]. Daedalic Entertainment (2017–2018)

King, M.: Procedural rhetorics-rhetoric's procedures: rhetorical peaks and what it means to win the game. Currents in Electronic Literacy (2010). Retrieved April 8, 2024, from https://currents.dwrl.utexas.edu/2010/king_procedural_rhetorics_rhetorics_procedures.html

Kiili, K., Moeller, K., Ninaus, M.: Evaluating the effectiveness of a game-based rational number training-In-game metrics as learning indicators. Comput. Educ. **120**, 13–28 (2018). https://doi.org/10.1016/j.compedu.2018.01.012

Koster, R.: Theory of Fun for Game Design. O'Reilly Media, Inc. (2013). http://ci.nii.ac.jp/ncid/BB15618405

Köbis, N., Mossink, L.D.: Artificial intelligence versus Maya Angelou: Experimental evidence that people cannot differentiate AI-generated from human-written poetry. Comput. Hum. Behav. **114**, 106553 (2021). https://doi.org/10.1016/j.chb.2020.106553

Kreps, S., Kriner, D.: How AI threatens democracy. J. Democr. **34**(4), 122–131 (2023). https://doi.org/10.1353/jod.2023.a907693

Luther, T., Kimmerle, J., Cress, U.: Co-writing with AI: How do people interact with ChatGPT in a writing scenario? In: Stephanidis, C., Antona, M., Ntoa, S., Salvendy, G. (ed.) HCI International 2024—Posters. HCII 2024. Communications in Computer and Information Science, vol. 2120, pp. 198–207. Springer (2024). https://doi.org/10.1007/978-3-031-62110-9_20

Metamorphosis [Video game]. Ovid Works (2020)

Müller, T., Hesse, F.W., Meyerhoff, H.S.: Two people, one graph: the effect of rotated viewpoints on accessibility of data visualizations. Cogn. Res.: Principles Implications **6**, 1–16 (2021). https://doi.org/10.1186/s41235-021-00297-y

Ninaus, M., Moeller, K., McMullen, J., & Kiili, K. (2017). Acceptance of game-based learning and intrinsic motivation as predictors for learning success and flow experience. Int. J. Serious Games **4**(3), 15–30. https://doi.org/10.17083/ijsg.v4i3.176

NVIDIA. NVIDIA ACE [Computer software] (2024). https://developer.nvidia.com/ace

OpenAI: ChatGPT [Large language model] (2024). https://chat.openai.com/chat

Plass, J.L., Homer, B.D., Kinzer, C.K.: Foundations of game-based learning. Educ. Psychol. **50**(4), 258–283 (2015). https://doi.org/10.1080/00461520.2015.1122533

Plass, J.L., et al.: The impact of individual, competitive, and collaborative mathematics game play on learning, performance, and motivation. J. Educ. Psychol. **105**(4), 1050–1066 (2013). https://doi.org/10.1037/a0032688

Playing Kafka [Video game]. Charles Games (2024)

Pereira, F.I., Badia, S.B., Jorge, C., da Silva Cameirão, M. (2019). Impact of game mode on engagement and social involvement in multi-user serious games with stroke patients. In: 2019 International Conference on Virtual Rehabilitation (ICVR), pp. 1–6. IEEE. https://doi.org/10.1109/ICVR46560.2019.8994505

Przybylski, A.K., Rigby, C.S., Ryan, R.M.: A motivational model of video game engagement. Rev. Gen. Psychol. **14**(2), 154–166 (2010). https://doi.org/10.1037/a0019440

Rick, J., Rogers, Y., Haig, C., Yuill, N.: Learning by doing with shareable interfaces. Child. Youth Environ. **19**(1), 320–341 (2009). https://doi.org/10.1353/cye.2009.0017

Ryan, R.M., Rigby, C.S., Przybylski, A.: The motivational pull of video games: a self-determination theory approach. Motiv. Emot. **30**, 344–360 (2006). https://doi.org/10.1007/s11031-006-9051-8

Sailer, M., Hense, J., Mayr, S.K., Mandl, H. How gamification motivates: an experimental study of the effects of specific game design elements on psychological need satisfaction. Comput. Human Behav. **69**, 371–380 (2017). https://doi.org/10.1016/j.chb.2016.12.033

Schraw, G.: Situational interest in literary text. Contemp. Educ. Psychol. **22**(4), 436–456 (1997). https://doi.org/10.1006/ceps.1997.0944

Shin, N., Sutherland, L.M., Norris, C.A., Soloway, E.: Effects of game technology on elementary student learning in mathematics. Br. J. Educ. Technol. **43**(4), 540–560 (2012). https://doi.org/10.1111/j.1467-8535.2011.01197.x

Ter Vrugte, J., De Jong, T., Vandercruysse, S., Wouters, P., Van Oostendorp, H., Elen, J.: How competition and heterogeneous collaboration interact in prevocational game-based mathematics education. Comput. Educ. **89**, 42–52 (2015). https://doi.org/10.1016/j.compedu.2015.08.010

Thoma, G., Moeller, K., Ninaus, M., Bahnmueller, J.: Collectible content—Towards a modular ecosystem of intrinsically integrated gameplay: the case of fractions. In: Dondio, P. et al. (eds.) Games and Learning Alliance. GALA 2023. Lecture Notes in Computer Science, vol. 14475. Springer (2024). https://doi.org/10.1007/978-3-031-49065-1_34

Van Veen, M., De Vries, A., Cnossen, F., Willems, R. (2009). Improving collaboration for children with PDD-NOS through a multi-touch based serious game. In: EDULEARN09 Proceedings, pp. 3559–3570. IATED (2009). https://www.rug.nl/staff/f.cnossen/2009_vanveen_devries_cnossen.pdf

Wouters, P., van Nimwegen, C., van Oostendorp, H., van der Spek, E.D.: A meta-analysis of the cognitive and motivational effects of serious games. J. Educ. Psychol. **105**(2), 249–265 (2013). https://doi.org/10.1037/a0031311

Yao, S., Rao, R., Hausknecht, M., Narasimhan, K.: Keep calm and explore: language models for action generation in text-based games (2020). arXiv:2010.02903

# The Application of Serious Games in Virtual Reality as Intervention for Sugar Addiction

Sophie Hascher[1]([✉]) [iD], Ori Ossmy[1,2] [iD], and Halley Pontes[1] [iD]

[1] Department of Psychological Sciences, University of London, Birkbeck WC1E 7HX, UK
shasch01@student.bbk.ac.uk
[2] Department of Psychological Sciences and Centre for Brain and Cognitive Development,
University of London, Birkbeck WC1E 7HX, UK

**Abstract.** The escalating global health crisis of obesity, diabetes and heart conditions linked to disordered eating needs the implementation of effective interventions. Serious games, especially in Virtual Reality (VR), offer promising avenues for addressing these challenges through embodiment and emotional reactivity. Integrating gamification and mindfulness techniques, serious games can target addictive behaviours associated with sugar consumption. We propose to test the application of VR as a tool to address addictive sugar cravings in an 8-week serious games mindfulness based intervention. We hypothesise that the VR group will experience greater reductions in sugar addiction symptoms compared to the 2D computer-based group.

**Keywords:** Wellbeing · Serious Game · Sugar Addiction · Virtual Reality · Mindfulness · MBRP

## 1 The Prevalence of Sugar Addiction

With the current health crisis, with more than 1 billion people in the world suffering from obesity and 43% of adults being overweight in 2022 [1], alongside the escalating prevalence of diabetes and heart conditions attributed to overweight problems, it is imperative to explore successful interventions to address these pressing challenges facing humanity.

According to the University of Michigan in 2023, about 1 in 8 Americans over 50 show signs of food addiction [2].

With the rise of processed and sugary food, this alarming number is predicted to only increase. Food addiction is characterised by individuals consuming larger amounts of certain foods than they intended, demonstrating an excessive preoccupation with specific foods, experiencing intense desires or urges for particular foods, and continuing to consume these foods despite being aware of their adverse consequences [3]. Mirroring other addiction forms, such as alcohol use disorder (AUD), a significant addiction craving feature as seen with AUD, are evident with food disorders [4].While these two disorders seem different at first glance, similar pathophysiological mechanisms exist, including the experiences of craving [4]. Specifically, in food addiction, individuals

J. L. Plass and X. Ochoa (Eds.): JCSG 2024, LNCS 15259, pp. 384–392, 2025.
https://doi.org/10.1007/978-3-031-74138-8_28

experience a compelling urge to consume highly palatable and sugar focused foods, indicating a profound psychological and behavioural overlap with traditional substance dependencies.

Sugar addiction, a subset of food addiction, specifically focuses on the addictive properties of sugar-containing foods. These foods, often highly processed and rich in added sugars, can trigger neurological responses similar to those seen with substance abuse [5]. Consequently, consuming high levels of sugar can lead to cravings, loss of control, overeating behaviours, as well as severe withdrawal symptoms when sugar intake is reduced. Therefore, it is crucial to develop effective interventions to help reduce sugar addictive tendencies.

It has been previously argued that food and SUD cravings are elicited via repetitive behaviours and the positive emotional reinforcement that follows these actions. This process is elucidated by the behaviourist theory of Pavlovian classical conditioning [6], where repeated associations of an unconditioned stimulus with a previously neutral stimulus, combined with positive reinforcement, culminate in the pairing of an emotional response with the neutral stimulus. For instance, individuals might resort to chocolate and other types of sugar consumption, as well as processed foods during moments of high stress or anxiety as a means to cope and mitigate negative feelings, a behaviour commonly referred to as self-medicating [7]. As a result of continual exposure, the brain begins to link these food items with intrinsic rewards, engendering cravings and impulsive desires for consumption, alongside changes in the brain's reward circuitry [7]. One treatment avenue to reduce sugar cravings is the use of serious games.

## 2 Serious Games as a Treatment Method for Mental Health

Serious games have been used in therapeutic settings to support the management of various mental health disorders, including anxiety [9], attention-deficit hyperactivity (ADHD) [11] and alcohol use disorder [13]. Results are promising, showing great improvement in the alleviation of symptoms, as well as the facilitation of deep learning [14] and behaviour change [15].

At the core of serious games lies a drive to modify behavioural patterns and a growing emphasis on education. Incorporating gaming elements into digital interventions offers numerous advantages, such as facilitating goal-driven, positive behavioural modifications and implementing reward systems [16]. Hence, serious games offer an incredible potential in developing successful interventions for mental health. This could result in the development of serious games centered around mindfulness techniques, which may include the adaptation of the Mindfulness-Based Relapse Prevention (MBRP) program to alleviate various mental health issues, including alcohol use disorder, internet gaming addiction and sugar addiction.

Mindfulness-based interventions offer promising avenues for treating mental health conditions, such as depression [17], obsessive compulsive disorder [18] and food addiction [19]. Methodologies behind mindfulness involve practices at fostering present moment awareness, acceptance and non-judgmental observations of one's thoughts, emotions and bodily sensations. By integrating a serious game approach and leveraging technology, especially virtual reality (VR), participants can experience a heightened sense of embodiment within the therapeutic environment. Ultimately, this immersive experience has the potential to enhance engagement by fostering connectedness to the content. Thus, drop-out rates may decline as participants may feel more motivated to actively participate in the intervention thanks to the immersive and embodied experience VR offers.

## 3 Serious Games in Virtual Reality

VR offers immersive interactivity in virtual environments by stimulating various senses, including visual, auditory and in some cases even haptic, [21]. This approach of immersiveness increases user engagement and may therefore lead to greater therapeutic impact, [23].

At the forefront of VR is the ability to transport users into a wide range of virtual worlds. By focusing on high-definition displays and incredible sophisticated environmental designs, VR scenes can look highly realistic, mirroring real-world scenes. This is especially important when creating a sense of embodiment [24] and creating serious games focused on the treatment of mental health [26].

Embodiment is referred to as a feeling of presence through different sensory signals arriving to the body, which the brain coherently interprets to create an accurate representation of the self [27]. Through integrating technology to applied neuroscience and psychology, especially through VR, subjects can experience embodiment in a virtual world. A study by Slater et al. [28] demonstrated that participants could experience a full-body transfer illusion in VR, where male participants were fully able to embody a virtual female bodily experience. Moreover, VR offers individuals the opportunity to experience the virtual world in a highly similar manner to the real world. González-Franco and colleagues [29] study highlighted identical brain responses in the motor cortex when moving their hand out of the way of a knife in VR compared to the same movement and neural responses in real life. Embodied simulations are especially crucial when designing effective psychological treatment methods for mental health disorders. Similar to the real world, VR experiences can predict sensory actions, concepts and emotions [30]. Thus, creating a similar physical and neural response within a virtual environment as one would encounter in the physical world.

A key consideration is whether engaging in mindfulness practices within a naturalistic VR environment would evoke stronger emotions and a more immersive full-body experience compared to practicing mindfulness in a traditional, non-VR setting, such as an indoor environment like an office. The immersive nature of VR, with its potential to create realistic and engaging nature environments, enhances sensory input and emotional engagement [31], making the mindfulness experience more vivid and impactful. This heightened level of immersion could amplify the emotional responses and physical sensations experienced during mindfulness practices, leading to more profound therapeutic outcomes. Previous studies on the application of VR in clinical populations with patients suffering from an eating disorders (ED), including anorexia nervosa (AN), bulimia nervosa (BN) and being eating disorder (BED), have shown effective outcomes in helping patients reduce food cravings and anxiety responses to food [32]. Additionally, journal articles investigating the efficacity of VR on compassion and self-compassion meditations have revealed that the use of virtual bodies can promote greater compassion and self-compassion, leading to a reduction of self-criticism [33].

Therapies like virtual exposure therapy or virtual social interactions heavily focus on the emotional reactions of the user when immersed in VR [34]. It may be possible that a similar emotional system is necessary in mindfulness VR interventions. Users experiencing a sense of presence when practicing mindfulness in VR may show greater changes compared to users practicing mindfulness in a 2D environment. Gall and colleagues [35] highlighted that virtual embodiment does affect emotional reactions to various stimuli. Hence, this supports our hypothesis that mindfulness VR interventions could be more efficient than mindfulness 2D environments, due to a sense of embodiment and emotional reactivity leading to greater significant therapeutic effects.

The immersive nature of VR shows great potential of application, especially for therapeutic purposes. Numerous studies using VR headsets, including exposure therapy for the treatment of post-traumatic stress disorders (PTSD) [36], cognitive-behavioural therapy (CBT) for the treatment of anxiety [37] and mindfulness for the treatment of alcohol abuse [38], have shown significant bettering of symptoms. For example, VR based interventions to treat PTSD are based on realistic environments that provoke fear or discomfort in a controlled environment, helping the user to successfully decrease their trauma.

By implementing VR in treatment methods for mental health, users have the possibility to alter their external and internal bodily experience, leading to a quicker and more significant reduction in sub-optimal mental health symptoms. Furthermore, patients might experience stronger emotions and more immersive full-body sensations through mindfulness practices in naturalistic VR environments than non-VR indoor environments like offices. Thus, this approach could potentially lead to enhanced therapeutic outcomes and deeper levels of relaxation and self-awareness, but also improved emotion regulation and stress management skills compared to the start of the intervention, while reducing stress responses over the course of the procedure.

## 4 Virtual Reality vS 2D Computer-Based Serious Game on Mindfulness to Alleviate Sugar Addiction

This section aims to outline a proposed study, which is looking at reducing sugar cravings by implementing an 8-week serious game mindfulness-based intervention (MBRP) in virtual reality compared to an 8-week 2D computer-based intervention. The aim is to understand whether embodiment VR is more effective in eliciting emotions related to mindfulness, as well as addiction, and whether this emotional reaction reduces sugar cravings more significantly than the 2D mindfulness intervention.

Eligible participants will be administered at random to one of the following groups: virtual reality (treatment condition) or computer based (control condition). Note that the protocol for both groups is identical, with the only exception of the delivery method, i.e., the intervention will either be delivered in virtual reality or through a computer screen. Virtual environments for the serious game on mindfulness will differ, with 20 participants (virtual reality intervention = 10 participants, computer based = 10 participants) being administered to a naturalistic mountain view, 20 participants (virtual reality intervention = 10 participants, computer based = 10 participants) being advised to a Japanese forest, and 20 participants (virtual reality intervention = 10 participants, computer based = 10 participants) assigned to a beach (see Fig. 1).

There is little literature on mindfulness and naturalistic environment highlight the benefits of nature in reducing rumination [39] and anxiety [27], two important comorbidities of addiction, [41]. However, research is limited and does not highlight which specific naturalistic environment is more effective. Therefore, this proposed study also aims at understanding this critical matter by utilising three distinct nature based virtual environments with highly different components.

**Fig. 1.** Virtual environments participants will undergo the 8-week serious game Mindfulness-Based Relapse Prevention (MBRP) intervention. Environments are as followed: Naturalistic mountain view (A), Japanese forest (B) and Beach (C).

Both treatment conditions will undergo an 8-week serious game MBRP intervention adapted from Bowen et al. [42] to address symptoms of sugar addiction. The new build intervention will comprise 8 different sessions. Each session will last approximatively 30 min and will have a central theme, based on meditation and mindfulness practices. Themes include, but are not limited to, being in auto-pilot, recognising thoughts and emotions when triggered, and the role of thoughts in relapse. The session on being on auto-pilot will focus on helping participants become aware of maladaptive habits and unconscious behaviours, while helping them to bring more intentionality into their daily actions. The session on recognisions thoughts and emotions when triggered, on the other hand, is aimed at teaching participants to identify immediate reactions to stressors, while teaching them to respond more mindfully rather than impulsively. Additionally, the role of thoughts in relapse session will explore how certain thoughts can contribute to the risk of relapse, at the same time as providing participants with strategies for reframing these maladaptive thoughts to support long-term recovery. This 8-week intervention implements aspects of gaming by introducing an earning point and 'level-up' system where participants have the opportunity to score points and receive rewards by going to the next level, i.e., after completion of a session, participants automatically get a reward by collecting points which will propel them to the next level/session. Note that the reward only occurs by completing the session. Any dropouts or non-completion are not rewarded.

Overall, this study aims to evaluate the effects of the serious game MBRP in virtual reality compared to a computer-based intervention. We hypothesise that a greater reduction in sugar addiction will occur in the virtual reality group than the computer-based group. This immersive quality of VR is expected to make the mindfulness practices more effective, thereby leading to better treatment outcomes. Secondary outcomes include among others cravings improvement for sugar addiction, mindfulness and perceived stress. Additionally, we are curious to compare the effects of the different natural-based environments. By exploring various natural elements, such as forests, beaches and mountains, we aim to determine which specific natural elements are most effective in enhancing mindfulness embodiment and eliciting strong emotional responses by analysing participant's mindfulness scores before and after the various naturalistic intervention. These initial findings will give us some direction into which environment might be most suitable for reducing sugar addiction.

**Acknowledgements.** This paper was supported by Birkbeck, University of London as part of a Ph.D. project.

**Disclosure of Interests** The authors declare no interests.

# References

1. One in eight people are now living with obesity. Accessed 12 July 2024. Available https://www.who.int/news/item/01-03-2024-one-in-eight-people-are-now-living-with-obesity
2. One in eight Americans over 50 show signs of food addiction. ScienceDaily. Accessed 03 June 2024. Available https://www.sciencedaily.com/releases/2023/01/230130090408.htm
3. Cassin, S., Leung, S., Hawa, R., Wnuk, S., Jackson, T., Sockalingam, S.: Food addiction is associated with binge eating and psychiatric distress among post-operative bariatric surgery patients and may improve in response to cognitive behavioural therapy. Nutrients **12**(10), 2905 (2020). https://doi.org/10.3390/nu12102905
4. Smith-Russell, D., Bowen, S.: Mediating effects of thought suppression in the relationship between mindfulness and substance use craving. Subst. Use Misuse **58**(10), 1196–1201 (2023). https://doi.org/10.1080/10826084.2023.2212277
5. Passeri, A., Municchi, D., Cavalieri, G., Babicola, L., Ventura, R., Di Segni, M.: Linking drug and food addiction: an overview of the shared neural circuits and behavioral phenotype. Front. Behav. Neurosci. **17** (2023). https://doi.org/10.3389/fnbeh.2023.1240748
6. Pavlov, P.: Conditioned reflexes: an investigation of the physiological activity of the cerebral cortex. Accessed 04 June 2024. Available https://psycnet.apa.org/record/1927-02531-000
7. Ravichandran, S., et al.: Alterations in reward network functional connectivity are associated with increased food addiction in obese individuals. Sci. Rep. **11**(1), 3386 (2021). https://doi.org/10.1038/s41598-021-83116-0

8. Wols, A., Lichtwarck-Aschoff, A., Schoneveld, E.A., Granic, I.: In-game play behaviours during an applied video game for anxiety prevention predict successful intervention outcomes. J. Psychopathol. Behav. Assess. **40**(4), 655–668 (2018). https://doi.org/10.1007/s10862-018-9684-4

9. Schoneveld, E.A., Malmberg, M., Lichtwarck-Aschoff, A., Verheijen, G.P., Engels, R.C.M.E., Granic, I.: A neurofeedback video game (MindLight) to prevent anxiety in children: a randomized controlled trial. Comput. Hum. Behav. **63**, 321–333 (2016). https://doi.org/10.1016/j.chb.2016.05.005

10. Bul, K., Doove, L., Franken, I.: A serious game for children with attention deficit hyperactivity disorder: who benefits the most? PLOS ONE. Accessed 03 Jun 2024. Available https://journals.plos.org/plosone/article?id=10.1371/journal.pone.0193681

11. García-Baos, A. et al.: Novel interactive eye-tracking game for training attention in children with attention-deficit/hyperactivity disorder. In: The primary care companion for CNS disorders. vol. 21, no. 4, p. 19m02428 (2019). https://doi.org/10.4088/PCC.19m02428

12. Flaudias, V., et al.: Reducing attentional bias in individuals with alcohol use disorders with a tablet application: a randomized controlled trial pilot study. Alcohol Alcohol. Oxf. Oxfs. **55**(1), 51–55 (2020). https://doi.org/10.1093/alcalc/agz080

13. Gamito, P., et al.: Executive functioning in alcoholics following an mHealth cognitive stimulation program: randomized controlled trial. J. Med. Internet Res. **16**(4), e102 (2014). https://doi.org/10.2196/jmir.2923

14. Dondlinger, M.: Educational video game design: a review of the literature. J. Appl. Educ. Technol. **4** (2007)

15. Read, J.L., Shortell, S.M.: Interactive games to promote behavior change in prevention and treatment. JAMA **305**(16), 1704–1705 (2011). https://doi.org/10.1001/jama.2011.408

16. Dewhirst, A., Laugharne, R., Shankar, R.: Therapeutic use of serious games in mental health: scoping review. BJPsych Open **8**(2), e37 (2022). https://doi.org/10.1192/bjo.2022.4

17. MacKenzie, M.B., Kocovski, N.L.: Mindfulness-based cognitive therapy for depression: trends and developments. Psychol. Res. Behav. Manag. **9**, 125–132 (2016). https://doi.org/10.2147/PRBM.S63949

18. Key, B.L., Rowa, K., Bieling, P., McCabe, R., Pawluk, E.J.: Mindfulness-based cognitive therapy as an augmentation treatment for obsessive-compulsive disorder. Clin. Psychol. Psychother. **24**(5), 1109–1120 (2017). https://doi.org/10.1002/cpp.2076

19. Bunio, L.K., Battles, J.A., Loverich, T.M.: The nuances of emotion regulation difficulties and mindfulness in food addiction. Addict. Res. Theory **29**(1), 11–17 (2021). https://doi.org/10.1080/16066359.2020.1714038

20. de Jong, J.R., Keizer, A., Engel, M.M., Dijkerman, H.C.: Does affective touch influence the virtual reality full body illusion? Exp. Brain Res. **235**(6), 1781–1791 (2017). https://doi.org/10.1007/s00221-017-4912-9

21. Summers, C., Jesse, M.: Creating immersive and aesthetic auditory spaces in virtual reality, p. 6 (2017). https://doi.org/10.1109/SIVE.2017.7938144

22. Gutiérrez-Maldonado, J., Wiederhold, B.K., Riva, G.: Future directions: how virtual reality can further improve the assessment and treatment of eating disorders and obesity. Cyberpsychol. Behav. Soc. Netw. **19**(2), 148–153 (2016). https://doi.org/10.1089/cyber.2015.0412

23. Laforest, M., Bouchard, S., Cretu, A.-M.: Frontiers. Inducing an anxiety response using a contaminated virtual environment: validation of a therapeutic tool for obsessive–compulsive disorder. Accessed 03 June 03 2024. Available https://www.frontiersin.org/articles/10.3389/fict.2016.00018/full

24. North, M.M., North, S.M.: A comparative study of sense of presence of traditional virtual reality and immersive environments. Aust. J. Inf. Syst. **20** (2016). https://doi.org/10.3127/ajis.v20i0.1168

25. Halldorsson, B., Hill, C., Waite, P., Partridge, K., Freeman, D., Creswell, C.: Annual research review: immersive virtual reality and digital applied gaming interventions for the treatment of mental health problems in children and young people: the need for rigorous treatment development and clinical evaluation. J. Child Psychol. Psychiatry **62**(5), 584–605 (2021). https://doi.org/10.1111/jcpp.13400

26. Sárkány, A., et al.: Maintain and improve mental health by smart virtual reality serious games, p. 229 (2016). https://doi.org/10.1007/978-3-319-32270-4_22

27. Matamala-Gomez, M., Donegan, T., Bottiroli, S.: Frontiers. Immersive virtual reality and virtual embodiment for pain relief. Accessed 03 June 2024. Available https://www.fronti ersin.org/articles/10.3389/fnhum.2019.00279/full

28. Slater, M., Spanlang, B., Sanchez-Vives, M.V., Blanke, O.: First person experience of body transfer in virtual reality. PLoS ONE **5**(5), e10564 (2010). https://doi.org/10.1371/journal. pone.0010564

29. González-Franco, M., Peck, T.C., Rodríguez-Fornells, A., Slater, M.: A threat to a virtual hand elicits motor cortex activation. Exp. Brain Res. **232**(3), 875–887 (2014). https://doi.org/ 10.1007/s00221-013-3800-1

30. Riva, G., Wiederhold, B.K., Mantovani, F.: Neuroscience of virtual reality: from virtual exposure to embodied medicine—PMC. Accessed: 03 June 2024. Available https://www.ncbi.nlm. nih.gov/pmc/articles/PMC6354552/

31. Naef, A.C., et al.: Investigating the role of auditory and visual sensory inputs for inducing relaxation during virtual reality stimulation. Sci. Rep. **12**(1), 17073 (2022). https://doi.org/ 10.1038/s41598-022-21575-9

32. Riva, G., Malighetti, C., Serino, S.: Virtual reality in the treatment of eating disorders. Clin. Psychol. Psychother. **28**(3), 477–488 (2021). https://doi.org/10.1002/cpp.2622

33. Cebolla, A., et al.: Putting oneself in the body of others: a pilot study on the efficacy of an embodied virtual reality system to generate self-compassion. Front. Psychol. **10** (2019). https://doi.org/10.3389/fpsyg.2019.01521

34. Riva, G., et al.: Affective interactions using virtual reality: the link between presence and emotions. In: Cyberpsychology & behavior: the impact of the internet, multimedia and virtual reality on behavior and society, vol. 10, no. 1, pp. 45–56 (2007). https://doi.org/10.1089/cpb. 2006.9993

35. Gall, D., Roth, D., Stauffert, J.-P., Zarges, J., Latoschik, M.E.: Embodiment in virtual reality intensifies emotional responses to virtual stimuli. Front. Psychol. **12** (2021). https://doi.org/ 10.3389/fpsyg.2021.674179

36. Rizzo, A., Reger, G., Gahm, G., Difede, J., Rothbaum, B.O.: Virtual reality exposure therapy for combat-related PTSD. In: Post-traumatic stress disorder: Basic science and clinical practice, pp. 375–399. Humana Press, Springer, Totowa, NJ, US (2009) https://doi.org/10.1007/ 978-1-60327-329-9_18

37. Geraets, C.N.W., Veling, W., Witlox, M., Staring, A.B.P., Matthijssen, S.J.M.A., Cath, D.: Virtual reality-based cognitive behavioural therapy for patients with generalized social anxiety disorder: a pilot study. Behav. Cogn. Psychother. **47**(6), 745–750 (2019). https://doi.org/10. 1017/S1352465819000225

38. Van Doren, N., Ng, H., Rawat, E., McKenna, K.R., Blonigen, D.M.: Virtual reality mindfulness training for veterans in residential substance use treatment: Pilot study of feasibility and acceptability. J. Subst. Use Addict. Treat. **161**, 209315 (2024). https://doi.org/10.1016/j.josat. 2024.209315

39. Bratman, G.N., Hamilton, J.P., Hahn, K.S., Daily, G.C., Gross, J.J.: Nature experience reduces rumination and subgenual prefrontal cortex activation. Proc. Natl. Acad. Sci. U. S. A. **112**(28), 8567–8572 (2015). https://doi.org/10.1073/pnas.1510459112

40. Hussenoeder, F.S., et al.: Anxiety and food addiction in men and women: results from the longitudinal LIFE-adult-study. Front. Psychiatry **13** (2022). https://doi.org/10.3389/fpsyt.2022.914358

41. Burrows, T., Kay-Lambkin, F., Pursey, K., Skinner, J., Dayas, C.: Food addiction and associations with mental health symptoms: a systematic review with meta-analysis. J. Hum. Nutr. Diet. Off. J. Br. Diet. Assoc. **31**(4), 544–572 (2018). https://doi.org/10.1111/jhn.12532

42. Bowen, S., Neha, C., Alan, M.: Mindfulness-based relapse prevention for addictive behaviors: a clinician's guide. Accessed 03 June 2024. Available https://psycnet.apa.org/record/2011-01707-000

# Exploring the Potential of Serious Games for Learning Mathematical Equations

Beatriz Moura Lima, Gabriel Pereira Tesch Sabaini,
Giovanna Micher Santana, Thiago Leandro Liporace$^{(\boxtimes)}$, Paula Torales Leite,
Pedro Henrique Cacique Braga, and Vera Lúcia Antônio Azevedo

Mackenzie Prebisterian University, Sao Paulo, Brazil
{10402432,10238782,10401330,10395816}@mackenzista.com.br,
{paula.leite,pedro.braga,veralucia.azevedo}@mackenzie.br

**Abstract.** This work proposes the development of a Serious Game for children and teens in Elementary II to teach the concept of first-degree mathematical equations. The goal is to help Brazilian students who face a widening educational gap intensified by the country's unpreparedness regarding COVID-19 in the area of mathematics. The proposed work was inspired by the Balance Scale Equation Game, a mathematical problem-solving activity that challenges participants to balance equations using weights on a scale. The application was developed using the CBL framework to systematically guide and document each of the steps necessary for its completion, including the ideation process with brainstorming sessions, prototyping, implementation and user testing with students to gather qualitative data on user experience and educational outcomes.

**Keywords:** Serious game · learning · mathematical equations · mobile

## 1 Introduction

The COVID-19 pandemic has highlighted deficiencies in Brazil's educational infrastructure, with emphasis on the unpreparedness of schools, especially public ones, to implement distance learning [1]. This scenario reflects on Brazil's performance in terms of school learning, as evidenced by the drop in the results of the Basic Education Assessment System (BEAS) in 2021 compared to 2019 in fundamental subjects such as Portuguese language and mathematics [2]. It was pointed out that there were greater average losses, estimated between 4 to 10 months of learning in mathematics and among younger children [2].

In addition to that, the results of the 2022 International Student Assessment Program (ISAP) indicated that 73% of 15-year-old Brazilian students—those who have just completed Elementary II—scored below level 2 in mathematical literacy. This means that these teens are unable to do simple operations, such as converting currencies or comparing distances [3].

In order to teach children and teens in Elementary II the concept of first-degree mathematical equations, as well as to bring students closer to this content

J. L. Plass and X. Ochoa (Eds.): JCSG 2024, LNCS 15259, pp. 393–399, 2025.
https://doi.org/10.1007/978-3-031-74138-8_29

in a practical way, this demo paper presents the creation of a serious game for iOS, developed in collaboration with Apple Developer Academy — Mackenzie and inspired by the Balance Scale Equation Game, developed and validated by the Mathematics Laboratory at Mackenzie Presbyterian University [4].

This work is structured into 5 sections. In addition to this first section, the theoretical framework of the work is presented in Sect. 2, which describes the documentation, methodologies, and concepts used for the development of the game. Section 3 includes the process of ideation, design, implementation, and descriptions of user testing. In Sect. 4, the results and discussions about the creation of the game are presented. In Sect. 5, final considerations are made about the results and limitations found in the proposal.

## 2    Theoretical Reference

Apple's Developer documentation [5] was the main theoretical foundation for the game's development. It represents the largest source of documentation on any subject related to the development of applications for Apple devices, offering a solid base for understanding and applying best practices in programming. It was used as a reference on topics such as programming in Swift—the native iOS language used in the project, SwiftUI [6] and SpriteKit [7] frameworks, which were used to compose the game's logic and interface.

The Human Interface Guidelines (HIG), as described in its document, "contains guidance and best practices that can help you design a great experience for any Apple platform" [9]. It was used as a guide for the implementation of UI and UX best practices in the creation of prototypes and construction of the final interface, to provide a pleasant experience for users. It was consulted for the creation of the Menu, Defeat screen, and the placement of elements on the main screens of the game.

Challenge Based Learning (CBL) [10] was the framework used to structure the research, the ideation process, and the game's development. It provides an efficient and effective way to solve real-world challenges. It is divided into three main stages: Engage, Investigate and Act. During the stages of ch1CBL, the development group may return to a prior stage to refine ideas and themes previously established.

Additionally, the concept of Serious Games was used as a part of the theoretical reference by the team. According to Blumberg et al. [11], "Serious Games are designed to entertain and educate players, and to promote behavioral change". It is a form of teaching students in an unconventional way compared to regular teaching methods. Research indicates that Serious Games ease students' understanding of a subject and improve their cognitive abilities [12]. Because of that, they are considered an effective pedagogical medium to cater for learners' requirements and expectations [13].

The Balance Scale Equation Game (see Fig. 1), developed by the Mathematics Laboratory at Mackenzie Presbyterian University, was the main inspiration for the system. It is a form of teaching elementary school students the principles of solving a first-degree equation. Through the game, students understand the Addition, Multiplication, Subtraction and Equivalence Principles [4]. The game works by presenting the equation as a balance scale, in which the sides of the balance scale represent the sides of the equation. The scale must remain balanced to show that what is done on one side of the equation must be done on the other side, in terms of mathematical operations.

**Fig. 1.** Balance scale equation game. Font: Matsui Yamamoto et al. [4].

The game begins by presenting an equation to the player, which has to organize the balance in order to isolate the unknown, "x". For example:

$$X + 5 = 7 \tag{1}$$

The balance scale is displayed with X + 5 on one side and 7 on the other side of the equal sign. If a subtraction operation of 5 occurs on one side, it needs to be done on the other. By doing this type of operation, the Equivalence Principle is put into practice and the equation is solved:

$$X = 2 \tag{2}$$

## 3  Methods

### 3.1  Ideation

The ideation process was executed during the Engage stage of CBL, in which the development group gathered potential ideas, themes, and math topics. The team started by brainstorming and exploring a diverse range of game mechanics employed by famous mobile games. After a two-week research period, the group elaborated the idea of "Tentálculos".

The game consists of solving a first-degree equation by adding fruits to plates, which represents both sides of an equation, and isolating the unknown factor to get the result—a similar process to the Balance Scale Equation Game by the Mathematics Laboratory. To make the learning process fun, the game is set in the bottom of the ocean with an octopus waiter as the main character, who is tasked with balancing customer's orders, represented as equations. The name of the game, Tentálculos, is a portmanteau of "Tentáculos" (tentacles) and "Cálculos" (calculations), reflecting its educational and marine themes (see Fig. 2). According to Mendonça and Mustaro [14], a story of a serious game can make the game much more exciting, and thus offering a motivational condition for its use.

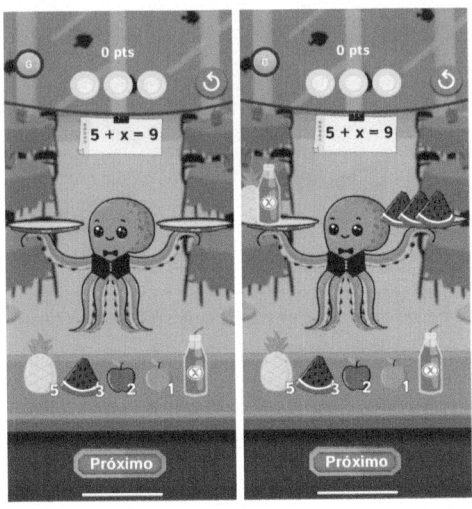

**Fig. 2.** Tentálculos' main screen. Font: Authors.

### 3.2   Design

During the character creation process, in the Investigate stage of CBL, a research on different octopus species was carried out as a reference for the creation of thumbnails—a common technique across design disciplines involving the creation of quick and straightforward drawings [15]. To elaborate the design, a Storyboard featuring a low-fidelity prototype on paper was made, simplifying potential user interactions and features. Subsequently, the development of the medium prototype began, following Apple's Human Interface Guidelines (HIG) [9] and taking into account the game's content, the layout of elements on the screen, and their interactive aspects.

In this process, mood boards and reference panels were created on Figma [15], acting as a support for the visual identity, which was based in a 2D vector style. The main software used for creating the illustrations was Adobe Illustrator [16]. At the end of the process, the design team developed a high-fidelity prototype featuring completed artwork, components, screens and their interactions (see Fig. 3).

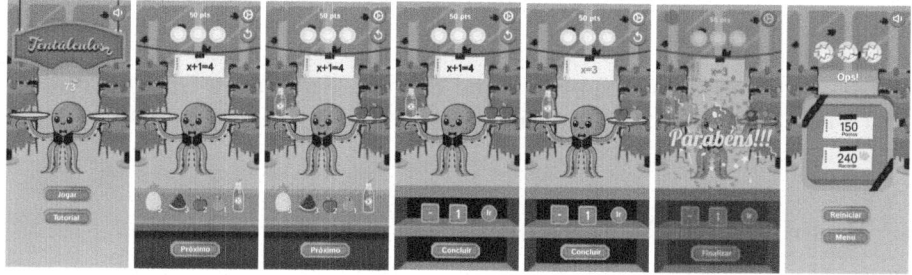

**Fig. 3.** High-fidelity prototype. Font: Authors.

### 3.3   Programming

The application was developed for iOS devices in the Swift programming language, with the SwiftUI library [6] to build the Menu screen and the SpriteKit library [7] to implement the logic and presentation of the game's visual elements.

The Swift language was used because, in addition to allowing the native development of applications on iOS devices, it facilitates user interaction with the software and the application development [8].

Behind the scenes, the game logic can be divided into three parts. The first is the generation of random equations the player has to solve. The second consists of the weight calculation, responsible for attributing values to both sides of the equation and calculating the value of the unknown factor. The third part is the logic for swapping fruits, that happens during the second stage of the game, in which subtraction or division happens and fruits from both sides of the plate are exchanged according to the mathematical operation performed.

### 3.4   User Testing

To evaluate the proposed work, interviews were carried out with 8 Elementary II students in order to gather qualitative data about the understanding of the functionalities, interaction and educational content, prompting the following questions: Do you know what an equation is? How would you begin to solve an equation? Do you know another way to solve equations?

Given these questions, almost half of the students did not know what an equation was, some of them would begin to solve it using the Equivalence Principle, which they referred to "passing the 'x' to the other side". All of them did not know another way to solve equations.

Subsequently, students were tasked to solve an equation by playing the game. At the end of the session, two more questions were asked to the participants: Can you summarize your experience using the app? If you could make any changes to the game, what would it be?

Overall, the answers to the first question were that the game was fun, challenging and the design was appealing, the interviewees also said they had a great experience and understood how to solve equations in a new way. For the second question, two interviewees said that it took a while to understand how the game worked at first, another interviewee said that he would like to get the fruit out of the plate by dragging it, the other interviewees reported they would not make any changes.

## 4   Results and Discussion

The interviews with Elementary II students uncovered certain questions and limitations regarding the game that are significant to be considered.

The game was created exclusively for iOS users, and a larger part of the target audience uses Android, a common operating system in mobile phones within the country [17]. This highlights the need to expand the game's compatibility to additional operating systems.

As the students played the game, solving first-degree equations became repetitive. Therefore, to maintain player engagement, implementing complex equations becomes increasingly valuable as players advance in knowledge.

Despite applying the Equivalence Principle to solve equations, it was observed that the students were unaware they were using it. This is a point to be taken into consideration because it contributes to the gap in learning mathematical logic as many students may have difficulties understanding this principle.

In spite of the previously stated limitations, all of the participants demonstrated progress in their mathematical knowledge after playing the game, as they were able to solve first-degree equations with greater ease and accuracy. It also remains essential to acknowledge the opportunity to use the game in the school environment, teachers could explain how it works and support students as they play individually. To facilitate this process, the game could provide documentation specifically tailored for teachers regarding its usage.

## 5   Conclusion

The purpose of the application is to teach first-degree mathematical equations for Brazilian Elementary II students, who face a delay in the grasp of mathematical concepts. For this, the Balance Scale Game was employed as the theoretical foundation to help the understanding of the basic principles of solving an equation: Addition, Multiplication, Subtraction and Equivalence Principles.

Some of the challenges found in the consolidation of the game were explored in this demo paper, which highlighted opportunities for expansion, such as the extension of compatibility to additional operating systems, potential use of the game in classrooms and implementation of complex equations as players advance in knowledge. The ability to grasp concepts through interactive gaming could transform classroom dynamics, shifting the focus from rote memorization to active problem-solving. As the game's reach expands, it could serve as a valuable tool in bridging the gap between abstract theory and practical application, making mathematics more accessible and engaging for students.

# References

1. Lichand, G., Doria, C.: The lasting impacts of remote learning in the absence of remedial policies: evidence from Brazil (2022)
2. BRASIL. MINISTERIO DA EDUCACAO, INSTITUTO NACIONAL DE ESTUDOS E PESQUISA EDUCACIONAIS ANISIO TEIXEIRA, Sabeb 2021. Brasilia, 16 de setembro de 2022, Disponível em https://download.inep.gov.br/institucional/apresentacao_saeb_ideb_2021.pdf. Last accessed 03 Nov 2022
3. 7 de cada 10 alunos brasileiros de 15 anos não sabem resolver problemas matemáticos simples, mostra Pisa, https://g1.globo.com/educacao/noticia/2023/12/05/7-de-cada-10-alunos-brasileiros-de-15-anos-nao-sabem-resolver-problemas-matematicos-simples-mostra-pisa.ghtml. Last accessed 02 Nov 2022
4. Matsui Yamamoto, E., Antonio Azevedo, V.L.: Material didático de apoio ao ensino e aprendizagem de Matemática no Ensino Fundamental II e Ensino Médio. Editora LiberArts, Sao Paulo (2023)
5. Apple Developer Documentation, https://developer.apple.com/documentation/. Last accessed 22 May 2024
6. SwiftUI Documentation: https://developer.apple.com/documentation/swiftui/. Last accessed 04 Nov 2022
7. SpriteKit Documentation: https://developer.apple.com/documentation/spritekit/. Last accessed 04 Nov 2022
8. Wysong, T.D.: Developing an iOS Game Application: Magnet Hockey (2022)
9. Human Interface Guidelines. https://developer.apple.com/design/human-interface-guidelines. Last accessed 03 Nov 2022
10. Challenge Based Learning. https://www.challengebasedlearning.org/. Last accessed 04 Nov 2022
11. Blumberg, F. C., Almonte, D. E., Anthony, J. S., Hashimoto, N.: Serious games: what are they? What do they do? Why should we play them? pp. 334–351 (2013)
12. Zhonggen, Y.: A meta-analysis of use of serious games in education over a decade (2019)
13. Lamb, R.L., Annetta, L., Firestone, J., Etopio, E.: A meta-analysis with examination of moderators of student cognition, affect, and learning outcomes while using serious educational games, serious games, and simulations. Comput. Hum. Behav. **80**, 158–167 (2018)
14. Mendonça, L.R., Mustaro, N.P.: Elementos imersivos e de narrativa como fatores motivacionais em serious games. In: SBC—Proceedings of SBGames, Salvador, BA, Brazil (2011)
15. Figma. https://www.figma.com. Last accessed 21 May 2024
16. Adobe Illustrator. https://www.adobe.com/products/illustrator.html. Last accessed 21 May 2024
17. Market share of mobile operating systems in Brazil from January 2019 to May 2023, https://www.statista.com/statistics/262167/market-share-held-by-mobile-operating-systems-in-brazil/. Last accessed 08 Nov 2022

# Game Design Prototype with GIMs: Fostering Neurodiverse Connections Through Storytelling

Yiqi Xiao[✉] [iD]

University of Illinois Urbana-Champaign, Champaign, IL 61802, USA
yiqix3@illinois.edu

**Abstract.** This ongoing experimental project investigates the use of Generative Image Models (GIMs) in crafting a picture book creation game designed to nurture social connections among autistic children and their neurotypical peers within a neuro-affirming environment. Moving away from traditional methods that often seek to condition neurodivergent children to socialize in prescribed ways, this project strives to cultivate a space where children can engage with one another naturally and creatively through art and storytelling, free from the pressure to adhere to standard social norms. Beyond merely "story-choosing," the research highlights the potential of GIMs to facilitate "story-creating," fostering peer social connections in a creative and structured collaborative learning experience.

**Keywords:** Autism Spectrum Disorder · Generative Image Models · Storytelling · Peer Relationship · Educational Game · Structured Collaborative Learning

## 1 Research Background

### 1.1 The Social Needs of Autistic Children

Peer relationships, which include acceptance, friendships, and participation in peer networks as characterized by Gifford-Smith and Brownell [1], are crucial for children's well-being [2] and cognitive growth [3] and would influence their school performance [1]. Just like other children, research suggests that autistic children often have a strong desire for friendships [4]. However, multiple studies indicate that they frequently encounter social challenges [5–7]. Ghanouni et al. [8] note that many autistic children struggle with language, sensory processing, and recognizing social cues, which include but are not limited to picking up on jokes, maintaining eye contact during conversation, or appropriately interpreting others' facial expressions or tone of voice [9], and these disadvantages may lead to reduced or atypical interactions with peers. In other words, not "thinking and acting like others" in a traditional social setting prevents autistic children from forming friendships naturally with their neurotypical peers, which can have detrimental impacts on their overall development and well-being.

While the social interactions of autistic children might differ from those of neurotypical peers, this does not preclude their ability to build friendships. Recent research challenged the long-held beliefs that being autistic prevents them from forming friendships,

J. L. Plass and X. Ochoa (Eds.): JCSG 2024, LNCS 15259, pp. 400–407, 2025.
https://doi.org/10.1007/978-3-031-74138-8_30

revealing that many of them can form bonds with both neurotypical and autistic peers, albeit with differing interaction styles [10]. Recognizing the challenges that autistic children face in forming friendships within traditional social environments while acknowledging their readiness and capability to engage in social relationships, necessitates greater attention to their social needs and the obstacles they encounter.

### 1.2 Bonding Between Autistic Children and Digital Games

Since autistic children usually face challenges in face-to-face communication, online spaces become an alternative for social expression and relaxation. Research shows that autistic children often show a pronounced inclination toward screen-based media, especially video games. Studies indicate that boys aged eight to eighteen on the autism spectrum average 2.4 h per day gaming, based on a study of 169 individuals [11]. Barrington Campbell [12], an autistic adult, shared his thoughts about autistic people staying online: "If you are autistic, this can feel more than stressful (interacting with people face-to-face). Online gaming means autistic people can play in an environment we feel comfortable in and can control—if it's not going well on screen, we can get into our safe spaces". Therefore, digital games present great opportunities to support the socialization of autistic children. By engaging with them through platforms they are comfortable with, designers and educators can create meaningful and effective interventions that align with autistic children's preferences.

## 2 Related Work with AI

The development of AI technology has significantly transformed and advanced practices in the educational context, for example, AI can assist teachers in designing and delivering personalized, timely, iterative, and enriching educational experiences, with predictive insights, making education more effective and inclusive [13–15]. Compared to the broader field of education, the application of AI in supporting special education, especially for autism, is relatively new. However, there are still many insightful ongoing projects and proposals. The National AI Institute for Exceptional Education is developing AI screeners designed to detect speech and language processing challenges in young children by analyzing video and audio recordings of classroom interactions. They are also working on AI Orchestrators, a sophisticated multi-agent reinforcement learning framework that assesses each student's learning progression and recommends the most suitable interventions [16]. Similarly, a project uses the inbuilt accelerometer of a smartwatch to detect autism stereotypic behaviors, including hand flapping, painting, and sibbing, to better inform teachers and parents about their kids' conditions [17]. In the field of serious games, the Film Detective game, designed by the AIVAS Lab at Vanderbilt University, helps autistic adolescents decode social situations and understand others' emotions by interacting with and teaching a virtual agent, which makes learning enjoyable [18].

### 2.1 More to Explore in Design with AI

While these projects employ various approaches to assist autistic individuals, they share some similarities. Many current approaches consider AI as an extension of the role of educators [18], caregivers [29], and other human experts [16, 17] aiming to achieve previously unimaginable efficiency. Although all these practices are valuable, they typically involve AI replicating existing adult roles without changing or enriching the forms of assistance available to children. An approach worth further exploring is using AI to empower children following their own wishes and creativity. While their capabilities are increased, their agency is also bolstered. This opens up more possibilities for children's learning and growth.

Another observation is that most research focuses on text, image, video analysis, and text generation, rather than image generation [16–18, 29]. This may be related to the previous fact that people typically use AI to replace adults' work with children while drawing pictures might not be the main part. It is important to address that, Generative Image Models (GIMs), a branch of generative AI technology designed to create images from natural language descriptions, have significant potential to contribute to special education and serious game design.

### 2.2 Opportunities that Generative Image Models Bring

In the field of autism education, image generation could offer tremendous opportunities for autistic children, especially in communication and social interaction. Many autistic children are visual thinkers. Dr. Temple Grandin [19–21], an autistic adult and advocate, wrote that many autistic individuals, including herself, think in pictures very efficiently [19]. Research also shows that some autistic children demonstrate high levels of visual-spatial skills [20] and visual memory [21]. These alternative strengths are sometimes revealed by young children with autism during the creative art-making process [22]. In these cases, GIMs can be an excellent tool for fostering visual expression and communication between autistic children with their peers, without being constrained by language and drawing skills.

In the context of "fair use" in education, AI-generated artwork can significantly accelerate game production and reduce labor costs. This enables educators and game designers with a forward-thinking vision to create without being limited by technical constraints. More importantly, AI could introduce new possibilities for game mechanics. Games with storytelling elements like Heavy Rain [23] and Detroit: Become Human [24] have fascinating storylines and visuals but still could only allow players to "choose" their path within pre-designed routes. With AI, players are allowed to "create" their own adventures. The capability for them to "create" the characters they are going to encounter, the tools that could help them solve problems, and the subsequent events in each playthrough will greatly increase the playability of the games.

## 3   Project Introduction

### 3.1   Research Question

How might we create an experience that fosters bonding among neurotypical and neurodivergent school-age children with the assistance of Generative AI?

## 3.2  Project Overview

This project is developing a hybrid learning experience designed to engage both autistic children and their neurotypical peers in a two-phase interactive process - creating a digital picture book online and telling the story together in person. The story setting is inspired by the well-known "Jack and Jill" rhyme, a narrative that depicts two children embarking on an adventure and experiencing the world together without relying on verbal communication. This story resonates with the concept of equal and diverse connections— a crucial idea to be emphasized when supporting autistic children in social scenarios. In the game, players first create and name their avatars, and start their adventure of fetching water by making a series of choices. The intention is to relate simple visual choices with realistic consequences, encouraging children to engage deeply with the narrative they're crafting. Some of the decisions will further impact the narrative's outcome, such as the location of the water source. All their decisions will be recorded and result in a digital storybook with a cover that showcases their avatars and includes their names as the title.

Upon completing the picture book activity, the digital book will be printed and sent to each child's home or classroom if they are classmates. This not only offers the children a tangible keepsake of their joint effort but also serves as a tool or 'seed' for further creative interaction. They can tell and even perform the story together under the guidance of the instructor, enhancing their collaborative experience.

## 3.3  Design Principles

This story-creating environment is built on three fundamental design principles.

- Firstly, it forgoes text and judgment. This work aims to create a space free from social pressure or fear of failure, enabling autistic children to express themselves and connect with others confidently.
- Secondly, it offers a visual experience that extends beyond mere images. With art elements generated by GIMs representing various objects, weather, actions, intentions, and sensations, players are invited to explore the implications of each visual choice and consider how it influences the story, for example, they choose the sky color to indicate the time of day, select characters to encounter (Fig. 1), and employ visual symbols in the dialogue box that influence the storyline.
- Thirdly, it is all about creation. Instead of "choosing" their adventure, players are "creating" their adventure. While initially, players may seem to be able to pick from pre-generated options as the game develops, it's anticipated to evolve, allowing AI to assist children directly, which will expand the possibilities for children to freely create their journeys, transforming the game into a genuinely open-ended experience.

## 3.4  Making All the Art Elements Using Generative AI

Utilizing generative AI for artwork creation has significantly enriched the game development process and has brought satisfying results. DALL·E [25], Midjourney [26], and Adobe Photoshop (Beta) [27] have been instrumental in producing the initial image prototypes and will further support players in generating unique story elements each time

**Fig. 1.** Players choose which character to encounter

they play. Additionally, the author has engaged with ChatGPT [28] for creative insights on narrative development and intends to further leverage its capabilities to assist with the game's coding phase.

### 3.5 Data Collection

Qualitative data will be collected from three sources: on-site observations of players' behavior while interacting with the game, the digital picture books completed by users online, and the observations or recordings of their telling the story they made together (Fig. 2), Additionally, follow-up questionnaires will be given to the caregivers of the participating children. These questionnaires will inquire about the children's experiences post-game, including questions like how many times they shared their picture book with others, how often they mentioned this experience, and whether they expressed a desire to design another book using this game. This approach aims to understand the children's experiences comprehensively, facilitating a thorough evaluation of the project. This evaluation is crucial for the project's future refinement.

## 4   Discussion

While it is designed for autistic children with social challenges, it can also benefit other neurodivergent children who encounter the same issue, as well as neurotypical children who are more inclined towards artistic creation compared to engaging in conventional social settings with their peers. Besides, the process collects extensive data

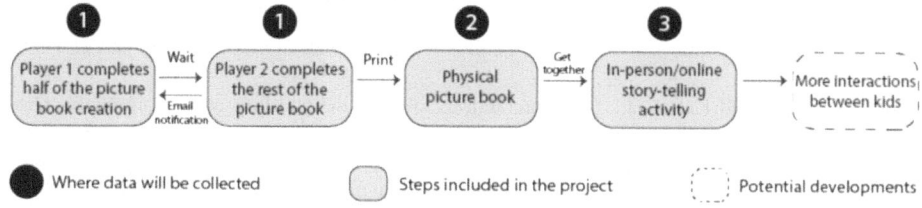

**Fig. 2.** The process of the project

about children's decision-making during gaming, which can potentially help scholars in neuroscience, education, and psychology to gain insight into the children's behaviors such as self-expression, creativity, learning, and social interactions.

Currently, this project is in the prototype stage, with all art elements pre-generated during the game design and then offered as choices to players. This game will keep evolving and explore the possibility of enabling children to interact directly with AI to generate their desired stories. This approach requires not only technical optimization but also careful consideration of safety. It is hoped that this work will spark further discussions about the application and safety of Generative Image Models (GIMs), aiding in its' development.

## 5 Conclusion

This paper identifies the potential of Game-Informed Methods (GIMs) in game design for autism education and proposes a prototype of a digital picture book-making game using GIMs. This game assists in creating a hybrid, structured, and collaborative learning experience between autistic children and their non-autistic peers. The digital platform of this game serves as a space that fosters their cocreation. A picture book they both contribute to allows autistic children to comfortably enter social interactions with peers. This innovative game-based approach fosters neurodiverse communication by providing a structured yet flexible environment where autistic children can creatively build peer relationships through creating and telling a story together.

**Acknowledgments.** The author would like to thank Juan Salamanca Garcia and Peizhen Wu for their valuable assistance in refining the language and improving the clarity of this paper.

## References

1. Gifford-Smith, M., Brownell, C.: Childhood peer relationships: social acceptance, friendships, and peer networks. J. Sch. Psychol. **41**, 235–284 (2003)
2. Laird, R., Pettit, G., Mize, J., Brown, E., Lindsey, E.: Mother–child conversations about peers: contributions to competence. Fam. Relat. **43**, 425 (1994)
3. Price, J., Brew, V.: Peer relationships of foster children: developmental and mental health service implications. J. Appl. Dev. Psychol. **19**, 199–218 (1998)

4. Rodda, A., Estes, A.: Beyond Social Skills: Supporting Peer relationships and friendships for school-aged children with autism spectrum disorder. Semin. Speech Lang. **39**, 178–194 (2018)
5. Lord, C., Magill-Evans, J.: Peer interactions of autistic children and adolescents. Dev. Psychopathol. **7**, 611–626 (1995)
6. Klin, A.: Young autistic children's listening preferences in regard to speech: a possible characterization of the symptom of social withdrawal. J. Autism Dev. Disord. **21**, 29–42 (1991)
7. Ghanouni, P., Jarus, T., Zwicker, J., Lucyshyn, J., Chauhan, S., Moir, C.: Perceived barriers and existing challenges in participation of children with autism spectrum disorders: 'he did not understand and no one else seemed to understand him'. J. Autism Dev. Disord. **49** (2019)
8. Ghanouni, P., Jarus, T., Zwicker, J.G., Lucyshyn, J., Chauhan, S., Moir, C.: Perceived barriers and existing challenges in participation of children with autism spectrum disorders: 'he did not understand and no one else seemed to understand him.' J. Autism Dev. Disord. **49**(8), 3136–3145 (2019)
9. Aherne, D.: The Pocket Guide to Neurodiversity. Jessica Kingsley Publishers (2023)
10. Rodda, A., Estes, A.: Beyond social skills: supporting peer relationships and friendships for school-aged children with autism spectrum disorder. Semin. Speech Lang. **39**, 178–194 (2018)
11. Mazurek, M.O., Engelhardt, C.R.: Video game use and problem behaviors in boys with autism spectrum disorders. Res. Autism Spectr. Disord. **7**(2), 316–324 (2013)
12. National Autistic Society: Stories from the Spectrum – Barrington. https://www.autism.org.uk/advice-and-guidance/stories/stories-from-the-spectrum-barrington. Last Accessed 22 May 2024
13. Ruiz-Rojas, L.I., Acosta-Vargas, P., De-Moreta-Llovet, J., Gonzalez-Rodriguez, M.: Empowering education with generative artificial intelligence tools: approach with an instructional design matrix. Sustainability **15**(15), 11524 (2023)
14. Nguyen, N.D.: Exploring the role of AI in education. Lond. J. Soc. Sci. (2023)
15. Baidoo-Anu, D., Owusu Ansah, L.: Education in the era of generative Artificial Intelligence (AI): understanding the potential benefits of ChatGPT in promoting teaching and learning. SSRN Electron. J. **7**(1), 52–62 (2023)
16. National AI Institute for Exceptional Education. Available at https://www.buffalo.edu/ai4exceptionaled.html. Last Accessed 25 Mar 2024
17. Amiri, A.M., et al.: WearSense: detecting autism stereotypic behaviors through smartwatches. Healthcare (Basel) **5**(1), 11 (2017)
18. Film Detective: Helping kids learn to decode social scenarios through a film-based game. Available at https://my.vanderbilt.edu/filmdetective/. Last Accessed 25 Mar 2024
19. Colorado State University: Grandin: The World Needs All Kinds of Minds, https://source.colostate.edu/grandin-the-world-needs-all-kinds-of-minds/. Last Accessed 22 May 2024
20. Wing, L.: The Autistic Spectrum: A Parent's Guide to Understanding and Helping Your Child. Ulysses Press, Berkeley, CA (2001)
21. Sacks, O.: An Anthropologist on Mars. Vintage Books, New York (1995)
22. Park, C.C.: Exiting Nirvana: A Daughter's Life with Autism. Back Bay Books, New York (2001)
23. Wikipedia: Heavy Rain. https://en.wikipedia.org/wiki/Heavy_Rain. Last Accessed 22 May 2024
24. Wikipedia: Detroit: Become Human. https://en.wikipedia.org/wiki/Detroit:_Become_Human. Last Accessed 22 May 2024
25. OpenAI: DALL-E 2. Available at https://openai.com/index/dall-e-2/. Last Accessed 20 July 2024

26. Midjourney: Home. Available at https://www.midjourney.com/home. Last Accessed 20 July 2024

27. Adobe: Photoshop Beta Community. Available at: https://community.adobe.com/t5/pho toshop-beta/ct-p/ct-photoshop-beta?page=1&sort=latest_replies&lang=all&tabid=all. Last Accessed 20 July 2024

28. OpenAI: ChatGPT. Available at https://openai.com/chatgpt/. Last Accessed 20 July 2024

# Eye Tracking in VR: A Case Study of "*Missing*"

Sercan Şengün[✉] [iD]

University of Central Florida, Orlando, FL 32816-1344, USA
sercan.sengun@ucf.edu

**Abstract.** In this paper, we present the highlights of our learnings with eye tracking in VR and their implementation in "*Missing*," a missing person thriller with a mental health message at its core, available in the Meta Store. By synthesizing current research and sharing insights gained from our practical implementations in the "*Missing*" project, this paper aims to provide a comprehensive overview of the opportunities and considerations surrounding eye tracking in VR design.

**Keywords:** Eye tracking · Virtual reality · VR · Serious games · Mental health

## 1 Introduction

Manipulation within a virtual environment (VE) involves the fundamental actions required to interact with virtual objects. These actions include core tasks such as pointing at, selecting, positioning, rotating, and scaling objects within the VE. From identifying objects of interest to adjusting their placement and modifying their size, these tasks form the basis of effective virtual element manipulation.

Eye gaze technology can significantly enhance selection processes in VEs, particularly for pointing and confirming choices [1]. Users can use their eye gaze to accurately indicate objects of interest, utilizing its precision and intuitive nature for efficient interactions. Once an object is targeted, selection can be confirmed through methods like dwell time or bi-modal mechanisms, ensuring precise and intentional choices [2]. From the lens of serious games, by incorporating eye gaze into the selection process, VEs can provide users with a more seamless and intuitive way to interact with digital elements, improving both usability and immersion, as well as ways to measure the intent and interests of users for researchers.

In "*Missing*" (see Fig. 1), users mobilize eye-tracking to search *Eleanor Parker*'s home for clues about what happened to her. As the users explore the surroundings, the environment responds to their gaze, and they begin to piece together a thought-provoking picture. The experience aims to cultivate empathy and understanding for mental health issues through a uniquely immersive, first-person narrative. As the protagonist of this narrative, guided by their inner thoughts, the users step into the shoes of someone living with a life-altering condition. The published version of this project stands as a work-in-progress, aiming to evolve with insights from leading scientists and medical professionals to deepen its impact.

J. L. Plass and X. Ochoa (Eds.): JCSG 2024, LNCS 15259, pp. 408–413, 2025.
https://doi.org/10.1007/978-3-031-74138-8_31

**Fig. 1.** *"Missing"* is available to download from the Meta Store: https://www.meta.com/en-gb/experiences/7078135438974343/.

## 2 Background Review

### 2.1 Gaze Tracking

Our eyes function effortlessly, naturally drawn to points of interest without the need for training. This inherent capability creates a clear control-display link within the brain. Consequently, a person's gaze reliably reflects their attention and intention, acting as a non-invasive indicator of focus [3]. Eyes not only contextualize our actions but also synchronize smoothly with hand movements. This coordination highlights the effectiveness of using eye movements as a rich source of information.

However, tracking the gaze using video technology presents some problems. First, eye movements are noisy, and they consist of both fixations and saccades. Fixations are stable gazes, while saccades are rapid transitions between different points. In the 1960s, Yarbus [3] discovered that even when individuals attempt smooth tracking, their eye movements still involve a mix of fixations and saccades, such as when following geometrical shapes. Second, eye movements behaviors can change according to the user and need to be calibrated [4]. For precise targets, this can result in a zone of uncertainty. Calibration is sometimes required just once, but accuracy may diminish over time due to changes in eye conditions and posture. Third, eyes are highly sensitive to visual changes, automatically directing attention to such changes. When providing feedback, it is essential to be cautious, as prominent feedback can unintentionally redirect users' gaze unless it is directly on the selected object.

Most of these problems converge on the concept of the Midas Touch Problem identified by Velichkovsky in 1997 [5]. Unlike the deliberate actions of controller inputs (such as mouse, keyboard, or VR controllers), eye movements are constantly active and serve visual perception. It is crucial to distinguish between eye movements intended for visual search and those for actions like pointing or selecting. The problem highlights the difficulty in differentiating unintentional gazes from deliberate actions, even with precise eye tracking. This challenge emphasizes the need for careful interaction design to minimize false activations and accurately interpret user intentions.

Finally, eye tracking is not accessible to a certain population of users due to vision problems such as low vision, as well as cognitive issues [6]. To address various accessibility needs, developers can offer alternatives to eye tracking or allow users to designate a primary eye for tracking. However, on the other hand, responsive user interfaces that track eye-gaze could empower users to make selections with limited or no physical interaction, enhancing other forms of accessibility and usability.

## 2.2  Serious Games

Serious games, a concept that emerged in the early 2000s, refer to games designed for purposes beyond mere entertainment [7]. They leverage the engaging and interactive nature of gaming to achieve specific educational, training, health, or social objectives. Unlike traditional games, serious games focus on delivering meaningful content and experiences that foster learning, skill development, or behavior change [8].

The roots of serious games can be traced back to military and educational simulations [9]. The military, for example, has used war games and simulations for training purposes for decades. However, an expanding application of serious games are present in industries such as education, healthcare, and corporate training among others. In the educational scene (see [10] for a meta-analysis), serious games are utilized to teach complex subjects in an interactive and engaging manner. They provide a hands-on learning experience, allowing students to experiment, make decisions, and see the consequences of their actions in a risk-free environment. In healthcare (see [11] for a systematic review), serious games are used for both patient education and professional training. For patients, these games can simulate disease management scenarios, helping them understand their condition and treatment better. For healthcare professionals, serious games provide a safe environment to practice surgical procedures, patient interactions, and emergency responses without the risk of real-world consequences. Finally, in corporate training (see [12] for a literature review), serious games are employed to enhance employee skills, from customer service to leadership training. These games can create immersive scenarios that mimic real-world challenges, allowing employees to practice and refine their skills.

Overall, serious games represent a powerful tool for learning and development across various fields. Their ability to combine engagement with practical application makes them an effective strategy for achieving educational, professional, and personal growth objectives. As technology continues to advance, the potential and scope of serious games are likely to expand further, offering even more innovative solutions for complex challenges.

# 3   Findings and Discussions

In this section we discuss our findings within the design and playtesting processes of building the app. Some of the findings may require larger scale user studies to verify our learnings which is our future direction.

## 3.1   User Assessment

Monitoring user behavior during assessments can range from basic remote evaluations to advanced setups involving physiological tracking equipment. Monitoring is also one of the cornerstones for assessing serious game design, especially to establish effect. Eye-tracking is a dependable indicator of attention, revealing where users focus during assessments and how they interpret task requirements. By analyzing eye-tracking data, developers can infer users' thought processes, even if the users themselves cannot remember them after completing the task. This ability improves assessment techniques, offering insights into user behavior and performance. Additionally, analyzing eye-tracking data enables developers to address key questions such as where users encounter difficulties, their anticipated next steps, which elements capture their attention, and what they might miss. This in-depth insight facilitates the refinement and optimization of applications, ensuring their effectiveness and improving the overall user experience.

## 3.2   Targeted Interactions

Particularly for virtual environments that use eye tracking, developers can create systems where objects within the user's line of sight become interactive, while those outside this area are automatically locked. This prevents unintended actions and ensures that users can only interact with objects they are directly looking at.

## 3.3   Soft Skills and Mechanical Operations Training

Skills training through serious games often requires a showing of effectiveness. VR offers a unique opportunity to transform these training approaches, with eye-tracking technology further enhancing their impact. For example, consider the subtle aspects of human interaction in situations like counseling, where eye contact duration and demeanor play crucial roles. VR simulations augmented with eye-tracking capabilities provide immersive experiences that emphasize these nuances, enabling users to understand the significance of their behavior firsthand. Features such as managing eye contact and interpreting contextual clues within scenes can instill a sense of relevance and accountability. Furthermore, eye-tracking data allows identifying individual strengths and areas needing improvement, ultimately increasing the effectiveness of soft skills training in VR environments.

In mechanical operations training, effective monitoring is crucial for maintaining procedural accuracy and safety. Therefore, it's essential to train users not only in performing tasks but also in monitoring critical aspects of these procedures. For example, tasks such as checking mirrors before driving or ensuring system pressure levels are within specified parameters require diligent monitoring for successful execution. Integrating eye-tracking technology can improve training methodologies by making monitoring tasks a key component of assessment criteria. This approach requires users to actively locate and observe components, with success depending on their ability to sustain focus and attention. Eye-tracking capabilities enable real-time monitoring and reinforce observational skills, ultimately enhancing user responsiveness and developing the muscle memory necessary for optimal performance.

### 3.4   User Interface and Experience

Given that users often look around a VR environment out of curiosity or for exploration, it's crucial to distinguish between intentional gaze interactions and casual glances, allowing time for thorough examination of each room and mystery. We minimized the use of traditional UI, relying instead on eye gaze mechanics with a semi-diegetic approach. In our experimentation, a smaller reticle made navigation more difficult due to the eyes' natural, constant movement, resulting in a shaky experience and a double reticle effect. A larger reticle provided more stability, enabling smoother and more controlled movements. However, in this project, it also diverted users' attention from the main objective, hindering task completion. Consequently, we implemented an eye gaze system that removed the need for a reticle, significantly enhancing the user experience.

Our experience indicates that larger objects facilitate easier and more intuitive eye-gaze interactions. Object size is particularly important for interactions from a distance, where larger objects ensure effortless engagement [13]. We learned that incorporating a subtle glistening effect to remind users of interactable objects after a period of inactivity effectively draws their attention back to the task. Prolonged use of eye-tracking in VR can cause strain and fatigue if the content requires constant focus or rapid eye movements [14]. We limited interactions in each section to keep users engaged and interested without causing boredom. Designated rest zones between eye-gaze-triggered objects allowed users to pause and explore without triggering interactions. Incorporating instant visual feedback, audio cues, and haptic responses supported a semi-diegetic approach, minimizing the need for traditional UI.

### 3.5   Environment Design

We highlight several learnings while designing an environment for gaze tracking. First, the presence of transparent objects or items with gaps can significantly impact gaze tracking, potentially leading to undesirable consequences. Second, interpreting prolonged focus on distant objects poses challenges. To address this, we organized gaze interactions into scenes based on distance, maintaining a consistent separation between all gaze-interactable objects. Third, eye-tracking magnetism serves as a method to address inaccuracies by prioritizing objects within the focal area. Strategic object placement and magnetism colliders effectively mitigate this issue. Fourth, while auditory cues can direct visual attention to relevant objects, they also pose challenges in discerning user intent. For instance, determining whether a user is looking at a clock due to interest or merely responding to its ticking sound can be problematic. Fifth, excessive head turning can disrupt gaze accuracy. Minimizing the need for large turning angles to access interactable items offers a potential solution to this issue. Finally, certain color schemes may induce pupillary unrest and high-density saccades. Users tend to focus on red and purple areas initially but prefer resting their eyes on yellow and orange areas as they continue exploring the scene. Overall, overly crowded or complex environments can hinder eye tracking. Incorporating windows and light sources can create the illusion of fullness without compromising eye-tracking performance.

In conclusion, our practical implementation of eye tracking in the serious game *"Missing"* has yielded valuable insights into design and user interaction. By leveraging eye-tracking technology, serious games can employ nuanced design patterns and behaviors, paving the way for enhanced outcomes.

**Acknowledgments & Disclosure of Interests.** We acknowledge the funding and the efforts of the team members of Born Immersive UK in building and publishing *"Missing."* Some of these findings have also been published as a public white paper by the company in addition to others[1].

# References

1. Adhanom, I.B., MacNeilage, P., Folmer, E.: Eye tracking in virtual reality: a broad review of applications and challenges. Virtual Reality **27**(2), 1481–1505 (2023)
2. Bowman, D.A., Kruijff, E., LaViola, J.J., Poupyrev, I.: An introduction to 3-D user interface design. Presence **10**(1), 96–108 (2001)
3. Yarbus, A.L.: Eye movements and vision. Springer (2013)
4. Nyström, M., Andersson, R., Holmqvist, K., Van De Weijer, J.: The influence of calibration method and eye physiology on eyetracking data quality. Behav. Res. Methods **45**, 272–288 (2013)
5. Velichkovsky, B., Sprenger, A., Unema, P.: Towards gaze-mediated interaction: collecting solutions of the "Midas touch problem." In: Proceedings of IFIP TC13 International Conference on Human-Computer Interaction, pp. 509–516. Springer, US (1997)
6. Molina, A.I., Arroyo, Y., Lacave C., Redondo, M.A., Bravo, C., Ortega, M.: Eye tracking-based evaluation of accessible and usable interactive systems: tool set of guidelines and methodological issues. In: Universal Access in the Information Society, pp. 1–24 (2024)
7. Susi, T., Johannesson, M., Backlund, P.: Serious Games: An Overview (2007)
8. Laamarti, F., Eid, M., El Saddik, A.: An overview of serious games. Int. J. Comput. Games Technol. **1**, 358152 (2014)
9. Wilkinson, P.: A brief history of serious games. In: Proceedings of the Entertainment Computing and Serious Games International Seminar, pp. 5–10. Springer (2016)
10. Zhonggen, Y.: A meta-analysis of use of serious games in education over a decade. Int. J. Comput. Games Technol. (2019)
11. Wang, R., DeMaria, Jr. S., Goldberg, A., Katz, D.: A systematic review of serious games in training health care professionals. Simul. Healthc. **11**(1), 41–51 (2016)
12. Larson, K.: Serious games and gamification in the corporate training environment: a literature review. TechTrends **64**(2), 319–328 (2020)
13. Microsoft Learn. https://learn.microsoft.com/en-us/windows/mixed-reality/design/gaze-and-commit-head. Last Accessed 27 May 2024
14. Lambooji, M., Ijsselstein, W., Fortuin, M., Heynderickx, I.: Visual discomfort and visual fatigue of stereoscopic displays: a review. J. Imaging Sci. Technol. **53**(5), 30201 (2009)

---

[1] https://www.born.net/eye-tracking-in-vr.

# Deceptive Algorithms in Massive Multiplayer Online Role Playing Games (MMOs)

Jason Starace$^{(\boxtimes)}$ ⓘ, Anmol Singh ⓘ, and Terence Soule ⓘ

University of Idaho, Moscow, ID 83844, USA
star0874@vandals.uidaho.edu ,
https://www.uidaho.edu/engr/departments/cs

**Abstract.** This paper proposes using a text-based dungeon crawler adventure as a case study to explore the methods to implement deception in video games. The study proposes a framework for integrating deception into gameplay, leveraging the alignment system from Dungeons and Dragons to define character behavior and motivation. The proposed approach would create an environment that allows researchers to observe AI-controlled characters in a dynamically generated environment that leverages LLMs. The framework is designed to address the issue of monotony in current games by training a deceptive agent, or villain, to recognize and exploit player beliefs and intentions. This adds complexity and depth to the gaming experience, making it more engaging and dynamic. Future research directions include integrating human players into the game environment and transitioning to 3-D gaming platforms, potentially leading to more immersive experiences, particularly in massive multiplayer online role-playing games (MMORPGs). By exploring the intersection of AI, deception, and gaming, this paper contributes to the evolving interactive entertainment landscape, paving the way for more sophisticated and captivating game experiences.

**Keywords:** Deception · Role Playing · Video Game

## 1 Introduction

The use of Artificial Intelligence (AI) in video games can be traced back to 1940 when Edward U. Condon [6] designed a computer game for the Westinghouse pavilion at the World's Fair. The Nimatron allowed patrons of the World's Fair a chance to play Nim against a machine. The computer would win 90% of the matches it played, but for those lucky few that did win, they would receive a token with the words "Nim Champ". Despite the early inclusion of AI in video games, there was little progress until the late 1980s when video games gained popularity.

As popularity grew, we saw the use of AI increase as well. AI has since been implemented into video games in many different ways, from dynamically

J. L. Plass and X. Ochoa (Eds.): JCSG 2024, LNCS 15259, pp. 414–420, 2025.
https://doi.org/10.1007/978-3-031-74138-8_32

adjusting the difficulty based on the player's demonstrated abilities to controlling the movement and responsiveness of non-playing characters in open-world games.

With the introduction of video game titles like 'AmongUs,' which encourage deception among the players to win, we have also observed increased research on deception in video games. We generalize the research into two methods: deception in dialogue and deception in asymmetric games based on actions taken. For example, in the work presented by Steputtis et al., they evaluate the detection of deception in dialogues in games where the good players must determine who the evil players are [1]. While in other works, like those performed by Sasahara, H. [2] and Li, L. & Shamma, J. [3], the research is performed using asymmetric signaling games in which deception can occur by both players, where:

1. The defender deceives attackers to believe they have successfully infiltrated the network (honeypot).
2. The attacker deceives defenders into believing they are an agent that should be allowed in the network.

In this work, we propose an environment that not only builds on the widely used and accepted alignment system created by Gary Gygax [5] for Dungeons & Dragons but introduces unique customizable motivations that help define an LLM-controlled player. This environment would be used to create and train a deceptive algorithm that leverages inverse reinforcement learning to determine the player's belief system and motivations. Based on that determination, the algorithm will identify opportunities for deception and which action would provide the highest chance of success in deceiving the player. In the next section, we will define deception and the player's attributes that the deceptive algorithm will recognize.

## 2   Laying the Foundation

Deception as formalized by Ward, F. et al. [8] is *"an agent S deceives another agent T if S intentionally causes T to believe $\phi$, where $\phi$ is false and S does not believe that $\phi$ is true"*. Ward et al. state in their work that the definition 'requires notions of intent and belief,' which is evident. With our proposed work, we do not intend to identify that *Agent T* maintains a specific belief and that *Agent S* intentionally tries to deceive *Agent T* into believing something else.

Instead, we intend to implement an inverse reinforcement learning algorithm to determine *Agent T's* belief system (alignment) and motivations. The alignments we will utilize are those available in the tabletop roleplaying game Dungeons & Dragons. These alignments were created in 1974 by Gary Gygax [5] and are widely accepted in the gaming community and considered 'game-ready.' In early testing, the alignments can be used by an LLM to provide the foundation needed to make decisions and navigate the dynamic environment; this is discussed more in Sect. 4.

The motivations defined below represent the *Agent T's* intent or goals (motivation). These motivations will not only add a layer of complexity to the players but also allow for additional testing and verification of the performance of the deceptive algorithm (villain). The motivations oppose their pair, so the contrast in actions taken is more obvious to the observer.

1. Wealth: The player seeks out riches regardless of risk.
2. Safety: The player values safety and minimizes risk when possible.
3. Wanderlust: The player is a completionist and wants to explore as much as possible.
4. Speed: The player wants out of the level.

Section 4 proposes a new system for creating an LLM-controlled player. The alignments expressed in the Players Handbook (Table 1) provide a general behavior pattern and structure that can be mapped to actions taken in a video game; there is room for variation within each alignment; however, these will act as guardrails that can be used to provide adequate structure.

**Table 1.** Alignments provided in the Players Handbook for Dungeons & Dragons

| Lawful Good | Neutral Good | Chaotic Good |
|---|---|---|
| Lawful Neutral | True Neutral | Chaotic Neutral |
| Lawful Evil | Neutral Evil | Chaotic Evil |

By pairing each alignment with each motivation available, the LLM can implement 36 different character profiles.

$$9 \; alignments \; * \; 4 \; motivations = 36 \; character \; profiles \qquad (1)$$

## 3   Creating the World

With the definitions for the player's alignment and motivation explained in the previous section, we now focus on creating the world with which the player will interact. The world is a text-based dungeon crawler that includes an observer (villain), which is discussed in Sect. 5.

To avoid having the villain overfit due to a limited environment, we plan to use the requirements listed below to create dungeons randomly. These requirements provide a map that will randomly test the players' behavior and help prevent the villain from learning behaviors based on limited routes, encounters, and loot.

Map Requirements:

1. 5 x 5 grid
2. 1 room dedicated as an entrance.
3. 1 room dedicated as an exit.

4. Entrance and Exit may not be the same square or directly adjacent. This allows for three possible scenarios:
   - Entrance is in a corner: 22 valid squares for the exit.
   - Entrance is on the side: 21 valid squares for the exit.
   - Entrance is in the map's interior: 20 valid squares for the exit.
5. Half of the remaining 23 rooms will have loot randomly assigned.
6. 9 of the remaining 23 rooms will have a random encounter assigned

Based on the provided requirements, we can estimate the number of potential maps using the equation below.

$$[(4 * 22) + (12 * 21) + (9 * 20)] * \frac{23!}{11!(23-11)!} * \frac{23!}{9!(23-9)!} = 5.7455 * 10^{14} \quad (2)$$

An example map generated with these requirements would force the player to have to navigate the map through at least one square (see Fig. 1)

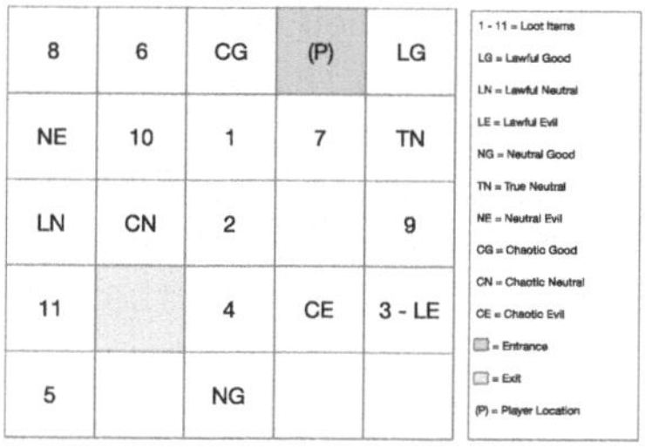
8
6
CG
(P)
LG
NE
10
1
7
TN
LN
CN
2
9
11
4
CE
3 - LE
5
NG
1 - 11 = Loot Items
LG = Lawful Good
LN = Lawful Neutral
LE = Lawful Evil
NG = Neutral Good
TN = True Neutral
NE = Neutral Evil
CG = Chaotic Good
CN = Chaotic Neutral
CE = Chaotic Evil
= Entrance
= Exit
(P) = Player Location

**Fig. 1.** An example map generated with the requirements listed in Sect. 3. Loot represented by numbers indicates rooms that test the player's motivation, while the abbreviation for that alignment indicates rooms designed to test alignments.

With this, we have a controlled environment that we can use to validate the player's behavior and train a model to determine the player's alignment (belief) and motivation (intent). We can further build on this structure and incorporate an LLM to handle the player's actions and decisions, which will be covered in the next section.

## 4 Creating a Player

With a system designed to allow the creation of random maps, pathways, encounters, and loot, we turn to the creation of the players. At the end of the paper, we will discuss the future works and possibilities of validating our system with human players; however, for the work at hand, we will focus on creating a system that can validate functionality with computer-generated and controlled players. We have designed two separate prompts to be sent to the LLM via API.

1. **Initial Prompt:** This template provides the LLM with the player's alignment as it relates to Dungeons and Dragons, their motivation, and the definition of their motivation. It also provides the form in which responses should be made. These responses are formatted to be parsed and stored for review and implementation in the game world.
2. **Recurrent Prompt:** This template will provide the LLM with each room's description, the items visible in and from the room, and a description of the surrounding area.

Responses are received from the LLM and processed in the game. Checks are made, and responses are stored for fine-tuning the templates.

### 4.1   Validating Player Behavior

The dungeon's random creation allows different scenarios to be presented to the LLM-controlled player. Each room will be assigned points based on how a player of a given alignment and motivation will react when passing through it. As the player navigates the dungeon, their behavior and actions in each room are tracked. Based on their interactions in the rooms, the player is assigned points related to the decisions made. The point values are never made available to the player so that they do not bias decisions or unintentionally train the player to obtain a specific 'score'. We will then refine and tune the templates and prompts until the interactions from the LLM align with the expected point value for the path taken through the dungeon.

With a system that allows for the auto-creation and validation of players, we can now focus on the game's deception component. The following section will cover the proposed solution for creating the observer(villain), who will ultimately determine if deception is possible and, in future works, attempt to deceive the player.

## 5   Creating the Villain

The model of the 'villian' who deceives the player will be based on the work completed by Shi, J. et al. [4]. For the villain to deceive the player it must build a 'profile' for the player in multiple phases - described in further detail in this section.

### 5.1   Evaluating the Player

We intend to train the model in three phases:

1. Alignment recognition with no motivator.
2. Motivation recognition with no alignment.
3. Combined alignment and motivation.

During each phase, the maps will only be populated with the corresponding loot or encounter types. We are taking a phased approach to fine-tune the model as needed and ensure each component can be validated as a standalone item. Our target is a 95% confidence in each phase. As defined in Sect. 2, not only must *Agent T* have a belief system and motivation but *Agent S* must be able to recognize these and act on them, in which *Agent S* convinces *Agent T* to believe something is true that they previously believe was false.

# 6    Opportunity to Deceive

The previous section describes how the villain will learn enough about the player to identify opportunities to deceive them. Once the target confidence mentioned in Sect. 5.2 has been met, the model will be trained to identify the method of deception. As no framework is built into the system that allows a dialogue between the player and villain, the methods the villain can choose from are limited to changing the room's description, adding loot, or an encounter to a room that does not have one.

For example, extending a room's description to indicate someone needs help in a dangerous room so that a Lawful Good character motivated by Safety disregards their motivations for Safety and ventures into the room to assist. The output of each run-through by a player would consist of the actual player profile, the profile as determined by the villain, the original map with loot & encounters, and the map modified by the villain. They will be programmatically compared to determine the successful isolation of opportunities for deception.

# 7    Future Works

Having proven that a model can be trained to recognize a player's belief system and motivations and successfully create a plan to deceive, we will expand on the interactions between the player and the villain. This will be achieved by integrating an in-game chat, allowing the player to interact with the villain and ask clarification questions. With this integration, we can determine if the deception was successful.

# 8    Conclusion

In this paper, we define deception as it relates to a dungeon crawler text-based adventure game and provides the basis for inclusion in future MMORPGs. We have provided the groundwork necessary to create an environment that allows an LLM-controlled player to navigate a dungeon and be observed and acted on by a deceptive agent. Our initial testing shows promising results that support LLMs mimicking human behavior by adhering to the guidelines set by defined belief systems and motivations.

**Disclosure of Interests.** The authors have no competing interests to declare relevant to this article's content.

# References

1. Stepputtis, S., Campbell, J., Xie, Y., Qi, Z., Zhang, W., Wang, R., Rangreji, S., Lewis, M., Sycara, K.: Long-horizon dialogue understanding for role identification in the game of Avalon with large language models (2023). https://doi.org/10.48550/arXiv.2311.05720

2. Sasahara, H., Sandberg, H.: Epistemic signaling games for cyber deception with asymmetric recognition. IEEE Control. Syst. Lett. **6**, 854–859 (2022). DOhttps://doi.org/10.1109/LCSYS.2021.3087097

3. Li, L., Shamma, J.: Efficient strategy computation in zero-sum asymmetric repeated games. ArXiv Preprint ArXiv:1703.01952. (2017), https://doi.org/10.48550/arXiv.1703.01952

4. Shi, J., Xu, J., Yao, Y., Xu, B.: Concept learning through deep reinforcement learning with memory-augmented neural networks. Neural Netw. **110**, 47–54 (2019). https://www.sciencedirect.com/science/article/pii/S0893608018303137 https://doi.org/10.1016/j.neunet.2018.10.018

5. Gygax, G.: Players Handbook. TSR Games, pp. 33. U.S.A. (1980)

6. Betsy Golden Kellem: The Nimatron. https://daily.jstor.org/the-nimatron/. Last Accessed 14 Apr 2024

7. Shi, C., Han, S., Fu, J.: Quantitative Planning with Action Deception in Concurrent Stochastic Games. *ArXiv.* **abs/2301.01349** (2023), https://api.semanticscholar.org/CorpusID:255416270

8. Ward, F., Everitt, T., Belardinelli, F., Toni, F.: Honesty Is the Best Policy: Defining and Mitigating AI Deception. *ArXiv.* **abs/2312.01350** (2023), https://api.semanticscholar.org/CorpusID:259341530

# Gaming on the Brain: Considerations for Designing Brain-Computer Interface Driven Gameplay

David King[✉], Tim Marsh, and Claudio Pizzolato

Griffith University, Brisbane, QLD, Australia
david.king4@griffithuni.edu.au, {t.marsh,
c.pizzolato}@griffith.edu.au

**Abstract.** One of the primary goals of Human-Computer Interaction (HCI) in game design has been the close coupling of players with the digital game system and an increasingly popular approach towards this is Brain-Computer Interaction (BCI). Recent improvements made to electroencephalogram-based (EEG) BCI technology have made it more widely available to researchers, more accessible to target end-users, and more viable for gameplay. However, the research has been limited to one side of serious games—the experiential and simulated environments—there has been little research into gameplay mechanics driven serious games. In this paper, we explore potential avenues for BCI-driven game and serious games gameplay design and development, as well as examining potential issues, conflicts and shortcomings that might arise from utilising BCI. This work informs our ongoing research and development of serious games utilising BCI-driven gameplay and can generalise to the development of other BCI-based games and serious games.

**Keywords:** brain-computer interface · experience · design · design strategies · game design · gameplay mechanics · serious games · virtual reality · purpose

## 1 Introduction

Serious games are games, simulations, and experiential and experimental environments for purpose [1]. In general, there is limited work in serious games that integrate the BCI into game mechanics and gameplay. They simulate environments and objects, and use the BCI to change the environment, but not to engage in gameplay mechanics with loops of interactive play. So far, most of the research is concerned with the possibility of the player interacting with a virtual environment through a BCI, rather than the brain being the controller for gameplay. This makes the existing research a fantastic foundation for that next logical step – what if the brain were the controller? What sorts of game mechanics, challenges, and playstyles could evolve from moving from a simulated environment to a game environment? What sort of transfer of purpose could a serious game controlled directly by the players brain achieve? How do the current limitations of the technology

© The Author(s), under exclusive license to Springer Nature Switzerland AG 2025
J. L. Plass and X. Ochoa (Eds.): JCSG 2024, LNCS 15259, pp. 421–426, 2025.
https://doi.org/10.1007/978-3-031-74138-8_33

limit design? This paper will address these questions by using existing research into BCI driven games, as well as propose a plan to test BCI driven serious game designs in further research.

## 2 Existing Games and Serious Games BCI Literature

### 2.1 Existing Serious Games Research

Brain-computer interface (BCI) technology allows direct interaction with a computational device by recording and translating the user's brain activity in real time. Electroencephalographic (EEG) signals are the most common non-invasive source of brain signals in BCIs [2]. Major problems facing development of BCI-driven systems are the inherent variability of EEG signals, as well as issues of signal noise. This hampers reliable detection and translation of on-going EEG patterns into messages that can be deciphered by a digital system, leading to bandwidth issues, input lag, and inconsistent detection. This issue is compounded by the fact that no default mappings between a digital device and human brain exist, and users and the device must be trained and calibrated before use [3]. Even with calibration, there is no way to truly know that a user is thinking correctly – a game design might call for them to concentrate on moving their arms, with that movement being reflected in game, but after calibration a user could be thinking about any completely unrelated task. It is for these reasons and more that some researchers have argued that the technology is still not ready for general public [4] use.

There has been a lot of research in BCI application in experimental and serious games. Several common methods have also arisen within the research. One popular method is using the EEG based BCI to track attention and non-attention [5], particularly for use in educational or training games, as well as to treat Attention-Deficit Hyperactivity Disorder (ADHD) [5, 6], or for use in a meditation application [7]. Another popular method is to use the BCI to track reactions. This is commonly used in various therapeutic applications, such as exposure therapy [8], where a participant is subjected to the source of their fear, anxiety, or distress in a virtual environment and the BCI is used (among other tools) to track levels of distress and automatically modulate the environment [9] to avoid overwhelming the participant. This is a technique not unlike dynamic difficult adjustment, which attempts to dynamically produce an experience unique to each user by adjusting to their play, intending to keep engagement throughout [10], has also been tested when linked to BCI, using the players brain activity to modulate the environment [11]. Finally, there are medical studies that use the BCI to respond to a person imagining moving their body and mapping those thought patterns to movement of an external object – this could be a digital object [12], a wheelchair [13], or even flying a virtual drone [14, 15].

While a large proportion of BCI research does not address gameplay elements, there is still some research that does. In their paper for Progressive Training for Motor Imagery Brain-Computer Interfaces, Skola et al. [16] used a progressive training system, not unlike any other games challenge curves, to challenge their users to get better at triggering the BCI using the Motor Imaging technique (motor imaging is defined as the state in which representations of a specific motor act are actively visualised without any motor output [17]). They also used some gamification techniques, chiefly score tracking and high scores, to keep players motivated to match the increasing challenge of the game. In addition to the high scores, the Virtual Reality (VR) environment adds context and feedback to the player's activities, making it more immersive and adding embodiment to the gameplay (with their research suggesting that embodiment and immersion makes triggering Motor Imaging easier).

## 2.2 BCI Limitations

One of the issues in designing for BCI include the inherent variability in EEG signals [3] - that is that even the same user will not have identical EEG signal on a session-to-session basis, even for an identical thought, focus or mental imagery pattern. Small environmental changes, as well as internal changes in the body of the player can negatively impact the quality of signals [18]. This variability, combined with the high signal-noise ratio [18] and inherent EEG signal variability making trying to detect specific actions or intent quite difficult. If designers want to avoid a lengthy and complex set of training sessions for each user, they are limited to using the BCI in an on/off fashion, triggered by activity level. This reduction in mechanical and input complexity could mean that the BCI component must supplement other types of gameplay or act as a function that magnifies or enhances another type of gameplay. Additionally, the players emotional and mental state can impact the ability to get accurate readings [19]. This is leveraged by virtual environments designed for exposure therapy, as mentioned earlier in the paper, however, unlike some other issues challenging game design this could potentially guide gameplay too. Using it to interlace with gameplay beyond dynamic difficulty adjustment does present an additional design challenge.

## 3 BCI-Driven Design Considerations

With the limitations inherent in using a non-invasive EEG driven BCI, a designer must first identify if their game can support the creation and synchronising of individual profiles for each user. With the time, complexity, and cost of doing so, as well as the risk that on a gameplay session-to-session basis that the profiles might not work, this framework will assume that the design will use more generic profiles. This will limit the BCI input to a most two states – either an on/off mode or the left/right model utilised by Skola et al. [16].

Second, due to the need for the player to actively concentrate or clear their mind to activate and deactivate the BCI, there is a need to identify which parts of the system need to be transparent to the player to avoid distractions, and which benefit from and being visible and the focus of players attention. For positive transfer of purpose, the loops of serious gameplay should typically be visible and provide player experience, while additional and emerging input systems such as, gaze and eye tracking, hand tracking, and so on should typically be made intuitive and transparent. This is similar to work such as Bolter and Gromala's Windows and Mirrors [20], however, we argue that the optimum blend of transparency and visibility provide a sense of agency.

Finally, additional controls need to be decided on, if any. While there is an interesting minimalist design challenge in limiting the game to a single on/off [18] or left/right control [16] and nothing else, more complex designs can be achieved by supplementing the

BCI's on/off with either traditional controls (coming from a keyboard, mouse, control pad, or other input device) or less traditional controls like gaze based, view direction based, gyroscopic, or limb tracking. As with the above, this needs to be taken in consideration with the user base, their potential knowledge of game inputs and controllers (or lack thereof), and how distracting these additional inputs might be, making it harder to utilise and control the BCI.

## 4   Proposed Research and Testing

### 4.1   BCI Driven Movement – Exploration Challenge 1.

In this creative artefact test, the player will use the BCI to control their forward momentum, and steer by looking in the direction they want to travel through a virtual environment. The gameplay loop will be the exploration of a virtual area and completion of navigation and exploration challenges, tracked and ranked by time and accuracy. This gamification challenges them to develop improved control over the BCI activation over multiple sessions. It is theorised that a combination of rewarding improvement and the variety of scaled challenges combined with the relative simplicity of an on/off BCI trigger should both encourage and allow for increasing mastery of the BCI input. The sense of agency given by the control over their movement and freedom to explore at their own pace should empower the player to devise their own strategies for better time and efficiency and develop their BCI activation strategy at their own pace.

### 4.2   BCI Activation – Timing Challenge 1.

In this creative artefact test, the player will a simple gameplay loop based on the children's game Red Light, Green Light. The player is allowed to move forward at specific intervals only, with movement controlled by the BCI. Players will have their results recorded in terms of reaction time, accuracy during moving / not moving phases, and challenged to improve their results. It is theorised that this artefact will work as an excellent educational game for Artefact 4.1, as it will help players trigger the right mental state faster and more on demand.

### 4.3   BCI Activation – Distraction Challenge 1.

In this creative artefact test, the gameplay loop is that of an on-rails shooter. The player will score points for targets shot, modulated by time taken. Instead of controlling movement, the BCI will control the games delta time function – if the player is activating the BCI, time flows normally, if they are not, the game freezes. Over time the number of targets will ramp up, increasing the level of distraction. This deliberately contradicts a lot of established research stating that BCI driven games need to minimise distractions by seeking to test exactly how distracting a game can get, and how much it can challenge the player, before the player becomes unable to concentrate on activating the BCI. It is theorised that repeated plays, with gamified encouragement for their progress (such as progress meters, best times, and high scores), will result in the player overcoming these distractions and becoming more focused over time, which will translate into both better scores in previous tests and better abilities to focus through distractions in the day-to-day life.

## 5  Discussion and Future Work

It is critical that all the design considerations from 3 need to be made in the context of the game's purpose. Novel game mechanics and experimenting with emergent technology is exciting, but if it lowers the quality of a serious game's positive transfer of purpose to the player then it was better off not being utilised. Likewise, if a BCI game with simpler mechanics achieves its purpose better than one with more complex mechanics, then the simpler design should be utilised, or if a simpler game fails to deliver on the games purpose, then complexity must by necessity be added.

We propose to develop and test these BCI-driven minigames with a wide variety of people, especially potential use cases for a BCI-driven serious game, and from the results modulate the design considerations from 3 and begin to develop a design framework for BCI driven serious games, to enable serious games designers to better leverage the BCI technology without compromising on the gameplay loops of the transfer of purpose for their serious games. This framework will then be iterated upon with more creative artefacts designed using the framework, to refine it into something useful and valuable for all serious game designers and developers.

**Acknowledgements.** This research is part of the BioSpine research project, which was funded by the Motor Accident Insurance Commission (MAIC), Queensland, Australia.

## References

1. Marsh, T.: Serious games continuum: between games for purpose and experiential environments for purpose. Entertainment Comp. 2(2), 61–68 (2011)
2. Mason, S.G., Bashashati, A., Fatourechi, M., Navarro, K.F., Birch, G.E.: A comprehensive survey of brain interface technology designs. Ann. Biomed. Eng. **35**, 137–169 (2007)
3. Scherer, R., Friedrich, E. C., Allison, B., Pröll, M., Chung, M., Cheung, W., et al.: Non-invasive brain-computer interfaces: Enhanced gaming and robotic control. In: Advances in Computational Intelligence: 11th International Work-Conference on Artificial Neural Networks, IWANN 2011, Torremolinos-Málaga, Spain, June 8–10, 2011, Proceedings, Part I 11, pp. 362–369. Springer Berlin Heidelberg (2011)
4. Cattan, G.: The use of brain–computer interfaces in games is not ready for the general public. Front. Comp. Sci. **3**, 628773 (2021)
5. Delisle-Rodriguez, D., et al.: Multi-channel EEG-based BCI using regression and classification methods for attention training by serious game. Biomed. Signal Process. Control **85**, 104937 (2023)
6. Gevensleben, H., et al.: Distinct EEG effects related to neurofeedback training in children with ADHD: a randomized controlled trial. Int. J. Psychophysiol. **74**(2), 149–157 (2009)
7. He, Y., et al.: Effectiveness of a mindfulness meditation app based on an electroencephalography-based brain-computer interface in radiofrequency catheter ablation for patients with atrial fibrillation: pilot randomized controlled trial. JMIR Mhealth Uhealth **11**, e44855 (2023)

8. Bender, S.M., Broderick, M., Bender, S.M., Broderick, M.: Virtual reality exposure therapy. In: Virtual Realities: Case Studies in Immersion and Phenomenology, 77–107 (2021)

9. Trappey, A., Trappey, C.V., Chang, C.M., Kuo, R.R., Lin, A.P., Nieh, C.H.: Virtual reality exposure therapy for driving phobia disorder: system design and development. Appl. Sci. **10**(14), 4860 (2020)

10. Hunicke, R.: The case for dynamic difficulty adjustment in games. In: Proceedings of the 2005 ACM SIGCHI International Conference on Advances in computer entertainment technology, pp. 429–433 (2005)

11. Bjørner, T.: Using EEG data as dynamic difficulty adjustment in a serious game about the plastic pollution in the oceans. In: Proceedings of the 2023 ACM Conference on Information Technology for Social Good, pp. 6–15 (2023)

12. McFarland, D.J., Sarnacki, W.A., Wolpaw, J.R.: Electroencephalographic (EEG) control of three-dimensional movement. J. Neural Eng. **7**(3), 036007 (2010)

13. Rebsamen, B., et al.: A brain controlled wheelchair to navigate in familiar environments. IEEE Trans. Neural Syst. Rehabil. Eng. **18**(6), 590–598 (2010)

14. Doud, A.J., Lucas, J.P., Pisansky, M.T., He, B.: Continuous three-dimensional control of a virtual helicopter using a motor imagery based brain-computer interface. PLoS ONE **6**(10), e26322 (2011)

15. LaFleur, K., Cassady, K., Doud, A., Shades, K., Rogin, E., He, B.: Quadcopter control in three-dimensional space using a noninvasive motor imagery-based brain–computer interface. J. Neural Eng. **10**(4), 046003 (2013)

16. Škola, F., Tinková, S., Liarokapis, F.: Progressive training for motor imagery brain-computer interfaces using gamification and virtual reality embodiment. Front. Hum. Neurosci. **13**, 329 (2019)

17. Decety, J.: The neurophysiological basis of motor imagery. Behav. Brain Res. **77**(1–2), 45–52 (1996)

18. Khademi, Z., Ebrahimi, F., Kordy, H.M.: A review of critical challenges in MI-BCI: from conventional to deep learning methods. J. Neurosci. Methods **383**, 109736 (2023)

19. Saha, S., et al.: Progress in brain computer interface: challenges and opportunities. Front. Syst. Neurosci. **15**, 578875 (2021)

20. Gromala, D., Bolter, J.D.: Windows and mirrors: interaction design, digital art, and the myth of transparency (2003)

# Generative AI-Enhanced Chatbot Design for Constructionist Gaming

Gyuri Byun[1]([✉]) [ID], Jewoong Moon[2]([✉]) [ID], Chen Sun[3] [ID], and Arezoo Ghooreian[2] [ID]

[1] Seoul National University, Seoul 08826, South Korea
gl3013@snu.ac.kr
[2] The University of Alabama, Tuscaloosa, AL, USA
jmoon19@ua.edu
[3] The University of Manchester, Manchester, UK

**Abstract.** This study presents the development of AI tutors that support learners in constructionist gaming environments. AI tutor-learning support is designed to offer direct answers to learners' questions, while AI tutor-feedback aims to evaluate code scripts based on computational thinking concepts. The AI tutors were designed through in-context learning with background prompts, ensuring tailored support and targeted feedback. The work-in-progress paper highlights the features of AI tutors and how AI alignment and tuning techniques can provide individual learning support.

**Keywords:** Generative AI · Constructionist Gaming · Chatbot · Feedback · Learning Support

## 1 Introduction

Constructionist gaming [1] involves open-ended problems that encourage active exploration and knowledge construction. In particular, during asynchronous online learning, learners face more challenges [2]. Accordingly, learning support and feedback are pivotal in promoting student learning in ill-structured domains [3, 4] and design-based tasks, which involve complex and open-ended problems and students actively build their artifacts to solve problems [5]. Learning support provides resources, tools, and strategies to facilitate understanding, engagement, and progress [6], while corrective and explanatory feedback identify errors and explain reasoning [7]. Given the complexity of game design and CT literacy, AI-enhanced tutors are hence considered. AI-enhanced tutors should be designed to provide contextualized learning support and feedback that aligns with learning objectives. AI-enhanced tutors should provide contextualized learning support and feedback aligned with learning objectives to effectively support CT [8] and design-based learning [9]. Hooshyar et al. [10] developed an AI-based virtual tutor to support students in learning programming through a digital learning environment. In recent days, since the promise of generative AI (GenAI) has emerged, it can significantly advance existing AI approaches in tutor design for constructionist gaming environments. GenAI can enable more natural and engaging interactions between the AI tutor and learners

© The Author(s), under exclusive license to Springer Nature Switzerland AG 2025
J. L. Plass and X. Ochoa (Eds.): JCSG 2024, LNCS 15259, pp. 427–432, 2025.
https://doi.org/10.1007/978-3-031-74138-8_34

by leveraging its ability to generate human-like responses and adapt to the learner's individual needs and preferences. GenAI can generate tailored explanations, hints, and guidance that align with the learner's current understanding and learning goals. However, a challenge remains regarding ways to ensure the accuracy and coherence of the feedback generated by GenAI-enhanced tutor, while retaining its naturalness of messages. Consequently, our research questions are (1) What features of an AI tutor can support learners in constructionist gaming environments? (2) How can AI alignment and tuning techniques be leveraged to provide individual feedback and learning support within the context of constructionist gaming?

## 2 Method

### 2.1 Research Context

We conceptualized and developed AI tutors for asynchronous CT learning (i.e., constructionist gaming) for undergraduates who are enrolled in a teacher education program. We developed a Roblox-supported constructionist gaming training program, with the purpose to enhance pre-service teachers' literacy in CT and the efficacy of game design activities to develop students' CT. The current study focused on developing the first prototype of AI tutors that feature key functions and interface architecture. With purposeful sampling pre-service teachers enrolled in digital literacy courses, following case studies are considered to test the current versions of AI tutors.

The learning environment is structured as a 4-week summer course, with 1–2 weeks dedicated to asynchronous learning activities. Fifteen pre-service teachers, purposefully sampled from digital literacy courses, engage in game design (constructionist gaming) exercises expected to take 5–10 h. These exercises serve as course assignments, with the AI tutors providing feedback to support their learning paths. This approach allows us to test the current version of AI tutors in a real educational context, bridging the gap between theoretical design and practical application in CT education. The intended learning outcomes of the module is the mastery of fundamental CT concepts, all within the context of game design. Students were expected to progress through a series of increasingly complex Roblox game design challenges. For example, they might start by creating simple in-game objects and progress to designing complex game mechanics that require nested conditional statements and loops. The AI tutors are designed to guide students through this learning path by providing contextualized feedback at each stage. For instance, when a student struggles with implementing a particular game feature, the AI tutor might suggest breaking the problem down into smaller steps (decomposition) or identify similar patterns in previously completed tasks (pattern recognition). This scaffolded approach aims to not only teach CT skills but also demonstrate how these skills apply in real-world game design scenarios.

# 3  Findings

## 3.1  What Features of an AI Tutor Can Support Learners in Constructionist Gaming Environments?

AI tutors, which are integrated with GPT-4 via an api, have been developed to deliver both individual learning support and feedback with the following features [11]. First, the learning support should be provided by the AI tutors. Students require assistance in navigating the diverse inquiries and obstacles that instructors may not anticipate. They may require assistance with a variety of learning encounters, such as the operation of the game-making tool, mathematical knowledge, and idea generation. As a result, the researchers designed **AI tutor-learning support**. Integrating GPT-4 with **AI tutor-learning support** leveraged the adaptive and synchronous nature of the GPT-4 models. The learners can enter their questions or the challenges that they are encountering into the query box, and ask **AI tutor-learning support** for providing learning support. The assistance would be provided in the form of text-based replies shown in the output box (Fig. 1). Second, the corrective and explanatory feedback about the codescript of the learners should be provided by the AI tutors. In the asynchronous online learning context, the learners might find it hard to look for the proper assistant who can analyze and give comments with their products. Regarding this, the researchers designed **AI tutor-feedback**. GPT-4 again was utilized to provide accurate evaluation about the codescripts. The learners can enter their code along with a description of the purpose of the code, then they will receive feedback on their code scripting. The feedback is generated by incorporating a variety of CT concepts (e.g., Algorithm & procedures, and automation logic) and the pedagogical functions of the corrective and explanatory feedback. It is then displayed in the output box in a bullet-pointed format for comprehension (Fig. 1). We conducted a pilot study to evaluate the functionality of tutor chatbots. Usability test participants (n = 4) noted that the AI tutor-learning support feature provided relevant assistance. Also, they accurately generated a comprehensive analysis of codes.

## 3.2  How Can AI Alignment and Tuning Techniques Be Leveraged to Provide Individual Feedback and Learning Support Within the Context of Constructionist Gaming?

Both types of the AI tutors, **AI tutor-learning support** and **AI tutor-feedback**, were designed through in-context learning with several background prompts. Basically, the prompt structure involves the context of the situation—who the learners are, what kind of projects they are involved in, the learning objective of this project, and what kind of computer language and game-making platform they are using. The information is delivered to the GPT-4, the generative model that the researchers utilized for the AI tutor. It is formatted in a way that uses bullet points, in order to make the meaning of the information more clear, leading to the better quality of the outputs.

In addition, there were specialized prompts for each AI tutors according to its specific goals. The prompt for **AI tutor-learning support** clarifies learners' objectives when they seek help, as they may need assistance with generating ideas, finding solutions for challenges, or seeking for alternative solutions. Regarding this, the researchers included question clarification prompts to optimize the learning support. This open-ended app-roach enables learners to get the specific type of support they need at any given moment. Here is a part of the prompt for AI tutor-learning support;

> *Your role: A tutor helping a student who is learning how to build a game...*
>
> *Situation: Your student is using a plugin called ... Your student requests your assistance in exploring alternative approaches, generating ideas*

AI **tutor-learning support** system is designed to clarify the learner's objectives through prompts, ensuring that the provided support is tailored to their specific needs. This differs from traditional help systems that often provide generic or predetermined support materials, which may not always address the learner's unique requirements. By focusing on the learner's objectives, AI tutor-learning support can offer more individual and effective assistance. **AI tutor-feedback** employs a different approach by providing targeted feedback based on the learner's submitted code scripts. The feedback mechanism is designed to be either corrective or explanatory, depending on the identified gaps or misconceptions in the learner's understanding of computational thinking (CT) concepts. Corrective feedback is provided when the AI tutor detects errors or inconsistencies in the code, guiding the learner towards the correct implementation. Explanatory feedback, in contrast, is offered when the learner's code is correct but there are opportunities to deepen their understanding of CT concepts. This feedback mechanism differs from general help seeking as it focuses specifically on the learner's application of CT concepts within their code through the CT concepts [12] inserted in the prompt, rather than addressing a broader range of project-related issues. By requiring learners to input the purpose of their code, AI tutor-feedback can provide more accurate and relevant feedback that helps learners bridge the gap between theory and practice.

> *Your role: You are a tutor who gives feedback about the Roblox code ...*
>
> *Situation: A student is using a plugin called ... The students ask for corrective and explanatory feedback of their own code ...*
>
> *What to do: give them the corrective or explanatory feedback and suggestions based on the aspect of Algorithm & procedures, Automation logic ... purpose of the code: ... code to be analyzed: ...*

Figure 1 shows the interface and a sample query-output for AI tutor-learning support and AI tutor-feedback. Preliminary qualitative data from student reflections illustrates increased engagement, skill development in game design and coding, and improved problem-solving persistence, despite early challenges. Students reported applying CT concepts like decomposition and algorithms, and expressed increased self-efficacy.

## 4   Discussion and Limitations

AI-enhanced tutors in constructionist gaming environments can support learners' CT development and engagement during design-based learning by navigating ill-structured problems and promoting meaningful artifact construction. Furthermore, the structure of the prompt (mentioned in Sect. 3.2) can reduce the barriers to building and utilizing AI tutors for educators by providing the tuning techniques that can adapt the LLM matching to the context of each instructor. Although the present study can provide the features and tuning techniques that can be included in the design of generative AI-enhanced chatbot for constructionist gaming, there are some limitations of this study. First, this study only considers the case of a single query of the learners through in-context learning, not considering the chat histories of inquiries and feedback. Better personalization can be achieved by providing additional user information through the chat history. Second, although this study provided a case of constructionist gaming, this study did not address the approaches and potentials of extending the AI-enhanced chatbot in further contexts with ill-structured problems. Since constructionist gaming is one of the learning contexts that deals with ill-structured problems [13], discussions about those potentials should be made.

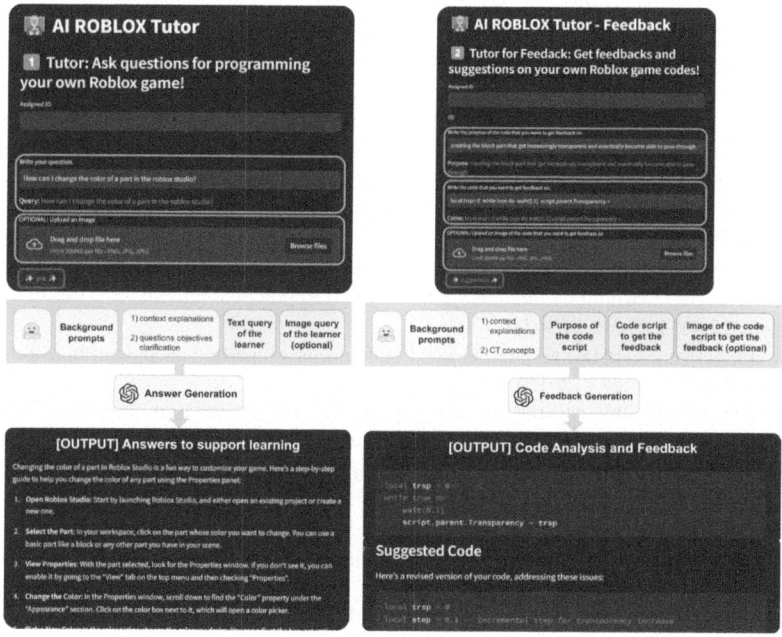

**Fig. 1.** A screen of AI tutor-learning support (*left*) and AI tutor-feedback (*right*).

Future research will aim at following areas. First, refining AI tutors for open-ended and dialogic interactions is essential. This refinement will involve developing more sophisticated natural language processing algorithms to better understand and respond to a wide range of student queries and comments. Key areas of improvement will include (1) context awareness: Enhancing the AI's ability to understand the broader context of a student's project and (2) guiding open-ended problem solving, which facilitate students' ill-structured problems, thereby encouraging creative thinking and multiple solution pathways. Second, integrating predictive models to create adaptive feedback systems for CT education will be considered. Among the models, specifically, Bayesian networks are probabilistic models that can represent relationships between different CT concepts. By analyzing probabilistic relationships, we could identify specific CT concepts a student struggles with, even if not immediately apparent from single task performance. This could inform targeted interventions, such as suggesting specific coding exercises to address conceptual gaps. Third, future research will design and integrate the efficacy measurement framework to rigorously evaluate the impact of AI tutors on CT development. It will involve a design-outcome matrix that maps specific AI tutors' interaction results with gained CT skills or efficacy improvements, enabling us to pinpoint which aspects of the system contribute most significantly to learning outcomes.

# References

1. Kafai, Y.B., Burke, Q.: Constructionist gaming: understanding the benefits of making games for learning. Education Psychol. **50**(4), 313–334 (2015)
2. Joksimović, S., Gašević, D., Kovanović, V., Riecke, B.E., Hatala, M.: Social presence in online discussions as a process predictor of academic performance. J. Comput. Assist. Learn. **31**(6), 638–654 (2015)
3. Jonassen, D.H.: Instructional design models for well-structured and III-structured problem-solving learning outcomes. Education Tech. Research Dev. **45**(1), 65–94 (1997)
4. Koehler, A.A., Vilarinho-Pereira, D.R.: Using social media affordances to support Ill-structured problem-solving skills: considering possibilities and challenges. Education Tech. Research Dev. **71**(2), 199–235 (2023)
5. Kolodner, J.L., Crismond, D., Fasse, B., Gray, J., Holbrook, J., Puntembakar, S.: Putting a student-centered learning by design™ curriculum into practice: lessons learned. J. Learning Sciences **12**(4), 495–548 (2003)
6. Plass, J.L., Homer, B.D., Kinzer, C.K.: Foundations of game-based learning. Education Psychol. **50**(4), 258–283 (2015)
7. Havnes, A., Smith, K., Dysthe, O., Ludvigsen, K.: Formative assessment and feedback: making learning visible. Stud. Education Eval. **38**(1), 21–27 (2012)
8. Grover, S., Pea, R.: Computational thinking in K–12: a review of the state of the field. Education Res. **42**(1), 38–43 (2013)
9. Gómez Puente, S.M., Van Eijck, M., Jochems, W.: A sampled literature review of design-based learning approaches: a search for key characteristics. Int. J. Technol. Des. Education **23**, 717–732 (2013)
10. Hooshyar, D., Ahmad, R. B., Yousefi, M., Fathi, M., Horng, S. J., & Lim, H.: SITS: a solution-based intelligent tutoring system for students' acquisition of problem-solving skills in computer programming. Innov. Education Teaching Int. **55**(3), 325–335 (2018)
11. OpenAI.: GPT-4 Technical Report (2023)
12. CSTA & ISTE: Computational Thinking in K-12 education—teacher resources, 2nd edition. CSTA & ISTE (2011)
13. Reynolds, R., Caperton, I.H.: Contrasts in student engagement, meaning-making, dislikes, and challenges in a discovery-based program of game design learning. Education Tech. Research Dev. **59**, 267–289 (2011)

# The INTENT Game: An Interactive Tool for Empathy in Neurotypicals

Varun Girdhar, Chao-Yang Tseng, Shiyu Wang, Ruoxi Yang, Zibo Ye,
Michael G. Christel[✉], Scott M. Stevens, and Morgan Evans

Carnegie Mellon University, Pittsburgh, PA 15213, USA
christel@cmu.edu, morganev@cs.cmu.edu

**Abstract.** This paper outlines the design and development of a browser-based game for neurotypicals to gain better understanding and empathy towards autistic people in the workplace. The game will be added to an arsenal of tools used by researchers planning to teach neurotypical people how to be better allies to their autistic colleagues.

**Keywords:** serious game · transformational game · autism spectrum disorder

## 1 Introduction

From a clinical point-of-view, autism spectrum disorder (ASD) is a neurodevelopmental disorder recognized as encompassing a wide variety of characteristics across a broad level of functioning [1]. Autistic people may be very dependent on routines and have restrictive or repetitive patterns of behavior, tend to have differences in communication and social interaction that may include conversation, non-verbal communication, and abilities related to maintaining and understanding relationships, and may find various environmental stimuli aversive due to hyperactive or hypoactive sensory processing. With a higher number of autistic individuals trying to enter the workforce, successfully employing autistic individuals is being addressed by society, for the benefit of the autistic worker, their colleagues, and the hiring organizations [2–4]. This paper documents the design and development of a browser-based game, INTENT, for neurotypicals to gain better understanding and empathy toward those with ASD in the workplace.

There have been, of course, games addressing autism. "Prism" was developed to help neurotypical children ages 8–10 empathize with their autistic classmates using a game plus workshop [5]. "Auti-sim" gives a first-person account of the sensory stimulation of an autistic child on the playground [6]. "Get the Job" provides a virtual reality experience of a day in an autistic person's life [7]. These three emphasize sensory overload simulation but not social/communication challenges of the workforce, while INTENT specifically focuses on establishing the context to be in a professional workplace. Findings of [7] suggest that the autism acceptance training program designed to increase autism knowledge and familiarity among neurotypical people holds promise for reducing explicit but not implicit biases toward autism. Hence, knowledge of ASD for neurotypicals will remain one of but not the only goal of the INTENT game.

© The Author(s), under exclusive license to Springer Nature Switzerland AG 2025
J. L. Plass and X. Ochoa (Eds.): JCSG 2024, LNCS 15259, pp. 433–439, 2025.
https://doi.org/10.1007/978-3-031-74138-8_35

With respect to workplace issues, communication is a central component that managers and autistic employees consistently indicated as an issue [4]. Different means of workplace interactions could increase the tension, ignore it, or overcome it. The game INTENT offers the player the ability to make consequential actions in an office setting with the chance to review them afterward.

## 2 Creating a Transformational Game

We used the Transformational Framework [8] in a one-semester (15 week) development timeline for five graduate students with two instructors. Weekly blog posts outline the progress of development on the project website, which also includes a playable link to the INTENT game [9]. We identified improvements in these four aspects as our transformational goals:

1. Knowledge: Knowledge of neurotypical people about autistic people
2. Disposition: Neurotypical person's feelings toward an autistic person
3. Behavior: How neurotypicals act when working with autistic people
4. Relationship: Bidirectional relationships between neurotypical people and autistic people

Throughout this paper, we make use of abbreviations NT for neurotypical people, and AP for autistic people. Interviews with AP gave insights into effective strategies for workplace inclusivity and helped with the authenticity of the episodes and narrative in our game. Subject matter experts (SMEs) and educational specialists, acknowledged at the end of the paper, kept the weekly iterations on track with respect to these goals.

**Knowledge** There are challenges that AP face in life and work, challenges that vary because ASD is a spectrum and each autistic individual will have their own abilities. In our game, we designed two autistic workers: Tony and Ash. Player interactions with the environment, other characters, and Tony and Ash directly move situations along, such as Tony's discomfort with overlapping environmental noises like conversation and a projector fan noise. Figure 1 illustrates two screen shots from the game where Tony puts on head phones and later makes the disclosure for his action.

Characters in the office are represented abstractly with different colors and accessories to distinguish them, and body and facial animations to communicate actions and messages. Tony, as one of the autistic characters, usually has a plain face that is not very expressive. Through iterations with both the autistic and neurotypical communities we refined to keep the facial animations authentic. Characters' colors were updated, avoiding stereotypes associated with the autism community. Animations such as "rub eyes" provide messages to the player about coworkers. The character art was intentionally simplified to not strongly signal gender, body shape, age, and other factors, keeping the distinction on AP and NT.

We designed three episodes each addressing different challenges. At the end of each episode, the learning panel displays (see Fig. 2), to recap the key moments and reinforce the interactive lesson.

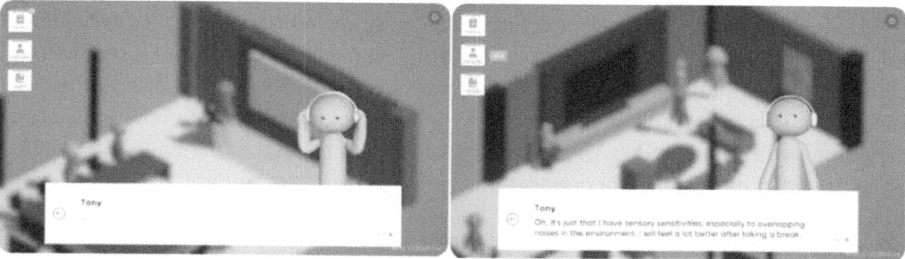

**Fig. 1.** An animation will have Tony putting on headphones at first, and then making a disclosure to the player about a need to deal with aural sensitivity.

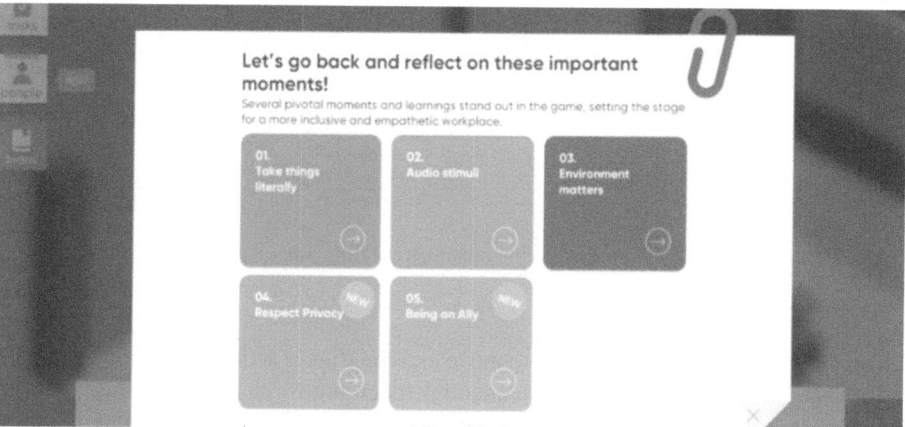

**Fig. 2.** Learning Panel to reinforce an episode's lesson.

**Disposition** We aimed to highlight AP's professional expertise and emphasize they are not a liability to their employer and colleagues. Tony demonstrates technical expertise in a brainstorming meeting. Ash demonstrates design professionalism. Screen shots are in Fig. 3. Their capabilities are also demonstrated in various interactions. For instance, in an agenda-making task, Tony shows his professionalism and organization skills. During the work distribution interaction, Tony leads the discussion.

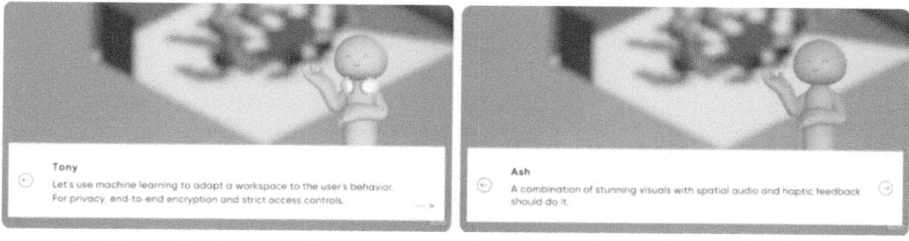

**Fig. 3.** Establishing the autistic characters as key contributors to the company.

This is a single player game, starting with the player entering their name which is addressed through dialogue with the nonplayable characters (NPCs), and through email in the game at the player's desk and computer in the office. The player character moves between the various rooms of the office to trigger, interact with, and conclude various interactions with other NPCs. By providing this personalized experience, we wanted players to feel a more personal connection with the characters. Figure 4 shows a few of these elements.

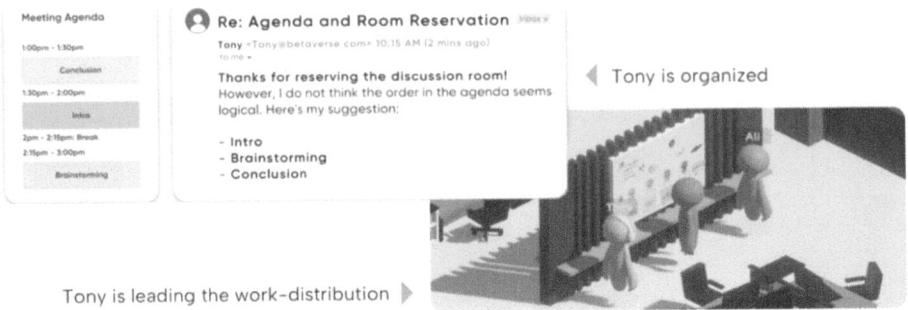

**Fig. 4.** Agenda-making episode revealing Tony's skills.

**Behavior** The player decides where to move and can trigger actions in the environment, from trivial (making coffee) to consequential (deciding to change window blinds to reduce the bright light in the room). The player also makes decisions in dialogue choices, with consequences for actions. By allowing the player to make choices that impact the story, the game aims to influence the player's behavior towards autistic individuals in a more understanding manner. Decisions are not always simple or binary; for example, the decision regarding the blinds as shown in Fig. 5 also brings up the option to disclose Ash's autism to co-worker Ming, which Ash did not grant permission to do. If the player supports Ash by adjusting the blinds, Ash will have a positive reaction. If they choose to disclose for Ash, then Ash will react negatively.

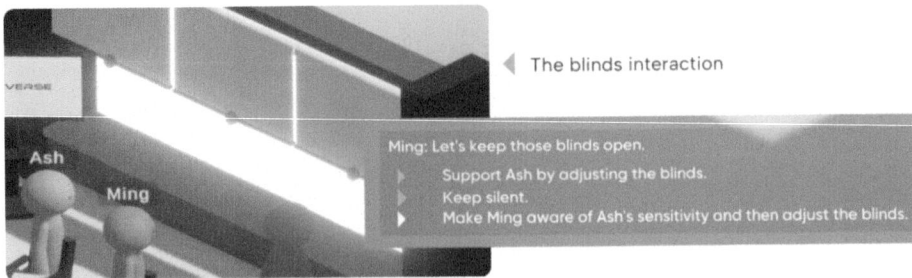

**Fig. 5.** Window blinds interaction (Ash prefers less glare).

Not only will the player's choice be reflected in the character's reaction, but it will also be visible in the dynamic Learning Panel (Fig. 2) to reinforce the positive behaviors. Under "Respecting Privacy", the player will see "you did a good job!" praise along with an explanation of this scenario if the player does not disclose for Ash. Other interactions that align with the behavior transformational goal include agenda-making, room reservation, and work distribution.

**Relationship** Building a positive relationship between the player and the co-workers Tony, Ming, Ali, and Ash is a gradual process achieved through three primary episodes with a number of interactions within them: (1) awareness; (2) active allyship; (3) result. INTENT takes players on a journey from awareness to active allyship where they learn to adapt their behaviors, communicate effectively, and build positive relationships with autistic individuals, ultimately creating a more inclusive and supportive social environment within the game and, ideally, in real-life interactions as well. The level of interaction escalated from basic awareness to making supportive movement, e.g., one narrative sequence has Tony requesting details and Ali then being obstructive (Fig. 6). The player can choose to intervene or hold back, with results shared in both the Learning Panel and in how the episodes play out and the different ending states for the game. As discussed with our SMEs, this progression mirrors the real-world process of building relationships and understanding, reinforcing the idea that transformation in social interactions is a gradual and evolving journey.

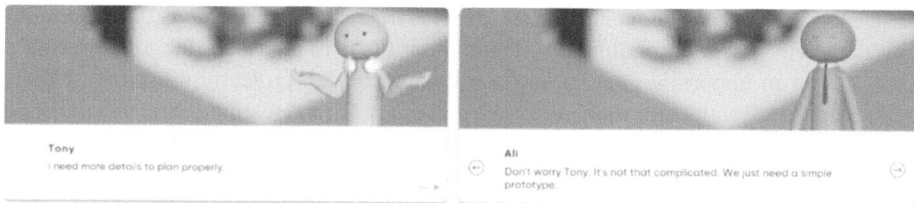

**Fig. 6.** Two consecutive text narrative panes, with Ali being obstructive.

## 3 Game Development Details

INTENT was built in Unity for WebGL deployment, i.e., running within desktop browsers. To accommodate future updates to the narrative text by those listed in the acknowledgments, the game used Yarn Spinner, an open-source narrative system plugin in Unity [10]. It is highly customizable with great expandability, allowing future variations of the narrative.

The user interface opens with a dynamic elevator rising animation, adding an element of visual interest. The opening scene features an elevator door and an office check-in screen, seamlessly introducing company information and the player's role. To enhance clarity, there are self-thought bubbles, simplifying the differentiation between a player's internal thoughts and actual conversations. A sound manager was implemented for an immersive auditory experience, with sound controls to keep or silence the background music and sound effects channels. The player walks through the office rooms and interacts with co-workers and the environment through mouse clicks. When a new task is introduced, as with the first task of making coffee, the player is shown where to move to with a highlight circle, and the tasks list has a cue as well regarding the new task. Figure 7 shows this state, with the coworkers' identities still unknown (as "???") until the player talks to them to discover their names as Tony and Ali.

**Fig. 7.** The user interface at the first task: make coffee in the breakroom.

Outside of the main narrative of the game, the player can interact with NPCs in the scene. These interactions change the flow of future dialogue strands. Some actions with the environment are required, to learn about the user interface (the making coffee action) or as an important interaction for a lesson (turning projector noise off). Others are "Easter Egg" actions to make the environment more interesting, such as a working interactive vending machine in the breakroom that will empty out as you play it. Players of INTENT typically finish the 3 episodes in 20 min (unless they get too involved with that vending machine).

## 4  Future Work and Conclusion

INTENT was designed and developed making use of the Transformational Framework [8]. It made use of interviews, art and game playtesting and reviews with SMEs, AP and NT to improve authenticity and the testing and communication of the game's goals. The transformational goals of knowledge, disposition, behavior, and relationship were covered through an interplay of character and environmental art, text dialogues, learning panels, and player choices. With the innovative and engaging nature of this project, it aims to facilitate future research that will formally assess whether it fosters greater understanding and empathy toward autistic individuals in professional environments.

**Acknowledgments.** This project worked with a team of subject matter experts led by Andrew Begel at Carnegie Mellon University, Jennifer Wessel, Elizabeth Redcay and Kathy Dow-Burger at the University of Maryland, and Steven Isaacson, Autistic Social Worker.

**Disclosure of Interests.** The authors have no competing interests to declare that are relevant to the content of this article.

# References

1. American Psychiatric Association: Diagnostic and statistical manual of mental disorders, 5th edn. American Psychiatric Publishing, Arlington, VA (2013)
2. Morath, E: America's hidden workforce returns. Wall Street Journal (2019). https://www.wsj.com/articles/americas-hidden-workforce-returns-11548478801
3. Austin, R.D., Pisano, G.P.: Neurodiversity as a competitive advantage. Harv. Bus. Rev. **95**(3), 96–103 (2017)
4. Whelpley, C.E., Banks, G.C., Bochantin, J.E., Sandoval, R.: Tensions on the spectrum: an inductive investigation of employee and manager experiences of autism. J. Business Psychol. (2020). https://doi.org/10.1007/s10869-019-09676-1
5. Ramesh, R., Wang, X., Wolpow, D., Zhu, Y., Zheng, Y., Christel, M., Stevens, S.: Prism, a Game to Promote Autism Acceptance Among Elementary School Students. In: Göbel, S. et al. (eds.) JCSG 2018, LNCS, vol. 11243, pp. 101–106. Springer Nature (2018)
6. Sarge, M.A., Kim, H.-S., Velez, J.A.: An auti-sim intervention: the role of perspective taking in combating public stigma with virtual simulations. Cyberpsychol., Behav., Social Netw. **23**(1) (2020). https://doi.org/10.1089/cyber.2019.0678
7. Pavanatto, L., et al.: Get the job! An immersive simulation of sensory overload. In: 2020 IEEE Conference on VR and 3D User Interfaces (VRW), pp. 509–510 (2020)
8. Culyba, S.: The Transformational Framework: A Process Tool for the Development of Transformational Games. ETC Press (2018). https://doi.org/10.1184/R1/7130594
9. INTENT: Carnegie Mellon University entertainment technology center project website. https://projects.etc.cmu.edu/intent/, last accessed 2024/07/10
10. Yarn Spinner. https://yarnspinner.dev/, last accessed 2024/07/10

# Puzzlegram: A Serious Game Designed for the Elderly in Group Settings

Sunny Choi(✉) 🄳

MusEdLab, New York University, New York, NY 10012, USA
ssc526@nyu.edu

**Abstract.** An original serious game prototype named 'Puzzlegram' is created for the elderly demographic in group settings as the target players. Puzzlegram is precisely designed to accentuate memory, auditory interaction as well as haptic response to visual signals with the use of music. Music is introduced as a key component for establishing the game design that provides a source of meaningful contextualization—familiar music from the past—for setting the game mechanics, which facilitated the construction of the serious game design process. The discussion topics raised include the need to design serious games for fostering meaningful interactions, as well as developing a thorough framework for constructing purposeful design for serious games. A potential integral of artificial intelligence to Puzzlegram may involve assigning a novel dimension to its existing problem-solving task by adapting to varying states of cognitive function for monitoring purposes based on an individual's interaction with the game.

**Keywords:** Music and game mechanics · Capability model · Serious game for the elderly

## 1 Introduction

While different games serve different purposes, video games are widely perceived as casual activities with entertainment value [1]. Serious games, on the other hand, are positioned with a goal to deliver beyond entertainment purposes, such as developing new skills, conveying meaning, and providing experiences and emotions or changing behavior and attitudes [2]. Just as general video games and serious games have depth-contrasting goals set to be met by the players, game design techniques can also be initially established with a goal to fulfill specific commercialization or academic/professional purposes [3].

When it comes to applying characteristics of serious games for a specific age group such as the elderly demographic, studies have said to primarily consider various physical and cognitive training to improve elderly people's deteriorating physiological functions [4]. Deteriorating bodily functions are evidently not conditions to be entertained with, thus creating a serious game for the elderly demographic requires a thoughtfully constructed game design process that can genuinely evoke a deeper purpose for the elderly people's fundamental well-being. For instance, obtaining a higher score in a generic

© The Author(s), under exclusive license to Springer Nature Switzerland AG 2025
J. L. Plass and X. Ochoa (Eds.): JCSG 2024, LNCS 15259, pp. 440–446, 2025.
https://doi.org/10.1007/978-3-031-74138-8_36

video game played by an elderly player does not necessarily reflect a healthy cognitive state of the player. Despite a wide range of new products introduced as serious games to serve the elderly population, the issue is that such products have already been classified as regular games with no specific aim to serve the elderly, lacking originality and rigorous game design research by leaving out the very target group that the product apparently claims to serve [4].

In this concisely formatted paper, the author introduces 'Puzzlegram': an original serious game prototype created for the elderly players in group settings as the target group. The game is specifically designed to accentuate memory, auditory interaction as well as haptic response to visual signals with the use of music as an essential component of the game design.

## 2 Methodology

The underpinning theoretical framework for Puzzlegram's design as a serious game stems from the capability approach [5], which highlights a person's capability to function, where a sense of functioning specifically refers to what the person can do or can be from recognizing the non-materialistic value from effective opportunities [6]. Previous study [7] discusses socially responsible design as a capability approach-driven design for societal development that takes human diversity into account. By deeply considering the moral values of elderly people towards designing for society, capability approach leads to capability expansion, promoting advancement in design for collaborative development between designers, engineers, sociologists and scientists. A shared cultural commonality, such as autobiographical memory of music, is said to promote anticipation and expectation – two key factors that drive motivation which have been described as fundamental for the musical experience to understand the effects of music on emotion [8] – towards increasing engagement with the game interface. In other words, familiar music from the past may play an impactful role in facilitating a purposeful game design to evoke meaningful interactions.

## 3 Design

### 3.1 Game Overview

Puzzlegram is built as a software-led hardware serious game where music plays an essential role in establishing the game design mechanics to yield meaningful interactions through gameplay [9]. As a three-player game, each player is individually assigned his/her own Puzzlegram hardware controller to elicit a sense of ownership and responsibility as a unique contributor:

**Goal** The goal of Puzzlegram is for all players to reach the end of the game as a team. By design as a non-competitive game, it is not possible for any one player to 'win' over other players (no ranking). Upon reaching the end of the game, players would have collaboratively constructed a familiar song from start to finish.

**Scope** Puzzlegram is intentionally designed to foster collaborative learning and design research process by directly involving the players and incorporating their interaction with the game mechanics for further design analysis [10]. The credibility of Puzzlegram's design is therefore to be determined by the players' subjective degree of capability as individuals derived by the embedded game mechanics.

**Game mode** Puzzlegram as a serious game is to be played with sound 'on', as sound plays an essential role in forming the game mechanics. If desired, the game may also be played muted, which would simply convert the game type as a memory game.

**Rule** Upon pairing the three individual hardware pieces connected via Bluetooth, Puzzlegram officially begins when a short musical excerpt from a well-known tune is played represented by a unique solid color display. The game interface is displayed on a separate monitor, which also shows the user's haptic input response with a corresponding color that is assigned to each haptic region as output, which is entirely initiated from each player's own Puzzlegram hardware controller. Once the anticipated color is discovered and matched by all players, the game proceeds to the next segment by unveiling the next excerpt of the same musical tune until all players collaboratively reach constructing the entire musical tune from start to finish (Figs. 1 and 2).

**Tutorial** Intentionally, there is no formal tutorial provided that explains the game rules. Instead, players are actively encouraged to explore the game hardware by freely touching any 16 unique haptic regions as the game is in active session. While there is only one haptic region that correctly corresponds to a matching reference color per 'level', there is no penalty associated with the user's game behavior for pressing any of the haptic regions where the corresponding color does not match the reference color.

**Level/Progress** The game does not increase or decrease in difficulty as it progresses. However, prior exposure to the color assigned to each haptic region as the game progresses may potentially make it easier to discover the matching color in a shorter time period.

**Challenge** There are no additional challenge or obstacle components added to the game design.

**Reward** When all three players press the expected haptic region that unveils the matching color display, the next musical excerpt is 'unlocked' and played in a loop, coupled with a new solid color display. As the game progresses, players reach closer to constructing the full song.

### 3.2 Music and Game Mechanics

Several digital audio station software (DAW) programs were used to design the sound component for Puzzlegram. A popular song title that is instantly recognizable among elderly people in North America was selected as the prototype song. The song was rearranged and composed with new instrumentation layers using Logic Pro (https://www.apple.com/logic-pro/). The creation of four distinct instrumentation layers composed of melody, harmony 1, harmony 2, and harmony 3. Using Ableton (https://www.ableton.

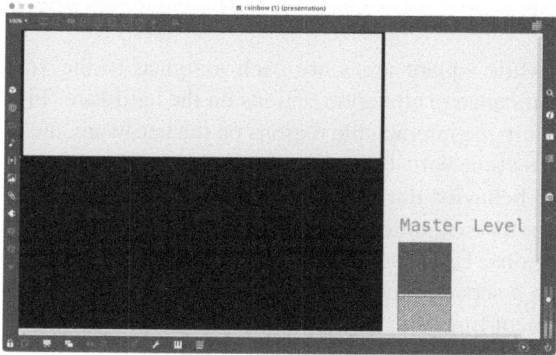

**Fig. 1.** Default visual display of Puzzlegram. The top rectangular solid color displays the corresponding color to be individually located and matched by each player.

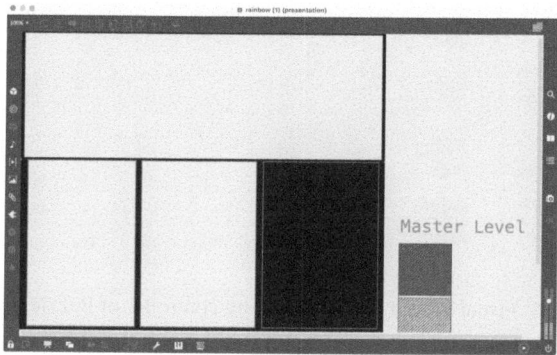

**Fig. 2.** User interface of Puzzlegram with two players waiting for the third player to locate the matching color.

com/), the exported audio layers were equally split to create a total of 16 distinct musical segments per instrumentation layer. Each audio file was randomly assigned an order between 1 and 16 and was paired to a haptic region.

Incorporating music to establish the game mechanics served an essential role in constructing Puzzlegram as a serious game. Multiple key components attached to music such as nostalgia, familiarity, and relatability have been considered to foster player motivation and add purpose to the serious game design. While it is possible to play Puzzlegram in a muted state with no music heard in the background, Puzzlegram would simply become a memory game to pair matching colors. In other words, making modifications to the original game may alter the function as a serious. Previous study also states that sound design can have a significant impact on user experience and attention in serious games [11].

### 3.3  Visual Design

Identically shaped white square areas are each assigned to the 16 haptic regions to distribute equal significance to all haptic regions on the hardware (Fig. 3). By assigning equal shape and color to the interactable regions on the hardware, the emphasis is placed on the player's interaction with the controller rather than on the design which may influence the player behavior during the game. Puzzlegram's controller as hardware serves no function on its own, unless the player engages with it by interacting with any of the 16 haptic regions. Each haptic region is associated with a specific solid color display, visible from a separate monitor that displays the game interface. A randomly assigned music segment from an assigned instrumentation layer is also associated with each haptic region.

**Fig. 3.** Visual design for the hardware controller of Puzzlegram

## 4  Discussion Topics for Future Research

### 4.1  Serious Game for Fostering Meaningful Interactions

The key elements used in establishing the game mechanics for Puzzlegram stemmed from incorporating a proximate source of familiarity through music, which acted as a gateway for players to have a reason to participate in the game. The game design for Puzzlegram also explored placing priority on the player's degree of freedom while keeping the game engaging and entertaining, rather than instructing to master the game environment as an end-goal in itself.

### 4.2  Framework for Designing Purposeful Serious Games

The digital interface for Puzzlegram was entirely empowered by each individual player's haptic input actions. Rather than letting the game rules or the visual environment dictate user's gameplay behavior, a critical need to consider the process of serious game design with the demographic it intends to serve is essential. To develop an effective serious game from its conception to execution phase, a clear need to establish a framework for designing purposeful serious games is crucial to justify its differentiation from regular games.

# 5   Conclusion

This paper described the design of Puzzlegram as a serious game. The game design attempted to highlight the value behind its purposeful design which fosters individual capability for the players, particularly for the elderly people in group settings. A potential integral of artificial intelligence to Puzzlegram may involve assigning a novel dimension to its existing problem-solving task by adapting to varying states of cognitive function for monitoring purposes based on an individual's interaction with the game. In conclusion, Puzzlegram sparks an important question about the need to create serious games that serve the elderly that promote a sense of empowerment by design, rather than positioning them as simply recipients of care or need. Reaching beyond the subject of quality of design, which is ultimately a subjective matter, this paper hopes to initiate further research work towards what it means to serve and aid the globally aging society.

**Disclosure of Interests.** The author has no competing interests to declare that are relevant to the content of this article.

# References

1. Shi, J., Renwick, R., Turner, N.E., Kirsh, B.: Understanding the lives of problem gamers: The meaning, purpose, and influences of video gaming. Comput. Hum. Behav. **97**, 291–303 (2019). https://doi.org/10.1016/j.chb.2019.03.023
2. Marsh, T.: Serious games continuum: Between games for purpose and experiential environments for purpose. Entertain. Comp. **2**(2), 61–68 (2011). https://doi.org/10.1016/j.entcom.2010.12.004
3. Pagulayan, R.J., Keeker, K., Wixon, D., Romero, R.L., Fuller, T.: User-centered design in games. In: The Human-Computer Interaction Handbook, pp. 915–938 (2002). https://doi.org/10.1201/9781410606723-41
4. Nguyen, T.T.H., Ishmatova, D., Tapanainen, T., Liukkonen, T.N., Katajapuu, N., Makila, T., Luimula, M.: Impact of serious games on health and well-being of elderly: a systematic review. In: Proceedings of the Annual Hawaii International Conference on System Sciences (2017). https://doi.org/10.24251/hicss.2017.447
5. Nussbaum, M., & Sen, A. (eds.).: The Quality of Life (1993). https://doi.org/10.1093/0198287976.001.0001
6. Nikou, S., Agahari, W., Keijzer-Broers, W., de Reuver, M.: Digital healthcare technology adoption by elderly people: a capability approach model. Telematics Inform. **53**, 101315 (2020). https://doi.org/10.1016/j.tele.2019.101315
7. Oosterlaken, I.: Design for development: a capability approach. Des. Issues **25**(4), 91–102 (2009). https://doi.org/10.1162/desi.2009.25.4.91
8. Vuust, P., Frith, C.D.: Anticipation is the key to understanding music and the effects of music on emotion. Behav. Brain Sci. **31**(5), 599–600 (2008). https://doi.org/10.1017/s0140525x08005542
9. Whittaker, L., Russell-Bennett, R., Mulcahy, R.: Reward-based or meaningful gaming? a field study on game mechanics and serious games for sustainability. Psychol. Market. **38**(6), 981–1000 (2021). https://doi.org/10.1002/mar.21476
10. Olsson, C.M., Björk, S., Dahlskog, S.: The conceptual relationship model: understanding patterns and mechanics in game design. In: Digital Games Research Association (DiGRA), Snowbird, Utah, USA, pp. 1–16. DIGRA (2014)

11. Cao, Z., Magalhães, E., & Bernardes, G.: Sound design impacts user experience and attention in serious game. In: Lecture Notes in Computer Science, 95–110 (2023). https://doi.org/10.1007/978-3-031-44751-8_7

# From Game-Based Simulation to Practice: The Challenges of Capturing, Modeling, and Transferring Multimodal Data for Chemistry Skill Mastery

Megan Wiedbusch[(✉)] [ID], Annamarie Brosnihan [ID], Tara Delgado [ID], Daryn Dever [ID], Cameron Marano [ID], Milouni Patel [ID], and Roger Azevedo [ID]

School of Modeling, Simulation, & Training, University of Central Florida, Orlando, FL 32826, USA
megan.wiedbusch@ucf.edu

**Abstract.** Game-based simulated learning environments that leverage extended reality technologies are expected to become a cornerstone of STEM workforce development as they offer accessible, flexible, and adaptable alternatives to traditional physical spaces. While these environments may be designed to provide social and experiential learning opportunities that can support students' acquisition, practice, and transfer of fundamental skills, there is much research needed to understand how to capture, model, and transfer trace data to inform these support scaffolds. Some conceptual theories and explanatory models of immersive virtual reality learning are beginning to emerge, but either fail to account for the role of trace data or still require empirical testing. This paper briefly describes an immersive virtual reality (IVR) study that examines the development of basic chemistry lab skills for (N = 45) high-school students using the VR game HoloLAB Champions. Participants completed multiple chemistry lab skill training exercises in a physical lab and in the game-based simulation lab space. During this experiment, participants' multimodal data were captured including self-reports, audio and video recordings, event-based data, and gestures. We discuss the challenges of modeling and transferring various trace data between the real and simulated world experiences and what this may entail for the future development of adaptive and intelligent scaffolds.

**Keywords:** Multimodal Data · Simulation-Based Training · Chemistry

## 1 Simulation-Based Games for Learning and Training

Simulations are synthetic environments or scenarios meticulously crafted to emulate specific facets of real-world phenomena that often emerge as a particular subset of game-based learning and training environments [1]. These simulated learning environments harnesses the capabilities of extended realities technologies (e.g., augmented, virtual, and mixed reality), alongside serious game elements including challenge, interaction, game objective, narrative, and gameplay mechanics [2]. These environments are

J. L. Plass and X. Ochoa (Eds.): JCSG 2024, LNCS 15259, pp. 447–454, 2025.
https://doi.org/10.1007/978-3-031-74138-8_37

increasingly recognized as pivotal to the advancement of STEM education and are anticipated to form the foundation for STEM workforce development [3, 4]. Chief among these are immersive virtual reality (IVR) laboratories, which offer an accessible, flexible, and adaptable alternative to traditional classroom settings that are adept at facilitating students' acquisition, practice, and transfer of fundamental skills to real-world contexts [5–7]. However, the effectiveness of these technologies varies significantly, often stemming from a fragmented understanding of how IVR affordances can be optimally utilized in K-12 STEM learning settings [8]. This gap is especially pronounced in areas requiring the acquisition of psychomotor and procedural skills, which are critical in STEM education [9, 10], especially in domains such as chemistry.

Within the past few years, there has been an influx of studies related to integrating simulation-based games with traditional learning contexts to supplement information, encourage discovery learning, and increase interest and engagement with complex topics and materials [11–13]. With this growth of literature on how learning occurs within simulation-based games for learning, conceptual theories, models, and frameworks for IVR learning have emerged, such as the Cognitive Affective Model of Immersive Learning (CAMIL [14, 15]). However, while these models have examined self-regulatory processes (e.g., planning, strategy implementation, reflection), these empirical studies rely on pretest-posttest self-report data, ignoring the processes and dynamics of learning as a process [14, 16]. Furthermore, these models tend to be more descriptive in nature, not prescriptive, therefore limiting educational applications. In other words, relationships between the learning process and learners' experiences within the IVR are typically described within the models based on the current field of work without providing pedagogical interventions or suggestions for supporting learning throughout learners' interactions with these environments. Finally, these models have been centered on the acquisition of knowledge, but fail to acknowledge the transfer of one's learning or training done between a virtual environment back and the real world. As others have identified, there is an extremely large challenge in studying the transfer (whether near or far) between environments that requires further investigation (Bossard et al., 2008; Levac et al., 2019).

As we have seen with other advanced learning technologies such as intelligent tutoring systems, multimodal data can offer insight into these learning processes and their dynamics as they unfold [17]. Multimodal data (e.g., self-reports, concurrent verbalizations, gestures, screen recordings; see [18]) captures *when, how,* and *where* learners engage in cognitive, affective, metacognitive, motivational, and social processes while learning with a simulation-based game. Recent studies have begun utilizing multimodal data [19–21]. However, these studies have not yet explored how these trace data can be used to augment simulation-based games, or how best to transfer multimodal data between the synthetic environment and the authentic environments they are replicating. Given that the availability of trace data across virtual and real-world contexts differ, can we continue to leverage the multimodal methods and analytics that are currently used in other advanced learning technologies (e.g., intelligent tutoring systems, multimedia, hypermedia) as well as traditional classroom environments to unobtrusively capture learning?

This paper explores the multifaceted challenges associated with modeling and transferring various trace data between real and simulated world experiences contextualized within an IVR chemistry lab game use case. It delves into the complexities of ensuring high fidelity and seamless integration of data across these distinct environments, a crucial aspect for the practical application and effectiveness of simulations-based learning environments.

## 2 Theoretical Framework

Hetzner et al.'s [22] Extended Self-Regulated Learning (SRL) model for learning in simulated and real world (see Fig. 1) expands upon the Zimmerman (2002) SRL model [23]. Within both, SRL is theorized to occur within three SRL phases (forethought, performance, and reflection). In the Hetzner et al. [22] expansion, these phases occur in both the simulated and real world. One's knowledge, skills, and abilities then transfer between the two after reflection into the other world's forethought phase. The forethought phase typically involves preparing for learning activities such as outcome expectation, intrinsic interest, goal setting, and self-efficacy. According to this model, it is informed by previous reflection cycles from either world. For example, a reflection within the virtual world (e.g., recognizing that using a pipette for repetitive behaviors is time consuming) may trigger planning or forethought in the real world (e.g., planning to batch the same pipetting action, when possible, to be more efficient). The performance phase occurs in the environmental context of the learning environment and is comprised of the deployment of various cognitive, affective, metacognitive, and motivational processes. During the reflection phase, learners undergo processes of self-evaluation and self-satisfaction that either feed back into future cycles within the same context or are carried over to the alternative world context.

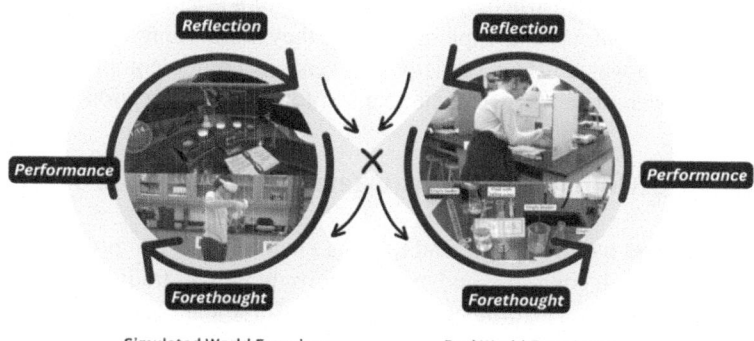

**Fig. 1.** Hetzner et al. [22] Extended Self-Regulated Learning Model for Learning in Simulated and Real Worlds with examples from HoloLAB Champions Case Study

# 3  Case Study – VR Chemistry Skill Training

We situate the discussion of capturing, modeling, and transferring multimodal data in IVR simulated chemistry lab game-based learning and training environment within a VR study that examines the development of basic chemistry lab skills for high-school students using the VR game HoloLAB Champions by Schell Games (https://hololabch ampions.schellgames.com/). HoloLAB Champions is a commercial IVR game developed to provide a playful learning environment where students use controller triggers to experiment with lab equipment, develop lab skills, and complete lab procedures in a safe and controlled domain. Players receive feedback while completing the virtual labs on the accuracy of their measurements, the degree of safety in which they use equipment, and their speed.

In this study, participants (N = 45) were asked to demonstrate lab skills both in real-world and simulated VR environments as we capture self-report measures, knowledge acquisition, and skill performance via audio and video recording. Participants were randomly assigned to one of two conditions: (1) IVR-based instruction (N = 25) and (2) non-IVR video-based instruction (N = 21). Students in both conditions completed a pre-test, a learning period, and a post-test. The pretest and posttest included several questionnaires[1] and 20 item knowledge assessment via Qualtrics, followed by a real-world wet-lab. All knowledge assessments were co-generated with STEM teacher experts. The timed wet-lab knowledge assessment was a 5-station physical lab completed by participants to assess their pre and post knowledge and skills correlating with the IVR mini-lab tasks. During the learning period, learners in the IVR-based instruction condition completed five mini-labs testing specific basic chemistry lab skills (e.g., using a Mohr's pipette to transfer measured liquid). Each mini-lab was equipped with instructions and a notebook that contains the mini-lab procedure. Learners were required to place their completed solution on a pedestal to receive feedback if their solution was correct or incorrect. Mini-lab materials could be reset at any time without penalty. Learners in the non-IVR video-based instruction watched a video of a teacher completing the same levels while thinking-aloud and explaining what they were doing and why. Once the learning assessment was finished, participants in each condition completed the posttest components and were then debriefed and thanked for their participation.

# 4  Capturing, Modeling, and Transferring Multimodal Trace Data

IVR simulated game-based learning and training environments can provide rich traces of affective, behavioral, cognitive, and metacognitive processes traditionally inferred in observation or self-report performance assessment. These data benefit from providing unobtrusive insight as they unfold in real time [18]. Below, we briefly review how multimodal data can be captured and modeled with trace data and the challenges of transferring that data between the synthetic and real world.

---

[1] Questionnaires measured metacognitive awareness [24], intrinsic motivation [25], self-efficiency [26], cognitive load [27], situational interest [28], agency [29], and presence [30].

### 4.1  Capturing and Modeling Trace Data

While, as we will show, many of these data can be utilized in IVR and the real-world, what they capture how they are modeled/interpreted can differ vastly between the two environments. This makes assessment across context challenging.

One of the major challenges first of capturing trace data in different environments is the difference in hardware. For example, eye-trackers can be imbedded within the head-mounted displays for IVR games, but their accuracy, precision, and even fixation detection algorithms can differ significantly from eye-tracking glasses worn in the real world [31].

Another challenge comes from the way we move and interact with objects. Controllers act as an IVR interface for human-computer interaction, allowing for simple button presses to replace fine-motor movements such as using the wheel on a pipette. This affects the duration of these actions during various procedures (making one-to-one comparisons between environments troublesome) and potentially the accuracy as a behavioral performance metric. In addition, grosser-level behavioral changes also differ, such as body positioning. IVR environments tend to bring most game elements to their optimal positioning for decreased barriers to use and improved utility. However, in the real world, this is not the case such as we see with the height of lab benches.

A third challenge is the availability and resource cost of these trace data in each of the environments. For example, performance is automatically calculated within IVR games, but instructors often must hand grade labs through observation or other timely and costly traditional methods. This inequality between worlds adds to the complexity in both assessment of learning and training/game design. Both require researchers and designers have actionable and insightful analytics derived from cognitive, affective, metacognitive, motivational, and behavioral data (i.e., learning analytics). Capturing and modeling trace data is often the first step for the development of learning analytics which are used to inform instructional decision making and within assessment [32]. These analytics allow one to understand and utilize the traces left behind during the learning process but require specific psychological constructs to be identified from those traces to be meaningful [32]. There is still much research that is needed to identify how universal these trace signals are across contexts, and where they diverge depending on environmental affordances and constraints.

### 4.2  Transferring Trace Data

When we imagine the future of game-based simulation learning and training environments, we imagine their impact on performance outside of synthetic environments. To truly understand their impact on the processes of learning and training, we must consider how our measures of these processes can be transferred between the two worlds. However, this transfer poses many open challenges that must be considered in the future design, development, and research of these environments. We argue that any comparison of non-contextualized metrics is ill advised as they are likely not equivalent in their capture or modeling (as described above). For example, perhaps we wish to add an adaptive element of training within HoloLAB Champions that asks students to practice their pouring technique prior to a mini-lab. This adaptivity would change the number of times the game asks the student to demonstrate the skill based off measures of jerk in their hand movements. To improve individualization and adaptivity, the game could have already a student model of the expected levels collected from a previous real-world lab session. However, this model would need to be based off data analytic granularity instead of raw accelerometer data. That is, it may be more appropriate to have a distribution of ratios of "smooth" to "jerky" movements instead of just jerk values to determine the current skill level of the student. This helps reduce any unintended noise caused by task difficulty, task time allotment, differences in collection methods, or comparisons of what "jerky" is classified as in the real world opposed to the synthetic one. This may result in added computational requirements of student modeling in which the data housed within the student model must be translated into the corresponding context every time it is to be referenced.

## 5    Discussion and Future Directions

Assuming we can accurately capture, model, and transfer trace data of SRL processes between simulated and real-world experiences, we then must consider how it can be utilized to develop intelligent adaptive scaffolding. The extended SRL model assumes that learning from the simulated world influences and triggers phases from the real-world SRL recursive forethought-performance-reflection cycle and vice-versa. This suggests that scaffolding embedded within an IVR must account for both cycles instead of treating them as separate. But what happens when scaffolding is introduced, especially scaffolding that only occurs within the simulated world? How best can we design these scaffolds to support the influence of SRL processes also occurring in the real world? This paper discusses these questions in addition to the theoretical, conceptual, and methodological challenges of such scaffold design informed by the capturing, modeling, and transfer of multimodal trace data.

**Acknowledgments.** The authors would like to thank the members from the SMART Lab at UCF for their assistance. Additionally, the authors would like to thank all of the support from NeoCity Academy and Trinity Preparatory Academy for their support.

**Disclosure of Interests.** The authors have no competing interests to declare that are relevant to the content of this article.

## References

1. Bell, B., Kanar, A., Kozlowski, S.: Current issues and future directions in simulation-based training in North America. Int. J. Human Res. Management **19**(8), 1416–1434 (2008)
2. Plass, J., et al.: Designing effective immersive VR learning experiences. Immersive Learn. Res.-Pract. **1**(1), 32–37 (2022)
3. OECD: OECD Work on Chemical Safety and Biosafety (2019)
4. Sanchez, J.: Are basic laboratory skills adequately acquired by undergraduate science students? how control quality methodologies applied to laboratory lessons may help us to find the answer. Anal. Bioanal. Chem. **414**(12), 3551–3559 (2022)

5. Jensen, L., Konradsen, F.: A review of the use of virtual reality head-mounted displays in education and training. Educ. Inf. Technol. **23**(4), 1515–1529 (2018)
6. Potkonjak, V., et al.: Virtual laboratories for education in science, technology, and engineering: A review. Comput. Educ. **95**, 309–327 (2016)
7. Sypsas, A., Kalles, D.: Virtual laboratories in biology, biotechnology and chemistry education: a literature review. In: Nikitas, K., Basilis, M. (eds.) Pan-Hellenic Conference on Informatics 2018. Association for Computing Machinery, pp. 70–75. ACM, New York (2018)
8. Wu, B., Yu, X., Gu, X.: Effectiveness of immersive virtual reality using head-mounted displays on learning performance: a meta-analysis. Br. J. Edu. Technol. **51**(6), 1991–2025 (2022)
9. McGowin, G., Fiore, S. M., Oden, K.: Learning affordances: theoretical considerations for design of immersive virtual reality in training and education. In: Proceedings of the human factors and ergonomics society annual meeting, pp. 883–887. Sage, Los Angeles, CA (2021)
10. McGowin, G., Fiore, S., Oden, K.: Me, myself, and the (virtual) world: a review of learning research in 4E cognition and immersive virtual reality. In: Chen, J., Fragomeni, G. (eds.) International Conference on Human-Computer Interaction, vol. 13318, pp. 59–73. Springer International Publishing, Washington, DC (2022)
11. Chernikova, O., Heitzmann, N., Stadler, M., Holzberger, D., Seidel, T., Fischer, F.: Simulation-based learning in higher education: a meta-analysis. Rev. Educ. Res. **90**(4), 499–541 (2020)
12. Ke, F., Xu, X.: Virtual reality simulation-based learning of teaching with alternative perspectives taking. Br. J. Edu. Technol. **51**(6), 2544–2557 (2020)
13. Walters, B., Potetz, J., Fedesco, H.N.: Simulations in the classroom: an innovative active learning experience. Clin. Simul. Nurs. **13**(12), 609–615 (2017)
14. Makransky, G., Petersen, G.B.: The Cognitive Affective Model of Immersive Learning (CAMIL): a theoretical research-based model of learning in immersive virtual reality. Educ. Psychol. Rev. **33**(3), 937–958 (2021)
15. Petersen, G.B., Petkakis, G., Makransky, G.: A study of how immersion and interactivity drive VR learning. Comput. Educ. **179**, 104429 (2022)
16. Makransky, G., Borre-Gude, S., Mayer, R.E.: Motivational and cognitive benefits of training in immersive virtual reality based on multiple assessments. J. Comput. Assist. Learn. **35**(6), 691–707 (2019)
17. Azevedo, R., et al.: Lessons learned and future directions of metatutor: leveraging multichannel data to scaffold self-regulated learning with an intelligent tutoring system. Front. Psychol. **13** (2022)
18. Azevedo, R., Gašević, D.: Analyzing multimodal multichannel data about self-regulated learning with advanced learning technologies: Issues and challenges. Comput. Hum. Behav. **96**, 207–210 (2019)
19. Lui, M., McEwen, R., Mullally, M.: Immersive virtual reality for supporting complex scientific knowledge: augmenting our understanding with physiological monitoring. Br. J. Edu. Technol. **51**(6), 2181–2199 (2020)
20. Mehler, A., et al.: A multimodal data model for simulation-based learning with Va. Si. Li-Lab. In: International Conference on Human-Computer Interaction, pp. 539–565. Springer Nature Switzerland, Cham (2023)
21. Sobocinski, M., Dever, D., Wiedbusch, M., Mubarak, F., Azevedo, R., Järvelä, S.: Capturing self-regulated learning processes in virtual reality: causal sequencing of multimodal data. Br. J. Edu. Technol. **00**, 1–21 (2023)
22. Hetzner, S., Steiner, C. M., Dimitrova, V., Brna, P., Conlan, O.: Adult self-regulated learning through linking experience in simulated and real world: A holistic approach. In: 6th Proceedings for Towards Ubiquitous Learning: European Conference of Technology Enhanced Learning EC-TEL 2011, pp. 166–180. Springer, Berlin Heidelberg (2011)
23. Zimmerman, B.: Becoming a self-regulated learner: an overview. Theory into practice **41**(2), 64–70 (2002)

24. Sperling, R., Howard, B., Miller, L., Murphy, C.: Measures of children's knowledge and regulation of cognition. Contemp. Educ. Psychol. **27**(1), 51–79 (2022)
25. Deci, E., Eghrari, H., Patrick, B., Leone, D.: Facilitating internalization: the self-determination theory perspective. J. Pers. **62**(1), 119–142 (1994)
26. Pintrich, P.R., De Groot, E.V.: Motivational and self-regulated learning components of classroom academic performance. J. Educ. Psychol. **82**(1), 33–40 (1990)
27. Eysink, T.H., de Jong, T., Berthold, K., Kolloffel, B., Opfermann, M., Wouters, P.: Learner performance in multimedia learning arrangements: an analysis across instructional approaches. Am. Educ. Res. J. **46**(4), 1107–1149 (2009)
28. Knogler, M., Harackiewicz, J.M., Gegenfurtner, A., Lewalter, D.: How situational is situational interest? investigating the longitudinal structure of situational interest. Contemp. Educ. Psychol. **43**, 39–50 (2015)
29. Eubanks, J.C., Moore, A.G., Fishwick, P.A., McMahan, R.P.: A preliminary embodiment short questionnaire. Front. Virtual Reality **2** (2021)
30. Makransky, G., Lilleholt, L., Aaby, A.: Development and validation of the multimodal presence scale for virtual reality environments: a confirmatory factor analysis and item response theory approach. Comput. Hum. Behav. **72**, 276–285 (2017)
31. Hutton, S.: Eye tracking methodology. In: Klein C., Ettinger, U. (eds.) Eye Movement Research. Studies in Neuroscience, Psychology and Behavioral Economics. Springer Chambers, pp. 277–308. Springer (2019)
32. Ochoa, X., Lang, C., Siemens, G., Wise, A., Gasevic, D., Merceron, A.: Multimodal learning analytics-Rationale, process, examples, and direction. In Lang, C., Siemens, G., Wise, A.F., Gasevic, D., Merceron, A. (eds.). The handbook of learning analytics, 2nd edn., pp. 54–65. SoLAR, Vancouver. (2022)

# The BlockQuest Game: Digital Behavioral Phenotyping of ADHD Using Embodied Serious Game in Virtual Reality

Marianna Muszynska[1,2(✉)] and Ori Ossmy[1,2]

[1] Center for Brain and Cognitive Development, Birkbeck, University of London, London, UK
marianna.muszynska@bbk.ac.uk
[2] School of Psychological Sciences, Birkbeck, University of London, London, UK

**Abstract.** Children with Attention-deficit-hyperactivity disorder (ADHD) exhibit higher levels of inattention, hyperactivity, and impulsivity compared to their typically developing peers, impacting their daily functioning. To characterize the effects of ADHD, traditional research methodologies have predominantly used an outcome-oriented approach—scoring at which ages children solve particular problems compared to typically developing children. However, such an approach neglects how children solve tasks and overlooks how perceptual, cognitive, and motor processes unfold from moment to moment during problem solving. Recent research attempted to address this knowledge gap using computerized gamification of tasks. However, most gamified paradigms are stationary and overlook the aspect of locomotion and embodiment, which are strongly related to daily functioning. Here, we argue that the effects of ADHD on daily living should be characterized through the use of virtual reality as a modernized embodied tool that provides digital behavioral phenotyping of ADHD. We present a novel embodied block-construction serious game paradigm in virtual reality that links ADHD characteristics and the real-time interaction between perception, cognition, and movement.

**Keywords:** Virtual Reality · Neurodevelopment · Locomotion · Attention-deficit-hyperactivity · Embodiment · Problem Solving · Digital Phenotyping

## 1 Introduction

Attention-Deficit-Hyperactivity-Disorder (ADHD) is a neurodevelopmental disorder that manifests in various ways among children. Children with ADHD exhibit varied levels of cognitive flexibility, attentional control, and impulse regulation. Their motor skills also often deviate from their typically developing peers, primarily evident in balance and coordination deficits during locomotor and manual tasks [1]. These differences have implications for daily functioning and learning outcomes. Critically, challenges in motor skills are not only physical but are intertwined with cognitive and sensory processing abilities, impacting academic outcomes and social behavior [2, 3].

Traditionally, developmental and cognitive research on the effect of ADHD has been driven by the perspective that cognition is a collection of learned rules and conventions, independent of the body's interaction with the environment [4, 5]. However, over the past few decades, an alternative perspective—embodied cognition—has gained prominence. The embodied cognition perspective argues that cognitive processes are fundamentally grounded in physical experiences with the environment [6–8].

However, research on the effects of ADHD over development is limited in examining embodiment. Most studies use an outcome-oriented approach in which children are tested in standard, non-embodied tests, and their outcomes are compared to those of typically developing children [4]. For example, in the cognitive domain, children with ADHD perform worse on standardized mathematical tests [9] and tend to be less accurate in spatial reasoning tests [10].

Few studies examined motor skills in children with ADHD, but those did not account for embodiment. For example, ADHD is associated with decreased motor control and lower performance in timed tasks (i.e. catching or throwing a ball [10, 11]). Children with ADHD also have more variable trajectories of arm movements [1] compared to their typically developing peers, suggesting ADHD leads to the use of trial-and-error strategies instead of response preparation and planning ahead [2]. Others found that ADHD is associated with alterations in perceptual functioning and its integration with motor movements [3, 9], which manifests in decreased performance in tasks that require coordinated visual-motor skills [13].

How are those perceptual-motor associations related to the effect of ADHD on cognitive development? To address this question, we argue that researchers should adopt a process-oriented perspective that tests how perception, action, and cognition interact and unfold from moment to moment. When solving problems, children first gather information from the environment (perceptual process), process this information (cognitive process), and then act upon the environment to solve the problem (motor process). Alterations in this interaction significantly impact children's behaviors and problem solving [3, 14, 15]. Therefore, ADHD should be characterized by tasks and environments spanning multiple domains. This approach will lead to a digital phenotyping of ADHD that will involve diverse measurements such as eye movements, facial expressions, detailed real-time motor behavior, and performance on embodied executive function tasks. We also argue that such digital phenotyping must rely on serious games because those provide an engaging and interactive platform that naturally integrates perceptual, cognitive, and motor processes, thereby allowing the detection of patterns and anomalies that may not be evident through traditional assessment methods.

## 2  Cognitive Evaluation of ADHD Effects Over Development

### 2.1  Continuous Performance Tests (CPTs)

Continuous Performance Tests (CPTs) are the main evaluation tests for cognitive functioning of children with ADHD. It was first developed in the early 1950s as a model for identifying sustained attention deficits in individuals with frontal lobe lesions [16]. CPTs require sustained attention over up to 10 min. Due to the variability in attention levels being a key characteristic of ADHD, early studies used the CPT paradigm to assess neuropsychological characteristics on task performance [17]. However, due to the differences in developmental trajectories in ADHD [18, 19], researchers are still limited in understanding the degree to which CPT corresponds to ADHD characteristics and how this correspondence changes over development [20]. Performance on some of these tests was found to improve over development but in a subset of children, specifically in inhibitory control measures [20, 21]. CPTs are also sensitive to ceiling effects due to their over reliance on cognitive stimuli that clearly indicate target or non-target cues. As a result, there is a high likelihood of either false positives or accidental flawless performance [20, 22]. Even when some CPTs are accurate, they are limited in measuring error rates and reaction times, often yielding conflicting results in the latter [23].

## 2.2  Gamified CPT Paradigms

With recent technological advances, alternative multimodal methods that are more engaging for children than traditional CPTs have emerged. Those were found effective in testing neurodevelopmental conditions and specifically ADHD [24]. For example, the use of computerized games as CPTs allowed researchers to customize the tests and capture additional measures, including mouse trajectory (serves as a specific measure of information seeking and reasoning [25]) or touch trajectory on tablet based games [26]. The gamified CPTs were validated against traditional CPTs [27], and although they were found beneficial in identifying new ADHD characteristics, they were also limited by their omission of interaction measures with the experimental environment and their focus on outcome-oriented metrics (e.g., reaction time and final task score). Finally, gamified CPTs have the benefit of being available on multiple platforms such as PC, PlayStation or mobile devices [28].

## 2.3  Immersive Virtual Reality (VR) Paradigms

The activities in gamified CPTs remained stationary, neglecting the crucial aspect of embodiment, which is essential for a full, multi-process characterization of ADHD. Therefore, VR has emerged in recent years as a popular and valuable research tool for studying the effects of ADHD. The embodied nature of using head-mounted VR displays offers a comprehensive evaluation of multiple domains confined within a single task [15, 16]. VR games are also highly customizable because they provide a rich, continuous behavioral data, including gaze tracking, decision-making, and movement. Such high-dimensional data provide insights into mechanisms underlying cognition when it is embedded within active behavior. Integrating VR with other technologies (e.g., bio- or neuro-sensors) and serious games offers the opportunity to examine behavior and physiology in highly engaging tasks.

However, similar to gamified CPT paradigms, researchers use VR primarily in sedentary tasks [17, 30]. Thus, its potential is not fully exploited, as it does not fully address embodiment as a concept to characterize ADHD.

## 3    BlockQuest—Embodied Serious Game to Characterize ADHD

Here, we introduce BlockQuest—a VR serious game to characterize ADHD over development. BlockQuest generates goal-oriented behavior in an engaging setting and requires full-body movement, including locomotion. The game is appropriate for school-aged children (aged 6 and above) and adults with and without ADHD.

### 3.1   Setup

BlockQuest consists of five difficulty levels, all sharing the same goal—constructing a structure from hidden elements (See Fig. 1). Players receive verbal instructions for each level and then complete the construction task in an immersive VR environment that includes boxes in two different colors and marked construction space (see Fig. 1). Players can move freely within the play boundary, measuring 320 cm by 406 cm, generated using the PICO Neo 3 Pro Eye's internal feature (other headsets can be used as well).

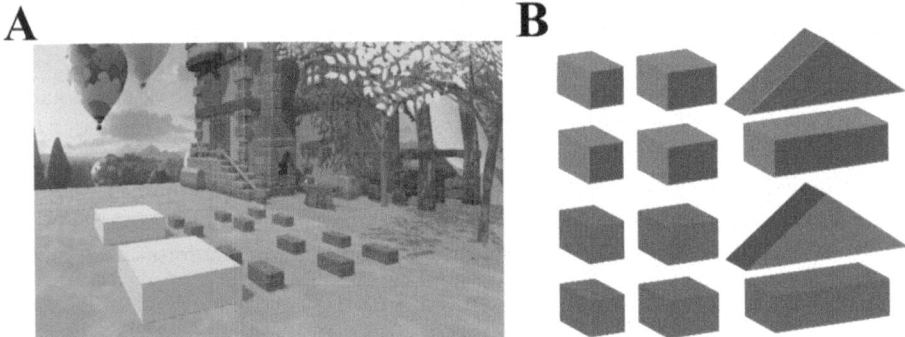

**Fig. 1.** BlockQuest serious game. (**A**) BlockQuest virtual environment. (**B**) Elements that are used for construction. Those elements are hidden within boxes in the virtual environment.

The environment follows real-world physical laws (e.g., terrestrial gravity) and the hidden elements have realistic physical properties. For example, smaller elements are lighter and are thrown further compared to bigger elements. Players are required to be precise when they open the boxes and grasp the hidden objects.

To succeed in the game, players must look ahead, coordinate their movements, demonstrate spatial awareness, and plan strategically. They need to integrate perceptual, motor, and cognitive skills simultaneously, and the interaction between these processes is recorded. Movement is recorded by three HD cameras and analyzed using computer vision, similar to previous research [23, 24]. Body position, hands position, eye gaze, and object dynamics are recorded via the headset. Object dynamics include object grasping and releasing, object movements, and box opening.

### 3.2   Task

The players are fully immersed in the colorful virtual world, and their quest is to locate and collect all hidden objects (See Fig. 1) which are scattered within the play area. From

Level 2 onward, players are asked to build a model object from collected hidden elements. Each level presents its own unique challenge associated with different processes affected by ADHD. The environment itself encourages exploration (there is no time limit for each level).

## 3.3  Procedure

Players start with practice activities to ensure comfort and understanding of the mechanics of the game. Subsequently, levels increase in difficulty. All levels include the initial information search aspect, where each hidden element must be collected from the box that hides it. An increase in difficulty changes cognitive load, which is associated with greater delay in response to real-time discounting tasks in children with ADHD. Additionally, an increase in difficulty was found to exacerbate impulsive behavior [31].

*Level 1.* Information search task. Each pink and blue cube hides an element (see Fig. 1). The goal is to collect all hidden elements and place them in a designated area, corresponding to each colored array of boxes. Searching for visual information is an integral part of everyday activities and is associated with problem-solving activities, in which children with ADHD exhibit different search behaviors when compared to their typically developing peers. Additionally, children with ADHD exhibit increased patterns of foraging, which is linked to lower attentional states that favor exploration over exploitation in tasks [32].

*Level 2.* The goal is to collect all hidden elements and build a model, starting with color blue and ensuring the 3D triangle, 'roof-like' element is on top of the modelled construction—players must use all hidden elements. Then, they need to repeat modelling the same construction in the pink colors. At this level, instructions are scarce, and construction is allowed without much constraint. The justification for this level is based on previous funding showing that children with ADHD tend to respond to problems differently based on the type of received instructions [28]; they performed better when given strategic instructions over tactical ones.

*Level 3.* The construction is placed within the environment in a neutral grey color (see Fig. 2). Players can use it as a reference model when constructing. This level introduces more structured instructions and puts more demand on higher-level working memory. Studies have shown that individuals with ADHD exhibit organizational problems in structuring tasks and maintaining order in their environment [22, 23], which are linked to inefficiencies in working memory.

*Level 4.* Similar goal to Level 3, but the reference construction is not placed within the virtual environment. Players must use recall to build the same model as in Level 3 without a visual cue. This level also addresses memory challenges in ADHD and adds cognitive load as an unexpected difficulty [32].

*Level 5.* The goal at this level is to build one construction model using all hidden elements from both colors. Players are shown a guiding animation (Fig. 2) on how to place the hidden elements. This is the last level and it involves the highest cognitive load. Players use all the skills that were required in previous levels simultaneously. Because children and adolescents with ADHD do not attempt to solve cognitively complex tasks where structuring and planning action is required [35], This level also examines players' ability to complete a construction in efficient manner.

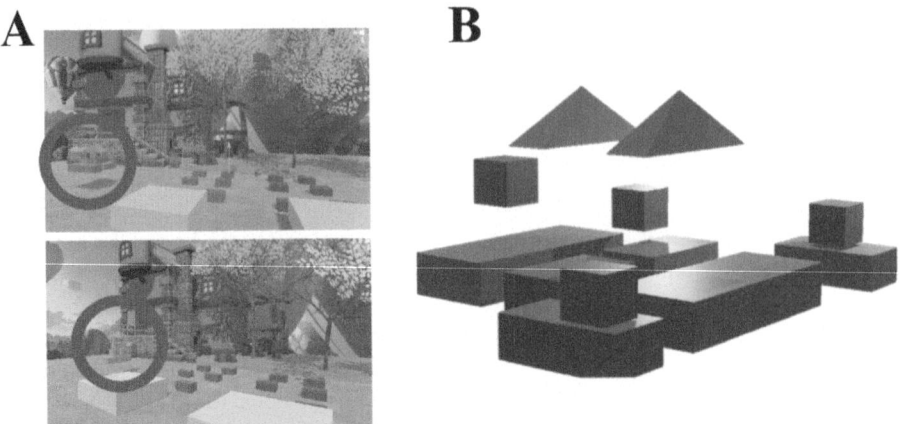

**Fig. 2.** (**A**) Reference object for Level 5 is placed outside the movement boundary to force mental representation of objects out of sight (Top), and Level 3 reference object in neutral grey color (Bottom). (**B**) Animation shown to players twice before starting level 5.

## 4 Final Remarks

The BlockQuest game provides a novel, digital-phenotyping approach to characterize ADHD [36, 37]. By integrating attention, working memory and sensorimotor measures, the game comprehensively assesses ADHD over development, which goes beyond the traditional outcome measures. BlockQuest aims to identify the underlying mechanisms associated with ADHD functional skills and their different developmental trajectories. By integrating measures from multiple domains into a single engaging task, BlockQuest pushes the envelope of ADHD characterization to an embodied experience which is more similar to daily life.

**Acknowledgements.** This work was supported by the Waterloo Foundation grant 917-4975 to OO.

**Disclosure of Interests.** The authors declare no interests.

## References

1. Dahan, A., Reiner, M.: Evidence for deficient motor planning in ADHD. Sci. Rep. **7**(1), 9631 (2017). https://doi.org/10.1038/s41598-017-09984-7
2. Eliasson, A.-C., Rösblad, B., Forssberg, H.: 'Disturbances in programming goal-directed arm movements in children with ADHD. Dev. Med. Child Neurol. **46**(1), 19–27 (2007). https://doi.org/10.1111/j.1469-8749.2004.tb00429.x
3. Carames, C.N., Irwin, L.N., Kofler, M.J.: 'Is there a relation between visual motor integration and academic achievement in school-aged children with and without ADHD? Child Neuropsychol. **28**(2), 224–243 (2022). https://doi.org/10.1080/09297049.2021.1967913
4. Newell, A., Simon, H.A.: Human problem solving. In: Human problem solving, p. 920. Prentice-Hall, Oxford (1972)

5.  Fodor, J.A.: The modularity of mind. The MIT Press (1983). https://doi.org/10.7551/mitpress/4737.001.0001

6.  Smith, L.B.: Action alters shape categories. Cogn. Sci. **29**(4), 665–679 (2005). https://doi.org/10.1207/s15516709cog0000_13

7.  Barsalou, L.W.: Grounding symbolic operations in the brain's modal systems. In: Embodied Grounding: Social, Cognitive, Affective, and Neuroscientific Approaches, pp. 9–42. Cambridge University Press, New York (2008). https://doi.org/10.1017/CBO9780511805837.002

8.  Glenberg, A.M.: Embodiment as a unifying perspective for psychology. Wiley Interdiscip. Rev. Cogn. Sci. **1**(4), 586–596 (2010). https://doi.org/10.1002/wcs.55

9.  Kanevski, M., et al.: The relationship between cognition and mathematics in children with attention-deficit/hyperactivity disorder: a systematic review. Child Neuropsychol. **28**(3), 394–426 (2022). https://doi.org/10.1080/09297049.2021.1985444

10. Johnson, K.A., et al.: Right-sided spatial difficulties in ADHD demonstrated in continuous movement control. Neuropsychologia **48**(5), 1255–1264 (2010). https://doi.org/10.1016/j.neuropsychologia.2009.12.026

11. Ziereis, S., Jansen, P.: Correlation of motor abilities and executive functions in children with ADHD. Appl. Neuropsychol. Child **5**(2), 138–148 (2016). https://doi.org/10.1080/21622965.2015.1038746

12. Fuermaier, A.B.M., et al.: Perception in attention deficit hyperactivity disorder. ADHD Atten. Deficit Hyperact. Disord. **10**(1), 21–47 (2018). https://doi.org/10.1007/s12402-017-0230-0

13. Fabio, R.A., Andricciola, F., Caprì, T.: Visual-motor attention in children with ADHD: the role of automatic and controlled processes. Res. Dev. Disabil. **123**, 104193 (2022). https://doi.org/10.1016/j.ridd.2022.104193

14. Ossmy, O., et al.: Real-time processes in the development of action planning. Curr. Biol. **32**(1), 190-199.e3 (2022). https://doi.org/10.1016/j.cub.2021.11.018

15. Ossmy, O., Han, D., Cheng, M., Kaplan, B.E., Adolph, K.E.: Look before you fit: the real-time planning cascade in children and adults. J. Exp. Child Psychol. **189**, 104696 (2020). https://doi.org/10.1016/j.jecp.2019.104696

16. Albrecht, B., Uebel-von Sandersleben, H., Wiedmann, K., Rothenberger, A.: ADHD history of the concept: the case of the continuous performance test. Curr. Dev. Disord. Rep. **2**(1), 10–22 (2015). https://doi.org/10.1007/s40474-014-0035-1

17. Neguţ, A., Jurma, A.M., David, D.: 'Virtual-reality-based attention assessment of ADHD: ClinicaVR: classroom-CPT versus a traditional continuous performance test. Child Neuropsychol. **23**(6), 692–712 (2017). https://doi.org/10.1080/09297049.2016.1186617

18. Miller, M., et al.: Delineating early developmental pathways to ADHD: setting an international research agenda. JCPP Adv. **3**(2), e12144 (2023). https://doi.org/10.1002/jcv2.12144

19. Murray, A.L., et al.: Developmental trajectories of ADHD symptoms in a large population-representative longitudinal study. Psychol. Med. **52**(15), 3590–3596 (2022). https://doi.org/10.1017/S0033291721000349

20. Berger, I., Slobodin, O., Cassuto, H.: Usefulness and validity of continuous performance tests in the diagnosis of attention-deficit hyperactivity disorder children. Arch. Clin. Neuropsychol. **32**(1), 81–93 (2017). https://doi.org/10.1093/arclin/acw101

21. Zeeuw, P.D., et al.: Inhibitory performance, response speed, intraindividual variability, and response accuracy in ADHD. J. Am. Acad. Child Adolesc. Psychiatry **47**(7), 808–816 (2008). https://doi.org/10.1097/CHI.0b013e318172eee9

22. Berlin, L., Bohlin, G., Nyberg, L., Janols, L.-O.: How well do measures of inhibition and other executive functions discriminate between children with ADHD and controls? Child Neuropsychol. **10**(1), 1–13 (2004). https://doi.org/10.1076/chin.10.1.1.26243

23. Huang-Pollock, C.L., Karalunas, S.L., Tam, H., Moore, A.N.: Evaluating vigilance deficits in ADHD: a meta-analysis of CPT performance. J. Abnorm. Psychol. **121**(2), 360–371 (2012). https://doi.org/10.1037/a0027205

24. Gizatdinova, Y., et al.: PigScape: an embodied video game for cognitive peer-training of impulse and behavior control in children with ADHD. In: Proceedings of the 24th International ACM SIGACCESS Conference on Computers and Accessibility, Athens Greece: ACM, pp. 1–4 (2022). https://doi.org/10.1145/3517428.3550401

25. Leontyev, A., Yamauchi, T.: Mouse movement measures enhance the stop-signal task in adult ADHD assessment. PLoS ONE **14**(11), e0225437 (2019). https://doi.org/10.1371/journal.pone.0225437

26. Perochon, S., et al.: A tablet-based game for the assessment of visual motor skills in autistic children. NPJ Digit. Med. **6**(1), 17 (2023). https://doi.org/10.1038/s41746-023-00762-6

27. Bioulac, S., Lallemand, S., Fabrigoule, C., Thoumy, A.-L., Philip, P., Bouvard, M.P.: Video game performances are preserved in ADHD children compared with controls. J. Atten. Disord. **18**(6), 542–550 (2014). https://doi.org/10.1177/1087054712443702

28. Peñuelas-Calvo, I., et al.: Video games for the assessment and treatment of attention-deficit/hyperactivity disorder: a systematic review. Eur. Child Adolesc. Psychiatry **31**(1), 5–20 (2022). https://doi.org/10.1007/s00787-020-01557-w

29. Seesjärvi, E., et al.: Quantifying ADHD symptoms in open-ended everyday life contexts with a new virtual reality task. J. Atten. Disord. **26**(11), 1394–1411 (2022). https://doi.org/10.1177/10870547211044214

30. Seesjärvi, E., Laine, M., Kasteenpohja, K., Salmi, J.: Assessing goal-directed behavior in virtual reality with the neuropsychological task EPELI: children prefer head-mounted display but flat screen provides a viable performance measure for remote testing. Front. Virtual Real. **4**, 1138240 (2023). https://doi.org/10.3389/frvir.2023.1138240

31. Seymour, K.E., Mostofsky, S.H., Rosch, K.S.: Cognitive load differentially impacts response control in girls and boys with ADHD. J. Abnorm. Child Psychol. **44**(1), 141–154 (2016). https://doi.org/10.1007/s10802-015-9976-z

32. Van den Driessche, C., Chevrier, F., Cleeremans, A., Sackur, J.: Lower attentional skills predict increased exploratory foraging patterns. Sci. Rep. **9**(1), 761 (2019). https://doi.org/10.1038/s41598-019-46761-0

33. Kofler, M.J., Larsen, R., Sarver, D.E., Tolan, P.H.: Developmental trajectories of aggression, prosocial behavior, and social–cognitive problem solving in emerging adolescents with clinically elevated attention-deficit/hyperactivity disorder symptoms. J. Abnorm. Psychol. **124**, 1027–1042 (2015). https://doi.org/10.1037/abn0000103

34. Kofler, M.J., et al.: Working memory and organizational skills problems in ADHD. J. Child Psychol. Psychiatry **59**(1), 57–67 (2018). https://doi.org/10.1111/jcpp.12773

35. Morsink, S., Sonuga-Barke, E., Van der Oord, S., Van Dessel, J., Lemiere, J., Danckaerts, M.: Task-related motivation and academic achievement in children and adolescents with ADHD. Eur. Child Adolesc. Psychiatry **30**(1), 131–141 (2021). https://doi.org/10.1007/s00787-020-01494-8

36. Onnela, J.-P.: Opportunities and challenges in the collection and analysis of digital phenotyping data. Neuropsychopharmacol. Off. Publ. Am. Coll. Neuropsychopharmacol. **46**(1), 45–54 (2021). https://doi.org/10.1038/s41386-020-0771-3

37. Insel, T.R.: Digital phenotyping: technology for a new science of behavior. JAMA **318**(13), 1215–1216 (2017). https://doi.org/10.1001/jama.2017.11295

# GalactiVote: Government in Action!
# An American Government Video Game

Hillary Gould(✉) ⓘ, Zach Lang ⓘ, and Victoria Mondelli ⓘ

University of Missouri, Columbia, MO 65211, USA
hgould@missouri.edu

**Abstract.** This demo paper presents *GalactiVote*, an educational game designed for introductory American Government undergraduate courses. The premise of the game is that students are astronauts starting their own government on a newly discovered planet. The goals of this game include bringing students' awareness of their own ideologies and political stances as well as an understanding of political party creation, campaigning, and elections.

**Keywords:** game-based learning · serious games · government · text-based games · education · political science · civics

## 1 Background

Introduction to American Government is a required course at the University of Missouri. Being a university of nearly 30,000 students, political science professors teach American Government to thousands of students every semester as part of the General Education requirement. This hybrid course is taught to mostly non-major and first year students across dozens of sections and is accompanied by weekly TA lead small-group discussion sections. In the past, student success in American Government was mixed and the faculty wanted to decrease the rate of students earning grades such as Ds, Fs, or Withdrawals (DFW rates) in the course. A Community of Practice with the Teaching for Learning Center empowered the faculty to co-inquire about a variety of modifications to improve the student experience, student learning, and the DFW rate. This turned into an opportunity to improve the course through Game-Based Learning. The Teaching for Learning Center enacted a unique model of faculty partnership with Adroit Studios, developing digital serious games, as well as empowering faculty to design learning games.

As part of this Community of Practice, the idea for the game, *GalactiVote: Government in Action!* (hereby, *GalactiVote*) was initiated. At this time, the game shows promise to become the cornerstone of a larger game-based learning grant project to enhance the student experience in American Government. *GalactiVote* is a text-based video game that students play together as part of their homework and in their discussion sections. In the game, students role-play as astronauts who are inhabiting a new planet and are faced with the task of creating their own government. Students complete "moons" or missions every week relating to the creation of their government: taking a personal ideology test, creating a political party, running an election campaign, and participating in an election.

J. L. Plass and X. Ochoa (Eds.): JCSG 2024, LNCS 15259, pp. 463–469, 2025.
https://doi.org/10.1007/978-3-031-74138-8_39

These missions in Kepler (the fictional planet where the game takes place) correspond to different themes in class each week, so students are learning about these political science topics, and investigating them personally with their classmates via the game.

This game is an important enhancement to the course experience because it will allow students to access the class material in new engaging ways. For example, the sound and graphic design is compelling to set the scene for play. The role-playing is designed to get them excited about learning and enable them to co-create course content with their peers.

## 1.1    Why Political Science is Critical for the General Education Curriculum

Political Science is a crucial topic for students and young adults to understand. Government affects nearly every aspect of Americans lives: where they live, the roads on which they drive, the taxes they pay, the goods and services they have access to, insurance plans, schools, emergency responders and more. Despite this massive impact, most Americans have very little information about the workings of American government. In fact, survey results indicate that a sobering 1 in 3 Americans could pass a U.S. citizenship test and in 49 out of 50 states, a majority of Americans would not pass (Institute for Citizens and Scholars 2018). The only exception is Vermont, with a narrow 53% of its population able to pass. These findings are exacerbated in younger generations, with those under the age of 45 knowing roughly 20% less about American government than those above 45.

The crucial lack of understanding about basic American civics only demonstrates the need for courses like American Government. In most universities, like the University of Missouri, American Government is an introductory level survey class meant to provide students with basic backgrounds on American government for their own development as citizens, or as introductions to topics that could be explored further in a political science major or minor. The class is divided into three sections around core conceptual themes in the field: political institutions, political behavior, and public policy. Political institutions surveys information and questions about structures of government like Congress, the executive branch, or the Constitution. Political behavior introduces concepts like political ideology, voting, campaigns, and elections. Public policy focuses on the actions and administration of government; laws, policies, regulations, and those who administer them.

While political science is crucial for a well-rounded student, citizen, and voter, it can at times be difficult for students to access. According to the instructors who teach the course, many who are not interested in this topic find learning about government complicated, boring, or confusing. A topic that students find boring is a good place to apply play (Bisz and Mondelli 2023). Additionally, some students have negative attitudes or misconceptions towards political topics (FIRE 2024), which is another reason that this is an ideal area to apply play (Bisz and Mondelli 2023). Therefore, it can be effective to pair political science education with a game-based learning approach to help students overcome these hurdles.

Video games have been described as powerful learning tools requiring players to respond to the environment, resulting in development of new knowledge and skills (Gee 2003; Pelletier 2009). Game-based learning can lead to substantial learning outcomes regarding content and skills across disciplines (Wouters et al. 2013) and can promote student motivation (Clark et al. 2016).

Given the confluence between the importance of learning about American government, the usefulness and success of game-based learning approaches, and the massive number of students who are exposed to American Government, this course made an excellent test case for which to create our American Government video game—*GalactiVote*.

*GalactiVote* focuses on one of the core themes in American Government: political behavior. While there have been tens of thousands of articles published in social science journals regarding political behavior, most college syllabi that encompass political behavior cover at least three core topics: ideology, political parties, and campaigns and elections. Each of these concepts also relate to seminal articles in the subfield of American politics (Abramowitz and Saunders 2005, Key 1958, Poole and Rosenthal 1984, Campbell 2008).

Political behavior was chosen specifically for students because it can be among the more tedious topics for students to learn about. For students who may have had little exposure in high school, learning about overlapping yet theoretically distinct groups like "liberals," "conservatives," "Republicans," "Democrats," "Libertarians," and more can seem daunting, confusing, and at times even contradictory. *GalactiVote* allows students to explore these topics together, while receiving instruction from their professor. By bringing these complex concepts into a fun learning-game environment, we have good reason to believe that students will become more willing to learn this information that will be useful to them throughout their lives.

## 2  Game Content

The setting of *GalactiVote* is a deserted planet in which a group of astronauts (the students) have landed on and need to create their own government in order to inhabit the planet. The game is organized into "moons" or missions that focus on one of these topics, progressing through four weeks of course content with each week correlating to a moon (see Fig. 1).

In the first moon, students take an ideology test developed by the political science faculty at the University of Missouri. The test contains a battery of statements that students rank their agreement with and the overall importance of the topic in question. Their answers to these questions classify them into constellations. Students are then shown their position in three dimensions, two on a Nolan Chart, which shows their views on personal and economic freedoms. The third dimension is represented by a slider between their concerns with regulatory versus distributive policies. They can view their results in relation to the class average on all three of these dimensions (see Fig. 2).

In the second moon, students create their own political parties by selecting the issue stances that matter to them the most, and then creating a party logo. Students are then automatically merged with other students in the class who select the same issues stances as them. Students can also join other political parties voluntarily, or combine one or more parties into a new political party (see Fig. 3).

In the third moon, students use the political parties they have created to run a simulated election campaign. In the campaign, students create memes that reflect their

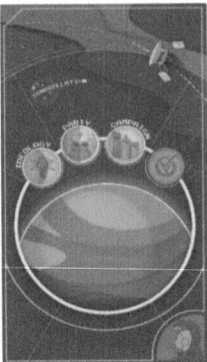

**Fig. 1.** Planet home screen showing all missions.

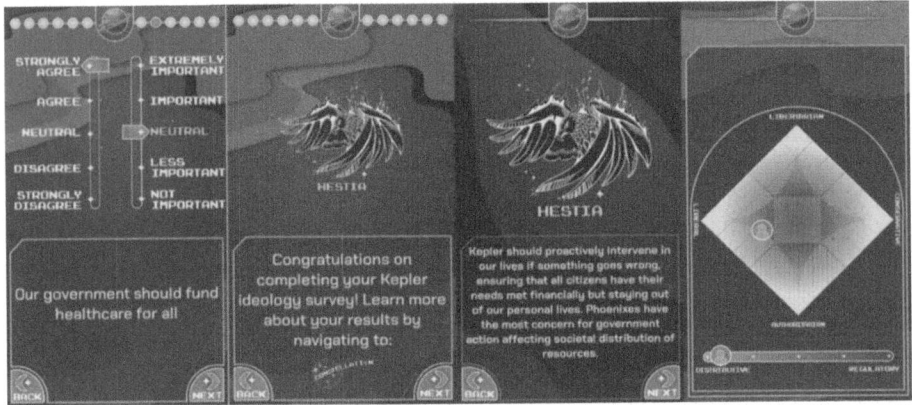

**Fig. 2.** Ideology, constellations, and nolan chart position.

political values, and compete with other parties to create the most popular meme. At this phase, students may also merge, join, or collapse parties (see Fig. 4).

In the fourth and final moon, students take part in an election to select the party (and candidate) that will govern the planet. The party candidate that receives the most votes wins. However, there is also an electoral college on the planet where students can observe the differences between that system and one with only plurality rule. In addition, there is also a ranked choice voting option that students use which displays the difference between single-vote systems and multi-vote systems like ranked choice voting.

## 3 Interactive Demo Feedback

In January 2024, we conducted an interactive demonstration at the CUNY Games conference. It provided an opportunity to collect informal feedback from faculty and graduate students knowledgeable about designing learning games. The demo allowed players to participate in the first through third missions. It is important to note that those who

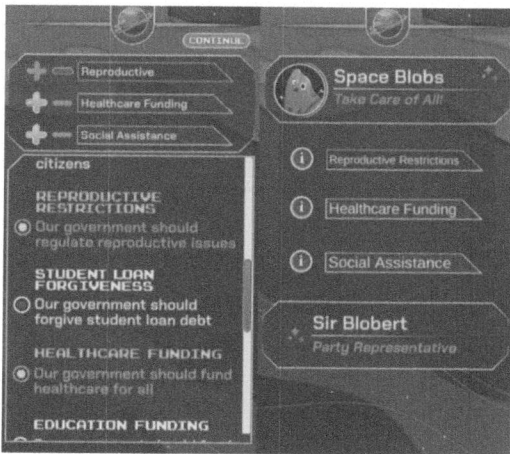

**Fig. 3.** Party creation screen and example student party.

**Fig. 4.** Meme creation screen and meme feed.

provided feedback did not get the full game experience since they played as individuals without in-game group interaction. *GalactiVote* is meant to be played collaboratively for campaigning and interacting with other players and their parties.

The demo allowed participants to complete the first moon and see their position on the ideology Nolan chart. In the second moon, participants were able to create their own political party and representative, choose the three values from their ideology that are most important to them, and customize their platform. However, they were not able to see other parties, as this collaborative aspect requires other players in the game. During the third moon, participants were able to create a meme to campaign for their party. In the finished game, students will have access to the meme feed (see Fig. 4) and be able to see the campaigns for other parties. Ideally, players would choose to merge parties in order to have a more successful campaign, but this aspect cannot be experienced without multiple players. The fourth moon was not developed at the time of this demo.

Some informal playtesting was conducted with a small group of participants playing through a demo of the currently finished aspects of the game. Participants stated that they "loved the imagery" and thought it was very valuable that this game helped students to determine their ideological positions. Another stated that they were "really invested in the party creation."

Most of the feedback from this informal group was around the user interface and instructions. They wanted more context around gameplay, which students would get in the classroom prior to playing through the game. Other suggestions were that the party creation screen suggest what the players' top values should be based on their responses to ideology, and that students decide what type of vote to take at the end rather than going through each type of voting. The team decided against implementing this, as it is an important part of the game to demonstrate ranked choice voting and how popular vote and electoral college votes differ to the students. Therefore, students will go through each type of voting process so that they can clearly infer how results differ based on the type of vote conducted.

## 4   Discussion

*GalactiVote* is expected to increase engagement and positively influence learning outcomes for the students enrolled in American Government. We expect *GalactiVote* to continue to improve the student experience in the course and have a positive indirect effect on the DFW rate. The game will be played by the students as homework in preparation for their discussion sections, and discussion section lessons will reinforce the concepts learned in the game.

Intrinsic and extrinsic motivation is important in any successful learning environment. *GalactiVote* taps into various aspects of what players might be motivated by: rivalry, rewards, and role (Bisz and Mondelli 2023) to achieve the important goal of winning an election. By creating a reward structure (a game where the ultimate goal is to win an election on a team), students will be encouraged to succeed and to work together with other students in order to complete the game. This collaborative learning will reinforce the concepts that they are learning in class while playing the game. We are confident that students who play *GalactiVote* will be more interested in the content and learn more deeply in this learning experience than in the former traditional format.

**Acknowledgments.** The co-authors wish to acknowledge the collaborative team at the University of Missouri which was comprised of faculty and staff from the Teaching for Learning Center, Adroit Studios, the Truman School of Government and Public Affairs, and the Kinder Institute for Constitutional Democracy. The collective effort with game design and development would not have been possible without: Bill Horner, Joe Griffin, Aaron Moss, Chelsea Bartlett, and Alex Unseth.

# References

1. Abramowitz, A., Saunders, K.: Why can't we all just get along? The reality of a polarized America. Forum **3**, 2 (2005)
2. Bisz, J., Mondelli, V.L.: The Educator's Guide to Designing Games and Creative Active-Learning Exercises: The Allure of Play. Teachers College Press (2023)
3. Campbell, J.: The American Campaign, 2nd edn. Texas A&M University Press, College Station (2008)
4. Clark, D.B., Tanner-Smith, E.E., Killingsworth, S.S.: Digital games, design, and learning: a systematic review and meta-analysis. Rev. Educ. Res. **86**(1), 79–122 (2016)
5. Foundation for Individual Rights and Expression: 2024 College free speech rankings: executive summary. FIRE (2024). https://www.thefire.org/research-learn/2024-college-free-speech-rankings. Accessed July 2024
6. Gee, J.P.: What Video Games have to Teach Us About Learning and Literacy. Macmillan (2003). https://doi.org/10.1145/950566.950595
7. Institute for Citizens and Scholars: National Survey Finds Just 1 in 3 Americans Would Pass a Citizenship Test. Princeton (2018). https://citizensandscholars.org/resource/national-survey-finds-just-1-in-3-americans-would-pass-citizenship-test/. Accessed 4 Dec 2024
8. Key, V.O.: Politics, Parties, and Pressure Groups, 4th edn. Thomas Crowell Publishing (1958)
9. Pelletier, C.: Games and learning: what's the connection. Int. J. Learn. Media **1**(1), 83–101 (2009)
10. Poole, K.T., Rosenthal, H.: U.S. presidential elections 1968–1980: a spatial analysis. Am. J. Polit. Sci. **28**(2), 282–312 (1984)
11. Wouters, P., Van Nimwegen, C., Van Oostendorp, H., Van Der Spek, E.D.: A meta-analysis of the cognitive and motivational effects of serious games. J. Educ. Psychol. **105**(2), 249–265 (2013). https://doi.org/10.1037/a0031311

# Venom CoLab: Exploring the Science of Venom for Middle School Learners

Corinne Brenner[1]([✉]) [iD], Jessica Ochoa Hendrix[1] [iD], Christopher Pollati[1],
Noelle Posadas Shang[1], TzuChin Chen[1] [iD], Oscar Barragan[1],
and Mandë Holford[1,2,3] [iD]

[1] Killer Snails, LLC, Brooklyn, NY, USA
corinne@killersnails.com
[2] Hunter College, The City University of New York, New York, NY, USA
[3] The American Museum of Natural History, New York, NY, USA

**Abstract.** Venom is a deadly adaptation that helps organisms thrive, but can also be separated into peptides and proteins with medically-relevant effects. Researchers studying venom have successfully used their understanding of these molecules to create drugs to treat health problems in humans. Inspired this field of study, Venom CoLab is a collaborative science experience for students in 6th to 8th grade (ages 11–14), where students take on roles as scientists. By completing activities on a website and in augmented reality (AR), each group studies a venomous organism (cone snails, scorpions, snakes, or sea anemones) to find new molecules to treat health problems such as pain, cancer, blood clotting, or autoimmune diseases. This demonstration will highlight how the project uses the website and augmented reality to support collaboration, implement interactive activities, and feature real scientists describing their work to encourage students' interest and build skills in science.

**Keywords:** STEM education · Augmented Reality · Collaboration

## 1 Background

Venom CoLab is a collaborative science experience for 6th–8th grade students. Inspired by—and featuring—the work of venom scientists, groups of up to four students study venom to create therapeutic medicines for humans. Over 5 class periods, students take on their distinct roles as scientists and work together to learn how venom is a deadly adaptation that helps organisms thrive, but can also be separated into peptides and proteins with medically-relevant effects. By completing activities on a website and in augmented reality (AR), each group studies a venomous organism (cone snails, scorpions, snakes, or sea anemones) to find new molecules to treat health problems such as pain, cancer, blood clotting, or autoimmune diseases.

Venom CoLab is inspired by the processes researchers have used to develop drugs like Captopril for blood pressure, Ozempic for diabetes, and Prialt for chronic pain. The connections between content knowledge, application of science and engineering

© The Author(s), under exclusive license to Springer Nature Switzerland AG 2025
J. L. Plass and X. Ochoa (Eds.): JCSG 2024, LNCS 15259, pp. 470–476, 2025.
https://doi.org/10.1007/978-3-031-74138-8_40

skills, and need for collaboration between experts in different areas uniquely addresses challenges that face middle school science learners. Studies have shown that students are interested in STEM subjects across gender and racial/ethnic categories during elementary school, but interest begins to wane in middle school, especially within underrepresented groups [1]. To help address these needs, Venom CoLab weaves multiple strands of research and evidence-based practice into its design, which will be explored in the demonstration.

## 2  Gamification and Game Elements

While the experience as a whole is not a game, elements of game design are used to varying degrees throughout the five chapters of Venom CoLab. For example, labeled models of cell types, cell receptors, and peptides are used to build knowledge of cell anatomy. Students then use those models in drag-and-drop activities with a goal such as blocking a cell receptor on a specific cell by finding interlocking peptide to demonstrate the effect of peptide binding to cell receptors.

Later interactions leverage additional game elements like time constraints, rules, resource management, and changes to the game mechanics so students achieve win states that represent the medical problems they are trying to solve. For the Snake group studying proteins to help create blood clots for people who have a blood clotting disorder, the interlocking shapes of proteins involved in blood clotting and platelet cells must be deployed in the right location and sequence to make a blood clot before time runs out. For the Scorpion group, early rounds of the game demonstrate how difficult it is to distinguish cancer cells from non-cancerous cells under a microscope. In a later round, the game mechanic changes: A useful peptide and glowing molecule can bind to a cell receptor that is only found on the cancer cells, making them easy to find and eliminate. The familiar framework of a game is meant to help make the unfamiliar molecular biology of peptides, proteins and cells more concrete, and the complex medical issues more comprehensible.

## 3  Individual Tasks in the Digital Science Journal

As a Zoologist, Biochemist, Molecular Biologist, or Pharmacologist, each student per-forms distinct tasks using personalized websites called their Digital Science Journal on laptops. Individual tasks include using interactive models to illustrate how peptides or proteins bind to cell receptors, demonstrate the principles behind analysis techniques like size exclusion chromatography, and minigames to explore the mechanisms causing different health problems (Fig. 1).

## 4  Collaborative Tasks in the Digital Science Journal

Students must learn from each other and collaborate during activities like lab meetings and experiments, working toward their goal of developing new treatments. This collab-orative design is inspired by the 'jigsaw' method for designing collaborative classroom

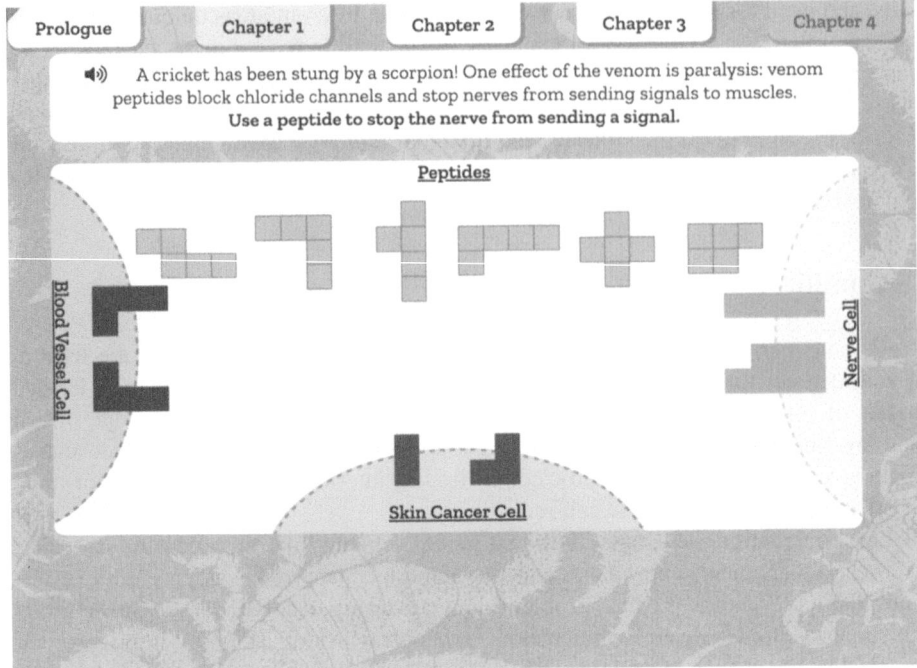

**Fig. 1.** A Chap. 1 task for the molecular biologist studying scorpions, demonstrating peptide-cell receptor binding.

activities, and models the collaborative practices of venom researchers. In a jigsaw task, students have distinct but interdependent roles in addressing a shared challenge [2]. Jigsaw tasks have been shown to enhance collaboration and science learning outcomes for students [3] (Fig. 2).

## 5  Representing Scientists

Throughout Venom CoLab, students hear from real scientists engaged in this work in brief videos and text chats, offering 'windows' into modern STEM workplaces [4]. Demonstrating counter-stereotypical examples of science and scientists positively impact middle school students' attitudes toward science and intent to pursue future studies. These factors are especially effective at engaging underrepresented students and increasing their beliefs about their skills and level of interest in STEM [5, 6] (Fig. 3).

## 6  Augmented Reality

Studies have shown that students are enthusiastic about and are motivated by augmented reality science lessons, but educators lack suitable, standards-aligned content [7, 8]. In Venom CoLab, students manipulate digital models of organisms and lab equipment to

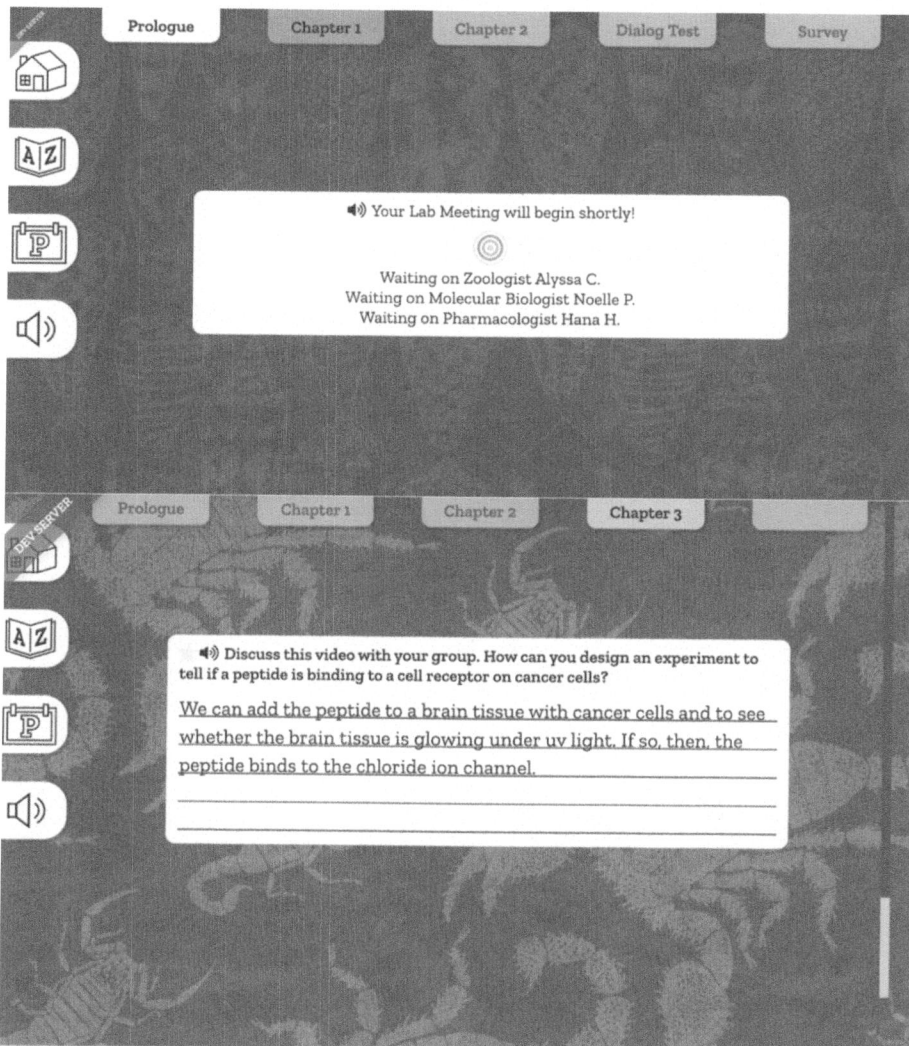

**Fig. 2.** Collaborative activities in Venom CoLab include coordinating lab meetings to share information acquired independently, editable open-ended text questions, and fill-in-the-blank statements.

engage in authentic science learning and take active roles as scientists investigating meaningful questions, using AR on an iPad, without the need for specialized lab equipment or dangerous venomous organisms. Students can use AR as common ground, sharing their device screens and comparing AR experiences to digital science journal content more easily than they could from within a VR headset. At the same time, only one student role uses the AR per chapter. Distinct AR content can be shown to each student based on their roles and needs, a feature which encourages collaborative actions like communicating, sharing information, and co-constructing solutions within groups [9] (Fig. 4).

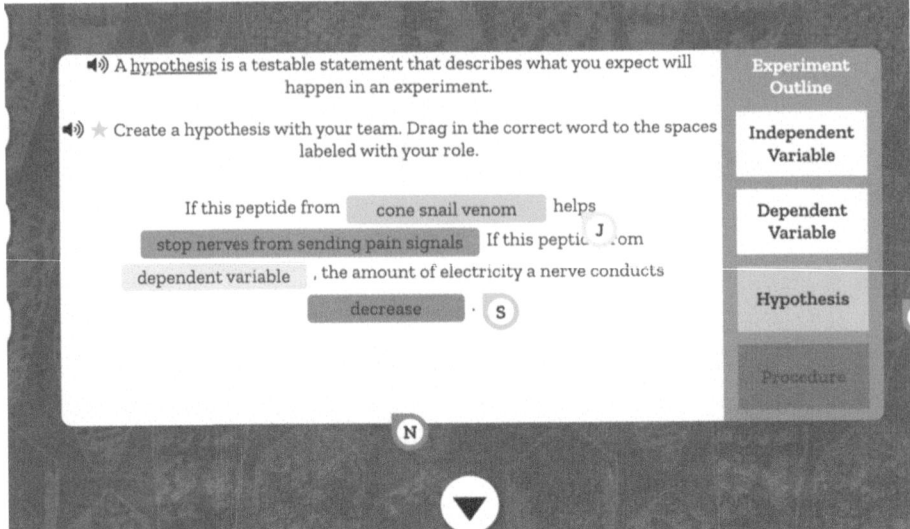

**Fig. 2.** (*continued*)

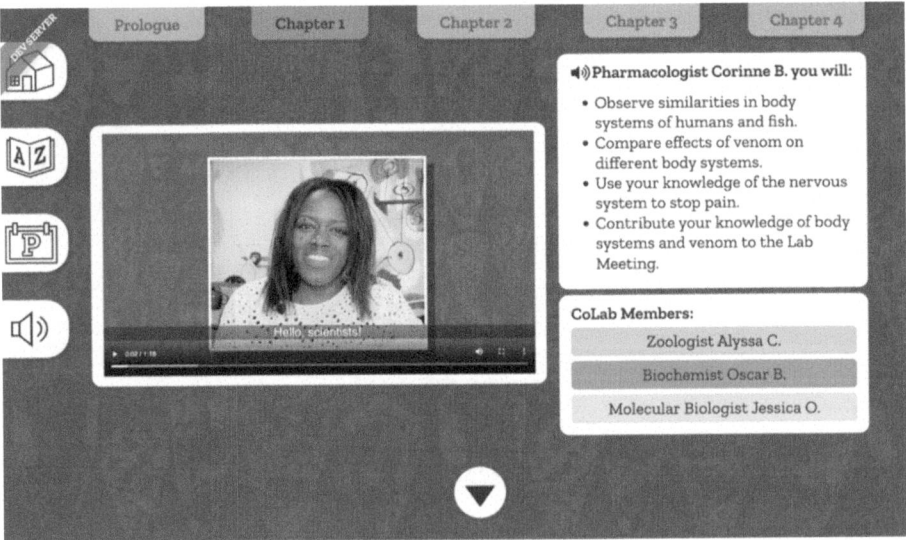

**Fig. 3.** Example of a digital science journal page for the pharmacologist, featuring a video of Dr. Mandë Holford.

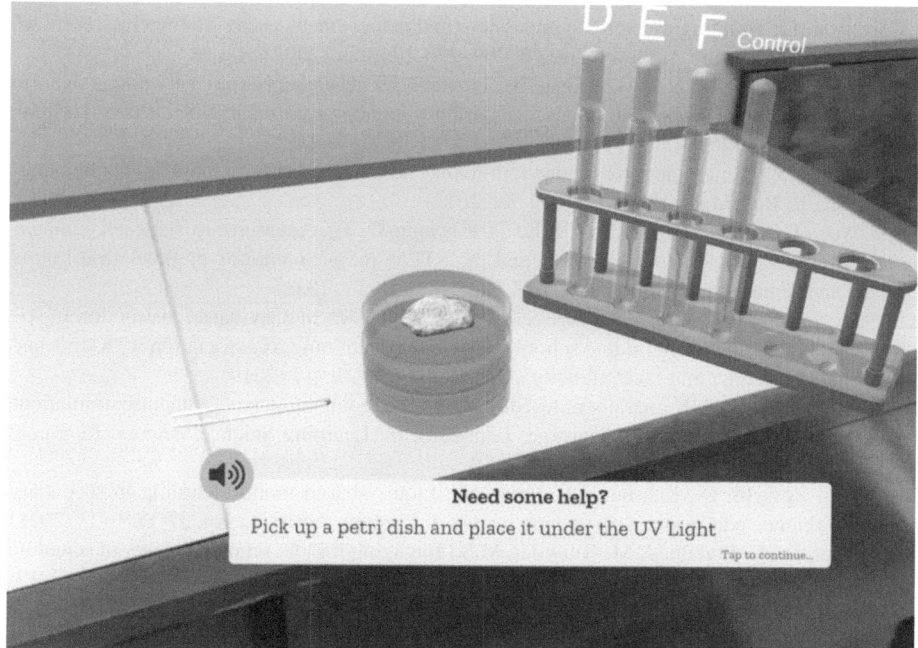

**Fig. 4.** Lab equipment set up in preparation for an experiment in Chap. 3.

## 7    Conclusion

Venom CoLab represents an effort to combine the affordances of digital technologies with collaborative learning: students build knowledge and skills by performing activities in a social setting, where meanings are negotiated between students with varying levels of skill. The long-term goal of material like this is for students to eventually transfer knowledge and skill from the classroom to applied contexts [7, 10].

In the proposed demonstration, conference attendees will be able to try out key elements of the experience and provide feedback on the usability of these features and the experience as a whole.

**Acknowledgments.** The product featured in this demonstration was supported by a grant from the National Institute of General Medical Sciences of the National Institutes of Health (5R44GM146490-03).

**Disclosure of Interests.** The authors have no competing interests.

## References

1. Andersen, L., Ward, T.J.: Expectancy-value models for the STEM persistence plans of ninth-grade, high-ability students: a comparison between black, hispanic, and white students. Sci. Educ. **98**(2), 216–242 (2014)

2. Aronson, E.: Building empathy, compassion, and achievement in the jigsaw classroom. In: Improving Academic Achievement, pp. 209–225. Elsevier (2002)
3. Bressler, D.M., Bodzin, A.M., Eagan, B., Tabatabai, S.: Using epistemic network analysis to examine discourse and scientific practice during a collaborative game. J. Sci. Educ. Technol. **28**(5), 553–566 (2019)
4. Gutiérrez, R.: Embracing Nepantla: rethinking "knowledge" and its use in mathematics teaching. J. Res. Math. Educ. **1**(1), 29–56 (2012)
5. Nguyen, U., Riegle-Crumb, C.: Who is a scientist? The relationship between counter-stereotypical beliefs about scientists and the STEM major intentions of Black and Latinx male and female students. Int. J. STEM Educ. **8**(1), 8–28 (2021)
6. Riegle-Crumb, C., Morton, K., Nguyen, U., Dasgupta, N.: Inquiry-based instruction in science and mathematics in middle school classrooms: examining its association with students' attitudes by gender and race/ethnicity. AERA Open **5**(3), 1–17 (2019)
7. Dede, C., Grotzer, T., Kamarainen, A., Metcalf, S.: Designing immersive authentic simulations that enhance motivation and learning: EcoLearn. In: Learning Science: Theory, Research, Practice, pp. 229–259. McGraw-Hill (2020)
8. Liu, C., Zowghi, D., Kearney, M., Bano, M.: Inquiry-based mobile learning in secondary school science education: a systematic review. J. Comput. Assist. Learn. **37**(1), 1–23 (2021)
9. Bressler, D.M., Bodzin, A.M., Tutwiler, M.S.: Engaging middle school students in scientific practice with a collaborative mobile game. J. Comput. Assist. Learn. **35**(2), 197–207 (2019)
10. Metcalf, S.J., Kamarainen, A.M., Torres, E., Grotzer, T.A., Dede, C.J.: EcoMUVE: a case study on the affordances of MUVEs in ecosystem science education. In: Integrating Multi-user Virtual Environments in Modern Classrooms, pp. 1–25. IGI Global (2018)

# Embodied Game Interactions: Somatosensation, Self-Identification, and the Potential of Alternative Game Controllers

Sara Jakubowicz$^{(\boxtimes)}$ (iD)

New York University, New York, NY 10012, USA
sarajakubowicz@nyu.edu

**Abstract.** Somatosensory experiences beyond the audio-visual, such as haptics, should be intentionally incorporated into pedagogical designs within serious games. Creating alternative controllers for serious games that externally represent domain-specific tools and concepts in their design can enhance learner competence within the field while fostering professional self-identification and belonging. Alternative game controllers that enable domain-specific embodied interactions can thus promote a learner's intrinsic motivation and technical knowledge as they digitally engage with the field of study. Embodied game interactions (EGIs) are mapped interactions that engage the learner directly and physically throughout gameplay, bridging game mechanics with learning mechanics. Applying the technological underpinnings of tangible user interfaces to learning theories and serious game design can augment how learners interact with and understand the material at hand, providing opportunities for near knowledge transfer in real-life situations.

**Keywords:** Interaction design · Embodiment · Somatosensation · Serious games · Alternative controllers · Professional self-identification

## 1 Introduction

Taking into account visual and auditory channels of information processing, whether that's through narrative, music, or signaling-game design aims to increase environment immersion. Currently, different game-based learning designs can be classified under four categories: cognitive, affective, motivational, and sociocultural [21]. Designers mold players' perceptions of the reality of a game environment, tacitly and explicitly. Game design can induce flow states and ease learners into a zone of proximal development by installing challenge states, like boss battles, and building player competence through proximal goal achievement [4, 25, 33]. However, theories regarding design around games and learning tend to focus on two-dimensional graphical user interfaces (GUIs) and interpretations rather than on three-dimensional experiences, a shortcoming of

J. L. Plass and X. Ochoa (Eds.): JCSG 2024, LNCS 15259, pp. 477–484, 2025.
https://doi.org/10.1007/978-3-031-74138-8_41

the Integrated Cognitive-Affective Model of Learning with Multimedia (ICALM) [22] and dual coding theory among others [20].

The design of serious games should attend to a wide range of sensory perceptions, including touch or haptics, to boost immersion, attention, multimodal representations, and multi-channel processing of information. Somatosensation and stimuli processing of physical information, through the haptic sense, have been shown to increase longitudinal recall and retention of information [17]. Object-based learning and experiential learning that leverage somatic processing channels in addition to visual ones have displayed heightened engagement and comprehension [32]. Designers intentionally accommodating for a somatic channel of information-processing when developing a product provides opportunities for somatosensory experiences to reduce extraneous cognitive load resulting from interactivity [19,23]. Applying expectancy-value theory and self-determination theory to serious games can create immersive experiences can boost game stickiness and player intrinsic motivation and desire for practice by increasing competency, self-efficacy, self-identity, and belonging through connected physical experiences [25,29,34].

Existing integrations of tactile experiences in games and simulations that incorporate the physical sensation of touch-in one study, through the use of vibrotactile feedback for a virtual reality cell simulation—foster a sense of presence within the simulated learning environment [6,18]. The use of haptics should be further explored and leveraged for learning; embodied cognition [24] and physical meaning-making through game interactions and the use of tangible user interfaces (TUIs) [12], can provide more multimodal learning experiences [12].

In practice, simulated experiences with objects can promote functional and mechanical knowledge about practical skills and technical tools, thus producing multimodal, multisensory mental models of information [26,28]. Furthermore, this allows for near transfer and physical memory retrieval of procedural, task knowledge from intra-game to exo-game situations [9]. Learning through the body heightens the chance for information selection and synaptic, schematic connections.

Designers can successfully embed learning content into the core mechanics of the game [2] by applying EGIs and haptic sensation into alternative controllers. This paper identifies alternative controllers as having important implications for the somatic design of serious games through embodied game interactions (EGIs) with embedded feedback. Through these EGIs, learners can understand the physical process that goes into more technical, practical fields that require hands-on learning.

Exploring past models of learning and engagement, this paper discusses how somatic learning differs from current models of information-processing theories. This leads to a discussion on the application of learning through games and the need for EGIs and tying them into intentional alternative controller design.

## 2   Embodied Game Interactions

Embodied Game Interactions (EGIs) are the connection between the physically mapped movements a player performs on a controller (the input) and the core mechanic a virtual agent completes on screen (the output). EGIs lay at the intersection between activity theory and interaction design [13,30], addressing the physical manipulation of the learning tool (controller) and a learners' integration into their mental models. Building upon the Learning Mechanic-Game Mechanic framework [2], EGIs unite the player with the game to achieve learning goals. With the added embodied game interactions, where physically controlled movements mimic those of a practitioner within the domain, one can increase their perceived and actual competence, driving higher levels of intrinsic motivation, task ability, and domain thinking [25,29].

Serious games often try to teach skills using cognitive apprenticeship [3]. By taking advantage of kinesthetic experiences and the physical experiences that stem from the original definition of apprenticeship, they provide more opportunities for skill practice, and near knowledge transfer whether that be art-making or practicing surgery. When the player is confronted with obstacles in the real world that resemble ones embedded in the game, they will be better equipped for novel situations. Players embody professional identities through their virtual agents and understand their roles and abilities through their interactions. As they work towards set goals, players shape task mental models around the game's learning content and discourse.

Pairing physical, technical abilities with concepts of a discipline with discourse in a game environment can shape how learners see themselves as practicing, participating members in the field. Through a perspective shift and practicing movements embedded within the jobs of the discipline, learners leave the peripheries of participation within their community of practice [16]and evolve their identity kits [7].

In a 4-year diary study, 378 dental students journaled about their journey in the field. The more those students practiced their skills in professional settings, as opposed to talking about concepts in class, their discourse surrounding dentistry shifted from more abstract ideas, like the dentistry field as a whole, to more concrete topics, such as care-strategy for patients [35].

However, years-long practical experience isn't always possible or accessible when the tools and technologies are expensive or failure may lead to dire consequences—like hurting themselves or others. It can take many years to grow professional self-identity within a domain. This is where serious games and embodied interactions come into play. They provide an airbag for failure; learners can gracefully fail with minimal risk [21]. Players can practice and learn from experience—from trial-and-error and educated strategic shifts based on the game's feedback. EGI design can provide nearer procedural knowledge transfer opportunities within safe spaces.

Serious games afford [8] the ability to manipulate temporal perception, speeding up or slowing down time. This effect is further magnified for players when they are in flow-state [4]. Learners can develop domain self-efficacy and attitudinal shifts at quicker rates than in real-life practice. There is the question, however, of how fast is too fast and the extent of the dosage needed within these digital experiences to enact similar effects on self-identity as was shown in the Wise et al. [35] dentistry study above.

Through simulated experiences, users don't have to rely on practicum opportunities, but can instead build upon skills and professional identity within gameplay. Increasing learners' understanding of self-trajectories within disciplines through serious games and embodied game interactions is a high-level goal for game design. For EGIs to manifest these changes in self-perception, the core mechanics must align with learning mechanics. In other words, the types of game interactions must represent the ones in the real world. But, what might these serious games with embodied interactions look like?

In a previous art simulation design, my team aimed to teach pre-operational and operational learners how to mix colors when painting, starting with primary colors and moving on to secondary and tertiary colors. By design, learners had to drag their fingers in a swirl to mix the colors in the same way they would do so with a paintbrush in real life. The digital interactions combine with other visual elements like environmental design to provide apprenticeship in learning painting. Current technologies—like the Kinect, Virtual Reality (VR) hardware, or other body-sensing and movement-tracking technologies—can be enhanced by integrating more tangible, tactile experiences in serious games, especially for disciplines where domain-unique tools, like rulers or paintbrushes, shape somatosensory interactions. Alternative controllers provide these tangible, modeled, exemplified interactions with real-world tools, playing with the conceptual knowledge in the process.

## 3  Alternative Game Controllers and Practicing Skills with Tangible Tools

Modern game controllers create a universal mode for system interaction, serving as both a benefit and a detriment to gaming. Upon playing on a new gaming console, one first needs to learn the controller, its anatomy, and how to use it, before being able to operate within the game world. These game system controllers allow a player to interact with all the games developed for the console, but each controller button may map to a different game mechanic in each game played.

Though there may be game mechanic heuristics and contiguity for button interactions within similar genres or game consoles (the $X$ button is the jump mechanic in many PlayStation games), users must adjust to the diverse and unique ways [5] these button-to-mechanic relations differ across games. The learning curve for unmapped interactions introduces an extraneous cognitive load, or task distraction, as users must learn the system before shifting the bulk of their mental effort toward the game's content.

Traditional controllers are usually limited to button-pressing interactions as opposed to spatial movements or other detectable actions that meaningfully engage players with the game content. More intuitive controllers can enable a more cohesive transition into the game with a reduced learning curve for control mastery, potentially leading to quicker spikes in-game engagement and motivation [25].

## 3.1 Emergent Themes on Controls in a User Research Study

When conducting a user research study for New York University's CREATE Lab on the Virtual Reality *Looking Inside Cells* Simulation ($N = 9$) [18], we observed users during audio-recorded think-aloud sessions as they performed two activities: building an animal cell and performing mitosis (splitting an animal cell). A theme emerged from the observations and transcripts around issues with the controls. Many users were confused as to which buttons corresponded with different player actions, leading them to press buttons that weren't in operation. One user expressed, "Some things were just, like, kind of [...] difficult to do with the controller." Others initially had trouble holding the controllers the right way. Users also struggled to vertically rotate a cell organelle to fit into a certain space. When different users tried to rotate their hand in the same fashion they wanted replicated on-screen and found that this didn't work, they experimented with different interactions, uttering, "How do you rotate it?"; "How do I rotate it that way?"; and "I thought I was supposed to rotate the pieces [horizontally]."

Even after completing the tutorial, many participants forgot about buttons closer aligned to player actions, such as using the toggle to move an organelle away from or toward the user. Instead, they opted for the more intuitive motion of moving their hand towards and away from them, despite the potential arm strain. To reduce the cognitive load on the learner during game initiation and enable a more immersive, embodied experience, more intuitive interactions should be heavily considered in the game design process.

During the tutorial phase, players enjoyed using the front trigger on their VR controllers to spritz the room with a spray bottle to practice pressing down on the front trigger control. The embodied game interaction heavily resembled the action users would take in real life to trigger a spray bottle. Over one-third of the users fixated or commented on the action, with one user uttering an expletive to express their excitement and enjoyment while engaging with the spray tool. Two users continually sprayed despite completing that tutorial section, one of whom started spraying with both hands simultaneously. Intuitive EGI design can lead to higher engagement, quicker mastery of controls, and reduction in cognitive load needed in learning how to interact with the game [25]. Learning through tangible objects tends to increase attention and longitudinal retention of information—something which these modeled, embodied controller interactions can facilitate [17].

Through alternative game controllers, we can map learning mechanics to game mechanics in the embedded interactions. This builds upon the applications of the learning mechanic-game mechanic (LM-GM) framework by taking the perspective that interactions, in addition to qualifying under the revised Bloom's taxonomic classification 'Apply,' can allow learners to 'Understand' the core learning objectives through physical manipulations of the input (game controller) if the interaction is designed for learning [2,15]. EGIs recognize the exchange between the player, the game, and the meaning-making medium within a Serious Game.

### 3.2 Embodied Game Interactions in Existing Games

Game controllers can provide a means for apprenticed learning and embodied cognition [24]. In the motorcycle racing arcade game, *MotoGP* [27], the motor-cycle serves as its own controller with in-game movements reflecting those of the user as they ride a stationary motorcycle in real life and build procedural knowl-edge. Another example is *Dance Dance Revolution* [14] where dancers move on a dance pad according to on-screen directional signals, practicing different dance routines in the process.

## 4    Limitations and Future Directions

Alternative controllers, or alt.ctrl (pronounced alt-control), have become more well known in gaming circles in recent years, popularized by conference exhibits such as *alt.ctrl.GDC* (Game Developers Conference) [11] and the *A Maze.* con-ference (International Games and Playful Media Festival) [1]. Databases such as Shake That Button [31], provide documentation and archival information for the different types of alternative controllers in existence.

Current alternative controllers are mostly single-purpose and require techni-cal skills for fabrication and implementation. A current question is how to mold alternative controllers to be more feasible and accessible to users and designers alike. Recently, some universal alternative controller designs have been developed that allow for the ability to switch out controller types for the same game, like the TinyCade project—a cardboard arcade gaming hardware that's connected to a plug-in software system called Beholder [10].

More research and dissemination into the design of universal, accessible alter-native controllers would allow for a better ability to implement these controllers in practice. Additionally, further evaluation is needed regarding the learning outcomes of alternative controllers with EGIs and their impact on domain self-identity.

## 5    Conclusion

When alternative controllers reflect the learning content a game depicts, the learning content can become more memorable and substantial to the learner, reducing extraneous cognitive load and fostering intrinsic cognitive load in inter-activity [23]. EGIs and interaction design should be more thoroughly considered in the intentional game design process. They can allow learners to move from the peripheries of participation within a field and increase their sense of competence, professional self-identity, and intrinsic motivation.

**Disclosure of Interests** The author has no competing interests to declare that are relevant to the content of this article.

# References

1. A MAZE.: A MAZE. In: Berlin 2024—13th International Games and Playful Media Festival (2024). https://2024.amaze-berlin.de/
2. Arnab, S., Lim, T., Carvalho, M.B., Bellotti, F., De Freitas, S., Louchart, S., Suttie, N., Berta, R., De Gloria, A.: Mapping learning and game mechanics for serious games analysis. Br. J. Edu. Technol. **46**(2), 391–411 (2015). https://doi.org/10.1111/bjet.12113
3. Collins, A.: Cognitive apprenticeship. In: The Cambridge Handbook of: The Learning Sciences, pp. 47–60. Cambridge University Press, New York (2006)
4. Csikszentmihalyi, M.: Flow: The Psychology of Optimal Experience, 1 edn. Harper & Row (1990)
5. Dotsenko, A.: Designing Game Controls (2017). https://www.gamedeveloper.com/design/designing-game-controls
6. Froehlich, F., Plass, J.L.: Can't touch this? Why vibrotactile feedback matters in educational VR. In: Proceedings of the 2024 IEEE Conference on Virtual Reality and 3D User Interfaces Abstracts and Workshops (VRW), pp. 755–756 (2024). https://doi.org/10.1109/VRW62533.2024.00174
7. Gee, J.P.: Literacy, discourse, and linguistics: introduction. J. Educ. **171**(1), 1–176 (1989)
8. Gibson, J.J.: The theory of affordances. In: The Ecological Approach to Visual Perception. Houghton Mifflin, Boston (1979)
9. Grush, R.: The emulation theory of representation: motor control, imagery, and perception. Behav. Brain Sci. **27**(3), 377–396 (2004). https://doi.org/10.1017/S0140525X04000093
10. Gyory, P.: Creating platforms to support craft and creativity in game controller design. In: Creativity and Cognition, pp. 708–710. ACM, Venice Italy (2022). https://doi.org/10.1145/3527927.3533733
11. Informa PLC: Alt.ctrl.GDC (2024). https://gdconf.com/alt-ctrl-gdc
12. Ishii, H.: The tangible user interface and its evolution. Commun. ACM **51**(6), 32–36 (2008). https://doi.org/10.1145/1349026.1349034
13. Kaptelinin, V., Nardi, B.A.: Acting with Technology: Activity Theory and Interaction Design. MIT Press, Cambridge (2006)
14. Konami: Dance Dance Revolution. Konami (1998)
15. Krathwohl, D.R.: A revision of bloom's taxonomy: an overview. Theory Into Pract. **41**(4), 212–218 (2002). https://doi.org/10.1207/s15430421tip4104_2
16. Lave, J., Wenger, E.: Situated Learning: Legitimate Peripheral Participation. Situated Learning: Legitimate Peripheral Participation. Cambridge University Press, New York (1991). https://doi.org/10.1017/CBO9780511815355
17. Novak, M., Schwan, S.: Does touching real objects affect learning? Educ. Psychol. Rev. **33**(2), 637–665 (2021). https://doi.org/10.1007/s10648-020-09551-z
18. NYU CREATE Lab, NYU Future Reality Lab, Verizon: Looking Inside: Cells (2024)
19. Paas, F., Sweller, J.: Implications of cognitive load theory for multimedia learning. In: The Cambridge Handbook of Multimedia Learning. Cambridge Handbooks in Psychology, 2nd edn., pp. 27–42. Cambridge University Press, New York (2014). https://doi.org/10.1017/CBO9781139547369.004

20. Paivio, A.: Dual coding theory: retrospect and current status. Can. J. Psychol. Revue canadienne de psychologie **45**(3), 255–287 (1991). https://doi.org/10.1037/h0084295
21. Plass, J.L., Homer, B.D., Mayer, R.E., Kinzer, C.K.: Theoretical foundations of game-based and playful learning. In: Handbook of Game-Based Learning., pp. 3–24. The MIT Press, Cambridge (2020)
22. Plass, J.L., Kaplan, U.: Emotional design in digital media for learning. In: Tettegah, S.Y., Gartmeier, M. (eds.) Emotions, Technology, Design, and Learning. Emotions and Technology, pp. 131–161. Academic Press, San Diego (2016). https://doi.org/10.1016/B978-0-12-801856-9.00007-4
23. Plass, J.L., Moreno, R., Brünken, R.: Cognitive Load Theory. Cambridge University Press, Cambridge (2010)
24. Pouw, W.T.J.L., Van Gog, T., Paas, F.: An embedded and embodied cognition review of instructional manipulatives. Educ. Psychol. Rev. **26**(1), 51–72 (2014). https://doi.org/10.1007/s10648-014-9255-5
25. Przybylski, A.K., Rigby, C.S., Ryan, R.M.: A motivational model of video game engagement. Rev. Gen. Psychol. **14**(2), 154–166 (2010). https://doi.org/10.1037/a0019440
26. Pujari, V.: Muscle memory and the brain: how physical skills are stored and retrieved. J. Adv. Med. Dent. Sci. Res. **7**(9), 21276 (2019) https://doi.org/10.21276/jamdsr https://doi.org/10.21276/jamdsr
27. Raw Thrills, Inc.: MotoGP—Raw Thrills, Inc (2024). https://rawthrills.com/games/motogp/
28. Remigereau, C., Roy, A., Costini, O., Osiurak, F., Jarry, C., Le Gall, D.: Involvement of technical reasoning more than functional knowledge in development of tool use in childhood. Front. Psychol. **7**, 1625 (2016)
29. Ryan, R.M., Deci, E.L.: Self-determination theory and the facilitation of intrinsic motivation, social development, and well-being. Am. Psychol. **55**(1), 68–78 (2000). https://doi.org/10.1037/0003-066x.55.1.68
30. Salvendy, G., Karwowski, W.: Handbook of Human Factors and Ergonomics. Wiley, Amsterdam (2021)
31. Shake That Button: Shake That Button—Alternative controllers, video game installations and playful performances (2024). https://shakethatbutton.com/
32. Sharp, A., Thomson, L., Chatterjee, H.J., Hannan, L.: The value of object-based learning within and between higher education disciplines. In: Chatterjee, H.J., Hannan, L. (eds.) Engaging the Senses: Object-Based Learning in Higher Education, pp. 97–116. Taylor and Francis, Farnham (2015)
33. Vygotsky, L.S.: Play and its role in the mental development of the child. Sov. Psychol. **5**(3), 6–18 (1967). https://doi.org/10.2753/RPO1061-040505036
34. Wigfield, A., Eccles, J.S.: Expectancy-value theory of achievement motivation. Contemp. Educ. Psychol. **25**(1), 68–81 (2000). https://doi.org/10.1006/ceps.1999.1015
35. Wise, A., Reza, S., Han, R.: Becoming a dentist: tracing professional identity development through mixed-methods data mining of student reflections. In: ICLS 2020 Proceedings, pp. 294–301. ISLS (2020)

# Author Index

J. L. Plass and X. Ochoa (Eds.): JCSG 2024, LNCS 15259, pp. 485–486, 2025.
https://doi.org/10.1007/978-3-031-74138-8

**SPRINGER NATURE**

# GPSR Compliance

*The European Union's (EU) General Product Safety Regulation (GPSR) is a set of rules that requires consumer products to be safe and our obligations to ensure this.*

*If you have any concerns about our products, you can contact us on ProductSafety@springernature.com*

In case Publisher is established outside the EU, the EU authorized representative is:

Springer Nature Customer Service Center GmbH
Europaplatz 3
69115 Heidelberg, Germany

The manufacturer's authorised representative in the EU is Springer
Nature Customer Service Centre GmbH, Europaplatz 3, 69115 Heidelberg,
Germany. If you have any concerns regarding our products, please
contact ProductSafety@springernature.com

Printed and bound by CPI Group (UK) Ltd, Croydon, CR0 4YY
29/04/2026
02099540-0002